Computer Science

21 Years 2025-2005

ISC

CHAPTERWISE - TOPICWISE QUESTION BANK

Computer Science

Class 12

Author
Neetu Gaikwad

arihant
SUCCESS AND NOTHING LESS

arihant
SUCCESS AND NOTHING LESS

ARIHANT PRAKASHAN
(School Division Series)

卐 ADMINISTRATIVE & PRODUCTION OFFICES

Regd. Office
'Ramchhaya' 4577/15, Agarwal Road, Darya Ganj, New Delhi -110002
Tele: 011- 47630600, 43518550

Head Office
Kalindi, TP Nagar, Meerut (UP) - 250002, Tel: 0121-7156203, 7156204

卐 SALES & SUPPORT OFFICES
Agra, Ahmedabad, Bengaluru, Bareilly, Chennai, Delhi, Guwahati, Hyderabad, Jaipur, Jhansi, Kolkata, Lucknow, Nagpur & Pune.

PO No : TXT-XX-XXXXXXX-X-XX

Published By Arihant Publications (India) Ltd.

For further information about the books published by Arihant, log on to www.arihantbooks.com or e-mail at info@arihantbooks.com

卐 **PRICE** ₹385.00

Follow us on

Achieving 99+
Marks in Board Exams

Achieving 99+ marks in board exams is definitely an ambitious goal, but with the right approach and these 7 tips from toppers, you can definitely increase your chances of success!

Here are the 7 Topper Tips to ace your board exams:

1. Master the art of consistency
Consistency builds understanding and confidence, both crucial for excelling in exams.

2. Build a winning study strategy
Create a personalised timetable that prioritises subjects based on your strengths and weaknesses.

3. Befriend the syllabus
Focus on high-weightage topics and prioritise mastering core concepts before moving on to advanced ones.

4. Embrace active learning
Explain concepts to yourself or in study groups to solidify understanding.

5. Conquer the past
Solve Past years' papers and Sample Papers under timed conditions to practice time management and understand paper pattern.

6. Seek help, when needed!
Don't hesitate to clarify doubts with teachers, tutors, or study groups. Asking questions strengthens your understanding and prevents confusion.

7. Prioritise well-being
Eat nutritious meals, get enough sleep, and regular exercise practice stress management techniques like meditation or to stay calm and focused during exams.

These tips are just a starting point, and you can personalise them to fit your learning style and preferences.

21 Years 2025-2005

ISC

CHAPTERWISE - TOPICWISE QUESTION BANK

Computer Science

Class 12

Description of

Newly Added Features

01

Propositional Logic

TREND ANALYSIS 4 YEARS

Propositional Logic

Average No. of Questions Across all Sets

Types of Questions	2024	2023	2020	2019
1 Mark	1	2	1	1
2 Marks	–	–	–	1
3 Marks	1	–	1	–
5 Marks	–	–	–	–
10 Marks	–	–	–	–

Trend Analysis

At the start of each chapter, Trend Analysis is given to indicate the types of questions asked from different topics of the chapter. This feature helps students to know the importance of different topics of the given chapter from exam point of view and helps them to prepare accordingly.

Key Idea

'Key Idea' is given with selected questions with the purpose to help students to get the approach 'to answer the question'. This feature help students to develop the systematic approach to answer difficult/complex questions.

32. Find the dual of

$$(A' + B).(1 + B') = A' + B$$

KEY idea

The principle of duality states that change every + by . and . by +.

Ans Take, LHS $= (A' + B).(1 + B')$

On applying principle of duality

6. Simplify the following expression using Boolean laws

$$F = [(X' + Y).(Y' + Z)]' + (X' + Z)$$ **ISC 2020**

Ans $F = [(X' + Y).(Y' + Z)]' + (X' + Z)$

$$= [(X' + Y)' + (Y' + Z)'] + (X' + Z)$$

$$= [(X')'.Y' + (Y')'.Z'] + (X' + Z)$$

$$= [XY' + YZ'] + X' + Z$$

$$= XY' + YZ' + X' + Z$$

Concept Enhancer Laws of Boolean algebra are helpful to simplify the expression and the best solution is which mention name of law at each step.

Concept Enhancer

Concept Enhancer gives the brief description of the concept, which has been used to answer the question. This feature provides revision of important concept along with practice of question solving.

Dream, Believe, Achieve Insights from ISC Toppers

Follow all the 5P's

• Persistence • Passion • Perseverance • Purpose • Practice

MANYA GUPTA
ISC Topper (99.75%)

"Aim for high marks, that's what I was doing. I convinced myself that if I aim for 100 I will at least get a 95. That was my logic, but I ended up getting a 100. "I studied with the help of my school and tuition classes. I didn't study daily much, but before the exams, I used to pull all-nighters and study".

ARYAAN
ISC Topper (99.75%)

"Studying for 3-4 hours every day along with six hours of school helped me secure 399 out of 400 marks, scoring 99.75%,"

I'm very active on all social media platforms but it has never hindered my studies. I strike a balance between hard work and fun,".

POOJA KEJRIWAL
ISC Topper (97.5%)

the degree of toughness of any subject is merely a subjective outlook. I made sure that I incentivised myself at times when I didn't feel like sitting at my study table, especially for theoretical subjects

I simply believe in revising the concepts which were taught at school or tuitions that very day and minimise backlogs as much as I could.

DEVANG KUMAR
ISC Topper

I believe there is no substitute to hard work. There was no fixed hours of preparation, I read a topic till the time I completely understood it. I had to be satisfied with the topic covered,"

See it is important to take breaks and everyone has their own way of entertainment. I do chat with friends on social media. I think it is fine until it becomes as addiction.

There is no secret formula as such, but one should not panic and have faith in his/her preparation.

DIMPLE KOTHARI
ISC Topper (97.5%)

- Don't run behind marks, crave for knowledge, experience because ultimately that's gonna help you.
- Don't let peer pressure dominate you.
- If you want to obtain good marks, leave all social media-This is a myth. I was active on Instagram & WhatsApp before my examinations, and even during my examinations. It's just that you need to remember that everyone has the same 24 hours, it's how you utilize it as well as enjoy it better than others.
- Both early morning and late night studies are best ~ you need to choose what's better for you.
- Don't hesitate to ask questions. If you have any doubts, please clarify. Everyone has different learning styles and speed, so it's nothing to be ashamed of.
- Never give up.

Please Note that all the information is collected from different websites.

Contents

ISC Chapterwise Question Bank 2025-2005

Latest Syllabus

Class XII (2026)

There will be two papers in the subject:

Paper I *Theory 70 Marks — 3 hours*

Paper II *Practical 30 Marks — 3 hours*

SECTION A

1. Boolean Algebra

(a) Propositional logic, well formed formulae, truth values and interpretation of well formed formulae (wff), truth tables, satisfiable, unsatisfiable and valid formulae. Equivalence laws and their use in simplifying wffs.

Propositional variables; the common logical connectives (~ (not)(negation), ∧ (and)(conjunction), ∨ (or)(disjunction), ⇒ (implication), ⇔ (biconditional); definition of a well-formed formula (wff); `representation of simple word problems as wff (this can be used for motivation); the values ***true*** *and* ***false;*** *interpretation of a wff; truth tables; satisfiable, unsatisfiable and valid formulae.*

Equivalence laws: commutativity of ∧, ∨; associativity of ∧, ∨; distributivity; De Morgan's laws; law of implication (p ⇒ q ≡ ~p ∨ q); law of biconditional ((p ⇔ q) ≡ (p ⇒ q) ∧ (q ⇒ p)); identity (p ≡ p); law of negation (~ (~p) ≡ p); law of excluded middle (p ∨ ~p ≡ true); law of contradiction (p ∧ ~p ≡ false); tautology and contingency simplification rules for ∧, ∨. Converse, inverse and contra positive. Chain rule, Modus Pones.

(b) Binary valued quantities; basic postulates of Boolean algebra; operations AND, OR and NOT; truth tables.

(c) Basic theorems of Boolean algebra (e.g. duality, idempotence, commutativity, associativity, distributivity, operations with 0 and 1, complements, absorption, involution); De Morgan's theorem and its applications; reducing Boolean expressions to sum of products and product of sums forms; Karnaugh maps (up to four variables).

Verify the laws of Boolean algebra using truth tables. Inputs, outputs for circuits like half and full adders, majority circuit etc., SOP and POS representation; Maxterms & Minterms, Canonical and Cardinal representation, reduction using Karnaugh maps and Boolean algebra

2. Computer Hardware

(a) Elementary logic gates (NOT, AND, OR, NAND, NOR, XOR, XNOR) and their use in circuits.

(b) Applications of Boolean algebra and logic gates to half adders, full adders, encoders, decoders, multiplexers, NAND, NOR as universal gates.

Show the correspondence between Boolean methods and the corresponding switching circuits or gates. Show that NAND and NOR gates are universal by converting some circuits to purely NAND or NOR gates.

SECTION B

The programming element in the syllabus (Sections B and C) is aimed at algorithmic problem solving and not merely rote learning of Java syntax. The Java version used should be 5.0 or later. For programming, the students can use any text editor and the javac and java programs or any other development environment: for example, BlueJ, Eclipse, NetBeans etc. BlueJ is strongly recommended for its simplicity, ease of use and because it is very well suited for an 'objects first' approach.

3. Implementation of algorithms to solve problems

The students are required to do lab assignments in the computer lab concurrently with the lectures. Programming assignments should be done such that each major topic is covered in at least one assignment. Assignment problems should be designed so that they are sufficiently challenging. Students must do algorithm design, address correctness issues, implement and execute the algorithm in Java and debug where necessary.

Self explanatory.

4. Programming in Java (Review of Class XI Sections B and C)

Note that items 4 to 13 should be introduced almost simultaneously along with classes and their definitions.

While reviewing, ensure that new higher order problems are solved using these constructs.

5. Objects

(a) Objects as data (attributes) + behaviour (methods); object as an instance of a class. Constructors.

(b) Analysis of some real-world programming examples in terms of objects and classes.

(c) Basic input/output using Scanner and Printer classes from JDK; input/output exceptions. Tokens in an input stream, concept of whitespace, extracting tokens from an input stream (String Tokenizer class).

6. Primitive values, Wrapper classes, Types and casting

Primitive values and types: byte, int, short, long, float, double, boolean, char. Corresponding wrapper classes for each primitive type. Class as type of the object. Class as mechanism for user defined types. Changing types through user defined casting and automatic type coercion for some primitive types.

7. Variables, Expressions

Variables as names for values; named constants (final), expressions (arithmetic and logical) and their evaluation (operators, associativity, precedence). Assignment operation; difference between left hand side and right hand side of assignment.

8. Statements, Scope

Statements; conditional (if, if else, if else if, switch case, ternary operator), looping (for, while, do while, continue, break); grouping statements in blocks, scope and visibility of variables.

9. Methods

Methods (as abstractions for complex user defined operations on objects), formal arguments and actual arguments in methods; different behaviour of primitive and object arguments. Static method and variables. The **this** Operator. Examples of algorithmic problem solving using methods (number problems, finding roots of algebraic equations etc.).

10. Arrays, Strings

Structured data types – arrays (single and multi-dimensional), address calculations, strings. Example algorithms that use structured data types (e.g. searching, finding maximum/minimum, sorting techniques, solving systems of linear equations, substring, concatenation, length, access to char in string, etc.).

Storing many data elements of the same type requires structured data types – like arrays. Access in arrays is constant time and does not depend on the number of elements. Address calculation (row major and column major), Sorting techniques (bubble, selection, insertion). Structured data types can be defined by classes – String. Introduce the Java library String class and the basic operations on strings (accessing individual characters, various substring operations, concatenation, replacement, index of operations). The class String Buffer should be introduced for those applications that involve heavy manipulation of strings.

11. Recursion

Concept of recursion, simple recursive methods (e.g. factorial, GCD, binary search, conversion of representations of numbers between different bases).

Many problems can be solved very elegantly by observing that the solution can be composed of solutions to 'smaller' versions of the same problem with the base version having a known simple solution. Recursion can be initially motivated by using recursive equations to define certain methods. These definitions are fairly obvious and are easy to understand. The definitions can be directly converted to a program. Emphasize that any recursion must have a base case. Otherwise, the computation can go into an infinite loop.

The tower of Hanoi is a very good example of how recursion gives a very simple and elegant solution where as non-recursive solutions are quite complex.

SECTION C

Inheritance, Interface, Polymorphism, Data structures, Computational Complexity

12. Inheritance, Interfaces and Polymorphism

(a) Inheritance; super and derived classes; member access in derived classes; redefinition of variables and methods in subclasses; abstract classes; class Object; protected visibility. Subclass polymorphism and dynamic binding.

Emphasize inheritance as a mechanism to reuse a class by extending it. Inheritance should not normally be used just to reuse some methods defined in a class but only when there is a genuine specialization (or subclass) relationship between objects of the super class and that of the derived class.

(b) Interfaces in Java; implementing interfaces through a class; interfaces for user defined implementation of behaviour.

Motivation for interface: often when creating reusable classes some parts of the exact implementation can only be provided by the final end user. For example, in a class that sorts records of different types the exact comparison operation can only be provided by the end user. Since only he/she knows which field(s) will be used for doing the comparison and whether sorting should be in ascending or descending order be given by the user of the class.

Emphasize the difference between the Java language construct interface and the word interface often used to describe the set of method prototypes of a class.

13. Data structures

(a) Basic data structures (stack, queue, circular queue, dequeue); implementation directly through classes; definition through an interface and multiple implementations by implementing the interface. Conversion of Infix to Prefix and Postfix notations.

Basic algorithms and programs using the above data structures.

Data structures should be defined as abstract data types with a well-defined interface (it is instructive to define them using the Java interface construct).

(b) Single linked list (Algorithm and programming), binary trees, tree traversals (Conceptual).

The following should be covered for each data structure:

Linked List (single): insertion, deletion, reversal, extracting an element or a sublist, checking emptiness.

Binary trees: apart from the definition the following concepts should be covered: root, internal nodes, external nodes (leaves), height (tree, node), depth (tree, node), level, size, degree, siblings, sub tree, completeness, balancing, traversals (pre, post and in-order).

14. Complexity and Big O Notation

Concrete computational complexity; concept of input size; estimating complexity in terms of methods; importance of dominant term; constants, best, average and worst case.

Big O notation for computational complexity; analysis of complexity of example algorithms using the big O notation (e.g. Various searching and sorting algorithms, algorithm for solution of linear equations etc.).

Analysis of Pupil Performance
ISC Computer Science

TOPICS FOUND DIFFICULT / CONFUSING BY STUDENTS

- Passing objects to functions
- Circular queue operations for push() and pop() operations
- Interfaces and its implementation using inheritance
- Degree of a node in a binary tree
- Properties of zero
- Dual and Compliment of a Boolean expression
- Infix to prefix notation
- Output using recursion
- Circular queue
- Concept of inheritance with interface and super class
- Degree of a node in a Binary tree
- Properties of zero in Boolean algebra
- Conversion from infix notation to prefix notation
- Best case and worst case for bubble sort
- Output using recursive function
- K-MAPS (grouping, redundant groups, map-rolling, place value)
- Drawing XOR gate using NOR gate
- Recursive technique

SUGGESTIONS FOR STUDENTS

- Apart from Textbook learning, surfing the net (Wikipedia, School net, etc.) and other reliable resources would be helpful to gather knowledge on the latest concepts and enhancements in programming. Proper definitions, output programs, algorithms, etc. can be downloaded directly from the internet.
- Prepare a summary for each chapter or use high lighters to highlight the important terms and definitions.
- Revise of the entire syllabus thoroughly.
- Relate everything taught in class with Real Life Environment examples which helps in remembering / recall of the concepts learnt.
- Practical work on the computer is necessary on regular basis to understand the syntax and to correct errors.
- Answers and definitions should be short and precise and according to the marks allocated.
- Solve ISC previous years' question papers.
- Underline/ Highlight Important words and terms.
- Show working at the side of each question, wherever required.
- Mention laws while reducing a Boolean Expression. Practice one form of K-Map with proper place value for both SOP and POS.
- In programming documentation is compulsory and should be mentioned with each program.
- Declare the class with data members and member functions.
- Expand or define each function according to the instructions given by the side of each function.
- Do not memorise the program, try to understand the logic.
- Practice constructors with every program. Treat each function of a class as a separate program.
- Do your preparations section-wise following the scope of the syllabus.

01 Propositional Logic

TREND ANALYSIS 4 YEARS

Propositional Logic

Average No. of Questions Across all Sets

Types of Questions	2024	2023	2020	2019
1 Mark	1	2	1	1
2 Marks	–	–	–	1
3 Marks	1	–	1	–
5 Marks	–	–	–	–
10 Marks	–	–	–	–

Logic

Logic is concerned with methods of reasoning. In other words, a logic is a trick or an analytical solution to solve a problem, generated by mental sharpness.

Besides the importance of logic in understanding mathematical reasoning, logic has numerous applications in computer science. Logic is used in the designing of computer circuits, in the construction of computer programs and in many other ways.

Propositional Logic

The propositional logic represents logic through propositions and logical connectives. A proposition is a declarative sentence that is either True or False but not both. Propositions are also called **sentences** or **statements**.

Consider the following examples:

1. Ottawa is the capital of Canada.
   (It is proposition, as it is True)
2. India is a continent.
   (It is proposition, as it is False)
3. What did you eat?
   (It is not proposition, as it does not result in True or False and also it is not a declarative sentence.)

In propositional logic, there are two types of propositions:

1. **Simple or Atomic Proposition** An atomic proposition (sentence) is the one whose truth or falsity does not depend on truth or falsity of any other proposition.
   In other words, a proposition consists a single propositional variable, i.e. they cannot be further subdivided is called atomic proposition, e.g. 5 is a prime number and it is a simple proposition.
2. **Compound or Composite Proposition** A proposition obtained from the combination of two or more propositions by means of connectives of two or more propositions or by negating a single proposition is called compound proposition. Compound propositions express logical relationships between simple sentences of which they are composed.
   Two or more simple propositions that forming the parts of compound proposition are called **components**. e.g. It is raining and wind is blowing., is a compound proposition.

Propositional Variables

Propositional variables (or statement variables) represent propositions as variables. These are used to denote numerical variables. The conventional letters used for propositional variables are p, q, r and s.

Connectives (or Operators)

A connective is a way of combining simple propositions into compound proposition and joins the compound propositions into larger compounds. In propositional logic, different types of connectives are used as follows

1. **Negation** (NOT) If p is any proposition, the negation of p, denoted by $\sim p$ or $\neg p$ or p' or $\overline{p}$ and read as not p. This proposition is false when p is true and proposition is true when p is false.

   e.g. p : Mumbai is in India.

   Then, the negation of p is

   $\neg p$: Mumbai is not in India.

Note Negation is not a connective because it effects only a single statement and does not join two or more statements. Hence, it is called an operator only.

2. **Conjunction** (AND) If p and q are two propositions, then conjunction of p and q is denoted by $(p \wedge q)$ or $(p \cdot q)$ and read as 'p and q'.

   The compound statement $p \wedge q$ is true when both p and q are true, otherwise it will be false.

3. **Disjunction** (OR) If p and q are two propositions, then disjunction of p and q is denoted by $(p \vee p)$ or $(p + q)$ and read as 'p or q'. The statement $p \vee q$ is always true if atleast one of p and q propositions is true, otherwise false.

4. **Conditional** (Implication) If p and q are two propositions, the compound proposition 'if p then q' denoted by $(p \Rightarrow q)$ or $(p \rightarrow q)$ or $(p \supset q)$ is called a conditional proposition. It means $p \Rightarrow q$ will be false, when p argument is true and q argument is false. For all other input combinations, it will be true.

5. **Bi-conditional** (Equivalence) If p and q are two statements, then the compound statement 'p if and only if q', denoted by $(p \Leftrightarrow q)$ or $(p \equiv q)$ is called a bi-conditional statement and the connective 'if and only if' is called the bi-conditional connective. It means either both arguments are true or both are false.

   e.g. If p represents 'This book is good' and q represents 'This book is cheap'.

   Here, some examples are given in symbolic form:

This book is good and cheap.	$(p \wedge q)$
This book is not good but cheap.	$((\neg p) \wedge q)$
This book is costly but good.	$((\neg q) \wedge p)$
This book is neither good nor cheap.	$(\neg p) \wedge (\neg q)$
This book is good or cheap.	$(p \vee q)$

Well Formed Formulae (WFF)

If a propositional variable is a symbol, representing any proposition, then a Well Formed Formulae can be defined recursively as follows:

1. If p is a propositional variable, then it is a wff.
2. If a is a wff, then $\neg a$ is a wff.
3. If α and β are wff, then $(\alpha \vee \beta)$, $(\alpha \wedge \beta)$, $(\alpha \rightarrow \beta)$, $(\alpha \leftrightarrow \beta)$ are wff.
4. A string of symbols is a wff, if and only if it is obtained by many applications of rules 1 to 3.

In simple terms, a formulae or Well Formed Formulae refers to simple proposition and compound proposition.

Truth Table

Truth tables are used to determine all the possible truth values regarding a propositional variable. Every simple or compound proposition may take value either True or False. These true values (denoted by 1) or false values (denoted by 0) are called **truth values**.

Earlier, we have introduced five important logical connectives: conjunctions, disjunctions, conditional, bi-directional and negation.

Now, with the help of truth table, we determine the truth values of these connectives as follow:

Truth Table for Connectives

p	q	$p \wedge q$	$p \vee q$	$\neg p$	$p \Rightarrow q$	$p \Leftrightarrow q$
0	0	0	0	1	1	1
0	1	0	1	1	1	0
1	0	0	1	0	0	0
1	1	1	1	0	1	1

Converse, Inverse and Contra Positive

Implications that can be formed from $p \Leftrightarrow q$

(i) The converse of $p \Leftrightarrow q$ is the implication $q \Leftrightarrow p$,

(ii) The inverse of $p \Leftrightarrow q$ is $\neg p \Rightarrow \neg q$,

(iii) The contra positive of $p \Rightarrow q$ is the implication $\neg q \Rightarrow \neg p$.

Consider the statement

p : it is raining

q : the home team wins.

The implication $p \Rightarrow q$ states that,
If it is raining then the home team wins.

The converse of this implication, namely $q \Rightarrow p$ states that,
If the home team wins then it must be raining.

The inverse of this implication, namely $\neg p \Rightarrow \neg q$ states that,

If it is not raining then home team does not win.

The contra positive of this implication, namely $\neg q \Rightarrow \neg p$ states that,

If the home team does not win then it is not raining.

Equivalence Laws of Proposition

In propositional logic, if any two propositions are joined up by the phrase 'if and only if', the result is a compound proposition called an **equivalence**. Two propositions forms are called equivalence if and only if, they have identical truth values for each possible propositions for their proposition variables.

Following are some equivalence laws used in propositional logic:

Equivalence	Illustrated
$(p \vee q) \Leftrightarrow (q \vee p)$ $(p \wedge q) \Leftrightarrow (q \wedge p)$	Commutative law
$[(p \vee q) \vee r] \Leftrightarrow [p \vee (q \vee r)]$ $[(p \wedge q) \wedge r] \Leftrightarrow [p \wedge (q \wedge r)]$	Associative law
$[p \wedge (q \vee r)] \Leftrightarrow [(p \wedge q) \vee (p \wedge r)]$ $[p \vee (q \wedge r)] \Leftrightarrow [(p \vee q) \wedge (p \vee r)]$	Distributive law
$\neg(p \vee q) \Leftrightarrow (\neg p \wedge \neg q)$ $\neg(p \wedge q) \Leftrightarrow (\neg p \vee \neg q)$	De-Morgan's law
$(p \vee p) \Leftrightarrow p$ $(p \wedge p) \Leftrightarrow p$	Idempotence law
$\neg\neg p \Leftrightarrow p$	Involution law
$p \vee (p \wedge q) \Leftrightarrow p$ $p \wedge (p \vee q) \Leftrightarrow p$	Absorption law
$p \wedge T = p$ $p \vee F = p$	Identity law
$p \vee T \Leftrightarrow T$ $p \wedge F \Leftrightarrow F$	Domination law
$p \vee \neg p \Leftrightarrow T$ $p \wedge \neg p \Leftrightarrow F$	Complementary law Excluded middle
$(p \Rightarrow q) = (\neg p \vee q)$	Implication
$p \leftrightarrow q = (p \rightarrow q) \wedge (q \rightarrow p)$ $p \leftrightarrow q = \neg p \leftrightarrow \neg q$	Bi-conditional

Chain Rule

In Boolean algebra, the chain rule is a fundamental property that allows you to simplify Boolean expressions by breaking them down into smaller, more manageable parts. The chain rule is closely related to the distributive law in Boolean algebra. The chain rule states that for any Boolean variables *A*, *B*, and *C*, the following holds true:

$$A \cdot (B + C) = (A \cdot B) + (A \cdot C)$$

However, in Boolean algebra, addition corresponds to logical OR (+) and multiplication corresponds to logical AND (·).

Here's a brief explanation of how the chain rule works:

1. Start with the expression $A \cdot (B + C)$.
2. Distribute the A across the terms inside the parentheses, using the distributive law.
3. You'll end up with $(A \cdot B) + (A \cdot C)$, which is the simplified form of the original expression.

Modus Pones

In Boolean algebra, "Modus Ponens" is a rule of inference used in deductive reasoning. It is also known as "implication elimination" or "conditional elimination." Modus Ponens is based on the logical implication (conditional statement) and asserts that if you have a statement of the form "If A, then B" (denoted as $A \rightarrow B$), and you know that A is true, then you can deduce that B is true. In Boolean algebra, where logical operations are represented by symbols, Modus Ponens can be explained in terms of logical expressions using the implication (→) and conjunction (·) operators. Let's say we have two Boolean variables A and B. Modus Ponens in Boolean algebra can be formulated as follows:

Given the expression $A \rightarrow B$ (if *A*, then *B*) and the fact that A is true, we can infer that B must also be true.

Symbolically:

$$A \rightarrow B, A \text{ entails } B$$

This rule reflects the logical notion that if the antecedent (the "if" part) of an implication is true, and the implication itself holds, then the consequent (the "then" part) must also be true.

Drawing Conclusion-Syllogism

An argument is a sequence of statements. All statements except the final one are called **premises**. The final statement is called **conclusion** and the logical process of drawing conclusions from given propositions is called **syllogism**.

The symbol '∴' read 'Therefore' is normally placed just before the conclusion.

An argument is said to be logically valid, if and only if the conjunction of its premises implies its conclusion, i.e. if all the premises are true, the conclusion also must be True.

There are two methods to draw conclusions that are as follows:

(i) Truth Table Method

To test an argument for validity using truth table method, follow the below mentioned steps:

***Step* 1** Identify the premises and conclusion of the argument.

***Step* 2** Construct a truth table showing the truth values of all premises and the conclusion.

***Step* 3** Find the rows in which all the premises are true.

***Step* 4** In each row (found in step 3), determine that conclusion of the argument is also true.

(a) If in each row, the conclusion is true, then the argument formed is **valid**.

(b) If there is atleast one such row in which conclusion is false, the argument formed is **invalid**.

e.g. Let us check $((p \Rightarrow q) \wedge (q \Rightarrow r)) \Rightarrow (p \Rightarrow r)$ is a valid argument or not.

Truth table for $((p \Rightarrow q) \wedge (q \Rightarrow r)) \Rightarrow (p \Rightarrow r)$ is as follows:

p	q	r	$p \Rightarrow q$	$q \Rightarrow r$	$(p \Rightarrow q) \wedge (q \Rightarrow r)$	$p \Rightarrow r$	$[(p \Rightarrow q) \wedge (q \Rightarrow r)] \Rightarrow (p \Rightarrow r)$
0	0	0	1	1	1	1	1
0	0	1	1	1	1	1	1
0	1	0	1	0	0	1	1
0	1	1	1	1	1	1	1
1	0	0	0	1	0	0	1
1	0	1	0	1	0	1	1
1	1	0	1	0	0	0	1
1	1	1	1	1	1	1	1

Since, in each case the conclusion is true, the argument is valid.

(ii) Algebraic Method

In this method, conditional elimination is carried out in order to draw conclusion from given premises. To test an argument for validity using algebraic method, do the following:

***Step* 1** In place of a conditional expression $(p \Rightarrow q)$, its equivalent expression $(\neg p \vee q)$ is substituted.

***Step* 2** Then, if the conjunction of the premises implying the conclusion, is a tautology then the argument is said to be valid, otherwise invalid.

e.g. from $p \Rightarrow q$ and $q \Rightarrow r$, infer $p \Rightarrow r$

where, $p \Rightarrow q$ and $q \Rightarrow r$ are premises

and $p \Rightarrow r$ is conclusion

Conditional expression is established

$[(p \Rightarrow q) \wedge (q \Rightarrow r)] \Rightarrow (p \Rightarrow r)$

$= [(\neg p \vee q) \wedge (\neg q \vee r)] \Rightarrow (\neg p \vee r)$ (conditional elimination)

$= \neg [(\neg p \vee q) \vee (\neg q \vee r)] \vee (\neg p \vee r)$

$= (\neg ((\neg p) \vee q)) \vee (\neg ((\neg q) \vee r)) \vee (\neg p \vee r)]$ (demorgan's law)

$= (\neg\neg p \wedge \neg q) \vee (\neg\neg q \wedge \neg r) \vee (\neg p \vee r)$ (demorgan's law)

$= (p \wedge \neg q) \vee (q \wedge \neg r) \vee (\neg p \vee r)$ (involution law)

$= \neg p \vee (p \wedge \neg q) \vee r \vee (q \wedge \neg r)$ (commutative law)

$= [(\neg p \vee p) \wedge (\neg p \vee \neg q)] \vee [(r \vee q) \wedge (r \vee \neg r)]$ (distributive law)

$\{\because (\neg p \vee p) = T \text{ or } (r \vee \neg r) = T\}$

$= [T \wedge (\neg p \vee \neg q] \vee [(r \vee q) \wedge T]$ (negation law)

$= (\neg p \vee \neg q) \vee (r \vee q)$ (identity law)

$= \neg p \vee r \vee (\neg q \vee q)$

$\{\because (\neg q \vee q) = T\}$ (negation law)

$= \neg p \vee (r \vee T)$ $(\because r \vee T = T)$

$= \neg p \vee T$ $(\because p \vee T = T)$

$= T$ (domination law)

Hence, argument is valid.

Some Related Terms

Some terms are given related to the compound propositions depending upon their truth or falsity.

Tautology A compound propositions that is always true is called a tautology.

Contradiction A compound proposition that is always false is called a contradiction.

e.g. **Truth Table**

p	$\neg p$	Tautology $p \vee \neg p$	Contradiction $p \wedge \neg p$
0	1	1	0
1	0	1	0

Contingency A compound proposition that is neither a tautology nor a contradiction is called a contingency.

Satisfiable A compound proposition is satisfiable, if there is an assignment of truth values to its variables that satisfies it. When a compound proposition is either tautology or contingency then it is called satisfiable.

Unsatisfiable When the compound proposition is false for all assignments of truth values, the compound proposition is known as unsatisfiable. When a compound proposition is a contradiction then it is called unsatisfiable.

PYQs Previous Years Questions

1 Mark Questions

1. **Assertion** For proposition $\sim A \Rightarrow B$, its contrapositive is $B \Rightarrow \sim A$

   Reason Contrapositive is the converse of inverse for any proposition. **ISC 2024**

   (a) Both Assertion and Reason are true, and Reason is the correct explanation for the Assertion.
   (b) Both Assertion and Reason are true, but Reason is not the correct explanation for the Assertion.
   (c) Assertion is true bu Reason is false
   (d) Assertion is false but Reason is true

Ans (d) Assertion is false but Reason is true

2. If $(\sim p \Rightarrow \sim q)$, then its contra positive will be **ISC 2023**

   (a) $p \Rightarrow q$ (b) $q \Rightarrow p$
   (c) $\sim q \Rightarrow p$ (d) $\sim p \Rightarrow q$

Ans (b) $q \Rightarrow p$

3. Verify if $(A + A')'$ is a tautology, contradiction or a contingency. **ISC 2023**

Ans

A	A'	$A + A'$	$(A + A')'$
0	1	1	0
1	0	1	0

From the above truth table, we can clearly see that all the values of last column are 0's. Hence, the given expression is a contradiction.

4. If $(x \Rightarrow \sim y)$, then its inverse will be **ISC SQP 2023**

   (a) $x \Rightarrow y$ (b) $y \Rightarrow x$
   (c) $\sim y \Rightarrow x$ (d) $\sim x \Rightarrow y$

Ans (d) $\sim x \Rightarrow y$

5. The propositional operator ^ represents **ISC 2022 (Sem I)**

   (a) Negation (b) Implication
   (c) Conjunction (d) Disjunction

Ans (c) Conjunction

6. Given the proposition $A \Rightarrow \sim B$, find the inverse of the proposition. **ISC 2022 (Sem I)**

   (a) $\sim A \Rightarrow B$
   (b) $B \Rightarrow \sim A$
   (c) $\sim A \Rightarrow \sim B$
   (d) $\sim B \Rightarrow A$

Ans (a) $\sim A \Rightarrow B$

7. Given the proposition $A \Rightarrow \sim B$, find the contra positive of the proposition. **ISC 2022 (Sem I)**

   (a) $\sim A \Rightarrow B$ (b) $B \Rightarrow \sim A$
   (c) $\sim B \Rightarrow A$ (d) $\sim A \Rightarrow \sim B$

Ans (b) $B \Rightarrow \sim A$

8. The proposition $(P \Rightarrow \sim Q) \vee (\sim P \Rightarrow Q)$ is a **ISC 2022 (Sem I)**

   (a) Contradiction (b) Tautology
   (c) Implication (d) Contingency

Ans (b) Tautology

9. The propositional operator $\Rightarrow$ represents **ISC SQP 2022 (Sem I)**

   (a) Conjunction (b) Implication
   (c) Disjunction (d) Negation

Ans (b) Implication

10. The proposition $(a \Leftrightarrow b)$ is represented by **ISC SQP 2022 (Sem I)**

    (a) $a'b' + ab$ (b) $(a' + b')\cdot(a + b)$
    (c) $(a + b)'$ (d) $(a \cdot b)'$

Ans (a) $a'b' + ab$

11. State whether the following proposition is a tautology, contradiction or contingency

$$F = (P \Rightarrow Q) \vee (Q \Rightarrow \sim P)$$ **ISC 2020**

Ans Given, $F = (P \Rightarrow Q) \vee (Q \Rightarrow \sim P)$

P	Q	$\sim P$	$P \Rightarrow Q$	$Q \Rightarrow \sim P$	$(P \Rightarrow Q) \vee (Q \Rightarrow \sim P)$
0	0	1	1	1	1
0	1	1	1	1	1
1	0	0	0	1	1
1	1	0	1	0	1

From the above truth table, we can clearly see that all the values of last column are 1's. Hence, the given expression is a tautology.

Common Mistake Some students think that $\vee$ is a conjunction and give the value of 0 and 1 is 0. While $\wedge$ is a disjunction and give the value of 0 and 1 is 1.

12. Draw the truth table to prove the proportional logic expression. **ISC SQP 2020**

$$(X \Rightarrow Y) \wedge (Y \Rightarrow X) = X \Leftrightarrow Y$$

Ans Here, we have two input variables, i.e. X and Y and take expression as

LHS = $(X \Rightarrow Y) \wedge (Y \Rightarrow X)$
RHS = $(X \Leftrightarrow Y)$

X	Y	$X \Rightarrow Y$	$Y \Rightarrow X$	$(X \Rightarrow Y) \wedge (Y \Rightarrow X)$	$X \Leftrightarrow Y$
0	0	1	1	1	1
0	1	1	0	0	0
1	0	0	1	0	0
1	1	1	1	1	1

$\therefore$ LHS = RHS

13. If A = "It is cloudy" and B = "It is raining", then write the proposition for
(i) Contra positive
(ii) Converse **ISC 2019**

Ans A = "It is cloudy"
B = "It is raining"
(i) **Contra positive** of $A \Rightarrow B$ is the implication
$\neg B \Rightarrow \neg A$
(ii) **Converse** of $A \Leftrightarrow B$ is the implication $B \Leftrightarrow A$

14. Verify the following proposition with the help of a truth table. **ISC 2018**

$$(P \wedge Q) \vee (P \wedge \sim Q) = P$$

Ans Here, we have two input variables, i.e. P and Q and take expression as
LHS = $(P \wedge Q) \vee (P \wedge \sim Q)$
RHS = P
Now, the truth table

P	Q	$\sim Q$	$(P \wedge Q)$	$(P \wedge \sim Q)$	$(P \wedge Q) \vee (P \wedge \sim Q)$
0	0	1	0	0	0
0	1	0	0	0	0
1	0	1	0	1	1
1	1	0	1	0	1
RHS					LHS

$\therefore$ LHS = RHS **Hence Proved**

15. State the law represented by the following proposition and prove it with the help of a truth table. **ISC 2017**

$$P \vee P = P$$

Ans $P \vee P = P$ proposition represents the idempotence law.
Truth table for $P \vee P = P$

P	P	$P = P \vee P$
0	0	0
1	1	1

$\therefore$ LHS = RHS **Hence Proved**

16. If $(\sim P \Rightarrow Q)$, then write its **ISC 2017**
(i) Inverse
(ii) Converse

Ans (i) To form the inverse of the statement, take the negation of both the antecedent and the consequent.
Given, $\sim P \Rightarrow Q$
Here, P is a antecedent and Q is a consequent
Hence, inverse would be $\sim(\sim P) \Rightarrow \sim Q$
$\therefore$ $P \Rightarrow \sim Q$
(ii) To form the converse of the statement, interchange the antecedent to consequent.
Hence, converse would be
$Q \Rightarrow \sim P$

17. Show that $X \vee \sim (Y \wedge X)$ is a tautology. **ISC 2016**

Ans Truth table for the given expression:

X	Y	$Y \wedge X$	$\sim(Y \wedge X)$	$X \vee \sim(Y \wedge X)$
0	0	0	1	1
0	1	0	1	1
1	0	0	1	1
1	1	1	0	1

From the above truth table, we can clearly see that all the values of last column are 1's. Hence, the given expression is a tautology.

2 Marks Questions

1. With reference to the given proposition $\sim P \Rightarrow Q$, answer the following questions (i) and (ii). **ISC SQP 2022 (Sem I)**
(i) The converse of the proposition is
(a) $\sim Q \Rightarrow P$ (b) $Q \Rightarrow \sim P$
(c) $\sim Q \Rightarrow \sim P$ (d) $\sim P \Rightarrow \sim Q$
(ii) The contra-positive of the proposition is
(a) $\sim P \Rightarrow Q$ (b) $Q \Rightarrow P$
(c) $\sim Q \Rightarrow P$ (d) $\sim P \Rightarrow \sim Q$

Ans (i) (b) $Q \Rightarrow \sim P$ (ii) (c) $\sim Q \Rightarrow P$

2. The proposition $\sim (a \wedge b) \vee (\sim a \Rightarrow b)$ is a **ISC SQP 2022 (Sem I)**
(a) contradiction (b) contingency
(c) tautology (d) implication

Ans (c) Truth table for $\sim (a \wedge b) \vee (\sim a \Rightarrow b)$ is

a	b	$\sim a$	$a \wedge b$	$\sim(a \wedge b)$	$(\sim a \Rightarrow b)$	$\sim(a \wedge b) \vee (\sim a \Rightarrow b)$
0	0	1	0	1	0	1
0	1	1	0	1	1	1
1	0	0	0	1	1	1
1	1	0	1	0	1	1

From the above truth table, we can clearly see that all the values of last column are 1's. Hence, the given expression is a tautology.

3. Using a truth table, state whether the following proposition is a tautology, contradiction or contingency. **ISC 2019**

$$\sim(P \Rightarrow Q) \Leftrightarrow (\sim P \vee Q)$$

Ans Given, $\sim(P \Rightarrow Q) \Leftrightarrow (\sim P \vee Q)$

P	Q	$\sim P$	$\sim P \vee Q$	$P \Rightarrow Q$	$\sim(P \Rightarrow Q)$	$\sim(P \Rightarrow Q) \Leftrightarrow (\sim P \vee Q)$
0	0	1	1	1	0	0
0	1	1	1	1	0	0
1	0	0	0	0	1	0
1	1	0	1	1	0	0

Column $\sim(P \Rightarrow Q) \Leftrightarrow (\sim P \vee Q)$ shows all zeroes, so it is contradiction.

4. State whether the following expression is a tautology, contradiction or a contingency with the help of a truth table. **ISC 2016**

$$(x \Rightarrow z) \vee \sim[(x \Rightarrow y) \wedge (y \Rightarrow z)]$$

KEY idea

Tautology is always true, Contradiction is always False and Contingency is neither tautology nor contradiction.

Ans Given, $(x \Rightarrow z) \vee \sim[(x \Rightarrow y) \wedge (y \Rightarrow z)]$

x	y	z	$x \Rightarrow z$	$x \Rightarrow y$	$y \Rightarrow z$	$[(x \Rightarrow y) \wedge (y \Rightarrow z)]$	$\sim[(x \Rightarrow y) \wedge (y \Rightarrow z)]$	$(x \Rightarrow z) \vee \sim [(x \Rightarrow y) \wedge (y \Rightarrow z)]$
0	0	0	1	1	1	1	0	1
0	0	1	1	1	1	1	0	1
0	1	0	1	1	0	0	1	1
0	1	1	1	1	1	1	0	1
1	0	0	0	0	1	0	1	1
1	0	1	1	0	1	0	1	1
1	1	0	0	1	0	0	1	1
1	1	1	1	1	1	1	0	1

From the above truth table, we can clearly see that all the values of last column are 1's. Hence, the given expression is a tautology.

5. Verify the following proposition with the help of a truth table. **ISC 2015**

$$P \vee (\sim P \wedge Q) = P \vee Q$$

KEY idea

Disjunction is denoted by $\vee$ and read as '*a* or *b*'. Conjunction is denoted by $\wedge$ and read as '*a* and *b*'.

Ans Given, $P \vee (\sim P \wedge Q) = P \vee Q$

P	Q	$\sim P$	$\sim P \wedge Q$	$P \vee (\sim P \wedge Q)$	$P \vee Q$
0	0	1	0	0	0
0	1	1	1	1	1
1	0	0	0	1	1
1	1	0	0	1	1
				LHS	RHS

$\therefore$ LHS = RHS **Hence Proved**

6. Write the truth table of 2-input proposition for conjunction and disjunction. ***ISC 2014***

Ans The truth table of 2-input proposition for conjunction $(A \wedge B)$ is represented as

Input		Output
A	**B**	**F**
0	0	0
0	1	0
1	0	0
1	1	1

The truth table of 2-input proposition for disjunction $(A \vee B)$ is represented as

Input		Output
A	**B**	**F**
0	0	0
0	1	1
1	0	1
1	1	1

7. Differentiate between a proposition and wff. ***ISC 2014***

Ans Differences between proposition and Well Formed Formulae (WFF) are as follows

Proposition	Well Formed Formulae
A proposition is a statement that has a truth value.	A well formed formulae would be any string composed of propositional variables and $\wedge, \vee, \Leftrightarrow, \Rightarrow$ or $\neg$.
A proposition is always true or false but not both.	Every propositional variable is a wff.

8. Using truth table, verify whether the following expression is true or false.

$$(p \Rightarrow q) = (q' \Rightarrow p')$$

ISC 2014, 2011

Ans In given expression, we have two input variables p and q. We consider as, LHS = $(p \Rightarrow q)$ and RHS = $(q' \Rightarrow p')$

p	q	$p \Rightarrow q$	p'	q'	$q' \Rightarrow p'$
0	0	1	1	1	1
0	1	1	1	0	1
1	0	0	0	1	0
1	1	1	0	0	1
		LHS			RHS

From the above truth table, we can see that LHS and RHS possess same truth values. So, it is verified that this expression is true.

9. Using the truth table, verify the expression $(\sim p \Rightarrow q) \wedge p = (p \wedge \sim q) \vee (p \wedge q)$ **ISC 2013**

Ans Here, we have two input variables, i.e. p and q and take expression as,

$$\text{LHS} = (\sim p \Rightarrow q) \wedge p \text{ and } \text{RHS} = (p \wedge \sim q) \vee (p \wedge q)$$

p	q	$\sim p$	$(\sim p \Rightarrow q)$	$(\sim p \Rightarrow q) \wedge p$	$\sim q$	$(p \wedge \sim q)$	$(p \wedge q)$	$(p \wedge \sim q) \vee (p \wedge q)$
0	0	1	0	0	1	0	0	0
0	1	1	1	0	0	0	0	0
1	0	0	1	1	1	1	0	1
1	1	0	1	1	0	0	1	1
				LHS				RHS

From the above truth table, we can see that LHS and RHS possess same truth values, therefore it is a verified expression.

10. If $(X \Rightarrow Y)$, then write its **ISC 2012**

(i) Converse

(ii) Contra positive

Ans In given expression, $(X \Rightarrow Y)$

(i) To determine the converse, we interchange the antecedent to consequent of a given expression.

if $(X \Rightarrow Y)$

Here, X is a antecedent, Y is a consequent

Hence, converse would be $(Y \Rightarrow X)$

(ii) To determine the contra positive, we derive this theorem on a given expression

i.e. $(p \Rightarrow q) = (\neg q \Rightarrow \neg p)$

On applying theorem, $(X \Rightarrow Y) = (\neg Y \Rightarrow \neg X)$

11. Verify it, $p.(\sim p + q') = (p \Rightarrow q)'$ using truth table. **ISC 2010**

Ans Here, we have two input variables, i.e. p and q. To satisfy this expression, take

$\text{LHS} = p.(\sim p + q')$

and $\text{RHS} = (p \Rightarrow q)'$

p	q	$\sim p$	q'	$(\sim p + q')$	$p.(\sim p + q')$	$p \Rightarrow q$	$(p \Rightarrow q)'$
0	0	1	1	1	0	1	0
0	1	1	0	1	0	1	0
1	0	0	1	1	1	0	1
1	1	0	0	0	0	1	0
					LHS		RHS

From the above truth table, we can see that both LHS and RHS possess same truth values. So, expression is verified.

Common Mistake Some students get confused that $\Rightarrow$ is an equivalence it means either both arguments are true or false. While $\Rightarrow$ is an implication, it means $p \Rightarrow q$ will be false when p is true and q is false, otherwise it will be true.

12. Draw the truth tables of the propositional logic expression $p \Rightarrow q$ and $p \Leftrightarrow q$. **ISC 2008**

Ans Here, we have two input variables, i.e. p and q.

(i) The truth table for $p \Rightarrow q$, i.e. implication between p and q.

p	q	$p \Rightarrow q$
0	0	1
0	1	1
1	0	0
1	1	1

(ii) The truth table for $p \Leftrightarrow q$, i.e. bi-directional between p and q.

p	q	$p \Leftrightarrow q$
0	0	1
0	1	0
1	0	0
1	1	1

13. Using the truth table, verify $p.q + p.q' = p$. **ISC 2007**

Ans Given expression is $p.q + p.q' = p$

Here, we have two input variables, i.e. p and q.

To satisfy the given expression, we take LHS = $p.q + p.q'$ and RHS = p.

Now, let us form the truth table,

p	q	$p.q$	q'	$p.q'$	$p.q + p.q'$
0	0	0	1	0	0
0	1	0	0	0	0
1	0	0	1	1	1
1	1	1	0	0	1
RHS					LHS

So, $p.q + p.q' = p$ **Hence Proved**

14. Using the truth table, prove that $(A + B)' + (A + B')' = A'$ **ISC 2006**

Ans Given expression, $(A + B)' + (A + B')' = A'$

Here, we have two input variables, i.e. A and B.

To satisfy this expression, we take LHS = $(A + B)' + (A + B')'$ and RHS = A'

Now, let us form the truth table,

A	B	$A + B$	$(A + B)'$	B'	$A + B'$	$(A + B')'$	$(A + B)' + (A + B')'$	A'
0	0	0	1	1	1	0	1	1
0	1	1	0	0	0	1	1	1
1	0	1	0	1	1	0	0	0
1	1	1	0	0	1	0	0	0
							LHS	RHS

From the above truth table, we can see that both LHS and RHS possess same truth values, therefore it is a verified expression.

15. Prove that $[(p'+q).(q'+r)]'+(p'+r)=1$ **ISC 2006**

Ans Here, we have three input variables, i.e. p, q and r. Now, let us form the truth table,

p	q	r	p'	q'	$p'+q$	$q'+r$	$(p'+q).(q'+r)$	$[(p'+q).(q'+r)]'$	$p'+r$	$[(p'+q).(q'+r)]'+(p'+r)$
0	0	0	1	1	1	1	1	0	1	1
0	0	1	1	1	1	1	1	0	1	1
0	1	0	1	0	1	0	0	1	1	1
0	1	1	1	0	1	1	1	0	1	1
1	0	0	0	1	0	1	0	1	0	1
1	0	1	0	1	0	1	0	1	1	1
1	1	0	0	0	1	0	0	1	0	1
1	1	1	0	0	1	1	1	0	1	1

From above truth table, last column has all 1's. Hence, it is proved.

3 Marks Questions

1. Verify if the following proposition is a Tautology, Contradiction or a Contingency, using a truth table **ISC 2024**

$$((A \Rightarrow B) \wedge (B \Rightarrow C)) \Rightarrow (A \Rightarrow C)$$

Ans

A	B	C	$A \Rightarrow B$	$B \Rightarrow C$	$(A \Rightarrow B)\wedge(B \Rightarrow C)$	$A \Rightarrow C$	$((A \Rightarrow B)\wedge(B \Rightarrow C)) \Rightarrow (A \Rightarrow C)$
T	T	T	T	T	T	T	T
T	T	F	T	F	F	F	T
T	F	T	F	T	F	T	T
T	F	F	F	T	F	F	T
F	T	T	T	T	T	T	T
F	T	F	T	F	F	T	T
F	F	T	T	T	T	T	T
F	F	F	T	T	T	T	T

Tautology, because all rows are true.

2. Verify if the following proposition is valid

$$(P \Rightarrow Q) \wedge (P \Rightarrow R) = P \Rightarrow (Q \wedge R)$$ **ISC SQP 2023**

Ans Here, we have three input variables, i.e. P, Q and R. Now, let us form the truth table.

P	Q	R	$P \Rightarrow Q$	$P \Rightarrow R$	$(P \Rightarrow Q) \wedge (P \Rightarrow R)$	$(Q \wedge R)$	$P \Rightarrow (Q \wedge R)$
0	0	0	1	1	1	0	1
0	0	1	1	1	1	0	1
0	1	0	1	1	1	0	1
0	1	1	1	1	1	1	1
1	0	0	0	0	0	0	0
1	0	1	0	1	0	0	0
1	1	0	1	0	0	0	0
1	1	1	1	1	1	1	1
					LHS		RHS

From the above truth table, we can see that LHS and RHS posses same truth values, therefore it is a verified expression.

3. Define proposition. How does tautology differ from contradiction? **ISC 2020**

Ans A proposition is a statement that has a truth value. It is always true or false but not both.
Difference between tautology and contradiction is

Tautology	Contradiction
A compound proposition that is always true.	A compound proposition that is always false.

4. Using the truth table, state whether the following proposition is a tautology, contingency or a contradiction **ISC 2018**

$$\sim(A \wedge B) \vee (\sim A \Rightarrow B)$$

Ans For the given expression, we have two input variables for truth table, i.e. *A* and *B*. Now, let us form the truth table,

A	B	$\sim A$	$(A \wedge B)$	$\sim(A \wedge B)$	$(\sim A \Rightarrow B)$	$\sim(A \wedge B) \vee (\sim A \Rightarrow B)$
0	0	1	0	1	0	1
0	1	1	0	1	1	1
1	0	0	0	1	1	1
1	1	0	1	0	1	1

From the above truth table, we can clearly see that all the values of last column are 1's. Hence, the given expression is a tautology.

5. Using a truth table, verify if the following proposition is valid or invalid.

$$(a \Rightarrow b) \wedge (b \Rightarrow c) = (a \Rightarrow c)$$ **ISC 2013**

Ans Here, we have three input variables, i.e. *a*, *b* and *c*.
To satisfy this expression, take LHS = $(a \Rightarrow b) \wedge (b \Rightarrow c)$ and RHS = $(a \Rightarrow c)$
Now, formed the truth table,

a	b	c	$a \Rightarrow b$	$b \Rightarrow c$	$(a \Rightarrow b) \wedge (b \Rightarrow c)$	$a \Rightarrow c$
0	0	0	1	1	1	1
0	0	1	1	1	1	1
0	1	0	1	0	0	1
0	1	1	1	1	1	1
1	0	0	0	1	0	0
1	0	1	0	1	0	1
1	1	0	1	0	0	0
1	1	1	1	1	1	1
					LHS	RHS

From the above truth table, we can see that $(a \Rightarrow b) \wedge (b \Rightarrow c)$ and $(a \Rightarrow c)$ do not possess same truth set value. So, it is proved that is invalid proposition.

6. Define the terms contingency, contradiction and tautology. **ISC 2012**

Ans **Contingency** A compound proposition that is neither a tautology nor a contradiction is called contingency.

Contradiction A compound proposition that is always false for all possible truth values of its variables is called a contradiction.

Tautology A compound proposition that is always true for all possible truth values of its variables is called tautology.

7. Verify if the following proposition is valid

$$(a \Rightarrow b) \wedge (a \Rightarrow c) = a \Rightarrow (b \wedge c)$$

ISC 2011

Ans From the given expression, we have three input variables, i.e. a, b and c. To satisfy this expression, take LHS = $(a \Rightarrow b) \wedge (a \Rightarrow c)$ and RHS = $a \Rightarrow (b \wedge c)$

Now formed the truth table,

a	b	c	$a \Rightarrow b$	$a \Rightarrow c$	$(a \Rightarrow b) \wedge (a \Rightarrow c)$	$(b \wedge c)$	$a \Rightarrow (b \wedge c)$
0	0	0	1	1	1	0	1
0	0	1	1	1	1	0	1
0	1	0	1	1	1	0	1
0	1	1	1	1	1	1	1
1	0	0	0	0	0	0	0
1	0	1	0	1	0	0	0
1	1	0	1	0	0	0	0
1	1	1	1	1	1	1	1
					LHS		RHS

From the above truth table, we can see that both LHS and RHS possess same truth values. So, it is a valid proposition.

Concept Enhancer To verify any proposition, first define the variables that will be used and solve whole expression by dividing into smaller expressions.

8. State whether the following expression is a tautology or contradiction with the help of truth table.

$$(X \Leftrightarrow Z).[(X \Rightarrow Y).(Y \Rightarrow Z)]$$

ISC 2010

Ans For the given expression, we have three inputs for truth table, i.e. X, Y and Z.

Truth table for given expression is

X	Y	Z	$X \Rightarrow Y$	$Y \Rightarrow Z$	$(X \Rightarrow Y).(Y \Rightarrow Z)$	$X \Leftrightarrow Z$	$(X \Leftrightarrow Z).[(X \Rightarrow Y).(Y \Rightarrow Z)]$
0	0	0	1	1	1	1	1
0	0	1	1	1	1	0	0
0	1	0	1	0	0	1	0
0	1	1	1	1	1	0	0
1	0	0	0	1	0	0	0
1	0	1	0	1	0	1	0
1	1	0	1	0	0	0	0
1	1	1	1	1	1	1	1

From the above truth table, we can clearly see that all the values of last column are neither all 1's nor 0's. Hence, the given expression is neither tautology nor contradiction.

CHAPTER TEST

1 Mark Questions

1 The proposition $\neg\neg p \Leftrightarrow p$ is represented by
(a) Distributive law (b) Associative law (c) Involution law (d) Commutative law

2 In propositional logic, how many types of proposition are there?
(a) 2 (b) 3 (c) 4 (d) 5

3 Let p be the statement 'You can take the flight' and let q be the statement 'You buy a ticket.' Then, find its contra positive.

2 Marks Questions

4 What are inverse of the implication that can be formed from $p \Leftrightarrow q$?

5 Construct the truth table of the compound proposition $(\neg p \Rightarrow q) \wedge (\neg p \vee q)$.

3 Marks Question

6 Write the negation of these propositions.
(a) Merry has an MP3 player.
(b) There is no pollution in New Jersey.

5 Marks Questions

7 Let p and q be the propositions 'The election is decided' and 'The votes have been counted', respectively. Express each of these compound propositions as an english sentence.
(a) $\neg p \wedge q$ (b) $\neg p \Leftrightarrow \neg q$ (c) $\neg q \Rightarrow \neg p$ (d) $\neg p \vee \neg q$
(e) $p \vee q$

8 Let p and q be the propositions
p : It is below freezing, q : It is snowing
Write these propositions using p and q and logical connectives (including negations)
(a) It is below freezing but not snowing.
(b) It is not below freezing and it is not snowing.
(c) If it is below freezing, then it is also snowing.
(d) Either it is below freezing or it is snowing, but it is not snowing if it is below freezing.

10 Marks Questions

9 What is propositional logic? Explain its types.

10 What is connectives? Also, explain its types.

02

Boolean Algebra

TREND ANALYSIS 4 YEARS

Average No. of Questions Across all Sets

	Types of Questions	2024	2023	2020	2019
Boolean Algebra	1 Mark	5	4	3	3
	2 Marks	2	1	2	1
	3 Marks	–	–	–	–
	5 Marks	3	1	1	1
	10 Marks	–	–	–	–

Algebra used for performing logical operations on binary variables is known as 'Boolean algebra'. It is the branch of mathematics that includes methods for manipulating logical variables and logical expressions or it was used to design the switching circuit of the computer that can do logical thinking very fast and very inexpensively. It provides the operations and the rules for working with the set {0, 1}. Here, we are introducing some terminology related to Boolean algebra.

Truth Functions or Logical Statements

The sentences which result either in true or false value called truth functions or logical statements.

Truth Table

It is a mathematical table, which is used to compute functional values of logical expressions.

Boolean Variable

It has only two values 0 and 1, where 0 stands for false value and 1 stands for true value. Boolean variables are also called **logical variables** or **binary valued variables** or **quantities**.

Logical Operation

A logical operation is an operation, which takes one or more logical values and produces another logical value. A logical operation that is done on a single logical value can deal with only two circumstances, i.e. True or False.

Before learning about these operations, you must know about compound logical functions and logical operators:

(i) **Logical Functions or Compound Statements** The logical statements or truth functions are combined with the help of logical operators like AND, OR and NOT to form a compound statement or logical function, e.g. I watch TV on Sunday or I go for swimming.

(ii) **Logical Operators** Boolean algebra has three logical operators, which are as follows:

(a) **AND Operator** This operator can have two or more inputs and one output. It performs an operation known as **logical multiplication**.

Expression for AND operator is:

$$F = X.Y$$

where, X and Y are the two inputs and F is an output of this operation.

Truth Table

X	Y	$F = X.Y$
0	0	0
0	1	0
1	0	0
1	1	1

(b) **OR Operator** This operator can have two or more inputs and one output. It performs an operation known as **logical addition**.

Expression for OR operator is: $F = X + Y$

where, X and Y are the two inputs and F is an output of this operation.

Truth Table

X	Y	$F = X + Y$
0	0	0
0	1	1
1	0	1
1	1	1

(c) **NOT Operator** It is also known as inverter. It performs the operation called **inversion** or **complementation,** where it changes 1 to 0 and 0 to 1. It has only one input and produces one output.

Expression for NOT operator is: $F = X'$

where, X is an input and F is an output of this operation.

Truth Table

X	$F = X'$
0	1
1	0

Basic Postulates of Boolean Algebra

- If one input of OR gate is always 0 and other input is X, then the output is always the value of X. i.e. $X + 0 = X$ or $0 + X = X$

  When, $X = 1$, $X + 0 = 1 + 0 = 1$

  $X = 0$, $X + 0 = 0 + 0 = 0$
- If one input of OR gate is always 1, then output is always 1. i.e. $X + 1 = 1$ or $1 + X = 1$

  When, $X = 0$, $X + 1 = 0 + 1 = 1$

  $X = 1$, $X + 1 = 1 + 1 = 1$
- If one input of AND gate is 0, then output is always 0.

  i.e. $X.0 = 0$
- If one input of AND gate is variable X and other input is 1, then the output is always the value of X

  $\therefore$ $X.1 = X$

  if $X = 0$, then $X.1 = 0.1 = 0 = X$

  if $X = 1$, then $X.1 = 1.1 = 1 = X$

Laws of Boolean Algebra

These are used to simplify the various complex problems of boolean expression. The laws of boolean algebra are

1. **Properties of 0 and 1** It states that
   (i) $A + 1 = 1$
   (ii) $A.0 = 0$
2. **Idempotence Law** It states that
   (i) $X + X = X$
   (ii) $X.X = X$
3. **Involution Law** It states that if a variable is complemented twice, the result is the variable itself, i.e. $\overline{\overline{X}} = X$
4. **Absorption Law** It states that
   (i) $X + X.Y = X$
   (ii) $X.(X + Y) = X$
5. **Commutative Law** It is the property (or law) associated with binary operations and functions. The commutative law is used for addition and multiplication of variables.
   It states that:
   (i) $X + Y = Y + X$
   (ii) $X.Y = Y.X$
6. **Associative Law** This property is used to perform the binary operation on three variables.
   It states that:
   (i) $X + (Y + Z) = (X + Y) + Z$
   (ii) $X.(Y.Z) = (X.Y).Z$
7. **Distributive Law** This law is used for expanding an equation containing OR and AND gates.
   It states that:
   (i) $X.(Y + Z) = X.Y + X.Z$
   (ii) $X + (Y.Z) = (X + Y).(X + Z)$
8. **Complementary Law** It states that:
   (i) $X + \overline{X} = 1$ (ii) $X.\overline{X} = 0$

De-Morgan's Theorem

Augustus De Morgan had certained the way to boolean algebra by discovering two important theorems. These are

(i) **The First De-Morgan's Theorem** "The complement of the sum of variables is equal to the product of the complements of individual variables, i.e. the complement of two or more OR variables is equivalent to the AND of the complements of the individual variables".

i.e. $(A+B+C+\ldots+F)'=A'.B'.C'\ldots F'$

e.g. $\overline{(X+Y)}=\overline{X}.\overline{Y}$

(ii) **The Second De-Morgan's Theorem** "The complement of the product of variables is equal to the sum of the complements of individual variables, i.e. the complement of two or more AND variables is equivalent to the OR of the complements of the individual variables", i.e.

$(A.B.C\ldots F)'=A'+B'+C'+\ldots+F'$

e.g. $\overline{X.Y}=\overline{X}+\overline{Y}$

Principle of Duality

The principle of duality states that a boolean relation can be derived by

(i) Changing every OR (+) by AND (.)

(ii) Changing every AND (.) by OR (+)

(iii) Changing every 0 by 1 and 1 by 0

e.g. $X+(X.Y)=X$

On applying the concept of duality, the expression would be: $X.(X+Y)=X$

Complement of a Boolean Function

Complement of a boolean function is the opposite nature of boolean function. If boolean function is X, then its complement is $\overline{X}$ or X'. In a boolean expression, the complement is obtained with the help of De-Morgan's theorem.

Boolean Expression and Standard Form

A boolean expression is an expression that results in a boolean value, i.e. either True or False. It is a logical expression that is used to compare boolean variables. It is also called **comparing expression, conditional expression** and **relational expression**.

In boolean expressions, a single variable or its complement is known as **literal**. In boolean expression, two important terms are used which are as follows

(i) **Minterms** A binary variable x can be represented in two different forms, normal form (x) or in its complement form (x'). Consider two variables x and y that are combined with an AND operation.

There are four possible combinations between them as $x'y'$, $x'y$, xy' and xy. These AND terms $x'y'$, $x'y$, xy' and xy are known as **minterms** or **standard form**.

(ii) **Maxterms** The variables are also combined to form a standard sum, when we take OR operation between the variables. These OR terms are known as **maxterms**.

Table of Minterms and Maxterms for Three Variables

			Maxterms (Π)		Minterms (Σ)	
x	y	z	Term	Designation	Term	Designation
0	0	0	$x+y+z$	M_0	$x'y'z'$	m_0
0	0	1	$x+y+z'$	M_1	$x'y'z$	m_1
0	1	0	$x+y'+z$	M_2	$x'yz'$	m_2
0	1	1	$x+y'+z'$	M_3	$x'yz$	m_3
1	0	0	$x'+y+z$	M_4	$xy'z'$	m_4
1	0	1	$x'+y+z'$	M_5	$xy'z$	m_5
1	1	0	$x'+y'+z$	M_6	xyz'	m_6
1	1	1	$x'+y'+z'$	M_7	xyz	m_7

Note
- Here, for maxterms, 0's are indicating normal form while 1's are indicating complementary form but for minterms, 1's are indicating normal form while 0's are indicating complementary form.
- Each maxterm is the complement of its corresponding minterm and *vice versa*.

Sum of Product (SOP)

It is a boolean expression in which product terms (AND terms) are connected by the OR operator. Each AND term contains one or more variables in complemented or nomral form.

e.g. $XY+XY'$

A SOP form can contain a term with a single variable form such as:

$$A+BCD+BC'D+CDE$$

A boolean function is in canonical SOP form, when each product term contain each of the literal.

Product of Sum (POS)

It is a boolean expression in which sum of terms (OR terms) are connected by the AND operator.

Each OR term contains one or more variables in complemented or normal form.

e.g. $(X+Y).(X'+Y')$

A POS can also contain a single variable form such as:

$$A(B+D+E)(C'+D)$$

A boolean function is an canonical POS form, when each sum term contains each of the literal.

Conversion from SOP Expression to Canonical SOP Expression

The following procedure is used to convert SOP expression into canonical SOP expression:

1. Check the missing variables in each term.
2. Perform AND operation with (e.g. $X+X'$) terms, which have missing variables.
3. Expand all terms and remove the duplicate terms such that $X+X=X$ or $X+X+X=X$
4. The produced SOP expression is the canonical SOP expression.

Conversion from POS Expression to Canonical POS Expression

The following procedure is used to convert POS expression into canonical POS expression:

1. Check the missing variables in each term.
2. Perform OR operation with (e.g. $X.X'$) missing variables.
3. Expand all terms and remove the duplicate terms such that $X.X=X$ or $X.X.X=X$.
4. The produced POS expression is the canonical POS expression.

Conversion from SOP Expression to Canonical POS Expression

The following procedure is used to convert the SOP expression into canonical POS expression

1. Check the given SOP expression is canonical SOP expression or not, if not then convert it into canonical SOP expression . If it is already in canonical SOP expression, then continue to step 2.
2. Use the duality theorem to convert SOP into canonical POS such that:
   (i) Change every OR sign (+) to AND sign (.).
   (ii) Change every AND sign (.) to OR sign (+).
   (iii) Change normal variable (A) into complement variable (A') and *vice versa*.
3. The produced expression is the canonical POS expression.

Conversion from POS Expression to Canonical SOP Expression

The following procedure is used to convert POS expression to canonical SOP expression:

1. Check the given POS expression is canonical POS expression or not, if not then convert it into canonical POS expression. If it is already in canonical POS expression, then continue step 2.
2. Use the duality theorem to convert POS expression into canonical SOP expression such that
   (i) Change every OR sign (+) to AND sign (.).
   (ii) Change every AND sign (.) to OR sign (+).
   (iii) Change normal variable (A) into complement variable (A') and *vice versa*.
3. The produced expression is the canonical SOP expression.

Differences between Cardinal Form and Canonical Form are as follows

	Cardinal Form	Canonical Form
1.	Cardinal form of a boolean expression in SOP $F(A, B, C) = \Sigma(1, 3, 5, 6, 7)$	Canonical form of a boolean expression in SOP $F(A, B, C) = A'B'C + A'BC + AB'C + ABC' + ABC$
2.	Cardinal form of a boolean expression in POS $F(A, B, C) = \Pi(0, 2, 4)$	Canonical form of a boolean expression in POS $F(A, B, C) = (A+B+C)(A+B'+C)(A'+B+C)$

Minimisation of Boolean Expression

The standard form of boolean expression is usually not a minimised expression. A minimised boolean expression means less number of boolean variables.

The following two methods used for the simplification of boolean expression are

1. Boolean algebra (Algebraic) method
2. Karnaugh map (K-map)

1. Boolean Algebra (Algebraic) Method

The algebraic method is used with the basic postulates and theorems to minimise boolean expression.

e.g. $x.(x+y)=x$

Take LHS,

$\Rightarrow \quad x.(x+y) = (x+0).(x+y)$ (by identity law)

$\Rightarrow \quad = x+0.y$ (by distributive law)

$\Rightarrow \quad = x+y.0$ (by commutative law)

$\Rightarrow \quad = x+0$ (by basic postulates)

$\Rightarrow \quad = x$ (by identity law)

So, LHS = RHS

2. Karnaugh Map (K-map)

K-map is a very popular technique used for the simplification of boolean expressions. It is drawn in the form of a diagram divided by rows and columns into squares and the number of square corresponds to a row number in the truth table.

K-map is composed of arrangement of cells each representing one particular combination of variables product form. For a total number of n variables, K-map consists of 2^n cells.

Two Variables K-Map

For two variables (A and B), K-map have $2^2 = 4$ cells. These are $A'B'$, $A'B$, AB' and AB, i.e. 00, 01, 10 and 11 respectively. The two variables K-map must have four cells as shown below

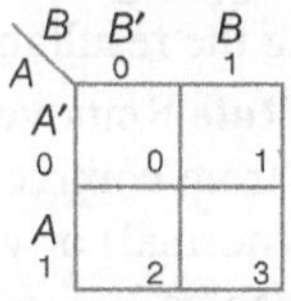

K-map is a graphical representation of a boolean function's truth table.

A	B	**Output** (F)
0	0	$A'B'$ or m_0
0	1	$A'B$ or m_1
1	0	AB' or m_2
1	1	AB or m_3

Two variables truth table

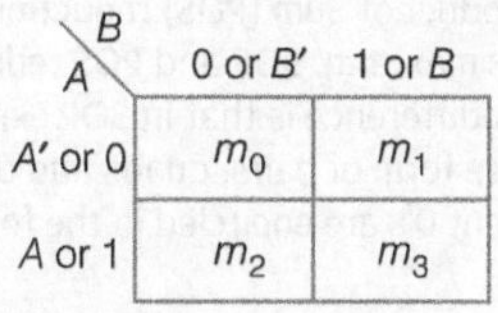

Three Variables K-Map

For three variables (A, B and C), K-map have $2^3 = 8$ cells. These are

$A'B'C'$, $A'B'C$, $A'BC$, $A'BC'$, $AB'C'$, $AB'C$, ABC and ABC'.

The three variables K-map represent in figure

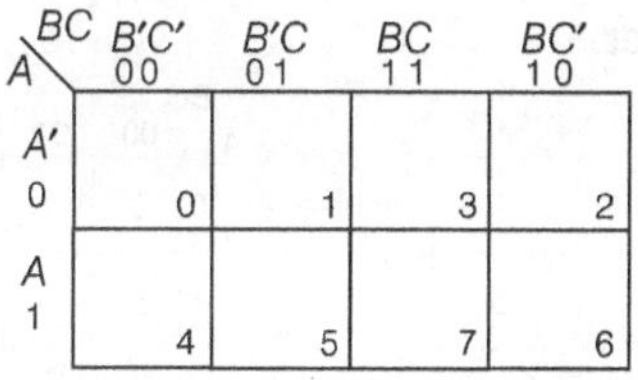

Four Variables K-Map

For four variables (A, B, C and D), K-map have $2^4 = 16$ cells. The four variables K-map with 16 cells as shown below

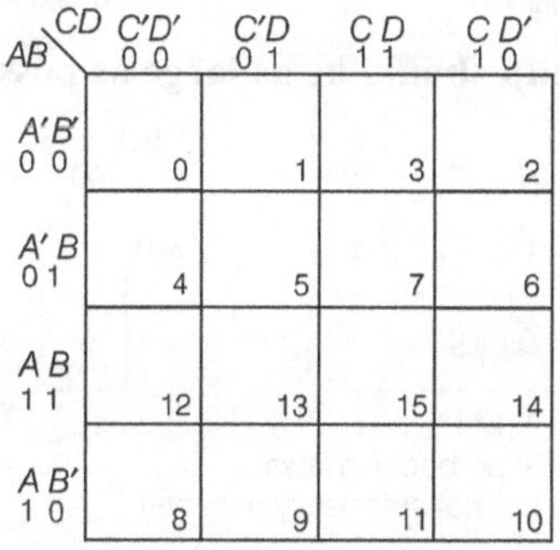

K-Map Simplification Rules

The K-map uses the following rules for the simplification of expressions by grouping together adjacent cells containing ones.

- **Groups may not include any cell containing a zero**

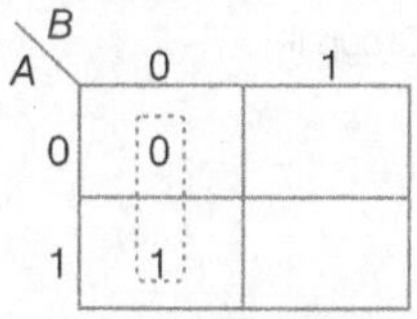

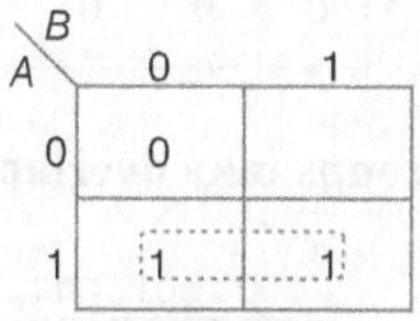

- **Groups may be horizontal or vertical, but not diagonal**

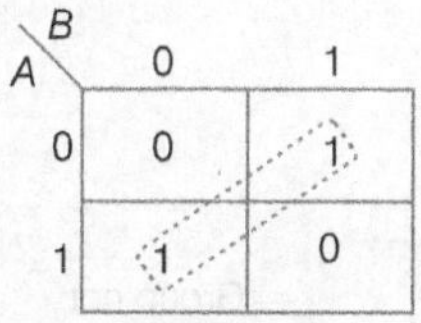

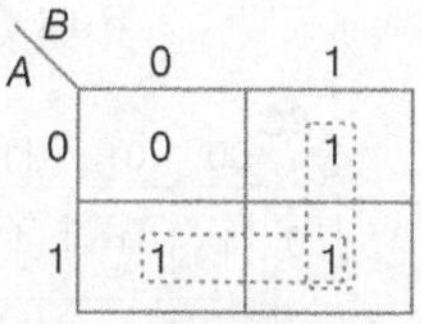

- Groups must contain 2, 4, 8 or in general 2^n cells. i.e. if n = 1, a group will contain two 1's since $2^1 = 2$, i.e. **pair**.
- If n = 2, a group will contain four 1's since $2^2 = 4$, i.e. **quad**.

- If $n = 3$, a group will contain eight 1's since $2^3 = 8$, i.e. **octet**.

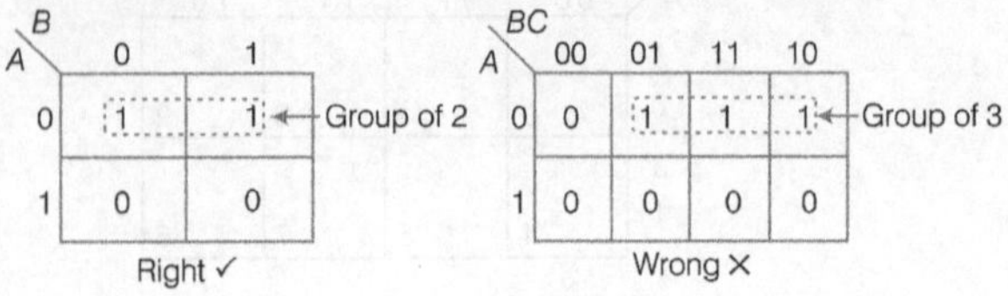

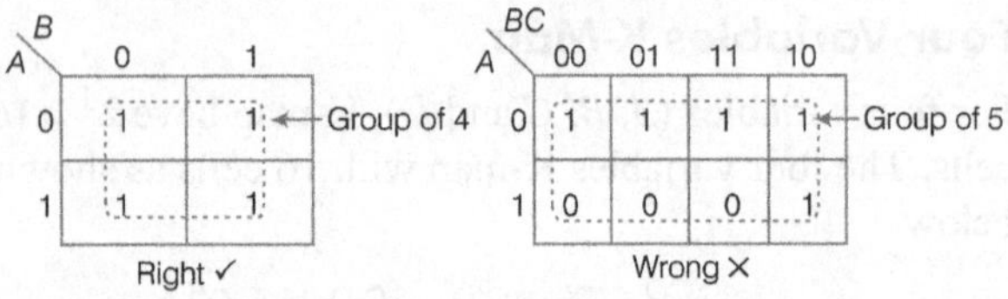

- **Each group should be as large as possible**

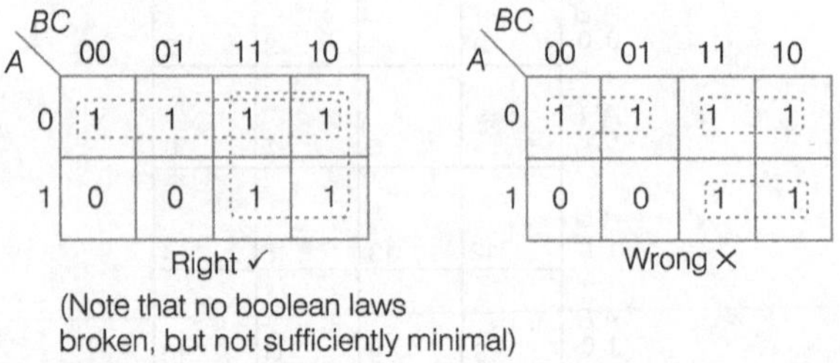

- **Each cell containing a one(1) must be in atleast one group**

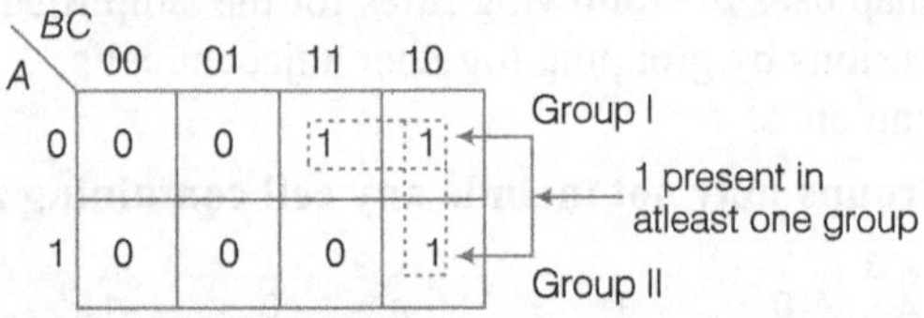

- **Groups may overlap**

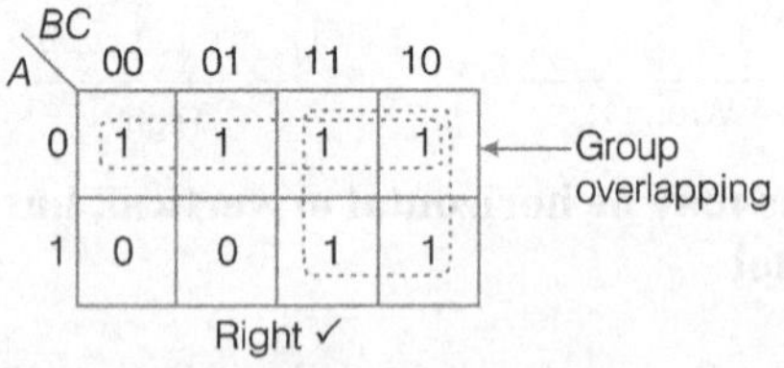

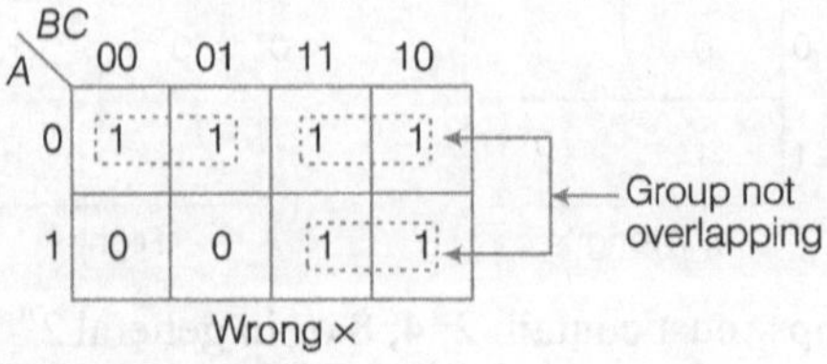

- **Groups may wrap around the table**
The leftmost cell in a row may be grouped with the rightmost cell and the top cell in a column may be grouped with the bottom cell.

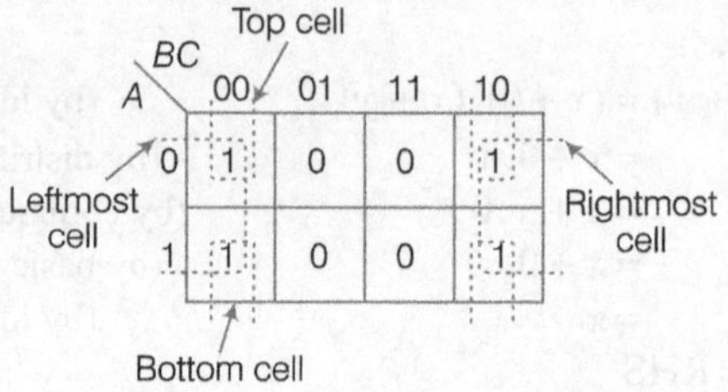

- **There should be as few groups as possible as long as this does not contradict any of the previous rules**

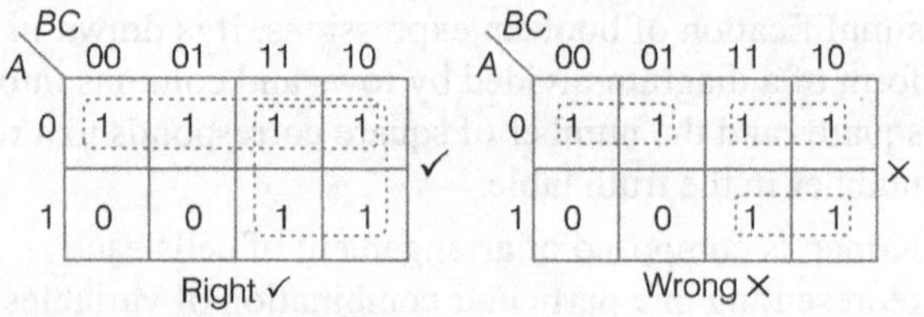

How to Reduce Boolean Expression in SOP form Using K-map

For reducing the expression, first we have to mark pairs, quads and octets.

While encircling groups of 1's, first search for octets and mark them, then for quads and mark them and lastly go for pairs. This is because a bigger group removes more variables thereby making the resultant expressions simpler.

- **Octet Reduction Rule** Removes the variables which change their state from complemented to uncomplemented (normal) or *vice versa*. An octet removes three variables.
- **Quad Reduction Rule** Removes the variables which change their states. A quad removes two variables.
- **Pair Reduction Rule** Removes the variables which change its state pair removes only one variable. Thus, reduced expression for entire K-map is sum of all the groups (i.e. pair, quad and octet).

Note Sum of Product (SOP) reduction each square of K-map represents a minterm while Product of Sum (POS) reduction each square of K-map represents maxterm. SOP and POS reduction follow same rules but the only difference is that in SOP expression adjacent 1's are encircled in the form of pairs, quads and octets and in POS expression adjacent 0's are encircled in the form of pairs, quads and octets.

Application of Boolean Algebra

Boolean algebra plays a vital role in computer science for designing logic circuits and simplifying circuits. In boolean algebra, the variable can take only two values, i.e. either True (1) or False (0) and hence it is compatible with binary arithmetic used in simplifying the designing of computer hardware.

PYQs Previous Years Questions

1 Mark Questions

1. According to the Principle of duality, the Boolean equation $(A + B') \cdot (A + 1) = A + B'$ will be equivalent to **ISC 2024**

(a) $(A' + B) \cdot (A' + 1) = A' + B$
(b) $(A \cdot B') + (A \cdot 0) = A \cdot B'$
(c) $(A' \cdot B) + (A' \cdot 1) = A' \cdot B$
(d) $(A' \cdot B) + (A' \cdot 0) = A' \cdot B$

Ans (b) $(A \cdot B') + (A \cdot 0) = A \cdot B'$

2. Idempotence law states that **ISC 2024**

(a) $X + X = X$ (b) $X + X' = 0$
(c) $X + X = 1$ (d) $X + X' = X$

Ans (a) $X + X = X$

3. The complement of the Boolean expression $(P' \cdot Q) + (R \cdot S')$ is **ISC 2024**

(a) $(P' + Q) \cdot (R' + S)$ (b) $(P + Q') \cdot (R' + S)$
(c) $(P' + Q) \cdot (R + S')$ (d) $(P + Q') \cdot (R + S')$

Ans (b) $(P + Q') \cdot (R' + S)$

4. Write the cardinal form of the maxterm $X + Y' + Z$. **ISC 2024**

Ans M_2

5. Write the canonical SOP expression for F (A, B) = A <=> B. **ISC 2024**

Ans $A' \cdot B' + A \cdot B$ (XNOR equivalent, that is either both or neither)

6. According to De Morgan's law $(a + b + c')'$ will be equal to **ISC 2023**

(a) $a' + b' + c'$ (b) $a' + b' + c$
(c) $a' \cdot b' \cdot c'$ (d) $a' \cdot b' \cdot c$

Ans (d) $a' \cdot b' \cdot c$

7. The dual of $(X' + 1) \cdot (Y' + 0) = Y'$ is **ISC 2023**

(a) $X \cdot 0 + Y \cdot 1 = Y$
(b) $X' \cdot 1 + Y' \cdot 0 = Y'$
(c) $X' \cdot 0 + Y' \cdot 1 = Y'$
(d) $(X' + 0) + (Y' + 1) = Y'$

Ans (c) $X' \cdot 0 + Y' \cdot 1 = Y'$

8. The reduced expression of the Boolean function $F(P, Q) = P' + PQ$ is **ISC 2023**

(a) $P' + Q$ (b) P
(c) P' (d) $P + Q$

Ans (a) $P' + Q$

9. Write the minterm of $F(A, B, C, D)$ when $A = 1, B = 0$ $, C = 0$ and $D = 1$. **ISC 2023**

Ans The minterm corresponding to the given values of the variables will be

$$AB'C'D$$

10. The law which states $a + (b \cdot c) = (a + b) \cdot (a + c)$ is **ISC SQP 2023**

(a) associative law (b) distributive law
(c) involution law (d) commutative law

Ans (b) distributive law

11. The dual of $(P + P') \cdot (Q + 0) = Q$ is **ISC SQP 2023**

(a) $P \cdot P' + Q \cdot 1 = Q$ (b) $P \cdot P' = Q \cdot 0 = Q$
(c) $P \cdot P + Q \cdot 1 = Q'$ (d) $P + P' + Q + 1 = Q$

Ans (a) $P \cdot P' + Q \cdot 1 = Q$

12. The complement of the Boolean expression $(P \cdot Q)' + R'$ is **ISC SQP 2023**

(a) $(P + Q) \cdot R$ (b) PQR
(c) $(P' + Q') \cdot R'$ (d) $(P' + Q') \cdot R$

Ans (b) PQR

13. Write the canonical sum of product form of the function $y(A, B) = A + B$. **ISC SQP 2023**

Ans
$$y(A, B) = A + B = A \cdot 1 + B \cdot 1$$
$$= A(B + B') + B(A + A') \quad [\because A + A' = 1]$$
$$= AB + AB' + BA + BA' \quad \text{[By distributive law]}$$
$$y(A, B) = AB + AB' + A'B$$

14. The Boolean equation which holds true for the Involution Law is **ISC 2022 (Sem I)**

(a) $A' + 1 = 1$ (b) $((A + B)')' = A + B$
(c) $(A + B)' = A' \cdot B'$ (d) $A \cdot (B + C) = (A + B) \cdot C$

Ans (b) $((A + B)')' = A + B$

15. The representation of the Boolean function $F(A, B) = p(1, 3)$ in canonical form is **ISC 2022 (Sem I)**

(a) $(A' + B) \cdot (A + B)$ (b) $S(0, 2)$
(c) $A'B + AB$ (d) $(A + B') \cdot (A' + B')$

Ans (d) $(A + B') \cdot (A' + B')$

16. If $P = 1, Q = 1, R = 0$ and $S = 1$, then the minterm will be **ISC 2022 (Sem I)**

(a) $P + Q + R' + S$ (b) $P'Q'RS'$
(c) $PQR'S$ (d) $P' + Q' + R + S'$

Ans (c) $PQR'S$

17. The dual of the Boolean equation $(X+Y)'+(X'\cdot Y')+1=1$ is **ISC 2022 (Sem I)**

(a) $(X\cdot Y)'\cdot(X'+Y')\cdot 0=0$
(b) $(X+Y)\cdot(X'\cdot Y')+1=1$
(b) $(X\cdot Y)\cdot(X+Y)\cdot 0=0$
(d) $(X\cdot Y)'\cdot(X'+Y')\cdot 1=1$

Ans (a) $(X\cdot Y)'\cdot(X'+Y')\cdot 0=0$

18. The group which eliminates the maximum variables in a Karnaugh's map is **ISC 2022 (Sem I)**

(a) Quad (b) Octet
(c) Pair (d) Redundant

Ans (b) Octet

19. The simplified expression for the Boolean expression $PQ\cdot(PQ+QR)$ is **ISC 2022 (Sem I)**

(a) P (b) 1
(c) PQ (d) QR

Ans (c) PQ

20. The Quad group in a Karnaugh's map eliminates **ISC SQP 2022 (Sem I)**

(a) One variable (b) Four variables
(c) Three variables (d) Two variables

Ans (d) Two variables

21. The compliment of the Boolean expression $F(P,Q,R)=(P+Q+R)$ is **ISC SQP 2022 (Sem I)**

(a) $P'Q'R'$ (b) $P'+Q'+R'$
(c) $P+(Q'+R')$ (d) $(P+Q)+R'$

Ans (a) $P'Q'R'$

22. The law which represents the Boolean equation $A+B=B+A$ is **ISC SQP 2022 (Sem I)**

(a) associative law (b) distributive law
(c) commutative law (d) absorption law

Ans (c) commutative law

23. The dual of the Boolean equation $(X+Y)\cdot 1=X+Y$ is **ISC SQP 2022 (Sem I)**

(a) $X+Y+0$ (b) $X\cdot Y+0=X\cdot Y$
(c) $(X\cdot Y)+1=X\cdot Y$ (d) $(X+Y)+0=X\cdot Y$

Ans (b) $X\cdot Y+0=X\cdot Y$

24. If $A=1, B=0, C=0$ and $D=1$, then the maxterm will be **ISC SQP 2022 (Sem I)**

(a) $AB'C'D$ (b) $A'BCD'$
(c) $A+B'+C'+D$ (d) $A'+B+C+D'$

Ans (d) $A'+B+C+D'$

25. State the properties of zero in Boolean algebra. **ISC 2020**

Ans Properties of zero in Boolean algebra are as follows

- If one input of OR gate is always 0 and other input is X, then the output is always the value of X.
  i.e. $X+0=X$ or $0+X=X$
- If one input of AND gate is 0, then output is always 0.
  i.e. $X.0=0$

26. Find the complement of the following Boolean expression using De-Morgan's law

$$F(P,Q,R)=P+(Q'.R)$$ **ISC 2020**

Ans Given expression is

$$F(P, Q, R) = P + (Q'.R)$$

Using De-Morgan's law,

$$F' = [P+(Q'.R)]' = P'.(Q'.R)'$$
$$= P'.((Q')'+R') = P'.(Q+R')$$

Common Mistake Students think that duality of principle is applied to find the complement of any Boolean expression. While, to find complement of any Boolean expression, De-Morgan's law is used.

27. Find the dual of

$$(A'+0).(B'+1)=A'$$ **ISC 2020**

Ans Take, LHS $=(A'+0).(B'+1)$

On applying principle of duality $=(A'.1)+(B'.0)$
$= A'+0 = A'$

Take, RHS $=A'$

On applying principle of duality $=A'$

$\therefore$ LHS = RHS

28. State Associative law and prove it with the help of a truth table. **ISC SQP 2020**

Ans Associative law is used to perform the binary operation on three variables. It states that

(i) $X+(Y+Z)=(X+Y)+Z$
(ii) $X\cdot(Y\cdot Z)=(X\cdot Y)\cdot Z$

Truth table for $X+(Y+Z)=(X+Y)+Z$

X	Y	Z	$Y+Z$	$X+Y$	$X+(Y+Z)$	$(X+Y)+Z$
0	0	0	0	0	0	0
0	0	1	1	0	1	1
0	1	0	1	1	1	1
0	1	1	1	1	1	1
1	0	0	0	1	1	1
1	0	1	1	1	1	1
1	1	0	1	1	1	1
1	1	1	1	1	1	1
					LHS	RHS

From the above truth table, we clearly see that LHS = RHS.

29. Find the dual for the Boolean equation

$$AB'+BC'+1=1$$ **ISC SQP 2020**

Ans Take, LHS = $AB' + BC' + 1$

On applying principle of duality

$$=(A+B')\cdot(B+C')\cdot 0=0$$

Take, RHS = 1

On applying principle of duality = 0

∴ LHS = RHS

30. Convert the Boolean expression $F(X,Y,Z)=X'Y'Z+X'YZ'+XYZ$ into its cardinal form. **ISC SQP 2020**

Ans Given, $F(X,Y,Z)=X'Y'Z+X'YZ'+XYZ$

$\Rightarrow$ 001 010 111

$\Rightarrow$ 1 2 7

So, cardinal form is $F(X,Y,Z)=\Sigma(1,2,7)$.

31. Minimize $F=XY+(XY)'+XY'Z$ using Boolean laws. **ISC SQP 2020**

Ans $F=XY+(XY)'+XY'Z$

$=XY+X'+Y'+XY'Z$

$=XY+X'(Y+Y')+Y'(X+X')+XY'Z$

$=XY+X'Y+X'Y'+XY'+X'Y'+XY'Z$

$=XY+X'Y+X'Y'+XY'+XY'Z$

$=XY+X'Y+X'Y'+XY'(1+Z)$

$=XY+X'Y+X'Y'+XY'$ $[\because 1+Z=1]$

$=Y(X+X')+Y'(X'+X)$

$=Y\cdot 1+Y'\cdot 1$ $[\because X+X'=1]$

$=Y+Y'=1$

32. Write the canonical POS expression of

$$F(P,Q)=\Pi(0,2)$$ **ISC 2019**

Ans Given expression is, $F(P,Q)=\Pi(0,2)$

Canonical POS expression = $(P+Q)(P'+Q)$

33. Find the dual of

$$X.Y+X.Y'=X+0$$ **ISC 2019**

Ans Given, $XY+X.Y'=X+0$

Take LHS $X.Y+X.Y'$

On applying duality, $=[X.Y+X.Y']'$

$=(X+Y).(X+Y')$

Now, again apply duality procedure = $(X.Y)+(X.Y')$

$=X(Y+Y')=X\cdot 1$

$=X+0=$ RHS

34. If $F(A,B,C)=A'B'C'+A'BC'$, then find F' using De-Morgan's law. **ISC 2019**

Ans Given, $F(A,B,C)=A'B'C'+A'BC'$

$F'=(A'B'C'+A'BC')'=(A'B'C')'(A'BC')'$

$=((A')'+(B')'+(C')')((A')'+B'+(C')')$

$=(A+B+C)(A+B'+C)$

35. State the Commutative law and prove it with the help of a truth table. **ISC 2018**

Ans **Commutative Law** is the property associated with binary operations and functions. It is used for addition and multiplication of variables.

It states that,

(i) $X+Y=Y+X$ (ii) $X.Y=Y.X$

Truth table for

(i) $X+Y=Y+X$

X	Y	$X+Y$	$Y+X$
0	0	0	0
0	1	1	1
1	0	1	1
1	1	1	1
		LHS	RHS

From the above truth table, it is verified that, LHS = RHS

36. Convert the following expression into its canonical POS form. **ISC 2018**

$$F(X,Y,Z)=(X+Y').(Y'+Z)$$

Ans Given expression is

$F(X,Y,Z)=(X+Y').(Y'+Z)$

$=(X+Y'+0).(0+Y'+Z)$

$=(X+Y'+ZZ').(XX'+Y'+Z)$

[by complement law]

$=(X+Y'+Z)(X+Y'+Z')(X+Y'+Z)(X'+Y'+Z)$ [by distributive law]

37. Find the dual of **ISC 2018**

$$(A'+B).(1+B')=A'+B$$

> **KEY idea**
>
> The principle of duality states that change every + by . and . by +.

Ans Take, LHS = $(A'+B).(1+B')$

On applying principle of duality

$=(A'.B)+(0.B')$

$=A'.B+0=A'.B$

Take RHS = $A'+B$

On applying principle of duality $=A'.B$

∴ LHS = RHS

38. If $F(A, B, C) = A'(BC' + B'C)$, then find F'. **ISC 2018**

Ans Given expression is,

$$F(A,B,C) = A'(BC' + B'C)$$
$$F'(A,B,C) = [A'(BC' + B'C)]'$$
$$= (A')' + (BC' + B'C)'$$
[by De-Morgan's law]
$$= A + (BC')'.(B'C)'$$
[by involution law]
$$= A + (B' + (C')')\cdot((B')' + C')$$
[by De-Morgan's law]
$$= A + (B' + C)(B + C')$$
[by involution law]
$$F'(A,B,C) = A + (B' + C)(B + C')$$

39. State the Principle of Duality. **ISC 2017**

Ans The principle of duality states that a boolean relation can be derived by

(i) Changing every OR (+) by AND (.)
(ii) Changing every AND (.) by OR (+)
(iii) Changing every 0 by 1 and 1 by 0

e.g. $X + (X.Y) = X$

On applying the concept of duality, the expression would be $X.(X + Y) = X$

40. Find the complement of the following Boolean expression using De-Morgan's law. **ISC 2017**

$$F(a,b,c) = (b' + c) + a$$

Ans Given expression is, $F(a, b, c) = (b' + c) + a$

The complement of F i.e. F'

$\Rightarrow F' = [(b' + c) + a]' = (b' + c)' . a'$
$= (b')' . c' . a' = b.c.'a'$
$F' = a' b c'$

41. State Involution law and prove it with the help of a truth table. **ISC 2016**

Ans The Involution law states that if a variable is complemented twice, the result is the variable itself $(A')' = A$

Truth Table

A	A′	(A′)′
0	1	0
1	0	1
RHS		LHS

LHS = RHS **Hence Proved**

42. Find the dual of **ISC 2016**

$$Y.X + X' + 1 = 1$$

Ans Take, LHS = $Y.X + X' + 1$

On applying principle of duality

$$= (Y + X).X'.0$$
$$= (Y + X).0 = 0 \qquad (\because X'.0 = 0)$$

Take, RHS = 1

Again, applying principle of duality = 0

$\therefore$ LHS = RHS

43. Write the maxterm and minterm, when the inputs are $A = 0, B = 1, C = 1$ and $D = 0$. **ISC 2016**

Ans The maxterm corresponding to the given values of the variables will be $= A + B' + C' + D$

The minterm corresponding to the given values of the variables will be $= A' B C D'$

2 Marks Questions

1. Find the complement of the following expression and reduce it by using Boolean laws. **ISC 2024**

$$P\cdot(P + Q)\cdot Q\cdot(Q + R')$$

Ans $[P\cdot(P+Q)\cdot Q\cdot(Q+R')]'$
$= [P\cdot(P+Q)]' + [Q\cdot(Q+R')]'$ since, $(A.B)' = A' + B'$
$= [P' + (P+Q)'] + [Q' + (Q+R')']$
$= P' + P'\cdot Q' + Q' + Q'\cdot(R')'$ since, $(A + B)' = A'.B'$
$= P' + P'\cdot Q' + Q' + Q'\cdot R$
$= P'(1 + Q') + Q'(1 + R)$, since $1 + A' = 1, 1 + A = 1$
$= P' + Q'$

2. Write the canonical form of the cardinal terms, m_3 and M_5 for F (A, B, C, D). **ISC 2024**

Ans $m_3 = A'B'CD$

$M_5 = (A + B' + C + D')$

3. Convert the following cardinal expression to its canonical form. **ISC 2023**

$$F(P,Q,R) = \pi(0, 1, 3, 4)$$

Ans Given expression is,

$$F(P,Q,R) = \pi(0, 1, 3, 4)$$

It is clear that, the function F is in POS form and contains four maxterm

i.e. $F(P,Q,R) = M_0 \cdot M_1 \cdot M_3 \cdot M_4$

To convert it into canonical form, we need to find the expression of the maxterm as

P	*Q*	*R*	Maxterm
0	0	0	M_0
0	0	1	M_1
0	1	0	M_2
0	1	1	M_3
1	0	0	M_4
1	0	1	M_5
1	1	0	M_6
1	1	1	M_7

From the above truth table,

$$F(P,Q,R) = M_0 \cdot M_1 \cdot M_3 \cdot M_4$$

$$F = (P+Q+R)\cdot(P+Q+R')\cdot(P+Q'+R')\cdot(P'+Q+R)$$

4. Simplify the following expression using Boolean laws

$$F = PQ + (P+Q)\cdot(P+PR) + Q$$ **ISC SQP 2023**

Ans Given,

$$F = PQ + (P+Q)\cdot(P+PR) + Q$$
$$= PQ + (P+Q)\cdot P(1+R) + Q$$
$$= PQ + (P+Q)\cdot P + Q \quad [\because 1+R=1]$$
$$= PQ + PP + PQ + Q$$
$$= PQ + PQ + P + Q$$
$$= PQ + P + Q \quad [\because A + A = A]$$
$$= P(Q+1) + Q$$
$$F = P + Q \quad [\because A + 1 = 1]$$

5. Write the maxterm and minterm for the function $F(A, B, C, D)$ when $A = 1$, $B = 1$, $C = 0$ and $D = 1$. **ISC SQP 2023**

Ans The maxterm corresponding to the given values of the variables will be $= A' + B' + C + D'$.

The minterm corresponding to the given values of the variables will be $= ABC'D$.

6. The reduced expression for the Boolean expression $F(X,Y,Z) = \Sigma(0, 1, 2, 3, 4, 5, 6, 7)$ is **ISC SQP 2022 (Sem I)**

(a) $XY' + X'Y$ (b) 1
(c) 0 (d) None of these

Ans (b)

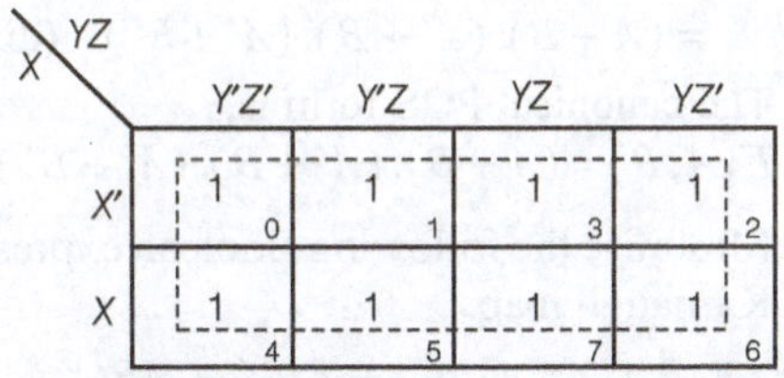

In a three variables K-map, octet means given expression will produce output 1, i.e. tautology. i.e. $F(X,Y,Z) = 1$

7. Convert the following expression to its cardinal SOP form

$$F(P, Q, R) = P'Q'R + P'QR + PQ'R' + PQR'$$ **ISC 2020**

Ans Given,

$$F(P, Q, R) = P'Q'R + P'QR + PQ'R' + PQR'$$

$\Rightarrow$ 001 011 100 110

$\Rightarrow$ 1 3 4 6

So, cardinal SOP form is

$$F(P, Q, R) = \Sigma(1, 3, 4, 6)$$

8. Simplify the following expression using Boolean laws

$$F = [(X'+Y).(Y'+Z)]' + (X'+Z)$$ **ISC 2020**

Ans $F = [(X'+Y).(Y'+Z)]' + (X'+Z)$

$$= [(X'+Y)' + (Y'+Z)'] + (X'+Z)$$
$$= [(X')'.Y' + (Y')'.Z'] + (X'+Z)$$
$$= [XY' + YZ'] + X' + Z$$
$$= XY' + YZ' + X' + Z$$

Concept Enhancer Laws of Boolean algebra are helpful to simplify the expression and the best solution is which mention name of law at each step.

9. Simplify the following expression using Boolean laws

$$(X+Z).(X.Y + Y.Z') + X.Z + Y$$ **ISC 2019**

Ans $F = (X+Z).(XY + YZ') + XZ + Y$

$$= (X+Z)Y(X+Z') + XZ + Y$$
$$= Y(X+Z)(X+Z') + XZ + Y$$
$$= XY(1+Z)(1+Z') + XZ + Y$$
$$= XY(1)(1) + XZ + Y$$
$$[\because (1+Z) = 1, (1+Z') = 1]$$
$$= XY + XZ + Y = XY + Y + XZ$$
$$= Y(X+1) + XZ = Y + XZ \quad [\because (X+1) = 1]$$

10. Simplify the following expression using Boolean laws **ISC 2018**

$$A.(A'+B).C.(A+B)$$

Ans Given expression $A.(A'+B).C.(A+B)$

$$= (AA' + AB).C.(A+B) \quad \text{[by distributive law]}$$
$$= (0 + AB).C.(A+B) \quad \text{[by complement law]}$$
$$= ABC(A+B)$$
$$= A.ABC + ABC.B \quad \text{[By distributive law]}$$
$$= ABC + ABC \quad \text{[by Idempotence law]}$$
$$= ABC \quad \text{[by Idempotence law]}$$

11. Convert the following Boolean expression into its canonical POS form **ISC 2017**

$$F(A, B, C) = (B+C').(A'+B)$$

Ans Given Boolean expression is

$$F(A,B,C) = (B+C').(A'+B)$$
$$= (A.A' + B + C').(A' + B + CC')$$
[by complement law]
$$= (A+B+C')(A'+B+C')(A'+B+C)(A'+B+C')$$
[by distributive law]
$$= (A+B+C')(A'+B+C')(A'+B+C)$$
[by idempotence law]

12. Define maxterms and minterms. Find the maxterm and minterm when **ISC 2017**

$$P=0, Q=1, R=1 \text{ and } S=0$$

Ans **Minterms** The variables are combined to form a standard product when we take AND operation between the variables. These AND terms are known as minterms.

Maxterms The variables are combined to form a standard sum when we take OR operation between the variables. These OR terms are known as maxterms.

When, $P=0, Q=1, R=1$ and $S=0$

Maxterm $P+Q'+R'+S$

Minterm $P'QRS'$

13. Differentiate between Canonical form and Cardinal form of expression. **ISC 2016**

Ans Refer to text on Page 18.

14. Simplify : $(A+C).(A+A.D)+A.C+C$ **ISC 2015**

Ans Given expression: $(A+C).(A+A.D)+A.C+C$

$=(A+C).A(1+D)+C(1+A)$ [by distributive law]

$=(A+C).A+C$ [by postulate law]

$=A.(A+C)+C$ [by distributive law]

$=A.A+A.C+C$ [by idempotence law]

$=A+A.C+C$

$=A+C(A+1)=A+C$

Common Mistake Some students get confused in laws of Boolean algebra. They used $A+1=A$ instead $A+1=1$. It is properties of 0 and 1 of which another law is $A.0=0$.

15. State De-Morgan's law and verify it using a truth table. **ISC 2015**

Ans According to De-Morgan's law, the complement of the product of two variables is equal to the sum of the complements of each variable.

e.g. $(A.B)'=A'+B'$

It is also state that, the complement of the sum of two variables is equal to the product of the complement of each variable.

e.g. $(A+B)'=A'.B'$

The truth table:

A	B	A'	B'	$A+B$	$A.B$	$(A+B)'$	$A'.B'$	$(A.B)'$	$A'+B'$
0	0	1	1	0	0	1	1	1	1
0	1	1	0	1	0	0	0	1	1
1	0	0	1	1	0	0	0	1	1
1	1	0	0	1	1	0	0	0	0

$(A.B)'=A'+B'$

$(A+B)'=A'.B'$ **Hence Proved**

16. Verify the following expression using Boolean laws. Also, mention the law used at each step of simplification. **ISC 2015**

$$X.Y.Z+X.Y'.Z+X.Y.Z'=X.(Y+Z)$$

Ans Given expression:

$$X.Y.Z+X.Y'.Z+X.Y.Z'=X.(Y+Z)$$

LHS $=X.Y.Z+X.Y'.Z+X.Y.Z'$

$=XZ(Y+Y')+X.Y.Z'$ [by distributive law]

$=XZ+X.Y.Z'$ [by complementary law]

$=X(Z+Y.Z')$ [by distributive law]

$=X((Z+Y)(Z+Z'))$ [by distributive law]

$=X(Z+Y)$ [by complementary law]

$=X(Y+Z)=$ RHS [by commutative law]

17. Convert the following expression into its canonical POS form

$F(A,B)=(A+B).A'$ **ISC 2014**

Ans Given expression is,

$$F(A,B)=(A+B).A'$$

As we know, in given expression there must be two maxterms but in one term a variable is missing like,

$$F(A,B)=\underbrace{(A+B)}_{\text{Maxterm}}.A'$$

Not maxterm (Missing B variable)

$F(A,B)=(A+B).(A'+(BB'))$

($\because BB'=0$, complementary law)

$=(A+B).(A'+B).(A'+B')$ (distributive law)

The canonical POS form is,

$F(A,B)=(A+B).(A'+B).(A'+B')$

18. Minimise the following Boolean expression using the Karnaugh map.

$F(A,B,C)=A'BC'+A'BC+ABC'+ABC$ **ISC 2014**

Ans Given expression is,

$$F(A,B,C)=A'BC'+A'BC+ABC'+ABC$$

Here, we have three inputs A, B and C. So, while draw the K-map we need $2^n=2^3=8$ squares.

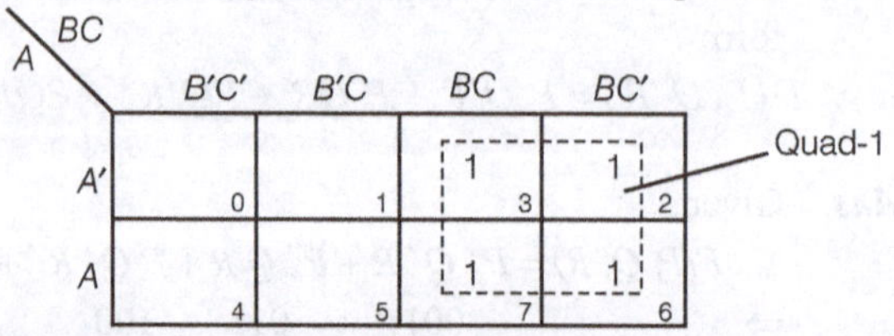

Quad-1 $=m_2+m_3+m_6+m_7=B$

So, minimised Boolean expression is

$$F(A,B,C)=B$$

19. Find the complement of $XY'Z + XY + YZ'$. **ISC 2014**

Ans Given expression, $F = XY'Z + XY + YZ'$

Complement of F is $F' = (XY'Z + XY + YZ')'$

$= (XY'Z)'.(XY)'.(YZ')'$

$= (X'+Y+Z').(X'+Y')(Y'+Z)$

20. State the principle of duality. Write the dual of $(P+Q').R.1 = PR + (Q'.R)$ **ISC 2013**

Ans Refer to text on page 24 Question 39 (1 Mark Questions).

Given expression, $(P+Q').R.1 = PR + (Q'.R)$

Take LHS, $(P+Q').R.1$

On applying duality $= (P.Q')+R+0$

$= P.Q'+R \quad (\because 0+R=R)$

Now, again apply duality procedure

$= (P+Q').R$

$= PR+Q'.R$

$=$ RHS

21. Minimise the expression using Boolean laws. **ISC 2013**

$$F = (A+B').(B+CD)'$$

Ans Given, $F = (A+B').(B+CD)'$

$F = (A+B').[B'.(CD)']$ (by De-Morgan's law)

$= (A+B').[B'.(C'+D')]$ (by De-Morgan's law)

$= (A+B').(B'C'+B'D')$ (by distributive law)

$= AB'C' + AB'D' + B'B'C' + B'B'D'$ (by distributive law)

$= AB'C' + AB'D' + B'C' + B'D'$ (by idempotence law)

$= AB'C' + B'.C' + AB'D' + B'D'$ (by commutative law)

$= B'C'(A+1) + B'D'(A+1)$ (by distributive law)

$= B'C' + B'D'$ (by property 1)

$F = B'(C'+D')$ (by distributive law)

22. Convert the following cardinal form of expression into its canonical form.

$F(P,Q,R) = \Pi(1, 3)$ **ISC 2013**

Ans Given expression is, $F(P,Q,R) = \Pi(1,3)$

It is clear that, the function F is in POS form and contains two maxterm,

i.e. $F(P,Q,R) = M_1 . M_3$

To convert it into canonical form, we need to find the expression of the maxterm as:

P	Q	R	Maxterm	Expression
0	0	0	M_0	$P+Q+R$
0	0	1	M_1	$P+Q+R'$
0	1	0	M_2	$P+Q'+R$
0	1	1	M_3	$P+Q'+R'$
1	0	0	M_4	$P'+Q+R$
1	0	1	M_5	$P'+Q+R'$
1	1	0	M_6	$P'+Q'+R$
1	1	1	M_7	$P'+Q'+R'$

From the above table, $F = M_1.M_3$

$F = (P+Q+R').(P+Q'+R')$

23. If $A=1$ and $B=0$, then find

(i) $(A'+1).B$

(ii) $(A+B')'$ **ISC 2013**

Ans (i) $(A'+1).B$

$\because$ Given, $A=1$ then $A'=0$

and $B=0$

$\Rightarrow (A'+1).B = (0+1).0 = 1.0 = 0$

(ii) $(A+B')'$

$\Rightarrow \because B=0,$

then $B'=1$

and $A=1$

$\Rightarrow (A+(B')')' = (1+1)' = (1)' = 0$

24. Using a truth table, verify the following expression

$x+(y+z) = (x+y)+z$

Also, state the law. **ISC 2012**

Ans Given expression is, $x+(y+z) = (x+y)+z$

Let's verify the given expression using truth table:

x	y	z	y + z	x + y	x + (y + z)	(x + y) + z
0	0	0	0	0	0	0
0	0	1	1	0	1	1
0	1	0	1	1	1	1
0	1	1	1	1	1	1
1	0	0	0	1	1	1
1	0	1	1	1	1	1
1	1	0	1	1	1	1
1	1	1	1	1	1	1
					LHS	RHS

From above truth table, it is verified that,

LHS = RHS

It is associative law.

25. Given $F(x, y, z) = (x' + y').(y + z')$

Write the function in canonical product of sum form. **ISC 2012**

Ans Given function is,

$$F(x, y, z) = (x' + y').(y + z')$$
$$= (x' + y' + 0).(0 + y + z')$$
$$= (x' + y' + zz').(xx' + y + z')$$
(by complement law)
$$F(x, y, z) = (x' + y' + z).(x' + y' + z')$$
$$.(x + y + z').(x' + y + z')$$
(by distributive law)

26. Find the complement of the following expression. **ISC 2012**

$$F = x' + xy'$$

> **KEY idea**
>
> Complement is obtained with the help of De-Morgan's theorem.

Ans Given expression is, $F = x' + xy'$

The complement of F, i.e. F'

$\Rightarrow$ $F' = [x' + xy']' = [x']' \cdot [xy']'$ (by De-Morgan's law)

$= x.[xy']'$ (by involution law)

$= x.[x' + (y')']$ (by De-Morgan's law)

$= x.[x' + y]$ (by involution law)

$= x.x' + xy = 0 + xy$

$F' = xy$ (by complement law, i.e. $x.x' = 0$)

27. State the two absorption laws. Verify any one of them using the truth table. **ISC 2011, 2006**

Ans Absorption law states that

(i) $x + xy = x$

(ii) $x(x + y) = x$ that

Now, let us proof $x + xy = x$ using truth table:

x	y	xy	$x + xy$
0	0	0	0
0	1	0	0
1	0	0	1
1	1	1	1
RHS			LHS

From the above truth table, it is verified that,

LHS = RHS

28. Reduce the following expression

$$F(A, B, C) = \Sigma(0, 1, 2, 3, 4, 5, 6, 7)$$

Also, find the complement of the reduced expression. **ISC 2011**

Ans Given expression is, $F(A, B, C) = \Sigma(0, 1, 2, 3, 4, 5, 6, 7)$

Now, draw the K-map according to the given minterms

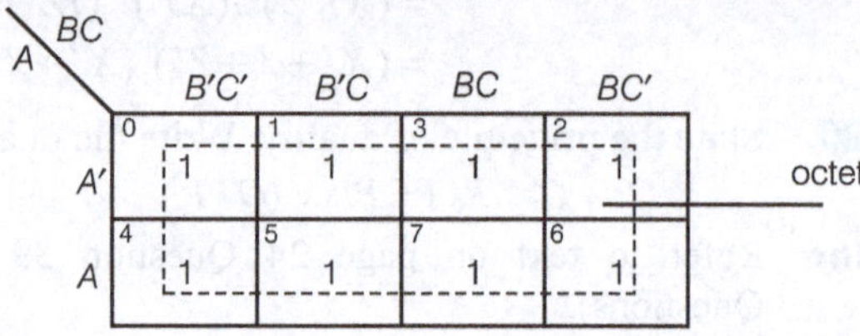

In a three variables K-map, octet means given function will produce output 1, i.e. tautology.

i.e. $F(A, B, C) = 1$

the complement of F, i.e. $F' = 1' = 0$

29. If $A = 1, B = 0, C = 1$ and $D = 1$, find its

(i) Maxterm (ii) Minterm **ISC 2011**

Ans (i) The maxterm corresponding to the given values of the variables will be:

$$= A' + B + C' + D'$$

(ii) The minterm corresponding to the given values of the variables will be:

$$= AB'CD$$

30. If $X = A'BC + AB'C + ABC + A'BC'$, then find the value of X when $A = 1, B = 0$ and $C = 1$. **ISC 2010**

Ans $\because$ $A = 1 \Rightarrow A' = 1' = 0$

$B = 0 \Rightarrow B' = 0' = 1$

$C = 1 \Rightarrow C' = 1' = 0$

Now, put the values of A, A', B, B', C and C' in the expression as

$$X = A'BC + AB'C + ABC + A'BC'$$
$$= 0.0.1 + 1.1.1 + 1.0.1 + 0.0.0$$
$$= 0 + 1 + 0 + 0$$
$$X = 1$$

31. Convert the following function into its canonical sum of product form.

$$F(x, y, z) = \Sigma(0, 1, 5, 7)$$ **ISC 2010**

Ans Given function is, $F(x, y, z) = \Sigma(0, 1, 5, 7)$

So, the canonical form of function F will be:

$$F = m_0 + m_1 + m_5 + m_7$$
$$= 000 + 001 + 101 + 111$$

So, $F(x, y, z) = x'y'z' + x'y'z + xy'z + xyz$

> **Concept Enhancer** There is another or easy method to convert any function to canonical SOP i.e. K-map. It is used three variables K-map which has 8 cells.

32. Show that the dual of $P'QR' + PQ'R + P'Q'R$ is equal to the complement of

$$PQ'R + Q.(P'R' + PR')$$ **ISC 2010**

Ans According to the principle of duality, interchange (+) with (.) and (.) with (+). So, the dual of expression $P'QR' + PQ'R + P'Q'R$, say X is,

$$X = (P' + Q + R').(P + Q' + R).(P' + Q' + R)$$

Now, let us assume the complement of

$$PQ'R + Q.(P'R' + PR') = Y.$$

So, $Y = [PQ'R + Q.(P'R' + PR')]'$

$= (PQ'R)'.[Q.(P'R' + PR')]'$

(by De-Morgan's law)

$= (P' + Q'' + R').[QP'R' + QPR']'$

(by De-Morgan's law)

$= (P' + Q'' + R').(QP'R')' \cdot (QPR')'$

(by De-Morgan's law)

$= (P' + Q'' + R').(Q' + P'' + R'').(Q' + P' + R'')$

(by De-Morgan's law)

$= (P' + Q + R').(Q' + P + R).(Q' + P' + R)$

(by involution law)

$= (P' + Q + R').(P + Q' + R).(P' + Q' + R)$

Now, we can see that $X = Y$, hence the dual of expression $P'QR' + PQ'R + P'Q'R$ is equal to the complement of $PQ'R + Q.(P'R' + PR')$.

33. Obtain the truth table to verify the following expression

$$x.(y+z) = x.y + x.z$$

Also, name the law stated above. **ISC 2009**

Ans Given expression is, $x.(y+z) = x.y + x.z$

To verify this expression using truth table,

x	y	z	$y+z$	$x.y$	$x.z$	$x.(y+z)$	$x.y+x.z$
0	0	0	0	0	0	0	0
0	0	1	1	0	0	0	0
0	1	0	1	0	0	0	0
0	1	1	1	0	0	0	0
1	0	0	0	0	0	0	0
1	0	1	1	0	1	1	1
1	1	0	1	1	0	1	1
1	1	1	1	1	1	1	1
						LHS	RHS

From the above table, LHS = RHS

$\therefore \quad x.(y+z) = x.y + x.z$

The law stated in the given expression is called distributive law.

34. Given $F = A + (B + C).(D' + E)$

Find F' and show the relevant working in steps. **ISC 2009**

Ans Given function is, $F = A + (B + C).(D' + E)$

We need to find the complement of F, i.e. F'.

First of all, we will simplify F

$$F = A + (B + C).(D' + E)$$
$$F = (A + B + C).(A + D' + E)$$

(by distributive law)

Now, complement of F is F'

$= [(A + B + C).(A + D' + E)]'$

$= (A + B + C)' + (A + D' + E)'$

(by De-Morgan's law)

$= A'B'C' + A'D''E'$

(by De-Morgan's law)

$= A'B'C' + A'DE'$ (by involution law)

$$F' = A'B'C' + A'DE'$$

35. For the given truth table where A, B, C are inputs and X is the output,

A	B	C	X
0	0	0	1
0	0	1	0
0	1	0	0
0	1	1	1
1	0	0	1
1	0	1	0
1	1	0	1
1	1	1	0

Write

(i) Canonical Sum of Product expression (SOP)

(ii) Canonical Product of Sum expression (POS) **ISC 2009**

Ans (i) Canonical Sum of Product expression is

$$A'.B'.C' + A'.B.C + A.B'.C' + A.B.C'$$

(ii) Canonical Product of Sum expression is

$$(A + B + C').(A + B' + C).(A' + B + C').(A' + B' + C')$$

36. Simplify the following expression by using the boolean laws. Show the working of each steps and also mention the laws used.

$$x'y'z' + x'y'z + x'yz + x'yz' + xy'z + xy'z$$ **ISC 2009**

Ans Given that,

$F = x'y'z' + x'y'z + x'yz + x'yz' + xy'z + xy'z$

$= x'y'z' + x'y'z + x'yz + x'yz' + xy'z$

(by idempotent law)

$= x'y'(z' + z) + x'y(z + z') + xy'z$

$= x'\,y'\,(1) + x'\,y\,(1) + xy'\,z$ (by complement law)

$= x'\,y' + x'\,y + xy'\,z = x'\,(y' + y) + xy'\,z$

$= x'\,(1) + xy'\,z$ (by complement law)

$= x'\,(1 + y'\,z) + xy'\,z$ (by basic postulates)

$= x' + x'\,y'\,z + xy'\,z = x' + y'\,z\,(x' + x)$

$= x' + y'\,z\,(1)$ (by complement law)

$F = x' + y'\,z$

37. Simplify the following boolean expression and state clearly the laws used for the simplification at each step

$xy + xz + xyz$ **ISC 2008**

Ans Given boolean expression is,

$F = xy + xz + xyz$

$= xy + xyz + xz$

$= xy\,(1 + z) + xz$ (by absorption law)

$= xy\,(1) + xz$ (by basic postulates)

$= xy + xz$

$F = x\,(y + z)$ (by distributive law)

38. State the two complement properties of boolean algebra. Verify any one of them using the truth table. **ISC 2008**

Ans According to the complement properties of boolean algebra, (i) $x + x' = 1$ (ii) $x \cdot x' = 0$

Now, we will verify the complement law using truth table as

x	x'	$x + x'$
0	1	1
1	0	1

So, it is verified that $x + x' = 1$.

39. Find the complement of $x \cdot (y' \cdot z' + y \cdot z)$ **ISC 2008**

Ans Given boolean function is, $F = x \cdot (y' \cdot z' + y \cdot z)$

Complement of F is

$F' = [x \cdot (y' \cdot z' + y \cdot z)]'$

$= x' + (y' \cdot z' + y \cdot z)'$ (by De-Morgan's law)

$= x' + (y' \cdot z')' \cdot (y \cdot z)'$ (by De-Morgan's law)

$= x' + (y'' + z'') \cdot (y' + z')$

(by De-Morgan's law)

$F' = x' + (y + z) \cdot (y' + z')$ (by involution law)

40. Convert the following Product of Sum (POS) form into its corresponding Sum of Product (SOP) form. **ISC 2008**

$F\,(x, y, z) = \Pi\,(2, 4, 6, 7)$

Ans Given function is, $F\,(x, y, z) = \Pi\,(2, 4, 6, 7)$

As we know, SOP and POS both are complement to each other.

Hence, sum of product of $F(x, y, z) =$ Complement of $\Pi(2, 4, 6, 7)$

i.e. $= \Sigma\,(0, 1, 3, 5)$

41. Given: $F\,(x, y, z) = \Sigma(1, 3, 7)$

Prove $F\,(x, y, z) = \Pi(0, 2, 4, 5, 6)$ **ISC 2008**

Ans Given expression is, $F(x, y, z) = \Sigma(1, 3, 7)$

$F' =$ Complement of $\Sigma(1, 3, 7)$

$= \Pi(0, 2, 4, 5, 6)$

$F'' =$ Complement of $\Pi(0, 2, 4, 5, 6)$

$= \Sigma\,(1, 3, 7)$

It is proved that SOP form, i.e. $\Sigma(1, 3, 7)$ and POS form, i.e. $\Pi(0, 2, 4, 5, 6)$ are complement to each other.

42. Simplify the following boolean expression using laws of boolean algebra. At each step, state clearly the law used for simplification. **ISC 2007**

$F = x.\,y\,(x.\,y + y.\,z)$

Ans Given boolean expression is,

$F = x.\,y\,(x.\,y + y.\,z)$

$= (x.\,y)\,(x.\,y) + (x.\,y)\,(y.\,z)$ (by distributive law)

$= (x.\,y) + (x.\,y)\,(y.\,z)$ (by idempotent law)

$= (x.\,y)\,(1 + y.\,z)$

$F = x.\,y$ (by absorption law)

43. Convert the following SOP expression into its corresponding POS expression.

$F\,(o, v, w) = o'v'w' + o'v'\,w + o'vw + ov'w$ **ISC 2007**

Ans Given function is,

$F\,(o, v, w) = o'v'w' + o'v'w + o'vw + ov'w$

To convert SOP expression into POS expression make a truth table as

o	v	w	Minterm	Minterm expression	Maxterm	Maxterm expression
0	0	0	m_0	$o'\,v'\,w'$	M_0	$o + v + w$
0	0	1	m_1	$o'\,v'\,w$	M_1	$o + v + w'$
0	1	0	m_2	$o'\,v\,w'$	M_2	$o + v' + w$
0	1	1	m_3	$o'\,v\,w$	M_3	$o + v' + w'$
1	0	0	m_4	$o\,v'\,w'$	M_4	$o' + v + w$
1	0	1	m_5	$o\,v'\,w$	M_5	$o' + v + w'$
1	1	0	m_6	$o\,v\,w'$	M_6	$o' + v' + w$
1	1	1	m_7	$o\,v\,w$	M_7	$o' + v' + w'$

From the above table,

$F = m_0 + m_1 + m_3 + m_5 = \Sigma\,(0, 1, 3, 5)$

Now, it is known that the complement of a minterm is equal to its corresponding maxterm.

$\therefore \quad F = M_2 . M_4 . M_6 . M_7$

So, the canonical POS form of F is,

$$F = (o + v' + w).(o' + v + w).(o' + v' + w).(o' + v' + w')$$

44. Find the complement of

$F\ (a, b, c, d) = [a + \{(b + c).(b' + d')\}]$ **ISC 2007**

Ans Given function is,

$F\ (a, b, c, d) = [a + \{(b + c).(b' + d')\}]$

On applying De-Morgan's theorem,

$F' = a' . \{(b + c).(b' + d')\}'$

$= a' . \{(b + c)' + (b' + d')'\}$ (by De-Morgan's law)

$= a' . \{b' . c' + b'' . d''\}$ (by De-Morgan's law)

$= a' \cdot \{b' \cdot c' + b \cdot d\}$ (by involution law)

$F' = a'\,b'\,c' + a'\,b\,d$ (by distributive law)

45. Find the complement of

$F\ (m, n, o) = m' . n . o' + m' . n' . o$ **ISC 2006**

Ans Given, $F\ (m, n, o) = m' . n . o' + m' . n' . o$

To find the complement of F, apply De-Morgan's law

$F' = (m' . n . o' + m' . n' . o)'$

$= (m' . n . o')' . (m' . n' . o)'$

$= (m'' + n' + o'').(m'' + n'' + o')$ (by De-Morgan's law)

$F' = (m + n' + o).(m + n + o')$ (by involution law)

46. Write the Product of Sum (POS) form for the boolean function $F\ (A, B, C)$ whose output is 0 only when **ISC 2006**

$A = 1, B = 0, C = 0$

$A = 0, B = 1, C = 0$

$A = 0, B = 0, C = 1$

$A = 1, B = 1, C = 1$

Ans From the given description, the truth table for three variables A, B and C is as follows:

A	B	C	F (A, B, C)	Maxterm	Maxterm expression
0	0	0	1	M_0	$A + B + C$
0	0	1	0	M_1	$A + B + C'$
0	1	0	0	M_2	$A + B' + C$
0	1	1	1	M_3	$A + B' + C'$
1	0	0	0	M_4	$A' + B + C$
1	0	1	1	M_5	$A' + B + C'$
1	1	0	1	M_6	$A' + B' + C$
1	1	1	0	M_7	$A' + B' + C'$

To find the POS form for F, we need to find those maxterms for which the value of F is 0 and these are M_1, M_2, M_4 and M_7.

So, $\quad F = M_1 . M_2 . M_4 . M_7$

$$F = (A + B + C').(A + B' + C).(A' + B + C).(A' + B' + C')$$

47. Simplify $a.b + a'.c + b.c$ using the laws of boolean algebra. At each step, state clearly the law used for simplification. **ISC 2006**

Ans Given expression is,

$F = a.b + a'.c + b.c$

$F = b(a + c) + a'.c$ (by distributive law)

$= a'.b.a + a'.b.c + b.c.a + b.c.c$ (by distributive law)

$= a'.a.b + a'.b.c + a.b.c + b.c$ (by idempotence law)

$= 0.b + a'.b.c + a.b.c + b.c$ (by zero property)

$= 0 + a'.b.c + a.b.c + b.c$ (by zero property)

$= a'.b.c + b.c\,(a + 1)$

$= a'.b.c + b.c.1$ (by basic postulates)

$= a'.b.c + b.c$

$= b.c\,(a' + 1)$ (by basic postulates)

$= b.\,c.1$

$F = b.c$ $\quad (\because b.c.1 = bc)$

48. Reduce the following three-input function into its simplest form.

$F\ (x, y, z) = \Sigma\ (0, 1, 3, 5)$ **ISC 2006**

Ans Given function, $F\ (x, y, z) = \Sigma\ (0, 1, 3, 5)$

i.e. $\quad F = m_0 + m_1 + m_3 + m_5$

As we know, $\quad m_0 = x'\,y'\,z'$

$m_1 = x'\,y'\,z$

$m_3 = x'\,yz$

$m_5 = xy'\,z$

$\therefore \quad F = x'\,y'\,z' + x'\,y'\,z + x'\,yz + xy'\,z$

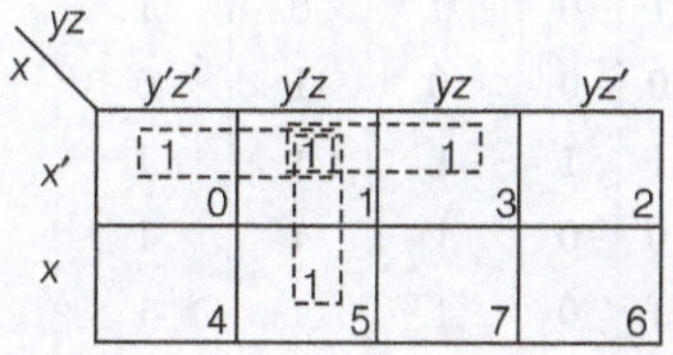

There are 3 pair

Pair 1 $= x'y'$

Pair 2 $= x'z$

Pair 3 $= y'z$

So, reduced expression will be $x'y' + x'z + y'z$.

49. Convert
$(x' + y + z').(x + y' + z).(x + y + z').(x + y + z)$
into SOP form. **ISC 2006**

Ans Given,
$F = (x' + y + z').(x + y' + z).(x + y + z').(x + y + z)$

Now, we will find the SOP form of F using truth table as

x	y	z	Maxterm	Maxterm expression	Minterm	Minterm expression
0	0	0	M_0	$x + y + z$	m_0	$x'y'z'$
0	0	1	M_1	$x + y + z'$	m_1	$x'y'z$
0	1	0	M_2	$x + y' + z$	m_2	$x'yz'$
0	1	1	M_3	$x + y' + z'$	m_3	$x'yz$
1	0	0	M_4	$x' + y + z$	m_4	$xy'z'$
1	0	1	M_5	$x' + y + z'$	m_5	$xy'z$
1	1	0	M_6	$x' + y' + z$	m_6	xyz'
1	1	1	M_7	$x' + y' + z'$	m_7	xyz

From the above truth table, $F = M_5 . M_2 . M_1 . M_0$

$\therefore \quad F = \Pi(0, 1, 2, 5)$

The SOP form for above expression is,

$$F = \Sigma(3, 4, 6, 7)$$
$$= m_3 + m_4 + m_6 + m_7$$
$$F = x'yz + xy'z' + xyz' + xyz$$

50. State the distributive law. Verify it using the truth table. **ISC 2005**

Ans The distributive law states that,

(i) $x + yz = (x + y).(x + z)$

(ii) $x.(y + z) = x.y + x.z$

Now, we will verify the first law using truth table as follows:

$$x + yz = (x + y).(x + z)$$

x	y	z	yz	$x + yz$	$x + y$	$x + z$	$(x + y).(x + z)$
0	0	0	0	0	0	0	0
0	0	1	0	0	0	1	0
0	1	0	0	0	1	0	0
0	1	1	1	1	1	1	1
1	0	0	0	1	1	1	1
1	0	1	0	1	1	1	1
1	1	0	0	1	1	1	1
1	1	1	1	1	1	1	1
				LHS			RHS

So, it is verified from the truth table that,

$$x + yz = (x + y).(x + z)$$

Now, we will verify the another law by truth table as follows

$$x.(y + z) = x.y + x.z$$

x	y	z	$y + z$	$x.(y + z)$	$x.y$	$x.z$	$x.y + x.z$
0	0	0	0	0	0	0	0
0	0	1	1	0	0	0	0
0	1	0	1	0	0	0	0
0	1	1	1	0	0	0	0
1	0	0	0	0	0	0	0
1	0	1	1	1	0	1	1
1	1	0	1	1	1	0	1
1	1	1	1	1	1	1	1
				LHS			RHS

So, it is verified from the truth table, that, $x.(y + z) = x.y + x.z$.

51. What is the canonical form of boolean expression? State the two types of canonical forms. **ISC 2005**

Ans A boolean expression is in canonical form when each sum or product term contain each of the literals.

There are two types of canonical forms:

(i) Canonical SOP expression

(ii) Canonical POS expression

52. What is the application of boolean algebra in computer science? **ISC 2005**

Ans Refer to text on Page 20.

53. Reduce the following expression to its simplest form using laws of boolean algebra. At each step clearly state the law used for simplification. **ISC 2005**

$$AB' + A'BC' + (AC)' + BC$$

Ans Given expression is, $F = AB' + A'BC' + (AC)' + BC$

Now, we will simplify the given expression by using boolean laws as below:

$$F = AB' + A'BC' + (AC)' + BC$$
$$= AB' + A'BC' + A' + C' + BC \quad \text{(by De-Morgan's law)}$$
$$= AB' + A' + A'BC' + C' + BC \quad \text{(by commutative law)}$$
$$= AB' + A'(1 + BC') + C' + BC \quad \text{(by distributive law)}$$
$$= AB' + A'.1 + C' + BC \quad \text{(by basic postulates)}$$
$$= AB' + A' + C' + BC \quad \text{(by identity law)}$$
$$= ((A + A').(B' + A')) + ((C' + C).(C' + B)) \quad \text{(by distributive law)}$$

$= 1.(B' + A') + 1.(C' + B)$ (by complement law)

$= (B' + A') + (C' + B)$ (by identity law)

$= B' + B + A' + C'$ (by commutative law)

$= 1 + A' + C'$ (by complement law)

$= 1 + C'$ (by basic postulates)

$F = 1$ (by basic postulates)

54. Verify that $(z + x)(z + x' + y) = (z + x)(z + y)$. *ISC 2005*

Ans Given expression,

$(z + x)(z + x' + y) = (z + x)(z + y)$

Take, LHS $= (z + x)(z + x' + y)$

$= (z + x)(z + x') + (z + x)y$ (by distributive law)

$= zz + zx' + xz + xx' + zy + xy$ (by distributive law)

$= z + zx' + xz + xx' + zy + xy$ (by idempotent law)

$= z + zx' + xz + 0 + zy + xy$ (by complement law)

$= z + zx' + xz + zy + xy$ (by identity law)

$= z(1 + x') + xz + zy + xy$

$= z + xz + zy + xy$ (by absorption law)

$= z(1 + x) + zy + xy$

$= z + zy + xy$ (by absorption law)

$= z(1 + y) + xy = z(1) + xy$

$= z + xy$ (by absorption law)

$= (z + x)(z + y)$ (by distributive law)

So, LHS = RHS **Hence verified**

3 Marks Questions

1. Prove the Boolean expression using Boolean laws. Also, mention the law used at each step. *ISC 2017*

$$F = (x' + z) + [(y' + z).(x' + y)]' = 1$$

Ans Given Boolean expression is,

$$F = (x' + z) + [(y' + z)\cdot(x' + y)]' = 1$$

LHS $(x' + z) + [(y' + z).(x' + y)]'$

$= (x' + z) + (y' + z)' + (x' + y)'$ [using De-Morgan's law]

$= (x' + z) + (y')'.z' + (x')'.y'$ [using De-Morgan's law]

$= (x' + z) + y.z' + x.y'$ [using involution law]

$= x' + z + yz' + xy'$

$= x'(y + y') + z(y + y') + yz' + xy'$ [using complementary law]

$= x'y + x'y' + yz + y'z + yz' + xy'$

$= x'y + y'(x' + x) + y(z + z') + y'z$ [using complementary law]

$= x'y + y' + y + y'z$

$= y(x' + 1) + y'(1 + z)$ [using postulates]

$= y + y' = 1 =$ RHS [using postulates]

Hence, LHS = RHS

2. State the complement properties. Find the complement of the following Boolean expression using De-Morgan's law: $AB' + A' + BC$ *ISC 2016*

Ans There exists an inverse, such that

(i) $X + X' = 1$

Truth table for $X + X' = 1$

X	X'	$X + X'$
0	1	1
1	0	1

(ii) $X.X' = 0$

Truth table for $X.X' = 0$

X	X'	$X.X'$
0	1	0
1	0	0

Given Boolean expression is,

$$F = AB' + A' + BC$$

Complement of F is,

$F' = [AB' + A' + BC]'$

$= (AB')'.(A')'.(BC)'$ (by De-Morgan's law)

$= (A' + B'').A.(B' + C')$ (by De-Morgan's law)

$F' = (A' + B).A.(B' + C')$ (by involution law)

3. Reduce the following expression using boolean laws. *ISC 2014*

$$F(A, B, C, D) = (A' + C)(A' + C')(A' + B + C'D)$$

Ans Given expression,

$F(A, B, C, D) = (A' + C)(A' + C')(A' + B + C'D)$

$= (A'A' + A'C' + CA' + CC')(A' + B + C'D)$ (by distributive law)

$= (A' + A'C' + CA' + CC')(A' + B + C'D)$

$= (A' + A'C' + CA')(A' + B + C'D)$ $[\because C\overline{C} = 0$ (by zero property)$]$

$= A'(1 + C' + C)(A' + B + C'D)$ $(\because 1 + C' = 1)$

$= A'(1 + C)(A' + B + C'D)$

So, $= A'(A' + B + C'D)$ (by distributive law)

$= (A'A' + A'B + A'C'D)$ $(\because A'A' = A')$

$= (A' + A'B + A'C'D)$

$= A'(1 + B + C'D)$ (by distributive law)

$= A'(1 + C'D)$ $(\because 1 + B = 1)$

$= A'$

$F(A, B, C, D) = A'$

4. Verify algebraically if,

$$x'y'z' + x'y'z + x'yz + x'yz' + xy'z' + xy'z = x' + y'$$ **ISC 2012**

Ans Given expression is, $x'y'z' + x'y'z + x'yz + x'yz' + xy'z' + xy'z = x' + y'$

LHS $= x'y'z' + x'y'z + x'yz + x'yz' + xy'z' + xy'z$

$= x'y'(z' + z) + x'y(z + z') + xy'(z' + z)$

$= x'y'(1) + x'y(1) + xy'(1)$ (by complement law)

$= x'y' + x'y + xy' = x'(y' + y) + xy'$

$= x'(1) + xy'$ (by complement law)

$= x' + xy' = (x' + x) \cdot (x' + y')$ (by distributive law)

$= 1.(x' + y')$ (by complement law)

$= x' + y'$

LHS = RHS

5. State the principle of duality. Give the dual of the following **ISC 2011**

$$(A'.B) + (C.1) = (A' + C).(B + C)$$

Or State the principle of duality. Give an example. **ISC 2008**

Ans Refer to text on page 24 Question 39 (1 Mark Questions).

Take, LHS $= (A'.B) + (C.1)$

On applying principle of duality,

$= (A' + B).(C + 0)$

$= (A' + B).C = A'C + BC$ $(\because C + 0 = C)$

Take, RHS $= (A' + C).(B + C)$

On applying principle of duality,

$= A'.C + B.C$

So, LHS = RHS **Hence Proved**

6. Convert the following cardinal expression into its canonical form and reduce it using boolean laws. **ISC 2011**

$$F(L, M, O, P) = \Pi(0, 2, 8, 10)$$

Ans Given function, $F(L, M, O, P) = \Pi(0, 2, 8, 10)$

It is clear that the function F is in POS form and contain the maxterm 0, 2, 8 and 10.

i.e. $F = M_0 . M_2 . M_8 . M_{10}$

Canonical POS form of F is,

$$F = (L + M + O + P).(L + M + O' + P).(L' + M + O + P).(L' + M + O' + P)$$

Now, we will simplify the above expression by using Boolean laws.

$F = (L + M + O + P).(L + M + O' + P).(L' + M + O + P).(L' + M + O' + P)$

$= (L + M + O.O' + P).(L' + M + O.O' + P)$ (by distributive law)

$= (L + M + 0 + P).(L' + M + 0 + P)$ (by complement law)

$= (L + M + P).(L' + M + P)$ (by identity law)

$= (L.L' + M + P)$ $(\because A.A' = 0)$

$= (0 + M + P)$ (by complement law)

$F = M + P$ (by identity law)

This is the simplified form of F.

7. What are maxterms? Convert the following function as a product of maxterms.

$$F(P, Q, R) = (P + Q).(P' + R')$$ **ISC 2010**

Ans The variables are also combined to form a standard sum when we take OR operation between the variables. These OR terms are known as maxterms.

Given function, $F(P,Q,R) = (P+Q).(P'+R')$

To convert the function F into product of maxterms, we need to add missing variable in these terms as,

$$F(P,Q,R) = (P+Q).(P'+R')$$
$$= (P+Q+0).(P'+0+R')$$
$$= (P+Q+RR').(P'+QQ'+R') \quad \text{(by complement law)}$$
$$= (P+Q+R).(P+Q+R').(P'+Q+R').(P'+Q'+R') \quad \text{(by distributive law)}$$

$\therefore \quad F(P,Q,R) = M_0.M_1.M_5.M_7$

8. Simplify the following expression and convert it to its canonical POS form.

$$((x.y)+z).(y+(z'.x))$$

ISC 2009

Ans Given expression, $F = (x.y+z)(y+z'.x)$

$$F = (x+z).(y+z).(y+z').(y+x) \quad \text{(by distributive law)}$$
$$= (x+z).(y+z).(y+z').(x+y) \quad \text{(by commutative law)}$$

Now, we will convert F into canonical form,

$$F = (x+0+z).(0+y+z).(0+y+z').(x+y+0)$$
$$= (x+yy'+z).(xx'+y+z).(xx'+y+z').(x+y+zz') \quad \text{(by complement law)}$$
$$= (x+y+z).(x+y'+z).(x+y+z).(x'+y+z).(x+y+z').(x'+y+z').(x+y+z).(x+y+z') \quad \text{(by distributive law)}$$
$$= (x+y+z).(x+y+z).(x+y+z).(x+y'+z).(x'+y+z).(x'+y+z').(x+y+z').(x+y+z')$$
$$F = (x+y+z).(x+y'+z).(x'+y+z).(x'+y+z').(x+y+z') \quad \text{(by idempotent law)}$$

9. Minimise the following expression and at each step state clearly the law used.

$$Y = (A+B').(B+CD)'$$

ISC 2009

Ans Given expression is,

$$Y = (A+B').(B+CD)' = (A+B').B'.(CD)' = (A+B').B'.(C'+D') \quad \text{(De-Morgan's law)}$$
$$= (A+B').(B'C'+B'D') \quad \text{(distributive law)}$$
$$= AB'C'+AB'D'+B'.B'C'+B'.B'D' \quad (A.A=A)$$
$$= AB'C'+AB'D'+B'C'+B'D'$$
$$= AB'C'+B'C'+AB'D'+B'D'$$
$$= B'C'(A+1)+B'D'(A+1) \quad (A+1=1)$$
$$= B'C'+B'D' = B'(C'+D')$$

10. Convert $A.B+B.C'$ to its canonical SOP form using Boolean algebra. **ISC 2008**

Ans The given function, $F = A.B+B.C'$

$$F = A.B.1+1.B.C' \quad \text{(by identity law)}$$
$$= A.B.(C+C')+(A+A').B.C' \quad \text{(by complement law)}$$
$$= ABC+ABC'+ABC'+A'BC'$$
$$F = ABC+ABC'+A'BC' \quad \text{(by idempotent law)}$$

11. Reduce the following boolean expression to the simplest form. **ISC 2008**

$$A.[(B+C).(AB+AC)']$$

Ans Given boolean expression, $F = A[(B+C).(AB+AC)']$

$$F = A.(B+C).(AB+AC)'$$
$$= A.[(B+C).((AB)'.(AC)')] \quad \text{(by De-Morgan's law)}$$
$$= A.[(B+C).((A'+B')(A'+C'))] \quad \text{(by De-Morgan's law)}$$

$= A.[(B+C).(A'.A'+A'.B'+A'.C'+B'.C')]$ (by distributive law)

$= A.[(B+C).(A'+A'B'+A'C'+B'C')]$ (by idempotent law)

$= A.[(B+C).(A'(1+B')+A'C'+B'C')]$ (by domination law)

$= A.[(B+C).(A'+A'C'+B'C')]$ (by absorption law)

$= A.[(B+C).(A'(1+C')+B'C')]$

$= A.[(B+C).(A'+B'C')]$ (by absorption law)

$= A(A'B+BB'C'+A'C+B'CC')$ (by distributive law)

$= A(A'B+0+A'C+B'CC')$ (by complement law)

$= A(A'B+A'C+0)$ (by complement law)

$= A(A'B+A'C)$

$= AA'B+AA'C$ (by distributive law)

$= 0+0=0$ (by complement law)

12. Prove that $F(A,B,C)=\Pi(2,3,4,7)=\Sigma(0,1,5,6)$.

ISC 2005

Ans Given that, $F(A,B,C)=\Pi(2,3,4,7)$

$F=\Pi(2,3,4,7)$

$\therefore$ $F'=\Pi(0,1,5,6)$

i.e. $F'=M_0.M_1.M_5.M_6$

By involution law, $F=(F')'$

$=(M_0.M_1.M_5.M_6)'$

$F=M_0'+M_1'+M_5'+M_6'$

(by De-Morgan's law)

It is known that the complement of a maxterm is equal to its corresponding minterm.

$\therefore$ $F=m_0+m_1+m_5+m_6$

$F=\Sigma(0,1,5,6)$ **Hence Proved.**

4/5 Marks Questions

1. To be recruited as the Principal in a renowned College, a candidate must satisfy any one of the following criteria: ***ISC 2024***

- The candidate must be a Postgraduate and should either possess a B.Ed. degree or a teaching experience of more than 15 years.

Or

- The candidate must be an employee of the same college with a teaching experience of more than 15 years.

Or
- The candidate must be a Postgraduate but not an employee of the same college and should have a teaching experience of more than 15 years.

The inputs are

Inputs	
P	Candidate is a Postgraduate
S	Candidate is an employee of the same College
E	Candidate has a teaching experience of more than 15 years.
B	Candidate possesses a B.Ed. degree

(In all the above cases, 1 indicates yes and 0 indicates no)

Output X - Denotes eligibility of a candidate [1 indicates eligibility and 0 indicates ineligibility in all cases]

Draw the truth table for the inputs and outputs given above and write the SOP expression for X (P, S, E, B)

Ans X = P(B + E) + SE + PS'E = PB + PE + SE + PS'E

P	S	E	B	S'	PB	SE	PE	PS'E	X		
0	0	0	0	1	0	0	0	0	0	0	
0	0	0	1	1	0	0	0	0	0	1	
0	0	1	0	1	0	0	0	0	0	2	
0	0	1	1	1	0	0	0	0	0	3	
0	1	0	0	0	0	0	0	0	0	4	
0	1	0	1	0	0	0	0	0	0	5	
0	1	1	0	0	0	1	0	0	1	6	P'SEB
0	1	1	1	0	0	1	0	0	1	7	P'SEB
1	0	0	0	1	0	0	0	0	0	8	
1	0	0	1	1	1	0	0	0	1	9	PS'E'B
1	0	1	0	1	0	0	1	1	1	10	PS'EB'
1	0	1	1	1	1	0	1	1	1	11	PS'EB
1	1	0	0	0	0	0	0	0	0	12	
1	1	0	1	0	1	0	0	0	1	13	PSE'B
1	1	1	0	0	0	1	1	0	1	14	PSEB'
1	1	1	1	0	1	1	1	0	1	15	PSEB

SOP Expression for F(P,S,E,B) = P'SEB' + P'SEB + PS'E'B + PS'EB' + PS'EB + PSE'B + PSEB' + PSEB

2. Reduce the above expression X (P, S, E, B) by using 4-variable Karnaugh map, showing the various groups (i.e., octal, quads and pairs)

Draw the logic gate diagram for the reduced expression. Assume that the variables and their complements are available as inputs. ***ISC 2024***

Ans K-map:

Quad(6,7,14,15) = SE

Quad(10,11,15,14) = PE

Quad(9,11,13,15) = PB

Reduced expression: X = SE + PE + PB

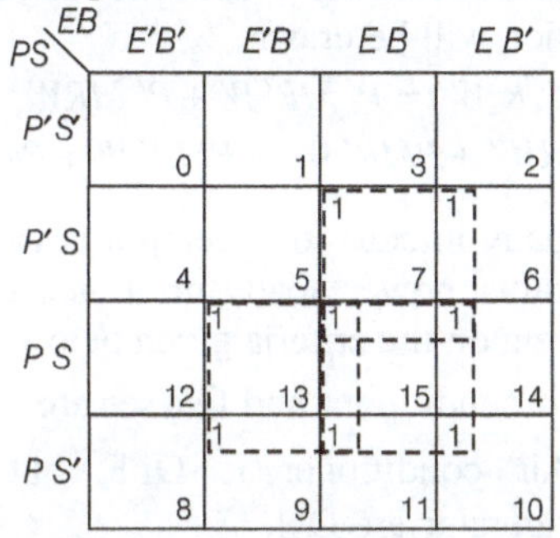

Logic gate of Reduced expression:

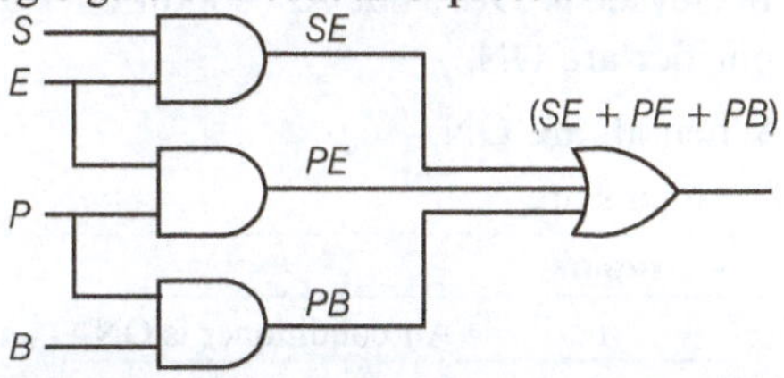

3. (a) Reduce the Boolean function F (A, B, C, D) = π (0, 2, 4, 6,8, 9, 10, 11, 14) by using 4-variable Karnaugh map, showing the various groups (i.e., octal, quads and pairs)

(b) Draw the logic gate diagram for the reduced expression. Assume that the variables and their complements are available as inputs. **ISC 2024**

Ans (a)

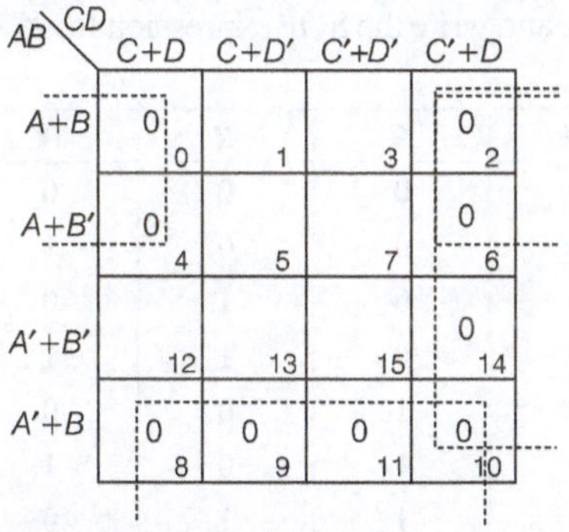

Quad(2,6,10,14) = C'+ D

Quad(0,2,4,6) = A + D

Quad(8,9,10,11) = A'+B

Reduced Boolean Expression: (A+D)(C'+D)(A'+B)

(b) Logic Gate of Reduced Boolean Expression:

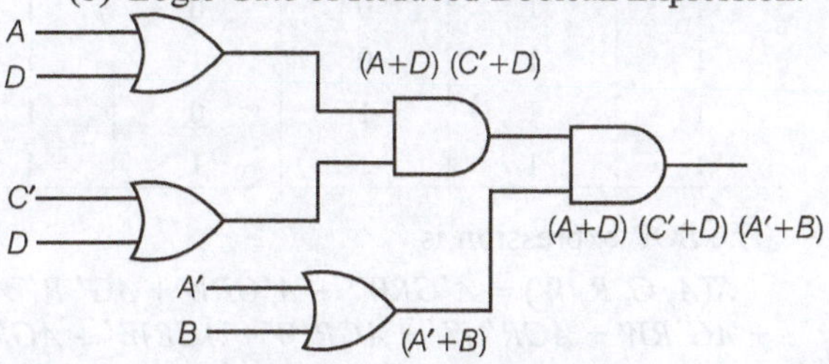

4. A shopping mall allows customers to shop using cash or credit card of any nationalised bank. It awards bonus points to their customers on the basis of criteria given below **ISC 2023**

- The customer is an employee of the shopping mall and makes the payment using a credit card

Or

- The customer shops items which carry bonus points and makes the payment using a credit card with a shopping amount of less than ₹ 10,000/-

Or

- The customer is not an employee of the shopping mall and makes the payment not through a credit card but in cash for the shopping amount above ₹ 10,000/-

The inputs are

INPUTS	
C	Payment through a credit card
A	Shopping amount is above ₹ 10,000/-
E	The customer is an employee of the shopping mall
I	Item carries a bonus point

(In all the above cases, 1 indicates yes and 0 indicates no)

Output: *X* [1 indicates bonus point awarded, 0 indicates bonus point not awarded for all cases]

Draw the truth table for the inputs and output given above and write the POS expression for $X(C, A, E, I)$.

Ans. The truth table for given inputs is

C	*A*	*E*	*I*	*X*
0	0	0	0	0
0	0	0	1	0
0	0	1	0	0
0	0	1	1	0
0	1	0	0	1
0	1	0	1	1
0	1	1	0	0
0	1	1	1	0
1	0	0	0	0
1	0	0	1	1
1	0	1	0	1
1	0	1	1	1
1	1	0	0	0
1	1	0	1	0
1	1	1	0	1
1	1	1	1	1

Using above truth table, the following POS expression will be drawn:

$$X(C,A,E,I) = (C+A+E+I)\cdot(C+A+E+I')\cdot(C+A+E'+I)\cdot(C+A+E'+I')\cdot(C+A'+E'+I)\cdot(C+A'+E'+I')\cdot(C'+A+E+I)\cdot(C'+A'+E+I)\cdot(C'+A'+E+I')$$

5. A family intends to purchase a smart phone depending on the criteria given below **ISC SQP 2023**

- Quad core processor with internal memory of 64 GB or more but not a resale phone

Or

- Resale phone with quad core processor but without warranty

Or

- Processor is not a quad core but with a warranty of 1 year and the internal memory is of 64 GB or more

The inputs are

INPUTS	
P	Quad core processor
M	Internal memory of 64 GB or more
R	Resale phone
W	Warranty of 1 year

(In all the above cases, 1 indicates yes and 0 indicates no)

Output: *X* [1 indicates purchased, 0 indicates not purchased for all cases]

Draw the truth table for the inputs and output given above and write the SOP expression.

Ans The truth table for given inputs is

P	*M*	*R*	*W*	*X*
0	0	0	0	0
0	0	0	1	0
0	0	1	0	0
0	0	1	1	0
0	1	0	0	0
0	1	0	1	1
0	1	1	0	0
0	1	1	1	1
1	0	0	0	0
1	0	0	1	0
1	0	1	0	1
1	0	1	1	0
1	1	0	0	1
1	1	0	1	1
1	1	1	0	1
1	1	1	1	0

Using above truth table, the following SOP expression will be drawn

$$X(P,M,R,W) = P'MR'W + P'MRW + PM'RW' + PMR'W' + PMR'W + PMRW'$$

6. A company intends to develop a device to show the high status power load for a household invertor depending on the criteria given below

- If Air conditioner and Geyser are ON.

Or

- If Air conditioner is OFF, but Geyser and Refrigerator are ON.

Or

- If Geyser is OFF, but Air conditioner and Water purifier are ON.

Or

- When all are ON.

The inputs are

Inputs	
A	Air conditioner is ON
G	Geyser is ON
R	Refrigerator is ON
W	Water purifier is ON

(In all the above cases 1 indicates yes and 0 indicates no.)

Output *X*[1 indicates high power, 0 indicates low power for all cases]

Draw the truth table for the inputs and outputs given above and write the SOP expression for *X*(*A*, *G*, *R*, *W*). **ISC 2020**

Ans

A	*G*	*R*	*W*	*X*
0	0	0	0	0
0	0	0	1	0
0	0	1	0	0
0	0	1	1	0
0	1	0	0	0
0	1	0	1	0
0	1	1	0	1
0	1	1	1	1
1	0	0	0	0
1	0	0	1	1
1	0	1	0	0
1	0	1	1	1
1	1	0	0	1
1	1	0	1	1
1	1	1	0	1
1	1	1	1	1

The SOP expression is

$$X(A,G,R,W) = A'GRW' + A'GRW + AG'R'W + AG'RW + AGR'W' + AGR'W + AGRW' + AGRW$$

7. Draw a truth table with a 3 input combination which outputs 1, if there are odd number of 0's. Also, derive an SOP expression for the output. Reduce the expression using Karnaugh Map. **ISC SQP 2020**

Ans

A	B	C	X
0	0	0	1
0	0	1	0
0	1	0	0
0	1	1	1
1	0	0	0
1	0	1	1
1	1	0	1
1	1	1	0

SOP expression of given truth table will be

$X(A,B,C) = A'B'C' + A'BC + AB'C + ABC'$

$= \Sigma(0, 3, 5, 6)$

K-map,

A \ BC	B'C'	B'C	BC	BC'
A'	1 (0)	(1)	1 (3)	(2)
A	(4)	1 (5)	(7)	1 (6)

8. The owner of a company pays bonus to his salesmen as per the criteria given below

- If the salesman works overtime for more than 4 hours but does not work on off days/holidays.

Or

- If the salesman works when festival sales are on and updates showroom arrangements.

Or

- If the salesman works on an off day/holiday when the festival sales are on.

The inputs are

Inputs	
O	Works overtime for more than 4 hours
F	Festival sales are on
H	Working on an off day/holiday
U	Updates showroom arrangements

(In all the above cases 1 indicates yes and 0 indicates no)

Output : *X*[1 indicates yes, 0 indicates no for all cases]

Draw the truth table for the inputs and output given above and write the POS expression for $X(O, F, H, U)$. **ISC 2019**

Ans Given expression $X(O, F, H, U)$ has four inputs and X represents output values.

The truth table for given inputs is

O	*F*	*H*	*U*	*X*
0	0	0	0	0
0	0	0	1	0
0	0	1	0	0
0	0	1	1	0
0	1	0	0	0
0	1	0	1	1
0	1	1	0	1
0	1	1	1	1
1	0	0	0	1
1	0	0	1	1
1	0	1	0	0
1	0	1	1	0
1	1	0	0	1
1	1	0	1	1
1	1	1	0	1
1	1	1	1	1

Using the truth table, the following POS expression will be drawn

$X(O, F, H, U) = (O + F + H + U)(O + F + H + U')(O + F + H' + U)(O + F + H' + U')(O + F' + H + U)(O' + F + H' + U)(O' + F + H' + U')$

9. A training institute intends to give scholarships to its students as per the criteria given below

- The student has excellent academic record but is financially weak.

Or

- The student does not have an excellent academic record and belongs to a backward class.

Or

- The student does not have an excellent academic record and is physically impaired.

The inputs are:

INPUTS	
A	Has excellent academic record
F	Financially sound
C	Belongs to a backward class
I	Is physically impaired

(In all the above cases 1 indicates yes and 0 indicates no).

Output : X [1 indicates yes, 0 indicates no for all cases]

Draw the truth table for the inputs and output given above and write the SOP expression for $X(A,F,C,I)$.

ISC 2018

Ans Truth table for given inputs in below

A	F	C	I	X
0	0	0	0	0
0	0	0	1	1
0	0	1	0	1
0	0	1	1	1
0	1	0	0	0
0	1	0	1	1
0	1	1	0	1
0	1	1	1	1
1	0	0	0	1
1	0	0	1	1
1	0	1	0	1
1	0	1	1	1
1	1	0	0	0
1	1	0	1	0
1	1	1	0	0
1	1	1	1	0

The SOP expression for the above truth table

$$X(A,F,C,I) = A'F'C'I + A'F'CI' + A'F'CI + A'FC'I + A'FCI' + A'FCI + AF'C'I' + AF'C'I + AF'CI' + AF'CI$$

10. A school intends to select candidates for an Inter-School Essay Competition as per the criteria given below

- The student has participated in an earlier competition and is very creative.

Or
- The student is very creative and has excellent general awareness, but has not participated in any competition earlier.

Or
- The student has excellent general awareness and has won prize in an inter-house competition.

The inputs are

INPUTS	
A	Participated in competition earlier
B	Is very creative
C	Won prize in an inter-house competition
D	Has excellent general awareness

(In all the above cases 1 indicates yes and 0 indicates no).

Output : X [1 indicates yes, 0 indicates no for all cases]

Draw the truth table for the inputs and output given above and write the POS expression for $X(A, B, C, D)$.

ISC 2017

Ans Truth table for given inputs in below

A	B	C	D	X
0	0	0	0	0
0	0	0	1	0
0	0	1	0	0
0	0	1	1	1
0	1	0	0	0
0	1	0	1	1
0	1	1	0	0
0	1	1	1	1
1	0	0	0	0
1	0	0	1	0
1	0	1	0	0
1	0	1	1	1
1	1	0	0	1
1	1	0	1	1
1	1	1	0	1
1	1	1	1	1

The POS expression for above truth table is

$$X(A,B,C,D) = (A+B+C+D).(A+B+C'+D).(A+B'+C+D)(A+B'+C'+D).(A'+B+C+D).(A+B+C+D')(A'+B+C+D').(A'+B+C'+D)$$

11. A passenger is allotted a window seat in an aircraft, if he/she satisfies the criteria given below:

- The passenger is below 15 years and is accompanied by an adult.

Or
- The passenger is a lady and is not accompanied by an adult.

Or
- The passenger is not below 15 years, but is travelling for the first time.

The inputs are

INPUTS	
A	The passenger is below 15 years age.
C	The passenger is accompanied by an adult.
L	The passenger is a lady.
F	The passenger is travelling for the first time.

(In all the above case 1 indicates yes and 0 indicates no).

Output : *W*-Denotes the passenger is allotted a window seat (1 indicates yes and 0 indicates no).

Draw the truth table for the inputs and output given above and write the SOP expression for *W*(*A*, *C*, *L*, *F*). **ISC 2016**

Ans The truth table for given inputs and ouput is

Inputs				Output
A	C	L	F	W
0	0	0	0	0
0	0	0	1	1
0	0	1	0	1
0	0	1	1	1
0	1	0	0	0
0	1	0	1	1
0	1	1	0	0
0	1	1	1	1
1	0	0	0	0
1	0	0	1	0
1	0	1	0	1
1	0	1	1	1
1	1	0	0	1
1	1	0	1	1
1	1	1	0	1
1	1	1	1	1

Required SOP expression is,

$$W(A,C,L,F) = A'C'L'F + A'C'LF' + A'C'LF + A'CL'F + A'CLF + AC'LF' + AC'LF + ACL'F' + ACL'F + ACLF' + ACLF$$

12. A combinational logic circuit with three inputs *P*, *Q*, *R* produces output 1 if and only if an odd number of 0's are inputs. **ISC 2013**

(i) Draw its truth table.

(ii) Derive a canonical SOP expression for the truth table.

(iii) Find the complement of the derived expression using De-Morgan's theorem and verify, if it is equivalent to its POS expression.

Ans (i)

P	*Q*	*R*	Output
0	0	0	1
0	0	1	0
0	1	0	0
0	1	1	1
1	0	0	0
1	0	1	1
1	1	0	1
1	1	1	0

(ii) The canonical SOP expression will be $P'Q'R' + P'QR + PQ'R + PQR'$.

(iii) The complement of derived SOP expression will be $(P'Q'R' + P'QR + PQ'R + PQR')'$

$$= (P+Q+R).(P+Q'+R').(P'+Q+R').(P'+Q'+R)$$

It is a POS expression of derived SOP expression because we know that SOP and POS expression are equivalent to each other.

13. Reduce the boolean expressions to the simplest forms. **ISC 2011**

(i) $\{(C.D)' + A\} + A + (C.D) + (A.B)$

(ii) $A.\{B + C(A.B + A.C)'\}$

Ans (i) Given expression,

$F = (C.D)' + A + A + (C.D) + (A.B)$

$F = 1 + A + A + A.B$ (by complementary law)

$F = 1 + A + A.B$ (by unit property)

$F = 1 + A.B$ (by domination law)

$F = (1+A).(1+B)$ (By domination law)

$F = (1).(1)$

$F = 1$

(ii) Given expression,

$F = A.\{B + C(A.B + A.C)'\}$

$F = A.\{B + C(A.B)'.(A.C)'\}$ (by De-Morgan's law)

$F = A.\{B + C(A' + B').(A' + C')\}$ (by De-Morgan's law)

$F = A.\{B + C(A'.A' + A'.C' + B'.A' + B'C')\}$ (by distributive law)

$F = A.\{B + C(A' + A'.C' + A'.B' + B'C')\}$ (by idempotent law)

$F = A.\{B + A'C + A'C'C + A'.B'.C + B'.C'.C\}$ (by distributive law)

$F = A.\{B + A'.C + 0 + A'.B'.C + 0\}$ (by complementary law)

$F = A.B + A.A'.C + A'.A.B'.C$ (by distributive law)

$F = A.B + 0 + 0$ (by complementary law)

$F = A.B$ (by identity law)

14. Verify if,

$x'.y.z + x.y'.z + x.y.z' + x.y.z = x.y + y.z + z.x$

At each step state the law used for simplification clearly. **ISC 2007**

Ans $LHS = x'.y.z + x.y'.z + x.y.z' + x.y.z$

$= x'.y.z + x.y'.z + x.y(z' + z)$ (by distributive law)

$= x'.y.z + x.y'.z + x.y(1)$ (by complement law)

$= x'.y.z + x.y'.z + x.y$ (by identity law)

$= x'.y.z + x.y + x.y'.z$ (by commutative law)

$= (x'.z + x)y + x.y'.z$ (by distributive law)

$= (x + z)y + x.y'.z$ ($\because A + A'B = A + B$)

$= x.y + y.z + x.y'.z$ (by distributive law)

$= x.y + (y + x.y').z$ (by distributive law)

$= x.y + (y + x).z$ ($\because A + A'B = A + B$)

$= x.y + y.z + z.x$ (by distributive law)

$\therefore$ LHS = RHS

Case Based Questions

1. Reduce the given Boolean function $F(A,B,C,D) = \Sigma(6, 7, 10, 11, 12, 14, 15)$ by using 4-variable Karnaugh map and answer the following questions **ISC 2022 (Sem I)**

(i) What will be the least number of groups and its types formed for reduction?
(a) 4 pairs (b) 2 quads and 1 pair
(c) 1 quad and 2 pairs (d) 3 quads

(ii) What is the reduced expression of the Boolean function given below?
(a) $ABD' + ACD' + BCD' + AC'D'$
(b) $(B+C)\cdot(A+C)\cdot(A+B+D')$
(c) $AC + ABD' + BCD'$
(d) $BC + AC + ABD'$

Ans (i) (b) 2 quads and 1 pair
(ii) (d) $BC + AC + ABD'$

Explanation For $F(A,B,C,D) = \Sigma(6, 7, 10, 11, 12, 14, 15)$

AB \ CD	C'D'	C'D	CD	CD'
A'B'	0	1	3	2
A'B	4	5	1 (7)	1 (6)
AB	1 (12)	13	1 (15)	1 (14)
AB'	8	9	1 (11)	1 (10)

There are 2 quads and 1 pair,

Ist quad $(m_6 + m_7 + m_{14} + m_{15}) = BC$

2nd quad $(m_{10} + m_{11} + m_{14} + m_{15}) = AC$

pair $(m_{12} + m_{14}) = ABD'$

So, final expression is

$F(A,B,C,D) = BC + AC + ABD'$

2. Reduce the given Boolean function $F(A,B,C,D) = \pi(3, 4, 5, 6, 7, 10, 12, 13, 14, 15)$ by using 4-variable Karnaugh map and answer the following questions **ISC 2022 (Sem I)**

(i) What will be the least number of groups and its types formed for reduction?
(a) 1 octet and 2 pairs
(b) 2 quads and 2 pairs
(c) 1 octet and 3 pairs
(d) 4 pairs

(ii) What is the reduced expression of the Boolean function given above?
(a) $(A'+C')\cdot(C'+D)\cdot(A'+C'+D)\cdot(A+C+D')$
(b) $B'\cdot(A'+C'+D)\cdot(A+C'+D')$
(c) $B'\cdot(A'+C')\cdot(C'+D')$
(d) $(A'+C'+D)\cdot(A+C+D')\cdot(A+B'+C)\cdot(B'+C+D')$

Ans (i) (a) 1 octet and 2 pairs
(ii) (b) $B'(A'+C'+D)(A+C'+D')$

Explanation For, $F(A,B,C,D) = \pi(3, 4, 5, 6, 7, 10, 12, 13, 14, 15)$

We get one octet and 2 pairs,

AB \ CD	C+D	C+D'	C'+D'	C'+D
A+B	0	1	0 (3)	2
A+B'	0 (4)	0 (5)	0 (7)	0 (6)
A'+B'	0 (12)	0 (13)	0 (15)	0 (14)
A'+B	8	9	11	0 (10)

Octet $(M_4 \cdot M_5 \cdot M_6 \cdot M_7 \cdot M_{12} \cdot M_{13} \cdot M_{14} \cdot M_{15}) = B'$

pair 1 $(M_3 \cdot M_7) = A + C' + D'$

pair 2 $(M_{10} \cdot M_{14}) = A' + C' + D$

Final expression, $F(A,B,C,D) = B'\cdot(A + C' + D')\cdot(A' + C' + D)$

3. Given the Boolean expression $F = P + ((Q + R).(Q' + S'))$ ISC 2022 (Sem I)

(i) Identify the complement of the expression

(a) $P' + (Q'R' + QS)$

(b) $P' \cdot (QR + Q'S')$

(c) $P' \cdot (Q'R' + QS)$

(d) $P'QR + P'QS$

(ii) De-Morgan's law states that the complement of a sum is equal to

(a) the complement of their product

(b) the product of their individual complements

(c) the sum of their individual complements

(d) the complement of their sum

Ans (i) (c) $P'.(Q'R' + QS)$

(ii) (b) the product of their individual complements

Explanation Given, $F = P + ((Q + R) \cdot (Q' + S'))$

Complement of F is $F' = [P + ((Q + R) \cdot (Q' + S'))]'$

$$= P' \cdot ((Q + R) \cdot (Q' + S'))'$$

$$= P'((Q + R)' + (Q' + S')')$$

$$= P'(Q'R' + QS)$$

De-Morgan's law states that the complement of a sum is equal to the product of their individual complements.

4. Reduce the given Boolean function $F(A, B, C, D) = \Sigma(0, 2, 4, 8, 9, 10, 12, 13)$ by using 4-variable Karnaugh map and answer the following questions. ISC SQP 2022 (Sem I)

(i) What will be the least number of groups and their types formed for reduction?

(a) 6 pairs

(b) 2 quad and 2 pairs

(c) 1 quad and 3 pairs

(d) 3 quads

(ii) The reduced expression of the Boolean function given above is

(a) $ACD' + B'D' + BD$

(b) $(A + C' + D') \cdot (B' + D') \cdot (A + C')$

(c) $C'D' + AC' + B'D'$

(d) $(C + D') \cdot (B' + D') \cdot (A + B + D)$

Ans. (i) (d) 3 quads

(ii) (c) $C'D' + AC' + B'D'$

Explanation For, $F(A, B, C, D) = \Sigma(0, 2, 4, 8, 9, 10, 12, 13)$

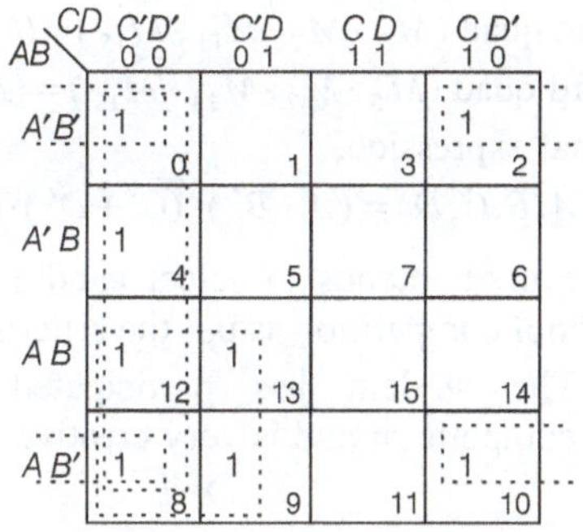

There are 3 quads as

Ist quad $(m_0 + m_2 + m_8 + m_{10}) = B'D'$

IInd quad $(m_0 + m_4 + m_8 + m_{12}) = C'D'$

IIIrd quad $(m_8 + m_9 + m_{12} + m_{13}) = AC'$

So, final expression is $F(A, B, C, D)$

$$= B'D' + C'D' + AC'$$

5. Reduce the given Boolean function $F(A, B, C, D) = \pi(3, 4, 5, 6, 7, 11, 13, 15)$ by using 4-variable Karnaugh map and answer the following questions: ISC SQP 2022 (Sem I)

(i) What will be the least number of groups and their types formed for reduction?

(a) 6 pairs (b) 3 quads

(c) 1 quad and 3 pairs (d) 2 quad and 3 pairs

(ii) The reduced expression of the Boolean function given above is

(a) $(B + C) \cdot (B + D) \cdot (A' + D)$

(b) $BC + BD + A'D$

(c) $AB' + C'D' + B'D'$

(d) $(A + B') \cdot (C' + D') \cdot (B' + D')$

Ans. (i) (b) 3 quads

(ii) (d) $(A + B') \cdot (C' + D') \cdot (B' + D')$

Explanation

Given, $F(A, B, C, D) = \pi(3, 4, 5, 6, 7, 11, 13, 15)$

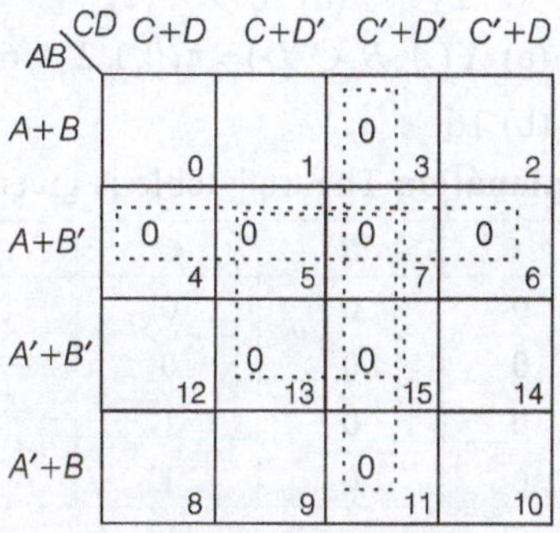

We get,

Ist quad $(M_4 \cdot M_5 \cdot M_6 \cdot M_7) = (A + B')$

IInd quad $(M_3 \cdot M_7 \cdot M_{11} \cdot M_{15}) = (C' + D')$
IIIrd quad $(M_5 \cdot M_7 \cdot M_{13} \cdot M_{15}) = (B' + D')$
Final expression,
$F(A,B,C,D) = (A + B') \cdot (C' + D') \cdot (B' + D')$

6. A school intends to select candidates for an inter school competition as per the criteria given below

- The student has participated in an earlier competition and is very creative

Or

- The student is very creative and has excellent general awareness, but has not participated in any competition earlier

Or

- The student has excellent general awareness and has won prize in an inter-house competition

The inputs are

Inputs	
A	Participated in a competition earlier
B	Is very creative
C	Won prize in an inter house competition
D	Has excellent general awareness

(In all the above cases 1 indicates yes and 0 indicates no).
Output: *X* [1 indicates yes and 0 indicates no for all cases].
Draw the truth table for the inputs and output given above and answer the following questions.
ISC SQP 2022 (Sem I)

(i) The POS expression for *X*(*A*, *B*, *C*, *D*) will be
(a) $X(A,B,C,D) = \Sigma(3, 5, 7, 11, 12, 13, 14, 15)$
(b) $X(A,B,C,D) = \pi(3, 5, 7, 11, 12, 13, 14, 15)$
(c) $X(A,B,C,D) = \pi(0, 1, 2, 4, 6, 8, 9, 10)$
(d) $X(A,B,C,D) = \Sigma(0, 1, 2, 4, 6, 8, 9, 10)$

(ii) The maximum input combinations for the above truth table will be
(a) 24 (b) 16 (c) 8 (d) 4

Ans (i) (c) $X(A,B,C,D) = \pi(0, 1, 2, 4, 6, 8, 9, 10)$
(ii) (b) 16

Explanation The truth table is given below

A	*B*	*C*	*D*	*X*
0	0	0	0	0
0	0	0	1	0
0	0	1	0	0
0	0	1	1	1
0	1	0	0	0
0	1	0	1	1
0	1	1	0	0
0	1	1	1	1
1	0	0	0	0
1	0	0	1	0
1	0	1	0	0
1	0	1	1	1
1	1	0	0	1
1	1	0	1	1
1	1	1	0	1
1	1	1	1	1

POS expression for
$X(A,B,C,D) = \pi(0, 1, 2, 4, 6, 8, 9, 10)$
In this expression, there are 4 variables i.e. $n = 4$
So, maximum input combinations for the above truth table will be $2^n = 2^4 = 16$

7. Given the Boolean expression
$F = (P + R) \cdot (P \cdot Q + Q \cdot R')$, identify
(i) The complement of the expression
ISC SQP 2022 (Sem I)
(a) $P'R' + (P' + Q') \cdot (Q' + R)$
(b) $(P' + R')(P' + Q') + (Q + R')$
(c) $P'R' \cdot (PQ' + Q'R)$
(d) $(P + R)' \cdot (P' + Q) \cdot (Q' + R)$

(ii) The law used
(a) Distributive Law
(b) De-Morgan Law
(c) Associative Law
(d) Idempotent Law

Ans. (i) (a) $P'R' + (P' + Q')(Q' + R)$
(ii) (b) De-Morgan Law

Explanation Given, $F = (P + R)(PQ + Q \cdot R')$

Complement of F is $F' = [(P + R) \cdot (PQ + QR')]'$
$= (P + R)' + (PQ + QR')'$
$= P'R' + (PQ)' \cdot (QR')'$
$= P'R' + (P' + Q') \cdot (Q' + R)$

The law used is De-Morgan Law.

CHAPTER TEST

1 Mark Questions

1. Which law is stated that $A + A.B = A$?

(a) Absorption law (b) Commutative law (c) Distributive law (d) Involution law

2. If $A = 1, B = 0, C = 0, D = 1$, find its minterm from given options.

(a) $A + B' + C' + D$ (b) $AB'C'D$ (c) $A' + B + C + D'$ (d) $A'BCD'$

2 Marks Questions

3. Express $P + Q'R$ in canonical SOP form.

4. Express $P + Q'R$ in POS form.

3 Marks Questions

5. Write the POS form of Boolean function G, which is represented in the truth table as follows

A	B	C	G
0	0	0	0
0	0	1	1
0	1	0	1
0	1	1	0
1	0	0	0
1	0	1	0
1	1	0	1
1	1	1	1

6. Verify the following Boolean expression using truth table

$$X + (Y.Z) = (X + Y).(X + Z)$$

7. Verify the following Boolean expression using truth table

(i) $X.X' = 0$ (ii) $X + 1 = 1$

8. State and verify distributive law in Boolean algebra.

9. Verify the following algebraically

$$X'.Y + X.Y' = (X' + Y').(X + Y)$$

5 Marks Questions

10. Reduce the following Boolean expression using K-map

$$F(P, Q, R, S) = \Sigma(1, 2, 3, 5, 6, 7, 9, 11, 12, 13, 15)$$

11. Reduce the following Boolean expression using K-map

$$H(U, V, W, Z) = \Pi(0, 1, 4, 5, 6, 7, 11, 12, 13, 14, 15)$$

10 Marks Question

12. What is minimisation of Boolean expression? Write two methods which is used for the simplification of Boolean expression.

03

Computer Hardware

TREND ANALYSIS 4 YEARS

Computer Hardware

Average No. of Questions Across all Sets

Types of Questions	2024	2023	2020	2019
1 Mark	1	–	1	1
2 Marks	–	1	–	–
3 Marks	1	2	2	2
5 Marks	–	3	3	3
10 Marks	–	–	–	–

A computer, or any other electronic device is made up of a number of circuits. Each circuit can be designed using the rules of boolean algebra.

The basic elements of circuits are called **gates**. Using these gates, we can apply the rules of boolean algebra to design circuits that performs a variety of tasks.

Logic Gates

A logic gate is an idealised or a physical device which is used to implement a boolean functions, i.e. it performs a logical operation on one or more logical inputs and produces a single logical output. In other words, logic gates are the building blocks of a computer system. A logic gate is an electronic circuit involving execution of a designed boolean/logical operation.

Gates are block of hardware that produces signals in a form of 1 or 0 when input logic requirements are satisfied.

Logic gates are helpful to design logic circuits include such devices as arithmetic logic units, multiplexers, registers, etc.

Elementary Logic Gates

A variety of logic gates are commonly used in digital computer system. Each gate has a distinct graphic symbol and its operation can be described by means of an algebraic expression. The logic gates represent electronic circuits in boolean algebra.

Elementary Logic Gates

Name	Graphical Symbol	Algebraic Function	Truth Table A	B	X
AND	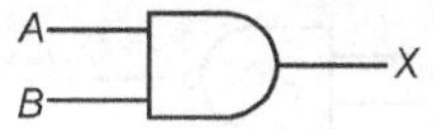	$X = A.B = AB$	0	0	0
			0	1	0
			1	0	0
			1	1	1
OR	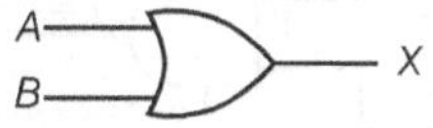	$X = A + B$	0	0	0
			0	1	1
			1	0	1
			1	1	1
NOT (Inverter)	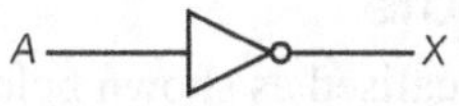	$X = A'$ or $\overline{A}$	0		1
			1		0
NAND	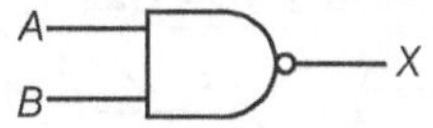	$X = (AB)'$	0	0	1
			0	1	1
			1	0	1
			1	1	0
NOR	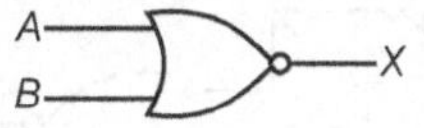	$X = (A + B)'$	0	0	1
			0	1	0
			1	0	0
			1	1	0
Exclusive OR (XOR)	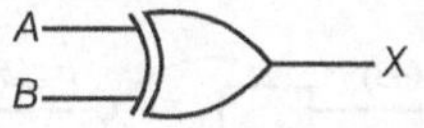	$X = A \oplus B$ or $X = A'B + AB'$	0	0	0
			0	1	1
			1	0	1
			1	1	0
Exclusive NOR (XNOR)	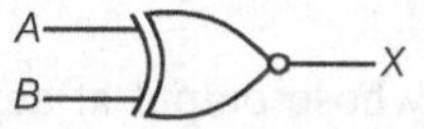	$X = A \odot B$ or $X = A'B' + AB$	0	0	1
			0	1	0
			1	0	0
			1	1	1

Universal Gates

A universal gate is a logic gate which can implement any Boolean function without the need to use any other type of logic gate.

NAND and **NOR** gates are known as universal gates because all the other gates (AND, NOT, OR) can be constructed using only these two gates. Any boolean or logic expression can be realised by using AND, OR and NOT gate. These two operations NAND and NOR are sufficient for realisation of any logic expression.

Realisation of Logic Gates using NAND Gate

Using NAND gate, the AND, OR and NOT gates can be realised as shown below:

Logic Gate	Symbol	Realisation using NAND Gate	Function Expression
NOT	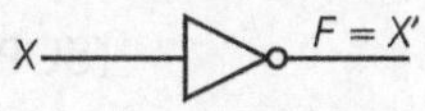	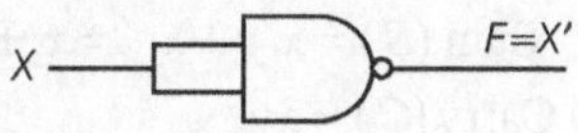	$F = X'$

Logic Gate	Symbol	Realisation using NAND Gate	Function Expression
AND	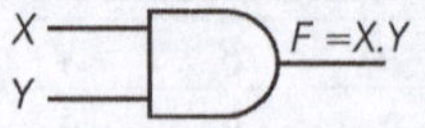	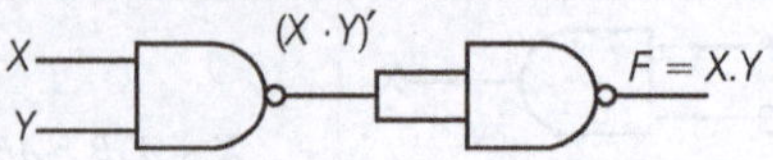	$F = X.Y$
OR	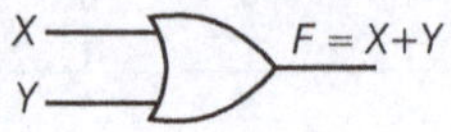	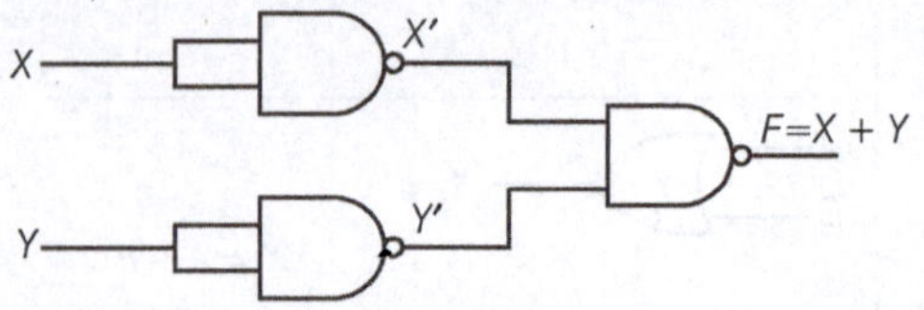	$F = X + Y$

Realisation of Logic Gates using NOR Gate

Using NOR gate, the AND, OR and NOT gates can be realised as shown below:

Logic Gate	Symbol	Realisation using NOR Gate	Function Expression
NOT	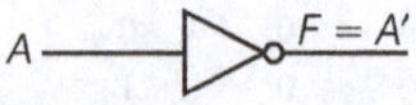	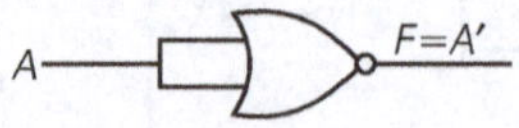	$F = A'$
AND	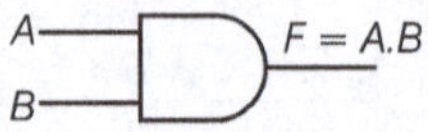	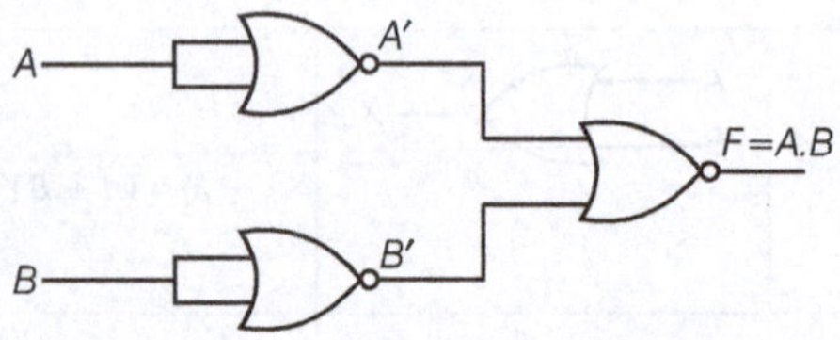	$F = A.B$
OR	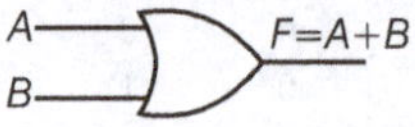	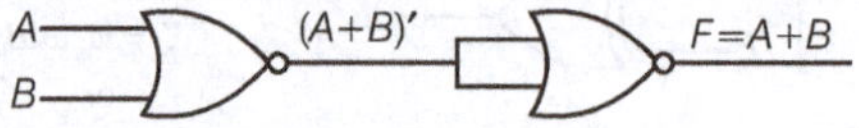	$F = A + B$

Combinational Circuits

A combinational circuit consists of related logic gates whose output at any time can be determined directly from the present combination of inputs irrespective of previous inputs. e.g. half adder, full adder, decoder, encoder, multiplexer, etc.

1. Half Adder

A combinational circuit that performs the addition of two bits is called a half adder. The two inputs are x and y and the two outputs are S (for sum) and C (for carry).

The truth table for half adder is shown in following table:

x	y	S	C
0	0	0	0
0	1	1	0
1	0	1	0
1	1	0	1

From the above truth table, we conclude that, when anyone input signal is equal to 1 and other is 0, then the output will be 1, otherwise output will be 0. The algebraic expression of Sum and Carry could be followed like:

$$\text{Sum } (S) = x'y + xy' = x \oplus y \quad \text{(SOP expression)}$$
$$\text{Carry } (C) = xy$$

The logic diagram for half adder is

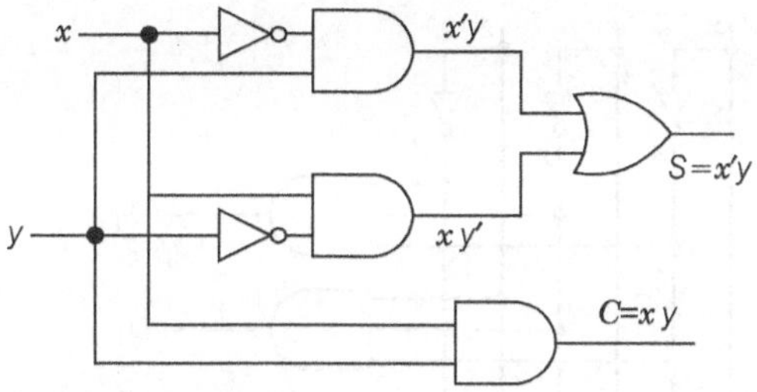

To simplify this logic diagram, we use XOR gate as shown in following circuit

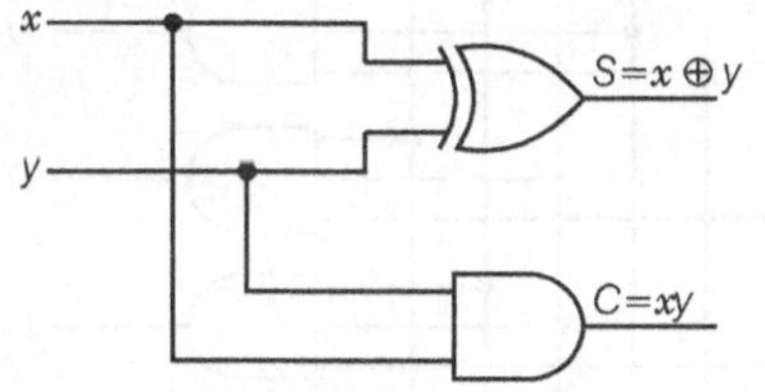

The POS expression of Sum and Carry for half adder is:

$$\text{Sum } (S) = (x + y).(x' + y')$$

$$\text{Carry } (C) = (x + y).(x' + y).(x + y')$$

2. Full Adder

A combinational circuit that performs the addition of three bits (two significant bits and one previous carry) is known as full adder.

Two of the input variables denoted by *x* and *y* represent two significant bits to be added and the third input *z* represents the previous carry. Two outputs are denoted by symbols *S* (for sum) and *C* (for carry).

The truth table for full adder is shown in following table:

x	*y*	*z*	*S*	*C*
0	0	0	0	0
0	0	1	1	0
0	1	0	1	0
0	1	1	0	1
1	0	0	1	0
1	0	1	0	1
1	1	0	0	1
1	1	1	1	1

From truth table, we conclude the expression of Sum and Carry as shown:

The SOP expression for Sum is,

$$S = x'y'z + x'yz' + xy'z' + xyz \quad \ldots\text{(i)}$$

$$= x'(y'z + yz') + x(y'z' + yz) \text{ (by distributive law)}$$

$$\Rightarrow \quad = x'(y \oplus z) + x(y \odot z)$$

($\because$ as per XOR gate, $F = x \oplus y = x'y + xy'$ and as per XNOR gate, $F = x \odot y = x'y' + xy$)

$$= x'(y \oplus z) + x(y \oplus z)'$$

($\because$ XNOR is the complement of XOR)

Now, $S = x \oplus (y \oplus z)$

($\because$ as per XOR, $x \oplus y = x'y + xy'$)

$$S = x \oplus y \oplus z$$

The SOP expression for Carry is,

$$C = x'yz + xy'z + xyz' + xyz \quad \ldots\text{(ii)}$$

$$= x'yz + xy'z + xyz' + xyz + xyz + xyz$$

(using idempotent law)

$$= x'yz + xyz + xy'z + xyz + xyz' + xyz$$

(using commutative law)

$$= (x' + x)yz + xz(y' + y) + xy(z' + z)$$

$$C = yz + xz + xy$$

(using complement law)

The logic diagram for full adder is:

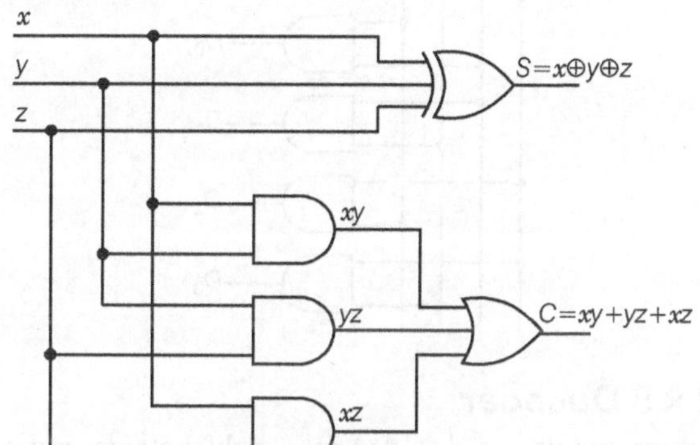

POS expression of Sum and Carry for full adder could be written as:

Sum (*S*)
$$= (x + y + z).(x + y' + z').(x' + y + z').(x' + y' + z)$$

Carry (*C*)
$$= (x + y + z).(x + y + z').(x + y' + z).(x' + y + z)$$

3. Decoder

A decoder is a typical combinational circuit that converts binary information from *n* input lines to a maximum of 2^n unique output lines.

This decoder is called as *n* to *m* line decoder, where $m \leq 2^n$.

The purpose of a general decoder is to generate 2^n or less minterms of *n* input variables. A decoder has *n* inputs and *m* outputs and is also referred as ***n* × *m* decoder**.

(i) 2 × 4 Decoder

For 2 × 4 decoder, we take $n = 2$

So, $m \leq 2^n$

$\Rightarrow$ $m \leq 2^2$

$\Rightarrow$ $m \leq 4$

So, the output lines will be 4. Now, we take, two input variables x and y and four output lines as D_0, D_1, D_2 and D_3.

The truth table for 2 × 4 decoder is:

x	y	D_0	D_1	D_2	D_3
0	0	1	0	0	0
0	1	0	1	0	0
1	0	0	0	1	0
1	1	0	0	0	1

The logic diagram for 2 × 4 decoder is:

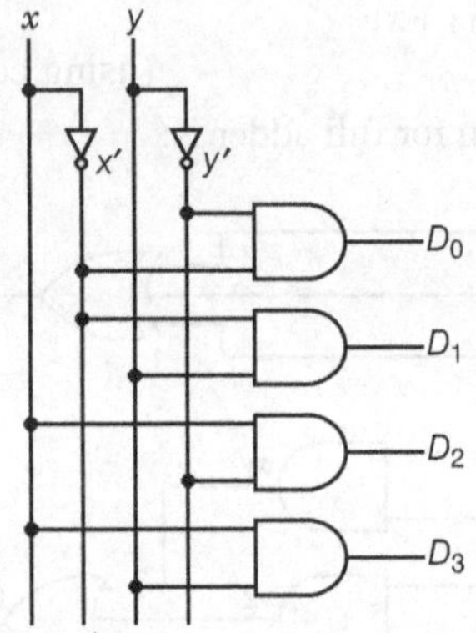

(ii) 3 × 8 Decoder

The three inputs are decoded into eight outputs and each output represents one of the combinations of three input variables.

The three inverters provide the complement of the input and each of the eight AND gates generate one of the binary combinations. A particular application of this decoder is binary to octal conversion.

The truth table for 3 × 8 decoder is shown in table:

x	y	z	D_0	D_1	D_2	D_3	D_4	D_5	D_6	D_7
0	0	0	1	0	0	0	0	0	0	0
0	0	1	0	1	0	0	0	0	0	0
0	1	0	0	0	1	0	0	0	0	0
0	1	1	0	0	0	1	0	0	0	0
1	0	0	0	0	0	0	1	0	0	0
1	0	1	0	0	0	0	0	1	0	0
1	1	0	0	0	0	0	0	0	1	0
1	1	1	0	0	0	0	0	0	0	1

The logic diagram for 3 × 8 decoder is shown below:

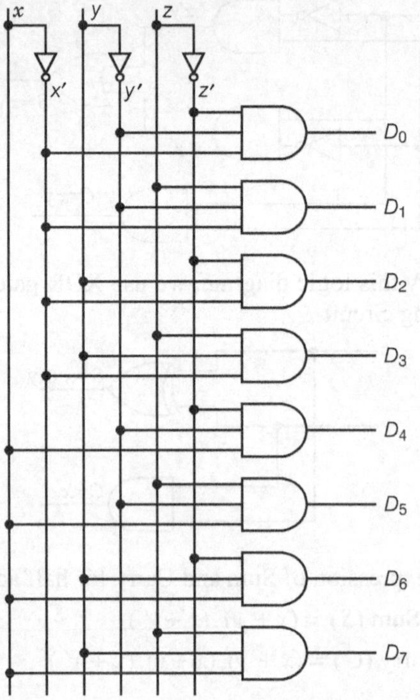

4. Encoder

An encoder is a combinational circuit that produces a reverse operation of decoder. Process of converting signals from one type to another type is called encoding. An encoder consists of 2^n (or less) input lines and n output lines, which generates the binary code for the 2^n input variables.

(i) Decimal to Binary Encoder

In decimal to binary encoder, we convert the decimal number from 0, 1, 2, 3… 9 to equivalent binary numbers. The method to determine number of output lines is, 2^n must be $\geq I$

Where, I represents the total numbers to be encoded. Here, I is 10 as (0-9) are to be encoded.

$$2^n \geq 10$$

to make it true, n must be 4 i.e. $2^4 \geq 10$.

Therefore, number of output lines is 4.

The truth table for decimal to binary encoder is:

Decimal Number	F_3	F_2	F_1	F_0
0	0	0	0	0
1	0	0	0	1
2	0	0	1	0
3	0	0	1	1
4	0	1	0	0
5	0	1	0	1

Decimal Number	F_3	F_2	F_1	F_0
6	0	1	1	0
7	0	1	1	1
8	1	0	0	0
9	1	0	0	1

From the above truth table, we conclude some function expression as:

$$F_0 = \Sigma(1,3,5,7,9),\quad F_1 = \Sigma(2,3,6,7)$$
$$F_2 = \Sigma(4,5,6,7),\quad F_3 = \Sigma(8,9)$$

Here, the output lines considered only those value where it produces 1 as output.

Now, to construct, the logic diagram for decimal to binary encoder is:

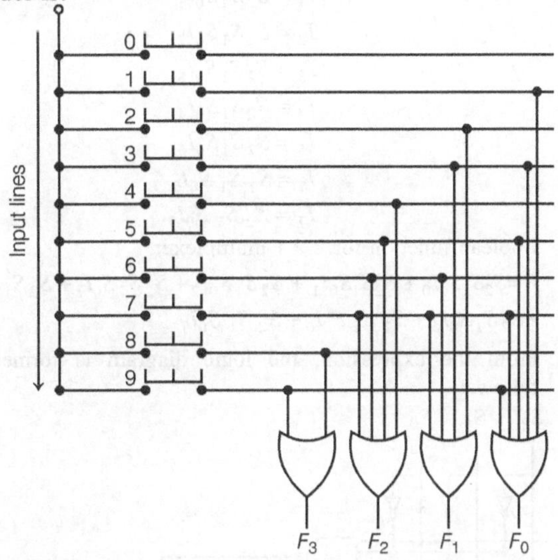

(ii) Hexadecimal to Binary Encoder

In hexadecimal to binary encoder, we convert $(0, 1, 2 \ldots 9, A = 10,\ B = 11 \ldots F = 15)$ into binary. To determine the output lines,

$$2^n \geq I$$

Here, $I = 16$

So, $2^n \geq 16$ (To make it true, put $n = 4$)

$\therefore$ 4 output lines are used

The truth table of hexadecimal to binary encoder is shown:

Input	Output			
Hex no.	B_3	B_2	B_1	B_0
0	0	0	0	0
1	0	0	0	1
2	0	0	1	0
3	0	0	1	1
4	0	1	0	0
5	0	1	0	1
6	0	1	1	0
7	0	1	1	1
8	1	0	0	0
9	1	0	0	1
A	1	0	1	0
B	1	0	1	1
C	1	1	0	0
D	1	1	0	1
E	1	1	1	0
F	1	1	1	1

From the above truth table, we conclude some boolean expression as:

$$B_0 = \Sigma(1,3,5,7,9,B,D,F)$$
$$B_1 = \Sigma(2,3,6,7,A,B,E,F)$$
$$B_2 = \Sigma(4,5,6,7,C,D,E,F)$$
$$B_3 = \Sigma(8,9,A,B,C,D,E,F)$$

Here, B_0, B_1, B_2 and B_3 are the output lines. The output lines will express this function only, where output is equal to 1.

Now, to construct, the logic diagram for hexadecimal to binary encoder is:

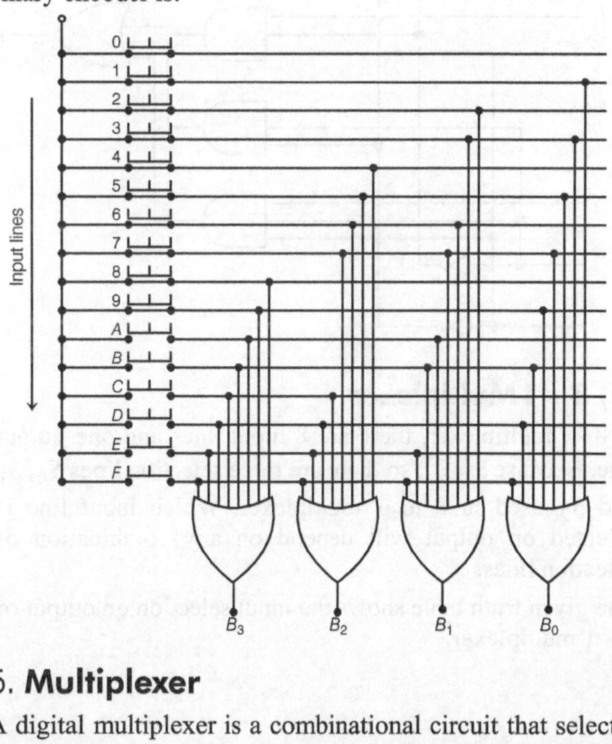

5. Multiplexer

A digital multiplexer is a combinational circuit that selects binary information from one of many input lines and directs it to a single output line. A multiplexer is also called a **data selector**, since it selects one of many inputs. The selection of a particular input line is controlled by a set of selection lines. For *n* selection lines, there are 2^n input lines.

(i) 4 × 1 Multiplexer

In 4 × 1 multiplexer, there are 4 input lines and one output line. Because $4 = 2^2$, so there are 2 selection lines S_0 and S_1 are used to select the particular input on output.

The truth table is shown for a 4 × 1 multiplexer:

S_1	S_0	Y
0	0	I_0
0	1	I_1
1	0	I_2
1	1	I_3

The size of the multiplexer is specified by the number 2^n of its data input lines and the single output line. The function expression drawn from diagram is:

$Y = I_0.S_1'.S_0' + I_1.S_1'.S_0' + I_2.S_1.S_0' + I_3.S_1.S_0$

Each of the four inputs I_0 to I_3 is applied to one input of an AND gate. Selection lines A and B are decoded to select a particular AND gate.

The logic diagram for 4 × 1 multiplexer is:

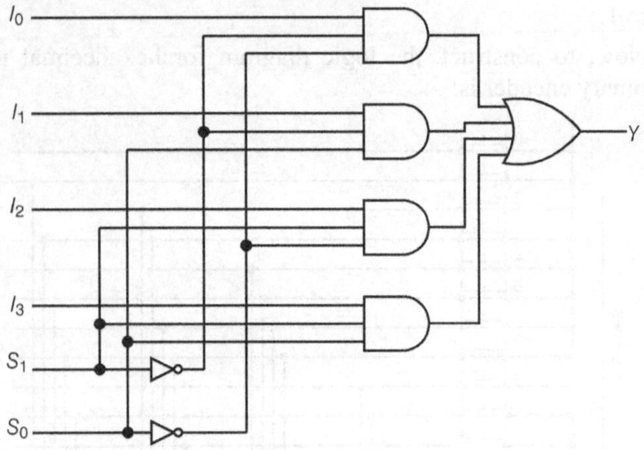

(ii) 8 × 1 Multiplexer

In 8 × 1 multiplexer, there are 8 input lines and one output line. Because $8 = 2^3$, so there are three selection lines S_0, S_1 and S_2 used in 8 to 1 multiplexer. Which input line is selected on output will depend on any combination of selection lines.

The given truth table shows the input selection on output of 8 × 1 multiplexer:

Selection Line			Output
S_2	S_1	S_0	F
0	0	0	I_0
0	0	1	I_1
0	1	0	I_2
0	1	1	I_3
1	0	0	I_4
1	0	1	I_5
1	1	0	I_6
1	1	1	I_7

From the given truth table, we conclude some expression as follows:

$$I_0 = S_2'S_1'S_0'I_0$$
$$I_1 = S_2'S_1'S_0I_1$$
$$I_2 = S_2'S_1S_0'I_2$$
$$I_3 = S_2'S_1S_0I_3$$
$$I_4 = S_2S_1'S_0'I_4$$
$$I_5 = S_2S_1'S_0I_5$$
$$I_6 = S_2\,S_1\,S_0'I_6$$
$$I_7 = S_2\,S_1\,S_0I_7$$

Boolean function for 8 × 1 multiplexer,

$$F = S_2'S_1'S_0'I_0 + S_2'S_1'S_0I_1 + S_2'S_1S_0'I_2 + S_2'S_1S_0I_3 + S_2S_1'S_0'I_4 + S_2S_1'S_0I_5 + S_2\,S_1\,S_0'I_6 + S_2\,S_1\,S_0I_7$$

From the expression, the logic diagram is formed as follows:

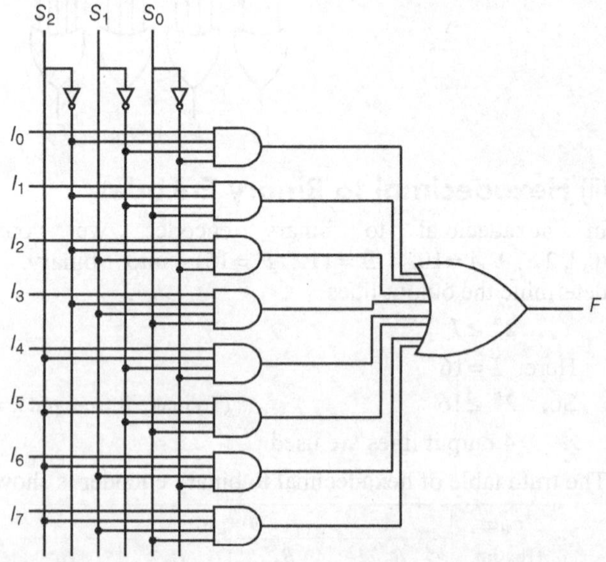

PYQs Previous Years Questions

1 Mark Questions

1. When a sequence of OR, NOT, NOR are connected in series, the logic gate obtained is *ISC 2024*

(a) AND (b) NOT (c) OR (d) XOR

Ans (c) OR

2. Name the basic gate that is equivalent to two NOR gates connected in series. *ISC SQP 2023*

Ans OR gate

3. A decoder is a combinational circuit which *ISC 2022 (Sem I)*

(a) inputs 2^n lines and output n lines
(b) converts parallel data into serial data
(c) inputs n lines and outputs 2^n lines
(d) adds more than two binary bits

Ans (c) inputs n lines and outputs 2^n lines

4. When three NAND gates are placed in series, it performs *ISC 2022 (Sem I)*

(a) NAND operation (b) AND operation
(c) OR operation (d) NOR operation

Ans (a) NAND operation

5. The expression for Sum of a Full adder is *ISC 2022 (Sem I)*

(a) $(a+b')\cdot(b+c')\cdot(a+c')$
(b) $a \oplus b \oplus c$
(c) $a'b + ab' + a'c$
(d) $a \oplus b$

Ans (b) $a \oplus b \oplus c$

6. Multiplexers are combinational circuits which are used for *ISC 2022 (Sem I)*

(a) converting High Level signals into Low Level signals
(b) data transmission
(c) converting binary to decimal
(d) adding binary bits

Ans (b) data transmission

7. The carry expression in cardinal form for a half adder is *ISC 2022 (Sem I)*

(a) $\pi(0, 1, 2)$ (b) $\Sigma(0, 1, 2)$ (c) $\pi(3)$ (d) $\Sigma(1, 2)$

Ans (c) $\pi(3)$

8. The reduced expression of the Boolean function $F = A(B + C(AB + AC)')$ is *ISC 2022 (Sem I)*

(a) 1 (b) AB
(c) 0 (d) $A'C + AB'C$

Ans (b) AB

9. Encoders are used for *ISC SQP 2022 (Sem I)*

(a) adding two bits
(b) converting decimal to binary
(c) converting binary to decimal
(d) data transmission

Ans (c) converting binary to decimal

10. NAND gate is formed by the combinations of *ISC SQP 2022 (Sem I)*

(a) AND gate and OR gate
(b) OR gate and NOT gate
(c) NAND gate and NOT gate
(d) AND gate and NOT gate

Ans (d) AND gate and NOT gate

11. The combinational circuit which adds two binary bits is *ISC SQP 2022 (Sem I)*

(a) full adder
(b) decoder
(c) half adder
(d) multiplexer

Ans (c) half adder

12. Study the diagram given below and answer the questions that follow *ISC 2020*

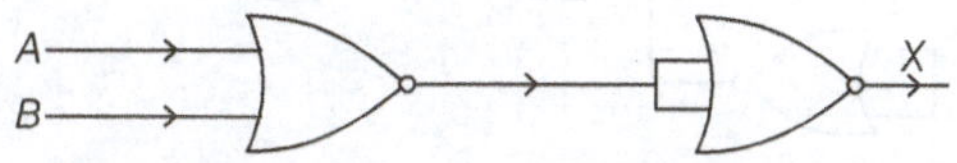

(i) Name the basic gate which is represented by the diagram.
(ii) What will be the value of X when $A = 1$ and $B = 0$?

Ans (i) OR gate using NOR gate

(ii)

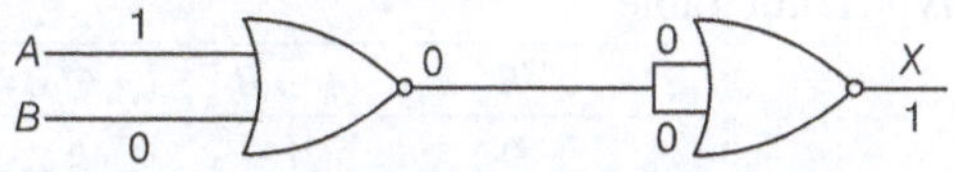

So, the output with inputs $A = 1$ and $B = 0$ is 1.

13. Name and draw the logic gate represented by the following truth table, where A and B are inputs and X is the output. *ISC 2019*

A	B	X
0	0	0
0	1	1
1	0	1
1	1	0

Ans XOR logic gate represented by the given truth table.

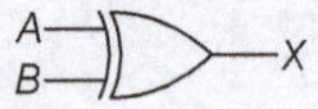

$X = A \oplus B$ or $X = A'B + AB'$

14. Draw the logic diagram and truth table for 2 inputs XNOR gate. **ISC 2017**

Ans Logic diagram for 2 inputs XNOR gate :

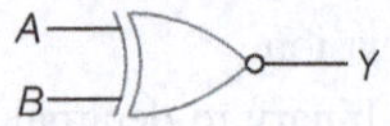

$Y = A \odot B = A'B' + AB$

Truth table for 2 inputs XNOR gate

A	B	Y
0	0	1
0	1	0
1	0	0
1	1	1

15. Draw the logic circuit of a NAND gate using NOR gates only. **ISC 2016, 2005**

Ans To draw the logic circuit of a NAND gate using NOR gates, we take two input variables x and y as shown below:

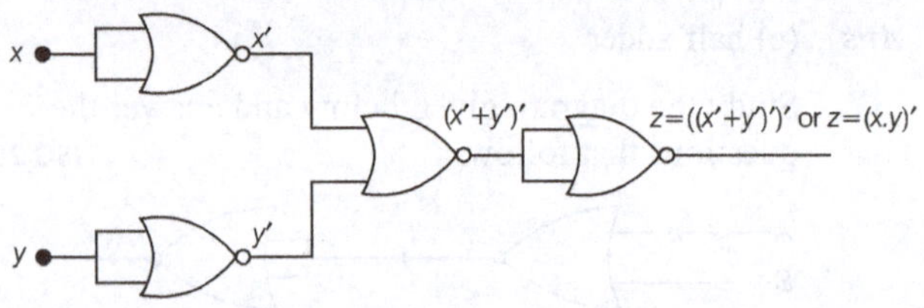

2 Marks Questions

1. Verify the following expression by using the truth table

$(A \odot B)' = (A \oplus B)$ **ISC 2023**

Ans Truth Table

A	B	$A \odot B$	$(A \odot B)'$	$A \oplus B$
0	0	1	0	0
0	1	0	1	1
1	0	0	1	1
1	1	1	0	0

From the above truth table, last two columns are same, hence the given expression is verified.

2. If the input in a decoder is $A'BC'D$, then the decimal equivalent output will be **ISC SQP 2022 (Sem I)**

(a) 8 (b) 10
(c) 5 (d) 6

Ans (c) When input in a decoder is $A'BC'D$

Its binary form is 0101

The decimal equivalent to binary

$$= 0 \times 2^3 + 1 \times 2^2 + 0 \times 2^1 + 1 \times 2^0$$
$$= 0 \times 8 + 1 \times 4 + 0 \times 2 + 1 \times 1$$
$$= 0 + 4 + 0 + 1$$
$$= 5$$

3. The basic logic gate that represents the simplification of the Boolean expression $A \cdot (A' + B) \cdot (A + B)$ is **ISC SQP 2022 (Sem I)**

(a) OR gate (b) NOT gate
(c) AND gate (d) None of these

Ans (c) Given expression $A(A' + B)(A + B)$

$= A(A'A + A'B + BA + BB)$ [by distributive law]

$= A(0 + A'B + AB + BB)$ [by complementary law]

$= A(A'B + AB + B)$ [by idempotence law]

$= AA'B + AAB + AB$ [by distributive law]

$= O + AAB + AB$ [by complementary law]

$= AAB + AB$

$= AB + AB$

$= AB$ [by idempotence law]

It represents the AND gate.

4. Define universal gates. Give one example and show how it works as an OR gate. **ISC SQP 2020**

Ans NAND and NOR gates are known as universal gates because all the other gates (AND, OR, NOT) can be constructed using only these two gates. Any Boolean or logic expression can be realised by using AND, OR and NOT gate.

e.g. NOR gate

OR gate can be replaced by NOR gate as

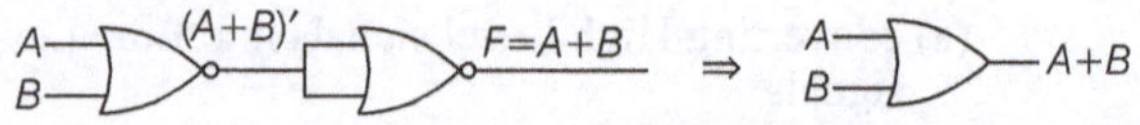

5. Draw the logic diagram of 4 : 1 multiplexer. **ISC SQP 2020**

Ans

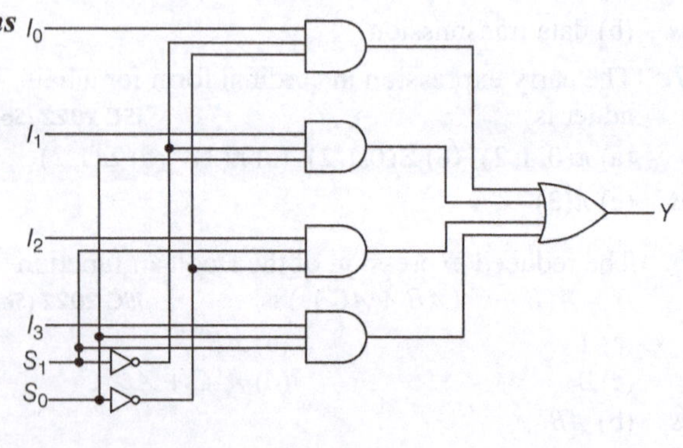

6. Using only NAND gates, draw the logic circuit diagram for $A' + B$. *ISC 2018*

Ans Expression $A' + B$

Logic circuit diagram using NAND gates only

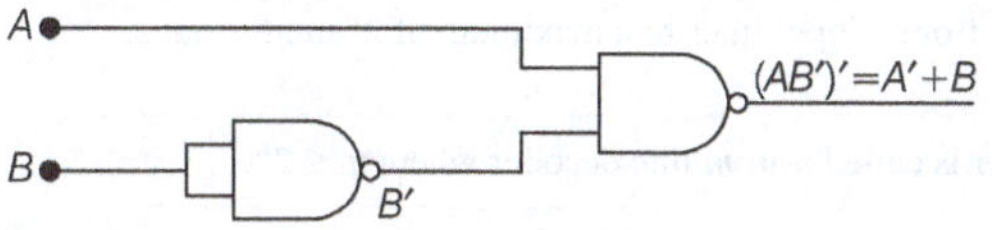

7. Answer the questions related to the circuit given below: *ISC 2015*

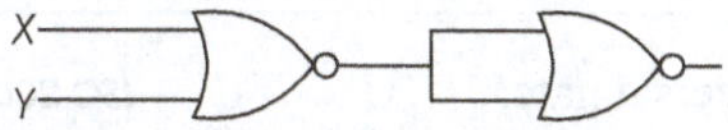

(i) Give the output if, $X = 1$ and $Y = 0$

(ii) Name the basic gate represented by the above diagram.

Ans (i)

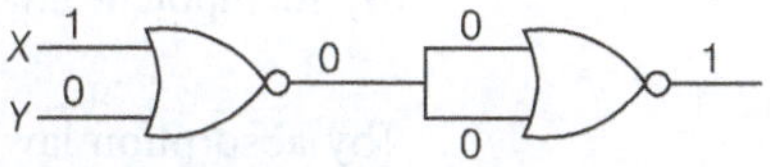

So, the output with $X = 1$ and $Y = 0$ is 1.

(ii) NOR gate.

8. From the logic circuit diagram given below, find output 'F' and simplify it. Also, state the law represented by the logic diagram. *ISC 2014*

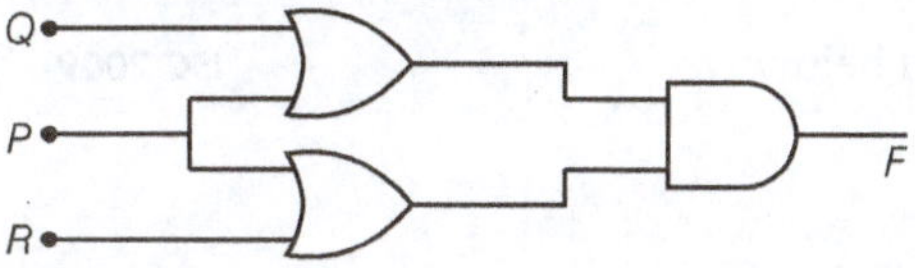

Ans From the logic diagram,

We have three input variables i.e. Q, P, R. To find the output F,

(i) We can see that Q and P input variables formed one OR gate and P and R input variables formed another OR gate.

(ii) On the output of both OR gate, an AND operation, is being performed.

(iii) So, output of $F = (Q + P) . (P + R)$

To simplify this expression,

$F = (Q + P)(P + R)$

$F = QP + QR + PP + PR$ (by distributive law)

$F = QP + QR + P + PR$

(by idempotent law i.e. $PP = P$)

$F = QP + QR + P(1 + R)$

$F = QP + QR + P$ (by absorption law)

$F = P(Q + 1) + QR$

$F = P + QR$ (by absorption law)

Logic diagram represented as distributive law.

9. What are Decoders? How are they different from Encoders? *ISC 2013*

Ans Refer to text on page 49.

An encoder is different from decoder because it produces a reverse operation from that of decoder i.e. an encoder provides various signals into binary form, whereas decoder provides various signals into decimal form.

10. Name the logic gate for the following circuit diagram and write its truth table. *ISC 2011*

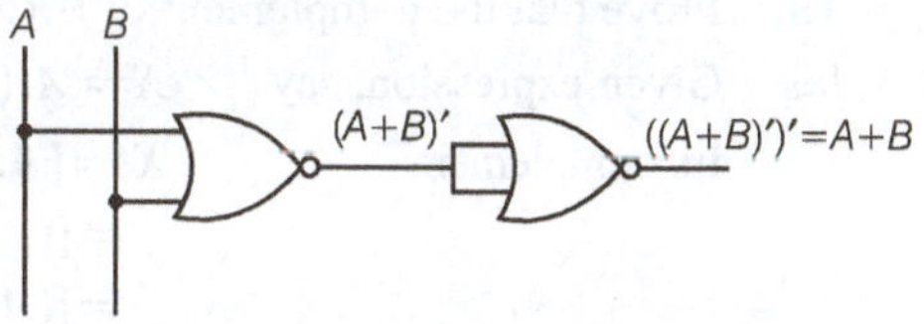

Ans In the given circuit diagram, there are two NOR gates

First NOR gate

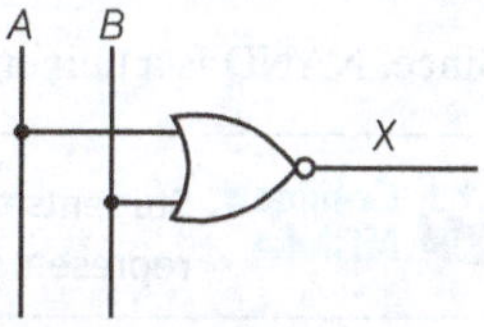

will produce output $X = (A + B)'$ and this output is being provided as input to second NOR gate i.e.

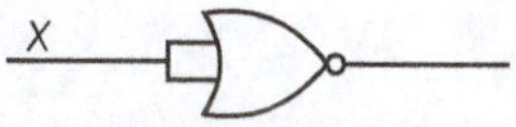

and second NOR gate being a single input NOR gate will work as a NOT gate only. Hence, it will produce $Y = X'$ i.e.

$= ((A + B)')'$

$= A + B$ (by involution law)

Hence, the given circuit diagram is just an OR gate.

11. Draw the logic circuit of NOR using NAND gate only. *ISC 2010*

Ans

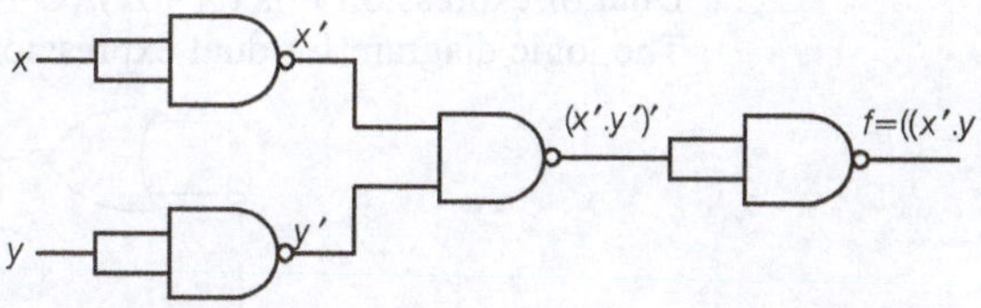

$F = ((x' \cdot y')')' = (x' \cdot y')$

$= (x + y)'$ (by involution law)

12. State the difference between multiplexer and decoder. ***ISC 2009***

Ans Differences between multiplexer and decoder are as follows:

Multiplexer	Decoder
A digital multiplexer is a combinational circuit that selects binary information from one of many input lines and directs it to a single output line.	A decoder is a combinational circuit that converts binary information from n input lines to a maximum of 2^n unique output lines.
It is called as data selector, since it selects one of many inputs.	This decoder is called n-to-m line decoder where $m \le 2^n$.
A multiplexer is used to share several signals to one device like A/D convertor.	Decoders are used to keep abstraction and modularity in hardware design.
e.g. 4-to-1 line multiplexer.	e.g. 3-to-8 decoder.

13. Prove that the complement of $A.(A+B).B(B+C')$ is a universal gate. ***ISC 2009***

Ans Given expression, say $X = A.(A+B).B(B+C')$

Its complement $X' = [A.(A+B).B(B+C')]'$

$= [(AA+AB).(BB+BC')]'$ [by distributive law]

$= [(A+AB).(B+BC')]'$ [by idempotent law]

$= [A(1+B)\cdot B(1+C')]'$

$= [A.B]'$ [by absorption law]

$=$ NAND gate

Since, NAND is a universal gate. Hence, the complement of given expression is a universal gate.

Common Mistake Students think that NAND gate is represented by $(A+B)'$ while NOR gate is represented by $(A+B)'$.

14. Answer the following questions related to the gate given below: ***ISC 2009***

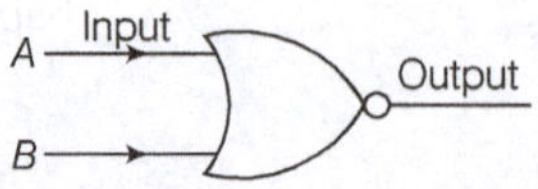

(i) What is the output of the above gate if input $A = 0, B = 1$?

(ii) What are the values of the inputs if output $= 1$?

Ans (i) The output of the NOR gate is 0.
if inputs $A = 0$ and $B = 1$.

(ii) $A = 0, B = 0$

15. State the dual for the following expression and also draw the logic gate diagram for the dual expression obtained using NOR gate only.

$$P = A.B + C.D$$ ***ISC 2009***

Ans $P = A.B + C.D$

Dual of expression P is $(A+B).(C+D)$

The logic diagram for dual expression is:

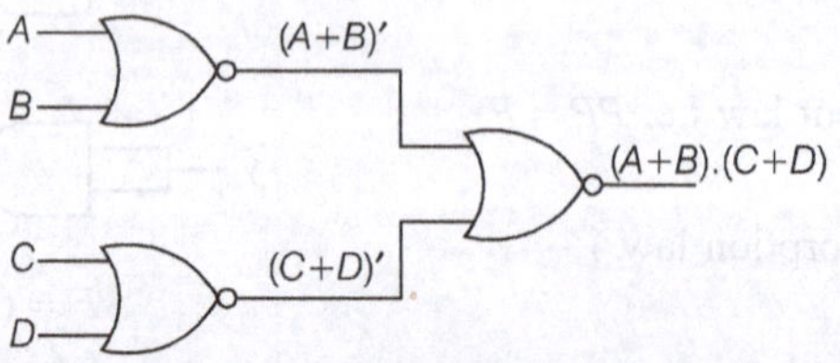

16. Draw the logic gate diagram and truth table for XOR gate. **ISC 2007**

Ans

Here, x and y are two inputs and F represents the output of XOR. The truth table of XOR is:

x	y	$F = x \oplus y$
0	0	0
0	1	1
1	0	1
1	1	0

The algebraic expression is $F = x \oplus y = x'y + xy'$

17. What is meant by a logic gate? State any one application of a logic gate circuit. **ISC 2007**

Ans A logic gate is simply an electronic circuit which operates on one or more input signals to produce an output signal. Logic gates can be constructed from diodes, transistors and resistors connected in such a way that circuit output is the result of a basic logic operations, performed on the input. Logic gates are used in bitwise boolean operations. The most popular application of logic gate is a switch.

18. Name the universal gates. **ISC 2007**

Ans Combinations of NOR and NAND gates may be arranged to create any other possible combination of gates, making them 'universal gate'.

The NAND and NOR gates are said to be the universal logic gates. These two gates are used to create all other logic gates.

NAND	NOR
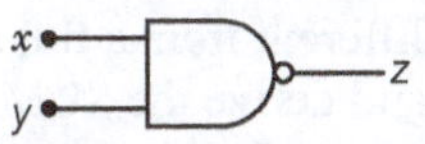	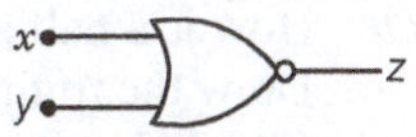
x y $z = (x \cdot y)'$ 0 0 1 0 1 1 1 0 1 1 1 0	x y $z = (x + y)'$ 0 0 1 0 1 0 1 0 0 1 1 0
Boolean expression $z = (x \cdot y)'$	**Boolean expression** $z = (x + y)'$

19. Why is the NOR gate regarded as a universal gate? Draw the logic gate symbol and make the truth table for the two input NOR gates. **ISC 2006**

KEY idea

NOR gate is the combination of NOT gate and OR gate.

Ans NOR gate is regarded as a universal gate because it can be used to construct many other gates like AND, OR, NOT.

NOR gate means NOT OR, i.e. the NOR function is complement of OR function as shown:

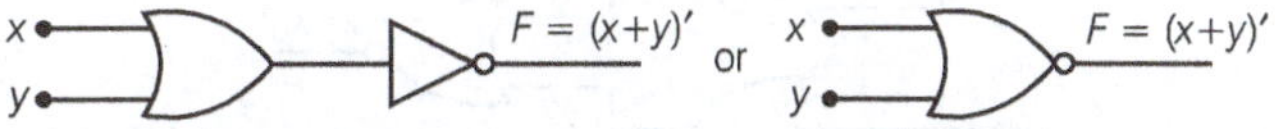

{Here, x and y are two inputs and F is output}

The truth table for 2-input NOR is:

x	y	$F = (x + y)'$
0	0	1
0	1	0
1	0	0
1	1	0

20. Write the SOP expression corresponding to the following truth table and draw its logic gate diagram. **ISC 2006**

A	B	C	F
0	0	0	0
0	0	1	0
0	1	0	1
0	1	1	1
1	0	0	0
1	0	1	0
1	1	0	1
1	1	1	1

Ans SOP expression of given truth table will be:

$$F = A'BC' + A'BC + ABC' + ABC$$

Logic gate diagram of above expression as shown below:

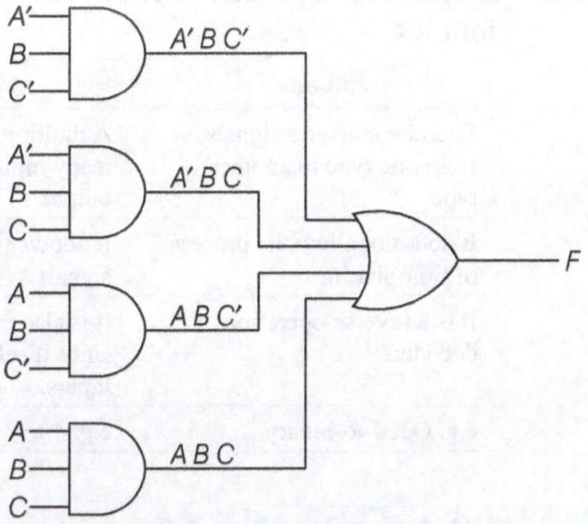

Concept Enhancer SOP (Sum of Product) is a Boolean expression in which product terms are connected by the OR operator.

21. Using NOR gates only, draw AND, OR and NOT gate. **ISC 2005**

Ans (i) Construction of AND gate using NOR gate:

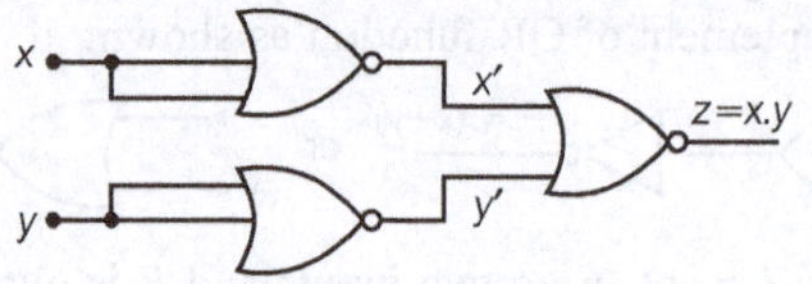

(ii) **Construction of OR gate using NOR gate:**

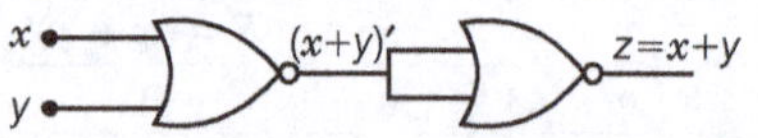

(iii) **Construction of NOT gate using NOR gate** Here, we have only one input variable *x* and it inverse using NOT gate produce *x*′. It passes through NOR, then the output will be:

$z = x'$

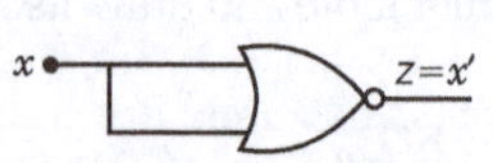

22. What is an encoder? State its application. **ISC 2005**

Ans An encoder is a logic circuit that converts signals of one type to another. An encoder consists of 2^n (or less) input lines and n output lines, which generate the binary code for the 2^n input variables.

Applications of Encoder

(i) It is used in conversion of decimal to binary, hexadecimal to binary, octal to binary system.

(ii) They are used in computer to convert the various input forms to binary form.

23. State the difference between an encoder and a multiplexer circuit. **ISC 2005**

Ans Differences between encoder and multiplexer are as follows:

Encoder	Multiplexer
Encoder converts signals from one type to another type.	A multiplexer is a circuit with many inputs but only one output.
It does not allow the process of time sharing.	It allows time sharing between signals.
It is a reverse operation of decoder.	It is also called data selector, since it selects one of many inputs.
e.g. Octal-to-binary.	e.g. 4-to-1 line Multiplexer.

3 Marks Questions

1. Draw the logic gate diagram for 2-input OR gate using NAND gates only. Show the expression at each step. **ISC 2024**

Ans

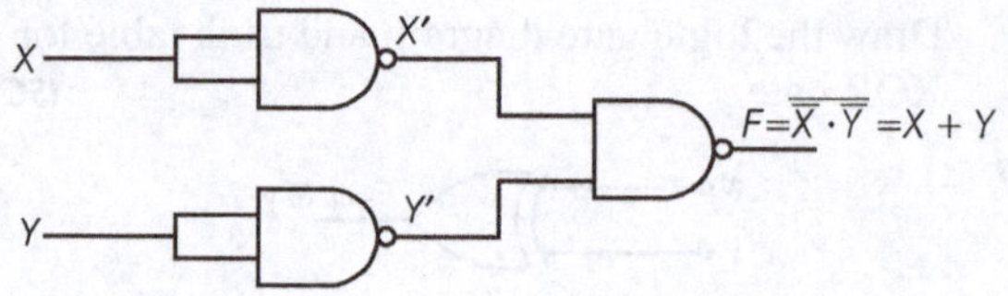

We implement this expression using three NAND gates

- First NAND gate : $\overline{X}$
- Second NAND gate : $\overline{Y}$
- Third NAND gate : $\overline{\overline{X} \cdot \overline{Y}}$

So, the final expression using NAND gates is $= \overline{\overline{X} \cdot \overline{Y}}$
$= X + Y$

2. From the logic diagram given below, write the Boolean expression for (1) and (2). Also, derive the Boolean expression (*F*) and simplify it. **ISC 2023**

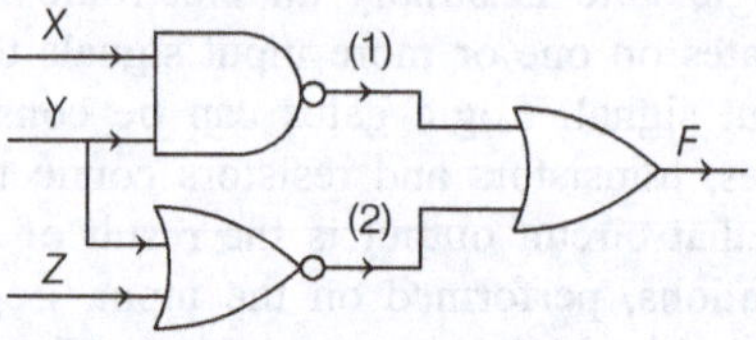

Ans Boolean expression for (1) $= (XY)'$
Boolean expression for (2) $= (Y + Z)'$
Boolean expression for $(F) = (XY)' + (Y + Z)'$

3. Differentiate between half adder and full adder. Write the Boolean expression and draw the logic circuit diagram for the SUM and CARRY of full adder. **ISC 2023**

Or Differentiate between half adder and full adder. Draw the logic circuit diagram for a full adder. **ISC 2018**

Or How is a half adder different from a full adder? Draw the truth table and derive the SUM and CARRY expression for a full adder. Also, draw the logic diagram for a full adder. **ISC 2016**

Or

State how a half adder is different from a full adder? Also, give their respective uses. **ISC 2012, 2005**

Ans Differences between half adder and full adder are as follows :

Half Adder	Full Adder
A combinational circuit that performs the addition of two bits is called a half adder.	A combinational circuit that performs the addition of three bits (two bits are significant and one is a previous carry) is called a full adder.
The half adder circuit needs two binary inputs and two binary outputs.	It consists of three binary inputs and two binary outputs.

Half Adder	Full Adder
Half adder does not have carry in input.	Full adder has carry in input.
It is used in calculators, computers, digital measuring devices etc.	It is used in multiple bit addition, digital processors etc.

Full Adder Refer to text on page 49.

4. What is half adder? Draw the logic circuit for the SUM and CARRY expression of a half adder using only NAND gates. **ISC SQP 2023**

Ans A combinational circuit that performs the addition of two bits is called a half adder. The two inputs are A and B and the two outputs are S (for sum) and C (for carry).

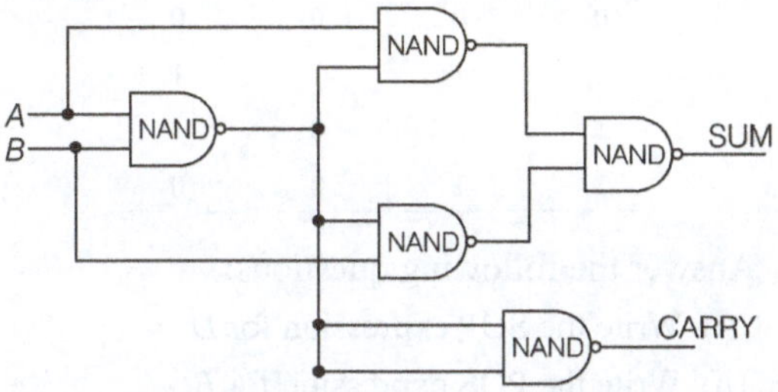

5. Draw the circuit of two inputs XOR gate with the help of NOR gate. **ISC 2020**

Ans XOR gate with the help of NOR gate

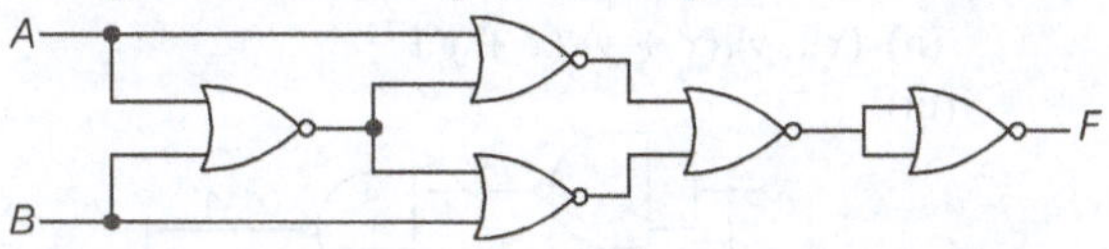

6. Draw the truth table and derive an SOP expression for sum and carry for a full adder. Also, draw the logic circuit for the carry of a full adder. **ISC 2020**

Or What is full adder? Write the SOP expressions for sum and carry simplify the expressions algebraically using boolean algebra. **ISC 2007**

Or What is full adder? Draw the truth table for a full adder. Also, derive SOP expression for a full adder and draw its logic diagram. **ISC 2011, 2009, 2006**

Ans Refer to text on page 49.

7. Simplify the following Boolean expression and draw the gate for the reduced expression

$F = A'B + AB'C + A$ **ISC SQP 2020**

Ans Given, $F = A'B + AB'C + A$

$= A'B + A + AB'C$ [by commutative law]

$= A'B + A(1+B'C)$

$= A'B + A$ [by absorption law]

$= A + A'B$ [by commutative law]

$= (A + A')(A + B)$ [by distributive law]

$F = A + B$ [by complementary law]

Gate for reduced expression

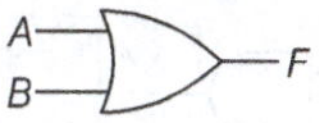

8. From the logic circuit diagram given below, derive the Boolean expression and simplify it to show that it represents a logic gate. Name and draw the logic gate. **ISC 2019**

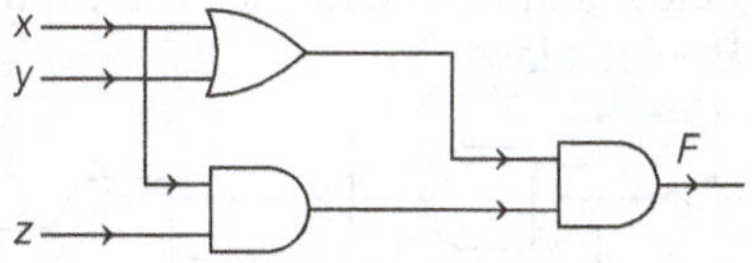

Ans

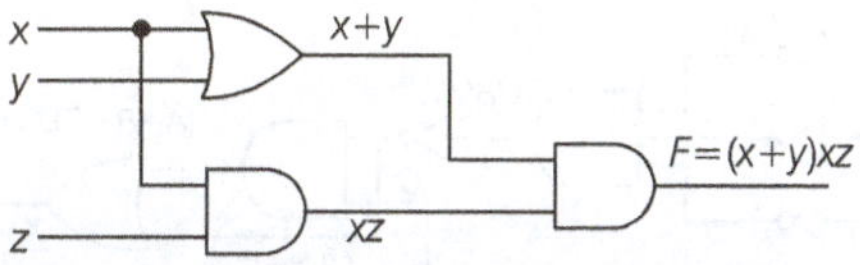

Final boolean expression = $(x + y)\, xz$

$\Rightarrow$ $xz + xyz$

$\Rightarrow$ $xz\,(1 + y)$

$\Rightarrow$ $xz\,(1)$ $[\because 1 + y = 1]$

$\Rightarrow$ xz

xz represents the AND gate and its logic gate is as follows

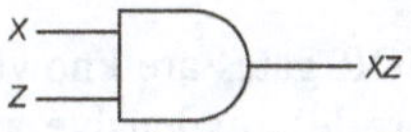

9. What is a half adder? Write the truth table and derive SOP expression for sum and carry for a half adder. **ISC 2019**

Ans Refer to text on pages 48 and 49.

10. State the application of a Half Adder. Draw the truth table and circuit diagram for a Half Adder. **ISC 2017, 2015, 2014, 2006**

Ans A combinational circuit that performs the addition of two bits is called a half adder.

Application of a Half Adder

The ALU of a computer uses half adder to compute the binary addition operation on two bits.

Truth table for a half adder

X	Y	S	C
0	0	0	0
0	1	1	0
1	0	1	0
1	1	0	1

Sum $(S) = X'Y + XY' = X \oplus Y$

Carry $(C) = XY$

The logic diagram for half adder is

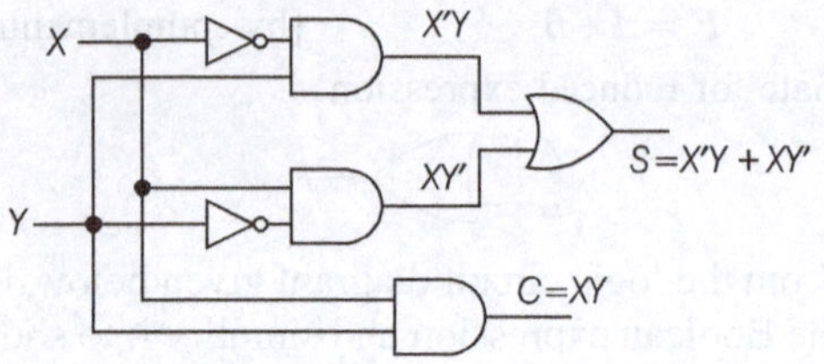

11. Derive a Boolean expression for the logic circuit given below and reduce the derived expression using Boolean laws. **ISC 2015**

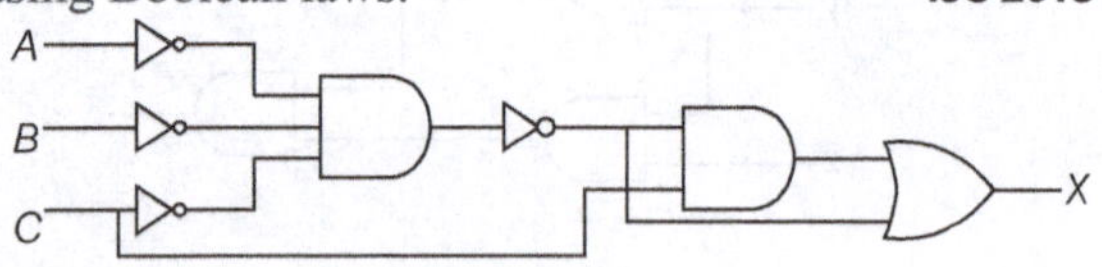

Ans

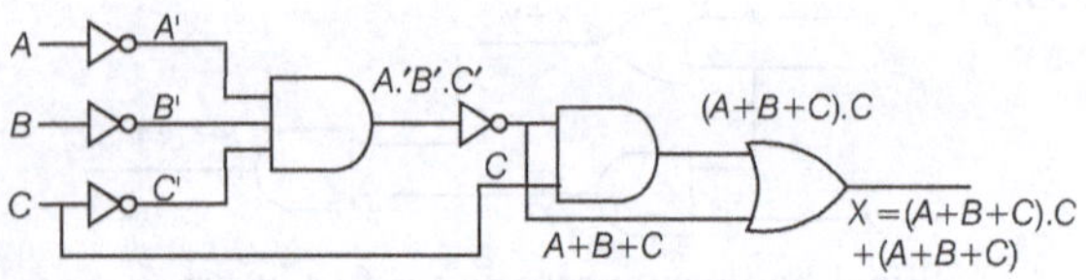

So, the expression will be

$X(A, B, C) = (A+B+C).C + (A+B+C)$

$= (A+B+C)(C+1) = A+B+C$

12. What are universal gates? Construct a logic circuit using NAND gates only for the expression : $A.(B+C)$ **ISC 2015**

Ans NAND and NOR gates are known as universal gates. These gates are less expensive and easier to design. Also, other switching functions (AND, OR) can easily be implemented using NAND/NOR gates.

The logic diagram for $A.(B+C)$ is as follows:

$A.(B+C) = AB + AC$

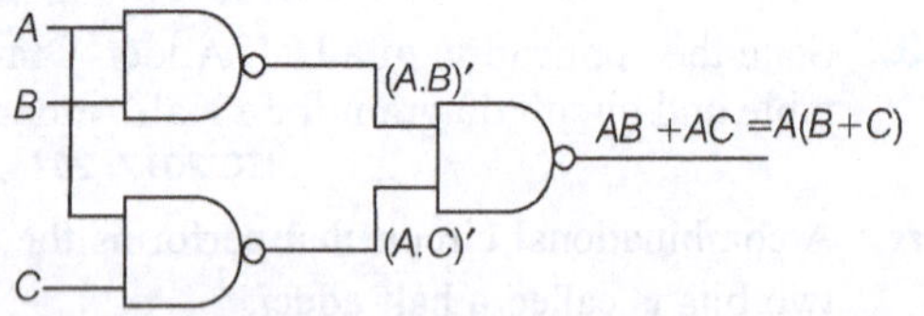

13. Derive a Boolean expression for the logic diagram given below and simplify it. **ISC 2014**

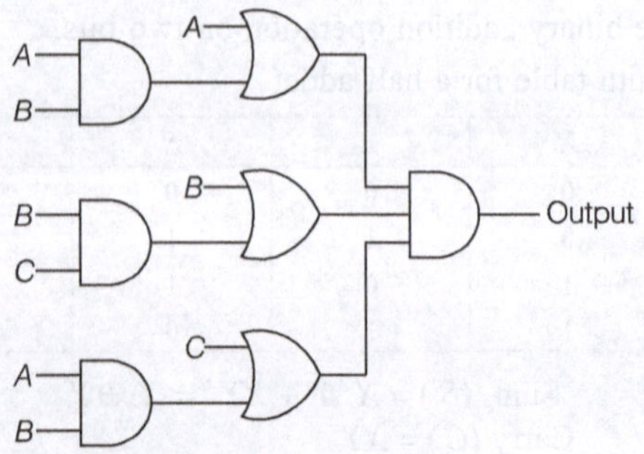

Ans The output will be:

$\Rightarrow (A+AB)(B+BC)(C+AB)$

$\Rightarrow A(1+B).B(1+C).(C+AB)$

$\Rightarrow A.B.(C+AB)$

$\Rightarrow ABC+ABAB$

$\Rightarrow ABC+AB$

$\Rightarrow AB(C+1) = AB$

14. In the following truth table, x and y are inputs and B and D are outputs: **ISC 2013**

Input		Output	
x	y	B	D
0	0	0	0
0	1	1	1
1	0	0	1
1	1	0	0

Answer the following questions:

(i) Write the SOP expression for D.

(ii) Write the POS expression for B.

(iii) Draw a logic diagram for the SOP expression derived for D using only NAND gates.

Ans (i) $x'y+xy'$

(ii) $(x+y).(x'+y).(x'+y')$

(iii)

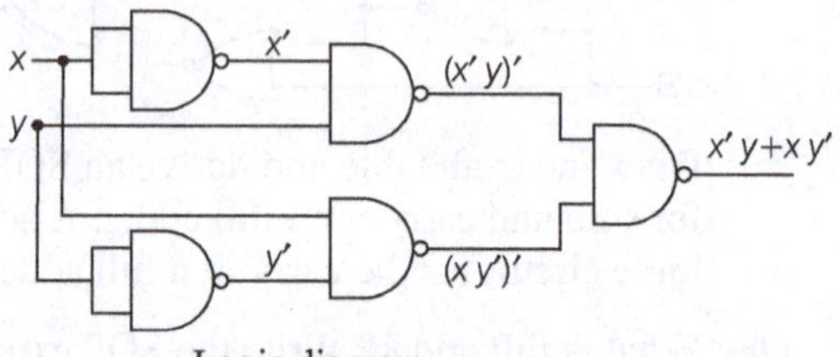

Logic diagram

15. Minimise the following expression using Boolean laws

$Q.(Q'+P).R.(Q+R)$

Also draw the logic gate for the reduced expression. **ISC 2012**

Ans Given expression is

$F = Q.(Q'+P).R.(Q+R)$

$F = (Q.Q'+Q.P).(R.Q+R.R)$

(using distributive law)

Next, $F = (0+Q.P).(R.Q+R.R)$

(using complement law)

Next, $F = (Q.P).(R.Q+R)$

(using zero property and idempotent law)

Next, $F = (Q.P).R\,(Q+1)$

Next, $F = (QP).R$ (using absorption law)

Next, $F = QP.R$

$F = Q.P.R$

Logic gate for $F = Q.P.R$ is

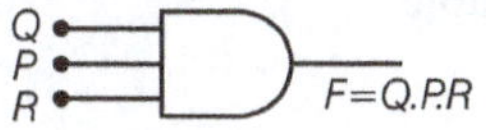

16. Represent the Boolean expression $X + YZ'$ with the help of NOR gates only. **ISC 2012**

Ans Expression $= X + YZ' = (X+Y).(X+Z')$

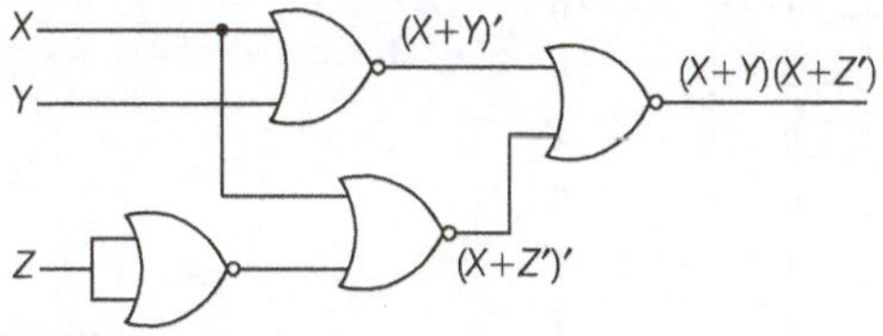

17. Consider the following truth table, where A and B are two inputs and X is the output.

A	*B*	*X*
0	0	0
0	1	1
1	0	1
1	1	0

(i) Name and draw the logic gate for the given truth table.

(ii) Write the POS of $X(A, B)$. **ISC 2012**

Ans (i) XOR gate

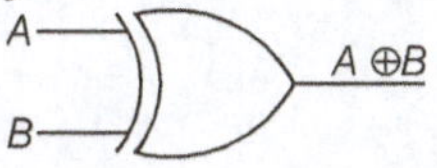

(ii) POS expression is $(A+B).(A'+B')$

18. Verify using a truth table, if **ISC 2011**

$$(A \odot B \odot C)' = A \oplus B \oplus C$$

Ans Given expression, $(A \odot B \odot C)' = A \oplus B \oplus C$

To construct the truth table, we need three input variables as shown in figure

A	*B*	*C*	$A \odot B$	$A \odot B \odot C$	$(A \odot B \odot C)'$	$A \oplus B \oplus C$
0	0	0	1	1	0	0
0	0	1	1	0	1	1
0	1	0	0	0	1	1
0	1	1	0	1	0	0
1	0	0	0	0	1	1
1	0	1	0	1	0	0
1	1	0	1	1	0	0
1	1	1	1	0	1	1
					LHS	RHS

From the above truth table, last two columns are same, hence the given expression $(A \odot B \odot C)' = (A \oplus B \oplus C)$ is verified.

19. State how a decoder is different from a multiplexer? Also state one use of each. **ISC 2011**

Ans Refer to text on page 56 Question 12 (2 Marks Questions).

20. Show with the help of a logic diagram how a NAND gate is equivalent to an OR gate. **ISC 2011**

Ans Let us take two input values A and B. Now, the implementation of OR gate using NAND gate is shown below:

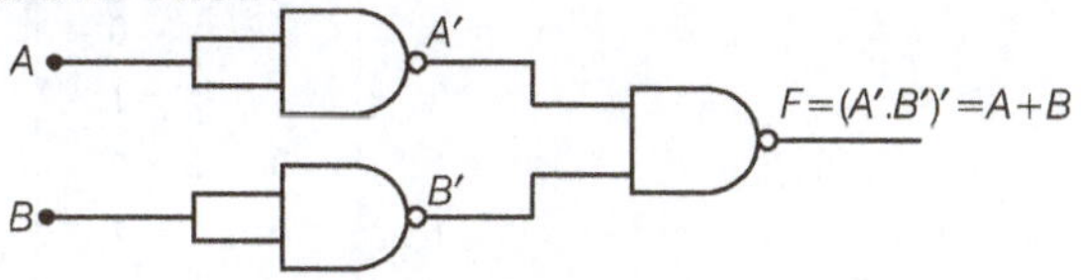

21. Draw the circuit diagram for a 3 to 8 decoder. **ISC 2010**

Ans Refer to text on page 50.

22. Draw the truth table for a half adder. Also, derive a POS expression for the half adder and draw its logic circuit. **ISC 2010**

Ans Truth Table for Half Adder

x	*y*	*S*	*C*
0	0	0	0
0	1	1	0
1	0	1	0
1	1	0	1

Its POS expression are Sum $= (x+y).(x'+y')$

Carry $= (x+y).(x+y').(x'+y)$

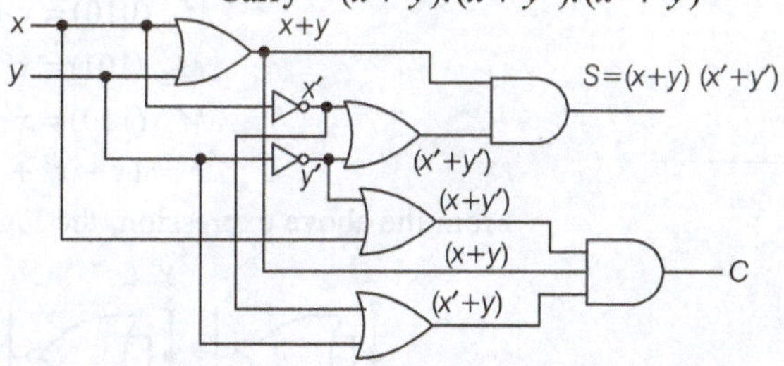

23. Draw the truth table representing 2 input XNOR gate and derive its SOP expression along with its logic gate diagram. **ISC 2010**

Ans Truth Table for XNOR gate

A	*B*	$A \odot B$
0	0	1
0	1	0
1	0	0
1	1	1

SOP expression will be $A'B'+AB$

The logic diagram for SOP expression is:

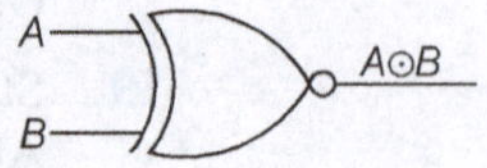

24. Verify the following Boolean expression with the help of a truth table. **ISC 2009**

$$A \oplus (B \odot C) = A \odot (B \oplus C)$$

Ans Given expression, $A \oplus (B \odot C) = A \odot (B \oplus C)$

A	B	C	$B \odot C$	$A \oplus (B \odot C)$	$B \oplus C$	$A \odot (B \oplus C)$
0	0	0	1	1	0	1
0	0	1	0	0	1	0
0	1	0	0	0	1	0
0	1	1	1	1	0	1
1	0	0	1	0	0	0
1	0	1	0	1	1	1
1	1	0	0	1	1	1
1	1	1	1	0	0	0
				LHS		RHS

From the above truth table, we can see that truth set of column $A \oplus (B \odot C)$ and column $A \odot (B \oplus C)$ are same. Hence, the given Boolean expression is verified.

25. Draw the logic gate diagram for the following three input function $F(x, y, z)$ using NOR gates only. **ISC 2008**

$$F(x, y, z) = \Sigma(0, 1, 3, 4, 7)$$

Ans Given expression,

$$F(x, y, z) = \Sigma(0, 1, 3, 4, 7)$$

For NOR implementation, we need to convert it to POS form

$\therefore$ $F(x, y, z) = \Sigma(0, 1, 3, 4, 7)$

$= \Pi(2, 5, 6) = M_2 . M_5 . M_6$

$M_2\ (010) = x + y' + z$

$M_5\ (101) = x' + y + z'$

$M_6\ (110) = x' + y' + z$

$\therefore$ $F = (x + y' + z)(x' + y + z')(x' + y' + z)$

From the above expression, the logic diagram is

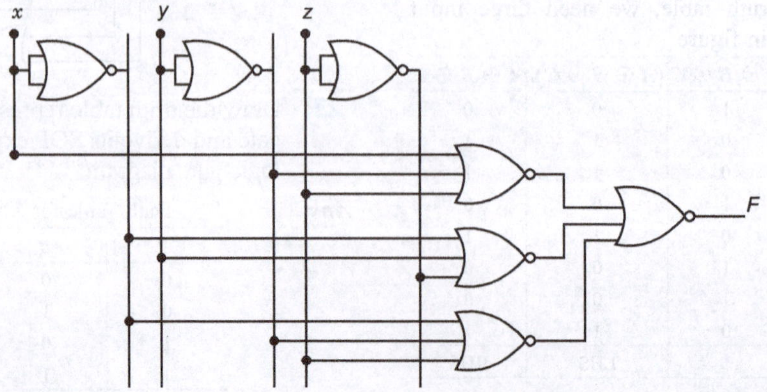

26. Draw the logic gate diagram for the Boolean function. **ISC 2006**

$$F(A,B,C)=(A'+B).(B'+C)$$

Making use of NOR gates only.

Ans $F(A,B,C)=(A'+B).(B'+C)$

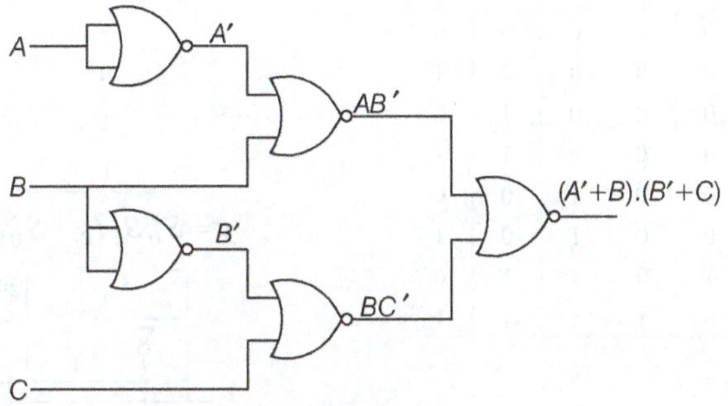

27. Using two half adder and an OR gate, construct full adder. **ISC 2007, 2005**

Ans As we know, the function expression of Sum and Carry of full adder are:

$$\text{Sum}\,(S)=x\oplus y\oplus z$$

$$\text{Carry}\,(C)=xy+yz+zx$$

To construct the full adder, using two half adder and an OR gate, we take three input variables *x*, *y* and *z* as shown in truth table:

x	*y*	*z*	*S*	*C*
0	0	0	0	0
0	0	1	1	0
0	1	0	1	0
0	1	1	0	1
1	0	0	1	0
1	0	1	0	1
1	1	0	0	1
1	1	1	1	1

From the above truth table, we formed a logic diagram using two half adder and OR gate.

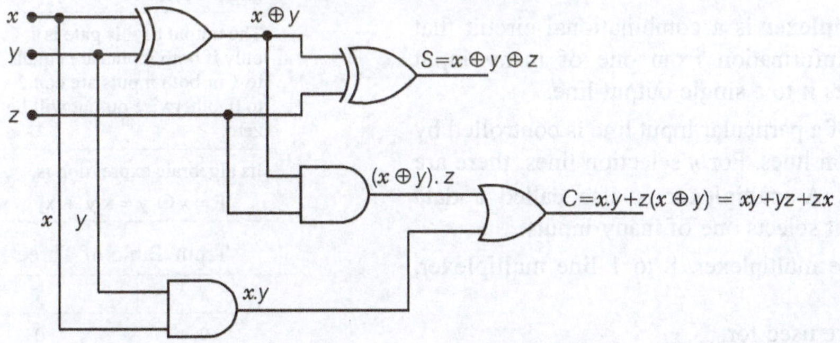

4 Marks Questions

1. Draw the truth table and logic circuit for a decimal to binary encoder. **ISC 2015**

Or With the help of a logic diagram and a truth table, explain a decimal to binary encoder. **ISC 2014**

Or Draw the truth table and logic circuit diagram for converting a decimal number to binary. Explain the working principle with an example. **ISC 2005**

Ans Refer to text on pages 50 and 51.

2. Draw the truth table and logic gate diagram for an octal to binary encoder. **ISC 2015**

Ans Truth table of Octal to Binary encoder is as follows:

I_0	I_1	I_2	I_3	I_4	I_5	I_6	I_7	Y_2	Y_1	Y_0
1	0	0	0	0	0	0	0	0	0	0
0	1	0	0	0	0	0	0	0	0	1
0	0	1	0	0	0	0	0	0	1	0
0	0	0	1	0	0	0	0	0	1	1
0	0	0	0	1	0	0	0	1	0	0
0	0	0	0	0	1	0	0	1	0	1
0	0	0	0	0	0	1	0	1	1	0
0	0	0	0	0	0	0	1	1	1	1

$$Y_0 = I_1 + I_3 + I_5 + I_7$$
$$Y_1 = I_2 + I_3 + I_6 + I_7$$
$$Y_2 = I_4 + I_5 + I_6 + I_7$$

The logic diagram of octal to binary encoder is,

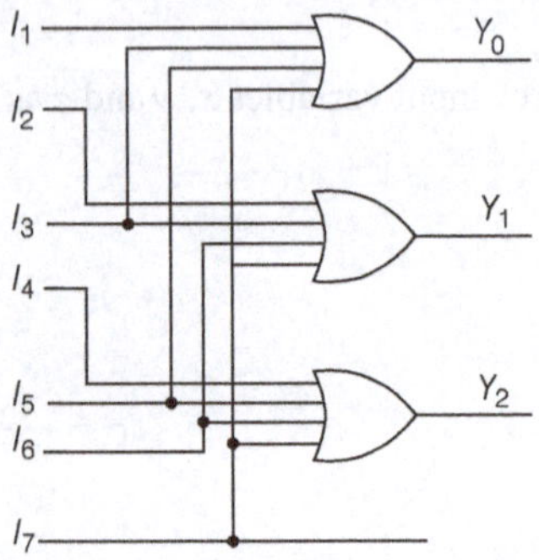

3. What is a multiplexer? State an application of a multiplexer. Also, draw the logic diagram of a 4:1 multiplexer. **ISC 2015, 2012**

Ans A digital **multiplexer** is a combinational circuit that select binary information from one of many input lines and directs it to a single output line.

The selection of a particular input line is controlled by a set of selection lines. For *n* selection lines, there are 2^n input lines. A multiplexer is also called a data selector, since it selects one of many inputs.

e.g. 4 to 1 line multiplexer, 8 to 1 line multiplexer, etc.

Multiplexers are used for:

(i) Routing several words to same destination such as bus.

(ii) Parallel to serial conversion.

Logic diagram of a 4 : 1 multiplexer:

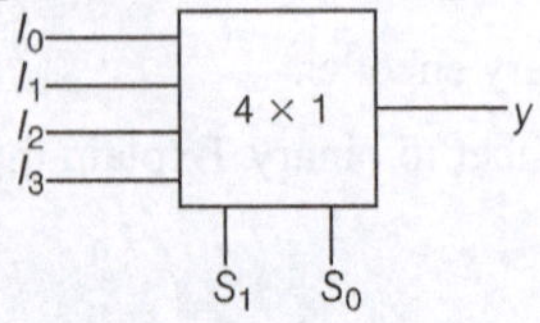

For 4 inputs multiplexer, we request 2 select lines, because $2^2 = 4$. Hence, select lines are S_0 and S_1.

Selection Lines		Input
S_0	S_1	I
0	0	I_0
0	1	I_1
1	0	I_2
1	1	I_3

$$y = S_0' S_1' I_0 + S_0' S_1 I_1 + S_0 S_1' I_2 + S_0 S_1 I_3$$

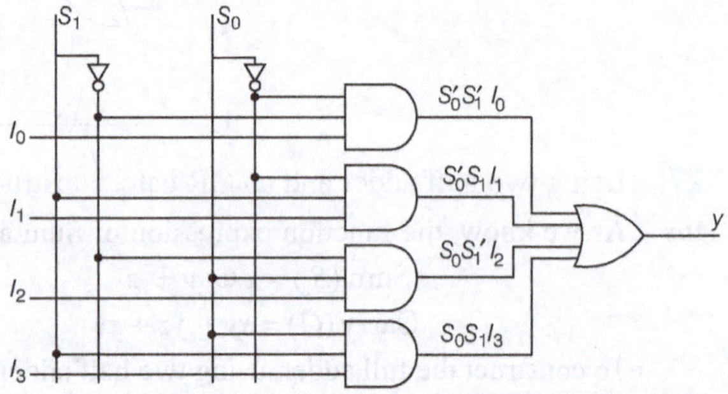

4. Differentiate between XNOR and XOR gates. Draw the truth table and logic diagrams of 3 input XNOR gates. **ISC 2014**

Ans The differences between XNOR and XOR gate are as follows:

XNOR	XOR
*X*NOR gate is also known as Exclusive NOR gate. It is the complement of Exclusive OR and indicated by the ⊙ graphic symbol.	The *X*OR is also known as Exclusive OR gate. It is indicated by the ⊕ graphic symbol.
The output of this gate is 1 only if both inputs are equal to 1 or both inputs are equal to 0, otherwise output will be zero.	The output of the *X*OR gate is 1 if any input is 1 but excludes the combination when both inputs are same.
Its algebraic expression is, $F = x \odot y = x'y' + xy$	Its algebraic expression is, $F = x \oplus y = xy' + x'y$

Truth Table of Three Inputs XNOR Gate

x	y	z	$F = x \odot y \odot z$
0	0	0	1
0	0	1	0
0	1	0	0
0	1	1	1
1	0	0	0
1	0	1	1
1	1	0	1
1	1	1	0

Logic diagram of XNOR for three-inputs is:

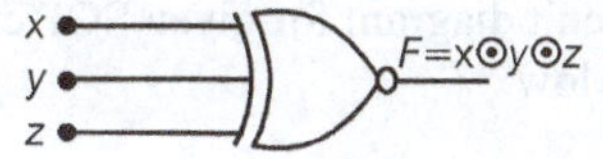

5. Draw the truth table and logic gate diagram for a 2 to 4 decoder and briefly explain its working. ***ISC 2013***

Or

What is a decoder? Draw the truth table and logic circuit diagram for a 2 to 4 decoder. ***ISC 2011, 2006***

Ans Decoder is a digital electronic circuit, which comments binary information from '*n*' input lines to a maximum of 2^n unique output lines.

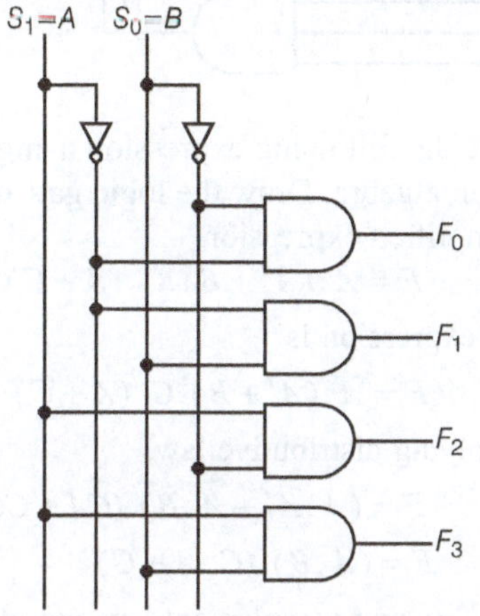

Here, *A* and *B* are two input variables and F_0, F_1, F_2 and F_3 are outputs.

The truth table for 2 to 4 decoder is

Truth Table of 2× 4 Decoder

A	*B*	F_0	F_1	F_2	F_3
0	0	1	0	0	0
0	1	0	1	0	0
1	0	0	0	1	0
1	1	0	0	0	1

From the given truth table,

(i) When both inputs are equal to 0, then F_0 produces 1 as output.

(ii) When Input $A = 0$ and $B = 1$, then F_1 produces 1 as output.

(iii) When Input $A = 1$ and $B = 0$, then F_2 produces 1 as output.

(iv) When both inputs *A* and *B* are equal to 1, then F_3 produces 1 as output.

6. From the logic circuit diagram given below, name the outputs (1), (2) and (3). Finally derive the Boolean expression and simplify it to show that it represents a logic gate. Name and draw the logic gate. ***ISC 2013***

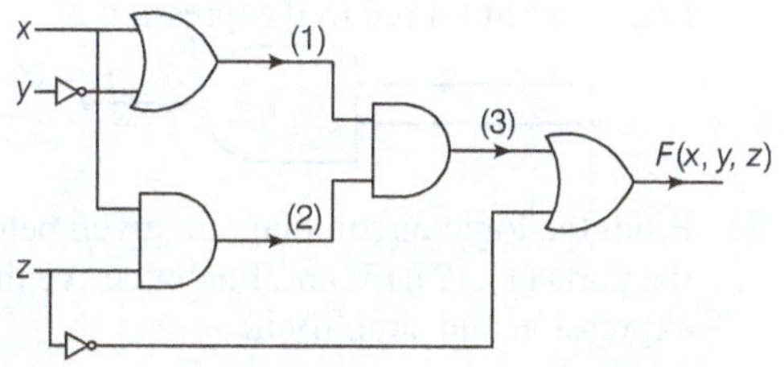

Ans (1) $X + Y'$

(2) $X.Z$

(3) $XZ.(X + Y')$

Final expression $= XZ(X + Y') + Z'$

$\Rightarrow \quad XZ + XY'Z + Z'$ (by distributive law)

$\Rightarrow \quad XZ(1 + Y') + Z'$ (by distributive law)

$\Rightarrow \quad XZ + Z'$ (by complement law)

$\Rightarrow \quad X + Z'$

It represents the OR gate, $X + Z'$

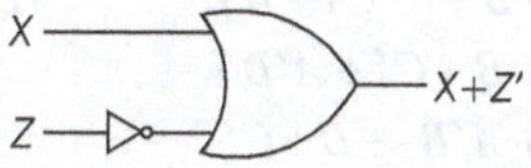

7. What is a multiplexer? Draw the truth table and logic diagram of a 8 × 1 multiplexer. ***ISC 2010***

Ans Refer to text on pages 51 and 52.

8. Simplify the following expression and also draw the circuit/gate for the reduced expression. [Show the stepwise working along with laws] ***ISC 2010***

$$F = X.(Y + Z.(X.Y + X.Z)')$$

Ans Given expression,

$$F = X.(Y + Z.(X.Y + X.Z)')$$
$$F = X.(Y + Z((X.Y) + (X.Z))')$$
$$F = X.(Y + Z((X' + Y').(X' + Z')))$$

{On applying De-Morgan's theorem, i.e.

$$(XY)' = X' + Y'\}$$

Next,

$F = XY + XZ[(X' + Y').(X' + Z')]$ (by distributive law)

$F = XY + XZ(X'X' + X'Z' + X'Y' + Y'Z')$ (using distributive law)

$= XY + XZ(X' + X'Z' + X'Y' + Y'Z')$ (using idempotent law)

$= XY + XZ(X' + X'Y' + Y'Z')$
(using absorption law)
$= XY + XZ(X' + Y'Z')$ (using absorption law)
$= XY + X'XZ + XZY'Z'$ (using distributive law)
$= XY$ (using complement law)

Logic circuit for reduced expression is:

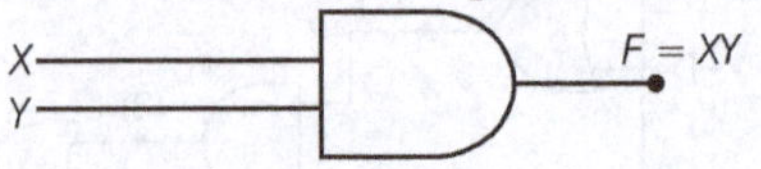

9. From the logic circuit diagram given below, name the parts (1), (2), (3) and finally derive the Boolean expression and simplify it: **ISC 2009**

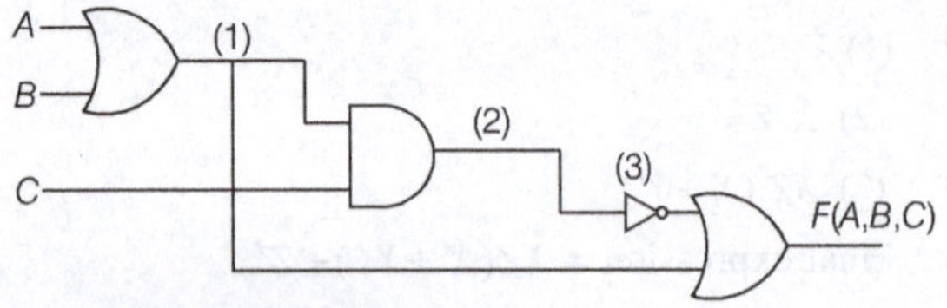

Ans (1) OR gate $A + B$
(2) AND gate $C(A + B)$
(3) NOT gate $[C(A + B)]'$

Final expression

$$F = [C(A+B)]' + A + B$$
$$= A + B + [C(A+B)]' \quad \text{(De-Morgan's law)}$$
$$= A + B + C' + A'B'$$
$$= A + A'B' + B + C'$$

10. How is an XOR gate different from an OR gate? Draw a truth table representing a three input XOR operation. Derive its SOP expression and draw the logic gate diagram for the SOP expression. **ISC 2008**

Ans OR gate produces output 1 for any input combination having one or more 1's, but XOR gate produces output 1 for only those input combinations that have odd number of 1's. Symbol ⊕ is used to denote XOR gate.

x	y	z	$F = x \oplus y \oplus z$	Minterms
0	0	0	0	$x'y'z'$
0	0	1	1	$x'y'z$
0	1	0	1	$x'yz'$
0	1	1	0	$x'yz$
1	0	0	1	$xy'z'$
1	0	1	0	$xy'z$
1	1	0	0	xyz'
1	1	1	1	xyz

$$F = x'y'z + x'yz' + xy'z' + xyz$$

Logic circuit diagram for given SOP expression (F) is shown below:

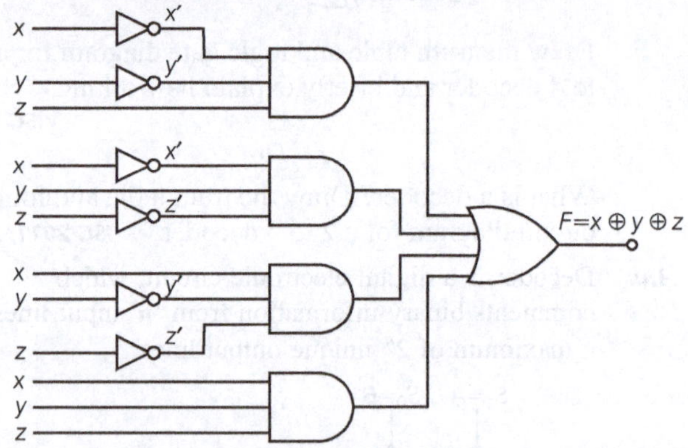

11. Reduce the following expression using the laws of Boolean algebra. Draw the logic gate diagram for the simplified expression. **ISC 2008**

$$F = A.(A' + B).C.(A + C)$$

Ans Given expression is

$$F = A.(A' + B).C.(A + C)$$

On applying distributive law,

$$F = (A.A' + A.B).(CA + CC)$$

So, $F = (A.B).(C.A + C)$

(using complement law and idempotent law)

$F = A.B(C)$ (using absorption law)

$$F = A.B.C$$

The required logic gate diagram for the reduced expression above is given below

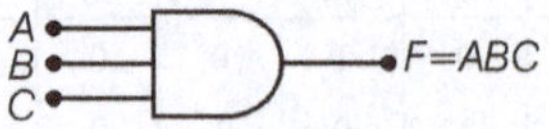

5/6 Marks Questions

1. Given the Boolean function $F(A, B, C, D) = \Sigma(2, 3, 6, 7, 8, 10, 12, 14, 15)$. **ISC 2023**

(i) Reduce the above expression by using 4-variable Karnaugh map, showing the various groups (i.e., octal, quads and pairs).

(ii) Draw the logic gate diagram for the reduced expression. Assume that the variables and their complements are available as inputs.

Ans Given, $F(A,B,C,D)=\Sigma(2, 3, 6, 7, 8, 10, 12, 14, 15)$

(i) From the K-map we conclude,

There are 3 quads.

Quad 1 $(m_2+m_3+m_6+m_7)=A'C$

Quad 2 $(m_6+m_7+m_{14}+m_{15})=BC$

Quad 3 $(m_8+m_{10}+m_{12}+m_{14})=AD'$

So, $F(A,B,C,D)=A'C+BC+AD'$

(ii) Logic gate diagram,

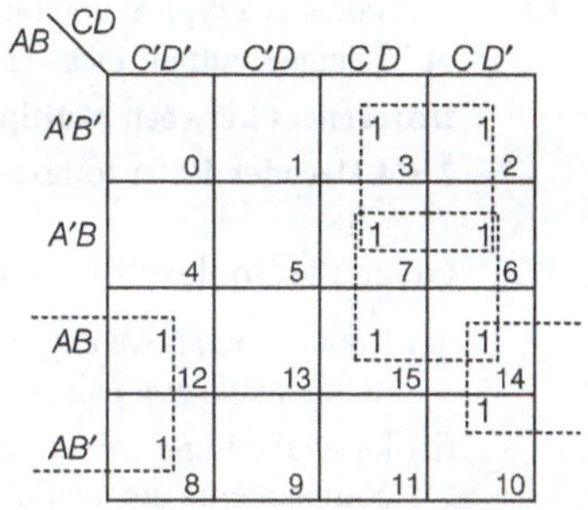

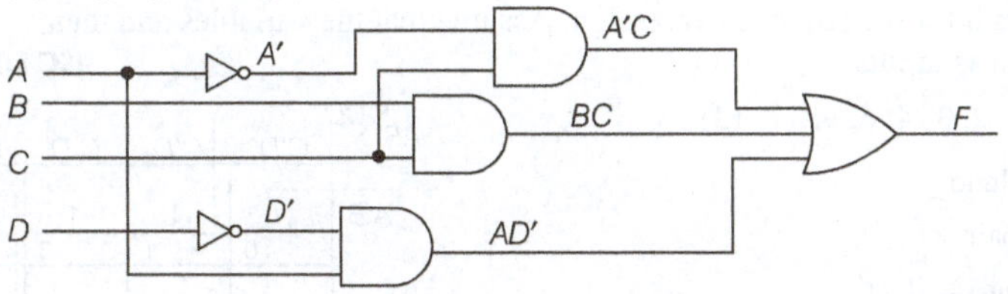

2. Given the Boolean function $F(A,B,C,D)=\pi(0, 1, 2, 4, 5, 8, 10, 11, 14, 15)$. **ISC 2023**

(i) Reduce the above expression by using 4 variable Karnaugh map, showing the various groups (i.e., octal, quads, and pairs)

(ii) Draw the logic gate diagram for the reduced expression. Assume that the variables and their complements are available as inputs.

Ans Given, $F(A,B,C,D)=\pi(0, 1, 2, 4, 5, 8, 10, 11, 14, 15)$

(i) From the K-map we conclude,

There are 3 quads,

Quad 1 $(M_0 \cdot M_1 \cdot M_4 \cdot M_5)=A+C$

Quad 2 $(M_0 \cdot M_2 \cdot M_8 \cdot M_{10})=B+D$

Quad 3$(M_{10} \cdot M_{11} \cdot M_{14} \cdot M_{15})=A'+C'$

So, $F(A,B,C,D)=(A+C)\cdot(B+D)\cdot(A'+C')$

(ii) Logic gate diagram,

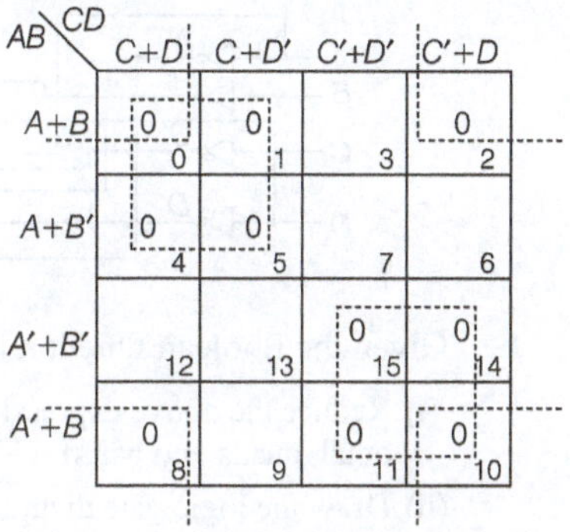

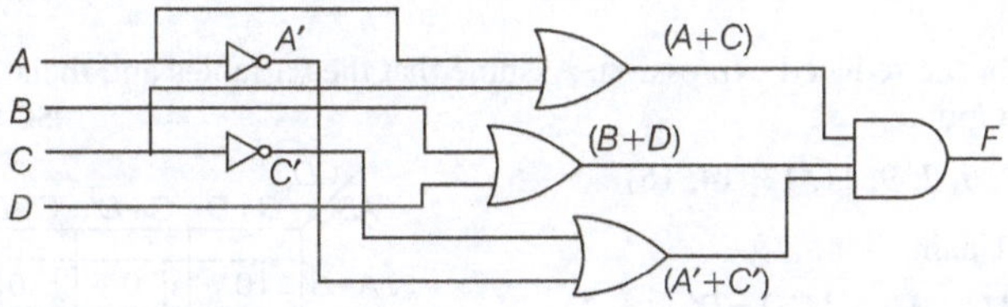

3. What is an encoder? How is it different from decoder? Draw the logic circuit for a 4 : 1multiplexer and explain its working. **ISC 2023**

Ans An encoder is a combinational circuit that produces a reverse operation of decoder. Process of converting signals from one type to another type is called encoding. An encoder consists of 2^n input lines and n output lines, which generates the binary code for the 2^n input variables.

Differences between Encoder and Decoder are as follows

Encoder	Decoder
Encoder circuit basically converts the applied information signal into a coded digital bit stream.	Decoder performs reverse operation and recovers the original information signal from the coded bits.
The number of inputs accepted by an encoder is 2^n.	The number of input accepted by decoder is only n inputs.

4 × 1 Multiplexer Refer to text on page 52.

4. What is a decoder? How is it different from a multiplexer? Draw the logic circuit for a 2 × 4 decoder and explain its working. **ISC SQP 2023**

Ans A decoder is a typical combinational circuit that converts binary information from n input lines to a maximum of 2^n unique output lines. This decoder is called as n to m line decoder, where $m \le 2^n$.

Differences between Multiplexer and Decoder Refer to text on page 56 Question 12 (2 Marks Questions).

2 × 4 Decoder Refer to text on page 50.

5. Given the Boolean function $F(A,B,C,D) = \Sigma(0, 1, 2, 3, 4, 6, 9, 11, 13)$.

(i) Reduce the above expression by using 4-variable Karnaugh map, showing the various groups (i.e. octal, quads and pairs).

(ii) Draw the logic gate diagram for the reduced expression. Assume that the variables and their complements are available as inputs. **ISC SQP 2023**

Ans Given, $F(A,B,C,D) = \Sigma$ (0, 1, 2, 3, 4, 6, 9, 11, 13)

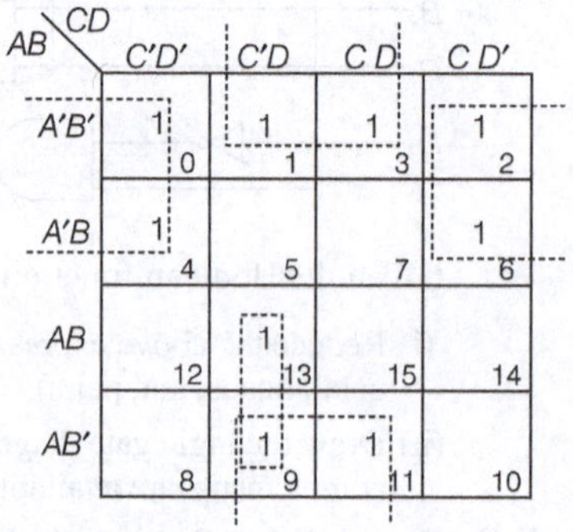

(i) From the K-map we conclude,

There are 2 quads and 1 pair

Quad 1 $(m_0 + m_2 + m_4 + m_6) = A'D'$

Quad 2 $(m_1 + m_3 + m_9 + m_{11}) = B'D$

Pair $(m_9 + m_{13}) = AC'D$

So, reduce expression

$F(A, B, C, D) = A'D' + B'D + AC'D$

(ii) Logic gate diagram,

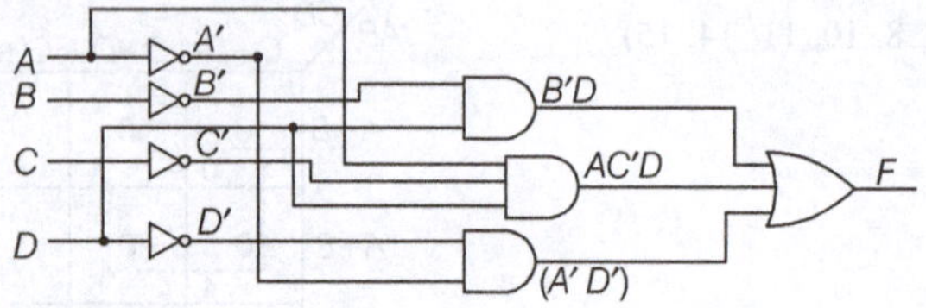

6. Given the Boolean function $F(A,B,C,D) = \pi(0, 1, 3, 5, 6, 7, 9, 11, 13, 14, 15)$.

(i) Reduce the above expression by using 4-variable Karnaugh map, showing the various groups(i.e. octal, quads and pairs).

(ii) Draw the logic gate diagram for the reduced expression. Assume that the variables and their complements are available as inputs. **ISC SQP 2023**

Ans Given, $F(A,B,C,D) = \pi(0, 1, 3, 5, 6, 7, 9, 11, 13, 14, 15)$

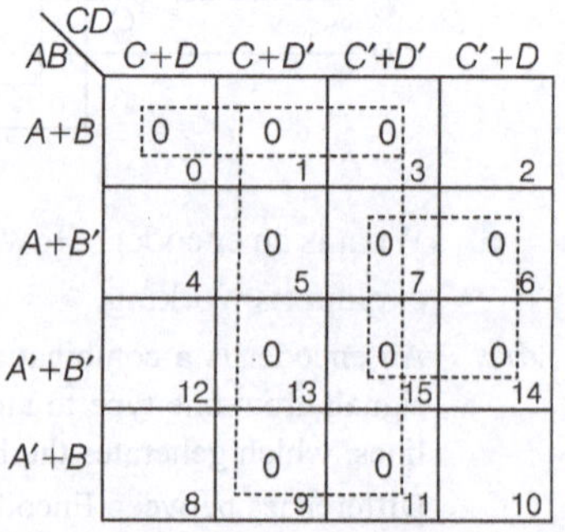

(i) There are 1 octet, 1 quad and 1 pair.

Octet $(M_1 \cdot M_3 \cdot M_5 \cdot M_7 \cdot M_9 \cdot M_{11} \cdot M_{13} \cdot M_{15}) = D'$

Quad $(M_6 \cdot M_7 \cdot M_{14} \cdot M_{15}) = B' + C'$

Pair $(M_0 \cdot M_1) = A + B + C$

So, reduced expression

$F(A,B,C,D) = D' \cdot (B' + C') \cdot (A + B + C)$

(ii) Logic circuit diagram

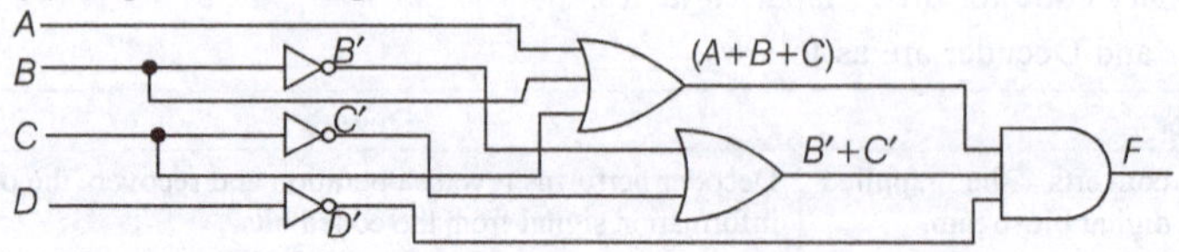

7. Given the Boolean function $F(A, B, C, D) = \Sigma$ (0, 1, 2, 3, 4, 5, 8, 9, 10, 11, 12, 13, 14).

(i) Reduce the above expression by using 4-variable Karnaugh map, showing the various groups (i.e. octet, quads and pairs).

(ii) Draw the logic gate diagram for the reduced expression. Assume that the variables and their complements are available as inputs. **ISC 2020**

Ans Given, $F(A,B,C,D) = \Sigma\,(0, 1, 2, 3, 4, 5, 8, 9, 10, 11, 12, 13, 14)$

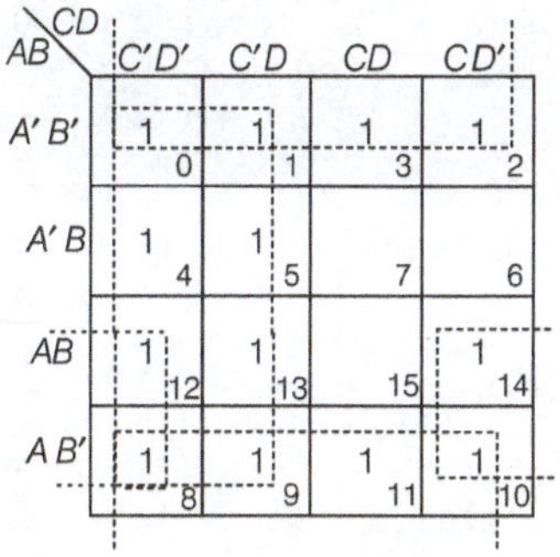

(i) From K - map,

There are 2 octets and 1 quad

Octet 1 $(m_0 + m_1 + m_4 + m_5 + m_8 + m_9 + m_{12} + m_{13}) = C'$

Octet 2 $(m_0 + m_1 + m_2 + m_3 + m_8 + m_9 + m_{10} + m_{11}) = B'$

Quad 1 $(m_8 + m_{10} + m_{12} + m_{14}) = AD'$

Hence, the final reduced expression

$F(A, B, C, D) = C' + B' + AD'$

(ii) Logic gate diagram for expression

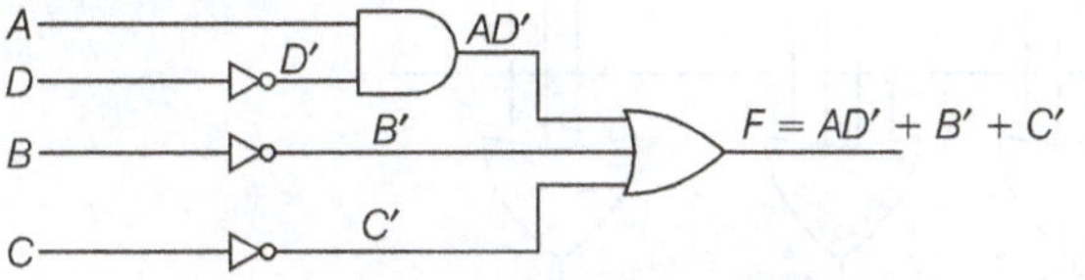

8. Given the Boolean function $F(A, B, C, D) = \Pi\,(3, 4, 6, 9, 11, 12, 13, 14, 15)$.

(i) Reduce the above expression by using 4-variable Karnaugh map, showing the various groups (i.e. octet, quads and pairs).

(ii) Draw the logic gate diagram for the reduced expression. Assume that the variables and their complements are available as inputs. ***ISC 2020***

Ans Given, $F(A, B, C, D) = \Pi\,(3, 4, 6, 9, 11, 12, 13, 14, 15)$

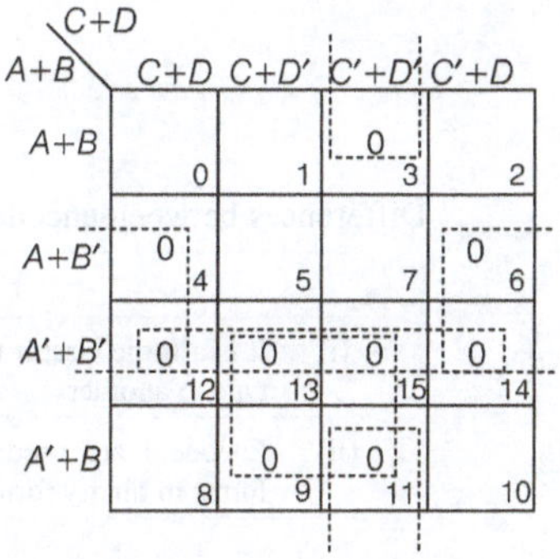

(i) From K-map,

There are 3 quads and 1 pair

Quad 1 $(M_{12} \cdot M_{13} \cdot M_{14} \cdot M_{15}) = A' + B'$

Quad 2 $(M_9 \cdot M_{11} \cdot M_{13} \cdot M_{15}) = A' + D'$

Quad 3 $(M_4 \cdot M_6 \cdot M_{12} \cdot M_{14}) = B' + D$

Pair 1 $(M_3 \cdot M_{11}) = C' + D' + B$

Final expression is

$F(A, B, C, D) = (A' + B')\cdot(A' + D')\cdot(B' + D)\cdot(C' + D' + B)$

(ii) Logic gate diagram for expression

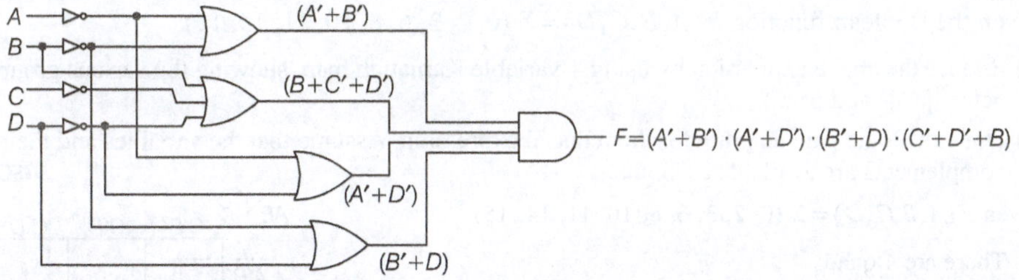

9. Draw the logic circuit diagram for an octal to binary encoder and explain its working when a particular digit is pressed. Also, state the difference between encoder and decoder. ***ISC 2020***

Ans Truth table for octal to binary encoder :

Inputs								Outputs		
D_7	D_6	D_5	D_4	D_3	D_2	D_1	D_0	A_2	A_1	A_0
0	0	0	0	0	0	0	1	0	0	0
0	0	0	0	0	0	1	0	0	0	1
0	0	0	0	0	1	0	0	0	1	0
0	0	0	0	1	0	0	0	0	1	1
0	0	0	1	0	0	0	0	1	0	0
0	0	1	0	0	0	0	0	1	0	1
0	1	0	0	0	0	0	0	1	1	0
1	0	0	0	0	0	0	0	1	1	

Logic gate diagram

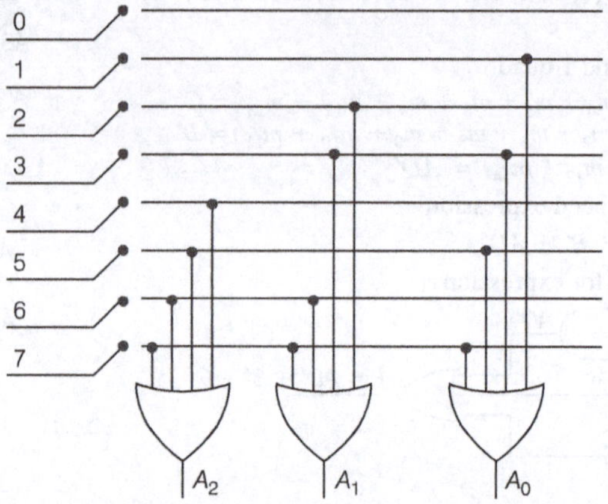

Working

The encoder can be implemented with OR gates whose inputs are determined directly from the truth table. Output $A_0 = 1$, if the input octal digit is 1 or 3 or 5 or 7.

Similar conditions apply for other two outputs.

These conditions can be expressed by the following Boolean functions :

$$A_0 = D_1 + D_3 + D_5 + D_7$$
$$A_1 = D_2 + D_3 + D_6 + D_7$$
$$A_2 = D_4 + D_5 + D_6 + D_7$$

Differences between encoder and decoder are as follows :

	Encoder	Decoder
(i)	It is a logic circuit that converts signal of one type to another.	It is a combinational circuit that converts binary information.
(ii)	Encoders are used to convert various input forms to binary form.	Decoders are used to keep abstraction and modularity in hardware design.

10. Given the Boolean function $F(A,B,C,D) = \Sigma\,(0, 2, 3, 6, 8, 10, 11, 14, 15)$

(i) Reduce the above expression by using 4-variable Karnaugh map, showing the various groups (i.e. octal, quads and pairs).

(ii) Draw the logic gate diagram for the reduced expression. Assume that the variables and their complements are available as inputs.

ISC SQP 2020

Ans Given $F(A,B,C,D) = \Sigma\,(0, 2, 3, 6, 8, 10, 11, 14, 15)$

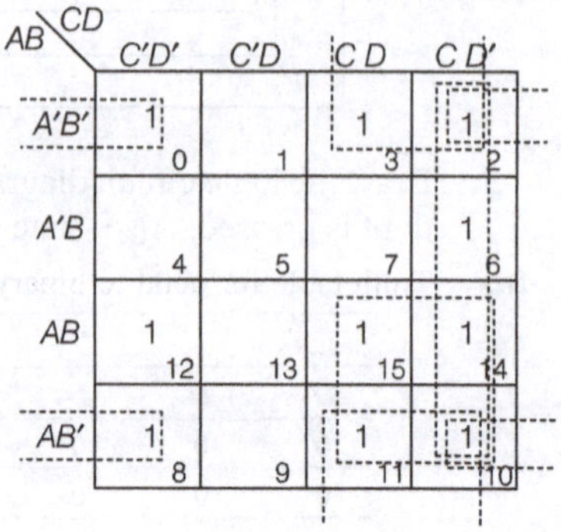

(i) There are 4 quads

Quad 1 $(m_0 + m_2 + m_8 + m_{10}) = B'D'$

Quad 2 $(m_2 + m_3 + m_{10} + m_{11}) = B'C$

Quad 3 $(m_2 + m_6 + m_{10} + m_{14}) = CD'$

Quad 4 $(m_{10} + m_{11} + m_{14} + m_{15}) = AC$

So, reduced expression

$F(A,B,C,D) = B'D' + B'C + CD' + AC$

(ii) Logic Gate diagram for reduced expression

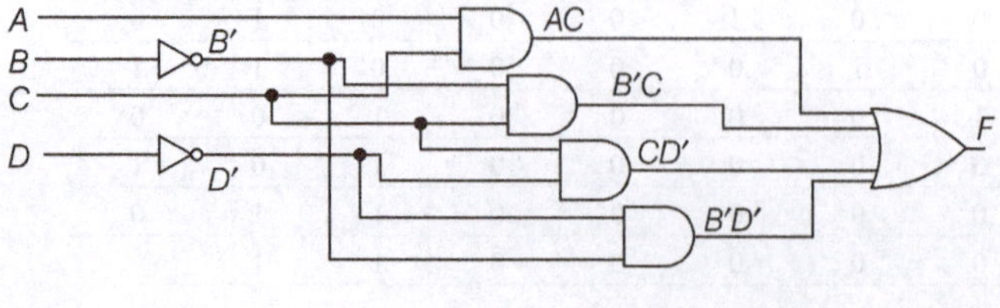

11. Given the Boolean function $F(P,Q,R,S) = \pi\,(5,7, 8, 10, 12, 14, 15\,)$

(i) Reduce the above expression by using 4-variable Karnaugh map, showing the various groups (i.e. octal, quads and pairs).

(ii) Draw the logic gate diagram for the reduced expression. Assume that the variables and their complements are available as inputs.

ISC SQP 2020

Ans Given,

$F(P,Q,R,S) = \pi(5, 7, 8, 10, 12, 14, 15)$

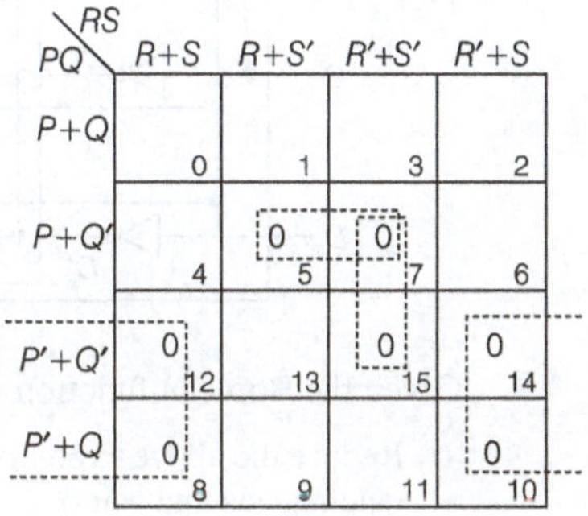

(i) From K-map we conclude,

There are 1 quad and 2 pair

Quad 1 $(M_8 \cdot M_{10} \cdot M_{12} \cdot M_{14}) = P' + S$

Pair 1 $(M_5 \cdot M_7) = P + Q' + S'$

Pair 2 $(M_7 \cdot M_{15}) = Q' + R' + S'$

So, reduced expression

$F(P,Q,R,S) = (P' + S) \cdot (P + Q' + S') \cdot (Q' + R' + S')$

(ii) Logic gate diagram

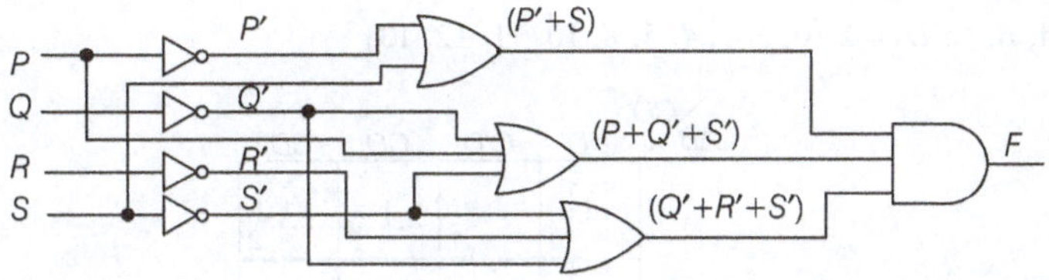

12. Draw the logic diagram and truth table to encode the decimal numbers (2, 3, 5, 7, 8) and briefly explain its working).

ISC SQP 2020

Ans Given $F(A,B,C,D) = \Sigma(2, 3, 5, 7, 8)$

A	*B*	*C*	*D*	F
0	0	0	0	0
0	0	0	1	0
0	0	1	0	1
0	0	1	1	1
0	1	0	0	0
0	1	0	1	1
0	1	1	0	0
0	1	1	1	1
1	0	0	0	1
1	0	0	1	0
1	0	1	0	0
1	0	1	1	0
1	1	0	0	0
1	1	0	1	0
1	1	1	0	0
1	1	1	1	0

SOP Expression,

$F(A,B,C,D) = A'B'CD' + A'B'CD + A'BC'D + A'BCD + AB'C'D'$

Logic gate diagram

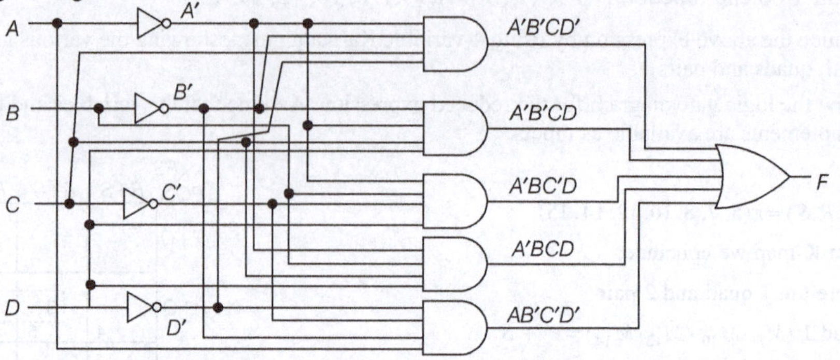

13. Given the Boolean function $F(A, B, C, D) = \Sigma\ (0, 2, 3, 4, 5, 8, 10, 11, 12, 13)$.

(i) Reduce the above expression by using 4-variable Karnaugh map, showing the various groups (i.e. octet, quads and pairs).

(ii) Draw the logic gate diagram for the reduced expression using only NAND gates. Assume that the variables and their complements are available as inputs. **ISC 2019**

Ans Given, $F(A, B, C, D) = \Sigma\ (0, 2, 3, 4, 5, 8, 10, 11, 12, 13)$

(i)

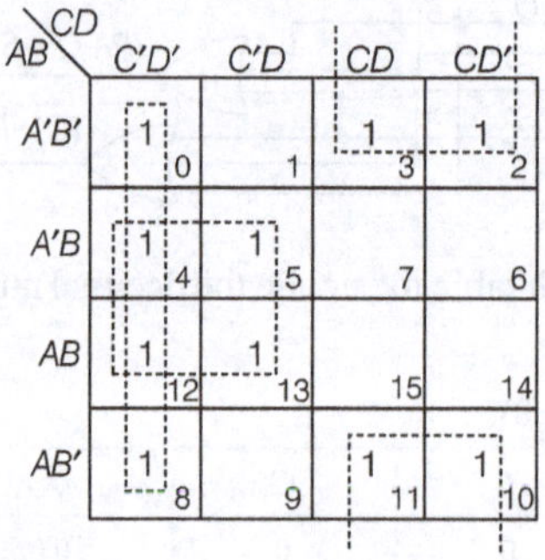

From the K-map, we conclude

Quad 1 = $C'D'$, Quad 2 = BC', Quad 3 = $B'C$

So, $F(A, B, C, D) = C'D' + BC' + B'C$

(ii) Logic gate diagram using NAND gates

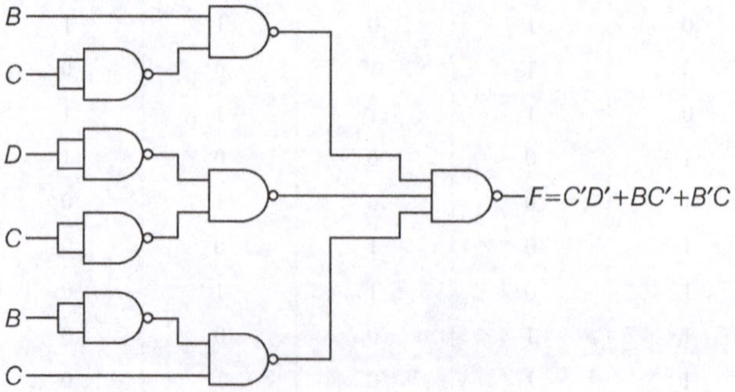

14. Given the Boolean function : $F(P, Q, R, S) = \Pi\ (0, 1, 2, 8, 9, 11, 13, 15)$.

(i) Reduce the above expression by using 4-variable Karnaugh map, showing the various groups (i.e. octet, quads and pairs).

(ii) Draw the logic gate diagram for the reduced expression using only NOR gates. Assume that the variables and their complements are available as inputs. **ISC 2019**

Ans Given, $F(P, Q, R, S) = \Pi\ (0, 1, 2, 8, 9, 11, 13, 15)$

(i)

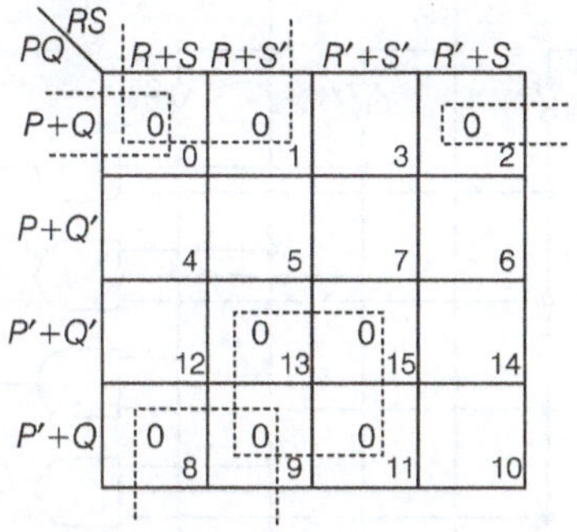

From the K-map, we conclude

Quad 1 = $P' + S'$, Quad 2 = $Q + R$, Pair 1 = $P + Q + S$

So, $F(P, Q, R, S) = (P' + S')\ (Q + R)\ (P + Q + S)$

(ii) Logic gate diagram using NOR gates

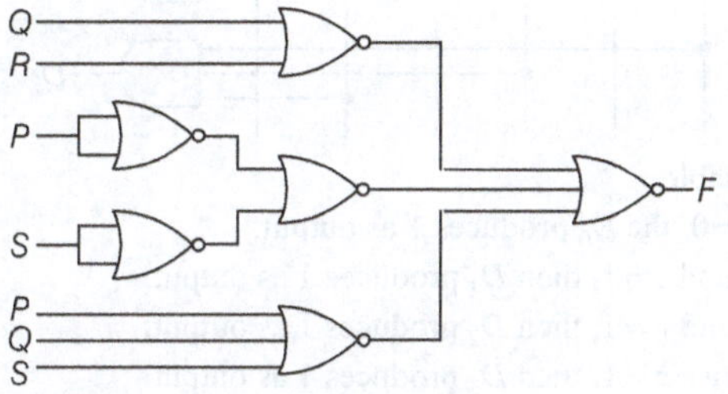

15. How is a decoder different from a multiplexer? Write the truth table and draw the logic circuit diagram for a 3 to 8 decoder and explain its working. ***ISC 2019***

Ans Differences between multiplexer and decoder are as follows

Multiplexer	Decoder
It is called as data selector, since it selects one of many inputs.	This decoder is called *n*-to-*m* line decoder, where $m \leq 2^n$
A multiplexer is used to share several signals to one device like A/D convertor.	Decoders are used to keep abstraction and modularity in hardware design.

Truth Table for 3 × 8 Decoder

x	y	z	D_0	D_1	D_2	D_3	D_4	D_5	D_6	D_7
0	0	0	1	0	0	0	0	0	0	0
0	0	1	0	1	0	0	0	0	0	0
0	1	0	0	0	1	0	0	0	0	0
0	1	1	0	0	0	1	0	0	0	0
1	0	0	0	0	0	0	1	0	0	0
1	0	1	0	0	0	0	0	1	0	0
1	1	0	0	0	0	0	0	0	1	0
1	1	1	0	0	0	0	0	0	0	1

The logic diagram for 3 × 8 decoder is shown below

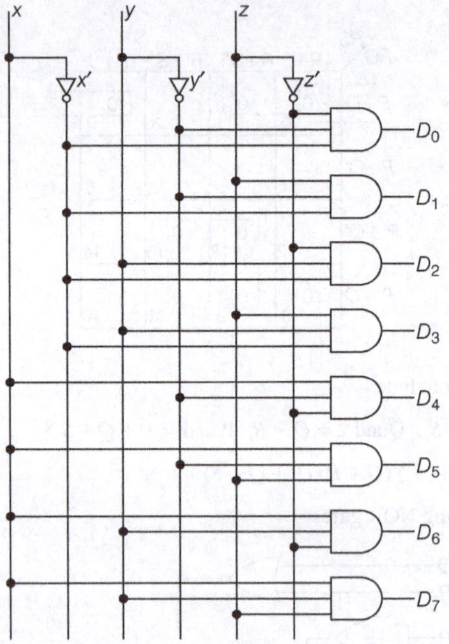

Working From the truth table,

(i) when inputs $x = y = z = 0$, the D_0 produces 1 as output.

(ii) when inputs $x = y = 0$ and $z = 1$, then D_1 produces 1 as output.

(iii) when inputs $x = z = 0$ and $y = 1$, then D_2 produces 1 as output.

(iv) when inputs $x = 0$ and $y = z = 1$, then D_3 produces 1 as output.

(v) when inputs $x = 1$ and $y = z = 0$, then D_4 produces 1 as output.

(vi) when inputs $x = z = 1$ and $y = 0$, then D_5 produces 1 as output.

(vii) when inputs $x = y = 1$ and $z = 0$, then D_6 produces 1 as output.

(viii) when inputs $x = y = z = 1$ then D_7 produces 1 as output.

16. What is an Encoder? Draw the Encoder circuit to convert A-F hexadecimal numbers to binary. State an application of a Multiplexer. ***ISC 2018***

Ans An encoder is a combinational circuit that produces a reverse operation of decoder. Process of converting signals from one type to another type is called encoding.

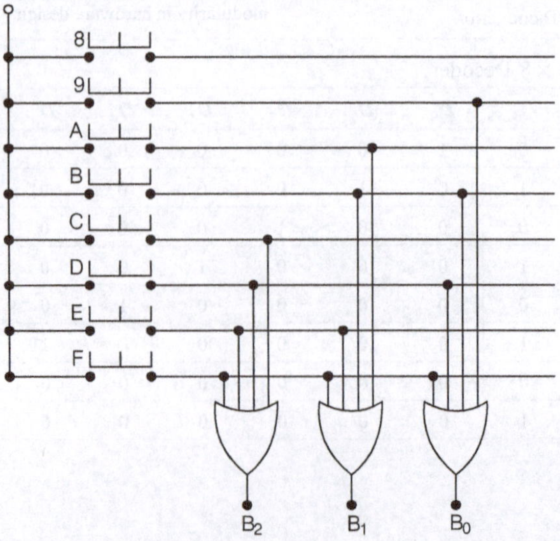

An encoder consists of 2^n input lines and n output lines, which generates the binary code for the 2^n input variables.

Here, B_0, B_1 and B_2 are the output lines. The output lines will express this function only, where output is equal to 1.

The logic diagram for hexadecimal to binary encoder is :

An application of a multiplexer is as :

- Routing several words to same destination such as bus.

17. Given the Boolean function $F(A, B, C, D) = \Sigma\,(0, 2, 4, 8, 9, 10, 12, 13)$.

(i) Reduce the above expression by using 4-variable Karnaugh map, showing the various groups (i.e. octet, quads and pairs).

(ii) Draw the logic gate diagram for the reduced expression. Assume that the variables and their complements are available as inputs. **ISC 2018**

Ans (i) Given, $F(A, B, C, D) = \Sigma(0, 2, 4, 8, 9, 10, 12, 13)$

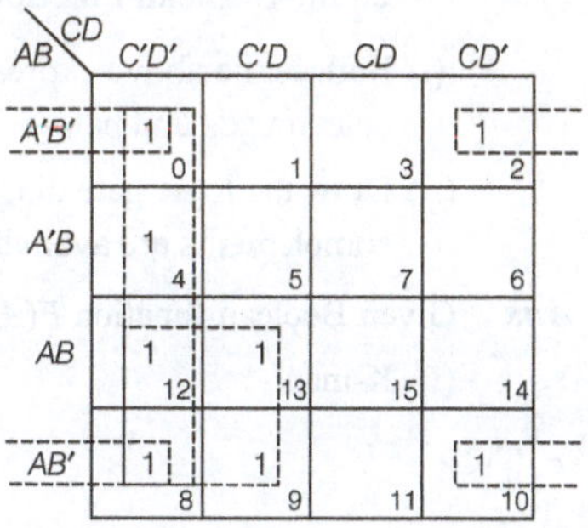

From the K-map we conclude,

Quad 1 $= C'D'$

Quad 2 $= AC'$

Quad 3 $= B'D'$

So, $F(A, B, C, D) = C'D' + AC' + B'D'$

(ii) Logic gate diagram,

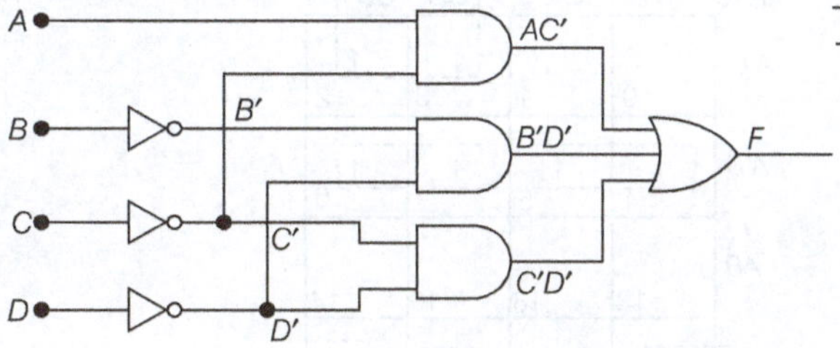

18. Given the Boolean function $F(A, B, C, D) = \Pi\,(3, 4, 5, 6, 7, 10, 11, 14, 15)$.

(i) Reduce the above expression by using 4-variable Karnaugh map, showing the various groups (i.e. octet, quads and pairs).

(ii) Draw the logic gate diagram for the reduced expression. Assume that the variables and their complements are available as inputs. **ISC 2018**

Ans (i) Given $F(A, B, C, D) = \Pi(3, 4, 5, 6, 7, 10, 11, 14, 15)$

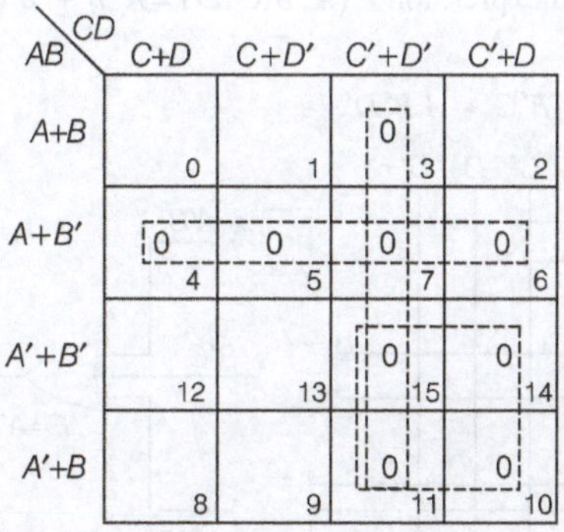

From the K-map, we conclude

Quad 1 $= A + B'$

Quad 2 $= C' + D'$

Quad 3 $= A' + C'$

So, $F(A, B, C, D) = (A + B')\cdot(C' + D')\cdot(A' + C')$

(ii) Logic gate diagram

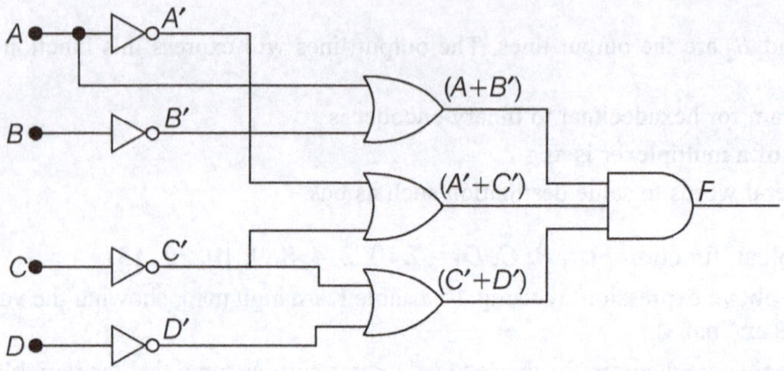

19. Given the Boolean function $F(A,B,C,D) = \Sigma(2,3,4,5,6,7,8,10,11)$.

(i) Reduce the above expression by using 4-variable Karnaugh map, showing the various groups (i.e. octet, quads and pairs).

(ii) Draw the logic gate diagram for the reduced expression. Assume that the variable and their complements are available as inputs. **ISC 2017**

Ans Given Boolean function $F(A, B, C, D) = \Sigma$ (2, 3, 4, 5, 6, 7, 8, 10, 11)

(i) K-map

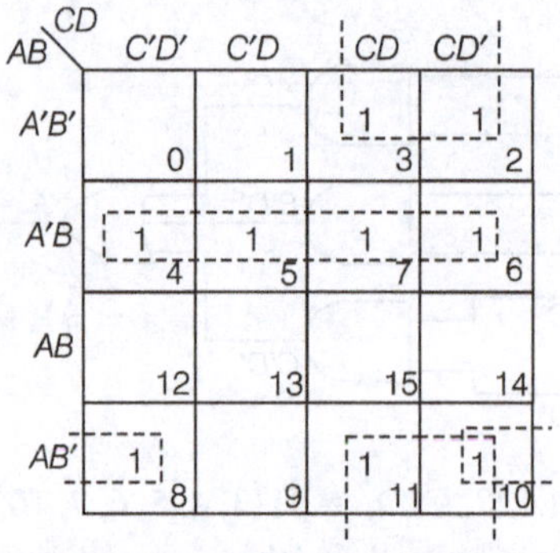

There are 2 quads and 1 pair

$$\text{Quad } 1(m_4 + m_5 + m_6 + m_7) = A'B$$

$$\text{Quad } 2\ (m_2 + m_3 + m_{10} + m_{11}) = B'C$$

$$\text{Pair } (m_8 + m_{10}) = AB'D'$$

Hence, the final reduced expression $F(A,B,C,D) = A'B + B'C + AB'D'$

(ii) Logic gate diagram for

$F(A,B,C,D) = A'B + B'C + AB'D'$

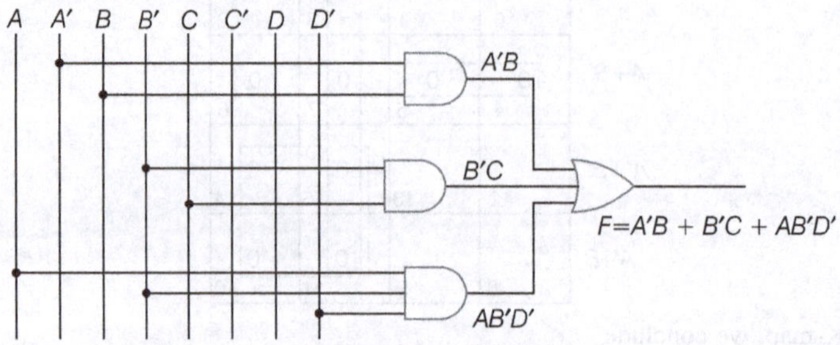

20. Given the Boolean function $F(P, Q, R, S) = \Pi(0, 1, 2, 4, 5, 6, 8, 10)$.

(i) Reduce the above expression by using 4-variable Karnaugh map, showing the various groups (i.e. octet, quads and pairs).

(ii) Draw the logic gate diagram for the reduced expression. Assume that the variable and their complements are available as inputs. **ISC 2017**

Ans Given, Boolean function $F(P,Q,R,S)=\Pi(0, 1, 2, 4, 5, 6, 8, 10)$

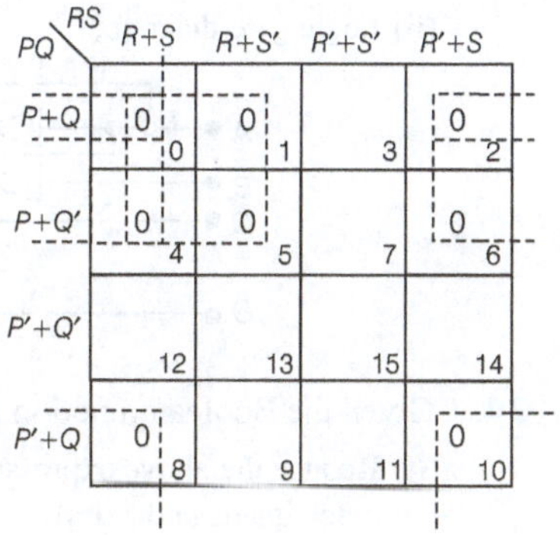

(i) K-map

There are 3 quads

Quad 1 $(M_0 + M_1 + M_4 + M_5) = P + R$

Quad 2 $(M_0 + M_2 + M_4 + M_6) = P + S$

Quad 3 $(M_0 + M_2 + M_8 + M_{10}) = Q + S$

Hence, the final reduced expression

$$F(P,Q,R,S) = (P + R) . (P + S) . (Q + S)$$

(ii) Logic gate diagram for

$$F(P,Q,R,S) = (P + R).(P + S).(Q + S)$$

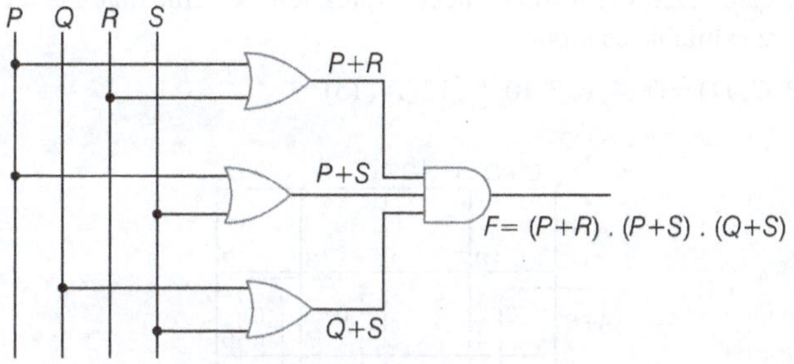

21. What is a multiplexer? How is it different from a decoder? Draw the circuit diagram for a 8 to 1 multiplexer. **ISC 2017**

Ans **Multiplexer and 8 × 1 multiplexer** Refer to text on page 51 and 52.

Differences between multiplexer and decoder Refer to text on page 56 Question 12 (2 Marks Questions).

22. What is a decoder? Draw the logic diagram for a binary to octal (3 to 8) decoder. **ISC 2016**

Ans Refer to text on pages 49 and 50.

23. Given the Boolean function $F(A, B, C, D) = \Sigma(1, 3, 5, 7, 8, 9, 10, 11, 14, 15)$.

(i) Reduce the above expression by using 4-variable Karnaugh map, showing the various group (i.e. octet, quads and pairs).

(ii) Draw the logic gate diagram for the reduced expression. Assume that the variables and their complements are available as inputs. **ISC 2016**

Ans (i) Given, $F(A, B, C, D) = \Sigma(1, 3, 5, 7, 8, 9, 10, 11, 14, 15)$

From the K-map we conclude,

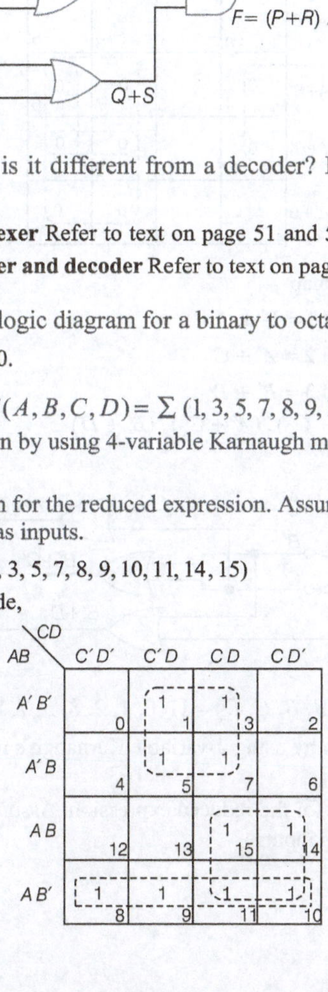

There are 3 quads,

Quad 1 = $A'D$

Quad 2 = AC

Quad 3 = AB'

So, $F(A, B, C, D) = A'D + AC + AB'$

(ii) Logic gate diagram,

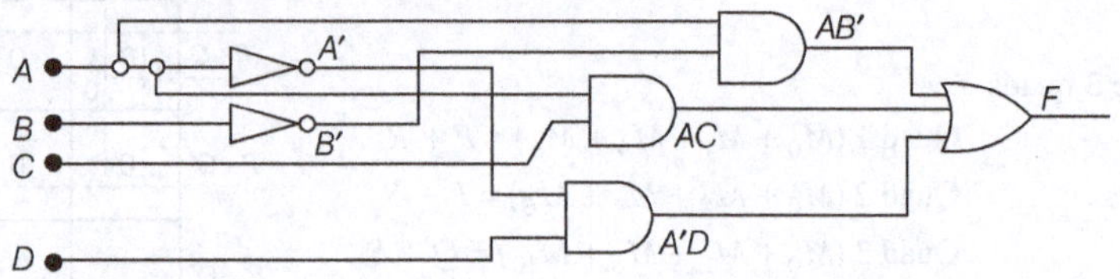

24. Given the Boolean function $F(A, B, C, D) = \Pi(4, 6, 7, 10, 11, 12, 14, 15)$.

(i) Reduce the above expression by using 4-variable Karnaugh map, showing the various groups (i.e. octet, quads and pairs).

(ii) Draw the logic gate diagram for the reduced expression. Assume that the variables and their complements are available as inputs. **ISC 2016**

Ans (i) Given, $F(A, B, C, D) = \Pi(4, 6, 7, 10, 11, 12, 14, 15)$

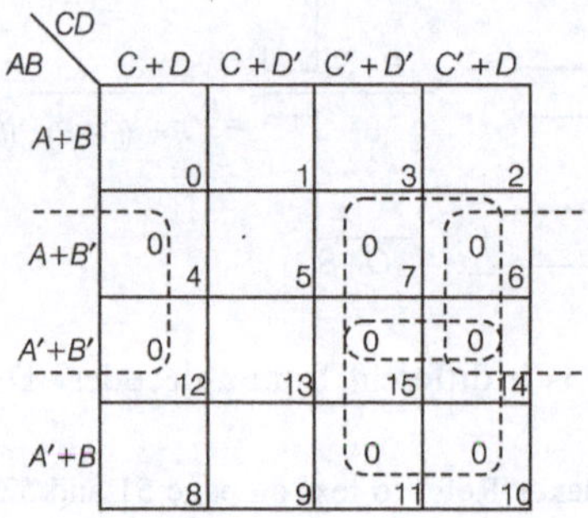

Reduced expression from K-map

Quad 1 = $B' + C'$

Quad 2 = $A' + C'$

Quad 3 = $B' + D$

So, $F(A, B, C, D) = (B' + C').(A' + C').(B' + D)$

(ii) Logic gate diagram,

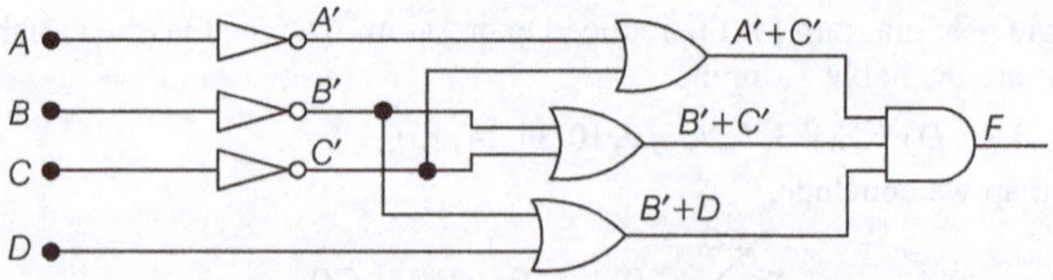

25. Given the Boolean function $F(A, B, C, D) = \Pi(0, 1, 2, 3, 5, 7, 8, 9, 10, 11)$.

(i) Reduce the above expression by using 4-variable Karnaugh's map, showing the various groups (i.e. octet, quads and pairs).

(ii) Draw the logic gate diagram for the reduced expression. Assume that the variables and their complements are available as inputs. **ISC 2015**

Ans (i) The given expression, $F(A, B, C, D) = \Pi(0, 1, 2, 3, 5, 7, 8, 9, 10, 11)$

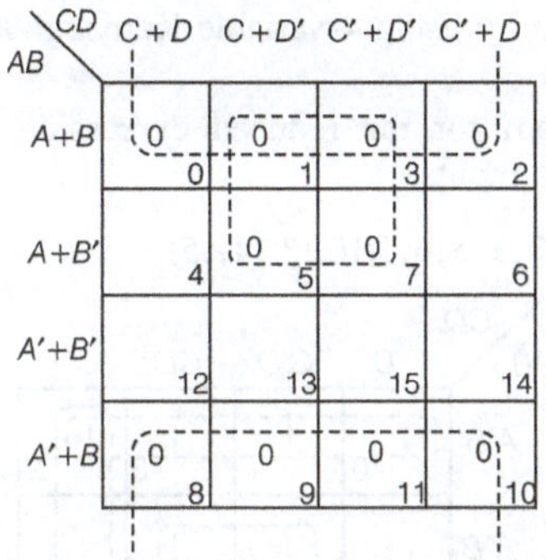

There are 1 octet and 1 quad

octet $= B$

quad $= A + D'$

Reduced Expression from K-map

$$F(A, B, C, D) = (A + D').B$$

(ii) The logic gate diagram for the reduced expression is as follows:

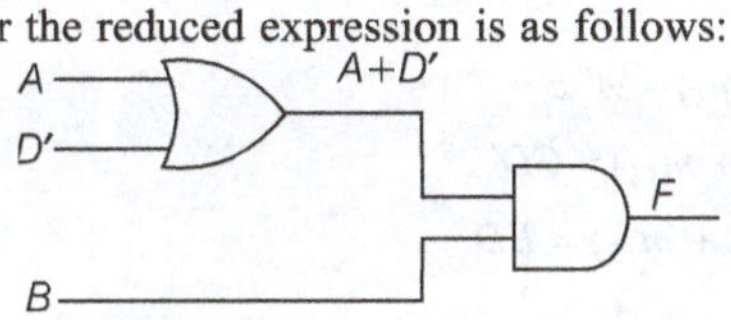

26. Given the Boolean function $P(A, B, C, D) = ABC'D' + A'BC'D' + A'BC'D + ABC'D + A'BCD + ABCD$

(i) Reduce the above expression by using 4-variable Karnaugh's map, showing the various groups (i.e. octet, quads and pairs).

(ii) Draw the logic gate diagram for the reduced expression. Assume that the variables and their complements are available as inputs. **ISC 2015**

Ans (i) Given expression $P(A, B, C, D) = ABC'D' + A'BC'D' + A'BC'D + ABC'D + A'BCD + ABCD$

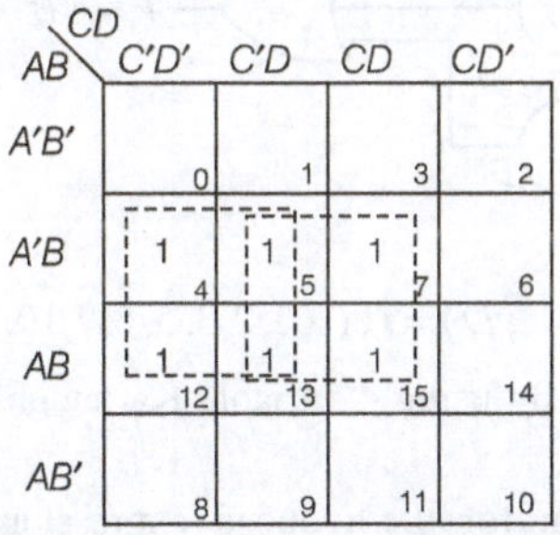

From the K-map,

Quad 1 $= BC'$

Quad 2 $= BD$

So, the reduced expression will be

$$P(A, B, C, D) = BC' + BD$$

(ii) The logic gate diagram for the reduced expression is as follows:

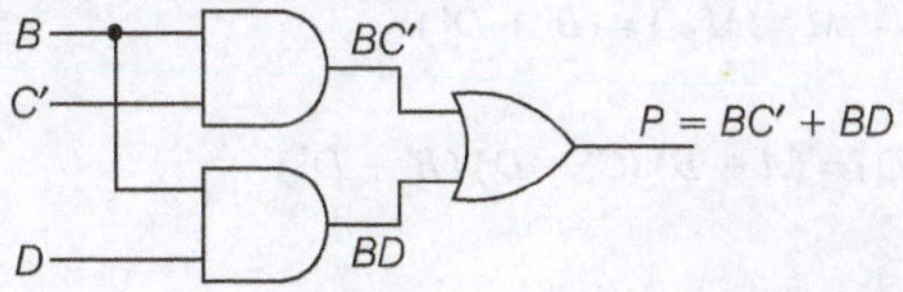

27. Given boolean function $F(A,B,C,D)= \Sigma(0,1,2,3,5,6,7,10,13,14,15)$

(i) Reduce the above expression by using 4-variable Karnaugh's map, showing the various groups (i.e. octet, quads and pairs).

(ii) Draw the logic gate diagram for the reduced expression. Assume that the variables and their complements are available as inputs. **ISC 2014**

Ans (i) Given $F(A,B,C,D)=\Sigma(0,1,2,3,5,6,7,10,13,14,15)$

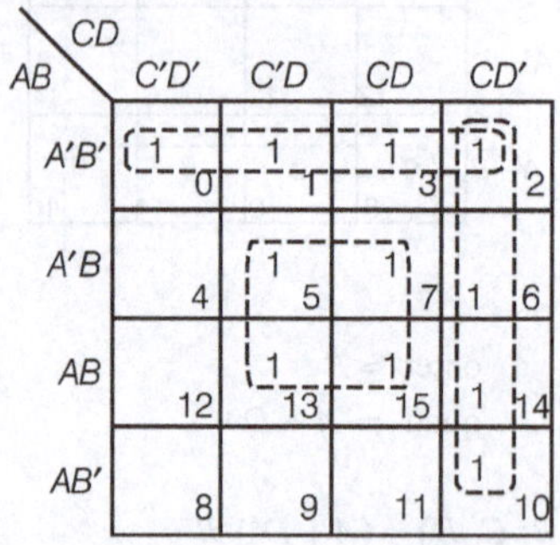

From K-map we conclude,

Ist quad $(m_0 + m_1 + m_2 + m_3) = A' B'$

IInd quad $(m_2 + m_6 + m_{10} + m_{14}) = CD'$

IIIrd quad $(m_5 + m_7 + m_{13} + m_{15}) = BD$

So, final expression is,

$$F(A, B, C, D) = A' B' + CD' + BD$$

(ii) **Logic gate diagram for expression**

$$F(A, B, C, D) = A' B' + CD' + BD$$

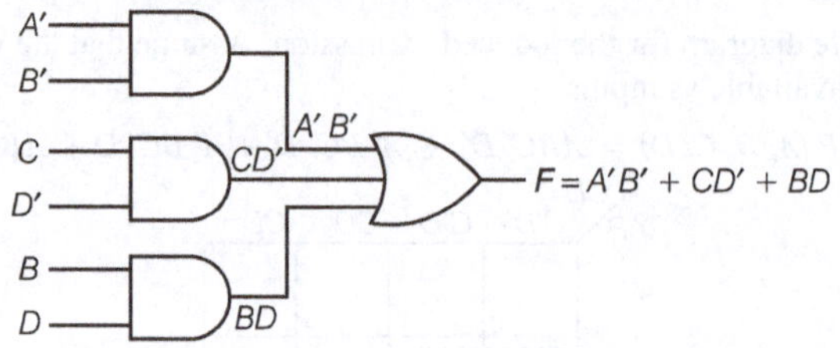

28. Given boolean function $P(A,B,C,D)=\Pi(0,1,2,3,5,6,7,10,13,14,15)$

(i) Reduce the above expression by using 4-variable Karnaugh's map, showing the various groups (i.e. octet, quads and pairs).

(ii) Draw the logic gate diagram for the reduced expression. Assume that the variables and their complements are available as inputs. **ISC 2014**

Ans (i) For $P(A, B, C, D) = \Pi\ (0, 1, 2, 3, 5, 6, 7, 10, 13, 14, 15)$

From K-map we conclude

Ist quad $(M_0 . M_1 . M_2 . M_3) = (A + B)$

IInd quad $(M_2 . M_6 . M_{10} . M_{14}) = (C' + D)$

IIIrd quad $(M_5 . M_7 . M_{13} . M_{15}) = (B' + D')$

So, final expression is,

$$P\ (A, B, C, D) = (A + B)\ (C' + D)\ (B' + D')$$

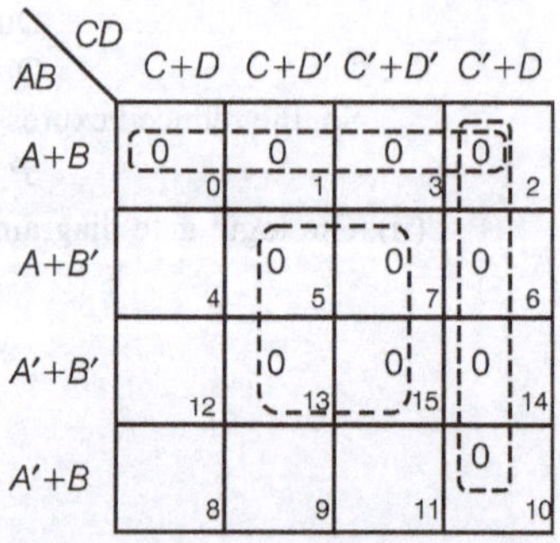

(ii) The logic diagram for the final expression is:

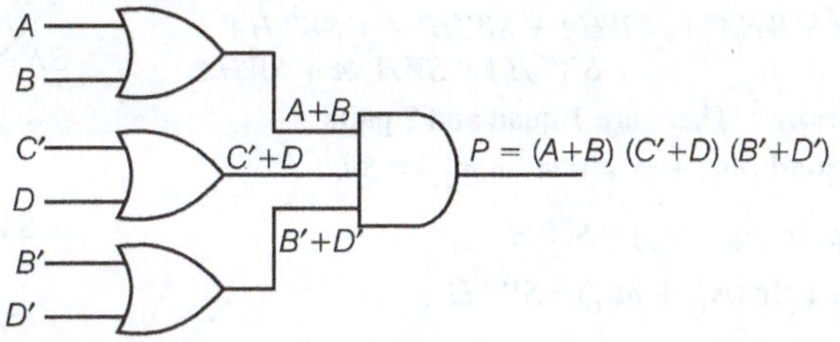

29. A school intends to select candidates for the Inter School Athletic Meet, as per the criteria given below:

- The candidate is from the Senior School and has participated in an Inter School Athletic Meet earlier.

Or

- The candidate is not from the Senior School, but the height is between 5 ft. and 6 ft. and weight is between 50 kg. and 60 kg.

Or

- The candidate is from the Senior School and has height between 5 ft. and 6 ft. but the weight is not between 50 kg. and 60 kg.

The inputs are:

Inputs	
S	Student is from the Senior School
W	Weight is between 50 kg. and 60 kg.
H	Height is between 5 ft. and 6 ft.
A	Taken part in Inter School Athletic Meet earlier

(In all of above cases 1 indicates yes and 0 indicates no)

Output: X-Denotes the selection criteria [1 indicates selected and 0 indicates rejected in all cases].

(i) Draw the truth table for the inputs and output given above and write the SOP expression for $X(S, W, H, A)$.

(ii) Reduce $X(S, W, H, A)$ using Karnaugh's Map.

Draw the logic gate diagram for the reduced SOP expression for $X(S, W, H, A)$ using AND and OR gate. You may use gates with two or more inputs. Assume that the variable and their complements are available as inputs. **ISC 2014**

Ans (i) The truth table for given inputs and output is:

Inputs				Output
S	W	H	A	X
0	0	0	0	0
0	0	0	1	0
0	0	1	0	0
0	0	1	1	0
0	1	0	0	0
0	1	0	1	0
0	1	1	0	1
0	1	1	1	1
1	0	0	0	0
1	0	0	1	1
1	0	1	0	1
1	0	1	1	1
1	1	0	0	0
1	1	0	1	1
1	1	1	0	0
1	1	1	1	1

Required SOP expression is,

$X(S, W, H, A) = S'WHA' + S'WHA + SW'H'A + SW'HA' + SW'HA + SWH'A + SWHA$

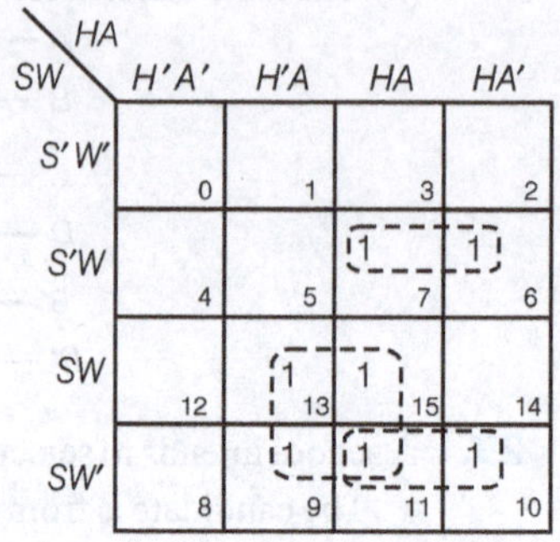

(ii) K-map representation There are 1 quad and 2 pairs

Ist quad $(m_{13} + m_{15} + m_9 + m_{11}) = SA$

Ist pair $(m_6 + m_7) = S'WH$

IInd pair $(m_{10} + m_{11}) = SW'H$

Final reduced expression is,

$X(S, W, H, A) = SA + S'WH + SW'H$

The logic diagram for the reduced expression is:

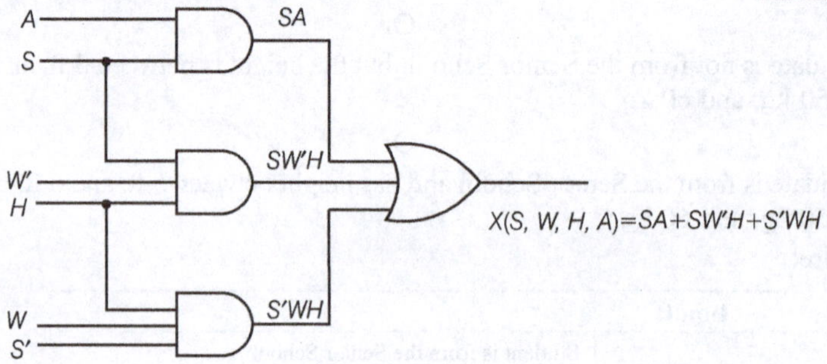

30. Given the boolean function $F(A, B, C, D) = \Sigma(0, 2, 4, 5, 8, 9, 10, 12, 13)$

(i) Reduce the above expression by using 4-variable K-map, showing the various groups (i.e. octet, quads and pairs).

(ii) Draw the logic gate diagram of the reduced expression. Assume that the variables and their complements are available as inputs.

ISC 2013

Ans (i) The given expression,

$F(A, B, C, D) = \Sigma(0, 2, 4, 5, 8, 9, 10, 12, 13)$

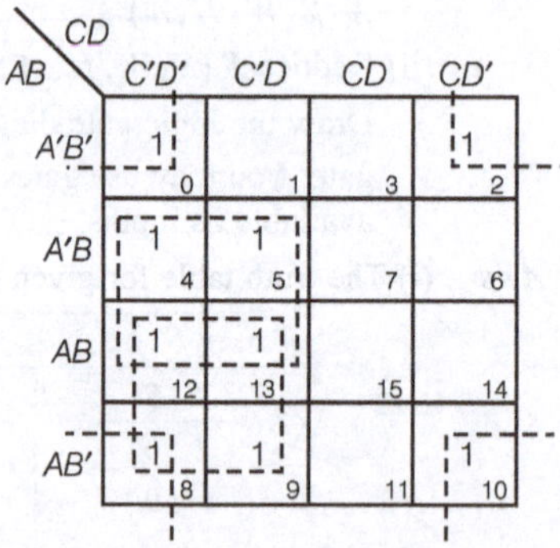

From K-map we conclude,

Ist Quad $(m_8 + m_9 + m_{12} + m_{13}) = AC'$

IInd Quad $(m_4 + m_5 + m_{12} + m_{13}) = BC'$

IIIrd Quad $(m_0 + m_2 + m_8 + m_{10}) = B'D'$

Hence, expression will be,

$F = B'D' + BC' + AC'$

(ii) **Logic diagram of expression** $F = B'D' + BC' + AC'$

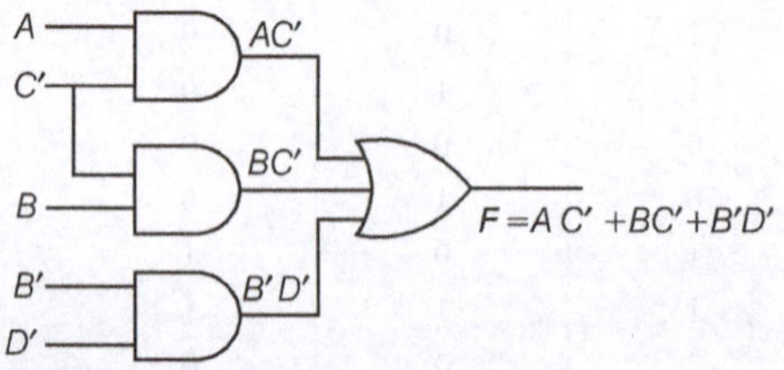

31. Given the boolean function $F(P, Q, R, S) = \Pi(0, 1, 3, 5, 7, 8, 9, 10, 11, 14, 15)$

(i) Reduce the above expression by using 4-variable K-map, showing the various group (i.e. octet, quads and pairs).

(ii) Draw the logic gate diagram of the reduced expression. Assume that the variable and their complements are available as inputs.

ISC 2013

Ans (i) The given expression,

$F(P, Q, R, S) = \Pi(0, 1, 3, 5, 7, 8, 9, 10, 11, 14, 15)$

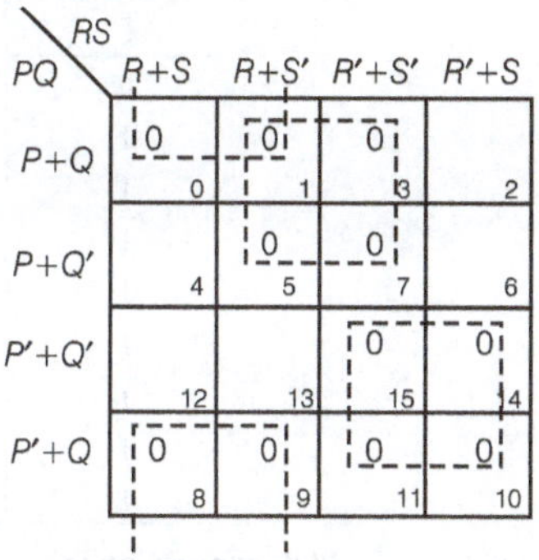

From K-map we conclude,

Ist Quad $(M_0 . M_1 . M_8 . M_9) = (Q + R)$

IInd Quad $(M_1 . M_3 . M_5 . M_7) = (P + S')$

IIIrd Quad $(M_{15} . M_{14} . M_{11} . M_{10}) = (P' + R')$

So, the reduced expression is,

$F(P,Q,R,S) = (Q + R).(P + S').(P' + R')$

(ii) Logic circuit diagram for $F(P,Q,R,S)$ is shown below:

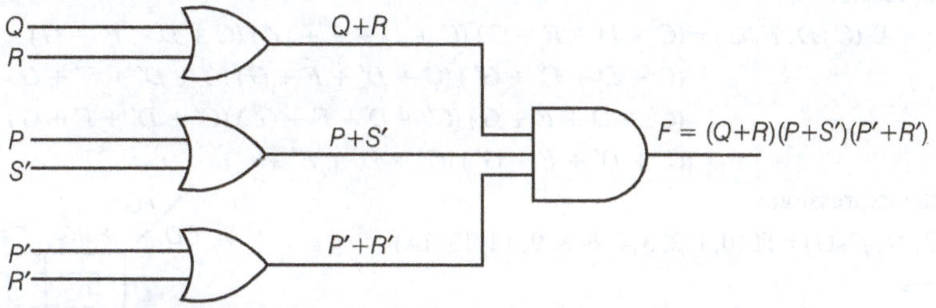

32. A Football Association coach analysis the criteria for a win/draw of his team depending on the following conditions:

- If the Centre and Forward players perform well but Defenders do not perform well.

Or

- If Goal keeper and Defenders perform well but the Centre players do not perform well.

Or

- If all the players perform well.

The inputs are:

Inputs	
C	Centre players perform well.
D	Defenders perform well.
F	Forward players perform well.
G	Goalkeeper performs well.

(In all of the above case 1 indicates YES and 0 indicates NO)

Output : X-Denotes the win/draw criteria [1 indicates win/draw and 0 indicates defeat in all the cases].

(i) Draw the truth table for the inputs and output given above and write the POS expression for $X(C, D, F, G)$.

(ii) Reduce $X(C, D, F, G)$ using Karnaugh's Map.

Draw the logic gate diagram for the reduced POS expression for $X(C,D,F,G)$ using AND and OR gate. You may use gates with two or more inputs. Assume that the variable and their complements are available as inputs.

ISC 2013

Ans (i) The truth table is shown below. Here C, D, F, G are the input variables of table while X is output variable.

C	D	F	G	X
0	0	0	0	0
0	0	0	1	0
0	0	1	0	0
0	0	1	1	0
0	1	0	0	0
0	1	0	1	1
0	1	1	0	0

C	*D*	*F*	*G*	*X*
0	1	1	1	1
1	0	0	0	0
1	0	0	1	0
1	0	1	0	1
1	0	1	1	1
1	1	0	0	0
1	1	0	1	0
1	1	1	0	0
1	1	1	1	1

POS expression is,

$$X(C,D,F,G)=(C+D+F+G)(C+D+F+G')(C+D+F'+G)$$
$$(C+D+F'+G')(C+D'+F+G)(C+D'+F'+G)$$
$$(C'+D+F+G)(C'+D+F+G')(C'+D'+F+G)$$
$$(C'+D'+F+G')(C'+D'+F'+G)$$

(ii) Using the expression,

$$X(C,D,F,G)=\Pi\,(0,1,2,3,4,6,8,9,12,13,14)$$

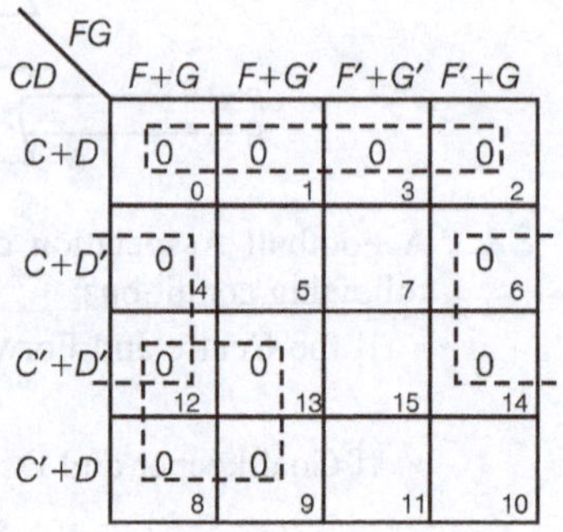

There are

Ist Quad $(M_0.M_1.M_2.M_3)=C+D$

IInd Quad $(M_4.M_6.M_{12}.M_{14})=D'+G$

IIIrd Quad $(M_8.M_9.M_{12}.M_{13})=F+C'$

Reduced expression is,

$$F=(C+D)(D'+G)(C'+F)$$

The logic circuit diagram for the reduced expression is given below:

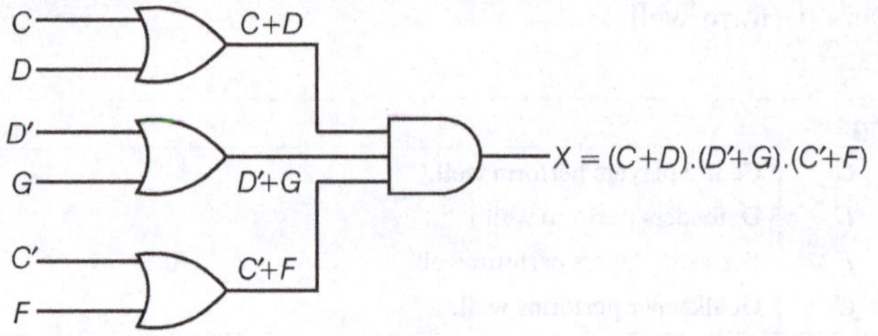

33. Given the boolean function $F(A,B,C,D)=\Sigma\,(4,6,7,10,11,12,14,15)$

(i) Reduce the above expression by using 4-variable K-map, showing the various groups (i.e. octet, quads and pairs).

(ii) Draw the logic gate diagram of the reduced expression. Assume that the variables and their complements are available as inputs. **ISC 2012**

Ans (i) Given expression,

$$F=(A,B,C,D)=\Sigma\,(4,6,7,10,11,12,14,15)$$

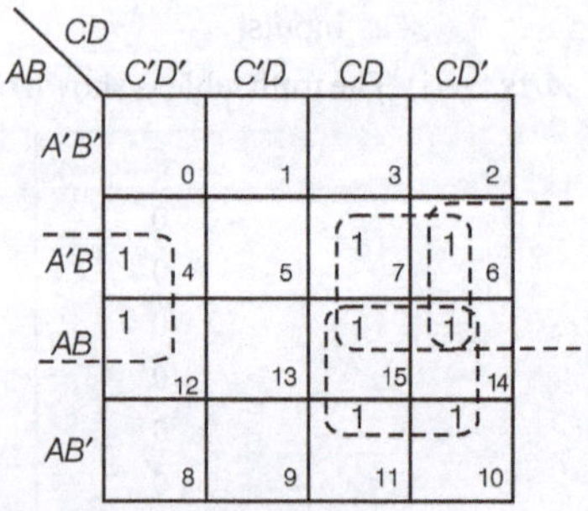

There are 3 quads,

Ist quad $(m_7+m_6+m_{15}+m_{14})=BC$

IInd quad $(m_{15}+m_{14}+m_{11}+m_{10})=AC$

IIIrd quad $(m_6+m_{14}+m_4+m_{12})=BD'$

Hence, reduced expression is,

$$F(A,B,C,D)=BC+AC+BD'$$

(ii) The logic gate diagram is shown below:

$$F(A, B, C, D) = BC + BD' + AC$$

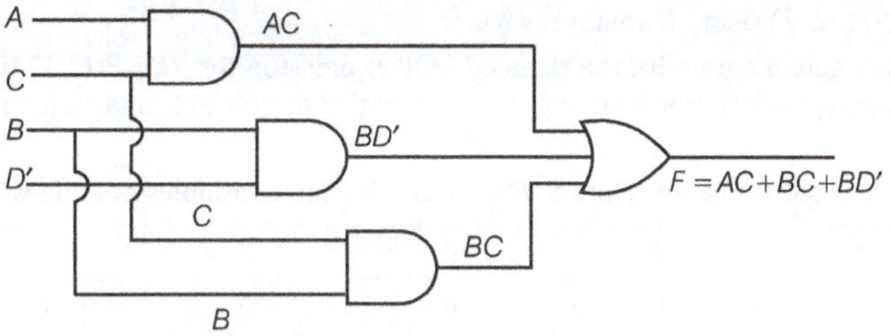

34. Given the boolean function $F(P, Q, R, S) = \Pi\ (0, 5, 7, 8, 10, 12, 13, 14, 15)$

(i) Reduce the above expression by using 4-variable K-map, showing the various groups (i.e. octet, quads and pairs).

(ii) Draw the logic gate diagram of the reduced expression. Assume that the variables and their complements are available as inputs.

ISC 2012

Ans (i) Given function,

$F(P, Q, R, S) = \Pi(0, 5, 7, 8, 10, 12, 13, 14, 15)$

There are 2 quads and 1 pair,

Ist Pair $(M_0 . M_8) = R + S + Q$

Ist Quad $(M_5 . M_7 . M_{13} . M_{15}) = S' + Q'$

IInd Quad $(M_8 . M_{10} . M_{12} . M_{14}) = S + P'$

Reduced expression is,

$F(P, Q, R, S) = (S' + Q').(S + P').(R + S + Q)$

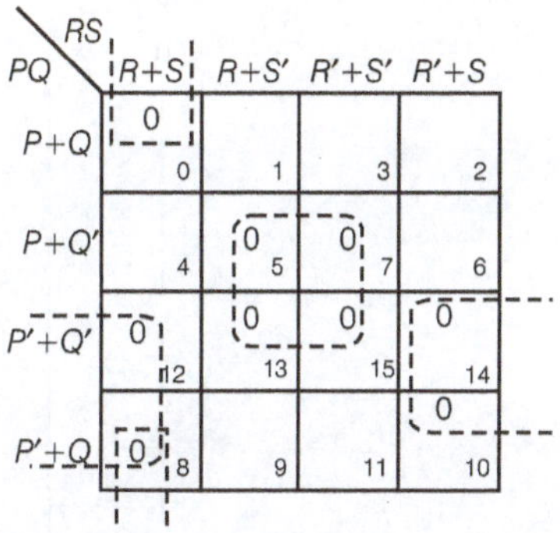

(ii) Logic diagram of reduced expression is:

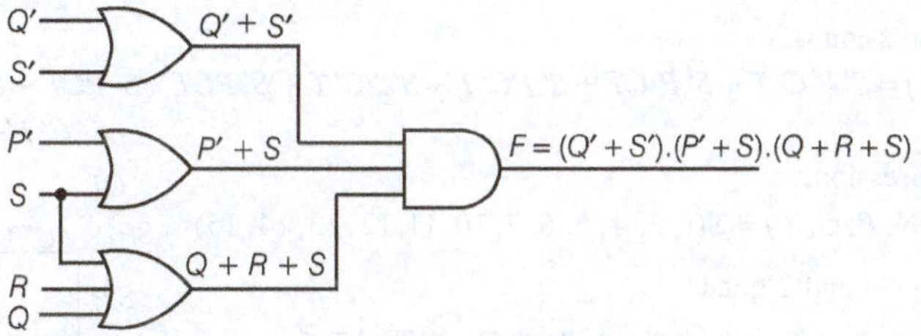

35. The principal of a school intends to select students for admission to class XI on the following criteria:

- Student is of the same school and has passed the class X Board Examination with more than 60% marks.

Or

- Student is of the same school, has passed the class X Board Examination with less than 60% marks but has taken active part in co-curricular activities.

Or

- Student is not from the same school but has either passed the class X Board Examination with more than 60% marks or has participated in sports at the national level.

The inputs are:

Inputs	
S	Student of the same school.
P	Has passed the class X Board Examination with more than 60% marks.
C	Has taken active part in co-curricular activities.
T	Has participated in sports at the national level.

Output X: Denotes admission status [1 indicates granted and 0 indicates refused in all the cases].

(i) Draw the truth table for the inputs and output given above and write the SOP expression.

(ii) Reduce $X(S, P, C, T)$ using Karnaugh's Map.

Draw the logic gate diagram for the reduced SOP expression for $X(S, P, C, T)$ using AND and OR gate. You may use gates with two or more inputs. Assume that the variable and their complements are available as inputs. ***ISC 2012***

Ans (i) The truth table is shown below. Here S, P, C, T are the input variables of table while X is output variable.

S	P	C	T	X
0	0	0	0	0
0	0	0	1	1
0	0	1	0	0
0	0	1	1	1
0	1	0	0	1
0	1	0	1	1
0	1	1	0	1
0	1	1	1	1
1	0	0	0	0
1	0	0	1	0
1	0	1	0	1
1	0	1	1	1
1	1	0	0	1
1	1	0	1	1
1	1	1	0	1
1	1	1	1	1

The SOP expression is,

$$X(S,P,C,T) = S'P'C'T + S'P'CT + S'PC'T' + S'PC'T + S'PCT' + S'PCT + SP'CT' + SP'CT + SPC'T' + SPC'T + SPCT' + SPCT$$

(ii) Using the expression,

$$X(S,P,C,T) = \Sigma(1, 3, 4, 5, 6, 7, 10, 11, 12, 13, 14, 15)$$

SP \ CT	C'T'	C'T	CT	CT'
S'P'	0	1 (1)	1 (3)	2
S'P	1 (4)	1 (5)	1 (7)	1 (6)
SP	1 (12)	1 (13)	1 (15)	1 (14)
SP'	8	9	1 (11)	1 (10)

There are 1 octet and 2 quads

Ist Octet $(m_4 + m_5 + m_6 + m_7 + m_{12} + m_{13} + m_{14} + m_{15}) = P$

Ist Quad $(m_1 + m_3 + m_5 + m_7) = S'T$

IInd Quad $(m_{10} + m_{11} + m_{14} + m_{15}) = SC$

Reduced expression is,

$$X = P + SC + S'T$$

The logic circuit diagram for the reduced expression is given below:

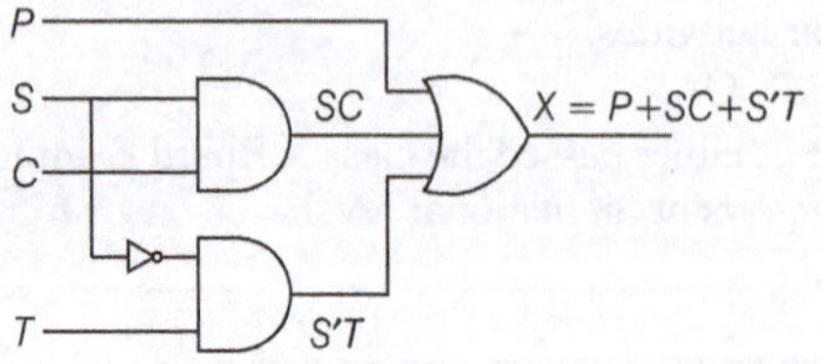

36. Given expression is $F(P,Q,R,S) = \Pi(2, 3, 6, 7, 9, 11, 12, 13, 14, 15)$.

Reduce the above expression by using four variable karnaugh's map. Draw the logic gate diagram of the reduced expression using NOR gate only. ***ISC 2011***

Ans The given expression is,

$$F(P, Q, R, S) = \Pi(2, 3, 6, 7, 9, 11, 12, 13, 14, 15)$$

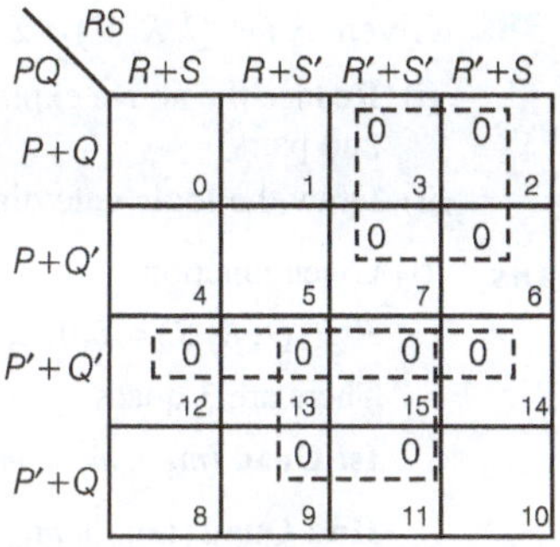

There are 3 quads

Ist Quad $(M_2 . M_3 . M_6 . M_7) = (R' + P)$

IInd Quad $(M_{13} . M_{15} . M_9 . M_{11}) = (P' + S')$

IIIrd Quad $(M_{12} . M_{13} . M_{15} . M_{14}) = (P' + Q')$

Reduced expression is,

$$F(P, Q, R, S) = (P + R').(P' + Q').(P' + S')$$

The logic diagram using NOR gate for above expression is:

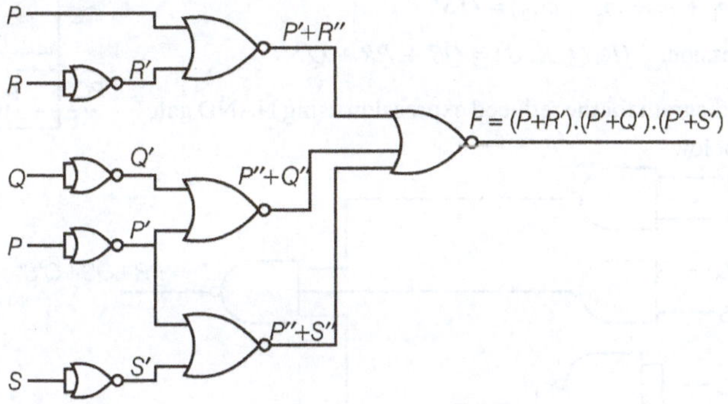

37. Given the expression

$F(A, B, C, D) = A'B'C'D' + A'B'C'D + AB'C'D' + AB'C'D + A'BC'D' + A'BCD'$.

Reduce the above expression by using 4-variable Karnaugh's map. Draw the logic gate diagram of the reduced expression using NAND gate only. ***ISC 2011***

Ans Given expression,

$$F(A, B, C, D) = A'B'C'D' + A'B'C'D + AB'C'D'$$
$$+ AB'C'D + A'BC'D' + A'BCD'$$

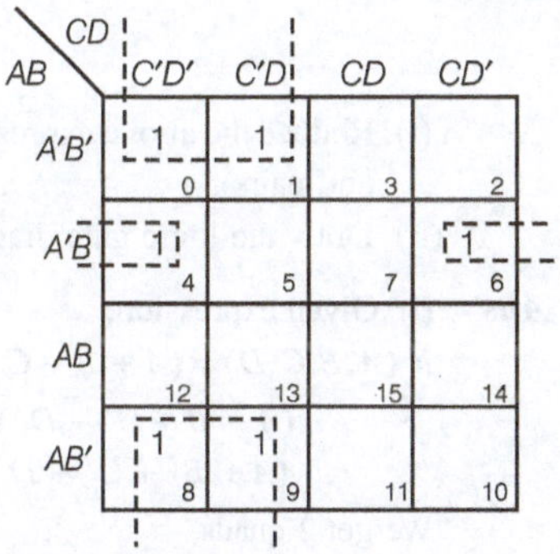

There are 1 quad and 1 pair

Ist Pair $(m_4 + m_6) = A'BD'$

Ist Quad $(m_0 + m_1 + m_8 + m_9) = B'C'$

Final reduced expression is,

$$F(A, B, C, D) = A'BD' + B'C'$$

Logic gate diagram for the reduced expression using NAND gate only is as follows:

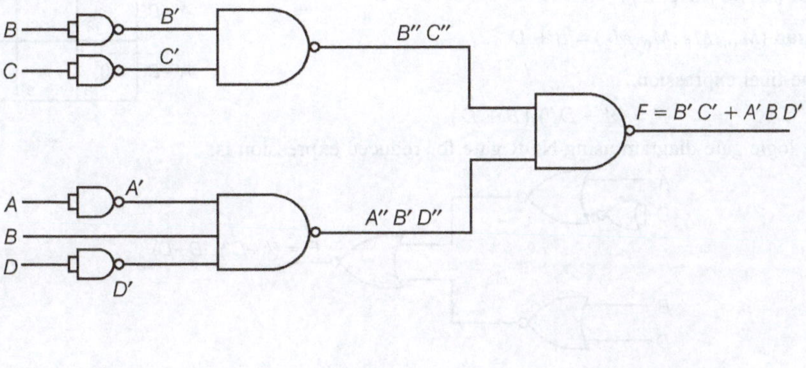

38. Given, $F(P,Q,R,S)=\Sigma(0,2,5,7,8,10,11,13,14,15)$

(i) Reduce the above expression by using 4 variable K-map, showing the various groups (i.e. octet, quads and pairs).

(ii) Draw the logic gate diagram of the reduced expression using NAND gate only. ***ISC 2010***

Ans (i) Given function is,

$F(P,Q,R,S)=\Sigma(0,2,5,7,8,10,11,13,14,15)$

There are 3 quads,

Ist Quad $(m_5+m_7+m_{13}+m_{15})=QS$

IInd Quad $(m_{15}+m_{14}+m_{11}+m_{10})=PR$

IIIrd Quad $(m_0+m_2+m_8+m_{10})=Q'S'$

Reduced expression, $F(P,Q,R,S)=QS+PR+Q'S'$

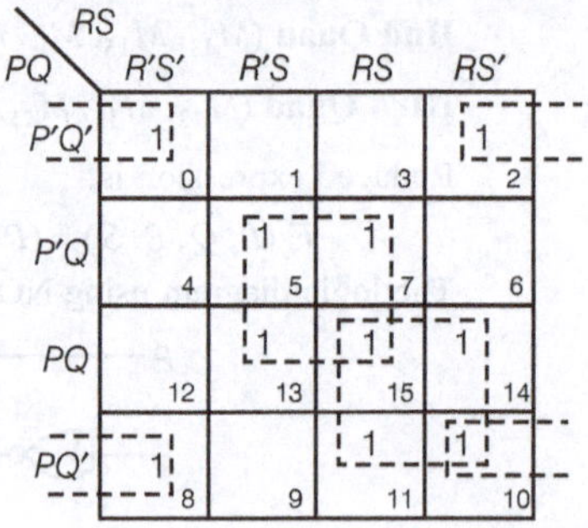

(ii) The logic gate diagram for the reduced expression using NAND gate only is given below:

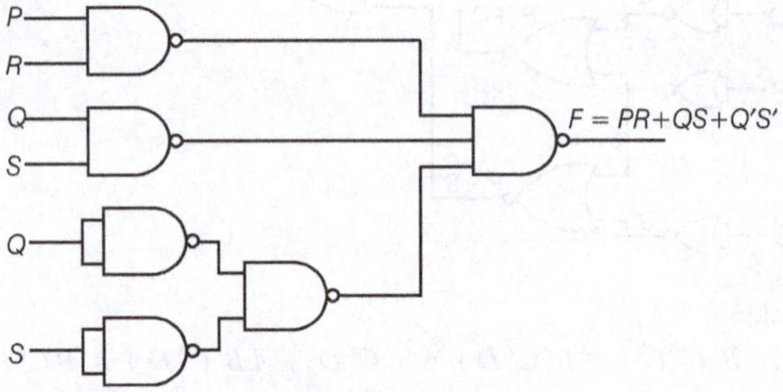

39. Given $F(A,B,C,D)=(A+B+C+D).(A+B+C+D').(A+B+C'+D')\cdot$

$(A+B+C'+D).(A+B'+C+D').(A+B'+C'+D').$

$(A'+B+C+D).(A'+B+C'+D)$

(i) Reduce the above expression by using 4-Variable K- Map, showing the various groups (i.e. octet, quads and pairs).

(ii) Draw the logic gate diagram of the reduced expression using NOR gate only. ***ISC 2010***

Ans (i) Given expression,

$F(A,B,C,D)=(A+B+C+D).(A+B+C+D').$

$(A+B+C'+D').(A+B+C'+D).(A+B'+C+D').$

$(A+B'+C'+D').(A'+B+C+D).(A'+B+C'+D)$

We get 2 quads,

Ist Quad $(M_1.M_3.M_5.M_7)=A+D'$

IInd Quad $(M_{10}.M_8.M_0.M_2)=B+D$

Thus, the final expression,

$F=(A+D').(B+D)$

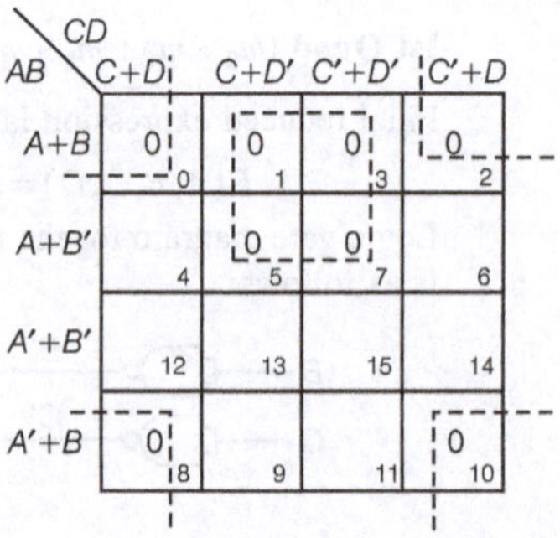

(ii) The logic gate diagram using NOR gate for reduced expression is:

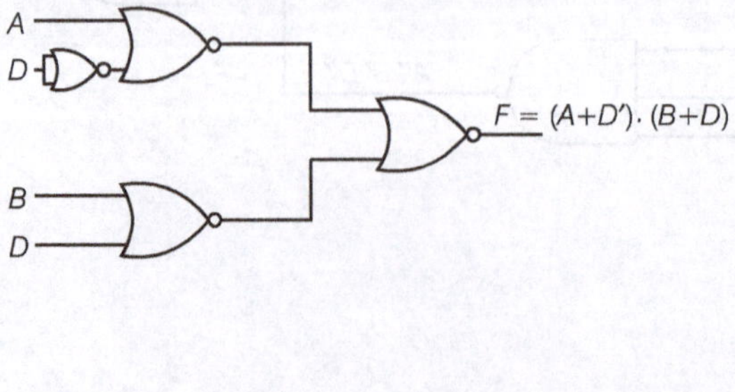

40. A Government Institution intends to award a medal to a person who qualifies any one of the following criteria:

- The person should have been an Indian citizen and had lost his/her life in a war but had not completed 25yr of service.

Or

- The person must be an Indian citizen and has served the nation for a continuous period of 25yr or more but has not lost his/her life in a war.

Or

- The person is not an Indian citizen but has taken active part in activities for the upliftment of the nation.

The inputs are:

Inputs	
A	The person is/was an Indian citizen.
B	Has a continuous service of more than 25 yr.
C	Lost his/her life in a war.
D	Taken part in activities for upliftment of the nation.

Output: X Denotes eligible for medal [1 indicates YES and 0 indicates NO in all cases].

(i) Draw the truth table for the inputs and output given above and write the POS expression for $X(A,B,C,D)$.

(ii) Reduce $X(A,B,C,D)$ using Karnaugh's map.
Draw the logic gate diagram for the reduced POS expression for $X(A,B,C,D)$.
You may use gates with two or more inputs. Assume that the variables and their complements are available as inputs.

ISC 2010

Ans (i) Given expression, $X(A,B,C,D)$ has four inputs and X represents output values.

The truth table for given inputs is,

A	B	C	D	X
0	0	0	0	0
0	0	0	1	1
0	0	1	0	0
0	0	1	1	1
0	1	0	0	0
0	1	0	1	1
0	1	1	0	0
0	1	1	1	1
1	0	0	0	0
1	0	0	1	0
1	0	1	0	1
1	0	1	1	1
1	1	0	0	1
1	1	0	1	1
1	1	1	0	0
1	1	1	1	0

Using above truth table, the following POS expression will be drawn:

$$X(A, B, C, D) = (A + B + C + D).(A + B + C' + D).(A + B' + C + D).$$
$$(A + B' + C' + D).(A' + B + C + D).(A' + B + C + D').(A' + B' + C' + D).$$
$$(A' + B' + C' + D')$$

(ii) From K-map, we get 1 quad and 2 pairs,

Ist Quad $(M_0 . M_2 . M_4 . M_6) = A + D$

Ist Pair $(M_{15} . M_{14}) = A' + B' + C'$

IInd Pair $(M_8 . M_9) = A' + B + C$

Thus, the final output is,

$F = (A + D).(A' + B' + C').(A' + B + C)$

The logic diagram for the expression is:

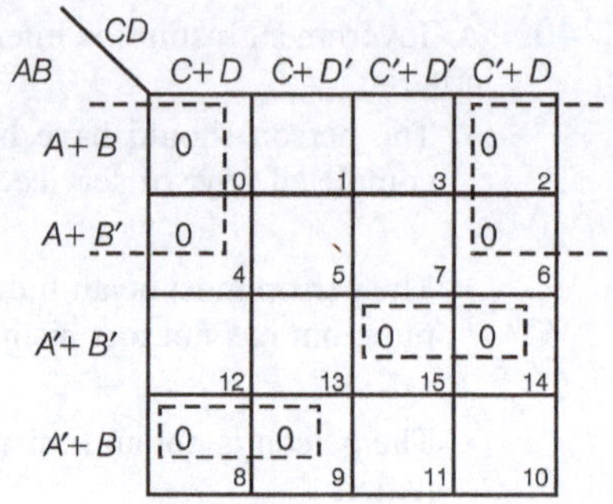

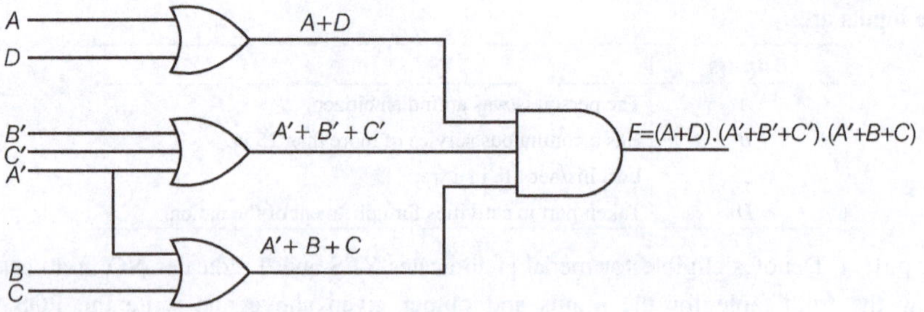

41. $F(P,Q,R,S) = P'Q'RS' + P'QRS' + PQ'R'S + PQ'RS' + PQ'RS + PQR'S + PQRS' + PQRS$

Use Karnaugh's map to reduce the given function F using the SOP form. Draw a logic gate diagram for the reduced SOP form. You may use gate with more than two inputs. Assume that the variables and their complements are available as inputs. **ISC 2009**

Ans Given expression,

$F(P,Q,R,S) = P'Q'RS' + P'QRS' + PQ'R'S + PQ'RS + PQR'S + PQRS' + PQRS + PQ'RS'$

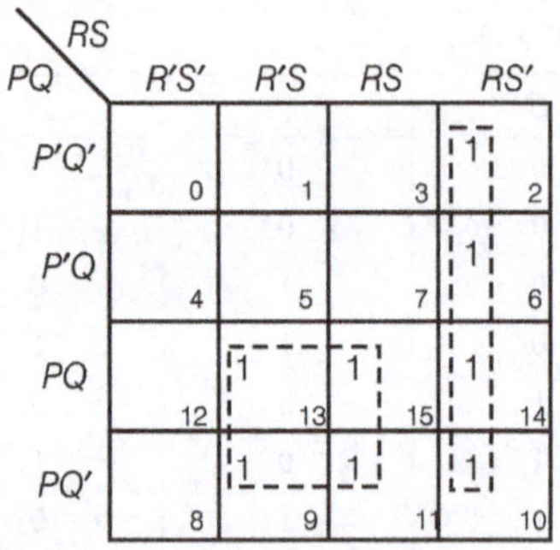

From K-map we conclude,

Ist Quad $(m_{13} + m_{15} + m_9 + m_{11}) = SP$

IInd Quad $(m_2 + m_6\ m_{14} + m_{10}) = RS'$

The reduced SOP expression, $F = SP + RS'$

From the given expression, the logic gate will be formed as:

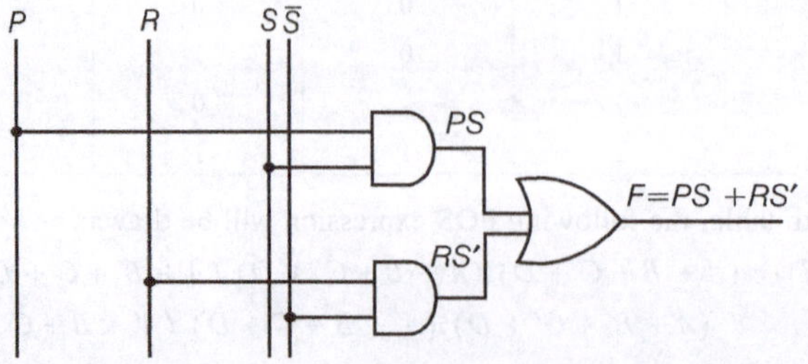

42. $F(A,B,C,D)=\Pi(0,1,2,3,5,7,9,13)$

Use Karnaugh's map to reduce the given function F using the POS form. Draw a logic gate diagram for the reduced POS form. You may use gate with more than two inputs. Assume that the variables and their complements are available as inputs. **ISC 2009**

Ans Given expression, $F(A,B,C,D)=\Pi(0,1,2,3,5,7,9,13)$

Now, to construct the K-map, we take four variable inputs

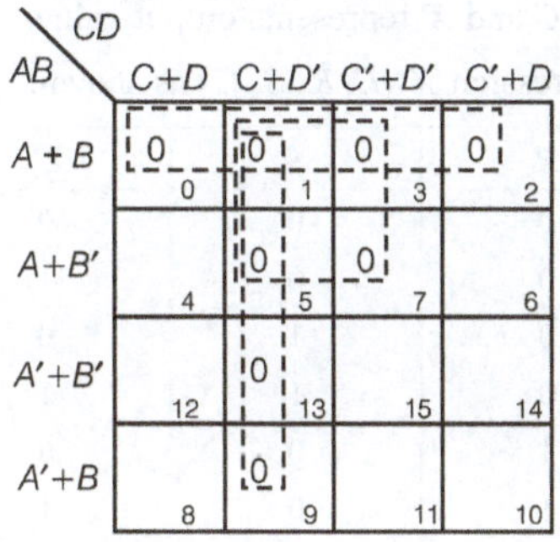

We conclude,

Ist Quad $(M_0 . M_1 . M_3 . M_2) = A + B$

IInd Quad $(M_1 . M_3 . M_5 . M_7) = A + D'$

IIIrd Quad $(M_1 . M_5 . M_{13} . M_9) = C + D'$

Thus, the final reduced POS expression is,

$$F = (A + B)(C + D')(A + D')$$

The logic diagram for above expression is:

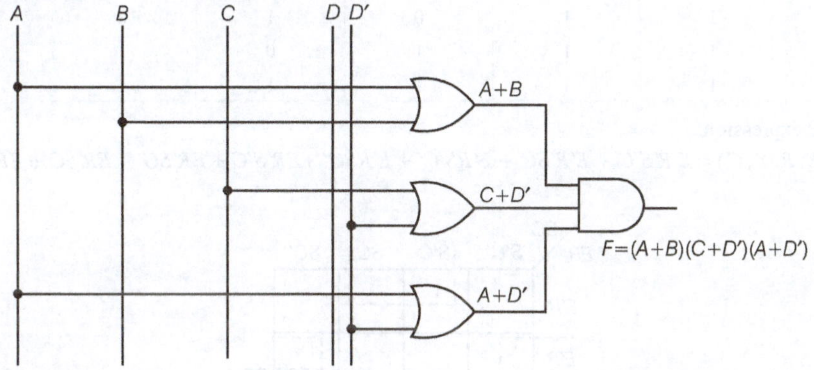

43. A provisional store announces a special discount on all its products as a festival offer only to those who satisfy any one of the following conditions:

- If he/she is an employee of the store and has a service of more than 10yr.

Or

- If he/she is a regular customer of the store whose age is less than 65yr and is not an employee of the store.

Or

- If he/she is a senior citizen but not a regular customer of the store.

The inputs are:

Inputs	
E	Employee of the store
R	Regular customer of the store
S	Service of the employee is more than 10yr
C	Senior citizen of 65yr or above

Output X: Denotes eligible for discount [1 indicates YES and 0 indicates NO in all cases].

(i) Draw the truth table for the inputs and output given above and write the SOP expression for $X(E, R, S, C)$.

(ii) Reduce $X(E, R, S, C)$ using Karnaugh's map.

Draw the logic gate diagram for the reduced SOP expression for $X(E, R, S, C)$ using AND and OR gates. You may use gates with two or more inputs. Assume that the variable and their complements are available as inputs.

ISC 2009

Ans (i) We have four inputs E, R, S, C and X represents output value.

The truth table for given expression $X(E, R, S, C)$ as shown:

E	R	S	C	X
0	0	0	0	0
0	0	0	1	1
0	0	1	0	0
0	0	1	1	1
0	1	0	0	1
0	1	0	1	0
0	1	1	0	1
0	1	1	1	0
1	0	0	0	0
1	0	0	1	1
1	0	1	0	1
1	0	1	1	1
1	1	0	0	0
1	1	0	1	0
1	1	1	0	1
1	1	1	1	1

SOP expression

$X(E, R, S, C) = E'R'S'C + E'R'SC + E'RS'C' + E'RSC' + ER'S'C + ER'SC' + ER'SC + ERSC' + ERSC$

(ii)

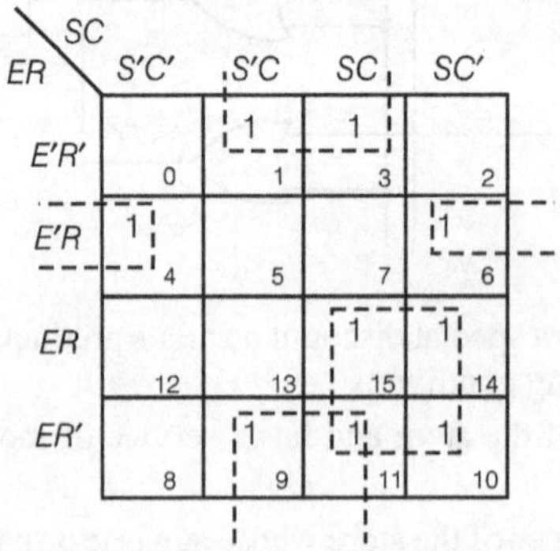

We get 2 quads and 1 pair,

Ist Quad $(m_1 + m_3 + m_9 + m_{11}) = R'C$

IInd Quad $(m_{10} + m_{11} + m_{14} + m_{15}) = ES$

Ist Pair $(m_4 + m_6) = E'RC'$

Reduced SOP expression, $X(E, R, S, C) = R'C + ES + E'RC'$

Logic gate diagram for above expression

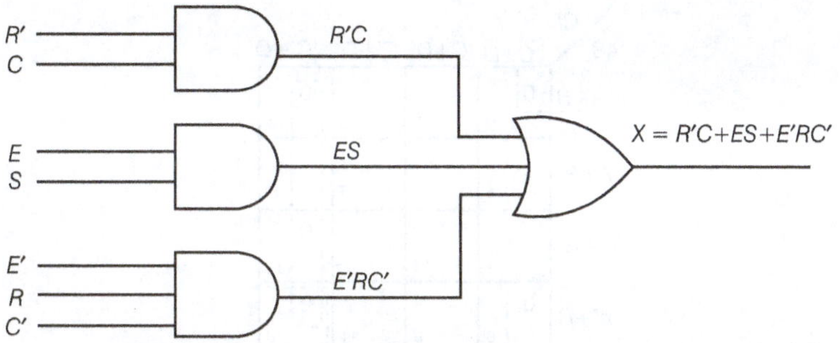

44. Draw the truth table and logic circuit diagram for a 3 × 8 decoder. State the difference between a multiplexer and a decoder. ***ISC 2008***

Ans **3 × 8 Decoder** Refer to text on page 50.

Difference between multiplexer and decoder Refer to text on page 56 Question 12 (2 Marks Questions).

45. Given the Boolean function $F(A, B, C, D) = \Sigma(5, 6, 7, 8, 9, 10, 14)$

Use Karnaugh's map to reduce the function F, using the SOP form. Draw a logic gate diagram for the reduced SOP form. You may use gates with more than two inputs. Assume that the variables and their complements are available as inputs. ***ISC 2008***

Ans Here, A, B, C and D are four variables. So we will use 4-variable K-map,

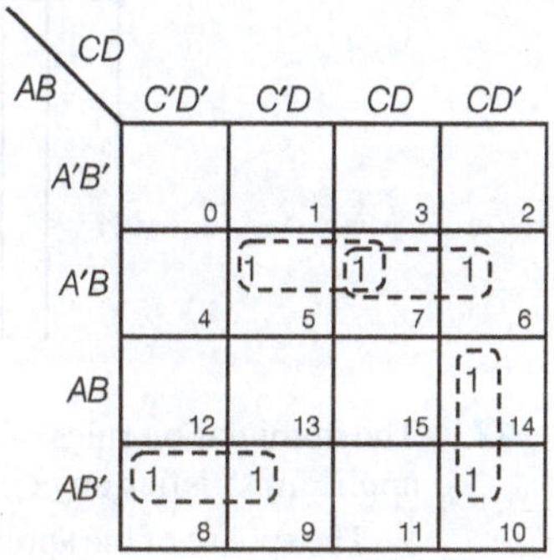

Ist Pair $(m_5 + m_7) = A'BD$

IInd Pair $(m_7 + m_6) = A'BC$

IIIrd Pair $(m_{10} + m_{14}) = ACD'$

IVth Pair $(m_8 + m_9) = AB'C'$

Hence, expression

$$F(A, B, C, D) = A'BD + A'BC + ACD' + AB'C'$$

Logic gate diagram for the expression is:

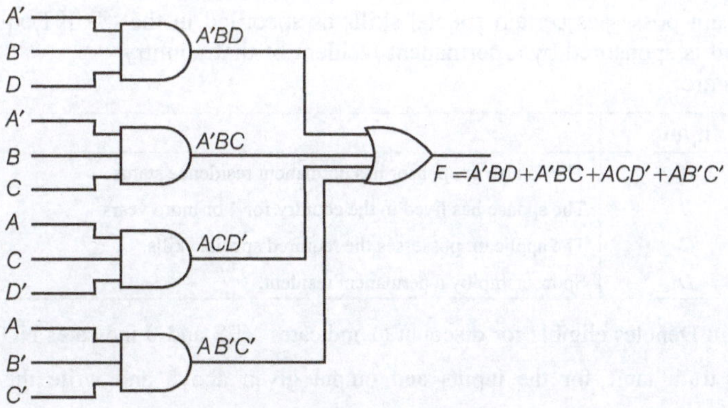

46. Given $X(A, B, C, D) = \Pi(0, 2, 6, 8, 10, 14)$

Use Karnaugh's map to reduce the given function X using the POS form. Draw a logic gate diagram for the reduced POS form. You may use gates with more than two inputs. Assume that the variables and their complements are available as inputs. ***ISC 2008***

Ans Here, given $X(A,B,C,D)=\Pi(0,2,6,8,10,14)$

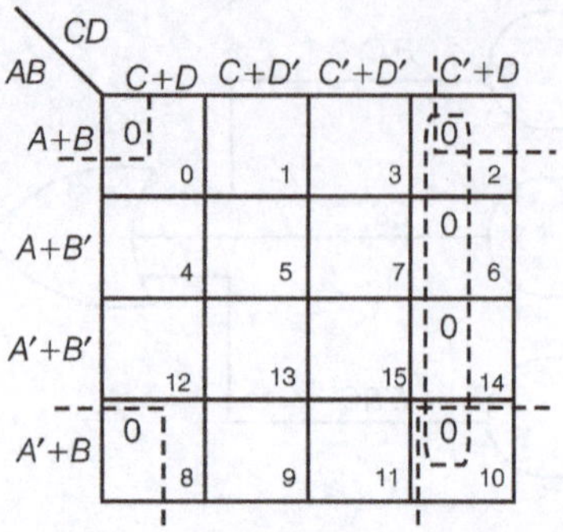

Here, we put all the maxterms of the given input and we conclude that,

Ist Quad $(M_2.M_0.M_{10}.M_8) = B + D$

IInd Quad $(M_2.M_6.M_{10}.M_{14}) = C' + D$

Hence, POS expression is $X = (B + D).(C' + D)$

Its logic circuit diagram is as follows:

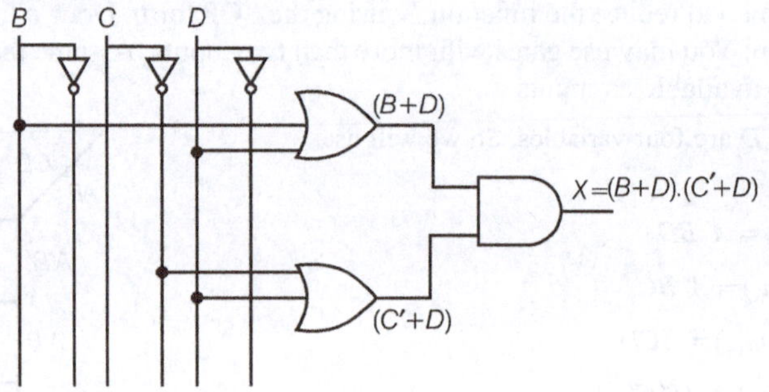

47. The immigration rules of a country allow the issue of work-cum-stay permits to an applicant only if the applicant satisfies any one of the following conditions.

- The spouse of the applicant is a permanent resident of that country, having lived there for at least 4yr.

Or

- The applicant possesses certain special skills as specified in the 'Skill Requirement List' of the country and is sponsored by a permanent resident of that country.

The inputs are:

Inputs	
A	The spouse or sponsor has permanent residence status.
B	The spouse has lived in the country for 4 or more years.
C	The applicant possesses the required special skills.
D	Sponsorship by a permanent resident.

Output X : Denotes eligible for discount (1 indicates YES and 0 indicates NO in all cases).

(i) Draw the truth table for the inputs and output given above and write the SOP expression for $X(A,B,C,D)$.

(ii) Reduce $X(A,B,C,D)$ using Karnaugh's map.
Draw the logic gate diagram for the reduced SOP expression for $X(A,B,C,D)$ using AND and OR gates. You may use gates with two or more inputs. Assume that the variable and their complements are available as inputs. ***ISC 2008***

Ans (i) From the above, we have four inputs *A, B, C* and *D* and one output *X*. The truth table for given variables is shown:

A	*B*	*C*	*D*	*X*
0	0	0	0	0
0	0	0	1	0
0	0	1	0	0
0	0	1	1	1
0	1	0	0	0
0	1	0	1	0
0	1	1	0	0
0	1	1	1	1
1	0	0	0	0
1	0	0	1	0
1	0	1	0	0
1	0	1	1	1
1	1	0	0	1
1	1	0	1	1
1	1	1	0	1
1	1	1	1	1

So, the SOP expression is,

$$X(A, B, C, D) = A'B'CD + A'BCD + AB'CD + ABC'D' + ABC'D + ABCD' + ABCD$$

(ii) K-map for above SOP expression is,

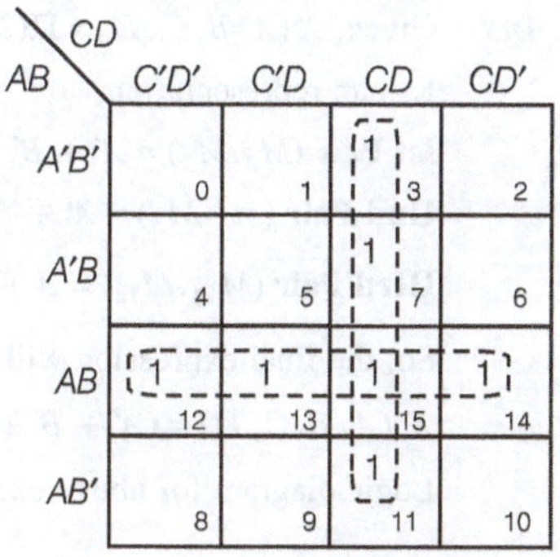

Ist Quad $(m_{12} + m_{13} + m_{14} + m_{15}) = AB$

IInd Quad $(m_3 + m_7 + m_{11} + m_{15}) = CD$

So, final expression $X(A, B, C, D) = AB + CD$

The logic diagram of expression is:

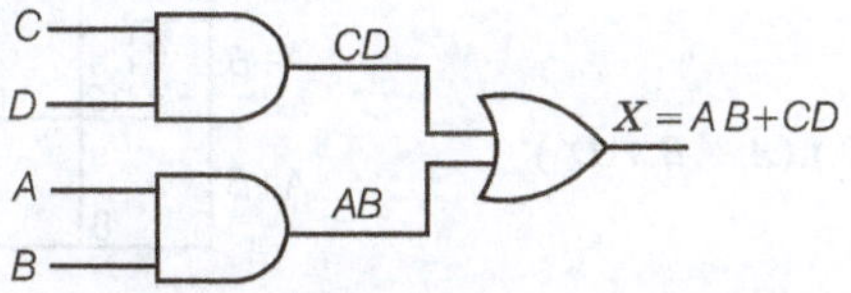

48. Given the Boolean function

$$F(A, B, C, D) = \Sigma\,(0, 2, 3, 4, 6, 7, 9, 13)$$

Use Karnaugh's map to reduce the function *F*, using the SOP form. Draw a logic diagram for the reduced SOP form. You may use gates with more than two inputs. Assume that the variables and their complements are available as inputs.
ISC 2007

Ans Given, $F(A, B, C, D) = \Sigma\,(0, 2, 3, 4, 6, 7, 9, 13)$

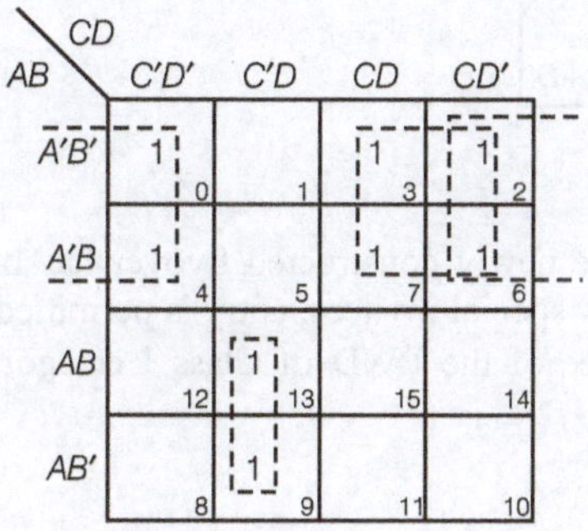

We get,

Ist Quad $(m_0 + m_2 + m_4 + m_6) = A'D'$

IInd Quad $(m_2 + m_3 + m_6 + m_7) = A'C$

Ist Pair $(m_9 + m_{13}) = AC'D$

So, the final expression will be,

$$F(A, B, C, D) = A'C + A'D' + AC'D$$

Logic diagram representation:

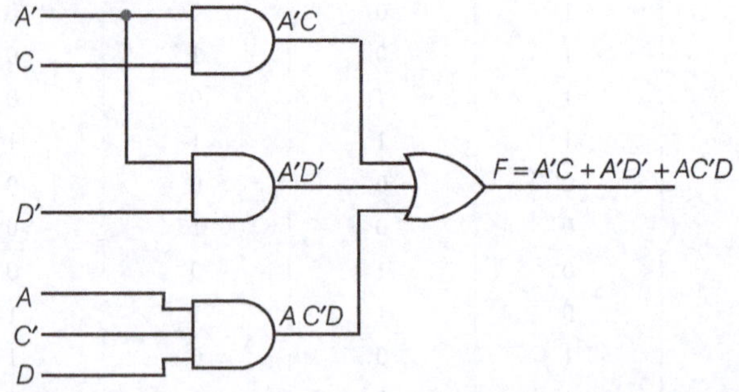

49. Given, $X(A, B, C, D) = \Pi(2, 3, 4, 5, 12, 14)$

Use Karnaugh's map to reduce this function X using the given POS form. Draw a logic gate diagram for the reduced POS form. You may use gates with more than two inputs. Assume that the variables and their complements are available as inputs. **ISC 2007**

Ans Given, $X(A, B, C, D) = \Pi(2, 3, 4, 5, 12, 14)$

K-map representation,

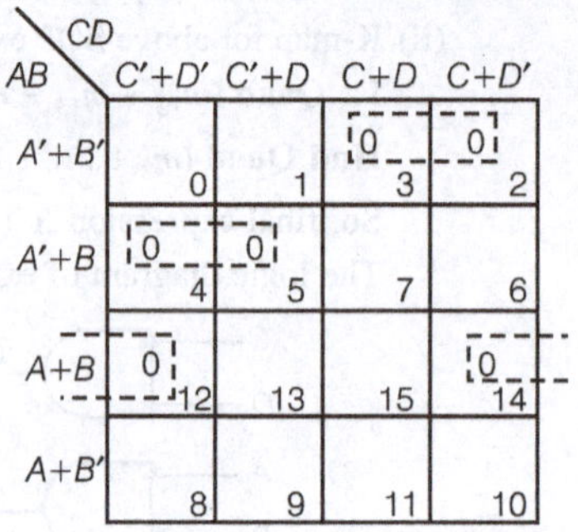

Ist Pair $(M_2 . M_3) = A' + B' + C$

IInd Pair $(M_4 . M_5) = A' + B + C'$

IIIrd Pair $(M_{12} . M_{14}) = A + B + D'$

So, the final expression will be

$X(A, B, C, D) = (A' + B' + C).(A' + B + C').(A + B + D')$

Logic diagram for above expression,

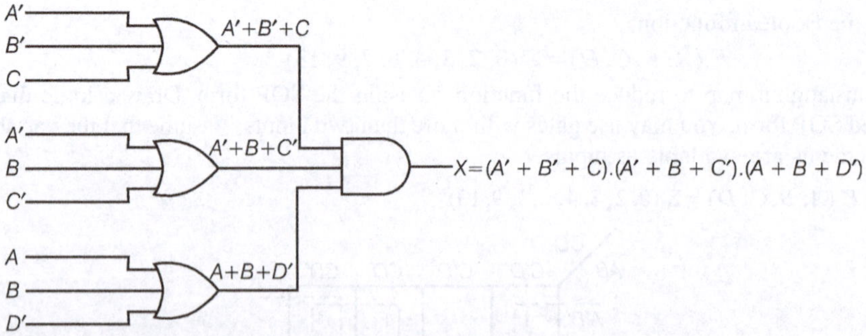

50. The inaugural function of the newly constructed flyover has been organised by the Public Works Department. Apart from a few special invitees, entry is permitted only, if:

- The person is an employee of the PWD of Class I category with more than 10yr of working experience.

Or

- The person is an employee of any other government or authorised private organisation either at the managerial level or with more than 10yr of working experience.

  The inputs are:

Inputs	
A	The person is a Class I employee of PWD.
B	The person is an employee of any other government or authorised private organisation.
C	The person has more than 10 yr of working experience.
D	The person is holding a managerial post.

Output:

X : Denotes eligible for entry [1 indicates YES and 0 indicates NO in all cases].

(i) Draw the truth tables for the inputs and output given above and write the SOP expression for $X(A, B, C, D)$.

(ii) Reduce $X(A, B, C, D)$ using Karnaugh's map.

Draw the logic gate diagram for the reduced SOP expression for $X(A, B, C, D)$ using AND and OR gates. You may use gates with two or more inputs. Assume that the variables and their complements are available as inputs. **ISC 2007**

Ans (i) Truth table for given inputs is given below:

A	B	C	D	X
0	0	0	0	0
0	0	0	1	0
0	0	1	0	0
0	0	1	1	0
0	1	0	0	0
0	1	0	1	1
0	1	1	0	1
0	1	1	1	1
1	0	0	0	0
1	0	0	1	0
1	0	1	0	1
1	0	1	1	1
1	1	0	0	0
1	1	0	1	1
1	1	1	0	1
1	1	1	1	1

SOP expression for (A, B, C, D)

$$= A'BC'D + A'BCD' + A'BCD + AB'CD' + AB'CD + ABC'D + ABCD' + ABCD$$

(ii) K-map representation

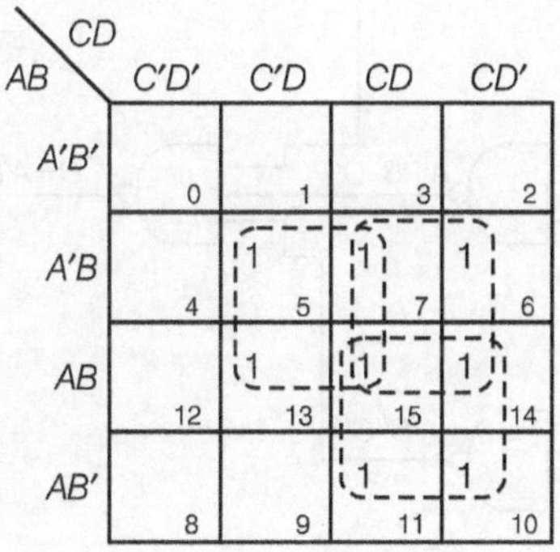

From K-map, we get

Ist Quad $(m_5 + m_7 + m_{13} + m_{15}) = BD$

IInd Quad $(m_7 + m_6 + m_{15} + m_{14}) = BC$

IIIrd Quad $(m_{15} + m_{14} + m_{11} + m_{10}) = AC$

So, the final expression will be

$$X\,(A, B, C, D) = BD + BC + AC$$

Logic diagram for above expression,

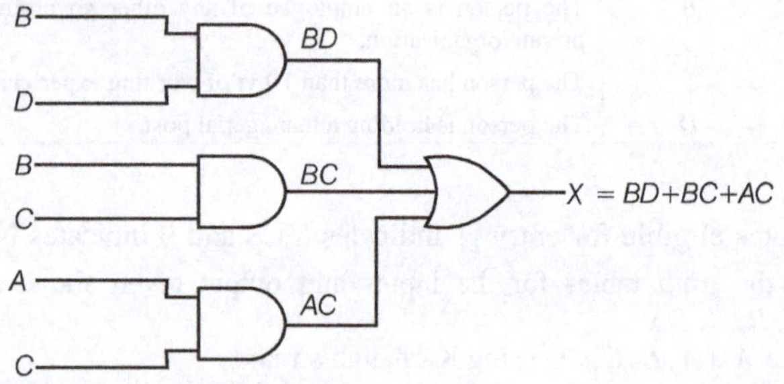

51. A combinational circuit with 3 inputs *A, B, C* detects an error during transmission of code and gives the output *D* as 1 if any two of the inputs are low (0).

(i) Write the truth table with inputs *A, B, C* and output *D*.

(ii) Write the SOP expression for $D(A, B, C)$ using minterms. Implements *D* using NAND gates only.

(iii) Write the POS expression for $D(A, B, C)$ using maxterms. Implement *D* using NOR gates only.

ISC 2007

Ans (i)

Inputs			Output
A	**B**	**C**	**D**
0	0	0	0
0	0	1	1
0	1	0	1
0	1	1	0
1	0	0	1
1	0	1	0
1	1	0	0
1	1	1	0

(ii) SOP expression, $D\,(A, B, C) = A'\,B'C + A'\,BC' + AB'C'$

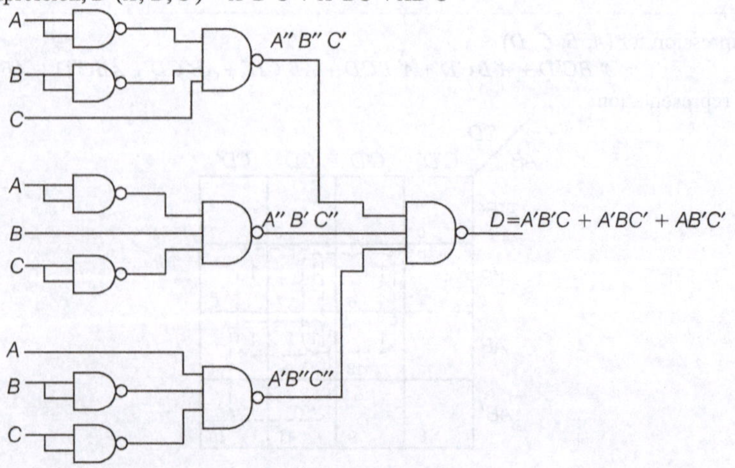

(iii) POS expression $D(A, B, C) = (A+B+C).(A+B'+C').(A'+B+C').(A'+B'+C).(A'+B'+C')$

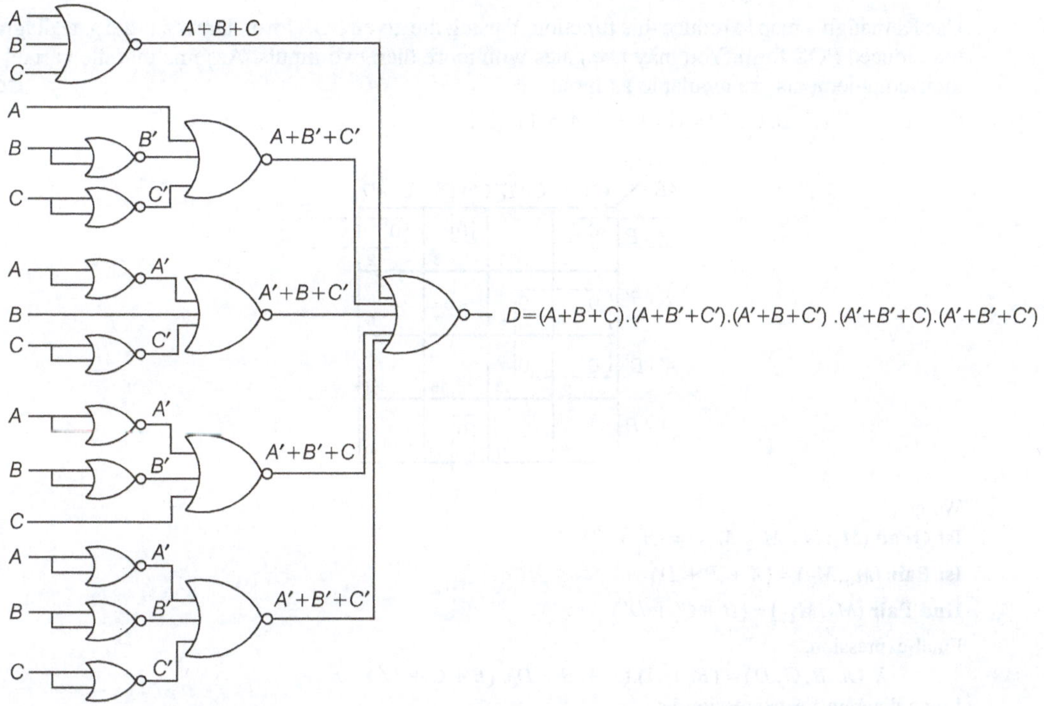

52. Draw the truth table and logic diagram for a hexadecimal to binary encoder. ***ISC 2007***

Ans Refer to text on page 51.

53. Given, the boolean function

$$F(A, B, C, D) = \Sigma(1, 6, 7, 8, 9, 10, 14, 15).$$

Use Karnaugh's map to reduce the function F, using the given SOP form. Draw a logic gate diagram for the reduced SOP form. You may use gates with more than two inputs. Assume that the variables and their complements are available as inputs. ***ISC 2006***

Ans Given,

$$F(A, B, C, D) = \Sigma(1, 6, 7, 8, 9, 10, 14, 15)$$

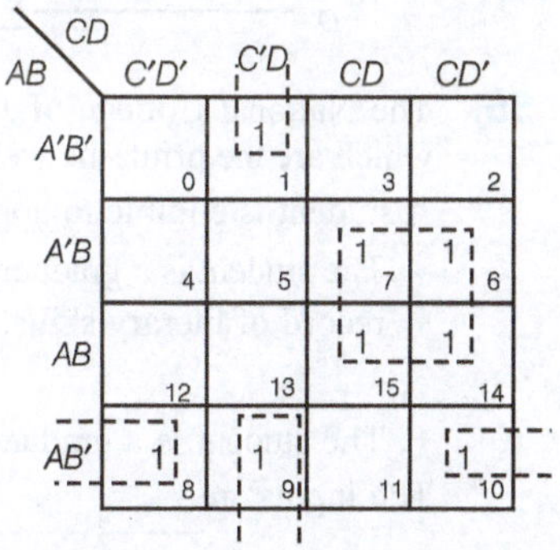

We get,

Ist Quad $(m_7 + m_6 + m_{15} + m_{14}) = BC$

Ist Pair $(m_1 + m_9) = B'C'D$

IInd Pair $(m_8 + m_{10}) = AB'D'$

So, the final expression will be

$$F(A, B, C, D) = B'C'D + AB'D' + BC$$

Logic diagram for final expression is:

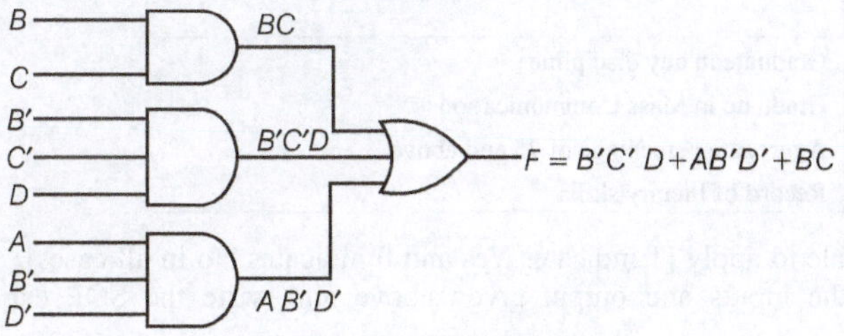

54. Given $X(A,B,C,D)=\Pi(0,2,3,4,5,11,12,13)$

Use Karnaugh's map to reduce this function X using the given POS form. Draw a logic gate diagram for the reduced POS form. You may use gates with more than two inputs. Assume that the variables and their complements are available as inputs. **ISC 2006**

Ans Given, $X(A,B,C,D)=\Pi(0,2,3,4,5,11,12,13)$

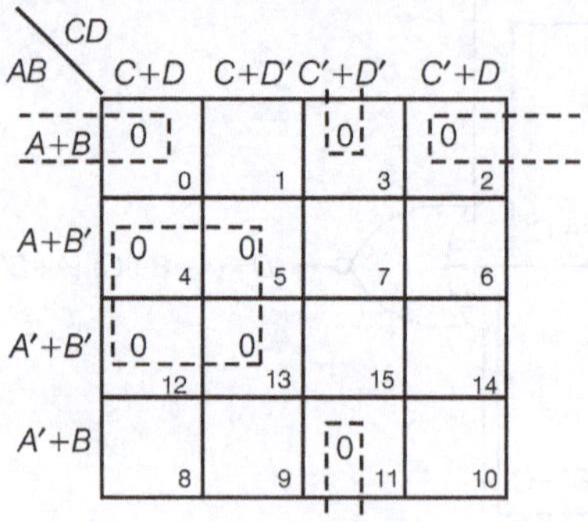

We get,

Ist Quad $(M_4.M_5.M_{12}.M_{13})=(B'+C)$

Ist Pair $(M_0.M_2)=(A+B+D)$

IInd Pair $(M_3.M_{11})=(B+C'+D')$

Final expression,

$$X(A,B,C,D)=(B'+C).(A+B+D).(B+C'+D')$$

Logic diagram for expression is:

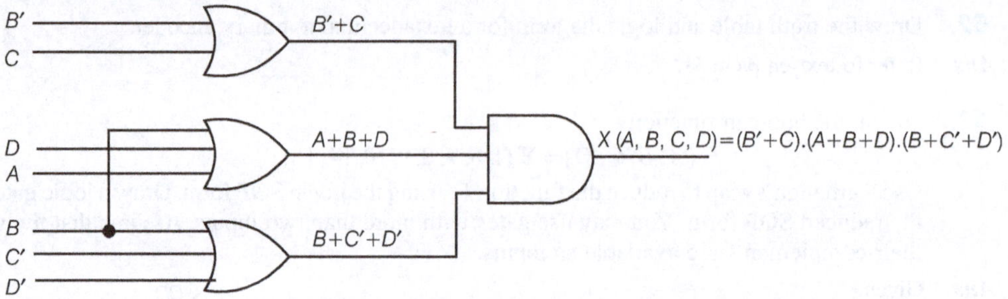

55. The National College of Journalism is offering courses in three different categories of journalism, which are the print, the web and the broadcasting media.

A student is eligible to apply, if he/she satisfies any one of the following conditions:

- The student is a graduate in any discipline with an aggregate percentage of 75 or above and with a record of literary skills.

Or

- The student is a graduate in Mass Communication with aggregate percentage of 75 or above:

The inputs are:

Inputs	
A	Graduate in any discipline
B	Graduate in Mass Communication
C	Aggregate percentage of 75 and above
D	Record of literary skills

Output: R : Denotes eligible to apply [1 indicates Yes and 0 indicates No in all cases].

(i) Draw the truth table for the inputs and output given above and write the SOP expression for $R(A,B,C,D)$.

(ii) Reduce $R(A, B, C, D)$ using Karnaugh's map.
Draw a logic gate diagram for the reduced SOP expression for $R(A, B, C, D)$ using AND and OR gates. You may use gates with two or more inputs. Assume that the variables and their complements are available as inputs. **ISC 2006**

Ans (i) The truth table is given below:

A	*B*	*C*	*D*	*R*
0	0	0	0	0
0	0	0	1	0
0	0	1	0	0
0	0	1	1	0
0	1	0	0	0
0	1	0	1	0
0	1	1	0	1
0	1	1	1	1
1	0	0	0	0
1	0	0	1	0
1	0	1	0	0
1	0	1	1	1
1	1	0	0	0
1	1	0	1	0
1	1	1	0	1
1	1	1	1	1

SOP form,

$R(A, B, C, D) = A'BCD' + A'BCD + AB'CD + ABCD' + ABCD$

(ii) **K-map representation**

$R(A, B, C, D) = \Sigma(6, 7, 11, 14, 15)$

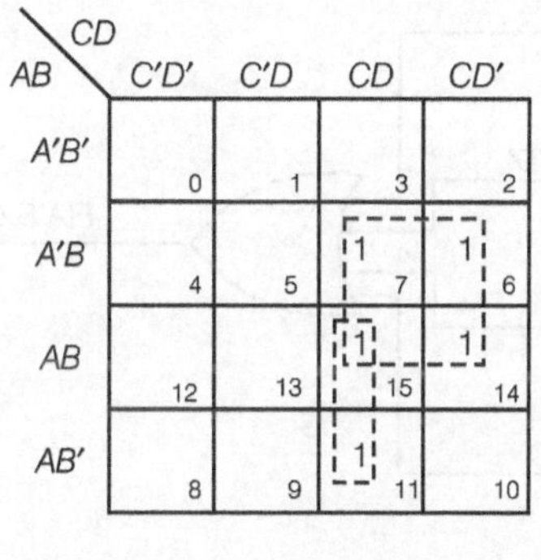

We get,

Ist Pair $(m_{15} + m_{11}) = ACD$

Ist Quad $(m_7 + m_6 + m_{15} + m_{14}) = BC$

So, final expression is $R(A, B, C, D) = BC + ACD$

Logic diagram for expression is:

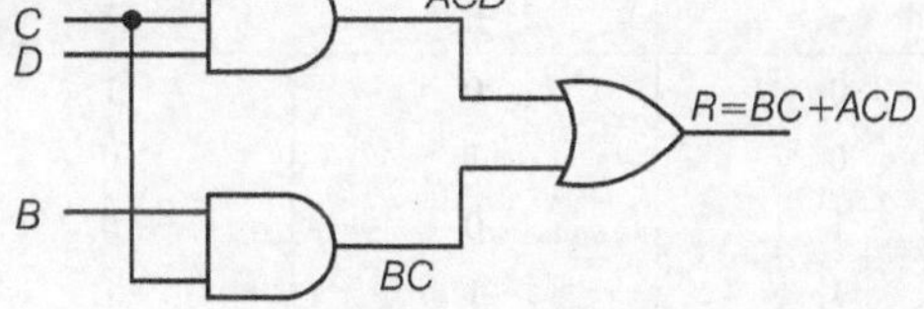

56. Given the Boolean function $F(A, B, C, D) = \Sigma(0, 1, 2, 4, 5, 7, 11, 13, 15)$.
Use Karnaugh's map to reduce this function F, using the given SOP form. Draw logic gate diagram for the reduced SOP form. You may use gates with more than two inputs. Assume that variables and their complements are available as inputs. **ISC 2006, 2005**

Ans The given expression is,

$$F(A, B, C, D) = \Sigma(0, 1, 2, 4, 5, 7, 11, 13, 15)$$

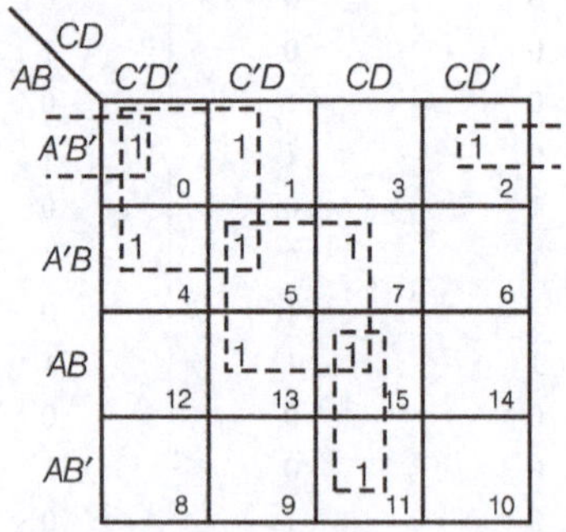

We get,

Ist Quad $(m_0 + m_1 + m_4 + m_5) = A'C'$

IInd Quad $(m_5 + m_7 + m_{13} + m_{15}) = BD$

Ist Pair $(m_0 + m_2) = A'B'D'$

IInd Pair $(m_{11} + m_{15}) = ACD$

So, the final SOP expression will be

$$F(A, B, C, D) = A'C' + BD + A'B'D' + ACD$$

Logic diagram for expression:

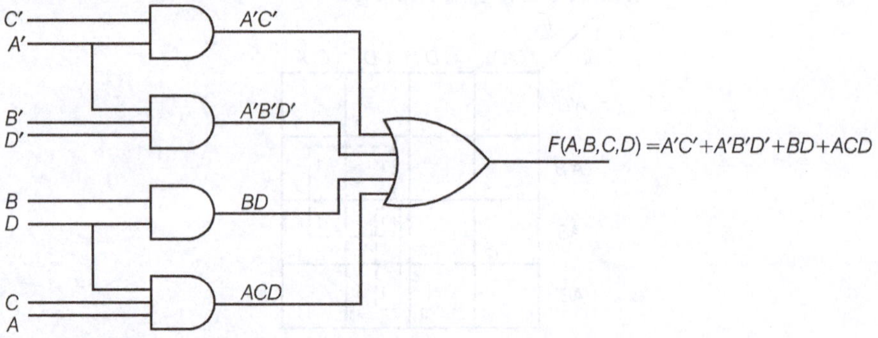

57. What is an XNOR gate? Draw a truth table representing a 2 input XNOR operation. Derive its SOP expression and draw its logic gate diagram. **ISC 2006**

Ans The XNOR gate is logically equivalent to an inverted XOR, i.e. XOR gate followed by a NOT gate. Thus XNOR gate produces 1 output when the input combination has even number of 1's.

Truth table for XNOR operation

A	*B*	*X*
0	0	1
0	1	0
1	0	0
1	1	1

SOP expression $X = A'B' + AB$

Logic gate for this SOP expression

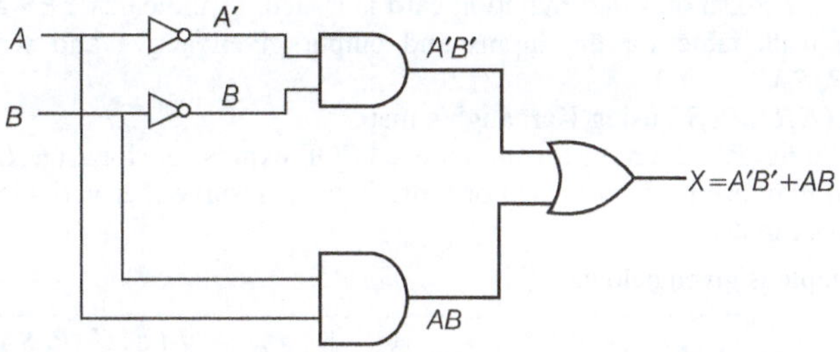

58. Given $X(A,B,C,D)=\Pi(2,3,4,7,9,10,11,12)$.

Use Karnaugh's map to reduce this function X using the given POS form. Draw logic gate diagram for the reduced POS form. You may use gates with more than two inputs. Assume that variables and their complements are available as inputs. **ISC 2005**

Ans Given expression,

$X(A,B,C,D)=\Pi(2,3,4,7,9,10,11,12)$

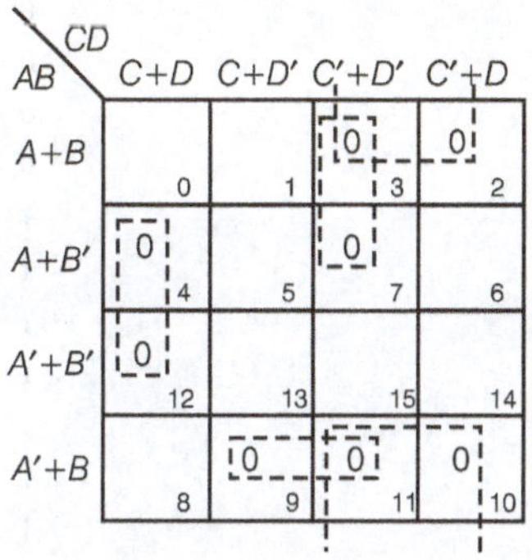

From K-map, we get

Ist Quad $(M_2 . M_3 . M_{10} . M_{11}) = B + C'$

Ist Pair $(M_4 . M_{12}) = B' + C + D$

IInd Pair $(M_3 . M_7) = A + C' + D'$

IIIrd Pair $(M_9 . M_{11}) = A' + B + D'$

So, the final POS expression will be

$X(A,B,C,D)=(B+C').(B'+C+D).$
$(A+C'+D').(A'+B+D')$

Logic diagram for expression:

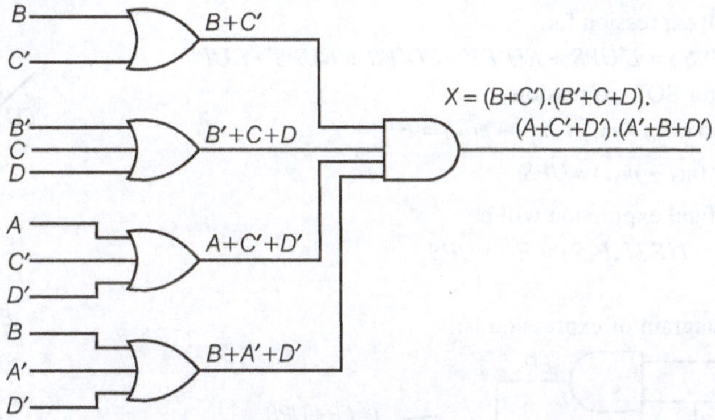

59. The Past Pupil Association of RK University Computer Science Department is organising a reunion function at the campus. The invitation card is to be issued to a person, if:

- The person is an ex-student of the department and had passed out in 1995.

Or

- The person is not an ex-student of the department but passed out from the same university in 1995 and has made a contribution of ₹ 1000.

The inputs are:

Inputs	
E	The person is ex-student of the department.
U	The person is not an ex-student of the department but a student of the same university.
P	The person passed out in 1995.
S	The person contributes ₹ 1000.

[1 indicates YES and 0 indicates NO in all the cases].

Output: I : Denotes the invitation card is issued. [1 indicates YES and 0 indicates NO.]

(i) Draw the truth table for the inputs and output given above and write the SOP expression for $I(E, U, P, S)$.

(ii) Reduce $I(E, U, P, S)$ using Karnaugh's map.
Draw the logic gate diagram for the reduced SOP expression for $I(E, U, P, S)$ using AND and OR gates. You may use gates with two or more inputs. Assume that variables and their complements are available as inputs. ***ISC 2005***

Ans (i) The truth table is given below:

E	U	P	S	$I(E, U, P, S)$
0	0	0	0	0
0	0	0	1	0
0	0	1	0	0
0	0	1	1	0
0	1	0	0	0
0	1	0	1	0
0	1	1	0	0
0	1	1	1	1
1	0	0	0	0
1	0	0	1	0
1	0	1	0	1
1	0	1	1	1
1	1	0	0	0
1	1	0	1	0
1	1	1	0	1
1	1	1	1	1

The SOP expression for,

$I(E,U,P,S) = E'UPS + EU'PS' + EU'PS + EUPS' + EUPS$

(ii) K-map for SOP expression

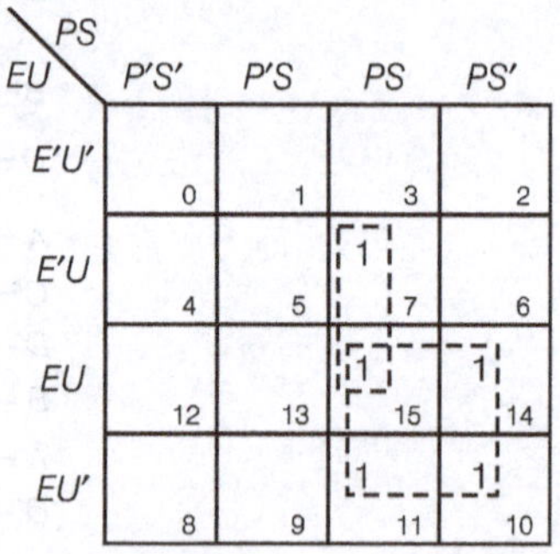

Ist Quad $(m_{10} + m_{11} + m_{14} + m_{15}) = EP$

Ist Pair $(m_7 + m_{15}) = UPS$

So, the final expression will be

$I(E,U,P,S) = EP + UPS$

Logic diagram of expression is:

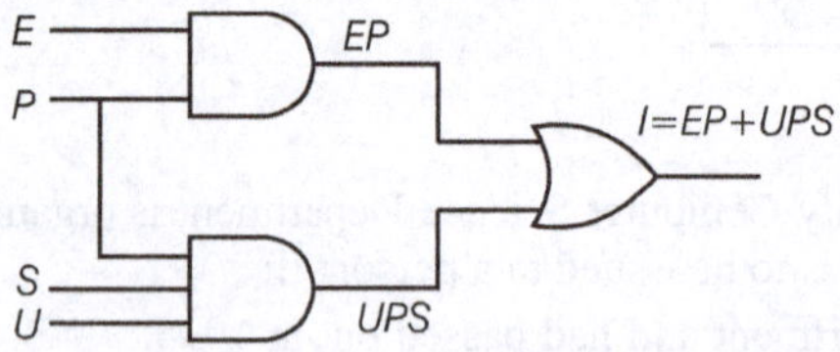

Case Based Questions

1.

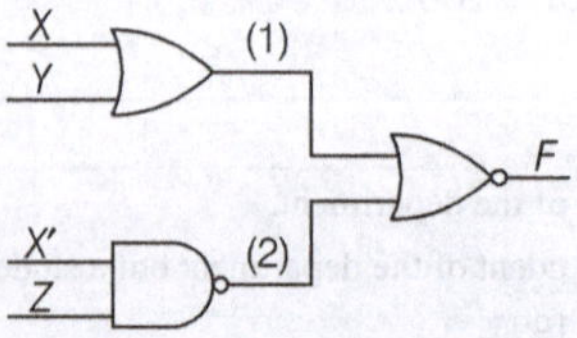

With reference to the logic diagram given above, where X, X', Y and Z are inputs and F is the output, answer the following questions. ***ISC 2022 (Sem I)***

(i) What is the expression at (1)?

(a) $X \cdot Y$ (b) $X' + Y'$ (c) $X + Y$ (d) $X + Y'$

(ii) What is the expression at (2)?

(a) $(X + Z)'$ (b) $(X + Z')$ (c) $X' + Z$ (d) $(X' \cdot Z)'$

(iii) What is the final expression $F(X, Y, Z)$?

(a) $(XY + X'Z)'$ (b) $((X + Y) + (X' \cdot Z)')'$
(c) $((X + Y) \cdot (X' \cdot Z)')'$ (d) $(X' + Z) + (XY)'$

Ans (i) (c) $X + Y$
(ii) (d) $(X' \cdot Z)'$
(iii) (b) $((X + Y) + (X' \cdot Z)')'$

2. 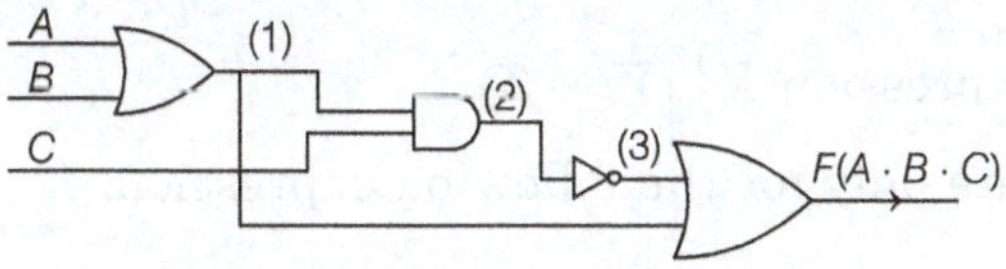

ISC SQP 2022 (Sem I)

From the logic diagram given above, where A, B and C are inputs and F is the output, answer the following questions.

(i) The expression at (1) is

(a) $A \cdot B$ (b) $A' + B'$ (c) $A + B'$ (d) $A + B$

(ii) The expression at (3) is

(a) $A + B \cdot C'$ (b) $((A + B)' \cdot C)'$ (c) $((A + B) \cdot C)'$ (d) $(A + B) \cdot C$

(iii) The final expression $F(A, B, C)$ is

(a) $F = ((A + B)' \cdot C)' + (A + B)$ (b) $F = (A + B)' \cdot (C + A + B)$
(c) $F = ((A + B) \cdot C)' + (A + B)$ (d) $F = (AB + C)' + (A + B)$

Ans (i) (d) $A + B$
(ii) (d) $(A + B) \cdot C$
(iii) (c) $F = ((A + B) \cdot C)' + (A + B)$

![CHAPTER TEST]

CHAPTER TEST

1 Mark Questions

1. If the input in a decoder is $P'QR'S'$, then the decimal equivalent output will be
   (a) 4 (b) 5 (c) 6 (d) 7
2. A combinational circuit that performs the addition of three bits is known as
   (a) half adder (b) full adder (c) encoder (d) decoder
3. Draw a logic circuit for a half adder using NAND gates only.

2 Marks Questions

4. Draw a logic circuit diagram for the Boolean expression $X'.(Y'+Z)$.
5. Draw the logic circuit diagram using NAND gate only for the following expression:
   $$AB + A'B + A'B'$$
6. Draw a logic circuit diagram for the Boolean expression $A'.(B+C)$ and truth table.

3 Marks Questions

7. Interpret the following logic circuit as Boolean expression

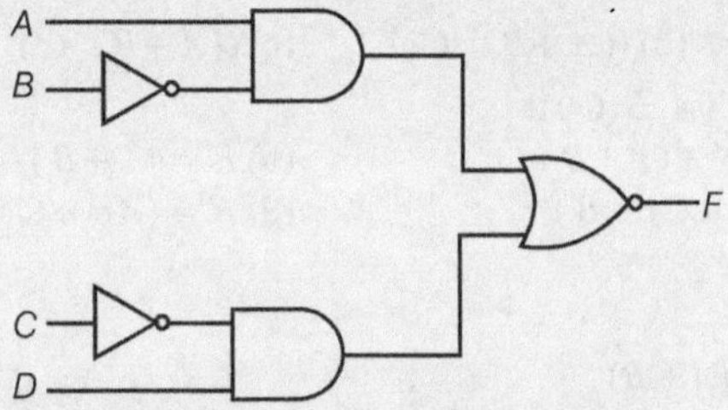

8. Draw a NOT gate with the help of NAND and NOR.

5 Marks Questions

9. Draw a logic circuit diagram for full adder. Give the truth table for full adder.
10. Draw a logic circuit diagram for the Boolean expression $A.(B+C')$, truth table and also give its SOP and POS form.

10 Marks Questions

11. Write the equivalent canonical Product of Sum (POS) expression for the following Sum of Product (SOP) expression
    $$F(X,Y,Z) = \Sigma(0,2,4,5)$$
    Also, draw a K-map and logic circuit.
12. Obtain the simplified form of a Boolean expression using K-map
    $$F(A,B,C) = \Pi(0,1,2,3,4)$$
    Also draw a logic gate from the reduced expression.
13. What is multiplexer? Also, write about 4 × 1 multiplexer and 8 × 1 multiplexer.

04 Fundamentals of Java

TREND ANALYSIS 4 YEARS

	Average No. of Questions Across all Sets				
	Types of Questions	2024	2023	2020	2019
Fundamentals of Java	1 Mark	–	–	–	–
	2 Marks	–	–	–	–
	3 Marks	–	–	–	–
	5 Marks	–	–	–	–
	10 Marks	–	–	–	–

Java is a portable, machine-independent, object oriented and multithreaded language. It was developed by James Gosling, Patrick Naughton, Ed Frank, Mike Sheridan at Sun Microsystems in year 1991. Java was initially called ''**Oak**'' but in 1996, it was renamed as ''Java'', which is now a part of Oracle Corporation.

Object

An object is an identifiable entity with some characteristics (attributes) and behaviour (methods). Objects are the key to understand object oriented programming approach.

e.g. **Student** is an object.

An object (Student) has some characteristics, which is used to distinguish it from other similar objects. They are:

(i) **Identity** (e.g. Student has name)

(ii) An object has **State** (e.g. Student is either studying or playing)

(iii) An object has **Behaviour** (e.g. Student studies, speaking, etc.)

(iv) An object has **Attributes** (e.g. age, name, etc.)

Class

A class is a group of objects that share common properties and relationships. It represents a group of similar objects. In other words, "An object is a runtime instance of a class". A class is a way to bind the data and its associated functions together.

e.g. Fruits is a class.

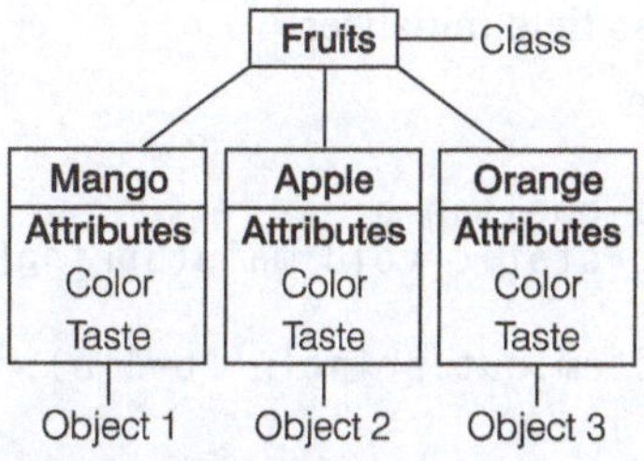

A class is a blue print or prototype for creating objects of a certain kind. e.g. it is clear that a class is the collection of only those objects, which have same characteristics or attributes.

Declaration and Initialization of a Class

In general, class declarations can include following components in order:

(i) Modifiers such as public, private, etc., shows the accessibility of class.

(ii) The class name with the initial letter capitalised by convention.

(iii) The name of the class's parent (super class), if any, preceded by the keyword extends.

(iv) The class body surrounded by braces {}.

Syntax
```
class class_name
{
   //class body
}
```

e.g.
```
class MyFirstClass
{
    public int gear;
       // Field
    public int speed;
    public MyFirstClass(int speedup,
                          int startgear)
       // Constructor
    {
       gear = startgear;
       speed = speedup;
    }
    public void setGear(int newValue)
       // Method
    {
       gear = newValue;
    }
}
```

Class initialization is the explicit initialization of the class fields to values. Each class field explicitly initializes to a value *via* a class field initializer.

e.g.
```
class once
{
    static boolean b;
    public static void main(String[] args)
    {
      System.out.println("b="+b);
    }
}
```

Output b = false

Class as Composite Types

Composite types are reference type, which hold the reference id of a memory location. A class is a composite data type because it requires a reference to use its attributes.

The class binds various primitive types together for using them as a unit.

These primitive types can be member variables (primitive type variables) or member methods (primitive type methods). e.g. A class abc has two variables x and y and the value of these variables cannot be assigned directly. They can be assigned with the help of reference

```
abc obj1;    //Creating an object of abc class
obj1.x = 5;  //Referencing the variable
obj1.y = 10;
```

Object as Instance of a Class

An object is an instance of a class or a class type variable that holds individual copy of data. An object can access all fields and methods of a class. The data type of an object is the class itself.

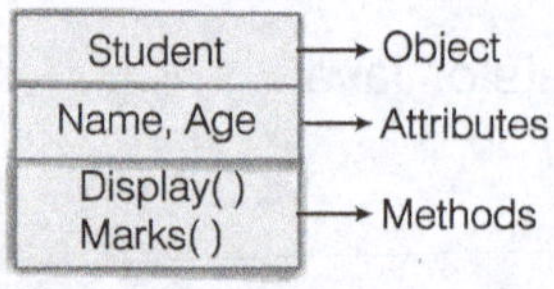

Creating Objects

In Java, you can create an object by creating an instance of a class or in other words, instantiating a class. Objects in Java are created using the **new** keyword.

The **new** keyword creates an object of the specified class and returns a reference of that object.

e.g.
```
Rectangle rect1;   //declare the object
 rect1 = new Rectangle();
                        //instantiate the object
```

Basic Concepts of Object Oriented Programming

Object oriented programming is a programming paradigm which deals with the concepts of object to build programs and software applications.

Every object has a well-defined identity, attributes and behaviour. The features of object oriented programming also map closely to the real-world features like, inheritance, abstraction, encapsulation and polymorphism. These are as follows:

Data Abstraction

"Data abstraction refers to the act of representing essential features without including the background details or explanations." It is the process that involves identifying the essential features without including the internal details.

Consider the example of data abstraction of Car shown in figure:

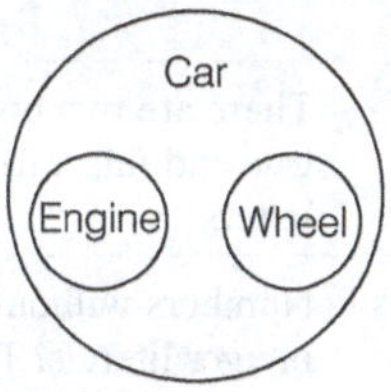

Data Abstraction of Car

In above figure, class Car represents the Engine and Wheel as two features of a Car, without showing their internal complexity as it is unnecessary.

Classes use the concept of abstraction to define a list of abstract attributes such as functions, size, etc., to operate on these objects.

The attributes are sometimes called **data members** because they hold information. Since the classes use the concept of data abstraction, they are known as **Abstract Data Types** (ADT).

Data Encapsulation

Encapsulation is the mechanism that binds code and the data together. Data encapsulation is,

(i) The wrapping up of data and methods into a single unit (called class).

(ii) Provide the interface between the object's data and the program.

(iii) Makes it possible for objects to be treated like "black boxes" each performing a specific task without any concern about internal implementation.

This insulation of the data from direct access by the program is called **data hiding**. In figure, Student is a class and its internal information like RollNo, Name, Marks all are hidden. The hidden attributes of a class are called **protected attributes.**

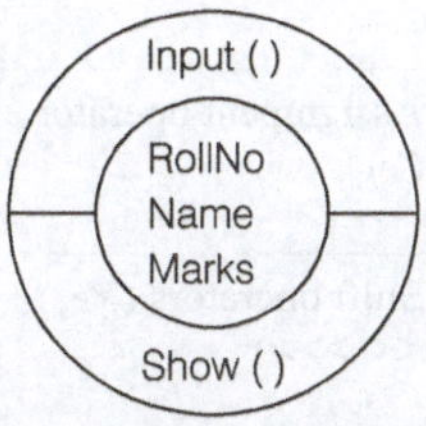

Data Encapsulation of Student Class

In object oriented programming, data encapsulation is concerned with:

(i) Hiding the details of how the object works.

(ii) The independence of each object.

(iii) Described as a protective barrier that prevents the code and data being randomly accessed by other code defined outside the class.

(iv) The ability to modify our implemented code without breaking the code of other classes.

Inheritance

Inheritance is the process by which one object acquires the properties of another objects. It supports the concept of hierarchical classification. Inheritance can

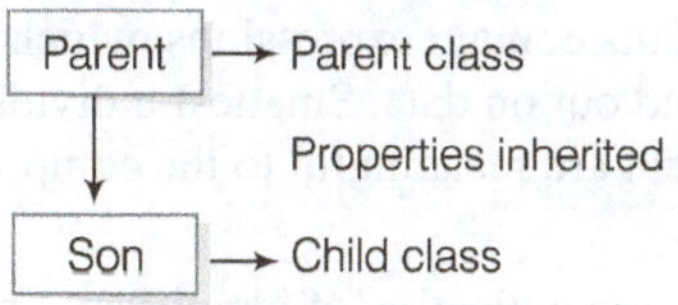

Inheritance

(i) Provide the idea of reusability.

(ii) Drive a new class from the existing one.

(iii) Have two types of class i.e. base class and subclass.

A class is derived from the base class, this concept is called inheritance.

The class which is derived from the another class is called **derived class** or **subclass** or **child class.** A class which derives another class is called **base class** or **superclass** or **parent class.**

Polymorphism

Polymorphism means the ability to take more than one form i.e. the same operation may behave differently in different situations as shown in figure.

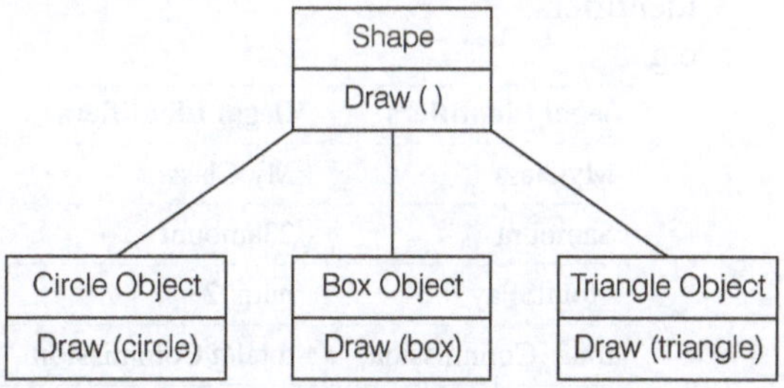

Polymorphism

Here, the same method name can be used to handle different number and different types of arguments.

Java Character Set

The smallest unit of Java language is the character, which is used to write Java tokens. These characters are defined by the **unicode** character set.

The unicode is a 16-bit character coding system and currently supports more than 34000 defined characters. A character represents any letter, digit or other sign.

e.g. `\40394 Δ The capital Greek letter delta`
`\40022 " The double quote`

Lexical Issues/Java Tokens

A Java program is basically a collection of classes. A class is defined by a set of declaration statements and methods containing executable statements.

Most statements contain expressions, which describe the actions carried out on data. Smallest individual elements in a program, that are meaningful to the compiler are known as tokens.

These tokens are collection of identifiers, literals, operators, separators and keywords.

These are described as below:

(i) **Identifiers** These are names assigned to variables, constants, methods, classes, packages and interfaces. An identifier may be any descriptive sequence of uppercase and lowercase letters, numbers, the underscore and dollar sign characters.

Java identifiers follow the following rules:

(a) They can have alphabets, digits, the underscore or dollar sign characters.
(b) They must not begin with a digit.
(c) Uppercase and lowercase letters are distinct because Java is case sensitive.
(d) They can be of any length.
(e) The whitespaces are not allowed within identifiers.

e.g.

Legal Identifiers	Illegal Identifiers
MyClass	My Class
$amount	23amount
_total$Pay	num^2
total_Commission	total@Commission

(ii) **Literals** A literal is a value that can be passed to a variable or constant in a program. It can be any number, text or other information that represents a value.

Literals can be integer, floating point, boolean, character, string notations or null literals. Java language specifies six major types of literals.

They are

Literals	Description
Boolean literals	There are two boolean literals namely true and false, formed from ASCII letters.
Integer literals	Numbers without any decimal places are integer literals. Three types of integer literals allowed in Java that are decimal (base 10), octal (base 8) and hexadecimal (base 16).
Floating literals	Numbers having fractional part are called floating literals.
Character literal	Single character enclosed in single quotes is called character literal.
String literals	Zero or more characters within double quotes are called string literals.
Null literal	The null reference is the only value coming under null literal.

(iii) **Operators** An operator is a symbol that takes one or more arguments and operates on them to produce a result. Following is the list of various operators available in Java:

Unary Operators	Increment operator (++)	Increments the value by one, i.e. a++ ⇒ a = a + 1
	Decrement operator (– –)	Takes one argument and decrements the value by one, i.e. a – – ⇒ a = a – 1
Binary Operators	Arithmetic operators (+, –, *, /, %)	Takes two operands and operates on them to generate the desired result.
	Relational operators (>, <, >=, ==, <=, !=)	Takes two operands, compares them and returns true or false, the result of comparison.
	Assignment operator (=)	Assigns right hand side value on left hand side.
	Shift operators (>>, <<, >>>)	Performs right shift or left shift on the binary equivalent of the operand and returns the resultant value.
Ternary Operator	Conditional operator (? :)	Works as a shorthand for if else construct.

Operator Precedence

It shows the order of operators in priority form top to bottom in different rows:

Precedence	Operator	Description	Associativity
1.	( )	Parenthesis	Left to Right
	[ ]	Array subscript	
	.	Access object method	
2.	++	Postfix prefix increment	Right to Left
	––	Postfix prefix decrement	
	+, –	Unary plus, Unary minus	
	!	Logical NOT	
	~	Bitwise NOT	
3.	(type) new	type cast object creation	Right to Left
4.	*	Multiplication	Left to Right
	/	Division	
	%	Modulus	
5.	+	Addition	Left to Right
	–	Subtraction	
	+	String concatenation	
6.	<<	Bitwise left shift	Left to Right
	>>	Bitwise right shift	
	>>>	Bitwise right shift with zero extension	
7.	<, <=	Less than, less than or equal to	Left to Right
	>, >=	Greater than, greater than or equal to	
	instanceof	For type comparison	
8.	= =	Equal to	Left to Right
	! =	Not equal to	
9.	&	Bitwise AND	Left to Right
10.	^	Bitwise XOR	Left to Right
11.	|	Bitwise OR	Left to Right
12.	& &	Boolean AND	Left to Right

Assignment Operation or Statement

Assignment statements consist of a left hand side and a right hand side separated by the assignment operator(=). The syntax of the assignment statement is:

```
lhsval = rhsval;
```

lhsval, i.e. left hand side of an assignment statement is either a variable, function, identifier or a property of an instance variable while rhsval, i.e. right hand side of an assignment statement is expression. When an assignment statement is executed, its right hand side expression is evaluated and its value is stored in the left hand side.

Note Assignment of primitive values through '=' operator creates a copy whereas assignment of object reference creates aliases.
e.g. x = 1 + 1; is a simple statement, when this statement is executed the right hand side 1 + 1 is evaluated and the resulting value, i.e. 2 is stored in the left hand side variable x.

(iv) **Separators** In Java, there are a few characters that are used as separators. The most commonly used separator in Java is the semicolon. It is used to terminate statements. The separators used in Java are ( ), { }, [ ], ; , etc.

(v) **Keywords** Keywords are essential part of a language definition. Keywords are predefined identifiers meant for a specific purpose and cannot be used for identifying classes, variables, methods, packages and interfaces. All keywords in Java are written in lowercase.
The lists of the keywords in Java are given below:

abstract	assert	boolean	break	byte	case
catch	char	class	continue	default	do
double	else	enum	extends	final	finally
float	for	if	implements	import	instanceof
int	interface	long	native	new	package
private	protected	public	return	short	static
strictfp	super	switch	synchronized	this	throw
throws	transient	try	void	volatile	while
const	goto				

Difference between this keyword and super keyword

this keyword	super keyword
this keyword is reference to the currently executing object on which the method or constructor was invoked.	super keyword is used to access methods or variables of an instance's superclass members.
It can not appear within static methods.	You can invoke the over-ridden method through the use of the keyword super.

Comments

A comment describes or explains the operation of the program to anyone who is reading its source code. The contents of a comment are ignored by the compiler. In real applications, comments are generally explain how some part of the program works or what a specific feature does.

Java supports three types of comments:

(a) Single line comment (Starts with // and makes the contents following // of that line a part of comment).

(b) Multiline comment (Starts with /* and ends with */ and makes everything written in between, whether in single or multiple lines).

(c) Demonstration or Java Doc comment (Starts with /** and ends with */).

Concepts of Whitespace

Java Character isWhitespace() Method

The isWhitespace(char ch) method of Character class determines whether the given character(Unicode code point) is a whitespace character or not.

A character in Java can be considered as a whitespace character if one of the following criteria is satisfied:

The character is a Unicode space character (either a SPACE_SEPARATOR, or a LINE_SEPARATOR, or a PARAGRAPH_SEPARATOR) but it must not be a non-breaking space.

- The character must be a HORIZONTAL TABULATION.
- The character must be a LINE FEED.
- The character must be a VERTICAL TABULATION.
- The character must be a FORM FEED.
- The character must be a CARRIAGE RETURN.
- The character must be a FILE SEPARATOR.
- The character must be a GROUP SEPARATOR.
- The character must be a RECORD SEPARATOR.
- The character must be a UNIT SEPARATOR.

Syntax

public static boolean isWhitespace(char ch)

Where,

ch The character that needs to be tested.

It returns a Boolean value, i.e., true if the given(or specified) character is a Java white space character. Otherwise, this method returns false.

Example 1

```
public class JavaCharacterisWhitespaceExample1 {
    public static void main(String[] args) {
        // Create three char primitives:ch1, ch2
                                            and ch3
        char ch1, ch2, ch3;
        // Assign the values to the char primitives.
        ch1 = '\n';
        ch2 = 'f';
        ch3 = '\b';
        //Create three boolean primitives.
        boolean b1, b2, b3;
        b1 =  Character.isWhitespace(ch1);
        b2 =  Character.isWhitespace(ch2);
        b3 =  Character.isWhitespace(ch3);
      System.out.println("The first character is a
                 white space character :"+b1);
      System.out.println("The second character is a
                   white space character :"+b2);
      System.out.println("The third character is a
                   white space character :"+b3);
    }
}
```

Output:

The first character is a white space character :true

The second character is a white space character :false

The third character is a white space character :false

StringTokenizer Class in Java

StringTokenizer class in Java is used to break a string into tokens. A StringTokenizer object internally maintains a current position within the string to be tokenized. Some operations advance this current position past the characters processed. A token is returned by taking a substring of the string that was used to create the StringTokenizer object. It provides the first step in the parsing process often called lexer or scanner.

Java String Tokenization

The String Tokenizer class allows an application to break strings into tokens. It implements the Enumeration interface. This class is used for parsing data. To use the String Tokenizer class we have to specify an input string and a string that contains delimiters. Delimiters are the characters that separate tokens. Each character in the delimiter string is considered a valid delimiter. Default delimiters are whitespaces, new lines, spaces, and tabs.

Constructors of StringToken

Let us consider 'str' as the string to be tokenized. In that case we have three constructor cases as mentioned below:

Constructor	Description
StringTokenizer(String str)	Default delimiters like newline, space, tab, carriage return, and form feed.
StringTokenizer(String str, String delim)	delim is a set of delimiters that are used to tokenize the given string.
StringTokenizer(String str, String delim, boolean flag)	The first two parameters have the same meaning wherein The flag serves the following purpose.

Data Types

Data types specify the size and types of values that can be stored. Java language is rich in its **data types**. In Java, two categories of data types are given below:

(i) Primitive Data Types

Primitive data types are the basic building blocks of any programming language. A primitive data type can have only one value at a time and is the simplest built-in form of data within Java.

Java supports following four categories of primitive data types:

Class	Data type	Size	Range
Integer Type	byte	1 byte	– 128 to + 127
	short	2 bytes	– 32768 to + 32767
	int	4 bytes	-2^{31} to $+(2^{31}-1)$
	long	8 bytes	-2^{63} to $+(2^{63}-1)$
Floating Point	float	4 bytes	1.4e – 045 to 3.4e + 0.38
	double	8 bytes	4.9e – 324 to 1.8e + 308
Character Type	char	2 bytes	0 to 65535
Boolean Type	boolean	Java reserves 8 bits but only uses 1 bit.	True or False

(ii) Non-Primitive (Reference) Data Type

In Java, a **reference data type** is a variable that can contain the reference or an address of dynamically created object.

These data types are not predefined like primitive data type. The reference data types are **arrays, classes** and **interfaces** that are made and handled according to a programmer in a Java program.

e.g. A **class** is an example of reference data type.

Consider the following class definition

```
class TypeDemo
{
    byte a;  //a, b and c are defined manually
    int b;
    float c;
}
```

The primitive data types of above class are int b, byte a, float c.

Variables

A variable is an identifier that holds values that are used in a Java program. e.g. Average, Height, Total_strength, etc. Variable names may consist of alphabets, digits, the underscore (_) and dollar characters subject to the rules for naming identifiers.

Declaration of Variables

A variable must be declared before it is used in the program. Declaration specified two things:

(i) It tells the compiler what the variable will hold.

(ii) It specifies size of the memory required for variable.

The general form of declaration of a variable is:

```
Data_Type variable1, variable2, ........ variableN;
```

Variables are separated by commas. A declaration statement must end with a semicolon, some valid declarations are:

```
int     count;
float   x, y;
double  p1;
char    C1, C2, C3;
```

Initialising the Variables

In a simple declaration, the initial value of the variable is undefined. We can combine a declaration with an assignment statement to provide an initial value for the variable.

e.g. int val = 10 ;

Here, variable **val** is initialised with the value 10.

If the variable is not initialised, then a default value is assigned to that variable according to its data type.

For the default values, consider the following table:

Type	Initial/Default value
byte	0 (Zero) of byte type
short	0 (Zero) of short type
int	0
long	0 L
float	0.0 f
double	0.0 d
char	Null character i.e. '\u0000'
boolean	False
All reference types	Null

Java Variable Types

Java programming language defines the following kinds of variables:

(i) **Instance Variable** Non-static variables are called instance variables. Instance variables are used to store the state of an object. Every object created from a class definition would have its own copy of variable.

Syntax `ObjectReference.VariableName`

(ii) **Class Variable** It is any field declared with the static modifier. It is a special type of class attribute (or class property, field, or data member). Class variable is created when the program starts and stops. It can be accessed by calling with the class name.

Syntax `ClassName.VariableName`

(iii) **Local Variable** These variables are declared in methods, constructors or blocks. These are implemented at stack level internally. There is no default value for local variable so, when local variable is declared, an initial value should be assigned to it before the first use.

Syntax `VariableName`

Scope of a Variable

The scope of a variable is the part of the program over which the variable name can be referenced. A variable cannot be referenced before its declaration. Variables in Java can be declared in several different places.

- In a class body as class fields. These variables are called classlevel variables.
- As parameters of a method.
- In a method body.
- Within a statement block such as a while or for block.

There are mainly two types of scope:

(i) **Class Scope** Sometimes, we need some variables that can be access from anywhere within a class. The scope of these variables will need to be at the class level and there is only one way to create these type of variables at class level only inside the class but outside the methods.

e.g.

```
public class A
{
     private int i;
}
```

(ii) **Method Scope** There are some variables that we want to make temporary and they are useful for only one method.

e.g.

```
public static void main(String[] args)
{
     int x=5;
}
```

The variable x is a local variable for main function, because it is created inside the main method. We cannot use the variable x outside the main method or we can say in another method because it only exists in the main method's scope.

When variables with the same name are defined in different scopes, visibility rules comes into focus.

Note We cannot declare two variables having same name in same scope but we can declare in different scope.

Constants

In Java, constants refer to fixed values that do not change during the execution of a program. The keyword **final** makes a variable as constant, i.e. whose value cannot be changed during program execution.

e.g. final double TAXRATE = 025;

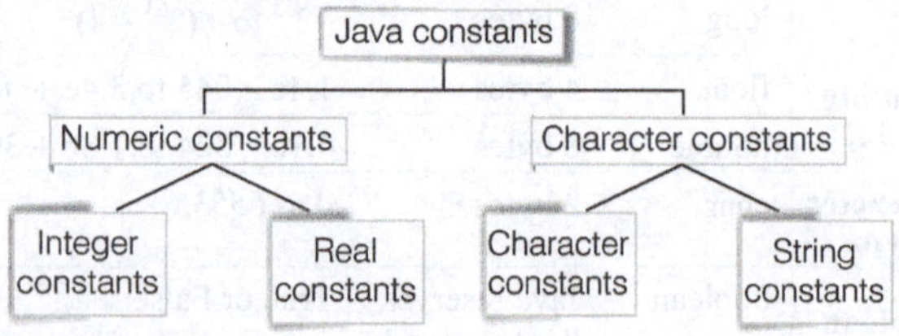

Expression

An expression is a combination of operators and/or operands. Java expressions are used to create objects, arrays, pass values to methods and call them, assigning value to variables and so on.

Broadly, Java's expressions can be categorised into following two categories:

(i) **Arithmetic Expression** An arithmetic expression is a combination of variables, constants and operators arranged as per the syntax of the language.

e.g.

Algebraic expression	Java expression
$ab - c$	$a*b - c$
$(m+n)(x+y)$	$(m+n)*(x+y)$
$\frac{ab}{c}$	$a*b/c$
$3x^2 + 2x + 1$	$3*x*x + 2*x + 1$
$\frac{x}{y} + c$	$x/y + c$

(ii) **Logical (Boolean) Expression** The boolean expression is a combination of constants, variables, logical and relational operators. The expressions that result into true or false are called boolean or logical expression.

The following are examples of some valid boolean expression:

(a) $x > y$

(d) $(y+z) \geq (x/z)$

(b) $(a+b) > c \&\& (c+d) > a$

(e) $(y>x) || (z<y)$

(c) $x || y \&\& z$

(f) (x)

Evaluation of Expressions Expressions are evaluated using an assignment statement of the form.

Variable = expression ;

All variables used in the expression must be assigned values before evaluation is attempted.

e.g.

$$x = a * b - c;$$

Type Casting/Type Conversion

Assigning a value of one type to a variable of another type is known as type casting.

In Java, type casting is classified into two parts:

(i) **Implicit Type Casting** When a data type of lower size is assigned to a data type of higher size, then Java compiler automatically upgrades lower type to higher type, it is called implicit type casting. It is also known as **widening casting**. It is shown as follows:

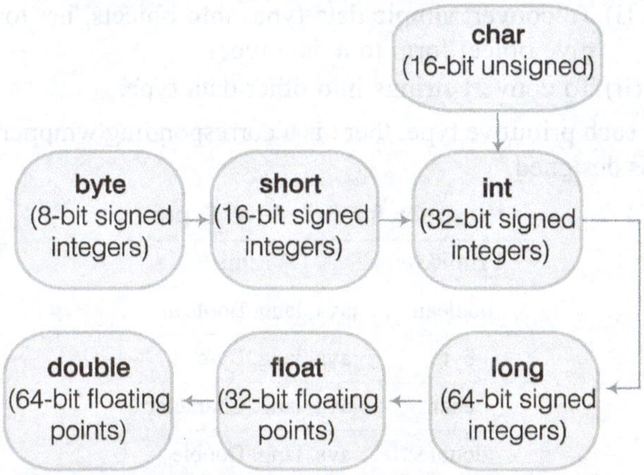

Orders of Implicit Type Casting for Primitive Data Types

The implicit type casting can take place when,

- The two types are compatible.
- The target type is larger than the source type.

e.g.
```
int x = 20;
float y = (x);
```

(ii) **Explicit Type Casting** A data type of higher size cannot be assigned to a data type of lower size implicitly. The higher size needs to be narrowed to lower size forcefully by programmer.

e.g.
```
int x = 10;
byte y = byte(x);
```

It is also known as **narrowing casting**.

The First Java Program

```
/*
comments
*/
import packagename;
class classname
{
     public static void main(String args[])
     {
          //statement block
     }
}
```

Section 1 /*comments */ is called a comment and is important for readability of the program from programmer's point.

Section 2 import packagename; In this statement, import is a keyword which is used for reusability purpose. Package is a collection of predefined classes and interfaces. So, you can mention the name of package from which you want to reuse a class in your program.

Section 3

```
class classname
{
}
```

use the keyword **class** to define a new class, which is a collection of data members and methods.

Section 4

```
public static void main(String args[ ])
{
     //statement block
}
```

main ( ) method is the entry point of control for any Java program i.e. execution of Java program starts from main function. Hence, every Java program must contain exactly one main ( ) method. Inside main ( ), you can write functionality of your program as statement block.

Constructors

It has the same name as the name of the class to which it belongs. Constructor's syntax does not include a return type, since constructors never return a value. It may include parameters of various types.

Types of Constructors

Constructors have different types and these are:

(i) **Default Constructor** It is the no-argument constructor that is automatically created by compiler in the absence of explicit constructor.

e.g.
```
public class Smart
{
   public Smart()
   {
      System.out.println("Default
                          cons.");
   }
   public static void main(String[]
                              args)
   {
      Smart sc=new Smart();
   }
}
```

(ii) **Parameterized Constructor** These constructors are required to pass parameters on creation of objects.

e.g.
```
public class Smart
{
   private String name;
   public Smart(String str)
   {
      this.name=str;
      System.out.println("The
         parameterized cons." +str);
   }
   public static void main(String
                           args[])
   {
      Smart sc=new Smart("Aaliya");
   }
}
```

(iii) **Constructor with Default Arguments** It is possible to define constructors with default argument.

e.g. `complex(float real, float imag=0);`

The default argument imag is zero.

Wrapper Classes

Java primitive types are not objects, i.e. we cannot say that Java is pure object oriented language. Hence, the concept of wrapper classes was introduced by Java designers.

A wrapper class wraps around a data type and gives it an object appearance.

Note Constructors of wrapper classes are used to convert data types into objects and the methods of the form XXXValue( ) and are used to retrieve back the data type from the object where XXX may be int, long, double, etc.

e.g. `int x = int object.intValue( );`

Methods in XXXValue( ) form

Method	Description
int intValue( )	Returns the value of the called object as an int.
long longValue( )	Returns the value of the called object as long.
short shortValue( )	Returns the value of the called object as short.
float floatValue( )	Returns the value of the called object as float.
double doubleValue( )	Returns the value of the called object as double.
byte byteValue( )	Returns the value of the called object as byte.

There are mainly two uses with wrapper classes:

(i) To convert simple data types into objects, i.e. to give object form to a data type.

(ii) To convert strings into other data type.

For each primitive type, there is a corresponding wrapper class designed.

Wrapper for Primitive Types

Primitive	Wrapper
boolean	java. lang. Boolean
byte	java. lang. Byte
char	java. lang. Character
double	java. lang. Double
float	java. lang. Float
int	java. lang. Integer
long	java. lang. Long
short	java. lang. Short

How to Create Object of the Wrapper Classes?

The following syntax is used to create object of wrapper classes.

```
wrapperclass object = new wrapperclass (parameter);
```

Methods of Java Wrapper Class

Class	Methods	Description
Integer	static int parseInt(String s)	Converts a String s to an int using base 10.
	static Integer valueOf(String s)	Converts a String s to an Integer object.
	static String toString(int n)	Converts an int n to a String object.
	String toString ( )	Converts an invoking object to a String.
Byte	static byte parseByte (String s)	Converts a String s to a byte.
	static Byte valueOf (String s)	Converts a String s to a Byte object.
	static String toString(byte n)	Converts a byte n to a String object.
	String toString ( )	Converts an invoking object to a String.
Short	static short parseShort(String s)	Converts a String s to a short.
	static Short valueOf(String s)	Converts a String s to a Short object.
	static String toString(short n)	Converts a short n to a String object.
	String toString( )	Converts an invoking object to a String.
Long	static long parseLong (String s)	Converts a String s to a long.
	static Long valueOf(String s)	Converts a String s to a Long object.
	static String toString(long n)	Converts a long n to a String object.
	String toString( )	Converts an invoking object to a String.
Float	static float parseFloat(String s)	Converts a String s to a float.
	static Float valueOf(String s)	Converts a String s to a Float object.
	static String toString(float n)	Converts a float n to a String object.
	String toString( )	Converts an invoking object to a String.
Double	static double parseDouble(String s)	Converts a String s to a double.
	static Double valueOf(String s)	Converts a String s to a Double object.
	static String toString(double n)	Converts a double n to a String object.
	String toString( )	Converts an invoking object to a String.
Character	static boolean isDigit(char ch)	Returns true if ch is a numeric digit between 0 and 9; otherwise returns false.
	static boolean isLetter(char ch)	Returns true if ch is letter otherwise returns a false.
	static boolean isLetterOrDigit(char ch)	Returns true if ch is a letter or a digit otherwise returns a false.
	static boolean isLowerCase(char ch)	Returns true if ch is in lowercase otherwise returns a false.
	static boolean isUpperCase(char ch)	Returns true if ch is in uppercase otherwise returns a false.
	static boolean isWhitespace(char ch)	Returns true if ch is a whitespace character otherwise returns a false.
	static char toLowerCase(char ch)	Returns a lowercase equivalent of ch.
	static char toUpperCase(char ch)	Returns a uppercase equivalent of ch.

Autoboxing and Unboxing

Autoboxing is the automatic conversion that the Java compiler makes between the primitive types and their corresponding object wrapper classes.

e.g. Converting an int to an Integer, a double to a Double.

If the conversion goes in reverse way, then it is called **unboxing.**

e.g. Integer i = 5; // primitive 5 autoboxed into an Integer object.

int j = i; // automatic unboxing of Integer into int.

PYQs Previous Years Questions

2 Marks Questions

1. What are Wrapper classes? Give any two examples. **ISC 2018**

Ans A wrapper class wraps around a data type and give it an object appearance. When we create an object to a wrapper class, it contains a field and in this field, we can store a primitive data type.

Examples of wrapper classes

(i) int intValue()

(ii) long longValue()

2. Differentiate between a constructor and a method of a class. **ISC 2017**

Ans Differences between constructor and method of a class are as follows :

Constructor	Method
It has no return type	It has a return type.
Constructor name should be same as the class name.	Method name can be any valid identifier.
Constructor is automatically called upon object creation.	Method is invoked explicitly.

Common Mistake Some students think that name of constructor is defined by programmer. While the constructor name should be same as the class name.

3. Define encapsulation and polymorphism. **ISC 2006**

Ans Refer to text on page 109.

Additional Questions

1. What are classes and objects?

Ans A class is a group of objects that share common properties and relationships. It represents a group of similar objects of a certain kind. An object is an instance of a class. It is an identifiable entity with some characteristics and behaviour.

2. Define the character set of Java.

Ans The smallest units of Java language are the characters that are used to write Java token. These characters are defined by the **Unicode** character set. The Unicode is a 16-bit character coding system that supports characters of any language across the world.

3. Write down the basic structure of a Java program.

Ans The basic structure of a Java program is as follows:

```
import package;
public className
{
    public static void main(String args[])
    {
        //Statements
    }
}
```

4. What are operators?

Ans An operator performs an action on one or more operands. An operator that performs an action on one operand is called a unary operator (+, –, ++, – –). An operator that performs an action on two operands is called a binary operator (+, –, /, *). An operator that performs an action on three operands is called a ternary operator (? :).

5. What's wrong with the following program?

```
public class SomethingIsWrong
{
   public static void main(String[ ]
                                  args)
   {
      Rectangle myRect;
      myRect.width = 40;
      myRect.height = 50;
      System.out.println("myRect's
                area is" + myRect.area());
   }
}
```

Ans In the given code, Rectangle myRect is declaring an object only and we are using this object in the code without instantiation. So, the above code will return an error at compile time.

6. Identify the following elements in the given class

(i) The name of the class

(ii) The names of the variables

(iii) The names of methods

```
public class Riddle
{
   private String question;
```

```
        private String answer;
        public String getQuestion()
        {
            return question;
        }
        public String getAnswer()
        {
            return answer;
        }
    }
```

Ans For the given class,

(i) The name of class : Riddle

(ii) The names of variables : question, answer

(iii) The names of methods : getQuestion ( ), getAnswer( )

7. What do you mean by type conversion? How is implicit conversion different from explicit conversion?

Ans Type conversion is changing a value from one data type to another type. Data type conversions are either implicit or explicit, it depends on the data capacities of the data type involved.

Differences between implicit conversion and explicit conversion are as follows

Implicit Conversion	Explicit Conversion
It is automatically type conversion.	It is completely defined within a program.
This method is used when upcasting is required like: int to long.	This method is used when downcasting is required like: double to byte.

8. How can declare variables in Java?

Ans A variable must be declared before it is used in the program. Declaration specified two things:

(i) It tells the compiler what the variable will hold.

(ii) It specifies size of the memory required for variable.

The general form of declaration of a variable is:

```
Data_Type variable1, variable2, ........
                                  variableN;
```

Variables are separated by commas. A declaration statement must end with a semicolon. Some valid declarations are:

```
int       count;
float     x, y;
double    p1;
char      C1, C2, C3;
```

CHAPTER TEST

1 Mark Questions

1. Which of the following is a group of objects that share common properties and relationships?
   (a) Class (b) Inheritance (c) Encapsulation (d) Data Abstraction
2. ………… is the process by which one object acquires the properties of another objects.
   (a) Polymorphism (b) Inheritance (c) Abstraction (d) Object
3. Which of the following data types are the basic building blocks of any programming language?
   (a) Non-primitive (b) Primitive (c) Tokens (d) None of these
4. Which of the following is incorrect string literal?
   (a) "HelloWorld" (b) "Hello\nWorld" (c) "\"HelloWorld" (d) "Helloworld"
5. Explain the types of data types.

2 Marks Questions

6. Explain constants with example.
7. What is wrapper classes in Java?

3 Marks Questions

8. Describe about the identifier. What are the identifier forming rules in Java?
9. What will be the value of following, if m = 5 initially?
   (i) (5 * ++m)%6 (ii) (5 * m ++)%6
10. Write the name of some primitive data types in Java.

5 Marks Questions

11. What is type casting?
12. How are parameterized constructor different from non-parameterized constructor?

10 Marks Questions

13. What will be the output of the following code?

```
class Equals
{
    public static void main(String[] args)
    {
        int x =100;
        double y = 100.1;
        boolean  b = (x = y); / * Line 1  * /
        System.out.println(b);
    }
}
```

14. State the difference between a boolean literal and character literal.

05

Statement and Control Structure

TREND ANALYSIS 4 YEARS

Average No. of Questions Across all Sets

	Types of Questions	2024	2023	2020	2019
Statement and Control Structure	1 Mark	–	–	–	–
	2 Marks	–	–	–	–
	3 Marks	–	–	–	–
	5 Marks	–	–	–	–
	10 Marks	–	–	–	–

A Java program is a set of statements, which are normally executed sequentially in order in which they appear. A statement is a single command that is executed by the Java interpreter.

Java statements can be broadly defined into three categories:

Single Statement

When one statement forms a complete unit of execution, it is called single statement. The following types can be made statements by terminating expression with semicolon (;).

1. Assignment expressions
2. Any use of ++ or -- operators.
3. Method invocations
4. Object creating expressions
5. Control flow statement
6. Null statement

Compound Statement

It is also known as **block of statements.** Packaging several statements into a single statement between two balanced braces { }, is called a compound statement.

e.g.
```
{
    x = 1;
    y = 0;
}
```

Control Statements

Control statements are used in programming languages to cause the flow of execution in advance. These statements are the branch based statements, where branches are depend on the state of a program.

In Java, control statements can be divided under the following three categories:

1. Selection Statements

Selection statements are used in a program to choose different paths of execution based upon the outcome of an expression or the state of a variable.

if Statement

The if statement is a powerful decision making statement and is used to control the flow of execution of statement. Its simplest form is:

```
if(condition)
{
    statement;
}
```

Here,

- condition is a boolean expression.
- if condition is true, then the statement will be executed.
- if condition is false, then the statement will be passed.

The control flow diagram of if statement is shown below:

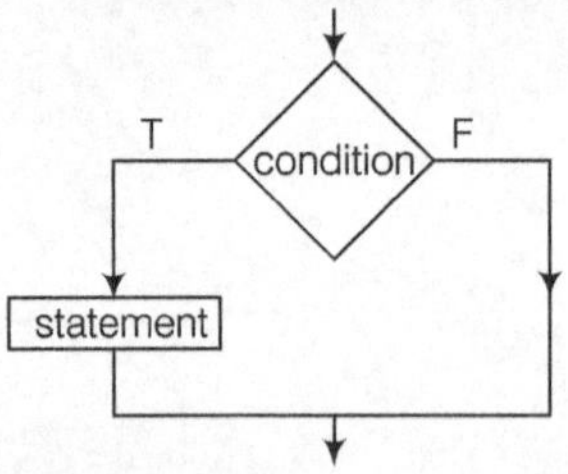

if-else Statement

The if-else statement can be used to route program execution through two different paths. The simplest form of if-else statement is:

```
if(condition)
{
    statement 1;   // if condition is true
}
else
{
    statement 2;  // if condition is false
}
```

Here,

- condition is a boolean expression.
- if condition is true, statement 1 or if block will be executed.
- if condition is false, statement 2 or else block will be executed.

The control flow diagram of if-else statement is shown below:

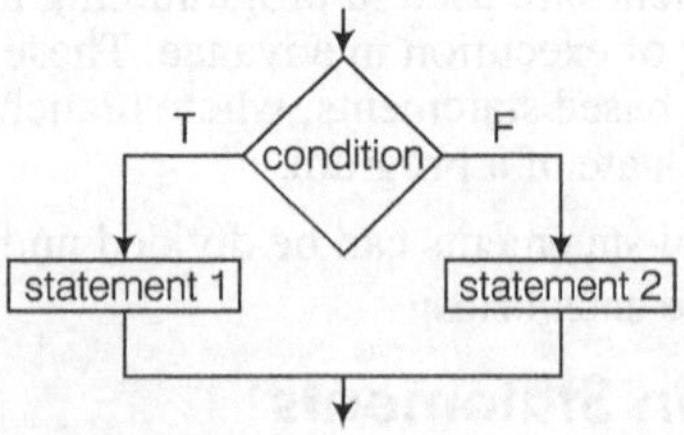

Nested if Statement

The if statement can be nested in Java, which means one if or if-else statement inside another if or if-else statement can be used. The simplest form of nested if statement is:

```
if(condition 1)
{
    if(condition 2)
    {
        statement 1;
    }
    else
    {
        statement 2;
    }
}
else
{
    if(condition 3)
    {
        statement 3;
    }
    else
    {
        statement 4;
    }
}
```

Here,

- if condition 1 is true, then condition 2 will be evaluated.
- if condition 2 is true, then statement 1 will execute.
- if condition 2 is false, then statement 2 will execute.
- if condition 1 is false, then in else block, condition 3 will be evaluated.
- if condition 3 is true, then statement 3 will execute.
- if condition 3 is false, then statement 4 will execute.

The control flow diagram of nested if statement is shown below:

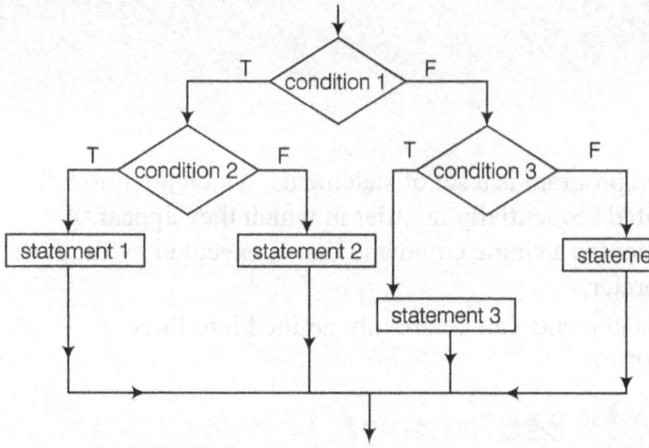

if else if Ladder

When a series of decisions are involved, we have to use more than one if else statement.

An if statement can be followed by an optional else if...... else statement, which is very useful to test various conditions. The simplest form is:

```
if(condition 1)
    statement 1;
else if(condition 2)
    statement 2;
else if(condition 3)
    statement 3;
:
else
    statement n+1;
```

Here,

- The if statements are executed from the top.
- As one of the conditions controlling the if is true, the statement will be executed.
- If none of the conditions is true, the final else statement will be executed.
- The final else acts as a default condition, if all the conditions become false, then it will be executed.

The control flow diagram of if else if ladder is shown below:

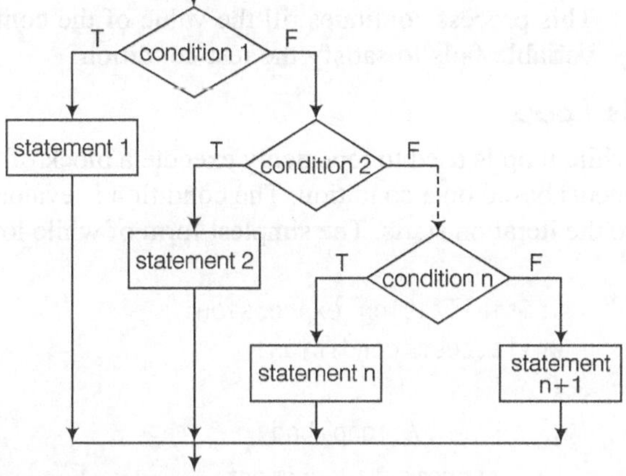

switch Statement

In Java, the switch statement is another selection statement that defines different paths of execution for a program. It can be used in place of chain of else statements. The simplest form of switch statement is:

```
switch(expression)
{
     case value 1:    // statement sequence
     break;
     case value 2:    // statement sequence
     break;
     :
     case value N:    // statement sequence
     break;
     default:   // default statement sequence
}
```

Here,

- The expression must be of type byte, short, int or char.
- Each case value must be a unique literal (that is, it must be a constant not a variable).
- The break statement is used inside the switch to terminate a statement sequence.
- If none of the constants matches with the value of the expression, then the default statement will be executed.

The control flow diagram of switch statement is given below:

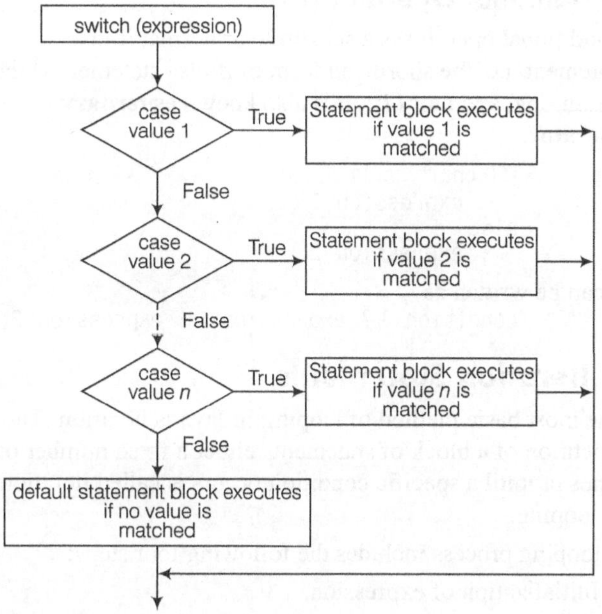

Nested switch Statements

A switch as part of the statement sequence of an outer switch is called a nested switch. The simplest form of nested switch statement is:

```
switch(expression 1)
{
     case value 1:
     switch(expression 2) // nested switch
     {
          case value 0:  // statement sequence
          break;
          case value 1:  // statement sequence
          break;
     }
     break;
     case value 2:       // statement sequence
     break;
     :
     default:   // default statement sequence
}
```

Here,

- The case value 1 statement in the inner switch does not conflict with the case value 1 statement in the outer switch.
- No two case constants in the same switch can have identical values.

Note Fall through is usually prevented with a break keyword at the end of the matching body, which exits execution of the switch block, but this can cause bugs due to unintentional fall through, if the programmer forgets to insert the break statement.

Conditional Operator (?:)

Conditional operator is a substitute of normal if-else statement, i.e. the shorthand form of if-else statement is the conditional operator (?:). It is also known as **ternary operator**.

e.g.
```
if(condition 1)
        expression 1;
else
        expression 2;
```

It can be written as
```
condition 1? expression 1 : expression 2;
```

2. Iteration Statements

The most basic method of looping in Java is iteration. The repetition of a block of statements either a fixed number of times or until a specific condition occurs is called iteration or looping.

A looping process includes the following four steps:

- Initialization of expression.
- Evaluation of the loop condition.
- Execution of the loop when the specified loop condition is true.
- Incrementing the expression.

Java provides three kinds of loops as follows

for Loop

When fixed number of iteration are to be performed, for loop is used.

The simplest form of for loop is:
```
for(initialization ; condition ;
                          increment/decrement)
{
    : // body of for loop
}
```

Here,

for loop grouped the following three common parts together into one statement:

(i) **Initialization** The control variables are initialized first, using assignment statement such as i = 1 and count = 0. The variables i and count are known as **loop-control variables.**
Initialization expression is executed only once.

(ii) **Condition** The value of the control variable is tested using test condition. If the condition is true, then the body of the loop is executed, otherwise the loop is terminated and the execution continues with the statement that immediately follows the loop.

(iii) **Increment** or **Decrement** When the body of the loop is executed, the control is transferred back to the for statement after evaluating the last statement in the loop. Now, the control variable is incremented/decremented using an assignment statement and the new value of the control variable is again tested to see whether it satisfies the loop condition or not. If the condition is satisfied, the body of the loop is again executed. This process continues till the value of the control variable fails to satisfy the test condition.

while Loop

The while loop is used to repeatedly execute a block of statements based on a condition. The condition is evaluated before the iteration starts. The simplest form of while loop is:
```
initialization expression;
while(test condition)
{
    :    // loop body
    increment/decrement;
}
```

Here,

- The test condition is evaluated and if the condition is true, then the body of the while loop is executed.
- When the condition becomes false, the program control passes to the statement written immediately after the loop body.

do-while Loop

The do-while loop always executes its body at least once, because its conditional expression is at the bottom of the loop. Its simplest form is:
```
do
{
    // body of loop
    increment/decrement;
} while(condition);
```

Here,

- Each iteration of the do-while loop first executes the body of the loop and then evaluates the conditional expression.
- If this expression is true, the loop will repeat. Otherwise, the loop will terminate.

3. **Jump Statements**

Java supports three jump statements break, continue and return. These statements transfer control to another part of the program.

break Statement

This statement is generally used to break the loop or switch statement.

It has three uses:

- It terminates a statement sequence in a switch statement.
- It can be used to exit a loop.
- It can be used as a 'civilised' form of goto statement.

```
     while(..........)                 do
     {                                 {
        ..........                        ..........
        ..........                        ..........
        if(condition)                     if(condition)
Exit      break;              Exit          break;
from    ..........            from        ..........
loop    ..........            loop        ..........
     }                                 } while(..........);
     ..........                        ..........
          (a)                               (b)

     for(..........)                   for(..........)
     {                                 {
        ..........                        ..........
        ..........                        for(..........)
        if (condition)                    {
Exit      break;                            ..........
from    ..........                          if(condition)
loop    ..........            Exit            break;
     }                        from          ..........
     ..........               innerloop   }
                                          ..........
                                       }
          (c)                               (d)
```

Uses of break Statement

By using break, you can force immediate termination of a loop by passing the conditional expression and any remaining code in the body of the loop. The break statement should be used to cancel a loop only when some sort of special situation occurs.

continue Statement

In Java, continue statement is used to skip the part of loop. Unlike break statement, it does not terminate the loop, instead it skips the remaining part of the loop and controls go back to check the condition again.

continue statement performs below mentioned actions:

- In while and do-while loops, a continue statement causes control to be transferred directly to the conditional expression that controls the loop.
- With the break statement, continue may specify a label to describe which enclosing loop to continue.

```
while(test condition)              do
{                                  {
     ............                       ............
     if(............)                   if(............)
       continue;                          continue;
     ............                       ............
     ............                       ............
}                                  } while(test condition);
        (a)                                 (b)

for(initialization; test condition; increment)
{
     ............
     if(............)
       continue;
     ............
     ............
}
        (c)
```

Uses of continue Statement

- It is a jumping statement and is used as keyword.
- It skips the loop and re-executes loop with new condition.
- In for loop, continue statement takes control to 'increment' step. i.e. After continue 'i++' will be get executed.

Labelled break and continue Statements

A label is any valid Java variable name. The break and continue statements can also be used with labels.

If we want to jump outside a nested loop or to continue a loop that is outside the current one, then we may have to use the labelled break and labelled continue statement.

e.g.

```
Outer:
for(int m = 1; m < 15; m++)
{
    for(int n = 1; n < 11; n++)
    {
        System.out.println(" " +m*n);
        if(n = = m)
            continue outer;
    }
}
```

Here, the continue statement terminates the inner loop when n == m and continues with the next iteration of the outer loop (counting m).

return Statement

It is used to explicitly return the expression from a method. It causes program control to transfer back to the caller of the method. The return statement immediately terminate the method in which it is executed.

Syntax

```
return(expression);
```

PYQs Previous Years Questions

2 Marks Questions

1. The following is an if-else code. *ISC 2022 (Sem I)*

```
if(x!=y)
  P=x + y;
else
  P=12;
```

What is the representation of the above code in ternary form?

> **KEY idea**
>
> Conditional operator is a substitute of normal if-else statement i.e. the shorthand form of if-else statement is the conditional operator (?:).

(a) P=(x!=y)?x+y,12;
(b) P=(x!=y)?P=x+y;P=12;
(c) P=(x!=y)?x+y:12;
(d) P=(x!=y)x+y,12;

Ans (c) P = (x! = y)? x + y : 12;

2. What is the output of the code given below? *ISC SQP 2022 (Sem I)*

```
int i, j;
for(i=1; i<=5;i++);
  for(j=i+1; j<1; j++);
      System.out.print(i+"+"+j);
```

(a) 67 (b) 1 + 2
(c) 6 + 7 (d) 12

Ans (c) 6 + 7

3. Define the term fall through condition with reference to switch () case. *ISC 2016*

Ans Fall through is usually prevented with a break keyword at the end of the matching body, which exits execution of the switch block, but this can cause bugs due to unintentional fall through, if the programmer forgets to insert the break statement.

e.g.

```
class Week
{
 public static void main (String[] args)
 {
   int wk = 4;
   switch (wk)
   {
     case 1: System.out.println("Sunday");
     case 2: System.out.println("Monday");
     case 3: System.out.println("Tuesday");
     case 4: System.out.println("Wednesday");
     case 5: System.out.println("Thursday");
     case 6: System.out.println("Friday");
     case 7: System.out.println("Saturday");
     break;
     default:
   }
 }
}
```

Output

Wednesday
Thursday
Friday
Saturday

> **Common Mistake** Some students will give output as Wednesday because it matches the case. While it will give output as Wednesday to Saturday because there is no break statement after case 4, so it will execute all statements till break statement found or end of code.

5 Marks Questions

1. State the final value of q at the end of following program segment. *ISC 2007*

```
int m, n, p, q = 0;
for(m = 2; m <= 3;  ++m)
{
    for(n = 1; n <= m; ++n)
    {
        p = m + n - 1;
        if(p%3 == 0)
           q += p;
        else
           q += p + 4;
    }
}
```

Ans The given program, iterates the values of m, n, p and q as given in table:

m	n	p = m + n − 1	if (p% 3 == 0)	q
for m = 2	1	p = 2 + 1 − 1 = 2	False, q = q + p + 4 = 0 + 2 + 4 = 6	q = 6
	2	p = 2 + 2 − 1 = 3	True, q = q + p = 6 + 3 = 9	q = 9
for m = 3	1	p = 3 + 1 − 1 = 3	True, q = q + p = 9 + 3 = 12	q = 12
	2	p = 3 + 2 − 1 = 4	False, q = q + p + 4 = 12 + 4 + 4 = 20	q = 20
	3	p = 3 + 3 − 1 = 5	False, q = q + p + 4 = 20 + 5 + 4 = 29	q = 29

Output = 29

2. Give the output of the following program segment.

ISC 2006

```
int x = 0;
do
{
  if(x < 3)
  {
     x += 2;
     System.out.println(x);
     continue;
  }
  else
  {
     System.out.println(++x);
     break;
  }
}while(x < 10);
```

Ans Initially x = 0;

Iteration 1 : if (x < 3)
condition true,
then x += 2 ⇒ x = x + 2
⇒ x = 0 + 2
⇒ x = 2
Print → 2

Iteration 2 : while(x < 10)
condition true,
if (x < 3) condition true,
then x += 2
⇒ x = 2 + 2 = 4
Print → 4

Iteration 3 : while(x < 10) condition true,
if (x < 3)
condition false,
then ++x = x + 1 = 4 + 1 = 5
Print → 5

Output = 2 4 5

Additional Questions

1. Find the output.

```
class ForDemo
{
  public static void main(String args[ ])
  {
     for(int i = 1; i <= 5; i++)
        System.out.println("Square of"+i+"
                              is " +(i*i));
  }
}
```

Ans The program will execute as given in table:

i	if i <= 5	i*i	Output
for i = 1	1 <= 5 True	1 × 1 = 1	Square of 1 is 1
for i = 2	2 <= 5 True	2 × 2 = 4	Square of 2 is 4
for i = 3	3 <= 5 True	3 × 3 = 9	Square of 3 is 9
for i = 4	4 <= 5 True	4 × 4 = 16	Square of 4 is 16
for i = 5	5 <= 5 True	5 × 5 = 25	Square of 5 is 25
for i = 6	6 <= 5 False	–	–

Output

Square of 1 is 1
Square of 2 is 4
Square of 3 is 9
Square of 4 is 16
Square of 5 is 25

2. Find the output of the following code

```
class IfElseNesting
{
  public static void main(String args[ ])
  {
     int a = 325, b = 712, c = 478;
     System.out.println("Largest value is:");
     if(a > b)
     {
        if(a > c)
        {
           System.out.println(a);
        }
        else
        {
           System.out.println(c);
        }
     }
     else
     {
        if(c > b)
        {
           System.out.println(c);
        }
        else
        {
           System.out.println(b);
        }
     }
  }
}
```

Ans for a = 325, b = 712, c = 478

Condition : if (a > b)

i.e. (325 > 712) (false)

jump to else statement, i.e.

if (c > b), i.e. 478 > 712 (false)

So, else block will execute, i.e. System.out.println(b), which will print 712 as value of b.

Hence, the final output will be

Largest value is : 712

3. Print the multiplication table from the following program as given.

```
class Table
{
  public static void main(String args[])
  {
     int row, column, y;
     System.out.println("Multiplication
                               Table");
     row = 1;
     do
     {
        column = 1;
        do
        {
           y = row * column;
           System.out.println(" " + y);
           column = column + 1;
        }
        while(column <= 3);
        System.out.println(" ");
        row = row + 1;
     }
     while(row <= 3);
  }
}
```

Ans Initially, row = 1;

***Step* 1** given, column = 1

now, y = row * column

So, y = 1 * 1 = 1

print (" " +y) = 1

Print = 1

***Step* 2** Now, column = column +1

= 1 + 1 = 2

So, y = row * column

= 1 * 2 = 2

Print = **2**

***Step* 3** Now, column = 2 + 1 = 3

y = row * column

= 1 * 3 = 3

Print = **3**

Now, output printed at this point will be **1 2 3**.

***Step* 4** Column = 3 + 1 = 4

Now, column < = 3

4 < = 3 (false)

So, in next line

row = row + 1

= 1 + 1 = **2**

***Step* 5** Next, row = 2

row < = 3

2 <= 3 (true)

Now, it will continue from do statement.

column = 1,

then,

y = row * column

= 2 * 1 = 2

Print = **2**

Next, column = column + 1

= 1 + 1 = 2

So, y = row * column

= 2 * 2 = 4

Print = **4**

Now, column = column + 1

= 2 + 1 = 3

y = row * column

= 2 * 3 = 6

Print = **6**

Now, output printed at this point will be

1 2 3

2 4 6

***Step* 6** Now, column = column +1

3 + 1 = 4

Now, column <=3

4 < = 3(False)

So, row = row + 1

∴ row = 2 + 1 = 3

column = 1

Now, y = row * column

= 3 * 1 = 3

Print = **3**

Now, column = column + 1

= 1 + 1 = 2

y = row * column

= 3 * 2 = 6

Print = 6

Now, column = column + 1

= 2 + 1 = 3

So, y = 3 * 3 = 9

Print = 9

The final output will be

Multiplication Table

1 2 3

2 4 6

3 6 9

CHAPTER TEST

1 Mark Questions

1. A switch as part of the statement sequence of an outer switch is called
(a) nested switch (b) flow switch (c) inner switch (d) selection switch

2. What is the output of the following code?

```
int i=0;
for (i=0; i<5; i++)
{
}
System.out.println(i);
```

(a) 5 (b) 0 (c) 4 (d) Compilation Error

3. Give the syntax of if-else statement.

2 Marks Questions

4. Name any two jump statements.

5. What is label?

6. What is iteration statement? Explain with example.

3 Marks Questions

7. Give the output of the following code.

```
public void fun( )
{
    int a, b;
    for(a = 1; i <= 10; i++)
    {
        for(b = 1; b <= a; b++)
        {
            System.out.println(a + b);
        }
    }
}
```

5 Marks Questions

8. Following is the code for printing a list of numbers using while loop. Modify the code to achieve the result.

```
class numberlist
{
    public static void main(String[ ] args)
    {
        int i = 1;
        while(i >= 10)
        {
            System.out.println(i);
            i++;
        }
    }
}
```

9. Explain the working of if-else with the help of an example program.

10 Marks Question

10. What is Jump statements? Also, write about break, continue return statements.

06

Methods and Recursion

TREND ANALYSIS 4 YEARS

Average No. of Questions Across all Sets

	Types of Questions	2024	2023	2020	2019
Methods and Recursion	1 Mark	1	1	–	–
	2 Marks	–	–	–	–
	3 Marks	2	2	–	–
	5 Marks	–	–	1	1
	10 Marks	1	1	1	1

A Java method is a collection of statements that are grouped together to perform an operation. Methods are declared inside the body of the class but immediately after the declaration of instance variables. Collectively, the methods and variables defined within a class are called **members of a class.**

Methods in Java are very useful because of the following reasons:

(i) To make the code reusable

(ii) To simplify the code

(iii) To break complex problem into simpler sub problems.

Definition of Method

Before using a method in a program, it must be defined.

Syntax for method definition is as follows:

```
[Access_modifier] [Non-Access_modifier]
    Return_type Method_name ([Parameter list])
{
    Method body
}
```

Above definition consists of:

(i) **Access Modifier** or **Access_specifier** can take private, protected or public values. If not specified then package friendly is the default specifier. These specify the visibility of the method.

(ii) **Non-Access_modifier** can take static, final, native, volatile, synchronised, transient as one of the value.

(iii) **Return_type** is used to specify the type of the value returned by the method.

(iv) **Method_name** is used to specify the name of the method.

(v) **Parameter list** is a comma separated list of variables used to provide input to the method.

(vi) **Method body** collection of statements, we want to execute as a single unit.

Method Prototyping

The method prototyping describes the method interface to the compiler by giving details such as the number of arguments, the type of arguments and the type of return value. With method prototyping, a template is always used when declaring and defining a method.

Method Call/Invocation

Methods cannot run on their own, they need to be invoked. Methods will be invoked by the objects of the class. It can be called by providing the method name, followed by the arguments being sent enclosed in parenthesis. A method whose prototype looks like as

Formal parameters

```
float volume(int a, float b, float c);
```

can be invoked in a program as follows:

Actual parameters

```
float x = volume(p, q, r);
```

The parameters, that appear in function definition are called **formal parameters** while the parameters, that appear in function calling are called the **actual parameters**.

There are two ways to call a method:

(i) Call by Value

It is also referred as **pass by value**. It is the value held in the variable that is passed as an argument is copied into the parameters, are defined in the method prototype. That is why, changes made to the variable within the method had no effect on the variable that was passed.

e.g.
```
public void meth(int num) //method prototype
int a = 34;
meth(a);                  //method invocation
```

(ii) Call by Reference

It is also known as **pass by reference.** This method is valid for passing an object reference to any method call. When we declare a reference type variable, the compiler allocates only space where the memory address of the object can be stored.

The space for the object is allocated at the time of object creation using the **new** keyword. A variable of reference type differs from a variable of a primitive type in the way that a primitive type variable holds the actual data while a reference type holds the address of the object, not the data.

```
public void meth(Number num)
Number a;
a = new Number(34);
meth(a);
```

Returning from a Method

- We can specify return type of the method as 'primitive data type' or 'class name'.
- Return type can be 'void' means it does not return any value.
- Method can return a value by using **'return'** keyword.
- The data type of the return value must match the method's declared return type, you cannot return a float value from a method declared to return an integer.

e.g.
```
//a method for computing the area of the
   rectangle can be written as
  public int getArea(int width, int height)
{
   return width * height;
}
```

Here, this getArea( ) method returns the integer value that the expression `width * height` evaluates too.

Access Specifier

Java provides a number of access specifiers to set access levels for classes, variables, methods and constructors. They can be used with a method declaration. It is also known as **access modifier**. There are four access specifiers as follows:

(i) **Private** access specifier denotes a variable or method as being private to the class and may not be accessed outside the class.

(ii) **Protected** access specifier denotes a variable or method as being public to subclasses of this class but private to all other classes outside the current package. So, derived classes have the ability to access protected variables of its parent.

(iii) **Public** access specifier denotes a variable or method as being directly accessible from all other classes.

(iv) **Default** access specifier is used when no access modifier is present. It denotes a variable or method as being public to all the classes within the same package.

Access Modifier

Access Modifier	Default	Private	Protected	Public
Accessible inside the class	yes	yes	yes	yes
Accessible within the subclass inside the same package	yes	no	yes	yes
Accessible outside the package	no	no	no	yes
Accessible within the subclass outside the package	no	no	yes	yes

The static Keyword

To create a member that can be used by itself without any object, we use the concept of static. When a member is declared static, it can be accessed before any objects of its class are created and without reference to any object. In Java, both variables and methods can be made static.

Instance variables declared as static are essentially global variables. When objects of its class are declared, no copy of static variable is made. Instead, all instances of the class share the same static variable. Methods declared as static can only call other static methods and access only static data members.

The following program demonstrates the use of 'static' keyword:

```
class Demostatic
{
    static int x = 3, y;
    static void fun(int p)
    {
        System.out.println("Static method
                            invoked");
        y = x*4;
        System.out.println("p = " +p);
        System.out.println("x = " +x);
        System.out.println("y = " +y);
    }
    public static void main(String args[])
    {
        fun(42);
    }
}
```

Output

Static method invoked

p = 42

x = 3

y = 12

The main() Method

`main()` method is the entry point for any Java program. In Java, execution of any program starts from main() method. This method has to strictly follow its syntax, as shown:

```
public static void main(String args[])
```

- `main()` method is public in Java because public can be accessible from outside of that class.
- It returns void, i.e. not supposed to return any value.
- `main()` method in Java must be static because it has to be called before the creation of any object of main() class.
- `main()` method can take arguments, which you need to supply before the program execution starts.

The this Keyword

The 'this' keyword is used in a method to refer to the object that invoked it, i.e. it refers to the current object. Whenever a reference to an object of the current class type is required, 'this' can be used.

It can also differentiate between instance variables and local variables.

The exact purpose of 'this' is to remove ambiguity between local and instance variables.

e.g.
```
public class Myclass
{
    int number;
    public Myclass(int number)
    {
        this.number = number;
    }
}
```

Algorithm

An algorithm is a procedure used for solving a problem or performing a computation. Algorithms act as a precise list of instructions that conduct specified actions step by step in either hardware- or software-based routines. Algorithmic programming is all about writing a set of rules with a finite number of steps that instruct the computer how to perform a task.

Advantages of Algorithm

- It is a step-wise representation of a solution to a given problem, which makes it easy to understand.
- An algorithm uses a definite procedure.
- It is not dependent on any programming language, so it is easy to understand for anyone even without programming knowledge.
- Every step in an algorithm has its own logical sequence so it is easy to debug.
- By using algorithm, the problem is broken down into smaller pieces or steps hence, it is easier for programmer to convert it into an actual program.

Disadvantages of Algorithm

- Algorithm is time consuming.
- Difficult to show branching and looping in algorithms.
- Big tasks are difficult to put in algorithms.

How to write an effective Algorithm?

Step 1 Obtain detailed information on the problem.

Step 2 Analyze the problem.

Step 3 Think of a problem solving approach.

Step 4 Review the problem solving approach and try to think of a better alternative.

Step 5 Develop a basic structure of the algorithm.

Step 6 Optimize, improve and refine.

Examples of Algorithm

Algorithm 1: Simple algorithm to reverse a number in Java:

Step 1. Take the number to be reversed as input.

Step 2. Initialize variables to hold the original number and the reversed number.

Step 3. Run a loop until the original number becomes 0.

Step 3.1 Extract the last digit of the original number using the modulo operator (%).

Step 3.2 Append this digit to the reversed number.

Step 3.3 Update the original number by removing the last digit using integer division (/).

Step 4. Print or return the reversed number.

Algorithm 2: Simple algorithm to find the roots of a quadratic equation:

Step 1. Read the coefficients a, b, and c of the quadratic equation $ax^2 + bx + c = 0$.

Step 2. Calculate the discriminant (D) using the formula: $D = b^2 - 4ac$.

Step 3. If the discriminant is negative ($D < 0$), the roots are complex, and the equation has no real roots.

Step 4. If the discriminant is zero ($D = 0$), the equation has one real root, which is -b/(2a).

Step 5. If the discriminant is positive ($D > 0$), the equation has two distinct real roots, which are (-b + sqrt(D))/(2a) and (-b - sqrt(D))/(2a), where sqrt() denotes the square root function.

Recursion

The idea of calling one function from another immediately suggests the possibility of a function calling itself. The function call mechanism in Java supports this possibility, which is known as recursion. A recursive method is a method that calls itself.

A recursive procedure must have the following two properties:

(i) There must be certain criteria, called **base criteria**, for which the procedure does not call itself.

(ii) Each time the procedure does call itself (directly or indirectly), it must be closer to the base criteria.

There are two types of recursion as follows:

(a) **Finite** Recursive procedure contains a valid test case.

(b) **Infinite** Recursive procedure does not contain any valid test case.

e.g.
```
public class RecursionDemo
{
    public void print(int n)
    {
        if(n<0)
            return;
        else
        {
            print(n - 1);
            System.out.println(n);
        }
    }
    public static void main(String
                                args[])
    {
        RecursionDemo obj = new
                        RecursionDemo();
        obj.print(3);
    }
}
```

In the above program method print(int n) is calling itself. Hence, the above procedure (method) is a recursive procedure.

At runtime, the recursive procedure uses stack data structure. Stack is a last-in-first-out data structure, i.e. the element coming last, goes out of stack first.

To understand the working of recursion, let us consider the following procedure:

- In the beginning, the program pushes a frame for `print(3)`. In this frame, the values of local variables is stored.
- As soon as `print(3)` will invoke `print(2)`, computer will place a new frame on the top of the stack, containing n value as 2.
- When `print(2)` will invoke `print(1)`, a new frame will be pushed onto the top of stack with n value being 1.
- When `print(1)` will invoke `print(0)`, a new frame will be pushed onto stack with $n = 0$.
- When `print(0)` will return as the test case becomes true, frame of `print(0)` will be popped out of the stack and output will be print 0.
- When `print(1)` will return as the termination condition the corresponding frame of `print(1)` will be popped off the stack and output 1 will print.

- Similarly when `print(2)` and `print(3)` will return one after another and consecutively output 2 and 3 will print, respectively. Now, stack will be empty.

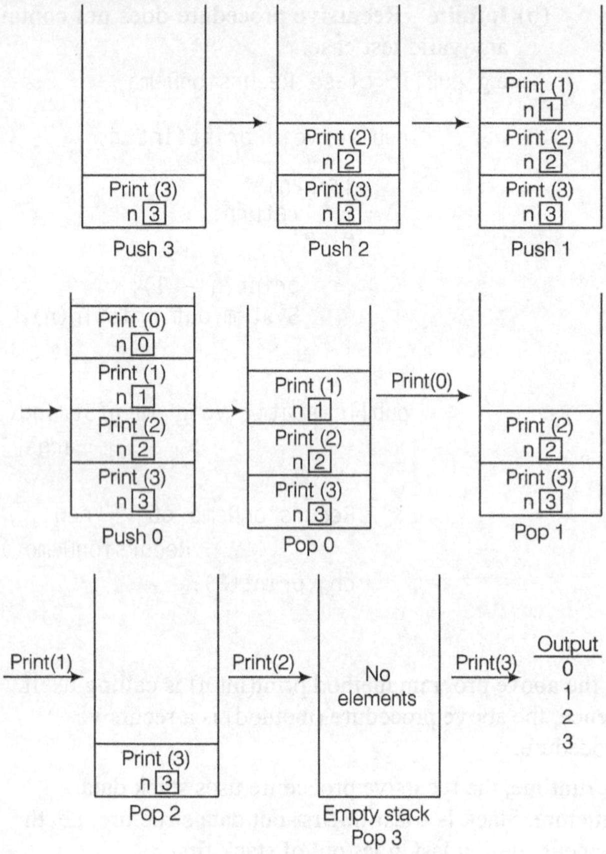

Steps to Operate a Stack

Program for Factorial Calculation

```
//Assume N is greater than 0
public int factorial(int N)
{
    if(N == 1)    //Test to stop or continue.
        return 1; //End case : recursion stops.
                                                  else
        return N * factorial (N-1);
/* Recursive case : recursion continues with
another recursive call */
}
```

Algorithm

Step 1 Start

Step 2 Declare variables n, factorial and i.

Step 3 Initialize variables

factorial ← 1

i ← 1

Step 4 Read value of n

Step 5 Repeat the steps until i = n

5.1 factorial ← factorial*i

5.2 i ← i+1

Step 6 Display factorial

Step 7 Stop

Program for Fibonacci Series Generation

The fibonacci sequence (usually denoted by F_0, F_1, F_2,...) is as follows:

0, 1, 1, 2, 3, 5, 8, 13, 21, 34, 55 ......

That is $F_0 = 0$ and $F_1 = 1$ and each succeeding term is the sum of the two preceding terms. e.g. the next two terms of the sequence are,

$$34 + 55 = 89 \text{ and } 55 + 89 = 144$$

Recursive procedure for fibonacci series generation is as follows:

```
public int fib(int n)
{
    if(n <= 1)
    {
        return n;
    }
    else
    {
        return fib(n - 1) + fib(n - 2);
    }
}
```

Algorithm

Step 1 Start

Step 2 Declare variables first_term,second_term and temp.

Step 3 Initialize variables first_term ← 0, second_term ← 1

Step 4 Display first_term and second_term

Step 5 Repeat the steps until second_term ≤ n

5.1 temp ← second_term

5.2 second_term ← second_term + first_term

5.3 first_term ← temp

5.4 Display second_term

Step 6 Stop

Program for Computing GCD Recursively

In mathematics, the Greatest Common Divisor (GCD), sometimes known as the **Highest Common Factor** (HCF) of two or more integers, is the largest positive integer that divides the numbers without a remainder. e.g. the greatest common divisor of 102 and 68 is 34 since both 102 and 68 are multiples of 34 but no integer larger than 34 that divides both 102 and 68.

The code below shows, how to implement GCD function recursively.

```
public long gcd(long a, long b)
{
    if (b==0)
        return a;
    else
        return gcd(b,a%b);
}
```

This recursive solution to the problem of computing the GCD is also known as **Euclid's algorithm**.

Towers of Hanoi

The towers of hanoi is a popular problem. You have three poles and n disks, which fit on the poles. All disks have different size. They are stacked on pole 1 in the orders of their size. The largest disk is on the bottom, the smallest is on the top.

The task is to move all disk from pole 1 to pole 3 under the following restrictions:

- Only one disk can be moved.
- A larger disk cannot be placed on a smaller disk.

The recursive algorithm works like the following; move n-1 disk from the starting pole to the pole, which is neither start nor target, move disk n to the target pole and then move n-1 disk from the intermediate pole to the target pole. The n-1 disks are moved recursively.

The recursive procedure implementing towers of hanoi problem is as follows:

```
public void move(int n,int L,int M,int R)
{
    if(n==1)
        System.out.println(L+"→"+R);
    else
    {
        move(n-1, L, R, M);
        System.out.println(L+"→"+R);
        move(n-1, M, L, R);
    }
}
```

Program for Binary Search

```
static int binarySearch(int[] arr, int left,
                        int right, int key)
{
  if (right >= left)
  {
    int mid = left + (right - left) / 2;
    // If the element is present at the middle
                                          itself
    if (arr[mid] == key)
    return mid;
    // If the element is smaller than the middle
         element, then it can only be present
                            in the left subarray
    if (arr[mid] > key)
      return binarySearch(arr, left, mid -
                                         1, key);
    // Else the element can only be present in the
                                  right subarray
    return binarySearch(arr, mid + 1, right,
                                          key);
  }
  // Element is not present in the array
  return -1;
}
```

This binarySearch method takes an array arr, the left and right indices of the subarray being searched (left and right), and the key being searched for. It recursively divides the array in half and searches the appropriate half until the key is found or the search range is exhausted. If the key is found, it returns the index of the key in the array. If the key is not found, it returns -1.

Program for Conversion of Representations of Numbers between Different Bases

```
static String convertToBase(int decimalNumber,
                                       int base)
{
    // Base case: if the number is 0, return "0"
                             in the target base
    if (decimalNumber == 0)
    {
      return "0";
    }
    // Recursive case: divide the number by the
       base and call the function recursively
    String result = "";
    int remainder = decimalNumber % base;
    if (remainder < 0) {
      // Make sure the remainder is positive for
                             negative numbers
      remainder += Math.abs(base);
    }
    result = convertToBase(decimalNumber / base,
                                        base);
    // Append the current remainder to the result
```

```
    if (remainder < 10) {
        result += (char) (remainder + '0');
    } else {
        result += (char) (remainder - 10 + 'A');
        // Convert remainder to character 'A'-'Z'
    }
    return result;
}
```

In this convertToBase method, the decimal number is repeatedly divided by the target base, and the remainders are used to construct the result string. The method calls itself recursively until the base case is reached (when the decimal number becomes 0).

Advantages of Recursion

Following are the advantages of recursion:

(i) Although at most of the times a problem can be solved without recursion, but in some situations in programming, it is must to use recursion. e.g. a program to display a list of all files of the system cannot be solved without recursion.

(ii) The recursion is very flexible in data structure like stacks, queues and linked list.

(iii) Using recursion, the length of the program can be reduced.

Disadvantages of Recursion

Following are the disadvantages of recursion:

(i) It requires extra storage space. The recursive calls and automatic variables are stored on the stack. For every recursive call, separate memory is allocated to automatic variables with the same name.

(ii) If the programmer forgets to specify the exit condition in the recursive function, the program will execute out of memory. In such a situation, user has to press Ctrl + break to pause or stop the function.

(iii) The recursion function is not efficient in execution speed and time.

Difference between Recursion and Iteration

Recursion	Iteration
Recursive function is a function that is partially defined by itself.	Iterative instructions are loop based repetitions of a process.
Recursion uses selection structure.	Iteration uses repetition structure.
Infinite recursion occurs, if the recursion step does not reduce the problem in a manner that converges on some condition (base case).	An infinite loop occurs with iteration, if the loop-condition test never becomes false.
Recursion terminates when a base case is recognised.	Iteration terminates when the loop-condition fails.
Recursion is usually slower than iteration due to overhead of maintaining stack.	Iteration does not use stack so it is faster than recursion.
Recursion uses more memory than iteration.	Iteration consumes less memory.
Infinite recursion can crash the system.	Infinite looping uses CPU cycles repeatedly.
Recursion makes code smaller.	Iteration makes code longer.

PYQs Previous Years Questions

1 Mark Questions

1. State any one difference between instance variable and class variable. ***ISC 2024***

Ans **instance variable** - a separate copy for each of the objects of the class

class variable - same copy of the variable is shared amongst all objects of the class

2. State any one purpose of using the keyword this in Java programming. ***ISC 2023***

Ans 'this' keyword helps to distinguish between local variable and variables passed in the method as parameters.

3. State any one purpose of using the keyword super in Java programming. ***ISC SQP 2023***

Ans super keyword can be used to invoke the parent class methods and constructors.

4. What is the output of the program code given below, when the value of x = 294?

```
int simple(int x)
{
    return (x<=0)? 0 : x + simple(x/10);
}
```

ISC 2022 (Sem II)

Ans **Output**

325

Common Mistake Some students think 0 will be answer when condition becomes false. While condition is True, 0 will be answer otherwise simple (x/10) function call.

5. State any one drawback of using recursive technique in a Java program. ***ISC 2022 (Sem II)***

Ans Recursive technique may require a lot of memory space to hold intermediate results on the system stacks.

6.

```
int Toy(int n)
{return (n<=0)? 1 : n%10+Toy(n/10);}
```

With reference to the program code given above, what will the function Toy() return when the value of n=56? ***ISC SQP 2022 (Sem II)***

(a) 65 (b) 12 (c) 651 (d) 11

Ans (b) 12

7. Give one reason, why iteration is better than recursion? ***ISC SQP 2022 (Sem II)***

Ans Recursion takes more memory and time to execute than its iterative counterpart.

2 Marks Questions

1. Differentiate between an infinite and a finite recursion. ***ISC 2022 (Sem II), 2010***

Ans Differences between finite recursion and infinite recursion are as follows

Finite Recursion	Infinite Recursion
When recursive procedure contains a valid test case, so that recursion can terminate after finite number of steps is called finite recursion.	When recursive procedure does not contain any valid test case to terminate recursion, then it is called infinite recursion.
Controlled recursion is called finite recursion.	Uncontrolled recursion is called infinite recursion.

2. Differentiate between direct recursion and indirect recursion. ***ISC SQP 2022 (Sem II)***

Ans Differences between direct recursion and indirect recursion are as follows

Direct recursion	Indirect recursion
Direct recursion called by the same function.	Indirect recursion called by the other function.
The base case and the recursive case are defined within the same function.	The base case and the recursive case are defined in separate functions.

3. State one advantage and one disadvantage of using recursion over iteration. ***ISC 2016***

KEY idea
The recursion method is a method that calls itself.
Iteration uses repetition structure.

Ans Advantage of using recursion over iteration is as follows:

- Simple and fast to code.

Disadvantage of using recursion over iteration is as follows:

- More memory consumption because of the recursion stack.

4. State difference between iteration and recursion. ***ISC 2014***

Ans Refer to text on page 136.

5. State any two disadvantages of recursion. ***ISC 2011***

Ans Refer to text on page 136.

6. Mention two points which distinguish a static data member from an ordinary data member in a class. ***ISC 2008***

Ans The difference between static and ordinary data member:

Static Data Member	Ordinary Data Member
It can be accessed in all the methods of a class.	It can be accessed in non-static methods of a class.
A single copy of static data is maintained for all objects.	For each object in a class, we maintain separate copy.

7. Why recursive functions result into slower execution of the program? **ISC 2005**

Ans Recursive procedures internally uses stack data structure for maintaining the correct sequence of method calls. For putting data into stack and take it out from there, addition functions need to be executed and because of this addition overhead of executing extra functions, the execution time of recursive procedures increases.

3/5 Marks Questions

1. The following function is a part of some class

```
int jolly(int[] x, int n, int m)
{
if (n < 0)
    return m;
else if(n<x.length)
    m=(x[n]>m)? x[n]: m;
return jolly(x, -- n, m);
}
```

(a) What will be the output of jolly() when the value of x[]={6, 3, 4, 7, 1}, n=4 and m=0?

(b) What function does jolly() perform, apart from recursion? **ISC 2024**

Ans (a) 7

(b) The jolly() function, apart from recursion, finds the maximum value in the array x[]. It recursively iterates through the array elements and updates m to the maximum encountered value.

2. The following function is a part of some class which is used to find the smallest digit present in a number. There are some places in the code marked by ?1?, ?2?, ?3? which must be replaced by an expression / a statement so that the function works correctly **ISC 2024**

```
int small_dig(int n)
{ int min = ?1?;
    while (n! =0)
    {
        int q=n/10;
        int r=?2? * 10;
        min = r > min ? ?3? : r;
        n=q;
    }
    return min;
}
```

(a) What is the expression or statement at ?1?

(b) What is the expression or statement at ?2?

(c) What is the expression or statement at ?3?

Ans (a) n%10

(b) n (just put n, question is wrong and the statement should be n%10 instead of n*10)

(c) min

3. With reference to the code given below, answer the questions that follow along with dry run / working. **ISC 2023**

```
boolean num(int x)
{ int a=1;
  for (int c=x; c>0; c/=10)
    a*=10;
  return (x*x%a)==x;
}
```

(a) What will the function num() return when the value of x=25?

(b) What is the method num() performing?

Ans (a) x = 25

a = 1

Iteration 1 c = 25; 25 > 0; c = 25/10 = 2

a = a * 10 = 1 * 10 = 10

Iteration 2 c = 2; 2 > 0; c = 2/10 = 0

a = 10 * 10 = 100

return (x * x % a) = = x;

⇒ 25 * 25% 100 = = 25

⇒ 625% 100 = = 25

⇒ 25 = = 25 True

(b) The method num ( ) is trying to check whether the number x is equal to the last two digits of its square.

4. The following function task() is a part of some class. Assume 'm' and 'n' are positive integers, greater than 0. Answer the questions given below along with dry run / working. **ISC 2023**

```
int task(int m, int n)
{
  if(m==n)
    return m;
  else if(m>n)
    return task(m-n, n);
  else
    return task(m, n-m);
```

}

(a) What will the function task() return when the value of m=30 and n=45?

(b) What function does task() perform apart from recursion?

Ans (a) m = 30, n = 45

Iteration 1 task (30, 45)

if (30 = = 45) False

else if (30 > 45) False

else

return task (30, 15)

Iteration 2 task (30, 15)

if (30 = = 15) False

else if (30 > 15) True

return task (15, 15)

Iteration 3 task (15, 15)

if (15 = = 15) True

return 15

(b) Apart from recursion, task ( ) function performs HCF of two numbers 30 and 45.

5. With reference to the code given below answer the questions that follow. ***ISC SQP 2023***

```
void Solve(int n)
{
  int a=1,b=1;
  for (int i=n;i>0;i=i/10)
  {
    int d=i%10;
    if (d%2==0)
      a=a*d;
    else
      b=b*d;
  }
  System.out.println(a+" "+b);
}
```

(a) What will the function Solve( ) return when the value of n=3269?

(b) What is the method Solve( ) computing?

Ans (a) a = 1, b = 1

Iteration 1for (i = 3269; i > 0; i = i/10) True

d = 3269% 10 = 9

if (9%2 = = 0) False

else

b = b * d = 1 * 9 = 9

Iteration 2 for (i = 326; i > 0; i = i/10) True

d = 326% 10 = 6

if (6%2 = = 0) True

a = a * d = 1 * 6 = 6

Iteration 3 for (i = 32; i > 0; i = i/10) True

d = 32% 10 = 2

if (2% 2 = = 0) True

a = a * d = 6 * 2 = 12

Iteration 4 for (i = 3; i > 0; i = i/10) True

d = 3% 10 = 3

if (3% 2 = = 0) False

else

b = b * d = 9 * 3 = 27

Iteration 5 for (i = 0; i > 0; i = i/10) False

Output 12 27

(b) Solve method computes product of odd and even digits from a number separately.

6. The following function quiz() is a part of some class. Assume 'n' is a positive integer, greater than 0. Answer the given questions along with dry run / working. ***ISC SQP 2023***

```
int quiz( int n)
{
  if (n <=1 )
    return n;
  else
    return (--n % 2) + quiz(n/10);
}
```

(a) What will the function quiz() return when the value of n=36922?

(b) State in one line what does the function quiz( ) do, apart from recursion?

Ans (a) **Iteration 1** quiz (36922)

if (36922 < = 1) False

else

return 1 + quiz (3692)

Iteration 2 quiz (3692)

if (3692 < = 1) False

else

return 1 + quiz (369)

Iteration 3 quiz (369)

if (369 < = 1) False

else

return 0 + quiz (36)

Iteration 4 quiz (36)

if (36 < = 1) False

else

return 1 + quiz (3)

Iteration 5 quiz (3)

if (3 < = 1) False

else

0 + quiz (0)

Iteration 6 quiz (0)
if (0 < = 1) True
return 0

So, when n = 36922, the function quiz ( ) will return 1 + 1 + 0 + 1 + 0 = 3.

(b) Apart from recursion, the function quiz ( ) calculates the sum of the digits of a given positive integer '*n*'.

7. The following function check() is a part of some class. What will the function check() return when the value of (i) n = 25 and (ii) n = 10? Show the dry run/working. ***ISC 2020***

```
int check (int n)
{
  if (n<= 1)
        return 1;
  if (n%2 = = 0)
        return 1 + check (n/2);
  else
        return 1 + check (n/2 + 1);
}
```

Ans (i) When n = 25

check(25)
→ 1 + check(13)
→ 1 + check(7)
→ 1 + check(4)
→ 1 + check(2)
→ 1 + check(1)
→ 1

= 1 + 1 + 1 + 1 + 1 + 1 = 6

(ii) When n = 10

check(10)
→ 1 + check(5)
→ 1 + check(3)
→ 1 + check(2)
→ 1 + check(1)
→ 1

= 1 + 1 + 1 + 1 + 1 = 5

8. The following is a function of some class. What will be the output of the function test () when the value of count is equal to 4 ? Show the dry run/ working. ***ISC SQP 2020***

```
void test (int count)
{
  if (count ==0)
     System.out.println(" ");
  else
     {
       System.out.println("Bye" + count);
       test( --count );
       System.out.println("" + count);
     }
}
```

Ans test (4)

Iteration 1 if (4 = = 0) False
else
print → Bye 4
test (3)
print → 3

Iteration 2 if (3 = = 0) False
else
print → Bye 3
test (2)
print → 2

Iteration 3 if (2 = = 0) False
else
print → Bye 2
test (1)
print → 1

Iteration 4 if (1 = = 0) False
else
print → Bye 1
test (0)
print → 0

Iteration 5 if (0 = = 0) True
print

Output
Bye 4
3
Bye 3
2
Bye 2
1
Bye 1
0

9. The following function Mystery () is a part of some class. What will the function Mystery () return when the value of num = 43629, x = 3 and y = 4, respectively? Show the dry run/working. ***ISC 2019***

```
int Mystery (int num, int x, int y)
{
  if(num < 10)
     return num;
```

```
    else
    {
        int z = num % 10;
        if (z % 2 = = 0)
            return z*x + Mystery (num/10, x, y);
        else
            return z*y + Mystery (num/10, x, y);
    }
}
```

Ans Given num = 43629, x = 3 and y = 4

Iteration 1 when (43629 < 10) False

else ↳
z = 43629%10 = 9
if (9%2 = = 0) False
else ↳
return [9*4 + Mystery (4362, 3, 4)]

Iteration 2 when (4362 < 10) False

else ↳
z = 4362%10 = 2
if (2%2 = = 0) True
return [2*3 + Mystery (436, 3, 4)]

Iteration 3 When (436 < 10) False

else ↳
z = 436%10 = 6
if (6%2 = = 0) True
return [6*3 + Mystery (43, 3, 4)]

Iteration 4 When (43 < 10) False

else ↳
z = 43%10 = 3
if (3%2 = = 0) False
else ↳
return [3*4 + Mystery (4, 3, 4)]

Iteration 5 if (4 < 10) True

return 4

Function Mystery will return 4.

10. The following function magicfun() is a part of some class. What will the function magicfun() return, when the value of n=7 and n=10, respectively? Show the dry run/working: ***ISC 2017***

```
int magicfun(int n)
{
    if (n==0)
        return 0;
    else
        return magicfun(n/2) * 10 + (n % 2);
}
```

Ans When n=7 then,

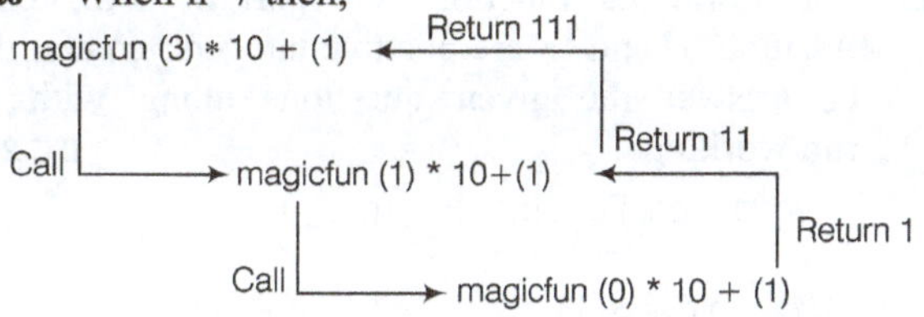

Hence, function magicfun( ) return 111, when the value of n=7

when n = 10 then,

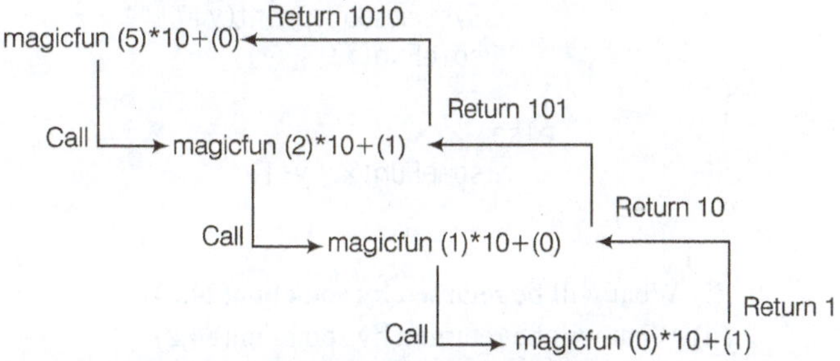

Hence, function magicfun( ) return 1010, when the value of n=10.

11. The following function **check()** is a part of some class. What will the function **check()** return when the values of both 'm' and 'n' are equal to 5? Show the dry run/working. ***ISC 2016***

```
int check (int m, int n)
{
    if (n== 1)
        return - m- - ;
    else
        return + + m+ check (m,-- n) ;
}
```

Ans Working of the given function check()

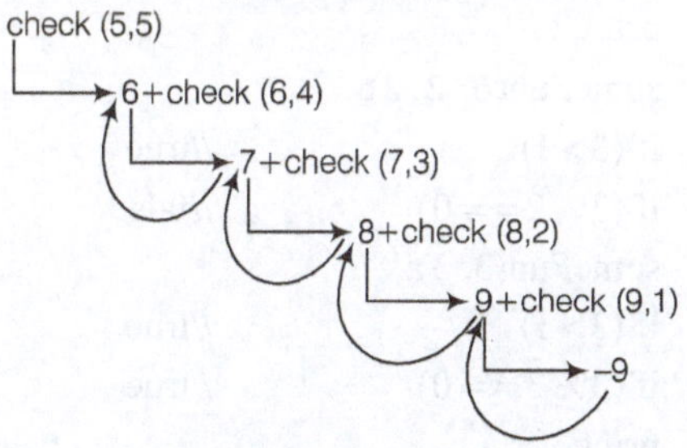

= 6 + 7 + 8 + 9 − 9

= 21

Common Mistake Some students write-9 as answer which will be the last value returned by function and they do not include previous returned value. While all returned values will be included at the end of function.

12. The following function is a part of some class. Assume '*x*' and '*y*' are positive integers, greater than 0. Answer the given questions along with dry run/working. ***ISC 2015***

```
void someFun(int x, int y)
{
     if(x > 1)
     {
          if (x%y == 0)
          {
               System.out.print(y+" ");
               someFun(x/y, y);
          }
          else
               someFun(x, y+1);
     }
}
```

(i) What will be returned by someFun(24,2)?
(ii) What will be returned by someFun(84,2)?
(iii) State in one line what does the function someFun() do, apart from recursion?

Ans (i) if (24 > 1) //true
if (24% 2==0) //true
print 2
someFun(24/2, 2);
if (12> 1) //true
if (12 % 2== 0) //true
print 2
someFun(12/2 , 2);
if (6> 1) //true
if (6% 2== 0) //true
print 2
someFun(6/ 2, 2);
if (3> 1) //true
if (3% 2== 0) //false
someFun(3, 3);
if (3> 1) //true
if (3% 3== 0) //true
print 3
someFun(3/ 3, 3);
if (1> 1) //false
So, the output will be 2 2 2 3.

(ii) if (84 > 1)//true
if (84% 2== 0) //true
print 2
someFun(84/2, 2);
if (42> 1) //true
if (42% 2== 0) //true
print 2
someFun(42/2, 2);
if (21> 1) //true
if (21 % 2== 0) //false
someFun(21, 3);
if (21> 1) //true
if (21% 3== 0) //true
print 3
someFun(21/3, 3);
if (7> 1) //true
if (7% 3== 0) //false
someFun(7, 4);
if (7> 1) //true
if (7% 4 == 0) //false
someFun(7, 5);
if (7> 1) //true
if (7% 5== 0) //False
someFun(7, 6);
if (7> 1) //true
if (7% 6== 0) //false
someFun(7, 7);
if (7> 1) //true
if (7% 7== 0) //true
print 7
someFun(7/7, 7);
if (1> 1) //false
So, the output will be 2 2 3 7.

(iii) The function someFun( ) print the factorization of value x.

13. The following function Recur() is a part of some class. What will be the output of the function Recur() when the value of n is equal to 10? Show the dry run/working. ***ISC 2013***

```
void Recur(int n)
{
     if(n > 1)
     {
          System.out.println(n+" ");
          if(n%2 != 0)
          {
               n = 3 * n + 1;
               System.out.println(n+" ");
          }
          Recur(n/2);
     }
}
```

Ans **Iteration 1.** 10 > 1 (True)
Print '10'
if (10%2 != 0) (False)
Recur(10/2) = Recur(5)

Iteration 2. 5 > 1 (True)
Print '5'
if (5% 2 != 0) (True)
n = 3 * 5 + 1;
n = 16
Print '16'
Now, n = 16
Recur(n/2) = Recur(8)

Iteration 3. 8 > 1 (True)
Print '8'
if (8% 2 != 0) (False)
Now, Recur(8/2) = Recur(4)

Iteration 4. 4 > 1 (True)
Print '4'
if (4%2 != 0) (False)
Recur(4/2) = Recur(2)

Iteration 5. 2 > 1 (True)
Print '2'
if (2%2! = 0) (False)
Now, Recur(2/2) = Recur(1)

Iteration 6. 1 > 1 (False)
So, final output will be,
10 5 16 8 4 2

14. The following function is a part of some class. Assume n is a positive integer. Answer the given questions along with dry run/working. ***ISC 2013***

```
int unknown(int n)
{
    int i, k=0;
    if(n%2 == 0)
    {
        i = n/2;
        k = 1;
    }
    else
    {
        k = n;
        n--;
        i = n/2;
    }
    while(i > 0)
    {
        k = k*i*n;
        i--;
        n--;
    }
    return k;
}
```

(i) What will be returned by unknown (5)?
(ii) What will be returned by unknown (6)?
(iii) What is being computed by unknown (int n)?

Ans (i) for n = 5

if (5% 2 == 0) (False)
Then,
k = 5
n = 4
∴ i = 4/2 = 2

Iteration 1. 2 > 0 (True)
$k = 5 * 2 * 4 \Rightarrow 40$
So, i = 1
n = 3

Iteration 2. 1 > 0 (True)
k = 40 * 1 * 3
= 120
i = 0
n = 2

Iteration 3. 0 > 0 (False)
Return k = 120

(ii) Similarly, as n is 6 which is even, so the condition under if will be executed.

∴ n = 6, i = 3, k = 1

condition (i > 0)	n	i	k
True	5	2	18
True	4	1	180
True	3	0	720
False	—	—	—

720 will be returned.

(iii) When n is even

n	i	k
n	n/2	1
(n – 1)	(n/2 – 1)	$1 * \frac{n}{2} * n = \frac{n^2}{2}$
(n – 2)	$\left(\frac{n}{2} - 2\right)$	$\frac{n^2}{2} * \left(\frac{n}{2} - 1\right) * (n-1)$
(n – 3)	$\left(\frac{n}{2} - 3\right)$	$\frac{n^2}{2} * \left(\frac{n}{2} - 1\right) * (n-1) * \left(\frac{n}{2} - 2\right)$ * (n – 2)

Output $\frac{n^2}{2}\left(\frac{n}{2} - 1\right)(n-1)\left(\frac{n}{2} - 2\right)(n-2)$........

Similarly, when n is odd

Output $n(n-1)\left(\frac{n}{2} - \frac{1}{2}\right)(n-2)\left(\frac{n}{2} - \frac{3}{2}\right)$

15. The following is a part of some class. What will be the output of function mymethod() when the value of counter is equal to 3? Show the run/working. **ISC 2011**

```
void mymethod(int counter)
{
    if(counter == 0)
        System.out.println(" ");
    else
    {
        System.out.println("Hello"+counter);
        mymethod(--counter);
        System.out.println(" "+counter);
    }
}
```

Ans mymethod(3)

print Hello3

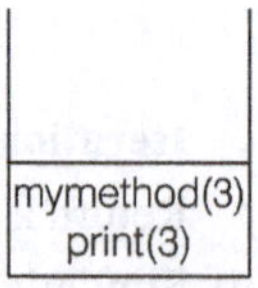

mymethod(2)

print Hello2

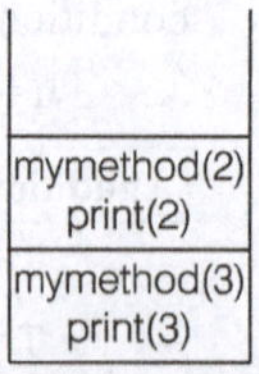

mymethod(1)

print Hello1

mymethod(0)

if (count = = 0) true

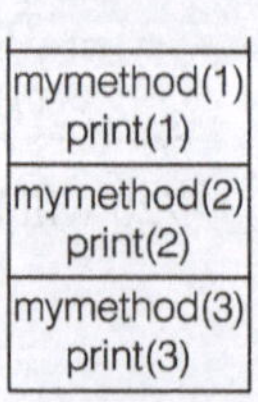

Recursion will stop at this point and frames from stack will be popped out in LIFO sequence. i.e. mymethod(1) frame will be popped out first and will complete its execution by printing 0, then mymethod(2) will print 1 and mymethod(3) will print 2.

Output is

Hello3

Hello2

Hello1

0

1

2

16. The following functions numbers(int) and numbers1(int) are a part of some class. Answer the questions given below showing the dry run/working. **ISC 2010**

```
public void numbers(int n)
{
    if(n > 0)
    {
        System.out.println(n+ " ");
        numbers(n - 2);
        System.out.println(n+ " ");
    }
}
public String numbers1(int n)
{
    if(n <= 0)
    {
        return " ";
        return numbers1(n - 1) +n+ " ";
    }
}
```

(i) What will be the output of the function numbers(int n) when n = 5?

(ii) What will the function numbers1(int n) return when n = 6?

(iii) State in one line what is the function numbers1(int) doing apart from recursion?

Ans (i) When n = 5 then

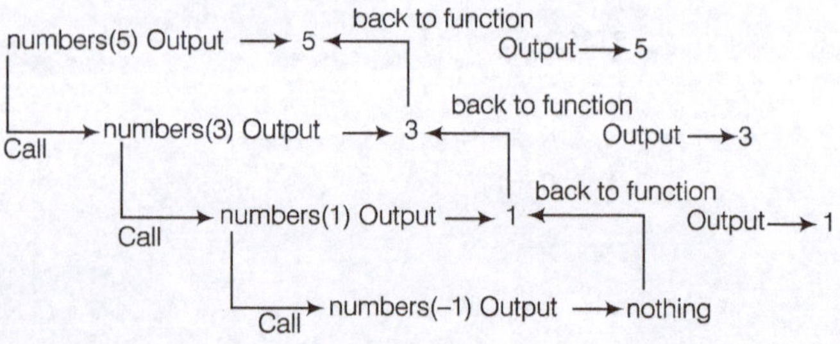

(ii) When n = 6 then

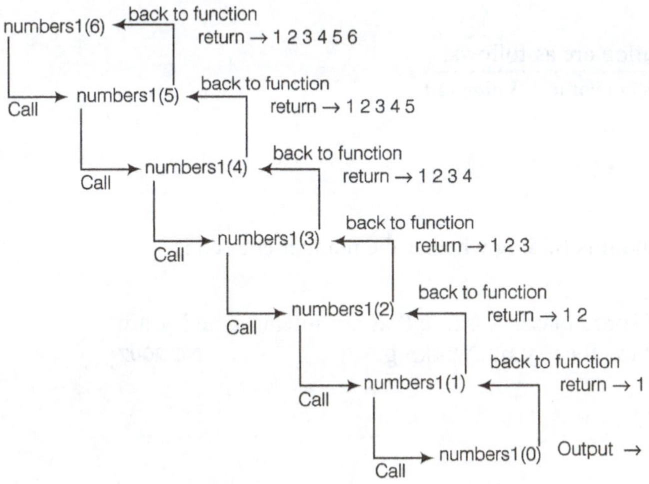

The final output will be 1 2 3 4 5 6.

(iii) Apart from recursion, the function number1(int) is performing the concatenation of numbers.

17. The following function trial() and perform() are a part of some class. Answer the following parts given below. Show the dry run/working. ***ISC 2009***

```
int trial(int n)
{
    if(n == 1)
        return 2 ;
    else if(n == 2)
        return 3 ;
    else
        return trial(n - 2) + trial(n - 1);
}
void perform(int p)
{
    int x;
    for(int i = 1; i <= p; i++)
    {
        x = trial(i);
        System.out.println(x+ " ");
    }
}
```

(i) What will the function trial() return when the value of n is 4?

(ii) What will be the output of the function perform() when the value of p is 5?

(iii) In one line state what the function trial() is doing, apart from recursion?

Ans (i) When the value of n is 4 the trial function will return 8.

(ii) When the value of p is 4 then the output is 2 3 5 8 13.

(iii) This function is finding fibonacci number at nth position starting from 2.

18. The following functions show() and calling() are a part of some class. Assume that the parameter n is greater than 1 when the function is invoked. It returns the value 1 when true otherwise it returns 0. Show the dry run/working. ***ISC 2008***

```
void calling(int i)
{
    int f = 2;
    show(n, f);
}
int show(int n, int f)
{
    if(n==f)
        return 1;
    if(n%f == 0 || n == 1)
        return 0;
    else
        return show(n, f + 1);
}
```

(i) What will the function show() return when the value of n is 11?

(ii) What will the function show() return when the value of n is 27?

(iii) In one line state, what the function show(...) is doing?

Ans (i) When the value of n = 11,

method show (11, 2) //function called

The change of values during execution is as follows:

Action	Value of n	Value of f
Function call	11	2
After 1st call	11	3
After 2nd call	11	4
After 3rd call	11	5
After 4th call	11	6
After 5th call	11	7
After 6th call	11	8
After 7th call	11	9
After 8th call	11	10
After final call	11	11

The value returned is 1.

(ii) When the value of n = 27,

show (27, 2) //function called

The change of values during function execution are as follows:

Action	Value of n	Value of f
Function call	27	2
After Ist and final call	27	3

The value returned is 0.

(iii) The function show is a recursive function and it is finding whether the number entered is PRIME or NOT.

19. In the following, function strange is a part of some class. Assume that arguments x and y are greater than 0 when the function is invoked. Show the dry run/working. ***ISC 2007***

```
int strange(int x, int y)
{
    // Assuming x >= 0 and y > 0
    if(x >= y)
    {
        x = x - y;
        return strange(x, y);
    }
    else
    {
        return x;
    }
}
```

(i) What will function strange (20, 5) return?

(ii) What will function strange (15, 6) return?

(iii) In one line state, what the function strange (…) is doing?

Ans (i) Initially, x = 20, y = 5

x >= y	x	y	Return
True	x = x − y = 15	5	strange (15, 5);
True	x = x − y = 10	5	strange (10, 5);
True	x = x − y = 5	5	strange (5, 5);
True	x = x − y = 0	5	strange (0, 5);
False	0	5	0

The function strange (20, 5) will return 0.

(ii) Initially, x = 15, y = 6

x >= y	x	y	Return
True	9	6	strange (9, 6);
True	3	6	strange (3, 6);
False	3	6	3

The function strange (15, 6) will return 3.

(iii) The function strange is determining the remainder of x/y.

6/8/10 Marks Questions

1. Design a class DeciHex to accept a positive integer in decimal number system from the user and display its hexadecimal equivalent. ***ISC 2024***

Example 1 : Decimal number = 25 Hexadecimal equivalent = 19

Example 2 : Decimal number = 28 Hexadecimal equivalent = 1C

Some of the members of the class are given below

Class name	**DeciHex**
Data members/Instance variables	
num	stores the positive integer
hexa	string to store the hexadecimal equivalent of num
Methods/Member functions	
DeciHex()	constructor to initialise the data members with legal initial values
void getNum()	to accept a positive integer
void convert(int n)	to find the hexadecimal equivalent of the formal parameter 'n' using the recursive technique
Void display()	to display the decimal number and its hexadecimal equivalent by invoking the function convert()

Specify the class DeciHex giving details of the constructor(), void getNum(), void convert(int) and void display(). Define a main() function to create an object and call all the functions accordingly to enable the task.

Ans
```
import java.util.Scanner;
class DeciHex
{
    private int num;
    private String hex;
    public DeciHex()
    {
        num = 0;
        hex = "";
    }
    public void getNum()
    {
        Scanner scanner = new Scanner(System.in);
        System.out.print("Enter an integer: ");
        num = scanner.nextInt();
    }
    public void convert(int n)
    {
        if (n == 0)
        {
            hex = "0" + hex;
            return;
        }
        int remainder = n % 16;
        if (remainder <= 9)
        {
            hex = remainder + hex;
        } else
         {
```

```
          char ch = (char) ('A' + (remainder- 10));
          hex = ch + hex;
       }
       convert(n / 16);
    }
    public void display()
    {
       System.out.println("Integer number: " + num);
       if (num == 0)
       {
          hex = "0";
       } else
         {
          convert(Math.abs(num)); // Handle negative integers
         }
       System.out.println("Hexadecimal equivalent: " + hex);
    }
}
public class ISC2024ComputerScienceBoardsQ6
{
    public static void main(String[] args)
    {
       DeciHex deciHex = new DeciHex();
       deciHex.getNum();
       deciHex.display();
    }
}
```

Output:

Enter an integer: 25

Integer number: 25

Hexadecimal equivalent: 019

2. Design a class NumDude to check if a given number is a Dudeney number or not. (A Dudeney number is a positive integer that is a perfect cube, such that the sum of its digits is equal to the cube root of the number.) ***ISC 2023***

Example: $5832 = (5+8+3+2)^3 = (18)^3 = 5832$

Some of the members of the class are given below

Class name	**NumDude**
Data member/instance variable	
num	to store a positive integer number
Methods / Member functions	
NumDude()	default constructor to initialise the data member with legal initial value
void input()	to accept a positive integer number
int sumDigits(int x)	returns the sum of the digits of number 'x' using recursive technique
void isDude()	checks whether the given number is a Dudeney number by invoking the function sumDigits() and displays the result with an appropriate message

Specify the class NumDude giving details of the constructor(), void input(), int sumDigits(int) and void isDude(). Define a main() function to create an object and call the functions accordingly to enable the task.

Ans

```
import java.util.Scanner;
class NumDude
{
   int num;
   NumDude()
   {
      num=0;
   }
   void input()
   {
      Scanner sc = new Scanner(System.in);
      System.out.println("Enter a positive number: ");
      num = sc.nextInt();
   }
   int sumDigits(int x)
   {
      if (x==0)
      {
         return 0;
      }
      else
      {
         return x%10+sumDigits(x/10);
      }
   }
   void isDude()
   {
      int number;
      number = sumDigits(num);
      if (number*number*number == num)
      {
         System.out.println("Entered number is Dudeney Number");
      }
      else
      {
         System.out.println("Entered number is not Dudeney Number");
      }
   }
   public static void main(String args[])
   {
      NumDude n = new NumDude();
      n.input();
      n.isDude();
   }
}
```

3. Design a class Pronic to check if a given number is a pronic number or not [A number is said to be pronic if the product of two consecutive numbers is equal to the number] ***ISC SQP 2023***

Example: $0 = 0 \times 1$

$2 = 1 \times 2$

$6 = 2 \times 3$

$12 = 3 \times 4$

thus, 0, 2, 6, 12... are pronic numbers.

Some of the members of the class are given below:

Class name	Pronic
Data members/instance variables:	
num	to store a positive integer number
Methods / Member functions	
Pronic()	default constructor to initialize the data member with legal initial value
void acceptnum()	to accept a positive integer number
boolean ispronic(int v)	returns true if the number num is a pronic number, otherwise returns false using recursive technique
void check()	checks whether the given number is a pronic number by invoking the function ispronic() and displays the result with an appropriate message

Specify the class Pronic giving details of the constructor(), void acceptnum( ), boolean ispronic(int) and void check(). Define a main() function to create an object and call the functions accordingly to enable the task.

Ans

```
import java.util.Scanner;
public class Pronic
{
  private int num;
  public Pronic()
  {
    num = 0;
  }
  public void acceptnum()
  {
    Scanner sc = new Scanner(System.in);
    System.out.print("Enter a positive integer: ");
    num = sc.nextInt();
    while (num <= 0)
    {
      System.out.print("Invalid input! Please enter a positive integer: ");
      num = sc.nextInt();
    }
  }
  public boolean ispronic(int v)
  {
    if (v == 0)
    {
      return true;
    }
    else
    {
      int i = 1;
      while (i*(i+1) <= v)
      {
        if (i*(i+1) == v)
        {
          return true;
        }
        i++;
      }
```

```
            return false;
         }
      }
      public void check()
      {
         if (ispronic(num))
         {
            System.out.println(num + " is a pronic number.");
         }
         else
         {
            System.out.println(num + " is not a pronic number.");
         }
      }
      public static void main(String[] args)
      {
         Pronic pr = new Pronic();
         pr.acceptnum();
         pr.check();
      }
   }
```

4. A class CalSeries has been defined to calculate the sum of the series

$$sum = 1 + x + x^2 + x^3 + ... + x^n$$

Some of the members of the class are given below

Class name	**CalSeries**
Data members/instance variables	
x	integer to store the value of *x*
n	integer to store the value of *n*
sum	integer to store the sum of the series
Member functions/methods	
CalSeries()	default constructor
void input ()	to accept the values of *x* and *n*
int power (int p, int q)	return the power of *p* raised to *q* (p^q) using recursive technique
void cal()	calculates the sum of the series by invoking the method power () and displays the result with an appropriate message

Specify the class CalSeries, giving details of the constructor, void input (), int power (int, int) and void cal (). Define the main () function to create an object and call the member function accordingly to enable the task. ***ISC 2022 (Sem II)***

Ans

```
import java.io.*;
class CalSeries
{
   public int x, n ;
   public int sum ;
   public CalSeries()
   {
      x = n = 0;
   }
   public void input() throws IOException
   {
```

```
        BufferedReader br = new BufferedReader(new InputStreamReader
                                                        (System.in));
        x = Integer. parseInt(br.readLine()) ;
        n = Integer. parseInt(br.readLine());
    }
    int power (int p, int q)
    {
        if (q == 1)
            return p ;
        else
            return (p* power (p, q - 1));
    }
    void cal()
    {
        sum = 1;
        for(int i = 1; i<=n; i + +)
        {
            sum = sum + power(p, i);
        }
    }
    public static void main (String args[])
    {
        CalSeries a = new CalSeries();
        a.input();
        a.cal();
    }
}
```

5. Design a class Revno which reverses an integer number.
Example 94765 becomes 56749 on reversing the digits of the number.
Some of the members of the class are given below

Class name	**Revno**
Data member/instance variable	
num	to store the integer number
Member functions/methods	
Revno()	default constructor
void inputnum()	to accept the number
int reverse(int nn)	returns the reverse of a number by using recursive technique
void display()	displays the original number along with its reverse by invoking the method reverse ()

Specify the class Revno, giving details of the constructor, void inputnum (), int reverse (int) and void display (). Define the main () function to create an object and call the functions accordingly to enable the task. **ISC 2022 (Sem II)**

Ans

```
import java. io. * ;
public class Revno
{
    int num ;
    Revno ()
    {
```

```
        num = 0 ;
    }
    void inputnum () throws IOException
    {
        InputStreamReader IR = new InputStreamReader (System.in);
        BufferedReader br = new BufferedReader (IR);
        System.out.println("Enter number");
        num = Integer.parseInt(br.readLine ());
    }
    int reverse(int nn)
    {
        int rev = 0, r ;
        if (nn == 0)
        {
            return rev ;
        }
        if (nn > 0)
        {
            r = nn% 10 ;
            rev = rev* 10 + r ;
            nn = reverse(nn/10);
        }
        return rev ;
    }
    void display ()
    {
        System.out.println("Original number:" + num);
        System.out.println("Reverse number :");
        reverse (num) ;
        System.out.println(rev);
    }
    public static void main (String args [])
    {
        Revno n = new Revno();
        n.inputnum ();
        n.display ();
    }
}
```

6. Design a class Check which checks whether a word is a palindrome or not (Palindrome words are those which spell the same from either ends). ***ISC SQP 2022 (Sem II)***

Example: MADAM, LEVEL etc.

The details of the members of the class are given below:

Class name	Check
Data members/instance variables	
wrd	stores a word
len	to store the length of the word
Methods/Member functions	
Check()	default constructor
void acceptword()	to accept the word
boolean palindrome ()	checks and returns true if the word is a palindrome otherwise returns false
void display()	displays the word along with an appropriate message

Specify the class Check giving details of the constructor, void acceptword(), boolean palindrome() and void display(). Define the main() function to create an object and call the functions accordingly to enable the task.

Ans

```
import java.util.Scanner;
public class Check
{
   String wrd;
   int len;
   public Check()
   {
      wrd = "";
      len = 0;
   }
   public void acceptword()
   {
      Scanner sc = new Scanner(System.in);
      System.out.print("Enter a word: ");
      wrd = sc.nextLine();
      len = wrd.length();
   }
   public boolean palindrome()
   {
      for (int i = 0; i < len / 2; i++)
      {
         if (wrd.charAt(i) != wrd.charAt(len - 1 - i))
         {
            return false;
         }
      }
      return true;
   }
   public void display()
   {
      if (palindrome())
      {
         System.out.println(wrd + " is a palindrome.");
      }
      else
      {
         System.out.println(wrd + " is not a palindrome.");
      }
   }
   public static void main(String[] args)
   {
      Check ck = new Check();
      ck.acceptword();
      ck.display();
   }
}
```

7. A class Fibo has been defined to generate the Fibonacci series 0, 1, 1, 2, 3, 5, 8, 13,.... (Fibonacci series are those in which the sum of the previous two terms is equal to the next term).
Some of the members of the class are given below: ***ISC SQP 2022 (Sem II)***

Class name	Fibo
Data members/instance variables	
start	integer to store the start value
end	integer to store the end value
Member functions/methods	
Fibo()	default constructor
void read()	to accept the numbers
int fibo(int n)	return the nth term of a Fibonacci series using recursive technique
void display()	displays the Fibonacci series from start to end by invoking the function fibo()

Specify the class Fibo giving details of the Constructor, void read(), int fibo(int), and void display(). Define the main() function to create an object and call the functions accordingly to enable the task.

Ans
```
import java.util.Scanner;
public class Fibo
{
    private int start;
    private int end;
    public Fibo()
    {
        start = 0;
        end = 0;
    }
    public void read()
    {
        Scanner sc = new Scanner(System.in);
        System.out.print("Enter the start value: ");
        start = sc.nextInt();
        System.out.print("Enter the end value: ");
        end = sc.nextInt();
    }
    public int fibo(int n)
    {
        if (n == 0)
            return 0;
        else if (n == 1)
            return 1;
        else
            return fibo(n-1) + fibo(n-2);
    }
    public void display()
    {
        System.out.println("The Fibonacci series from " + start + " to " + end + " is:");
        for (int i = start; i <= end; i++)
        {
            System.out.print(fibo(i) + " ");
        }
        System.out.println();
    }
```

```
    public static void main(String[] args)
    {
        Fibo f = new Fibo();
        f.read();
        f.display();
    }
}
```

8. A class Gcd has been defined to find the Greatest Common Divisor of two integer numbers. Some of the members of the class are given below ***ISC SQP 2022 (Sem II)***

Class name	**Gcd**
Data members/instance variables	
num1	integer to store the first number
num2	integer to store the second number
Member functions/methods	
Gcd()	default constructor
void accept()	to accept the numbers
int gcd(int x,int y)	return the GCD of the two number x and y using recursive technique
void display()	displays the result with an appropriate message

Specify the class Gcd, giving details of the Constructor, void accept(), int gcd(int,int), and void display(). Define the main() function to create an object and call the functions accordingly to enable the task.

Ans

```
import java.util.*;
class Gcd
{
    int num1, num2;
    Gcd()
    {
        num1 = 0;
        num2 = 0;
    }
    void accept()
    {
        Scanner sc = new Scanner(System.in);
        System.out.print("Enter the first number: ");
        num1 = sc.nextInt();
        System.out.print("Enter the second number: ");
        num2 = sc.nextInt();
    }
    int gcd(int x, int y)
    {
        if (y == 0)
        {
            return x;
        }
        else
        {
            return gcd(y, x % y);
        }
    }
```

```
    void display()
    {
       int result = gcd(num1, num2);
       System.out.println("The GCD of " + num1 + " and " + num2 + " is " + result);
    }
    public static void main(String[] args)
    {
       Gcd gc = new Gcd();
       gc.accept();
       gc.display();
    }
}
```

9. Design a class Convert to find the date and the month from a given day number for a particular year.

e.g. If day number is 64 and the year is 2020, then the corresponding date would be March 4, 2020 i.e. (31 + 29 + 4 = 64)

Some of the members of the class are given below :

Class name	Convert
Data members/instance variables	
n	integer to store the day number
d	integer to store the day of the month (date)
m	integer to store the month
y	integer to store the year
Methods/Member functions	
Convert()	constructor to initialize the data members with legal initial values
void accept()	to accept the day number and the year
void day_to_date()	converts the day number to its corresponding date for a particular year and stores the date in 'd' and the month in 'm'
void display()	displays the month name, date and year

Specify the class Convert giving details of the constructor, void accept(), void day_to_date() and void display(). Define a main() function to create an object and call the functions accordingly to enable the task. ***ISC 2020***

Ans

```
import java.io.*;
class Convert
{
    int n, d, m, y;
    public Convert()
    {
        n = 0;
        d = 0;
        m = 0;
        y = 0;
    }
    public void accept()throws IOException
    {
        BufferedReader br = new BufferedReader(new InputStreamReader(System.in));
```

```
            System.out.print("Day number: ");
            d = Integer.parseInt(br.readLine());
            System.out.print("Year: ");
            y = Integer.parseInt(br.readLine());
            if((y % 100 == 0 && y % 400 == 0) || y % 4 == 0)
            {
                if(d > 366)
                {
                    System.out.println("Invalid day number!");
                    System.exit(0);
                }
            }
            else if(d > 365)
            {
                System.out.println("Invalid day number!");
                System.exit(0);
            }
        }
        public void day_to_date()
        {
            int a[] = {31, 28, 31, 30, 31, 30, 31, 31, 30, 31, 30, 31};
            if((y % 100 == 0 && y % 400 == 0) || y % 4 == 0)
                a[1] = 29;
                int sum = 0;
                if(d <= 31)
                    m = 0;
            else
            {
                while(d > 0)
                {
                    d -= a[m];
                    m++;
                    if(d <= a[m])
                        break;
                }
            }
        }
        public void display()
        {
            String months[] = {"January", "February", "March", "April", "May",
             "June", "July", "August", "September", "October", "November", "December"};
            System.out.println(months[m] + " " + d + ", " + y);
        }
        public static void main(String args[])throws IOException
        {
            Convert ob = new Convert();
            ob.accept();
            ob.day_to_date();
            ob.display();
        }
    }
```

10. A Special number is a number in which the sum of the factorial of its digits is equal to the number. Example: 145 (1! + 4! + 5! = 145). Thus, 145 is a Special number.

Design a class Special to check if the given number is a Special number or not. Some of the members of the class are given below: ***ISC SQP 2020***

Class name	Special
Data member/instance variable	
n	integer to store number
Member functions/methods	
Special()	default constructor
void read()	to accept the number
int factorial(int x)	return the factorial of a number using recursive technique
boolean isSpecial()	checks for the special number by invoking the function factorial() and returns true if Special, otherwise returns false
void display()	displays the result with an appropriate message

Specify the class Special, giving details of the Constructor, void read(), int factorial(int), boolean isSpecial() and void display(). Define the main() function to create an object and call the member function according to enable the task.

Ans

```
import java.util.Scanner;
class Special
{
   int n;
   public Special()
   {
      n = 0;
   }
   public void read()
   {
      Scanner sc = new Scanner(System.in);
      System.out.print("Enter a number: ");
      n = sc.nextInt();
   }
   public int factorial(int x)
   {
      if (x == 0 || x == 1)
      {
         return 1;
      }
      else
      {
         return x * factorial(x - 1);
      }
   }
   public boolean isSpecial()
   {
      int temp = n;
      int sum = 0;
      while (temp > 0)
      {
         int digit = temp % 10;
```

```
            sum += factorial(digit);
            temp /= 10;
        }
        return (sum == n);
    }
    public void display()
    {
        if (isSpecial())
        {
            System.out.println(n + " is a Special number.");
        }
        else
        {
            System.out.println(n + " is not a Special number.");
        }
    }
    public static void main(String[] args)
    {
        Special sp= new Special();
        sp.read();
        sp.display();
    }
}
```

11. Design a class ArmNum to check, if a given number is an Armstrong number or not. [A number is said to be Armstrong, if sum of its digits raised to the power of length of the number is equal to the number]

Example : $371 = 3^3 + 7^3 + 1^3$

$1634 = 1^4 + 6^4 + 3^4 + 4^4$

$54748 = 5^5 + 4^5 + 7^5 + 4^5 + 8^5$

Thus, 371, 1634 and 54748 are all examples of Armstrong numbers.
Some of the members of the class are given below:

Class name	ArmNum
Data members/instance variables	
n	to store the number
length	to store the length of the number
Methods/Member functions	
ArmNum (int nn)	parameterised constructor to initialise the data member *n* = nn
int sum_pow(int i)	returns the sum of each digit raised to the power of the length of the number using recursive technique. eg. 34 will return $3^2 + 4^2$ (as the length of the number is 2)
void isArmstrong ( )	checks whether the given number is an Armstrong number by invoking the function sum_pow() and displays the result with an appropriate message

Specify the class ArmNum giving details of the constructor, int sum_pow(int) and void isArmstrong(). Define a main() function to create an object and call the functions accordingly to enable the task. **ISC 2019**

Ans
```
import java.util.*;
class ArmNum
{
  int n;
  int length;
  ArmNum(int nn)
  {
    n = nn;
    length = String.valueOf(n).length();
  }
  int sum_pow(int i)
  {
    if (i == 0)
    {
      return 0;
    }
    else
    {
      int digit = i % 10;
      return (int) Math.pow(digit, length) + sum_pow(i / 10);
    }
  }
  void isArmstrong()
  {
    int sum = sum_pow(n);
    if (sum == n)
    {
      System.out.println(n + " is an Armstrong number");
    }
    else
    {
      System.out.println(n + " is not an Armstrong number");
    }
  }
  public static void main(String[] args)
  {
    Scanner sc = new Scanner(System.in);
    System.out.print("Enter the positive number: ");
    int num = sc.nextInt();
    ArmNum an = new ArmNum(num);
    an.isArmstrong();
  }
}
```

12. Design a class Perfect to check, if a given number is a perfect number or not. [A number is said to be perfect, if sum of the factors of the number excluding itself is equal to the original number]
Example : 6 = 1 + 2 + 3 (where 1, 2 and 3 are factors of 6, excluding itself)
Some of the members of the class are given below:

Class name	Perfect
Data member/instance variable	
num	to store the number

Methods/Member functions	
Perfect (int nn)	parameterised constructor to initialize the data member num=nn
int sum_of_factors(int i)	returns the sum of the factors of the number(num), excluding itself, using recursive technique
void check( )	checks whether the given number is perfect by invoking the function sum_of_factors( ) and displays the result with an appropriate message

Specify the class **Perfect** giving details of the constructor( ), int sum_of_factors(int) and void check( ). Define a main( ) function to create an object and call the functions accordingly to enable the task. ***ISC 2018***

Ans

```
import java.util.Scanner;
class Perfect
{
int num;
  Perfect(int nn)
  {
    num = nn;
  }
  int sum_of_factors(int i)
  {
    if (i <= 1)
      return 0;
    else if (num % i == 0)
      return i + sum_of_factors(i - 1);
    else
      return sum_of_factors(i - 1);
  }
  void check()
  {
    int sum = sum_of_factors(num - 1);
    if (sum == num)
    {
      System.out.println(num + " is a perfect number.");
    }
    else
    {
      System.out.println(num + " is not a perfect number.");
    }
  }
  public static void main(String[] args)
  {
    int n;
    Scanner s = new Scanner (System.in);
    System.out.println("Enter any integer you want to check");
    n= s.nextInt();
    Perfect obj = new Perfect (n);
    obj.check();
  }
}
```

13. A class Palin has been defined to check whether a positive number is a Palindrome number or not. The number 'N' is palindrome if the original number and its reverse are same. Some of the members of the class are given below:

Class Name	Palin
Data members/instance variables	
num	integer to store the number
revnum	integer to store the reverse of the number
Methods/Member functions	
Palin()	constructor to initialize data members with legal initial values
void accept()	to accept the number
int reverse(int y)	reverses the parameterized argument 'y' and stores it in 'revnum' using recursive technique
void check()	checks whether the number is a Palindrome by invoking the function reverse() and display the result with an appropriate message

Specify the class Palin giving details of the constructor, void accept(), int reverse(int) and void check(). Define the main() function to create an object and call the functions accordingly to enable the task. ***ISC 2017***

Ans

```
import java.io.*;
class Palin
{
    int num;
    int revnum;
    int reverse = 0;
    Palin()
    {
        num=0;
        revnum=0;
    }
    void accept() throws IOException
    {
        InputStreamReader IR=new InputStreamReader(System.in);
        BufferedReader br=new BufferedReader(IR);
        System.out.println("Enter the number");
        num=Integer.parseInt(br.readLine());
    }
    int sum=0,rem;
    int reverse(int y)
    {
        if(y>0)
        {
            rem=y%10;
            sum=sum*10+rem;
            reverse(y/10);
        }
        else
            return sum;
```

```
        return sum;
    }
    void check()
    {
        revnum=reverse(num);
        if(num==revnum)
            System.out.println(num+" is a palindrome number");
        else
            System.out.println(num+" is not a palindrome number");
    }
    public static void main(String args[]) throws IOException
    {
        Palin P = new Palin();
        P.accept();
        P.check();
    }
}
```

14. A disarium number is a number in which the sum of the digits to the power of their respective position is equal to the number itself.

Example : $135 = 1^1 + 3^2 + 5^3$

Hence, 135 is a disarium number.

Design a class Disarium to check if a given number is a disarium number or not. Some of the members of the class are given below:

Class name	Disarium
Data members/instance variables	
num	stores the number
size	stores the size of the number
Methods/member functions	
Disarium(int nn)	parameterised constructor to initialise the data members num = nn and size = 0
void countDigit()	counts the total number of digits and assigns it to size
int sumofDigits(int n, int p)	returns the sum of the digits of the number(n) to the power of their respective positions(p) using recursive technique
void check()	checks whether the number is a disarium number and displays the result with an appropriate message

Specify the class Disarium giving the details of the constructor, void countDigit(), int sumofDigits(int, int) and void check(). Define the main() function to create an object and call the functions according to enable the task. *ISC 2016*

Ans

```
import java.io.*;
class Disarium
{
        int num;
        int size;
        public Disarium(int nn)
        {
            num = nn;
            size = 0 ;
        }
```

```
    public void countDigit()
    {
        for(int i = num; i ! = 0; i /= 10)
            size++;
    }
    public int sumofDigits(int n, int p)
    {
        if(p = = 1)
                return n;
        return n*sumofDigits(n, - -p);
    }
    public void check()
    {
        int sum = 0 ;
        int n = num;
        for(int i = size; i >= 1; i--)
        {
                sum + = sumofDigits(n % 10, i);
                n/= 10;
        }
        if(sum == num)
                System.out.println(num+'' is a Disarium Number.'');
        else
                System.out.println(num+'' is not a Disarium Number.'');
    }
    public static void main(String args[])throws IOException
    {
        InputStreamReader isr = new InputStreamReader (System.in);
        BufferedReader br = new BufferedReader(isr);
        System.out.print(''Enter the number:'');
        int n = Integer.parseInt(br.readLine());
        Disarium obj = new Disarium(n);
        obj.countDigit();
        obj.check();
    }
}
```

15. A class Merger concatenates two positive integers that are greater than 0 and produces a new merged integer.

e.g. If the first number is 23 and the second is 764, then the concatenated number will be 23764.

Some of the members of the class are given below:

Class name	Merger
Data members/Instance variables	
n1	long integer to store first number
n2	long integer to store second number
mergNum	long integer to store the merged number
Member functions/Methods	
Merger()	constructor to initialise the data members
void readNum()	to accept the values of the data members n1 and n2
void joinNum()	to concatenate the numbers n1 and n2 and store it in mergNum
void show()	to display the original numbers and the merged number with appropriate messages

Specify the class Merger giving the details of the constructor, void readNum(), void joinNum() and void show(). Define the main() function to create an object and call the functions accordingly to enable the task. **ISC 2015**

Ans
```
import java.io.*;
public class Merger
{
    long n1,n2,mergNum;
    Merger()
    {
       n1=0;
       n2=0;
       mergNum=0;
    }
    void readNum() throws IOException
    {
       InputStreamReader IR=new InputStreamReader(System.in);
       BufferedReader br=new BufferedReader(IR);
       System.out.println("Enter first number");
       n1=Long.parseLong(br.readLine());
       System.out.println("Enter second number");
       n2=Long.parseLong(br.readLine());
    }
    void joinNum()
    {
       mergNum = Long.parseLong(Long.toString(n1) + Long.toString(n2));
    }
    void show()
    {
       System.out.println("First number is "+n1);
       System.out.println("Second number is "+n2);
       System.out.println("Concatenated number will be "+mergNum);
    }
    public static void main(String args[]) throws IOException
    {
       Merger M=new Merger();
       M.readNum();
       M.joinNum();
       M.show();
    }
}
```

16. A class SeriesSum is designed to calculate the sum of the following series

$$\text{Sum} = \frac{x^2}{1!} + \frac{x^4}{3!} + \frac{x^6}{5!} + \cdots \frac{x^n}{(n-1)!}$$

Some of the members of the class are given below:

Class Name	**SeriesSum**
Data members/instance variables	
x	to store an integer number
n	to store number of terms
sum	double variable to store the sum of the series

Member functions	
SeriesSum (int xx, int nn)	constructor to assign $x = xx$ and $n = nn$
double findfact (int m)	to return the factorial of m using recursive technique.
double findpower (int x, int y)	to return x raised to the power of y using recursive technique.
void calculate ( )	to calculate the sum of the series by invoking the recursive functions respectively.
void display ( )	to display the sum of the series

Specify the class SeriesSum, giving details of the constructor(int, int), double findfact(int), double findpower(int, int), void calculate() and void display(). Define the main() function to create an object and call the functions accordingly to enable the task. ***ISC 2014***

Ans

```
import java.io.*;                          //class library of Java
class SeriesSum                            //class name SeriesSum
{
    public int x, n;                       //variable declaration
    public double sum;
    public SeriesSum(int xx, int nn)       //parameterized constructor
    {
        x = xx;
        n = nn;
    }
    public double findfact(int m)          //to return the factorial of m
    {
        if(m <= 1)
        {
            return 1;
        }
        else
        {
            return(m * findfact(m - 1));
        }
    }
    double findpower(int x, int y) //to return x raised to the power of y
    {
        if(y == 1)
            return x;
        else
            return(x * findpower(x, y - 1));
    }
    public void calculate() //to calculate the sum
    {
        sum = 0;
        for(int i = 2; i<= n; i = i + 2)
        {
            sum = sum + (findpower(x, i)/findfact(i - 1));
        }
    }
    void display() //to display the sum of series
    {
        System.out.println("Sum of series : " +sum);
    }
    public static void main(String args[]) throws IOException
    {
```

```
            BufferedReader br = new BufferedReader(new InputStreamReader(System.in));
            System.out.println("Enter the value of x :");
            int x = Integer.parseInt(br.readLine());
            System.out.println("Enter the value of n :");
            int n = Integer.parseInt(br.readLine());
            SeriesSum ob = new SeriesSum(x, n);
            ob.calculate();
            ob.display();
        }
    }
```

17. An emirp number is a number which is prime backwards and forwards. Example : 13 and 31 are both prime numbers. Thus, 13 is an emirp number. Design a class Emirp to check if a given number is Emirp number or not.

Some of the members of the class are given below:

Class name	**Emirp**
Data members/instance variables	
n	store the number
rev	store the reverse of the number
f	store the divisor
Member functions/methods	
Emirp (int nn)	to assign n = nn, rev = 0 and f = 2
int isprime (int x)	check if the number is prime using the recursive technique and return 1 if prime otherwise return 0.
void isEmirp ( )	reverse the given number and check if both the original number and the reverse number are prime, by invoking the function isprime (int) and display the result with an appropriate message.

Specify the class Emirp giving details of the constructor(int), int isprime(int) and void isEmirp(). Define the main() function to create an object and call the methods to check for Emirp number.

ISC 2013

Ans

```
import java.io.*;
class Emirp                             //class Emirp
{
    int n, rev, f;
    Emirp(int nn)                       //constructor Emirp
    {
        n = nn;
        rev = 0;
        f = 2;
    }
    public int isprime(int x)       //method
    {
        for(int  i = 2; i <= x-1; i++)
        {
            if(x%i == 0)
            {
                return 0;
            }
        }
```

```
            return 1;
        }
        void isEmirp()                      //method
        {
            int C=n, rev=0; int R;
            while(C!=0)
            {
                R = C%10;
                rev = rev * 10 + R;
                C = C/10;
            }
            int a = isprime(n);
            int b = isprime(rev);
            if(a == 1 && b == 1)
                System.out.println(n+" number is Emirp");
            else
                System.out.println(n+" number is not Emirp");
        }
        public static void main(String args[]) throws IOException
        {
            System.out.println("Enter value of n");
            BufferedReader br = new BufferedReader(new InputStreamReader(System.in));
            int n = Integer.parseInt(br.readLine());
            Emirp e = new Emirp(n);
            e.isEmirp();
        }
    }
```

18. A Happy number is a number in which the eventual sum of the square of the digits of the number is equal to 1.

e.g. $28 = (2)^2 + (8)^2 = 4 + 64 = 68$

$68 = (6)^2 + (8)^2 = 36 + 64 = 100$

$100 = (1)^2 + (0)^2 + (0)^2 = 1 + 0 + 0 = 1$

Hence, 28 is a happy number.

e.g. $12 = (1)^2 + (2)^2 = 1 + 4 = 5$

Hence, 12 is not a happy number.

Design a class Happy to check if a given number is a happy number.

Some of the members of the class are given below:

Class name	Happy
Data member/instance variable	
n	store the numbers
Member functions	
Happy ( )	constructor to assign 0 to n
void getnum (int nn)	to assign the parameter value to the number n = nn
int sum_sq_digits (int x)	returns the sum of the square of the digits of the number x, using the recursive technique.
void ishappy( )	checks if the given number is a happy number by calling the function sum_sq_digits(int) and displays an appropriate message.

Specify the class Happy giving details of the constructor, void getnum(int), int sum_sq_digits(int) and void ishappy(). Also define a main() function to create an object and call the methods to check for happy number. ***ISC 2012***

Ans

```
import java.io.*;
class Happy
{
    int n;
    Happy()                              //constructor
    {
        n = 0;
    }
    void getnum(int nn)                  //method
    {
        n = nn;
    }
    int sum_sq_digits(int x)             //method
    {
        if(x >= 0 && x <= 9)
            return x * x;
        else
            return(sum_sq_digits(x%10) + sum_sq_digits(x/10));
    }
    void ishappy()                       //method
    {
        int a = 0, num = 0;
        a = sum_ sq_ digits(n);
        while(a>9)
        {
            num = sum_sq_digits(a);
            a = num;
        }
        if(num == 1)
            System.out.println("Happy no.");
        else
            System.out.println("Not a Happy no.");
    }
    public static void main(String args[]) throws IOException
    {
        System.out.println("Enter a number");
        BufferedReader br=new BufferedReader(new InputStreamReader(System.in));
        int n = Integer.parseInt(br.readLine());
        Happy ob = new Happy();  //object creation
        ob.getnum(n);
        ob.ishappy();
    }
}
```

19. A class DeciOct has been defined to convert a decimal number into its equivalent octal number. Some of the members of the class are given below:

Class name	DeciOct
Data members/instance variables	
n	stores the decimal number
oct	stores the octal equivalent number

Class name	DeciOct
Member functions	
DeciOct ( )	constructor to initialise the data members n = 0, oct = 0
void getnum (int nn)	assign nn to n
void deci_oct ( )	calculates the octal equivalent of 'n' and stores it in oct using the recursive technique.
void show ( )	displays the decimal number 'n', calls the function deci_oct( ) and displays its octal equivalent.

Specify the class DeciOct, giving details of the constructor, void getnum(int), void deci_oct() and void show(). Also define a main() function to create an object and call the functions accordingly to enable the task. ***ISC 2011***

Ans

```
class DeciOct
{
    int n, oct;
    public DeciOct()
    {
        n = oct = 0;
    }
    void getnum(int nn)
    {
        n = nn;
    }
    void deci_oct()
    {
        int x = n;
        if(n > 8)
        {
            n = n/8;
            deci_oct();
        }
        oct = oct * 10 + x%8;
    }
    void show()
    {
        System.out.println("Number "+n);
        deci_oct();
        System.out.println("Its octal equivalent "+oct);
    }
    public static void main(String args[])
    {
        DeciOct d1 = new DeciOct();
        d1.getnum(25);
        d1.show();
    }
}
```

20. The coordinates of a point *P* on a two dimensional plane can be represented by *P*(*x*, *y*) with *x* as the *x*-coordinate and *y* as the *y*-coordinate. The coordinates of mid-point of two points *P*1(*x*1, *y*1) and *P*2(*x*2, *y*2) can be calculated as *P*(*x*, *y*) where:

$$x = \frac{x1 + x2}{2}, y = \frac{y1 + y2}{2}$$

Design a class Point with the following details:

Class name	Point
Data Members/instance variables	
x	stores the x-coordinate
y	stores the y-coordinate
Member functions/methods	
Point( )	constructor to initialise $x = 0$, $y = 0$
void readpoint( )	accepts the coordinates x and y of a point.
Point midpoint (Point A, Point B)	calculates and returns the mid-point of the two points A and B
void displaypoint( )	displays the coordinates of a point.

Specify the class Point giving details of the constructor, member functions void readpoint( ), Point midpoint(Point, Point) and void displaypoint( ) alongwith the main( ) function to create an object and call the functions accordingly to calculate the mid-point between any two given points.

ISC 2010

Ans

```
import java.io.*;
class Point
{
    double x,y;
    Point()
    {
        x=y=0;
    }
    void readpoint() throws IOException
    {
        BufferedReader br=new BufferedReader(new InputStreamReader(System.in));
        System.out.println("Enter coordinates");
        x=Double.parseDouble(br.readLine());
        y=Double.parseDouble(br.readLine());
    }
    Point midpoint(Point A, Point B)
    {
        Point C=new Point();
        C.x=(A.x+B.x)/2;
        C.y=(A.y+B.y)/2;
        return C;
    }
    void displaypoint()
    {
        System.out.println(x+","+y);
    }
    public static void main(String args[]) throws IOException
    {
        Point P1=new Point();
        Point P2=new Point();
        Point P3=new Point();
        P1.readpoint();
        P2.readpoint();
```

```
            P3=P3.midpoint(P1,P2);
            P3.displaypoint();
        }
    }
```

21. A magic number is a number in which the eventual sum of digits of the number is equal to 1.

e.g. 172 = 1 + 7 + 2 = 10

10 = 1 + 0 = 1

Then, 172 is a magic number.

Design a class Magic to check if a given number is a magic number. Some of the members of the class are given below

Class name	Magic
Data member/instance variable	
n	stores the number
Member functions	
Magic ( )	constructor to assign 0 to n
void getnum (int nn)	to assign the parameter value to the number, n = nn
int Sum_of_digits (int)	returns the sum of the digits of a number.
void ismagic ( )	checks if the given number is a magic number by calling the function Sum_of_digits(int) and displays appropriate message.

Specify the class Magic giving the details of the constructor, void getnum(int), int Sum_of_digits(int) and void ismagic(). You need not to write the main function. **ISC 2009**

Ans

```
class Magic
{
    int n;
    Magic()                         //Constructor
    {
        n = 0;
    }
    void getnum(int nn)             //Method getnum
    {
        n = nn;
    }
    int Sum_of_digits(int x)        //Method Sum_of_digits
    {
        int s = 0;
        while(x != 0)
        {
            s = s + x%10;
            x = x/10;
        }
        return s;
    }
    void ismagic()                  //Method ismagic
    {
        while(n > 9)
        {
```

```
            int sum = Sum_of_digits(n);
            n = sum;
        }
        if(n == 1)
        {
            System.out.println("The number is Magic Number");
        }
        else
        {
            System.out.println("The number is not Magic Number");
        }
    }
}
```

22. A special number is a number in which the sum of the factorial of each digit is equal to the number itself.

e.g. $145 = 1! + 4! + 5! = 1 + 24 + 120$

Design a class Special to check, if a given number is a special number.

Some of the members of the class are given below

Class name	**Special**
Data member/instance variable	
n	Integer
Member functions	
Special ( )	constructor to assign 0 to n
Special (int)	parameterized constructor to assign a value to 'n'
void sum ( )	calculate and display the sum of the first and the last digit of 'n'
void isSpecial ( )	check and display if the number 'n' is a special number.

Specify the class Special giving the details of the constructors, void sum() and void isSpecial(). You need not to write the main function. ***ISC 2008***

Ans

```
class Special
{
    int n;
    Special()                        //constructor without arguments
    {
        n = 0;
    }
    Special(int x)                   //constructor with argument
    {
        n = x;
    }
    void sum()                       //method sum
    {
        int n1 = n;
        int rev = 0;
        if(n > 9)                    //if n is more than single digit
        {
            while(n1 != 0)
            {
```

```
                rev = rev * 10 + n1% 10;
                n1 = n1/10;
            }
            int sum = n%10 + rev%10;
            System.out.println("The sum of First and Last Digit of n is "+sum);
        }
        else
        {
            System.out.println("The number "+ n +" is a Single Digit");
        }
    }
    void isSpecial()                //Method isSpecial
    {
        int n1 = n;
        int sum = 0;
        while(n1 != 0)
        {
            int f = 1;
            for(int i = 1; i <= n1%10; i++)
            {
                f = f * i;
            }
            sum = sum + f;
            n1 = n1/10;
        }
        if(sum==n)
        {
            System.out.println(n+" is a Special Number");
        }
        else
        {
            System.out.println(n+" is not a Special Number");
        }
    }
}
```

23. A class Hifact has been defined to find the HCF of two numbers using the recursive technique. This HCF is used to find the LCM of the two numbers. Some members of the class are given below:

Class name	**Hifact**
Data members/Instance variables	
a, b, hcf, lcm	integers
Member functions/methods	
Hifact ( )	constructor to assign initial values to the data members
void getdata ( )	to input values of a and b
void change ( )	to swap a and b if a > b
int rechcf (int, int)	to find hcf using the recursive technique
int fn_lcm (int, int, int)	to find lcm using a, b and hcf
void result ( )	to invoke rechcf ( ) and fn_lcm ( ) and to print lcm, hcf of the two numbers a and b

Specify the class Hifact giving the details of constructor, void getdata(), void change(), int rechcf() and int fn_lcm(). Write the main function and find the hcf and lcm of any two integers, a and b.

ISC 2006

Ans

```
import java.io.*;
class Hifact
{
    int a, b, hcf, lcm;
    Hifact()
    {
        a = 0;
        b = 0;
        hcf = 0;
        lcm = 0;
    }
    void getdata() throws IOException
    {
        InputStreamReader in = new InputStreamReader(System.in);
        BufferedReader br = new BufferedReader(in);
        System.out.println("Enter any two numbers");
        a = Integer.parseInt(br.readLine ());
        b = Integer.parseInt(br.readLine());
    }
    void change()
    {
        int t;
        if(a > b)
        {
            t = a;
            a = b;
            b = t;
        }
    }
    int rechcf(int a, int b)
    {
        if(b!=0)
            return rechcf(b, a%b);
        else
            return a;
    }
    int fn_lcm(int a, int b, int h)
    {
        int l;
        l=(a*b)/h;
        return l;
    }
    void result()
    {
        hcf=rechcf(a,b);
        lcm=fn_lcm(a,b,hcf);
```

```
        System.out.println("HCF of these numbers is "+hcf);
        System.out.println("LCM of these numbers is "+lcm);
    }
    public static void main(String args[]) throws IOException
    {
        Hifact hf = new Hifact();
        hf.getdata();
        hf.change();
        hf.result();
    }
}
```

24. A ticket at a ticket selling booth at a fair is priced at ₹ 2.50/-. The booth keeps track of the total number of people who have visited the booth, the number of people who have actually purchased a ticket and the total amount of money collected. Design a class called Ticbooth, which includes the following members:

Class name	Ticbooth
Data members	
no_people	number of people who have visited the booth.
amount	total amount of money collected.
Member functions	
void initial( )	to assign initial values to data members.
void notsold( )	increment total number of people only visiting the booth and not purchasing a ticket.
void sold( )	increment total number of people purchasing a ticket and the amount collected when a ticket is sold.
void disp_totals ( )	to display the total number of people visiting the booth (the total number of people purchasing the tickets as well as those not purchasing a ticket).
void disp_ticket ( )	to display the total number of ticket sold and the amount collected.

Specify the class Ticbooth giving details of the functions void initial(), void sold(), void notsold(), void disp_totals() and void disp_ticket(). The main() function need not to be written. ***ISC 2006***

Ans
```
class Ticbooth                              //class Ticbooth
{
    int no_people;
    float amount;
    void initial()                          //method initial
    {
        no_people = 0;
        amount = 0;
    }
    void notsold()                          //method notsold()
    {
        no_people++;
    }
    void sold()                             //method sold
    {
        no_people++;
        amount = (float) (amount+2.50);
    }
```

```
    void disp_totals()              //method disp_total()
    {
        System.out.println("no. of peoples visited the booth "+ no_people);
    }
    void disp_ticket()                //method disp_ticket
    {
        System.out.println("amount collected " +amount);
        System.out.println("total no. of tickets sold " +amount/2.50);
    }
}
```

25. A class Telcall calculates the monthly phone bill of a consumer. Some of the members of the class are given below

Class name	**Telcall**	
Data members/instance variables		
phno	phone number	
name	name of consumer	
n	number of calls made	
amt	bill amount	
Member functions/methods		
Telcall (String, String, int)	parameterized constructor to assign values to data members.	
void compute( )	to calculate the phone bill amount based on the slabs given below.	
	Number of calls	**Rate**
	1-100	Rs. 500/-rental charge only
	101-200	Rs. 1.00/-per call rental charge
	201-300	Rs. 1.20/-per call rental charge
	above 300	Rs. 1.50/-per call rental charge
void dispdata( )	to display the details in the specified format.	

The calculations need to be done as per the slabs.

Specify the class Telcall, giving the details of the constructor, void compute( ) and void dispdata( ). In the main function, create an object of type Telcall and display the phone bill in the following format:

Phone Number	Name	Total calls	Amount
XXXXXXXX	XXX	XXXXX	XXXX

ISC 2006

Ans.
```
class Telcall
{
  String phno,name;
  int n;
  double amt;
  Telcall(String ph, String na, int nc)
  {
      phno=ph;
      name=na;
      n=nc;
      amt=0.00;
  }
  void compute()
  {
```

```
            if(n<=100)
            {
                amt=500.0;
            }
            if(n>100  &&  n<=200)
            {
                amt=(n-100)*1+500;
            }
            if(n>200 && n<=300)
            {
                amt=(500+100*1+(n-200)*1.2);
            }
            if(n>300)
            {
                amt=(500+100*1+100*1.2+(n-300)*1.5);
            }
        }
        void dispdata()
        {
            System.out.println("Phone Number\tName\t\tTotal calls\tAmount");
            System.out.println(phno+"\t"+name+"\t"+n+"\t\t"+amt);
        }
        public static void main(String args[])
        {
            Telcall t=new Telcall("9897205588","Amit Sharma",250);
            t.compute();
            t.dispdata();
        }
    }
```

26. A class quad contains the following data members and member functions to find the roots of quadratic equation:

Class name	quad
Data members	a, b, c (float), x1, x2 (float)
Member functions/methods	
quad (float, float, float)	constructor to assign values to the data members.
float discriminant ( )	to return the discriminant [$b^2 - 4ac$]
void root_equal ( )	to display the root if both roots are equal.
void imag ( )	to display the roots, if roots are imaginary.
void root_real ( )	to display the two real, unequal roots.
void root ( )	to call other appropriate functions to find the solution of the problem.

If $ax^2 + bx + c = 0$ is the quadratic equation, then if $b^2 - 4ac > 0$ roots are real, unequal

Where, $x1 = \dfrac{-b + \sqrt{b^2 - 4ac}}{2a} \Rightarrow x2 = \dfrac{-b - \sqrt{b^2 - 4ac}}{2a}$

If $b^2 - 4ac = 0$ roots are real, equal

$x1 = x2 = -b/2a$

If $b^2 - 4ac < 0$ roots are imaginary.

Specify the class quad giving the details of the functions

```
quad(float, float, float)
float discriminant()
void root_equal()
void root_real()
void root()
```

You may assume that other functions are written for you. You need not to write the main function.

ISC 2005

Ans

```
class quad
{
    float a, b, c, x1, x2, d;
    quad(float x, float y, float z)          //constructor with argument
    {
        a = x; b = y; c = z;
    }
    float discriminant()                     //method discriminant
    {
        return(b*b)-(4*a*c);
    }
    void root_equal()                        //method root_equal
    {
        x1 = -b/(2 * a);
        x2 = -b/(2 * a);
        System.out.println(x1 + " " + x2);
    }
    void root_real()                         //method root_real
    {
        x1 = (float)((-b + Math.sqrt(d))/2 * a);
        x2 = (float)((-b - Math.sqrt(d))/2 * a);
        System.out.println(x1 + " " + x2);
    }
    void root()                              //method root
    {
        d = discriminant();
        if(d == 0)
            root_equal();
        if(d > 0)
            root_real();
        if(d < 0)
            System.out.println("Imaginary");
    }
}
```

27. $\text{Sum} = 1 + \frac{x}{1!} + \frac{x^3}{2!} + \frac{x^5}{3!} + \cdots + \frac{x^{2n-1}}{n!}$

A class sumseries has been defined to calculate sum of the above series. Some of the members of the class are given below:

Class name	sumseries
Data members/instance variables	x, n (integer), sum (double)
Member functions/methods	
sumseries ( )	constructor
int factorial (int n)	calculates and returns factorial of n where $n! = 1 \times 2 \times 3 \times \ldots \times n$
double term (int p, int q)	calculates and return the value of p/q! by making use of factorial (int)
void accept ( )	inputs the value of data member x, n
void displaysum ( )	displays the value of data member sum.
double calsum ( )	calculates the sum of the given series using the appropriate data and other member function.

(i) Specify the class sumseries giving details of constructor, int factorial(int), double term(int, int), void displaysum(). You may assume that other member functions are written for you. You do not need to write the main function.

(ii) What do you need to take while designing double term (int, int)? ***ISC 2005***

Ans (i)
```
class sumseries
{
    int x, n;
    double sum;
    sumseries( )                     //constructor sumseries
    {
        x = 0;
        n = 0;
        sum = 0.0;
    }
    int factorial(int n)             //method factorial
    {
        if(n == 1)
            return(n);
        else
            return(n * factorial(n - 1));
    }
    double term(int p, int q)        //method term
    {
        double d;
        double f;
        if(q==0)
        {
            System.out.println("Division by zero");
```

```
            return 0;
        }
        else
        {
            f = factorial(q);
            d = p/f;
        }
        return(d);
    }
    void displaysum()                       //method displaysum
    {
        System.out.println("sum is" +sum);
    }
}
```

(ii) When we design double term (int, int), care should be taken that a division operation should not be done by zero. Therefore, first we should check whether the divisor is zero. If so, then we should exit the program.

28. A class recursion has been defined to find the fibonacci series upto a limit.
Some of the members of the class are given below:

Class name	recursion
Data members	
a, b, c, limit	all integers
Member functions/methods	
recursion ( )	constructor to assign a, b, c with the appropriate values.
void input ( )	to accept the limit of the series.
int fib (int n)	to return the nth fibonacci term using recursive technique.
void generate_fibseries ( )	to generate fibonacci series upto the given limit.

Specify the class recursion, giving the details of the constructor, int fib(int), void generate_fibseries(). You may assume other functions are written for you and you need not write the main function.
ISC 2005

Ans

```
class recursion
{
    int a, b, c, limit;
    public recursion()                      //constructor recursion
    {
        a = 0;
        b = 1;
        c = 1;
    }
    int fib(int n)                          //method fib
    {
        if(n == 1)
            return 0;
        else if(n == 2)
            return 1;
```

```
            else
                return(fib(n- 1)+ fib(n- 2));
        }
        void generate_fibseries()           //method generate_fibseries
        {
            int x = 1;
            while(x <= limit)
            {
                c = fib(x);
                System.out.println(c);
                x++;
            }
        }
    }
```

Case Based Questions

1. With reference to the following program code, answer the questions that follow: ***ISC 2022 (Sem I)***

```
void trick (int a, int b)
{ int p=1;
  for (int j=1; j<=b;j++,p*=a) ;
  System.out.println (p);
}
```

(i) What will be the output of the method trick() when the values of a=3 and b=4?

(a) 12 (b) 127

(c) 81 (d) 64

(ii) What is the method trick() computing?

(a) Factorial of a number

(b) Product of the number

(c) Power of a number raised to a number

(d) HCF of the two numbers

Ans (i) (c) trick (3, 4) , p = 1

j	Condition j < = b	p * = a
1	1 < = 4 (True)	p = 1 * 3 = 3
2	2 < = 4 (True)	p = 3 * 3 = 9
3	3 < = 4 (True)	p = 9 * 3 = 27
4	4 < = 4 (True)	p = 27 * 3 = 81
5	5 < = 4 (True)	

Output 81

(ii) (c) Method trick ( ) computes power of a number raised to a number.

2. With reference to the following program code, answer the questions that follow ***ISC 2022 (Sem I)***

```
void funny (int p, int m, int n)
{
  for (int i=p;i<=p;i++)
  {
    switch (i)
    {
      case 1: m+=10;
      case 2: n-=1; break;
```

```
            case 3: m+=n; n+=3; break;
            default: m+=2;
        }
        System.out.println (m+ " : "+n);
    }
}
```

(i) What will be the output of the method funny() when the values of p=1, m=12 and n=6?

(a) 20:4 (b) 22:5 (c) Error (d) 24:7

(ii) What is the keyword used in Java to avoid a fall through condition?

(a) case (b) continue (c) switch (d) break

Ans (i) (b) funny (1, 12, 6)

Iteration 1 for (i = 1; i <= 1; i ++) True

switch (1)

m = m + 10 = 12 + 10 = 22

n = n − 1 = 6 − 1 = 5

print 22 : 5

Iteration 2 for (i = 2; i <= 1; i ++) False

Output 22 : 5

(ii) (d) break keyword is used to avoid a fall through condition in Java.

3. With reference to the following program code, answer the questions that follow: ***ISC 2022 (Sem I)***

```
void play (int n)
{
   int s=0;
   while (n!=0)
   {
      s=s*10+n-(n/10) *10;
      n/=10;
   }
   System.out.println (s);
}
```

(i) What will be the output of the method play() when the value of n=6957?

(a) 27 (b) 695

(c) 5679 (d) 7596

(ii) What is the method play() performing?

(a) Arranging the digits in ascending order (b) Reversing the number

(c) Extracting the first 3 digits (d) Sum of the digits

Ans (i) (d) play (6957)

Iteration 1 s = 0

```
while (6957 ! = 0) True
    s = s * 10 + n - (n/10) * 10
    s = 0 * 10 + 6957 - (6957/10) * 10
    s = 6957 - 695 * 10 = 6957 - 6950 = 7
    n = n/10 = 6957/10 = 695
```

Iteration 2 s = 7

```
while (695 ! = 0) True
    s = s * 10 + n - (n/10) * 10
      = 7 * 10 + 695 - (695/10) * 10
      = 70 + 695 - 69 * 10
      = 70 + 695- 690 = 75
    n = n/10 = 695/10 = 69
```

Iteration 3
```
s = 75
while (69 ! = 0) True
    s = s * 10 + n − (n/10) * 10
      = 75 * 10 + 69 − (69/10) * 10
      = 750 + 69 −  6 * 10
      = 750 + 69 − 60
    s = 759
    n = n/10 = 69/10 = 6
```
Iteration 4
```
while (6! = 0) True
s = s * 10 + n − (n/10) * 10
  = 759 * 10 + 6 − (6/10) * 10
s = 7590 + 6 − 0 = 7596
n = 6/10 = 0
```
Iteration 5
```
while (0 ! = 0) False
```
Output will be 7596

(ii) (b) Method play ( ) performs reversing the number.

4. With reference to the program code given below, answer the questions that follow:

ISC SQP 2022 (Sem I)

```
void fun(int n)
{
  int i,f;
  for( i=1,f=1;i<=n;i++,f*=i);
  System.out.print(f);
}
```

(i) What is the output of the method fun() when the value of n=4?

(a) 24
(b) 72
(c) 120
(d) ERROR

(ii) What is the method fun() performing?

(a) Checking for prime numbers
(b) Product of odd numbers
(c) Factors of a number
(d) Finding the factorial

Ans fun (4)

i	f	Condition i < = n	f * = i
1	1	1 < = 4 (True)	f = 1 * 1 = 1
2	1	2 < = 4 (True)	f = 2 * 1 = 2
3	2	3 < = 4 (True)	f = 3 * 2 = 6
4	6	4 < = 4 (True)	f = 4 * 6 = 24
5	24	5 < = 4 (False)	

(i) (a) Output
24

(ii) (d) Method fun ( ) performs to find the factorial.

5. With reference to the program code given below, answer the questions that follow

ISC SQP 2022 (Sem I)

```
int test(int n)
{
  if(n==1) return 0;
    for (int i=2;i<=(int) (Math.sqrt(n));i++)
  if( n%i==0)
    return 0;
  return 1;
}
```

(i) What will the method test() return when the value of n=9?

(a) 1 (b) true (c) 0 (d) Error

(ii) What is the method test() performing?

(a) Prime number/Composite number (b) Armstrong number

(c) Palindrome number (d) Perfect number

Ans test (9)

Iteration 1 if (9 = = 1) False

for (i = 2; i < 3; i + +) True

if (9% 2 = = 0) False

return 1

Iteration 2 for (i = 3; i <= 3; i ++) True

if (9% 3 = = 0) True

return 0

Iteration 3 for (i = 4; i < = 3; i ++) False

(i) (c) Output is 0

(ii) (a) Method test ( ) performs prime number/composite number.

6. With reference to the program code given below, answer the questions that follow

ISC SQP 2022 (Sem I)

```
int solve(int a, int b)
{
   int i,l=0;
   for(i=1;i<=a*b;i++)
   {
      if(i%a==0&& i%b==0)
      {
         l-i; break;
      }
   }
   return l;
}
```

(i) What will be the output of the method solve() when the value of a=8 and b=12?

(a) 4 (b) 96 (c) 0 (d) 24

(ii) What is the method solve() performing?

(a) HCF of 'a' and 'b' (b) Prime Factors of 'a' and 'b'

(c) LCM of 'a' and 'b' (d) None of these

Ans (i) (d) For value i = 24, both conditions i% a = = 0 and i % b = = 0 are true. So, output will be 24.

(ii) (c) Method solve ( ) computes the LCM of a and b.

7. The following program code checks if the positive integer 'N' is a palindrome number by returning true or false. There are some places in the code marked as ?1?, ?2?, ?3?, ?4? and ?5? which are to be replaced by a statement/expression so that the code works properly. ***ISC SQP 2022 (Sem I)***

```
boolean Palindrome (int N)
{
   int rev =?1?;
   int num =N;
   while (num>0)
   {
      int f= num/10;
      int s = ?2?;
      int digit = num-?3?;
      rev =?4? + digit;
```

```
        num /= ?5?;
    }
    if(rev == N)
        return true;
    else
        return false;
}
```

Answer the following questions.

(i) What is the statement or expression at ? 1 ?

(a) – 1 (b) 0 (c) 10 (d) 2

(ii) What is the statement or expression at ? 2 ?

(a) s *10 (b) f/10 (c) rev (d) f * 10

(iii) What is the statement or expression at ? 3 ?

(a) s (b) rev (c) f (d) digit * 10

(iv) What is the statement or expression at ?4?

(a) s * 10 (b) rev *10 (c) f (d) rev

(v) What is the statement or expression at ? 5 ?

(a) 1 (b) 100 (c) 10 (d) rev

Ans (i) (b) 0 (ii) (d) f*10 (iii) (a) s
(iv) (b) rev*10 (v) (c) 10

8. The following is a function of some class which checks, if a positive integer is a Palindrome number by returning true or false. (A number is said to be palindrome, if the reverse of the number is equal to the original number.) The function does not use modulus (%) operator to extract digit. There are some places in the code marked by ?1?, ?2?, ?3?, ?4?, ?5? which may be replaced by a statement / expression so that the function works properly. ***ISC 2018***

```
boolean PalindromeNum( int N )
{
    int rev= ?1?;
    int num=N;
    while( num>0)
    {
        int f= num/10;
        int s = ?2?;
        int digit = num-?3?;
        rev= ?4? + digit;
        num /= ?5?;
    }
    if( rev= =N )
        return true;
    else
        return false;
}
```

(i) What is the statement or expression at ?1?

(ii) What is the statement or expression at ?2?

(iii) What is the statement or expression at ?3?

(iv) What is the statement or expression at ?4?

(v) What is the statement or expression at ?5?

Ans Statement or expression at

(i) ? 1 ? = 0 (ii) ? 2 ? = f * 10 (iii) ? 3 ? = s
(iv) ? 4 ? = rev *10 (v) ? 5 ? = 10

9. The following is a function of some class which checks if a positive integer is an Armstrong number by returning true or false. (A number is said to be Armstrong if the sum of the cubes of all its digits is equal to the original number). The function does not use modulus (%) operator to extract digit. There are some places in the code marked by ?1?, ?2?, ?3?, ?4?, ?5? which may be replaced by a statement/expression, so that the function works properly. ***ISC 2015***

```
boolean ArmstrongNum(int N)
{
    int sum=?1?;
    int num=N;
    while(num>0)
    {
        int f= num/10;
        int s = ?2?;
        int digit = num-s;
        sum+ = ?3?;
        num = ?4?;
    }
    if(?5?)
        return true;
    else
        return false;
}
```

(i) What is the statement or expression at ?1?
(ii) What is the statement or expression at ?2?
(iii) What is the statement or expression at ?3?
(iv) What is the statement or expression at ?4?
(v) What is the statement or expression at ?5?

Ans (i) 0 (ii) num % 10 (iii) Math. pow (s, 3)
(iv) num/10 (v) sum == N

10. The following function is a part of some class which computes and returns greatest common divisor of any two numbers. There are some places in the co-marked ?1?, ?2?, ?3?, ?4? and ?5? which must be replaced by statement expression so that the function works correctly. ***ISC 2011***

```
int gcd(int a, int b)
{
    int r;
    while(?1?)
    {
        r = ?2?;
        b = ?3?;
        a = ?4?;
    }
    if(a == 0)
        return ?5?;
    else
        return -1;
}
```

(i) What is the expression or statement at ?1?
(ii) What is the expression or statement at ?2?
(iii) What is the expression or statement at ?3?
(iv) What is the expression or statement at ?4?
(v) What is the expression or statement at ?5?

Ans (i) a > 0 (ii) b%a (iii) a (iv) r (v) b

11. The following is a function of some class. It returns 1 if the number is a perfect number otherwise it returns 0.

/*A perfect number is a number which is equal to the sum of its factors other than the number itself.*/ **ISC 2008**

```
int perfectNo(int n)
{
    int ?1?;
    for(int j = 1; ?2?; j++)
    {
        if(?3?)
            sum ?4?;
    }
    if(?5?)
        return 1;
    else
        return 0;
}
```

(i) What is the expression/value at ?1?
(ii) What is the expression/value at ?2?
(iii) What is the expression/value at ?3?
(iv) What is the expression/value at ?4?
(v) What is the expression/value at ?5?

Ans (i) sum = 0
(ii) j < n
(iii) n % j = = 0
(iv) sum + = j
(v) sum = = n

CHAPTER TEST

1 Mark Questions

1. Which of these will happen, if recursive method does not have a base case?
   (a) An infinite loop occurs
   (b) System stops the program after some time
   (c) After 100 calls, it will be automatically stopped
   (d) None of the above
2. What is the return type of a method that does not return any value?
   (a) int (b) float (c) void (d) double
3. What are the members of a class?

2 Marks Questions

4. Define finite recursion in one line.
5. What is the use of 'new' keyword?
6. What do you mean by call by value?

3 Marks Questions

7. Give the example of default access modifier.
8. Define method and how to declare it?
9. How to declare the main() method in program? Give a suitable example.

5 Marks Question

10. The following function is a function of some class. It computes x raised to the power n. Here, x is the base value and n is the power. There are five places in the code marked by ?1?, ?2?, ?3?, ?4?, ?5? that must be replaced by expression or statement so that the program works correctly.

```
double integralPower(double x, int n)
{
    int inverse=0;
    double result=1.0;
    if(n==0)
        return ?1?;
    else if(n<0)
    {
        inverse=1;
        n=?2?;
    }
    for(int i=1; ?3?; i++)
        result ?4?;
    if(inverse==1)
        result=?5?;
    return result;
}
```

(i) What is the expression or statement at ?1?
(ii) What is the expression or statement at ?2?
(iii) What is the expression or statement at ?3?
(iv) What is the expression or statement at ?4?
(v) What is the expression or statement at ?5?

10 Marks Question

11. Design a class HotelBooking with the following description.

Class name	HotelBooking	
Instance variables/Data members		
string name	To store the name of the customer	
string type	To store the type of room that customer wants to	
double mobno	To store customer's mobile number	
int amt	To store basic amount of room	
int totalamt	To store the amount to be paid after updating the original amount	
Member Methods		
void accept()	To take input for name, type, mobile number and amount	
void update()	To update the amount as per the type selected	
	Extra amount to be added in the amount	
	Type of room	**Amount**
	Full AC	4000
	Partial AC	3000
	Cooler	2000
	Normal	1000
void display()	To display all details of a customer such as name, type, total amount and mobile number	

Also, define a main() method to create an object of the class and call the above member methods.

07

Arrays and Strings

TREND ANALYSIS 4 YEARS

Arrays and Strings

Average No. of Questions Across all Sets

Types of Questions	2024	2023	2020	2019
1 Mark	–	–	–	–
2 Marks	1	1	1	1
3 Marks	–	–	–	–
5 Marks	–	–	–	–
10 Marks	3	2	2	2

An array is a data structure that stores a fixed-size sequential collection of elements of the same type. It is used to store a collection of data. It is a group of contiguous or related data items that share a common name. In other words, an array is a collection of variables of the same type all of which are referred by a common name. The specific element of an array is accessed by an index.

The array can be classified into two types:

One-dimensional Array

In one-dimensional array, a single subscript or index is used, where each index value refers to an individual array element. The index of an array starts from 0 and goes upto $n-1$, i.e. the first value of the array will have an index of 0, here n is the number of elements in the array. Figure shows the Marks array with data elements.

60	58	50	78	89
Marks [0]	Marks [1]	Marks [2]	Marks [3]	Marks [4]

Creating an Array

A creation of an array is similar to an object creation, which can inherently involve three steps:

(i) Declaring an array
(ii) Memory allocation in array
(iii) Initialising/assigning an array

Declaring an Array

An array declaration is very similar to a variable declaration. The syntax of declaring an array is:

```
      data_type Array_name[];
or    data_type[] Array_name;
or    data_type []Array_name;
```

```
e.g. int marks[];
or   int[] marks;
or   int []marks;
```

Memory Allocation in Array

Amount of memory utilised by array is estimated by specifying its size. Java allows us to create arrays using **new** operator only, as shown below:

```
      Array_name = new type[size];
e.g.  number = new int[5];
      average = new float[5];
```

Here, the variable number refers to an array of 5 integers and average refers to an array of 5 floating point values.

Initialising/Assigning an Array

Initialising an array can be done as follows:

```
      Array_name[index] = value;
```

```
e.g. class Array
     {
         public static void main(String[ ] args)
```

```
    {
        int[ ] marks = new int[5];
        // declaration of an array dynamically
        marks[0] = 60;
        marks[1] = 78;
        marks[2] = 50;
        marks[3] = 54;
        marks[4] = 89;
    }
}
```

Arrays can be assigned or initialised values in the same way as the variables, i.e. at the time of declaration itself. The syntax for the same can be:

```
type ArrayName[ ] = {value1, value2, …, valuen};
```

e.g. `int marks[ ] = {60, 78, 50, 54, 89};`

Memory Representation in One-dimensional Array

Internally, arrays are stored as a special object containing:

- A group of contiguous memory locations that all have the same name and same data type.
- A reference that stores the beginning address of the array elements.
- A separate instance variable containing the number of elements in the array.

Figure shows the memory arrangement of arrays:

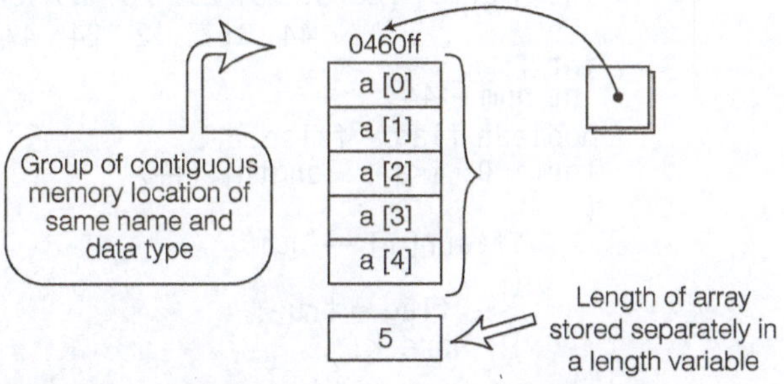

Length of an Array

In Java, allocated length or size of an array store in a variable, i.e. length.

e.g.
```
students = new int[10];
int size = students.length;
```

Two-dimensional Array

A two-dimensional array can be a table containing rows and columns. It contains the other properties of an array with respect to the indices, capacity and data types.

Let us consider the following data table, which shows the value of sales of items by four Salesgirls:

	Item 1	**Item 2**	**Item 3**
Salesgirl # 1	310	275	365
Salesgirl # 2	210	190	325
Salesgirl # 3	405	235	240
Salesgirl # 4	260	300	380

In mathematics, we represent a particular value in a matrix by using two subscripts such as v_{ij}. Here, v denotes the entire matrix and v_{ij} refers to the value in the ith row and jth column.

The above table can be represented as:

`v[4][3];` {where, row = 4 and column = 3}

Syntax for Two-dimensional Arrays

```
type[][] array_reference_name
        = new type[row_length][column_length];
```

(mandatory) (optional)

We may create a two-dimensional array like this:

```
int array[][];
array = new int[3] [4];
```

or,

```
int array[][] = new int[3][4];
```

Memory Representation in Two-dimensional Array

Two-dimensional arrays are stored in a row-column matrix, where the first index indicates the row and the second index indicates the column.

This means the second index (i.e. column) changes faster than the first index (i.e. row) when accessing the elements in the array in the order in which they are actually stored in memory.

If you have declared an array the syntax is as follows:

```
short[][] pay = new short[5][7];
```

It will have $5 \times 7 = 35$ elements, which will be represented in memory as shown below in figure:

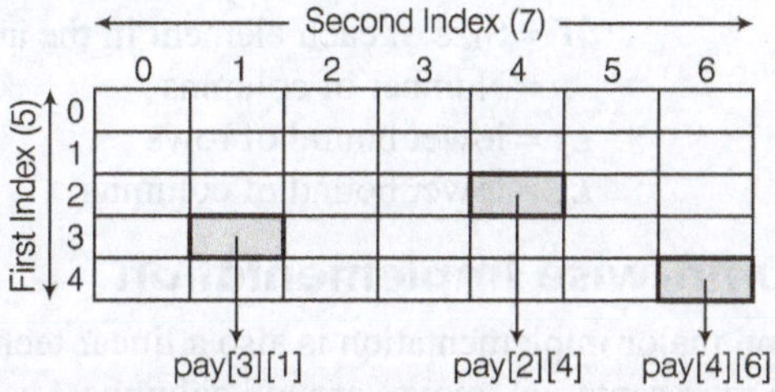

The amount of storage required to hold a two-dimensional array is also dependent upon its base type, number of rows and number of columns. The formula to calculate total number of bytes required by a two-dimensional array is given below:

Total bytes = number of rows × number of columns × size of base type.

Implementation of Two-dimensional Array

While storing the elements of a two-dimensional array in memory, contiguous locations are allocated to them. The elements of a two-dimensional array are declared as,

```
int[][] a = new int[3][3];
```

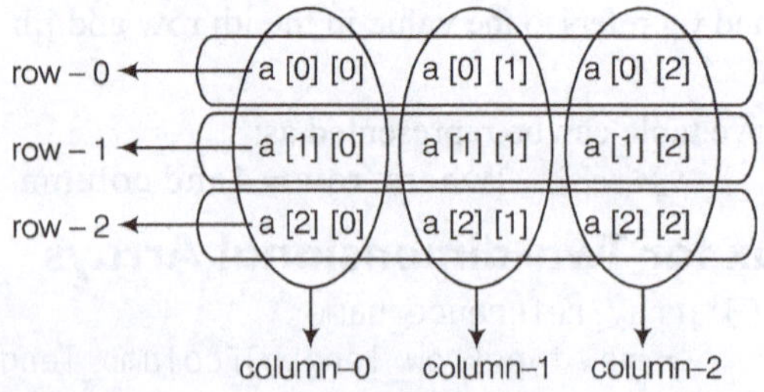

3 × 3 Two-dimensional Array

Address Calculation

Row-wise Implementation

Row major implementation technique is a linear technique in which representation moves around forward or we can say that the whole array is implemented row wise i.e. the complete first row is stored then complete second row is stored and so on.

Let us consider an example of matrix form of 3 × 3 dimensions then in the form of row major implementation, we represent it as:

R_0			R_1			R_2		
a_{00}	a_{01}	a_{02}	a_{10}	a_{11}	a_{12}	a_{20}	a_{21}	a_{22}

One can evaluate the address of an element in row major implementation by the following formula:

Address of element a $[i][j] = B + W[n \times (i - L_r) + (j - L_c)]$

Where, B = Base address of the array

W = Size of each element in the array

n = Number of columns

L_r = lower bound of rows

L_c = lower bound of columns

Column-wise Implementation

Column major implementation is also a linear technique in which representation moves around columns, i.e. to implement the whole array column-wise, i.e. first the elements of the complete first column is stored, then elements of complete second column is stored and so on.

So, one can evaluate the address of an element in column major implementation by the following formula:

Address of element $a[i][j] = B + W[m \times (j - L_c) + (i - L_r)]$

Where, B = Base address of the array

W = Size of each element in the array

m = Number of rows

L_r = lower bound of rows

L_c = lower bound of columns

Operations on a One-dimensional Array

A one-dimensional array performed mainly two operations:

Searching

It involves searching for the specific data element in an array. Searching can be done in two ways:

(i) **Linear Search** In linear search, each element of array is compared with the each value of the list, one at a time and in sequence, until the desired one is found. The method which transverses the array sequentially to locate the given item, is called linear search or sequential search.

e.g.
```
public class LinearSearch
{
    public static void main(String[] args)
    {
        System.out.println("Linear Search
                                        List");
        int[] arr = {2879, 15, 29, 78, 26, 24,
                            44, 167, 12, 24, 47};
        int i;
        int num = 44;
        boolean flag = false;
        for(i=0; i<arr.length; i++)
        {
            if(arr[i] == num)
            {
                flag = true;
            }   break;
        }
        if(flag == true)
        {
            System.out.println(num+" index
                                  position" +i);
        }
        else
        {
            System.out.println(num+" number
                                      not found");
        }
    }
}
```

Output

Linear Search List

44 index position 6

(ii) Binary Search Binary search relies on divide and conquer strategy in a sorted list. In this searching, first of all the desired element is compared with the middle most elements of the list, then in this situation, three conditions aries:

(i) If the element is equal to middle most element's value, then the search is complete and the location of middle most element is return.

(ii) If the element is smaller than middle most element, then the whole process is repeated with the first half of the list.

(iii) If the element is greater than the middle element, then the whole process is repeated with the second half of the list.

e.g.
```
public class BinarySearch
{
    public static void main(String[] args)
    {
        int array[] = {10,15,20, 25, 40, 45, 63, 70, 77, 90};
        int key = 77;  //item to be searched for
        binary_search(array,0,9, key);
    }
    public static void binary_search(int[]array, int lowerbound, int
                                                   upperbound, int key)
    {
        int position;
        int compare_count = 1;
        position = (lowerbound + upperbound)/2;
        // calculate initial search position.
        while((array[position]!= key)&&(lowerbound < upperbound))
        {
            compare_count++;
            // if the value in the search position is greater than the
            // number for which we are searching, then change upperbound to
            // search position minus one.
            if(array[position]>key)
            {
                upperbound = position-1;
            }
            else
            {
                lowerbound = position+1;
                //else, change lowerbound to search position plus one
            }
            position = (lowerbound + upperbound)/ 2;
        }
        if(lowerbound < upperbound)
        {
            System.out.println("A binary search found the number in "+
                                       compare_count +" comparisons.");
            System.out.println("The number was found in array
                                           subscript "+ position);
        }
        else
            System.out.println("Number not found by binary search after "
                                     +compare_count + " comparisons.");
    }
}
```

Output

A binary search found the number in 3 comparisons.

The number was found in array subscript 8

Finding Maximum/Minimum in an Array

An array stores values in a sequence form, its starting index 0 th place towards. It is easy to find the maximum and minimum value in an array. There are two methods to find the maximum and minimum value in an array-with sorted array and unsorted array.

Let us consider an example to find the minimum and maximum element in an array.

```
public class findArray
{
    public static void main(String args[ ])
    {
        int array[] = {10, 15, 8, 3, 1, 93, 85, 98, 7};
        int max, min;
        max = Maximum(array);
        min = Minimum(array);
        System.out.println("Maximum number in the array is : "+max);
        System.out.println("Minimum number in the array is : "+min);
    }
    public static int Maximum(int[] t)
    {
        int maxim =t[0];    //start with first value
        for(int i=1; i<t.length; i++)
        {
            if(t[i]> maxim)
            {
                maxim = t[i]; //start with the first value
            }
        }
        return maxim;
    }
    public static int Minimum(int[ ] t)
    {
        int minim = t[0];
        for(int i = 1; i < t.length; i++)
        {
            if(t[i]< minim)
            {
                minim = t[i]; // new minimum
            }
        }
        return minim;
    }   //minimum method finish
}
```

Output

Maximum number in the array is : 98
Minimum number in the array is : 1

Sorting

Sorting is defined as arranging data in a certain order, is a very common activity in data processing. Sorting of an array means arranging the array elements in a specified order i.e. either in ascending or descending order. Sorting can be done as:

(i) **Selection Sort** Selection sort is probably the easiest sort to understand. The basic idea of a selection sort is to repeatedly select the smallest or largest key in the remaining unsorted array and placing it at the first position of the array. Then the process is repeated with rest of the array, i.e. the next smallest/largest element is selected and put onto the next slot and so on till the last of elements. In this sorting, largest element is selected if the user wants to sort the list from largest to smallest element and smallest element is selected for *vice-versa*.

Let us consider a program of using array for applying selection sort as shown below:

```
public static void selection_sort(int[] array) throws Exception
{
  int i, j, small, temp, pos =0, k =0;
  for(i = 0; i < array.length;i++)
  {
      small = array[i];
      pos = i;
      for(j = i + 1;j < array.length;j++)
      {
      //find smallest element between the positions i and last position
          if(array[j] < small)
          {
              small = array [j];
              pos = j;
          }
      }
      temp = array[pos];        // swap smallest element found in position of i
      array[pos]= array[i];
      array[i]=temp;
  }
}
```

(ii) **Bubble Sort** The basic idea of bubble sort is to compare two adjoining values and exchange them, if they are not in proper order. Let us consider a program of using array for applying bubble sorting as shown below:

```
public static void bubble_sort(int[] num)
{
  int j;
  boolean flag = true;          // set flag to true to begin initial pass
  int temp ;                    // holding variable
  while(flag)
  {
      flag = false;             // set flag to false awaiting a possible swap
      for(j = 0; j < num.length-1; j++)
      {
          if(num [j]> num[j+1])
          {
                                // change to > for ascending sort
              temp = num[j];    // swap elements
              num[j] = num[j+1];
              num[j+1]= temp;
              flag = true;      //indicates that a swap occurred
          }
      }
  }
}
```

(iii) **Insertion Sort** In this sort, initially the first element is picked up in the unsorted part and then appropriately inserted in the sorted part, this process will repeat till the final list is orderd accordingly.

Let us consider a program using array for applying insertion sort as shown below:

```
void insertion_sort(int a[], int n)
{
    int i, j, current, pos;
    for(i=1; i<n; i++)
    {
        current = a[i];
        pos=0;
        while((pos<i)&&(a[pos]<=current))
            pos++;
        if(pos!=i)
        {
            for(j=i-1; j>=pos; j--)
                a[j+1]=a[j];
            a[pos]=current;
        }
    }
}
```

Operations on a Two-dimensional Array

Following operations can be implemented on a two-dimensional array:

Transpose of a Matrix

To demonstrate the two-dimensional arrays, we would consider the problem of finding a transpose of a matrix.

```
void TranspMat(int A[ ][ ], int rows, int cols)
{
    for(int i = 0; i< cols; i++)
    {
        for(int j = i+1; j < rows; j++)
        {
            int temp = A[i][j];
            A[i][j]= A[j][i];
            A[j][i]= temp;
        }
    }
}
```

String

String represents a sequence of characters. The easiest way to represent string in Java is by using a character array. e.g.

```
char charArray [] = new char[4];
charArray [0] = 'J';
charArray [1] = 'a';
charArray [2] = 'v';
charArray [3] = 'a';
```

Strings are class objects and implemented by using two classes, that is **String** and **StringBuffer**. A Java string is an instantiated object of the String class. It is not a character array and not NULL terminated. Strings may be declared and created as follows:

```
String stringName;
stringName = new String("string");
```

e.g. Java offers three classes to work with character data:

1. Character Class can hold single character data.
2. String Class can hold unchanging string, i.e. once initialised, its contents cannot be modified.
3. StringBuffer Class can hold mutable strings, i.e. can be changed or modified.

Declaring and Allocating Strings

To create a String through assignment, we does not require the use of **new** operator. The most direct way to create a string is to write:

```
String greeting = "Hello world!";
```

The String class supports several constructors. To create an empty string, we call a default constructor.

e.g.

```
String s = new String();
```

This will create an instance of String with no character in it.

To create a String initialised by an array of characters, use the constructor shown here:

```
String(char Chars[ ])
```

e.g.

```
char Chars[ ] = {'a', 'b', 'c'};
String s = new String(Chars);
```

Here, this constructor initialises `s` with the string `"abc"`.

Methods of String Class

The String class provides many access or methods that may be used to perform operation on string as shown in table:

Method	Description
char charAt(int index)	Returns the character at the specified index.
int compareTo(Object o)	Compares this string to another object.
int compareTo(String anotherString)	Compares two strings lexicographically.
int compareToIgnoreCase(String str)	Compares two strings lexicographically, ignoring case differences.
String concat(String str)	Concatenates the specified string to the end of this string.
boolean endsWith(String suffix)	Tests if this string ends with the specified suffix.
int indexOf(int ch)	Returns the index within this string of the first occurrence of the specified character.
int indexOf(int ch, int fromIndex)	Returns the index within this string of the first occurrence of the specified character, starting the search at the specified index.
int indexOf(String str)	Returns the index within this string of the first occurrence of the specified substring.
String intern( )	Returns a canonical representation for the string object.
int lastIndexOf(int ch)	Returns the index within this string of the last occurrence of the specified character.
int length( )	Returns the length of this string.
String replace(char oldChar, char newChar)	Returns a new string resulting from replacing all occurrences of oldChar in this string with newChar.
String[ ] split(String regex)	Splits this string around matches of the given regular expression.

Method	Description
String[ ] split(String regex, int limit)	Splits this string around matches of the given regular expression.
boolean startsWith(String prefix)	Tests if this string starts with the specified prefix.
String toLowerCase( )	Converts all of the characters in this string to lower case using the rules of the default locale.
String toLowerCase(Locale locale)	Converts all of the characters in this string to lower case using the rules of the given locale.
String toString( )	This object (which is already a string!) is itself returned.
String toUpperCase( )	Converts all of the characters in this string to upper case using the rules of the default locale.
String toUpperCase(Locale locale)	Converts all of the characters in this String to upper case using the rules of the given locale.
String trim( )	Returns a copy of the string, with leading and trailing whitespace omitted.

StringBuffer Class

StringBuffer is a peer class of string that provides much of the functionality of strings. The StringBuffer class is used to create mutable (modifiable) string i.e. it can be changed.

StringBuffer defines these three constructors:

(i) `StringBuffer()` creates an empty string buffer.

(ii) `StringBuffer(int size)` creates a string buffer with specified string.

(iii) `StringBuffer(string str)` creates an empty string buffer with the specified length. StringBuffer reduces the number of reallocations that take place.

(iv) `StringBuffer (Charsequence[]ch)` creates a string buffer that contains the same characters as the specified char sequence.

Methods of StringBuffer class

(a) **`length()` and `capacity()`** The current length of a StringBuffer can be found *via* the `length()` method, while the total allocated capacity can be found through the capacity(). They have the following general forms:

```
int length();
int capacity();
```

(b) **`setLength()`** To set the length of the buffer within a StringBuffer object, used `setLength()`. Its general form is:

```
void setLength(int len)
```

(c) **`insert()`** The `insert()` method inserts one string into another. It calls string valueOf() to obtain the string representation of the value it is called with. This string is then inserted the invoking StringBuffer object.

e.g. `StringBuffer insert(int index, String str)`

(d) **`reverse()`** To reverse the characters within a StringBuffer object using `reverse()`, as shown,

```
StringBuffer reverse()
```

(e) **`setCharAt()`** The setCharAt(), specifies the index of the character being set, and ch specifies the new value of the character. The general form is shown:

```
void setCharAt(int where, char ch)
```

(f) **`delete()`** The general form of delete() method is:

```
StringBuffer delete (int startIndex, int endIndex)
```

Here, `delete()` method deletes a sequence of characters from the invoking object where `startIndex` specifies the index of the first character to remove and endIndex specifies an index one past the last character to remove.

Operations on Strings

Following are some operations that can be performed on the strings:

Substring

The substring() method extracts the characters from a string between two specified indices and returns the new sub string.

```
import java.util.Scanner;
class SubstringsOfAString
{
    public static void main(String args[])
    {
        String string, sub;
        int i, c, length;
        Scanner in = new Scanner(System.in);
        System.out.println("Enter a string to print it's all substrings");
        string  = in.nextLine();
        length = string.length();
        System.out.println("Substrings of \""+string+"\" are :-");
        for( c = 0 ; c < length ; c++ )
        {
            for( i = 1 ; i <= length - c ; i++ )
            {
                sub = string.substring(c, c+i);
                System.out.println(sub);
            }
        }
    }
}
```

Output

Enter a string to print it's all substrings
Mango
Substrings of "Mango" are:-
M
Ma
Man
Mang
Mango
a
an
ang
ango
n
ng
ngo
g
go
o

String Concatenation

Concatenation of two substrings can be performed by using concat() method of string class as,

```
class JavaStringConcat
{
    public static void main(String args[])
    {
        String str1 = "Hello";
```

```
            String str2 = "World";     //1. Using + operator
            String str3 = str1 + str2;
            System.out.println("String concat using + operator :"+ str3);
                                       //2. Using String.concat() method
            String str4 = str1.concat(str2);
            System.out.println("String concat using String concat method : " + str4);
                                       //3. Using StringBuffer.append method
            String str5 = new StringBuffer().append(str1).
            append(str2).toString();
            System.out.println("String concat using StringBuffer append method : "
                                                                        + str5);
        }
    }
```

Output

String concat using + operator : HelloWorld
String concat using String concat method: HelloWorld
String concat using StringBuffer append method: HelloWorld

String Length

length() returns the number of characters contained in the string object. The `length()` method of string class can be used as:

```
    public class Test
    {
        public static void main(String args[])
        {
            String Str1 = new String("Welcome to string");
            String Str2 = new String("Class");
            System.out.print(" First String Length : ");
            System.out.println(Str1.length());
            System.out.print(" Second String Length : ");
            System.out.println(Str2.length());
        }
    }
```

Output

First String Length : 17
Second String Length : 5

Accessing each Character from a String

Each character from a string, can be retrieved using `charAt()` method of String class as follows:

```
    import java.io.*;
    public class Test
    {
        public static void main(String args[])
        {
            String str = new String("Hello");
            for(int i=0;i<str.length();i++) System.out.println(str.charAt(i));
        }
    }
```

Output

H
e
l
l
o

PYQs Previous Years Questions

1 Mark Questions

1. The output of the statement given below

```
System.out.println("Computer
Science".lastIndexOf('E'));
```

ISC 2022 (Sem II)

(a) 8 (b) 7 (c) –1 (d) 15

Ans (c) – 1

2. Write a statement in Java to extract the last four characters from the word "SIMPLICITY".

ISC 2022 (Sem II)

Ans

```
System.out.println(str. substring
                  (str.length() -4));
```

3. Write the statement in Java to extract the word "MISS" from the word "SUBMISSION".

ISC SQP 2022 (Sem II)

Ans

```
System.out.println("SUBMISSION".substring(3,7));
```

4. What is the output of the statement given below?

```
System.out.print("FAN"+("AUTOMATIC"
                .charAt(5)));
```

ISC SQP 2022 (Sem II)

Ans FANA

2 Marks Questions

1. An array ARR [–5 ...15, 10 ... 20] stores elements in Row Major Wise with each element requiring 2 bytes of storage. Find the address of ARR [10] [15] when the base address is 2500. *ISC 2024*

Ans Given $B = 2500$, $W = 2$ bytes, $i = 10$, $j = 15$, $U_r = 15$, $U_c = 20$, $L_r = -5$, $L_c = 10$

n (Number of columns) $= U_c - L_c + 1$
$= 20 - 10 + 1 = 11$

According to row major

$= B + W[n(i - L_r) + (j - L_c)]$

Address of ARR [10] [15]

$= 2500 + 2[11(10 + 5) + (15 - 10)]$

$= 2500 + 2[11 \times 15 + 5]$

$= 2500 + 2[165 + 5]$

$= 2500 + 2 \times 170 = 2840$

2. A matrix M [–6... 10, 4...15] is stored in the memory with each element requiring 4 bytes of storage. If the base address is 1025, find the address of M [4] [8] when the matrix is stored in column major wise. *ISC 2023*

Ans Given, $B = 1025$, $W = 4$, $i = 4$, $j = 8$, $L_c = 4$, $L_r = -6$

$m = 10 - (-6) + 1 = 10 + 6 + 1 = 17$

Column major wise,

$M[i][j] = B + W[m(j - L_c) + (i - L_r)]$

$M[4][8] = 1025 + 4[17(8 - 4) + (4 + 6)]$

$= 1025 + 4[17 * 4 + 10]$

$= 1025 + 4[68 + 10]$

$= 1025 + 4(78)$

$= 1025 + 312$

$M[4][8] = 1337$

3. A matrix N [11] [8] is stored in the memory with each element requiring 2 bytes of storage. If the base address at N [2] [3] is 2140, find the address of N [7] [5] when the matrix is stored in row major wise.

ISC SQP 2023

Ans Given, $B = 2140$, $W = 2$ bytes, $L_r = 2$, $L_c = 3$, $m = 11$, $n = 8$, $i = 7$, $j = 5$

For row major wise,

$N[i][j] = B + W[n(i - L_r) + (j - L_c)]$

$N[7][5] = 2140 + 2[8(7 - 2) + (5 - 3)]$

$= 2140 + 2[8(5) + (2)]$

$= 2140 + 2[40 + 2]$

$= 2140 + 2(42)$

$= 2140 + 84$

$= 2224$

4. A matrix MAT[10][15] is stored in the memory in row major wise with each element requiring 2 bytes of storage. If the base address at MAT[1][2] is 2215, then the address of MAT[3][7] will be

ISC SQP 2022 (Sem I)

(a) 2285 (b) 2315
(c) 2319 (d) None of these

Ans Given, $W = 2$ bytes, $B = 2215$, $L_r = 1$, $L_c = 2$, $i = 3$, $j = 7$, $n = 15$, $m = 10$

Row major wise,

$MAT[i][j] = B + W[n(i - L_r) + (j - L_c)]$

$MAT[3][7] = 2215 + 2[15(3 - 1) + (7 - 2)]$

$= 2215 + 2[15(2) + (5)]$

$= 2215 + 2(30 + 5)$

$= 2215 + 2(35)$

$= 2215 + 70$

$= 2285$

5. What is the conditional statement to check for the Non-boundary elements in a double dimensional array of 'M' number of rows and 'N' number of columns? The row index is represented by 'r' and the column index is represented by 'c'.

ISC SQP 2022 (Sem I)

(a) (r>0 || r<M-1 && c>0 || c<N-1)
(b) (r>0 && r<M-1 || c>0 && c<N-1)
(c) (r>0 && r<M-1 && c>0 && c<N-1)
(d) (r>0 || r<M-1 || c>0 || c<N-1)

Ans (c) (r>0 && r<M-1 && c>0 && c<N-1)

6. What is the output of the statement given below?

```
System.out.print('A'+'1'+'C');
```

ISC SQP 2022 (Sem I)

(a) 65 + 1 + 66 (b) 10 + 1 + 67
(c) 181 (d) 65 + 49 + 67

Ans (c) 181

7. What is the output of the statement given below?

```
System.out.print(Integer.parseInt("234")+'A');
```

ISC SQP 2022 (Sem I)

(a) 234 + 65 (b) 234A
(c) 299 (d) ERROR

Ans (c) 299

8. A matrix $B[10][20]$ is stored in the memory with each element requiring 2 bytes of storage. If the base address at $B[2][1]$ is 2140, find the address of $B[5][4]$ when the matrix is stored in column major wise.

ISC 2020

Ans Given,

$$m = 10, n = 20, i = 5, j = 4, L_r = 2, L_c = 1$$
$$B = 2140, W = 2 \text{ bytes}$$

Column wise,

$$B[i][j] = B + W[(i - L_r) + m\,(j - L_c)]$$
$$B[5][4] = 2140 + 2\,[(5 - 2) + 10\,(4 - 1)]$$
$$= 2140 + 2[3 + 30] = 2140 + 2[33]$$
$$= 2140 + 66 = 2206$$

9. Each element of an array arr[15][20] requires 'W' bytes of storage. If the address of arr[6][8] is 4440 and the Base Address at arr[1][1] is 4000, find the width 'W' of each cell in the array arr[ ] [ ] when the array is stored as column major wise.

ISC SQP 2020

Ans Given $B = 4000$, arr [6] [8] = 4440, $i = 6$, $j = 8$, $L_r = 1$, $L_c = 1$, $m = 15$, $n = 20$

Column major wise,

$$arr[i][j] = B + W[(j - L_c) + (i - L_r)]$$
$$4440 = 4000 + W[15\,(8 - 1) + (6 - 1)]$$
$$4440 - 4000 = W[15 * 7 + 5]$$
$$440 = W[105 + 5]$$
$$440 = W[110]$$
$$W = \frac{440}{110} = 4$$
$$W = 4 \text{ bytes}$$

10. A matrix ARR [–4…6, 3…8] is stored in the memory with each element requiring 4 bytes of storage. If the base address is 1430, find the address of ARR[3][6] when the matrix is stored in row major wise.

ISC 2019

Ans Given, $B = 1430$, $W = 4$ bytes, $i = 3, j = 6, U_r = 6$, $U_c = 8, L_r = -4, L_c = 3$

n(number of columns) $= U_c - L_c + 1$

$$= 8 - 3 + 1 = 5 + 1 = 6$$

According to row-major, $B + W[n(i - L_r) + (j - L_c)]$

Address of ARR [3][6]

$$= 1430 + 4[6(3 - (-4)) + (6 - 3)]$$
$$= 1430 + 4[6(7) + 3]$$
$$= 1430 + 4[42 + 3]$$
$$= 1430 + 4[45]$$
$$= 1430 + 180 = 1610$$

11. A matrix $A[m][m]$ is stored in the memory with each element requiring 4 bytes of storage. If the base address at $A[1][1]$ is 1500 and the address of $A[4][5]$ is 1608, determine the order of the matrix when it is stored in column major wise.

ISC 2018, 2016

Ans Given $i = 4$, $j = 5$, $B = 1500$, $L_r = 1$, $L_c = 1$, $W = 4$, $m = ?$

Add[4][5] = 1608

Column wise,

$$Add[i][j] = B + W[m(j - L_c) + (i - L_r)]$$
$$1608 = 1500 + 4[m(5 - 1) + (4 - 1)]$$
$$1608 - 1500 = 4[4m + 3]$$
$$108 = 4[4m + 3]$$
$$\frac{108}{4} = 4m + 3$$
$$27 = 4m + 3$$
$$4m = 27 - 3$$
$$4m = 24$$
$$m = 6$$

12. A matrix $P[15]$ [10] is stored with each element required 8 bytes of storage. If the base address at $P[0][0]$ is 1400, determine the address at $P[10][7]$ when the matrix is stored in row major wise.

ISC 2017

Ans Given, $B = 1400$, $W = 8$, $L_r = 0$, $L_c = 0$, $m = 15$, $n = 10$, $I = 10$, $J = 7$

For row major wise,

$$A[I][J] = B + W[n(I - L_r) + (J - L_c)]$$
$$A[10][7] = 1400 + 8[10(10 - 0) + (7 - 0)]$$
$$= 1400 + 8[10(10) + 7]$$
$$= 1400 + 8[100 + 7]$$
$$= 1400 + 8[107]$$
$$= 1400 + 856 = 2256$$

13. The array $D[-2......10][3.....8]$ contains double type elements. If the base address is 4110, find the address of $D[4][5]$, when the array is stored in column major wise. **ISC 2015**

Ans For the given question, $i = 4,\ j = 5,\ L_r = -2,\ U_r = 10,$ $L_c = 3,\ U_c = 8,\ B = 4110,\ W = 8$

Number of rows (m)

$$= U_r - L_r + 1 = 10 - (-2) + 1 = 13$$

For column wise,

$$\text{Address } [i, j] = B + W[m(j - L_c) + (i - L_r)]$$
$$D[4][5] = 4110 + 8[13(5 - 3) + (4 - (-2))]$$
$$= 4110 + 8[13 \times 2 + 6] = 4110 + 8 \times 32$$
$$= 4366$$

14. An array AR[-4...6, -2...12] stores element in row major wise, with the address AR[2][3] as 4142. If each element requires 2 bytes of storage, find the base address. **ISC 2014**

Ans Given, $i = 2, j = 3,\ W = 2$ bytes, $U_c = 12,\ L_c = -2,$ $U_r = 6,\ L_r = -4$

$$AR[i][j] = 4142,$$

To find n,

$$n = U_c - L_c + 1$$
$$= (12 - (-2)) + 1 = 12 + 2 + 1 = 15$$
$$n = 15$$

Row wise order,

$$AR[2][3] = B + W[n(i - L_r) + (j - L_c)]$$
$$B = ?$$

Now,

$$4142 = B + 2[15(2 - (-4)) + (3 - (-2))]$$
$$4142 = B + 2[15(2 + 4) + (3 + 2)]$$
$$4142 = B + 2[90 + 5]$$
$$4142 = B + 190$$
$$B = 4142 - 190 = 3952$$

15. A square matrix $M[\ ][\ ]$ of size 10 is stored in the memory with each element requiring 4 bytes of storage. If the base address at $M[0][0]$ is 1840, determine the address at $M[4][8]$ when the matrix is stored in row major wise. **ISC 2013**

Ans Given, $W = 4$ bytes, $i = 4,\ j = 8$

$$\text{Add } [i][j] = ?$$
$$B = 1840$$
$$n = 10 \qquad [\because L_r = L_c = 0]$$

So, row wise address

$$\text{Add } [i][j] = B + W[n(i - L_r) + (j - L_c)]$$
$$M[4][8] = 1840 + 4[10(4 - 0) + (8 - 0)]$$
$$= 1840 + 4(10 \times 4 + 8)$$
$$= 1840 + 4(48)$$
$$= 1840 + 192$$
$$= 2032$$

16. A matrix $B[10][7]$ is stored in the memory with each element requiring 2 bytes of storage. If the base address at $B[x][1]$ is 1012 and the address at $B[7][3]$ is 1060, determine the value 'x' where the matrix is stored in column major wise. **ISC 2012**

Ans Given, $i = 7,\ j = 3,\ W = 2,\ B = 1012,\ m = 10,$ $L_r = x, L_c = 1$

$$\text{Add } [i][j] = 1060$$

Column wise, Add

$$[i][j] = B + W[m(j - L_c) + (i - L_r)]$$
$$\Rightarrow 1060 = 1012 + 2[(3 - 1) * 10 + (7 - x)]$$
$$\Rightarrow \quad 1060 = 1012 + 2[20 + (7 - x)]$$
$$1060 - 1012 = 40 + 14 - 2x$$
$$48 - 40 - 14 = -2x$$
$$8 - 14 = -2x$$
$$2x = 6$$
$$x = 3$$

17. A square matrix $A[m \times m]$ is stored in the memory with each element requiring 2 bytes of storage. If the base address $A[1][1]$ is 1098 and the address at $A[4][5]$ is 1144, determine the order of the matrix $A[m \times m]$ when the matrix is stored column major wise. **ISC 2011**

Ans Given, $i = 4, j = 5, B = 1098,\ L_r = 1, L_c = 1, W = 2,$ $m = ?$

$$A[4][5] = 1144$$

Column wise,

$$A[4][5] = B + W[m(j - L_c) + (i - L_r)]$$
$$\Rightarrow \quad 1144 = 1098 + 2[(m(5 - 1) + (4 - 1)]$$
$$\Rightarrow \quad 1144 - 1098 = 2[(m(4) + (3))]$$
$$\Rightarrow \quad \frac{46}{2} = 4m + 3$$
$$\Rightarrow \quad 23 - 3 = 4m$$
$$\Rightarrow \quad \frac{20}{4} = m$$
$$\Rightarrow \quad m = 5$$

18. A character array $B[7][6]$ has a base address 1046 at 0,0. Calculate the address at $B[2][3]$, if the array is stored column major wise. Each character requires two bytes of storage. **ISC 2010**

Ans Given,

$i=2,\ j=3,\ L_r=0,\ B=1046,\ L_c=0$

$W=2,\ m=7$

Column wise,

$$B\,[2][3]=B+W[(i-L_r)+m(j-L_c)]$$
$$=1046+2\,[(2-0)+7\,(3-0)]$$
$$=1046+2\,(2+21)$$
$$=1046+46$$
$$=1092$$

19. Each element of an array $A[20][10]$ requires two bytes of storage. If the address of $A[6][8]$ is 4000, find the base address at $A[0][0]$ when the array is stored as row major wise. **ISC 2009**

Ans Given, Address of $A[6][8]=4000$

$n=10$

$W=2,\ i=6,\ j=8,\ L_r=L_c=0$

The base address of A[0][0] row major wise is calculated as follows:

$$A[6,8]=B+W[n(i-L_r)+(j-L_c)]$$
$$\Rightarrow\quad 4000=B+2[10(6-0)+(8-0)]$$
$$\Rightarrow\quad 4000=B+2[10\times 6+8]$$
$$\Rightarrow\quad 4000=B+136$$
$$\Rightarrow\quad B=4000-136=3864$$

20. A two dimensional array defined as $X[3...6,\ -2...2]$ requires 2 bytes of storage space for each element. If the array is stored in row-major order, determine the address of $X[5,\ 1]$ given the base addresses as 1200. **ISC 2008**

Ans Given,

$B=1200,\ W=2$ byte, $i=5,\ j=1,\ U_r=6,\ U_c=2,$

$L_r=3,\ L_c=-2$

n(number of columns) $=U_c-L_c+1$

$n=2-(-2)+1=5$

According to row-major, $B+W[n(i-L_r)+(j-L_c)]$

$$\text{Address of } X\,[5][1]=1200+2[5(5-3)+(1-(-2))]$$
$$=1200+2[5(2)+3]$$
$$=1200+2\times(10+3)$$
$$=1200+2\times 13$$
$$=1200+26=1226$$

21. Each element of an array $X[-15...10,\ 15...40]$ requires one byte of storage. If the array is stored in column major order with the beginning location 1500, determine the location of [5, 20]. **ISC 2007**

Ans Given, Base Address $(B)=1500$

Element Size $(W)=1,\ L_r=-15,\ L_c=15,\ U_r=10,$ $U_c=40$

Number of Rows $(m)=U_r-L_r+1=10-(-15)+1$ $=26$

Therefore, the address of $X[5,\ 20]$ in column major order

$$=B+W\,[m(j-L_c)+(i-L_r)]$$
$$=1500+1[26(20-15)+(5-(-15))]$$
$$=1500+1(130+20)$$
$$=1500+130+20$$
$$X\,[5][20]=1650$$

22. In an array of real numbers ARR[25][25], ARR [1][1] is stored at the location 1000. Find the address of ARR[12][12] when the array is stored row major wise. Assume each real number requires 4 bytes. **ISC 2006**

Ans Given, ARR [25][25]

$i=12,\ j=12,\ W=4,\ B=1000,\ n=25$

Row wise,

$$\text{ARR}[12][12]=B+W\,[n(i-L_r)+(j-L_c)]$$
$$=1000+4\,[25(12-1)+(12-1)]$$
$$=1000+4\,[25\times 11+11]$$
$$=1000+4\,[275+11]$$
$$=1000+1144$$
$$=2144$$

23. An array ARR[10][5] is stored in memory with each element requiring 2 bytes of storage. If the first element ARR[0][0] is stored at the location 1250, calculate the location of ARR[5][3] when the array is stored row major wise. **ISC 2005**

Ans Given,

$B=1250,\ W=2$ bytes, $i=5,\ j=3,\ L_r=0,\ L_c=0,$ $n=5$

Row major wise

$$\text{ARR}[i][j]=B+W\,[n(i-L_r)+(j-L_c)]$$
$$\therefore\quad \text{ARR}\,[5][3]=1250+2\,[5(5-0)+(3-0)]$$
$$=1250+2(25+3)$$
$$=1250+2\times 28$$
$$=1250+56$$
$$=1306$$

6/10 Marks Questions

1. A class InsSort contains an array of integers which sorts the elements in a particular order.

   Some of the members of the class are given below

Class name	InsSort
Data members/Instance variables	
arr[]	stores the array elements
size	stores the number of elements in the array
Methods/Member functions	
InsSort(int s)	constructor to initialise size = s
void getArray()	accepts the array elements
void insertionSort()	sorts the elements of the array in descending order using the **Insertion Sort technique**
double find()	calculates and returns the average of all the odd numbers in the array
void display()	displays the elements of the array in a sorted order along with the average of all the odd numbers in the array by invoking the function find() with an appropriate message.

Specify the class InsSort giving details of the constructor(), void getArray(), void insertionSort(), double find() and void display(). Define a main() function to create an object and call all the functions accordingly to enable the task. ***ISC 2024***

Ans

```
import java.util.Scanner;
class InsSort
{
   private int arr[];
   private int size;
   public InsSort(int s)
   {
      size = s;
      arr = new int[s];
   }
   public void getArray()
   {
      Scanner scanner = new Scanner(System.in);
      System.out.print("Enter " + size +
                                 " integers: ");
      for( int i=0; i<size; i++ )
      {
         arr[i] = scanner.nextInt();
      }
   }
   public void insertionSort()
   {
      for( int i=1; i<size; i++ )
      {
         int j = i-1;
         int temp = arr[i];
         while( j>=0 && arr[j]<temp )
         {
            arr[j+1] = arr[j];
            j--;
         }
         arr[j+1] = temp;
      }
   }
   public double find()
   {
      double total = 0;
      int numOdd = 0;
      for( int i=0; i<size; i++ )
      {
         if( arr[i]%2!=0 )
         {
            total += arr[i];
            numOdd++;
         }
      }
      double average = total/numOdd;
      return average;
   }
   public void display()
   {
      insertionSort();
      System.out.print("Sorted elements: ");
      for( int i=0; i<size; i++ )
      {
         System.out.print(arr[i] + " ");
      }
      System.out.println();
      System.out.println("Average of all
                           odd numbers: " + find());
   }
}
public class Q7
{
   public static void main(String[] args)
   {
      InsSort insSort = new InsSort(10);
      insSort.getArray();
      insSort.display();
   }
}
```

Output

Enter 10 integers: 3 4 5 6 5 4 3 4 4 2

Sorted elements: 6 5 5 4 4 4 4 3 3 2

Average of all odd numbers: 4.0

2. Design a class Coding to perform some string related operations on a word containing alphabets only.

Example Input: "Java"
Output: Original word: Java
J = 74
a = 97
v = 118
a = 97
Lowest ASCII code: 74
Highest ASCII code : 118

Some of the members of the class are given below

Class name	Coding
Data members/Instance variables	
wrd	stores the word
len	stores the length of the word
Method/Member functions	
Coding()	constructor to initialise the data members with legal initial values
void accept()	to accept a word
void find()	to display all the characters of 'wrd' along with their ASCII codes. Also display the lowest ASCII code and the highest ASCII code in 'wrd'
void show()	to display the original word and all the characters of 'wrd' along with their ASCII codes. Also display the lowest ASCII code and the highest ASCII code in 'wrd', by invoking the function find().

Specify the class Coding giving details of the constructor(), void accept(), void find() and void show(). Define a main() function to create an object and call all the functions accordingly to enable the task. ***ISC 2024***

Ans

```
import java.util.Scanner;
class Coding
{
   private String wrd;
   private int len;
   public Coding()
   {
      wrd = "";
      len = 0;
   }
   public void accept()
   {
      Scanner scanner = new Scanner(System.in);
      System.out.print("Enter a string: ");
      wrd = scanner.nextLine();
      len = wrd.length();
   }
   public void find()
   {
      char lowestASCII = wrd.charAt(0);
      char highestASCII = wrd.charAt(0);
      for( int i=0; i<len; i++ )
      {
         char ch = wrd.charAt(i);
         int ascii = ch;
         System.out.println(ch + " = " + ascii);
         if( lowestASCII>ch )
         {
            lowestASCII = ch;
         }
         if( ch>highestASCII )
         {
            highestASCII = ch;
         }
      }
      System.out.println();
      System.out.println("Lowest ASCII Code: " +
                                  (int)lowestASCII);
      System.out.println("Highest ASCII Code: " +
                                  (int)highestASCII);
   }
   public void show()
   {
      System.out.println("Original Word:  " +
                                              wrd);
      find();
   }
}
public class Q8
{
   public static void main(String[] args)
   {
      Coding coding = new Coding();
      coding.accept();
      coding.show();
   }
}
```

Output:

Enter a string: Primitive data types
Original Word: Primitive data types
P = 80
r = 114
i = 105
m = 109
i = 105
t = 116
i = 105
v = 118

e = 101
= 32
d = 100
a = 97
t = 116
a = 97

3. CardGame is a game of mental skill, built on the simple premise of adding and removing the cards from the top of the card pile.

The details of the class CardGame are given below

Class name	CardGame
Data members/Instance variables	
cards[]	array to store integers as cards
cap	to stores the maximum capacity of array
top	to store the index of the topmost element of the array
Method/member functions	
CardGame(int cc)	constructor to initialise cap=cc and top= –1
void addCard(int v)	to add the card at the top index if possible, otherwise display the message "CARD PILE IS FULL"
int drawCard()	to remove and return the card from the top index of the card pile, if any, else return the value – 9999
void display()	to display all the cards of card pile.

(a) Specify the class CardGame giving details of the functions void addCard(int) and int drawCard(). Assume that the other function have been defined.
The main() function and algorithm need NOT be written.

(b) Name the entity described above and state its principle. ***ISC 2024***

Ans (a)

```
class CardGame
{
   private int cards[];
   private int cap;
   private int top;
   public CardGame(int cc)
   {
      cap = cc;
      top = -1;
      cards = new int[cap];
   }
   public void addCard(int v)
   {
      if( (top+1)==cap )
      {
         System.out.println("CARD PILE IS FULL");
         return;
      }
      cards[++top] = v;
   }
   public int drawCard()
   {
      if( top==-1 )
      {
         return -9999;
      }
      int topCard = cards[top];
      top--;
      return topCard;
   }
   public void display()
   {
      if( top!=-1 )
      {
         System.out.println("Cards on the pile: ");
         System.out.print("Top ==> ");
         System.out.println(cards[top]);
         for( int i=top-1; i>=0; i-- )
         {
            System.out.println("         " +
                                        cards[i]);
         }
      }
      else
      {
         System.out.println("Card Pile is
                                         empty!");
      }
   }
}
public class Q9
{
   public static void main(String args[])
   {
      CardGame cardGame = new CardGame(5);
      // display - empty
      cardGame.display();
      System.out.println();
      // add 3 cards
      cardGame.addCard(12);
      cardGame.addCard(4);
      cardGame.addCard(7);
      // display
      cardGame.display();
      System.out.println();
      // draw card
      System.out.println("Top card drawn: " +
                               cardGame.drawCard());
```

```
        System.out.println();
        // display
        cardGame.display();
        System.out.println();
        // draw card
        System.out.println("Top card drawn: " +
                                cardGame.drawCard());
        System.out.println();
        // display
        cardGame.display();
        System.out.println();
        cardGame.addCard(12);
        cardGame.addCard(4);
        cardGame.addCard(7);
        cardGame.addCard(12);
        cardGame.addCard(4);
        cardGame.addCard(7);
    }
}
```

Output

Card Pile is empty!
Cards on the pile:
Top ==> 7
4
12
Top card drawn: 7
Cards on the pile:
Top ==> 4
12
Top card drawn: 4
Cards on the pile:
Top ==> 12
CARD PILE IS FULL
CARD PILE IS FULL

(b) The entity stack is described in the above code. The principle it follows is that of a stack data structure, where cards are added and removed from the top of the pile (last in, first out - LIFO).

4. A class Trans is defined to find the transpose of a square matrix. A transpose of a matrix obtained by interchanging the elements of the rows and columns.

Example: If size of the matrix = 3, then

ORIGINAL		
11	5	7
8	13	9
1	6	20

TRANSPOSE		
11	8	1
5	13	6
7	9	20

Some of the members of the class are given below:

Class name	Trans
Data members/Instance variables	
arr [ ] [ ]	to store integers in the matrix
m	integer to store the size of the matrix
Methods / Member functions	
Trans(int mm)	parameterised constructor to initialise the data member m = mm
void fillarray( )	to enter integer elements in the matrix
void transpose( )	to create the transpose of the given matrix
void display( )	displays the original matrix and the transposed matrix by invoking the method transpose ()

Specify the class Trans giving details of the constructor ( ), void fillarray ( ), void transpose( ) and void display ( ). Define a main( ) function to create an object and call the functions accordingly to enable the task.
ISC 2023

Ans

```
import java.util.*;
class Trans
{
    int[][] arr;
    int m;
    Trans(int mm)
    {
        m = mm;
        arr = new int[m][m];
    }
    void fillarray()
    {
        Scanner sc = new Scanner(System.in);
        System.out.println("Enter " + m*m + "
                            elements of the matrix: ");
        for (int i = 0; i < m; i++)
        {
            for (int j = 0; j < m; j++)
            {
                arr[i][j] = sc.nextInt();
            }
        }
    }
    void transpose()
    {
        for (int i = 0; i < m; i++)
        {
            for (int j = i+1; j < m; j++)
            {
                int temp = arr[i][j];
                arr[i][j] = arr[j][i];
```

```
            arr[j][i] = temp;
         }
      }
   }
   void display()
   {
      System.out.println("ORIGINAL MATRIX");
      for (int i = 0; i < m; i++)
      {
         for (int j = 0; j < m; j++)
         {
            System.out.print(arr[i][j] + " ");
         }
         System.out.println();
      }
      transpose();
      System.out.println("TRANSPOSE MATRIX");
      for (int i = 0; i < m; i++)
      {
         for (int j = 0; j < m; j++)
         {
            System.out.print(arr[i][j] + " ");
         }
         System.out.println();
      }
   }
   public static void main(String[] args)
   {
      Scanner sc = new Scanner(System.in);
      System.out.print("Enter the size of the
                                        matrix: ");
      int size = sc.nextInt();
      Trans t = new Trans(size);
      t.fillarray();
      t.display();
   }
}
```

5. A class SortAlpha has been defined to sort the words in the sentence in alphabetical order.

Example: Input: THE SKY IS BLUE

Output: BLUE IS SKY THE

Some of the members of the class are given below

Class name	**SortAlpha**
Data members/Instance variables	
sent	to store a sentence
n	integer to store the number of words in a sentence
Methods / Member functions	
SortAlpha()	default constructor to initialise data members with legal initial values
void acceptsent( )	to accept a sentence in UPPER CASE
void sort(SortAlpha P)	sorts the words of the sentence of object P in alphabetical order and stores the sorted sentence in the current object
void display( )	displays the original sentence along with the sorted sentence by invoking the method sort( )

Specify the class SortAlpha giving details of the constructor( ), void acceptsent( ), void sort(SortAlpha) and void display( ). Define a main( ) function to create an object and call the functions accordingly to enable the task. ***ISC 2023***

Ans

```
import java.util.*;
class SortAlpha
{
   String sent;
   int n;
   SortAlpha()
   {
      sent = "";
      n = 0;
   }
   void acceptsent()
   {
      Scanner sc = new Scanner(System.in);
      System.out.print("Enter a sentence in
                                UPPER CASE: ");
      sent = sc.nextLine();
      n = sent.split(" ").length;
   }
   void sort(SortAlpha P)
   {
      String[] words = P.sent.split(" ");
      Arrays.sort(words);
      sent = String.join(" ", words);
   }
   void display()
   {
      System.out.println("Original Sentence: "
                                 + sent+"\n");
      sort(this);
      System.out.println("Sorted Sentence  : "
                                     + sent);
   }
   public static void main(String[] args)
   {
      SortAlpha sa = new SortAlpha();
      sa.acceptsent();
      sa.display();
   }
}
```

6. Design a class OddEven to arrange two single dimensional arrays into one single dimensional array, such that the odd numbers from both the arrays are at the beginning followed by the even numbers.

Example: Array 1: {2, 13, 6, 19, 26, 11, 4 }

Array 2: {7, 22, 4, 17, 12, 45 }

Arranged Array = { 13, 19, 11, 7, 17, 45, 2, 6, 26, 4, 22, 4, 12}

Some of the members of the class are given below:

Class name	OddEven
Data members/Instance variables	
a[]	to store integers in the array
m	integer to store the size of the array
Methods / Member functions	
OddEven(int mm)	parameterised constructor to initialize the data member m=mm
void fillarray()	to enter integer elements in the array
OddEven arrange(OddEven P, OddEven Q)	stores the odd numbers from both the parameterized object arrays followed by the even numbers from both the arrays and returns the object with the arranged array
void display()	displays the elements of the arranged array

Specify the class OddEven giving details of the constructor( ), void fillarray( ), OddEven arrange(OddEven, OddEven) and void display( ). Define a main( ) function to create objects and call the functions accordingly to enable the task.

ISC SQP 2023

Ans

```
import java.util.*;
public class OddEven
{
   int[] a;
   int m;
   public OddEven(int mm)
   {
      m = mm;
      a = new int[m];
   }
   public void fillarray()
   {
      Scanner sc = new Scanner(System.in);
      System.out.println("Enter " + m + "
                                    integers:");
      for (int i = 0; i < m; i++)
      {
         a[i] = sc.nextInt();
      }
   }
   public static OddEven arrange(OddEven P,
                                    OddEven Q)
   {
      OddEven R = new OddEven(P.m + Q.m);
      int rIndex = 0;
      for (int i = 0; i < P.m; i++)
      {
         if (P.a[i] % 2 != 0)
         {
            R.a[rIndex] = P.a[i];
            rIndex++;
         }
      }
      for (int i = 0; i < Q.m; i++)
      {
         if (Q.a[i] % 2 != 0)
         {
            R.a[rIndex] = Q.a[i];
            rIndex++;
         }
      }
      for (int i = 0; i < P.m; i++)
      {
         if (P.a[i] % 2 == 0)
         {
            R.a[rIndex] = P.a[i];
            rIndex++;
         }
      }
      for (int i = 0; i < Q.m; i++)
      {
         if (Q.a[i] % 2 == 0)
         {
            R.a[rIndex] = Q.a[i];
            rIndex++;
         }
      }
      return R;
   }
   public void display()
   {
      System.out.println("Arranged Array:");
      for (int i = 0; i < m; i++)
      {
         System.out.print(a[i] + " ");
      }
      System.out.println();
   }
   public static void main(String[] args)
   {
      OddEven arr1 = new OddEven(7);
      arr1.fillarray();
      OddEven arr2 = new OddEven(6);
      arr2.fillarray();
      OddEven arr3 = OddEven.arrange(arr1, arr2);
      arr3.display();
   }
}
```

7. A class Encrypt has been defined to replace only the vowels in a word by the next corresponding vowel and forms a new word. i.e. A→ E, E→ I, I→ O, O→ U and U→ A

Example: Input: COMPUTER

Output: CUMPATIR

Some of the members of the class are given below:

Class name	Encrypt
Data members/Instance variables	
wrd	to store a word
len	integer to store the length of the word
newwrd	to store the encrypted word
Methods / Member functions	
Encrypt()	default constructor to initialize data members with legal initial values
void acceptword()	to accept a word in UPPER CASE
void freqvowcon()	finds the frequency of the vowels and consonants in the word stored in '*wrd*' and displays them with an appropriate message
void nextVowel()	replaces only the vowels from stored in '*wrd*' by the next corresponding vowel and assigns it to '*newwrd*', with the remaining alphabets unchanged
void disp()	Display the original word along with the excrypted word

Specify the class Encrypt giving details of the constructor( ), void acceptword(), void freqvowcon(), void nextVowel() and void disp(). Define a main( ) function to create an objects and call the functions accordingly to enable the task. ***ISC SQP 2023***

Ans

```
import java.util.Scanner;
class Encrypt
{
    String wrd;
    int len;
    String newwrd;
    Encrypt()
    {
        wrd = "";
        len = 0;
        newwrd = "";
    }
    void acceptword()
    {
        Scanner sc = new Scanner(System.in);
        System.out.print("Enter a word in UPPER
                                            CASE: ");
        wrd = sc.nextLine();
        len = wrd.length();
    }
    void freqvowcon()
    {
        int vowCount = 0;
        int conCount = 0;
        for(int i = 0; i < len; i++)
        {
            char ch = wrd.charAt(i);
            if(ch == 'A' || ch == 'E' || ch == 'I' ||
                         ch == 'O' || ch == 'U')
            {
                vowCount++;
            }
            else
            {
                conCount++;
            }
        }
        System.out.println("Frequency of vowels: "
                                      + vowCount);
        System.out.println("Frequency of
                     consonants: " + conCount);
    }
    void nextVowel()
    {
        newwrd = "";
        for(int i = 0; i < len; i++)
        {
            char ch = wrd.charAt(i);
            switch(ch)
            {
                case 'A': newwrd += 'E'; break;
                case 'E': newwrd += 'I'; break;
                case 'I': newwrd += 'O'; break;
                case 'O': newwrd += 'U'; break;
                case 'U': newwrd += 'A'; break;
                default: newwrd += ch; break;
            }
        }
    }
    void disp()
    {
        System.out.println("Original Word: " +
                                            wrd);
        System.out.println("Encrypted Word: " +
                                         newwrd);
    }
    public static void main(String[] args)
    {
        Encrypt e = new Encrypt();
        e.acceptword();
        e.freqvowcon();
        e.nextVowel();
        e.disp();
    }
}
```

8. Design a class Unique, which checks whether a word begins and ends with a vowel.
Example : APPLE, ARORA etc.
The details of the members of the class are given below:

Class name	Unique
Data members/Instance variables	
word	stores a word
len	to store the length of the word
Methods / Member functions	
Unique ()	default constructor
void acceptword()	to accept the word in UPPER CASE
boolean checkUnique ()	checks and returns true if the word starts and ends with a vowel otherwise returns false
void display ()	displays the word along with an appropriate message

Specify the class Unique, giving details of the constructor, void acceptword (), boolean checkUnique () and void display (). Define the main () function to create an object and call the functions accordingly to enable the task. *ISC 2022 (Sem II)*

Ans
```
import java.util.* ;
class Unique
{
   String word ;
   int len ;
   Unique ()
   {
      word = " " ;
      len = 0;
   }
   void acceptword ()
   {
      Scanner sc = new Scanner
                                 (System.in);
      System.out.println("Enter the word
                            to be check :");
      word = sc.nextLine ();
      len = word.length () ;
   }
   boolean checkUnique ()
   {
      char ch = n.charAt(0) ;
      char ch2 = n.charAt (n.length() -1);
      if ((ch == 'A' ||  ch == 'E' || ch
       == 'I' || ch == 'O' || ch == 'U') &&
                (ch2 == 'A' || ch2 == 'E' ||
             ch2 == 'I' || ch 2 == 'O' ||
                                 ch2 == 'U'))
         return true ;
      else
         return false;
   }
   void display ()
   {
      if (checkUnique () == true)
         System.out.println(word
                     + "starts with vowel and
                            ends with vowel");
      else
         System.out.println(word + "does
                     not start with vowel and
                             end with vowel");
   }
   public static void main (String args [])
   {
      Unique u = new Unique();
      u.acceptword () ;
      u.display () ;
   }
}
```

9. Design a class NoRepeat which checks whether a word has no repeated alphabets in it.
Example : COMPUTER has no repeated alphabets but SCIENCE has repeated alphabets.
The details of the class are given below

Class name	NoRepeat
Data members/Instance variables	
word	to store a word
len	to store the length of the word
Methods/member functions	
NoRepeat (String wd)	parameterised constructor to initialise word = wd
boolean check()	checks whether a word has no repeated alphabets and returns true else returns false
void prn()	displays the word along with an appropriate message

Specify the class NoRepeat, giving details of the constructor(String), boolean check() and void prn (). Define the main () function to create an object and call the functions accordingly to enable the task.
ISC 2022 (Sem II)

Ans
```
import java.io.* ;
class NoRepeat
{
   String word ;
   int len;
   public NoRepeat (String wd)
   {
      word = wd;
      len = word.length();
   }
   public boolean check()
   {
      int count ;
      char string [] = word.
                                toCharArray();
```

```
    for (int i = 0; i < string.length ;
                               i + +)
    {
       count = 1 ;
       for (int j= i+ 1; j<
                   string.length ; j + +)
       {
          if (string [i] == string [j]
                   && string [i] ! =‘’)
          {
             count + +;
             string [j] = ‘0’;
          }
       }
       if(count>1 &&string[i]! = ‘0’)
          return true;
       else
          return false;
    }
  }
  void prn()
  {
    System.out.println(“Repeated
                alphabet in given word”);
    check();
  }
  public static void main(String args[])
  {
    InputStreamReader IR = new
        InputStreamReader (System.in);
    BufferedReader br = new
                   BufferedReader (IR);
    System.out.println(“Enter any word”);
    String s = br.readLine ();
    NoRepeat r=new NoRepeat(s);
    r. prn();
  }
}
```

10. Design a class Toggle which toggles a word by converting all upper case alphabets to lower case and vice *versa*.

Example: The word "mOTiVATe" becomes "MotIVatE"

The details of the members of the class are given below:

Class name	Toggle
Data members/Instance variables	
str	stores a word
newstr	stores the toggled word
len	to store the length of the word
Methods/Member functions	
Toggle()	default constructor
void readword()	to accept the word
void toggle ()	converts the upper case alphabets to lower case and all lower case alphabets to upper case and stores it in newstr
void display()	displays the original word along with the toggled word

Specify the class Toggle giving details of the constructor, void readword(), void toggle( ) and void display(). Define a main( ) function to create an object and call the functions accordingly to enable the task.

ISC SQP 2022 (Sem II)

Ans

```
import java.util.*;
class Toggle
{
   String str, newstr;
   int len;
   Toggle()
   {
      str = "";
      newstr = "";
      len = 0;
   }
   void readword()
   {
      Scanner sc = new Scanner(System.in);
      System.out.print("Enter a word: ");
      str = sc.nextLine();
      len = str.length();
   }
   void toggle()
   {
      for (int i = 0; i < len; i++)
      {
         char c = str.charAt(i);
         if (Character.isUpperCase(c))
         {
            newstr += Character.toLowerCase(c);
         }
         else if (Character.isLowerCase(c))
         {
            newstr += Character.toUpperCase(c);
         }
         else
         {
            newstr += c;
         }
      }
   }
   void display()
   {
      System.out.println("Original word: " +
                                  str+"\n");
      System.out.println("Toggled word: " +
                                    newstr);
   }
   public static void main(String[] args)
   {
      Toggle t = new Toggle();
      t.readword();
      t.toggle();
      t.display();
   }
}
```

11. Design a class BinSearch to search for a particular value in an array.

Some of the members of the class are given below :

Class name	BinSearch
Data members/Instance variables	
arr[]	to store integer elements
n	integer to store the size of the array
Member functions/methods	
BinSearch (int nn)	parameterized constructor to initialize n = nn
void fillArray()	to enter elements in the array
void sort ()	sorts the array elements in ascending order using any standard sorting technique
int bin_Search(int l,int u,int v)	searches for the value 'v' using binary search and recursive technique and returns its location if found otherwise returns –1

Define the class BinSearch giving details of the constructor, void fillarray(), void sort() and int bin_Search(int,int,int). Define the main() function to create an object and call the functions accordingly to enable the task. ***ISC 2020***

Ans

```
import java.io.*;
class BinSearch
{
    int arr[];
    int n;
    public BinSearch(int nn)
    {
        n = nn;
        arr = new int[n];
    }
    public void fillArray()throws IOException
    {
        BufferedReader br = new BufferedReader(new
                                    InputStreamReader(System.in));
        System.out.println("Enter array elements:");
        for(int i = 0; i < n; i++)
            arr[i] = Integer.parseInt(br.readLine());
    }
    public void sort()
    {
        for(int i = 0; i < n; i++)
        {
            for(int j = 0; j < n - 1 - i; j++)
            {
                if(arr[j] > arr[j + 1])
                {
                    int temp = arr[j];
                    arr[j] = arr[j + 1];
                    arr[j + 1] = temp;
                }
            }
        }
    }
    public int bin_Search(int l, int u, int v)
    {
```

```
            int mid = (l + u) / 2;
            if(v == arr[mid])
                return mid;
            else if(l > u)
                return -1;
            else if(v > arr[mid])
                return bin_Search(mid + 1, u, v);
            else
                return bin_Search(l, mid - 1, v);
        }
        public static void main(String args[])throws IOException
        {
            BufferedReader br = new BufferedReader(new
                                    InputStreamReader(System.in));
            System.out.print("Enter the size of array: ");
            int num = Integer.parseInt(br.readLine());
            BinSearch obj = new BinSearch(num);
            obj.fillArray();
            obj.sort();
            System.out.print("Enter value to be searched: ");
            int value = Integer.parseInt(br.readLine());
            int index = obj.bin_Search(0, num - 1, value);
            if(index == -1)
                System.out.println(value + " is not found.");
            else
                System.out.println(value + " is found at index " + index);
        }
    }
```

12. A class Mix has been defined to mix two words, character by character, in the following manner :

The first character of the first word is followed by the first character of the second word and so on. If the words are of different length, the remaining characters of the longer word are put at the end.

e.g. If the first word is "JUMP" and the second word is "STROLL", then the required word will be "JSUTMRPOLL".

Some of the members of the class are given below :

Class name	**Mix**
Data members/Instance variables	
wrd	to store a word
len	to store the length of the word
Member functions/methods	
Mix()	default constructor to initialize the data members with legal initial values
void feedword ()	to accept the word in UPPER case
void mix_word (Mix P, Mix Q)	mixes the words of objects P and Q as stated above and stores the resultant word in the current object
void display()	displays the word

Specify the class Mix giving the details of the constructor, void feedword(), void mix_word(Mix, Mix) and void display(). Define the main() function to create objects and call the functions accordingly to enable the task. ***ISC 2020***

Ans

```
import java.io.*;
class Mix
{
    String wrd;
    int len;
    public Mix()
    {
        wrd = " ";
        len = 0;
    }
    public void feedword()throws IOException
    {
        BufferedReader br = new BufferedReader(new
                                 InputStreamReader(System.in));
        wrd = br.readLine();
        wrd = wrd.toUpperCase();
        if(wrd.indexOf(' ') > 0)
            wrd = wrd.substring(0, wrd.indexOf(' '));
        len = wrd.length();
    }
    public void mix_word(Mix P, Mix Q)
    {
        int i = 0;
        int j= 0;
        while(true)
        {
            if(i < P.len && j < Q.len)
            {
                this.wrd += P.wrd.charAt(i);
                this.wrd += Q.wrd.charAt(j);
            }
            else
                break;
                i++;
                j++;
        }
        if(i < P.len)
            this.wrd += P.wrd.substring(i);
        if(j < Q.len)
            this.wrd += Q.wrd.substring(i);
    }
    public void display()
    {
        System.out.println(wrd);
    }
```

```
public static void main(String args[])throws IOException
{
    Mix ob = new Mix();
    Mix ob1 = new Mix();
    Mix  ob2 = new Mix();
    System.out.print("First word: ");
    ob.feedword();
    System.out.print("Second word: ");
    ob1.feedword();
    ob2.mix_word(ob, ob1);
    System.out.print("Required word: ");
    ob2.display();
}
}
```

13. A class Composite contains a two dimensional array of order [m × n]. The maximum value possible for both 'm' and 'n' is 20. Design a class Composite to fill the array with the first (m × n) composite numbers in column wise. The details of the members of the class are given below:

Class name	Composite
Data members/Instance variables	
arr[] []	stores the composite numbers column wise
m	integer to store the number of rows
n	integer to store the number of columns
Member functions/methods	
Composite(int mm, int nn)	to initialize the size of the matrix m=mm and n=nn
int isComposite(int p)	returns 1 if number is composite otherwise returns 0
void fill ()	to fill the elements of the array with the first (m × n) composite numbers in column wise
void display ()	display the array in a matrix form

Specify the class Composite giving details of the constructor(int, int), int is Composite(int), void fill() and void display(). Define a main( ) function to create an objects and call the functions accordingly to enable the task. ***ISC SQP 2020***

Ans

```
import java.util.*;
public class Composite
{
   private int[][] arr;
   private int m, n;
   public Composite(int mm, int nn)
   {
      m = mm;
      n = nn;
      arr = new int[m][n];
   }
     public int isComposite(int p)
   {
      int count = 0;
      for (int i = 1; i <= p; i++)
      {
         if (p % i == 0)
         {
            count++;
         }
```

```
        }
        if (count > 2)
        {
            return 1;
        }
        else
        {
            return 0;
        }
    }
    public void fill()
    {
        int num = 4;
        for (int j = 0; j < n; j++)
        {
            for (int i = 0; i < m; i++)
            {
                while (isComposite(num) == 0)
                {
                    num++;
                }
                arr[i][j] = num;
                num++;
            }
        }
    }
    public void display()
    {
        for (int i = 0; i < m; i++)
        {
            for (int j = 0; j < n; j++)
            {
                System.out.print(arr[i][j] + " ");
            }
            System.out.println();
        }
    }
    public static void main(String[] args)
    {
        Composite c = new Composite(3, 4);
        c.fill();
        c.display();
    }
}
```

14. Design a class Sort which enables a word to be arranged in alphabetical order. The details of the members of the class are given below :

Class name	**Sort**
Data members/Instance variables	
str	stores a word
len	to store the length of the word
Methods/Member functions	
Sort()	default constructor
void readword()	to accept the word
void arrange ()	to arrange the word in alphabetical order using any standard sorting technique.
void display( )	displays the original word along with the sorted word

Specify the class Sort giving details of the constructor, void readword(), void arrange() and void display(). Define a main( ) function to create an object and call the functions accordingly to enable the task.
ISC SQP 2020

Ans
```
import java.util.*;
class Sort
{
   String str;
   int len;
   public Sort()
   {
      str = "";
      len = 0;
   }
   public void readword()
   {
      Scanner sc = new Scanner(System.in);
      System.out.print("Enter a word: ");
      str = sc.nextLine();
      len = str.length();
   }
   public void arrange()
   {
      char[] arr = str.toCharArray();
      Arrays.sort(arr);
      str = new String(arr);
   }
   public void display()
   {
      System.out.println("Original word: " + str);
      arrange();
      System.out.println("Sorted word: " + str);
   }
   public static void main(String[] args)
   {
      Sort sr = new Sort();
        sr.readword();
        sr.display();
    }
}
```

15. Design a class MatRev to reverse each element of a matrix.

Example

72	371	5		27	173	5
12	6	426	becomes	21	6	624
5	123	94		5	321	49

Some of the members of the class are given below:

Class name	MatRev
Data members/Instance variables	
arr[ ][ ]	to store integer elements
m	to store the number of rows
n	to store the number of columns

Member functions/methods	
MatRev (int mm, int nn)	parameterised constructor to initialise the data members m = mm and n = nn
void fillarray( )	to enter elements in the array
int reverse(int x)	returns the reverse of the number x
void revMat(MatRev P)	reverses each element of the array of the parameterised object and stores it in the array of the current object
void show( )	display the array elements in matrix form

Define the class MatRev giving details of the constructor, void fillarray(), int reverse(int), void revMat (MatRev), and void show(). Define the main() function to create objects and call the functions accordingly to enable the task. ***ISC 2019***

Ans

```
import java.util.Scanner;
public class MatRev
{
   int arr[][];
   int m;
   int n;
   public MatRev(int mm, int nn)
   {
      m = mm;
      n = nn;
      arr = new int[m][n];
   }
   public void fillarray()
   {
      Scanner sc = new Scanner(System.in);
      System.out.println("Enter the elements of the matrix:");
      for (int i = 0; i < m; i++)
      {
         for (int j = 0; j < n; j++)
         {
            arr[i][j] = sc.nextInt();
         }
      }
   }
   public int reverse(int x)
   {
      int rev = 0;
      while (x != 0)
      {
         int digit = x % 10;
         rev = rev * 10 + digit;
         x /= 10;
      }
      return rev;
   }
   public void revMat(MatRev P)
   {
      for (int i = 0; i < m; i++)
      {
```

```
            for (int j = 0; j < n; j++)
            {
                arr[i][j] = P.reverse(P.arr[i][j]);
            }
        }
    }
    public void show()
    {
        System.out.println("The reversed matrix is:");
        for (int i = 0; i < m; i++)
        {
            for (int j = 0; j < n; j++)
            {
                System.out.print(arr[i][j] + " ");
            }
            System.out.println();
        }
    }
    public static void main(String[] args)
    {
        Scanner sc = new Scanner(System.in);
        System.out.println("Enter the number of rows and columns:");
        int m = sc.nextInt();
        int n = sc.nextInt();
        MatRev obj1 = new MatRev(m, n);
        obj1.fillarray();
        MatRev obj2 = new MatRev(m, n);
        obj2.revMat(obj1);
        obj2.show();
    }
}
```

16. A class Rearrange has been defined to modify a word by bringing all the vowels in the word at the beginning followed by the consonants.

Example : ORIGINAL becomes OIIARGNL

Some of the members of the class are given below:

Class name	Rearrange
Data members/Instance variables	
wrd	to store a word
newwrd	to store a rearranged word
Member functions/methods	
Rearrange( )	default constructor
void readword( )	to accept the word in UPPER case
void freq_vow_con( )	finds the frequency of vowels and consonants in the word and displays them with an appropriate message
void arrange( )	rearranges the word by bringing the vowels at the beginning followed by consonants
void display( )	displays the original word along with the rearrange word

Specify the class Rearrange, giving the details of the constructor, void readword(), void freq_vow_con(), void arrange() and void display(). Define the main() function to create an object and call the functions accordingly to enable the task. ***ISC 2019***

Ans

```
import java.io.Scanner;
class Rearrange
{
   private String wrd;
   private String newwrd;
   public Rearrange()
   {
      wrd = "";
      newwrd = "";
   }
   public void readword()
   {
      Scanner scanner = new Scanner(System.in);
      System.out.print("Enter a word in uppercase: ");
      wrd = scanner.nextLine();
      scanner.close();
   }
   public void freq_vow_con()
   {
      int vowelCount = 0;
      int consonantCount = 0;
      for (int i = 0; i < wrd.length(); i++)
      {
         char ch = wrd.charAt(i);
         if (ch == 'A' || ch == 'E' || ch == 'I' || ch == 'O' || ch == 'U')
         {
            vowelCount++;
         }
         else
         {
            consonantCount++;
         }
      }
      System.out.println("Frequency of vowels: " + vowelCount);
      System.out.println("Frequency of consonants: " + consonantCount);
   }
   public void arrange()
   {
      StringBuilder vowels = new StringBuilder();
      StringBuilder consonants = new StringBuilder();
      for (int i = 0; i < wrd.length(); i++)
      {
         char ch = wrd.charAt(i);
         if (ch == 'A' || ch == 'E' || ch == 'I' || ch == 'O' || ch == 'U')
         {
            vowels.append(ch);
         }
         else
         {
```

```
                consonants.append(ch);
            }
        }
        newwrd = vowels.toString() + consonants.toString();
    }
    public void display()
    {
        System.out.println("Original word: " + wrd);
        System.out.println("Rearranged word: " + newwrd);
    }
    public static void main(String[] args)
    {
        Rearrange Obj = new Rearrange();
        Obj.readword();
        Obj.freq_vow_con();
        Obj.arrange();
        Obj.display();
    }
}
```

17. Two matrices are said to be equal if they have the same dimension and their corresponding elements are equal.

For example the two matrices A and B given below are equal:

Matrix A

1	2	3
2	4	5
3	5	6

Matrix B

1	2	3
2	4	5
3	5	6

Design a class EqMat to check if two matrices are equal or not. Assume that the two matrices have the same dimension.

Some of the members of the class are given below:

Class name	EqMat
Data members/Instance variables	
a[ ][ ]	to store integer elements
m	to store the number of rows
n	to store the number of columns
Member functions/methods	
EqMat(int mm, int nn)	parameterised constructor to initialise the data members m = mm and n = nn
void readarray( )	to enter elements in the array
int check(EqMat P, EqMat Q)	checks if the parameterized objects P and Q are equal and returns 1 if true, otherwise returns 0
void print( )	displays the array elements

Define the class EqMat giving details of the constructor, void readarray(), int check(EqMat, EqMat) and void print(). Define the main() function to create object and call the functions accordingly to enable the task. ***ISC 2018***

Ans

```
import java.util.Scanner;
public class EqMat
{
    int n,m;
    public EqMat(int mm, int nn)
    {
        m=mm;
        n=nn;
    }
    public void readarray()
    {
        Scanner sc = new Scanner(System.in);
        System.out.println("First Matrix");
        System.out.println("Enter the number of rows : ");
        int m = sc.nextInt();
        System.out.println("Enter the number of columns : ");
        int n = sc.nextInt();
        int a[][] = new int[m][n];
        System.out.println("Enter the elements :");
        for (int i = 0; i < m; i++)
        {
            for (int j = 0; j < n; j++)
            {
                a[i][j] = sc.nextInt();
            }
        }
        Scanner sc1 = new Scanner(System.in);
        System.out.println("Second Matrix");
        int b[][] = new int[m][n];
        System.out.println("Enter the elements :");
        for (int i = 0; i <m; i++)
        {
            for (int j = 0; j < n; j++)
            {
                b[i][j] = sc1.nextInt();
            }
        }
    }
    public int check(EqMat P, EqMat Q)
    {
        int flag=1;
        for(int i=0; i <m; i++)
        {
            for(int j=0; j<n; j++)
            {
                if(a[i][j] != b[i][j])
                {
                    flag=0;
                    break;
                }
            }
        }
        if(flag==0)
```

```
                System.out.println("Not identical matrices");
            else
                System.out.println("Identical matrices");
        }
        public void print()
        {
            System.out.println("Printing the First matrix :");
            for (int i = 0; i < m; i++)
            {
                for (int j = 0; j < n; j++)
                {
                    System.out.print(a[i][j]+"\t");
                }
                System.out.println();
            }
            System.out.println("Printing the Second matrix :");
            for (int i = 0; i < m; i++)
            {
                for (int j = 0; j < n; j++)
                {
                    System.out.print(b[i][j]+"\t");
                }
                System.out.println();
            }
        }
        public static void main(String[] args)
        {
            EqMat e=new EqMat();
            e.readarray();
            e.check();
            e.print();
        }
    }
```

18. A class Capital has been defined to check whether a sentence has words beginning with a capital letter or not.

Some of the members of the class are given below:

Class name	**Capital**
Data members/Instance variables	
sent	to store a sentence
freq	stores the frequency of words beginning with a capital letter
Member functions/methods	
Capital( )	default constructor
void input( )	to accept the sentence
boolean isCap(String w)	checks and returns true if word begins with a capital letter, otherwise returns false
void display( )	displays the sentence along with the frequency of the words beginning with a capital letter

Specify the class Capital, giving the details of the constructor, void input(), boolean isCap(String) and void display(). Define the main() function to create an object and call the functions accordingly to enable the task.
ISC 2018

Ans
```
import java.util.Scanner;
class Capital
{
   private String sent;
   private int freq;
   public Capital()
   {
      sent = "";
      freq = 0;
   }
   public void input()
   {
      Scanner scanner = new Scanner(System.in);
      System.out.print("Enter a sentence: ");
      sent = scanner.nextLine();
      scanner.close();
   }
   public boolean isCap(String w)
   {
      if (w.length() > 0)
      {
         char firstChar = w.charAt(0);
         return Character.isUpperCase(firstChar);
      }
      return false;
   }
   public void display()
   {
      String[] words = sent.split(" ");
      freq = 0;
      System.out.println("Sentence: " + sent);
      for (String word : words)
      {
         if (isCap(word))
         {
            freq++;
         }
      }
      System.out.println("Frequency of words beginning with a capital letter: " + freq);
   }
   public static void main(String[] args)
   {
      Capital capitalObj = new Capital();
      capitalObj.input();
      capitalObj.display();
   }
}
```

19. A class Adder has been defined to add any two accepted time
Example :

Time A - 6 hours 35 minutes
Time B - 7 hours 45 minutes
Their sum is - 14 hours 20 minutes (where 60 minutes = 1 hour)

The details of the members of the class are given below

Class Name	Adder
Data member/Instance variable	
a[ ]	integer array to hold two elements (hours and minutes)
Member functions/methods	
Adder()	constructor to assign 0 to the array elements
void readtime()	to enter the elements of the array
void addtime(Adder X, Adder Y)	adds the time of the two parameterized objects X and Y and stores the sum in the current calling object
void disptime()	displays the array elements with an appropriate message (i.e. hours = and minutes =)

Specify the class Adder giving details of the constructor, void readtime(), void addtime(Adder, Adder) and void disptime(). Define the main function to create object and call the functions accordingly to enable the task. ***ISC 2017***

Ans

```
import java.io.*;
class Adder
{
    int a[] = new int[2];
    Adder()
    {
        a[0]=0;
        a[1]=0;
    }
    void readtime() throws IOException
    {
        InputStreamReader IR=new InputStreamReader(System.in);
        BufferedReader br=new BufferedReader(IR);
        System.out.println("Enter the Time in Hours and Minutes");
        a[0]=Integer.parseInt(br.readLine());
        a[1]=Integer.parseInt(br.readLine());
    }
    void addtime(Adder X, Adder Y)
    {
        a[0]=X.a[0]+Y.a[0];
        a[1]=X.a[1]+Y.a[1];
        if(a[1]>=60)
        {
            a[0]=a[0]+a[1]/60;
            a[1]=a[1]%60;
        }
    }
    void disptime()
```

```
    {
        System.out.println(a[0]+" hours "+a[1]+" minutes");
    }
    public static void main(String args[]) throws IOException
    {
        Adder A = new Adder();
        Adder B = new Adder();
        Adder C = new Adder();
        A.readtime();
        B.readtime();
        C.addtime(A, B);
        System.out.println("Time A - ");
        A.disptime();
        System.out.println("Time B - ");
        B.disptime();
        System.out.println("Their sum is - ");
        C.disptime();
    }
}
```

20. A class SwapSort has been defined to perform string related operations on a word input. Some of the members of the class are as follows

Class Name	**SwapSort**
Data members/Instance variables	
wrd	to store a word
len	integer to store length of the word
swapwrd	to store the swapped word
sortwrd	to store the sorted word
Member functions\Methods	
SwapSort( )	default constructor to initialize data members with legal initial values
void readword( )	to accept a word in UPPER CASE
void swapchar( )	to interchange/swap the first and last characters of the word in 'wrd' and stores the new word in 'swapwrd'
void sortword( )	sorts the character of the original word in alphabetical order and stores it in 'sortwrd'
void display( )	displays the original word, swapped word and the sorted word.

Specify the class SwapSort, giving the details of the constructor, void readword(), void swapchar(), void sortword() and void display(). Define the main() function to create an object and call the functions accordingly to enable the task. ***ISC 2017***

Ans

```
import java.io.*;
public class SwapSort
{
    char [] wrd;
    int len;
    char [] swapwrd;
    char [] sortwrd;
```

```
SwapSort()
{
    len=0;
}
void readword() throws IOException
{
    InputStreamReader IR=new InputStreamReader(System.in);
    BufferedReader br=new BufferedReader(IR);
    System.out.println("Enter the word in UPPER CASE");
    String t=br.readLine();
    len=t.length();
    wrd = new char[len];
    for(int i=0; i<len;i++)
        wrd[i]=t.charAt(i);
    swapwrd = new char[len];
    sortwrd = new char[len];
}
void swapchar()
{
    for(int i=0;i<len;i++)
    {
        if(i==0)
            swapwrd[i]=wrd[len-1];
        else if(i==len-1)
            swapwrd[len-1]=wrd[0];
        else
            swapwrd[i]=wrd[i];
    }
}
void sortword()
{
    for(int i=0;i<len;i++)
    {
        sortwrd[i]=wrd[i];
    }
    for(int i=0;i<len;i++)
    {
        for(int j=0;j<len-i-1;j++)
        {
            if(sortwrd[j]>sortwrd[j+1])
            {
                char t = sortwrd[j];
                sortwrd[j]=sortwrd[j+1];
                sortwrd[j+1]=t;
            }
        }
    }
}
```

```
    void display()
    {
        System.out.print("Original Word : ");
        for(int i=0;i<len;i++)
            System.out.print(wrd[i]);
        System.out.println();
        System.out.print("Swapped Word : ");
        for(int i=0;i<len;i++)
            System.out.print(swapwrd[i]);
        System.out.println();
        System.out.print("Sorted Word : ");
        for(int i=0;i<len;i++)
            System.out.print(sortwrd[i]);
        System.out.println();
    }
    public static void main(String args[]) throws IOException
    {
        SwapSort S = new SwapSort();
        S.readword();
        S.swapchar();
        S.sortword();
        S.display();
    }
}
```

21. A class Shift contains a two dimensional integer array of order $(m \times n)$ where the maximum values of both m and n is 5. Design the class Shift to shuffle the matrix (i.e. the first row becomes the last, the second row becomes the first and so on). The details of the members of the class are given below:

Class name	Shift
Data members/Instance variables	
mat[ ][ ]	stores the array element
m	integer to store the number of rows
n	integer to store the number of columns
Member functions/methods	
Shift(int mm, int nn)	parameterised constructor to initialise the data members m = mm and n = nn
void input( )	enters the elements of the array
void cyclic(Shift P)	enables the matrix of the object(P) to shift each row upwards in a cyclic manner and stores the resultant matrix in the current object
void display( )	displays the matrix elements

Specify the class Shift giving details of the constructor, void input(), void cyclic(Shift) and void display(). Define the main() function to create an object and call the methods accordingly to enable the task of shifting the array elements. ***ISC 2016***

Ans

```
import java.io.*;
class Shift
{
    int mat[][];
    int m;
    int n;
    public Shift(int mm, int nn)
    {
        m = mm;
        n = nn;
        mat = new int[m][n];
    }
    public void input()throws IOException
    {
        InputStreamReader isr = new InputStreamReader(System.in);
        BufferedReader br = new BufferedReader(isr);
        for(int i = 0; i < m; i++)
        for(int j = 0; j < n; j++)
        {
            System.out.print("Element"+i+", "+j+":");
            mat[i][j] = Integer.parseInt(br.readLine());
        }
    }
    public void cyclic(Shift P)
    {
        for(int i = 0; i < m; i++)
        for(int j = 0; j < n; j++)
        {
            if(i == 0)
                this.mat[m-1][j] = P.mat[i][j];
            else
                this.mat[i-1][j] = P.mat[i][j];
        }
    }
    public void display()
    {
        for(int i = 0; i < m; i++)
        {
            for(int j = 0; j < n; j++)
                 System.out.print(mat[i][j]+"\t");
            System.out.println();
        }
    }
    public static void main(String args[])throws IOException
    {
        InputStreamReader isr = new InputStreamReader(System.in);
        BufferedReader br = new BufferedReader (isr);
```

```
            System.out.println("Enter the number of rows and columns below or
                                                                    equal to 5");
            int r = Integer.parseInt(br.readLine());
            int c = Integer.parseInt(br.readLine());
            Shift obj1 = new Shift(r, c);
            Shift obj2 = new Shift (r, c);
            obj1.input();
            System.out.println("ORIGINAL MATRIX");
            obj1.display();
            obj2.cyclic(obj1);
            System.out.println("NEW MATRIX");
            obj2.display();
        }
    }
```

22. A class ConsChange has been defined with the following details:

Class name	ConsChange
Data members/Instance variables	
word	stores the word
len	stores the length of the word
Member functions/methods	
ConsChange()	default constructor
void readword()	accepts the word in lowercase
void shiftcons()	shifts all the consonants of the word at the beginning followed by the vowels (e.g. spoon becomes spnoo)
void changeword()	changes the case of all occurring consonants of the shifted word to uppercase, e.g. (spnoo becomes SPNoo)
void show()	displays the original word, shifted word and the changed word

Specify the class ConsChange giving the details of the constructor, void readword(), void shiftcons(), void changeword() and void show(). Define the main() function to create an object and call the functions accordingly to enable the task. ***ISC 2016***

Ans

```
import java.io.*;
class ConsChange
{
    String word;
    int len;
    public ConsChange()
    {
        word = new String();
        len = word.length();
    }
    public void readword()throws IOException
    {
        InputStreamReader isr = new InputStreamReader(System.in);
        BufferedReader br = new BufferedReader(isr);
        System.out.print("Enter the word in lowercase:");
        word = br.readLine();
```

```
        len = word.length();
    }
    public void shiftcons()
    {
        String cons = new String();
        String vowel = new String();
        for(int i = 0; i < len; i++)
        {
            char ch = word.charAt(i);
            switch(ch)
            {
                case 'a':
                case 'e':
                case 'i':
                case 'o':
                case 'u':
                    vowel + = ch;
                    break;
                default:
                    cons + = ch;
            }
        }
        word = cons + vowel;
    }
    public void changeword()
    {
        int pos = - 1;
        for(int i = 0; i < len; i+ +)
        {
            char ch = word.charAt(i);
            switch(ch)
            {
                case 'a':
                case 'e':
                case 'i':
                case 'o':
                case 'u':
                    break;
                default:
                    pos = i;
            }
            word = word.substring(0, pos+1).toUpperCase()
                                        + word.substring(pos+1);
        }
    }
    public void show()
    {
        System.out.println(''Original Word:''+word);
        shiftcons();
        System.out.println(''Shifted Word:''+word);
        changeword();
        System.out.println(''Changed Word:''+word);
    }
    public static void main(String args[])throws IOException
    {
        ConsChange obj = new ConsChange();
        obj.readword();
        obj.show();
    }
}
```

23. A class Admission contains the admission numbers of 100 students. Some of the data member/member functions are given below:

Class name	Admission
Data member/Instance variable	
Adno[ ]	integer array to store admission numbers
Member functions/methods	
Admission( )	constructor to initialise the array elements
void fillArray( )	to accept the elements of the array in ascending order
int binSearch(int l, int u, int v)	to search for a particular admission number (v) using binary search and recursive technique and returns 1 if found otherwise returns - 1

Specify the class Admission giving details of the constructor, void fillArray() and int binSearch(int, int, int). Define the main() function to create an object and call the functions accordingly to enable the task. ***ISC 2015***

Ans

```
import java.io.*;
public class Admission
{
    int Adno[]=new int[100];
    Admission( )
    {
        for(int i=0;i<100;i++)
        {
            Adno[i]=0;
        }
    }
    void fillArray( ) throws IOException
    {
        InputStreamReader isr = InputStreamReader(System.in);
        BufferedReader br = new BufferedReader(isr);
        System.out.println("Enter the elements of array in ascending order");
        for(int i = 0; i< 100 ; i+ +)
        {
            Adno[i] = Integer.parseInt(br.readLine( ));
        }
    }
    int binSearch(int l, int u, int v)
    {
        int m = -1;
        while(l <= u)
        {
            m=(l+u)/2;
            if(Adno[m]==v)
            {
                return 1;
            }
            else if(Adno[m]>v)
            {
                u = m - 1;
                m = binSearch(l, u, v);
            }
            else
            {
```

```
                l = m + 1;
                m = binSearch(l, u, v);
            }
        }
        return -1;
    }
    public static void main(String args[]) throws IOException
    {
        Admission A=new Admission( );
        A.fillArray( );
        InputStreamReader IR=new InputStreamReader(System.in);
        BufferedReader br=new BufferedReader(IR);
        System.out.println("Enter an admission number to be search");
        int v=Integer.parseInt(br.readLine( ));
        int r=A.binSearch(0, 99, v);
        if(r==1)
            System.out.println("Item found");
        else
            System.out.println("Item is not found");
    }
}
```

24. A class TheString accepts a string of a maximum of 100 characters with only one blank space between the words.

Some of the members of the class are as follows:

Class name	TheString
Data members/Instance variables	
str	to store a string
len	integer to store the length of the string
wordcount	integer to store the number of words
cons	integer to store the number of consonants
Member functions/Methods	
TheString( )	default constructor to initialise the data members
TheString(String ds)	parameterized constructor to assign str=ds
void countFreq( )	to count the number of words and the number of consonants and store them in wordcount and cons respectively
void Display( )	to display the original string, alongwith the number of words and the number of consonants

Specify the class TheString giving the details of the constructors, void countFreq() and void Display(). Define the main() function to create an object and call the functions accordingly to enable the task. **ISC 2015**

Ans

```
import java.io.*;
public class TheString
{
    String str;
    int len, wordcount,cons;
    TheString( )
    {
        str=" ";
```

```
        len=0;
        wordcount=0;
        cons=0;
    }
    TheString(String ds)
    {
        str=ds;
        len=str.length( );
        wordcount=0;
        cons=0;
    }
    void countFreq( )
    {
        char c;
        for(int i=0; i<len; i++)
        {
            c=str.charAt(i);
            if(c == ' ')
                wordcount++;
            else
            {
                c=toUpperCase(c);
                if(!(c=='A'||c=='E'||c=='I'||c=='O'||c=='U'))
                    cons++;
            }
        }
    }
    void Display()
    {
        System.out.println("The original string is "+str);
        System.out.println("The number of words in the string is "
                                                            +(wordcount+1));
        System.out.println("The number of consonants in the string is "+cons);
    }
    public static void main(String args[]) throws IOException
    {
        InputStreamReader IR = new InputStreamReader(System.in);
        BufferedReader br = new BufferedReader(IR);
        System.out.println("Enter any string");
        String S = br.readLine();
        TheString TS = new TheString(S);
        TS.countFreq();
        TS.Display();
    }
}
```

25. A class Mixer has been defined to merge two sorted integer arrays in ascending order. Some of the members of the class are given below:

Class name	Mixer
Data members/Instance variables	
int arr [ ]	to store the elements of an array.
int n	to store the size of the array.
Member functions	
Mixer (int nn)	constructor to assign n = nn
void accept ( )	to accept the elements of the array in ascending order without any duplicates.
Mixer mix(Mixer A)	to merge the current object array elements with the parameterised array elements and return the resultant object.
void display( )	to display the elements of the array.

Specify the class Mixer giving details of the constructor, void accept(), Mixer mix(Mixer) and void display(). Define the main() function to create an object and call the functions accordingly to enable the task. ***ISC 2014***

Ans

```
import java.io.*;
class Mixer                                    //class name Mixer
{
    public int arr[] = new int[20];
    public int n;
    public Mixer(int nn)                       //constructor with argument
    {
        n = nn;
    }
    void accept() throws IOException
    {
        BufferedReader br = new BufferedReader(new
                                    InputStreamReader(System.in));
                                       //BufferedReader used to input
        System.out.println("Enter elements of array in ascending
                                 order and without duplication :");
        for(int i = 0; i < n; i++)
        {
            arr[i] = Integer.parseInt(br.readLine( ));
                                       // to read the line
        }
    }
    Mixer mix(Mixer A) throws IOException
    {
        int p = 0, q = 0, x = 0;
        Mixer M = new Mixer(n + A.n);  //declaration
        while(p < n && q < A.n)
        {
```

```
            if(arr[p] < A.arr[q])
            {
                M.arr[x++] = arr[p];
                p++;
            }
            else
            {
                M.arr[x++] = A.arr[q];
                q++;
            }
        }
        if(p < n)
        {
            for(int i = p; i < n; i++)
            {
                M.arr[x++] = arr[i];
            }
        }
        else if(q < A.n)
        {
            for (int i = q; i < A.n; i++)
            {
                M.arr[x++] = A.arr[i];
            }
        }
        return M;
    }
    void display()
    {
        for(int i = 0; i < n; i++)
        {
            System.out.println(arr[i]);
        }
    }
    public static void main(String args[]) throws IOException
    {
        BufferedReader br = new BufferedReader
        (new InputStreamReader(System.in));            //input the value
        System.out.println("Enter the size of array:");
        int n = Integer.parseInt(br.readLine());
        Mixer ob = new Mixer(n);                   //declaration and initialising
        Mixer k = new Mixer(n);
        Mixer J = new Mixer((ob.n)+(k.n));
        ob.accept();                                      //calling function
        k.accept();
        J=ob.mix(k);
        J.display();
    }
}
```

26. A class Matrix contains a two-dimensional integer array of order [m × m]. The maximum value possible for both 'm' and 'n' is 25. Design a class Matrix to find the difference of two matrices. The details of the members of the class are given below:

Class name	Matrix
Data members/Instance variables	
arr[ ][ ]	stores the matrix element
m	integer to store the number of rows
n	integer to store the number of columns
Member functions	
Matrix (int mm, int nn)	parameterized constructor to initialise the size of the matrix m = mm and n = nn
void fillarray( )	to enter the elements of the matrix
Matrix SubMat(Matrix A)	subtract the current object from the matrix of parameterised object and return the resulting object
void display ( )	display the matrix elements

Specify the class Matrix giving details of the constructor(int,int), void fillarray(), Matrix SubMat(Matrix) and void display(). Define the main() function to create object and call the methods accordingly to enable the task. ***ISC 2013***

Ans
```
import java.io.*;
class Matrix                                    //class name
{
    int arr[][];
    int m, n;
    Matrix(int mm, int nn)                      //constructor
    {
        m = mm;
        n = nn;
        arr = new int[m][n];
    }
    void fillarray() throws IOException     //method
    {
        BufferedReader br = new BufferedReader (new
                                        InputStreamReader(System.in));
        System.out.println("Enter the elements of the matrix");
        for(int i = 0; i < m; i++)
        {
            for(int j = 0; j < n; j++)
            {
                arr[i][j] = Integer.parseInt(br.readLine());
            }
        }
    }
    Matrix SubMat(Matrix A)
    {
        Matrix B = new Matrix(m, n);
        for(int i = 0; i < m; i++)
        {
            for(int j = 0; j < n; j++)
            {
```

```
                B.arr[i][j] = arr[i][j] - A.arr[i][j];
            }
        }
        return B;
    }
    void display()
    {
        System.out.println("The difference of both two matrices is");
        for(int i = 0; i < m; i++)
        {
            for(int j = 0; j < n; j++)
            {
                System.out.print(arr[i][j] + "\t");
            }
            System.out.println();
        }
    }
    public static void main(String[] args) throws IOException
    {
        int m=0, n=0;
        BufferedReader br=new BufferedReader(new InputStreamReader(System.in));
        System.out.println("Enter number of rows and columns: (Maximum
                                                             limit=25)");
        m=Integer.parseInt(br.readLine());
        n=Integer.parseInt(br.readLine());
        Matrix M = new Matrix(m, n);
        M.fillarray(); //calling method
        Matrix K = new Matrix(m, n);
        K.fillarray(); //calling method
        Matrix P = new Matrix(m, n);
        P = M.SubMat(K);
        P.display(); //calling method
    }
}
```

27. A class Combine contains an array of integers which combines two arrays in a single array including the duplicate elements, if any, and sorts the combine array. Some of the members of the class are given below:

Class name	**Combine**
Data members/Instance variables	
com[ ]	integer array
size	size of the array
Member functions/methods	
Combine (int nn)	parameterised constructor to assign size = nn
void inputarray( )	to accept the array elements
void sort ( )	sorts the elements of combined array in ascending order using the selection sort technique
void mix (Combine A, Combine B)	combines the parameterised object arrays and stores the result in the current object array along with duplicate elements, if any
void display ( )	displays the array elements

Specify the class Combine giving details of the constructor(int), void inputarray(), void sort(), void mix(Combine,Combine) and void display(). Also, define the main() function to create an object and call the methods accordingly to enable the task. **ISC 2012**

Ans

```
import java.io.*;
class Combine                              //class name Combine
{
      int com[ ], size;
      Combine(int nn)                      //constructor
      {
          size = nn;
          com = new int[nn];
      }
      void inputarray() throws IOException
      {
          BufferedReader br = new BufferedReader(new InputStreamReader(System.in));
          //BufferedReader used to input the value
          //InputStreamReader reads bytes and decodes them into
          //character
          for(int  i = 0; i < com.length; i++)
          {
              com[i] = Integer.parseInt(br.readLine());
          }
      }
      void sort()
      {
          for(int i = 0; i < com.length; i++)
          {
              for(int j = i + 1; j< com.length; j++)
              {
                  if(com[i] > com[j])
                  {
                      int temp = com[i];
                      com[i] = com[j];
                      com[j] = temp;
                  }
              }
          }
      }
      void display()
      {
          for(int i = 0; i<com.length; i++)
          {
              System.out.println(com[i]);
          }
      }
      void mix(Combine A, Combine B)
      {
          int len1, len2;
          len1 = A.com.length;
          len2 = B.com.length;
          com = new int[len1 + len2];
          int i, j, k;
          i = 0; j = 0; k = 0;
```

```
            while(i < len1 && j < len2)
            {
                if(A.com[i] < B.com[j])
                {
                    com[k] = A.com[i];
                    i++;
                }
                else
                {
                    com[k] = B.com[j];
                    j++;
                }
                k++;
            }
            if(i < len1)
            {
                while(i < len1)
                {
                    com[k++] = A.com[i];
                    i++;
                }
            }
            if(j < len2)
            {
                while(j < len2)
                {
                    com[k++] = B.com[j];
                    j++;
                }
            }
        }
        public static void main(String[] args) throws IOException
        {
            Combine obj = new Combine(2);           //creating object
            Combine obj1 = new Combine(3);
            Combine obj2 = new Combine( );
            System.out.println("Enter First Array");
            obj.inputarray();                        //calling method
            System.out.println("Enter Second Array");
            obj1.inputarray();
            obj.sort();
            obj1.sort();
            System.out.println("Display Array 1 is:");
            obj.display();
            System.out.println("Display Array 2 is:");
            obj1.display();
            obj2.mix(obj, obj1);
            System.out.println("Sorted Array is:");
            obj2.display();
        }
    }
```

28. Class Binary contains an array of n integers (n <= 100) that are already arranged in ascending order. The subscripts of the array elements vary from 0 to n – 1. The data members and member functions of the class Binary are given below:

Class name	Binary
Data members/Instance variables	
a [ ]	integer array of 100 elements
n	size of the array
l	location of the lower bound
u	location of the upper bound
Member functions	
Binary (int nn)	constructor to initialise in size n = nn and the other instance variables
void readdata ( )	to fill the elements of the array in ascending order
int binary_search(int v)	returns the location of the value (v) to be searched in the list by binary search method using the Recursive technique. The function returns-1, if the number is not present in the given list

(i) Specify the class Binary giving the details of the constructor, void readdata() and int binary_search(int). You need not to write the main function.

(ii) State the Best Case in the recursive function binary_search(). *ISC 2009*

Ans (i)
```
import java.io.*;
class Binary                    //class name Binary
{
        int a[];
        int n, l, u;
        Binary(int nn)
        {
            a = new int [100];
            n = nn;
            for(int i = 0; i < n; i++)
            {
                a[i] = 0;
            }
            l = 0;
            u = n - 1;
        }
        void readdata() throws IOException
        {
            BufferedReader br = new BufferedReader
                                (new InputStreamReader(System.in));
            // to input the value of array
            System.out.println("Enter the value in ascending order");
            for(int i = 0; i < n ; i++)
            {
                a[i] = Integer.parseInt(br.readLine());
            }
        }
        int binary_search(int v)
        {
            int m=-1;
            while(l!=0||u<=n-1)
            {
                m = (l + u)/2;
```

```
                if(a[m] > v)
                {
                    u = m - 1;
                    m = binary_search(v);
                }
                else if(a[m] < v)
                {
                    l = m + 1;
                    m = binary_search(v);
                }
                else
                {
                    break;
                }
            }
            return m;
        }
    }
```

(ii) The best case in the function binary_search is the condition if (l < u) when condition is evaluated to be false, then function will not call itself and return statement will be executed.

29. A class SortWord has been defined with the following details:

Class Name	**SortWord**
Data members/Instance variables	
txt	stores the word
len	stores the length of the word
Member functions	
SortWord( )	default constructor
void readTxt( )	to accept the word in lower case
void sortTxt( )	to sort the word in alphabetical order of characters using bubble sort technique and display it
void changeTxt( )	to change the case of vowels in the word to UPPER case (e.g. school becomes schOOl)
void disp( )	to display the changed string

Specify the class SortWord giving the details of the functions constructor, void readTxt(), void sortTxt(), void changeTxt() and void disp(). You need not to write the main function. **ISC 2009**

Ans

```
import java.io.*;
class SortWord                    //class name SortWord
{
    char txt[];
    int len;
    SortWord()
    {
        len = 0;
    }
    void readTxt() throws IOException
    {
        BufferedReader br = new BufferedReader
                             (new InputStreamReader(System.in));
        System.out.println("Enter the word in lower case");
        String t = br.readLine();
        len = t.length();
```

```
        txt = new char[len];
        for(int i = 0; i < len; i++)
        {
            txt[i] = t.charAt(i);
        }
    }
    void sortTxt()
    {
        char a, b;
        for(int i = 0; i < len; i++)
        {
            for(int j = 0;j < len-i-1;j++)
            {
                a = txt[j];
                b = txt[j + 1];
                if(a > b)
                {
                    char t = txt[j];
                    txt[j] = txt[j + 1];
                    txt[j+1] = t;
                }
            }
        }
    }
    void changeTxt()
    {
        for(int i = 0; i < len; i++)
        {
            switch(txt[i])
            {
                case 'a' : txt[i]= (char)(txt[i]-32); break;
                case 'e' : txt[i]= (char)(txt[i]-32); break;
                case 'i' : txt[i]= (char)(txt[i]-32); break;
                case 'o' : txt[i]= (char)(txt[i]-32); break;
                case 'u' : txt[i]= (char)(txt[i]-32); break;
            }
        }
    }
    void disp()
    {
        System.out.println(txt);
    }
}
```

30. A transpose of an array is obtained by interchanging the elements of the rows and columns. A class Transarray contains a two-dimensional integer array of order [m × n]. The maximum value possible for both 'm' and 'n' is 20. Design a class Transarray to find the transpose of a given matrix. The details of the members of the class are given below:

Class name	Transarray
Data members/Instance variables	
arr [ ][ ]	stores the matrix elements
m	integer to store the number of rows
n	integer to store the number of columns

Member functions	
Transarray ( )	default constructor
Transarray (int mm, int nn)	to initialise the size of the matrix, m = mm, n = nn
void fillarray ( )	to enter the elements of the matrix
void transpose (Transarray A)	to find the transpose of a given matrix
void disparray( )	displays the array in a matrix form

Specify the class Transarray giving the details of the constructors, void fillarray(), void transpose(Transarray) and void disparray(). You need not to write the main function. ***ISC 2009***

Ans

```
import java.io.*;
class Transarray                    //class name
{
        int arr[][];                //declare array
        int m, n;
        Transarray()                //default constructor
        {
            arr = new int[20][20];  //initialise array
            m = 20;
            n = 20;
        }
        Transarray(int mm, int nn)  //parameterized constructor
        {
            int i,j;
            m = mm;
            n = nn;
            arr = new int[mm][nn];
            for(i = 0; i < m; i++)
            {
                for(j = 0; j < n; j++)
                {
                    arr[i][j] = 0;
                }
            }
        }
        void fillarray() throws IOException
        {
            int i, j;
            BufferedReader br = new BufferedReader
                             (new InputStreamReader(System.in));
            System.out.println("Enter the values");
            for(i = 0; i < m; i++)
            {
                for(j = 0; j < n; j++)
                    arr[i][j] = Integer.parseInt(br.readLine());
            }
        }
        void transpose(Transarray A)
        {
            int i, j;
            if(n == A.m && m == A.n)
```

```
            {
                for(i = 0; i < A.m; i++)
                {
                    for(j = 0; j < A.n; j++)
                    {
                        arr[i][j] = A.arr[j][i];
                    }
                }
            }
        }
        void disparray()
        {
            int i, j;
            System.out.println("The transported value of array");
            for(i = 0; i < m; i++)
            {
                for(j=0; j < n; j++)
                {
                    System.out.print("\t" +arr[i][j]);
                }
                System.out.println();
            }
        }
    }
```

31. A class PrimeFac contains an array of 50 integers. Some of the members of the class are given below:

Class name	PrimeFac
Data members/Instance variables	
num[ ]	array to store integers
freq[ ]	array to store the frequency of prime factors of numbers
Member functions	
PrimeFac( )	constructor to initialise array elements to 0
void enter( )	to enter values into array num[ ]
void frefac( )	to determine the frequency of prime factors of the numbers stores in num[ ] and assign it to freq[ ]
void disp( )	to display both the arrays

Specify the class PrimeFac giving the details of constructor, void enter(), void frefac() and void disp(). You need not to write main function. ***ISC 2009***

Ans

```
import java.io.*;
class PrimeFac
{
    int num[ ];
    int freq[ ];
    PrimeFac()                  //constructor
    {
        num = new int[50];      //declaration array dynamically
        freq = new int[50];
        for(int i = 0; i < 50; i++)
        {
```

```
            num[i]++;
            freq[i] = 0;
        }
    }
    void enter() throws IOException
    {
        BufferedReader br = new BufferedReader(new InputStreamReader(System.in));
        int i;
        for(i = 0; i < 50; i++)
        {
            System.out.println("Enter the number");
            num[i] = Integer.parseInt(br.readLine());
        }
    }
    void frefac()
    {
        int i;
        for(i = 0; i < 50; i++)
        {
            freq[i] = 0;
            for(int j = 1; j < num[i]; j++)
            {
                if(num[i]%j == 0 && isprime(j) == 1)
                {
                    freq[i] += 1;
                }
            }
        }
    }
    int isprime(int n)                //method
    {
        for (int i = 2; i < n; i++)
        {
            if(n % i == 0)
              return 0;
        }
        return 1;
    }
    void disp()                       //method
    {
        System.out.println("Number\t frequency");
        for(int i = 0; i < 50; i++)
        {
            System.out.println(num[i] + "\t"+freq[i]);
        }
    }
}
```

32. A class Collection contains an array of 100 integers. Using the following class description create an array with common elements from two integer arrays. Some of the members of the class are given below:

Class name	Collection
Data members/Instance variables	
arr[ ]	integer array
len	length of the array
Member functions	
Collection ( )	default constructor
Collection (int)	parameterised constructor to assign the length of the array
void inparr ( )	to accept the array elements
Collection common (Collection)	returns a Collection containing the common elements of current Collection object and the Collection object passed as a parameter
void arrange ( )	sort the array elements of the object containing common elements in ascending order using by sorting technique
void display ( )	displays the array elements

Specify the class Collection giving the details of the constructors, void inparr() and void arrange(), Collection common(Collection). You need not to write the main function. *ISC 2008*

Ans

```
import java.io.*;
class Collection                                    //class name
{
        int arr[];
        int len;
        Collection()                                //default constructor
        {
            arr = new int[100];                     //initialisation of arr
            len = 100;
        }
        Collection(int x)                           // parameterized constructor
        {
            len = x;
            arr = new int[len];
        }
        void arrange()                              //method
        {
            for(int i = 0; i < len; i++)
            {
                for(int j = i + 1; j < len; j++)
                {
                    if(arr[i] > arr[j])
                    {
                        int t = arr[i];
                        arr[i] = arr[j];
                        arr[j] = t;
                    }
                }
            }
        }
        void display()                              //method
        {
            for(int  i = 0; i < len; i++)
            {
                System.out.println(arr[i]);
```

```
        }
    }
    void inparr() throws IOException
    {
        InputStreamReader ip = new InputStreamReader(System.in);
        //convert byte to char
        BufferedReader br = new BufferedReader(ip);
        //create default input size
        System.out.println("Enter the "+ len+" elements");
        for(int i = 0; i < len; i++)
        {
            arr[i] = Integer.parseInt(br.readLine());
        }
    }
    Collection common(Collection a)        //method
    {
        Collection b = new Collection(len);
        //creating object
        int num, k = 0;
        for(int i = 0; i < a.len; i++)
        {
            num = a.arr[i];
            for(int j = 0; j < len; j++)
            {
                if(num == arr[j])
                {
                    b.arr[k] = num;
                    k++;
                    break;
                }
            }
        }
        b.len = k;
        return b;
    }
}
```

33. A class Revstr defines a recursive function to reverse a string and check whether it is a Palindrome. The details of the class are given below:

Class name	Revstr
Data members/Instance variables	
Str	stores the string
Revst	stores the reverse string
Member functions/methods	
void getStr( )	to accept the string
void recReverse (int)	to reverse the string using the recursive technique
void check( )	to display the original string, its reverse and whether the string is a Palindrome or not

Specify the class Revstr giving the details of the functions void getStr(), void recReverse(int) and void check(). The main function need not to be written. ***ISC 2008***

Ans

```
public class Revstr
{
    private String str;
    private String revst;
    public void getstr()
    {
        Scanner scanner = new Scanner(System.in);
        System.out.println("Enter a string: ");
        str = scanner.nextLine();
        scanner.close();
    }
    public void recreverse(int index)
    {
        if (index < str.length())
        {
            char ch = str.charAt(index);
            recreverse(index + 1);
            revst += ch;
        }
    }
    public void check()
    {
        revst = "";
        recreverse(0);
        System.out.println("Original string: " + str);
        System.out.println("Reversed string: " + revst);
        if (str.equals(revst))
        {
            System.out.println("The string is a palindrome.");
        }
        else
        {
            System.out.println("The string is not a palindrome.");
        }
    }
}
```

34. Design a class Change to convert a decimal number to its equivalent in base 16 and to convert it back to its decimal form. e.g.

(i) The decimal number 35 is 23 in base 16.

(ii) The decimal number 107 is 6B in base 16.

Some of the members of the class are given below:

Class name	Change
Data members/Instance variables	
a [ ]	integer type array
n	integer to be converted to base 16
Member functions/methods	
Change ( )	constructor to assign 0 to instance variables
void input ( )	accept integer to be converted to base 16
void hexadeci (int)	to convert decimal integer 'n' to hexadecimal form
void decihexa ( )	to convert hexadecimal number back to decimal form

Specify the class Change giving the details of the constructor and the functions void input(), void hexadeci(int) and void decihexa(). The main() function need to be written. ***ISC 2007***

Ans

```
import java.io.*;
class Change                                              //class name
{
    int a[];
    int n;
    Change()                                              //constructor
    {
        a = new int[10];
        n = 0;
        for(int i = 0; i <= 9; i++)
            a[i] = 0;
    }
    void input() throws IOException
    {
        BufferedReader br=new BufferedReader(new InputStreamReader(System.in));
        System.out.println("Enter the integer number to be converted to base 16");
        n=Integer.parseInt(br.readLine());
    }
    void hexadeci(int n)                                  //method
    {
        int r, i = 9;
        while(n > 16)
        {
            r = n%16;
            n = n/16;
            a[i--] = r;
        }
        a[i] = n;
        for(int k = i; k <= 9; k++)
        {
            if (a[k] > 9)
            {
                int t = a[k] - 10;
                System.out.print((char)(65 + t));
            }
            else
                System.out.print(a[k]);
        }
        System.out.println();
    }
    void decihexa()                                       //method
    {
        int s = 0, i;
        for(i = 0; i <= 9; i++)
        {
            if(a[i] > 0)
                break;
        }
        if(i < 10)
        {
```

```
                for(int k = i; k <= 9; k++)
                {
                    s = s + a[k] * ((int) Math.pow(16, 9 - k));
                }
                System.out.println(s);
            }
        }
        public static void main(String args[]) throws IOException
        {
            Change c=new Change();
            c.input();
            c.hexadeci(c.n);
            c.decihexa();
        }
    }
```

35. A class Rearrange has been defined to insert an element and to delete an element from an array. Some of the members of the class are given below:

Class name	Rearrange
Data members/Instance variables	
a [ ]	integer type array
n	size of array (integer)
Pos1	position of insertion (integer)
Pos2	position of deletion (integer)
item	item to be inserted (integer)
Member functions/methods	
void enter( )	to enter size, array elements and to display the entered elements
void insert( )	to accept element (item) to be inserted, position of insertion and insert the element (item) at the position of insertion
void disp1( )	to display array after item is inserted
void disp2( )	to display array after item is deleted
void remove( )	to accept the position of deletion and delete element (item) at the position of deletion

Specify the class Rearrange giving details of the functions void enter(), void insert(), void displ(), void disp2() and void remove(). The main function need to be written. ***ISC 2007***

Ans

```
import java.io.*;
class Rearrange
{
    int a[],n,Pos1, Pos2, item;
    void enter() throws IOException
    {
        InputStreamReader in = new InputStreamReader(System.in);
        BufferedReader br = new BufferedReader(in);
        System.out.println("Enter size of array");
        n = Integer.parseInt(br.readLine());
        a = new int[20];
        System.out.println("Enter elements of array");
        for(int i = 0; i < n; i++)
            a[i] = Integer.parseInt(br.readLine());
```

```
        System.out.println("Elements of array are");
        for(int i = 0; i < n; i++)
            System.out.println(a[i]);
    }
    void disp1()
    {
        System.out.println("Array after Insertion");
        for(int i = 0; i < n; i++)
            System.out.println(a[i]);
    }
    void disp2()
    {
            System.out.println("Array after Deletion");
            for(int i = 0; i < n; i++)
                System.out.println(a[i]);
    }
    void insert() throws IOException
    {
        InputStreamReader in = new InputStreamReader(System.in);
        BufferedReader br = new BufferedReader(in);
        System.out.println("Enter item to insert");
        item = Integer.parseInt(br.readLine());
        System.out.println("Enter position");
        int Pos1 = Integer.parseInt(br.readLine());
        if(Pos1 > n)
        {
            System.out.println("Invalid position");
        }
        else
        {
            n++;
            for(int k = n; k > Pos1 - 1; k--)
            {
                a[k] = a[k-1];
            }
            a[Pos1-1] = item;
            disp1();
        }
    }
    void remove() throws IOException
    {
        InputStreamReader in = new InputStreamReader(System.in);
        BufferedReader br = new BufferedReader(in);
        System.out.println("Enter position to delete item");
        Pos2 = Integer.parseInt(br.readLine());
        if(Pos2 < 0 || Pos2 > n)
        {
            System.out.println("Invalid Position");
        }
        else
```

```
            {
                n--;
                for(int k = Pos2-1; k < n; k++)
                {
                    a[k] = a[k+1];
                }
                disp2();
            }
        }
        public static void main(String args[]) throws IOException
        {
            Rearrange r=new Rearrange();
            r.enter();
            r.insert();
            r.disp1();
            r.remove();
            r.disp2();
        }
    }
```

36. A class Mystring has been defined for the following methods/functions:

Class name	Mystring
Data members/Instance variables	
str [ ]	to store a string
len	length of the given string
Member functions/methods	
Mystring ( )	constructor
void readString ( )	reads the given string from the input
int code (int index)	returns, ASCII code for the character at position index
void word ( )	displays longest words in the string

Specify the class Mystring giving the details of the constructor, void readString(), int code(int) and void word() only. The main function need not to be written. ***ISC 2007***

Ans

```
import java.io.*;
class Mystring                    //class name
{
    String str;
    int len;
    Mystring()
    {
        str = " ";
        len =0;
    }
    void readString() throws IOException
    {
        InputStreamReader in = new InputStreamReader(System.in);
        BufferedReader br = new BufferedReader(in);
        System.out.println("Enter string");
        str = br.readLine();
        len = str.length();
```

```
    }
    int code(int index)
    {
        if(index >= len)
        {
            System.out.println("Invalid Index");
            return-1;
        }
        else
            return((int)str.charAt(index));
    }
    void word()
    {
        char c;
        String s, p;
        s = " ";
        p = " ";
        for(int i = 0; i <= len-1; i++)
        {
            c = str.charAt(i);
            if(c ==' '|| c == len-1)
            {
                if(s.length() > p.length())
                {
                    p = s;
                    s = " ";
                }
            }
            else
                s = s + c;
        }
        System.out.println("longest word is" +s);
    }
}
```

37. A class Sort contains an array of 50 integers. Some of the member functions/data members are given below:

Class name	Sort
Data members/Instance variables	
arr [ ]	integers
item	numbers to be searched in the array
Member functions/methods	
void inpdata ( )	to input 50 integers (no duplicate numbers are to be entered)
void bubsort ( )	to sort the array in ascending order using the bubblesort technique and to display the sorted list
void binsearch ( )	to input item and search for it using the binary search technique, if found to print the item searched and its position in the sorted list, otherwise to print an appropriate message

Specify the class Sort giving the details of the functions void inpdata(), void bubsort() and void binsearch(). The main function need not to be written. ***ISC 2006***

Ans
```
import java.io.*;
class Sort                          //class name
{
       int item;
       int arr [ ];
       Sort()                       //constructor
       {
           arr = new int[50];       //declare array size dynamically
       }
       void inpdata() throws IOException
       {
           InputStreamReader inp = new InputStreamReader(System.in);
           BufferedReader br = new BufferedReader(inp);
           int x, k;
           for(int i = 0; i <= 49; i++)
           {
               k = 0;
               x = Integer.parseInt(br.readLine());
               for(int m = 0; m <= i; m++)
               {
                   if(arr [m] == x)
                   {
                       System.out.println("Duplicate Item");
                       k = 1;
                       i--;
                       break;
                   }
               }
               if(k == 0)
               {
                   arr[i] = x;
               }
           }
       }
       void bubsort()                                   //method
       {
           int t, i;
           for(i = 0; i < 49; i++)
           {
               for(int j = 0; j < 49 - i; j++)
               {
                   if(arr [j] > arr[j + 1])
                   {
                       t = arr[j];
                       arr[j] = arr[j+1];
                       arr[j+1] = t;
                   }
               }
           }
           System.out.println("Sorted Array");
           for(i = 0; i <= 49; i++)
           {
```

```
            System.out.println(arr [i]);        //printing the array
        }
    }
    void binsearch() throws IOException
    {
        InputStreamReader inp = new InputStreamReader(System.in);
        BufferedReader br = new BufferedReader(inp);
        int b, e, m, pos = -1;
        b = 0;
        e = arr.length -1;
        System.out.println("Enter Item to be search");
        item = Integer.parseInt(br.readLine());
        while(b <= e)
        {
            m = (b+e)/2;
            if(arr[m] == item)
            {
                pos = m+1;
                break;
            }
            else
            {
                if(arr[m] < item)
                    b=m+1;
                else
                    e = m -1;
            }
        }
        if( pos == -1)
            System.out.println("Item Not Found");
        else
            System.out.println("Item found at " +pos);
    }
}
```

38. Design a class Stringfun to perform various operations on strings without using built in functions for finding the length of the string. Some of the member functions/data member are given below:

Class name	**Stringfun**
Data member/Instance variable	
str	to store the string
Member functions/methods	
void input ( )	to accept the string
void words ( )	to find and display the number of words, number of vowels and number of uppercase characters in the string
void frequency ( )	to display frequency of each character within the string

Specify the class Stringfun giving the details of the functions void input(), void words() and void frequency(). You do not need to write the main function. **ISC 2006**

Ans

```
import java.io.*;
class Stringfun                         //class name
{
    String str;
```

```
void input() throws IOException
{
    InputStreamReader in = new InputStreamReader(System.in);
    //convert byte to character
    BufferedReader br = new BufferedReader(in);
    //create default size of input
    str = br.readLine();
}
void words()                //method
{
    char c;
    int i , w = 1, v = 0, u = 0;
    for(i = 0; i < str.length(); i++)
    {
        c = str.charAt(i);
        if(c == ' ')
            w++;
        else
        {
            if(c=='a'||c=='e'||c=='i'||c=='o'||
                c=='u'||ch='A'||ch=='E'||ch=='I'||ch=='O'||ch=='U')
                v++;
            if(c >= 'A' && c <= 'Z')
                u++;
        }
    }
    System.out.println("No of words " + w);
    System.out.println("No of uppercase letter " + u);
    System.out.println("No of vowels " + v);
}
void frequency()
{
    int i;
    int c[]=new int[26];
    for(i=0;i<26;i++)
        c[i]=0;
        for(i =0;i<str.length();i++)
        {
            char ch;
            ch = str.charAt(i);
            for(int j = 0; j < str.length(); j++)
            {
                if(ch == str.charAt(j))
                    c[i]++;
            }
        }
        for(i=0;i<26;i++)
        {
            char ch1=(char)(65+i);
            char ch2=(char)(97+i);
```

```
                for(int j=0;j<str.length();j++)
                if(ch1==str.charAt(j)||ch2==str.charAt(j))
                {
                    System.out.println("frequency of "+str.charAt(j)+" 
                                                              is " +c[j]);
                   break;
                }
            }
        }
    }
```

39. Class indexedarray contains the employee code of 100 employees. Some of the member functions/data member are given below:

Class name	**indexedarray**
Data member	
ar [ ]	integer
Member functions/methods	
indexedarray ( )	to assign the code to 0
void fillarra ( )	to input the code in the arr [ ]
void sortarr ( )	to sort the array variable using selection sort technique
int binarysearch (int [ ], int)	to search and return 1 if an employee code is found in the array object otherwise return 0

Specify the class indexedarray giving details of the constructor, void sortarr() and int binarysearch(). You may assume, other functions are written for you and you do not need to write the main function. ***ISC 2005***

Ans

```
class indexedarray              //class name
{
        int ar[];
        indexedarray()                  //constructor
        {
            int i;
            ar = new int[100];
            for(i = 0; i <= 99; i++)
                ar[i] = 0;
        }
        void sortarr()
        {
            int N = ar.length;
            int i, j, pos, temp;
            for(i = 0; i < N-1; i++)
            {
                pos = i;
                for(j = i+1; j < N; j++)
                {
                    if(ar[j] < ar[pos])
                    {
                        pos = j;
                    }
                }
                temp = ar[i];
                ar[i] = ar[pos];
                ar[pos] = temp;
            }
```

```
    }
    int binarysearch(int ar[], int c)
    {
        int beg, end, pos = -1, mid;
        beg = 0;
        end = 99;
        while(beg<=end)
        {
            mid = (beg+end)/2;
            if(ar[mid] == c)
            {
                pos = mid+1;
                break;
            }
            else if(ar[mid] < c)
                beg = mid + 1;
            else
                end = mid - 1;
        }
        if( pos == -1)
            return 0;
        else
            return 1;
    }
}
```

40. A class Stringop is designed to handle string related operations. Some members of the class is given below:

Class name	Stringop
Data member	
txt	to store the given string of maximum length 100.
Member functions	
Stringop ( )	constructor
void readstring	To accept the string.
char caseconvert (int)	To convert the letter to other case.
void circulardecode	To decode the string by replacing each …next character in a circular way. Hence, "Abz" will be decoded as "bCa".

Specify the class giving the details of the char caseconvert(int) and void circulardecode() only you may assume that other functions are written for you. You do not need to write the main().

ISC 2005

Ans

```
class Stringop
{
    String txt;
    char caseconvert(int a)
    {
      if(a>='A'&&a<='Z')
          return (char) (a+32);
       if(a>='a'&&a<='z')
          return (char) (a-32);
      return 0;
    }
    void circulardecode()
    {
        String K = "";
```

```
        char c;
        int l = txt.length();
        for(int i = 0; i < l; i++)
        {
            c = caseconvert(txt.charAt(i));
            if(c >= 'A' && c <= 'Y')
                c = (char) (c + 1);
            else if(c == 'Z')
                c = 'A';
            else if(c == 'z')
                c = 'a';
            else if(c >= 'a' && c <= 'y')
                c = (char)(c + 1);
            else
                c = 'a';
            K = K + c;
        }
        System.out.println("String is"+K);
    }
}
```

Case Based Questions

1. With reference to the program code given below, answer the questions that follow

ISC SQP 2022 (Sem I)

```
void dimen(int n[] [])
{
  int p=0;
  for (int i=0;i<n.length;i++)
  for(int j=0;j<n[0].length;j++)
  {
    if(i==0||i==n.length-1 ||j==0||j==n[0].length-1)
    p=p+n[i][j];
  }
  System.out.print(p);
}
```

(i) What will be the output of the method dimen() when the value of n[ ][ ] = {{2,3,7},(1,5,9}, {10,-3,8} } ?

(a) 42 (b) 33 (c) 5 (d) 37

(ii) What is the method dimen() performing?

(a) Finding the product of the boundary elements
(b) Finding the sum of the non-boundary elements
(c) Finding the sum of the boundary elements
(d) Finding the sum of the matrix elements

Ans (i) (d) 37 (ii) (c) Finding the sum of the boundary elements

2. With reference to the program code given below, answer the questions that follow

ISC SQP 2022 (Sem I)

```
void single(int x[])
{
  int w=1;
  for(int y=0:y<x.length; y++)
  {
    if(x[y]%2==0 && x[y]>0)
      w=w*x[y];
  }
```

```
    System.out.print(w);
}
```

(i) What will be the output of the method single() when the value of x[ ] = {10, 2, 9,– 6, 5, 6}?
(a) 120 (b) 45 (c) 720 (d) 18

(ii) What is the method single() performing?
(a) Sum of the positive odd elements (b) Product of the even elements
(c) Product of the positive even elements (d) Sum of the positive even elements

Ans **(i) (a) 120**

(ii) (c) Product of the positive elements

3. The following program code sorts a single dimensional array in ascending order using Insertion Sort technique. There are some places in the code marked as ?1?, ?2?. ?3?, ?4? and ?5? which are to be replaced by a statement/expression so that the code works properly. ***ISC SQP 2022 (Sem I)***

```
void insertionSort(int array[])
{
  int n = ?1 ?;
  for (int j = 1;j<n; j++)
  {
    int key = ?2?;
    int i = j-1;
    while ( (i>-1) && ( array [i] >?3? ) )
    {
      array [i+1]=?4?;
      i--;
    }
    ?5? = key;
  }
}
```

Answer the following questions.

(i) What is the statement or expression at ?1?
(a) array.length() (b)array.length (c) length (d) – 1

(ii) What is the statement or expression at ?2?
(a) j (b) array[j+1] (c) array[j] (d) 0

(iii) What is the statement or expression at ?3?
(a) key (b) array[j] (c) i+l (d) n

(iv) What is the statement or expression at ?4?
(a) j+l (b) key (c) array[j] (d) array[i]

(v) What is the statement or expression at ?5?
(a) array[i+1] (b) i+l (c) j (d) array[i]

Ans **(i) (b) array.length (ii) (c) array[j] (iii) (a) key**

(iv) (d) array[i] (v) (a) array[i+1]

4. The following is a function of some class which sorts an integer array a[ ] in ascending order using selection sort technique. There are some places in the code marked by ?1?, ?2?, ?3?, ?4?, ?5? which may be replaced by a statement/expression so that the function works properly.

```
void selectsort(int []a)
{
    int i, j, t, min, minpos;
    for(i=0;i<?1?;i++)
    {
        min = a[i];
```

```
            minpos = i;
            for(j = ?2?; j<a.length;j++)
            {
                if(min > a[j])
                {
                    ?3? = j;
                    min = ?4?;
                }
            }

            t = a[minpos];
            a[minpos] = a[i];
            a[i]= ?5?
        }
        for(int k=0; k>a.length; k++)
            System.out.println(a[k]);
    }
```

(i) What is the expression or statement at ?1?
(ii) What is the expression or statement at ?2?
(iii) What is the expression or statement at ?3?
(iv) What is the expression or statement at ?4?
(v) What is the expression or statement at ?5? ***ISC 2014***

Ans (i) `a.length-1` (ii) `i + 1` (iii) `minpos`
(iv) `a[j]` (v) `t`

5. The following function is a part of some class. It sorts the array a[ ] in ascending order using insertion sort technique. There are some places in the code marked by ?1?, ?2?, ?3?, ?4?, ?5? which must be replaced by expression/statement so that the function works correctly.

```
void insertsort(int a[])
{
    int m=?1?;
    int b, i, t;
    for(i = ?2?; i<m; i++)
    {
        t = a[i];
        b = i-1;
        while(?3?>=0 && t<a[b])
        {
            a[b+1] = a[b];
            ?4?
        }
        ?5? = t;
    }
}
```

(i) What is the expression or statement at ?1?
(ii) What is the expression or statement at ?2?
(iii) What is the expression or statement at ?3?
(iv) What is the expression or statement at ?4?
(v) What is the expression or statement at ?5? ***ISC 2010***

Ans (i) `a.length` (ii) 1 (iii) `b`
(iv) `b--;` (v) `a[b]`

CHAPTER TEST

1 Mark Questions

1. Java allows us to create arrays using .... operator only.
(a) new (b) this (c) super (d) static

2. Which of the following relies on divide and conquer strategy in a sorted list?
(a) Linear search (b) Binary search (c) Insertion sort (d) Selection sort

3. Define append( ) method with syntax.

2 Marks Questions

4. How to use loop with arrays?

5. How to declare an array? Define with syntax.

3 Marks Questions

6. Give a one-dimensional array A[45] with base address A as 100 and each element occupies 2 bytes, find the location of A[10].

7. Explain the linear search and binary search processes using example program.

8. Define the structure of one-dimensional array. Explain its initialisation.

5 Marks Questions

9. An array [5][10] is stored in memory with each element requiring & bytes of storage. If the first element ARR[0][0] is stored at the location 1455, calculate the location if ARR[6][5] when the array is row major wise.

10. Name some operations on string. Define any one.

11. What are different types of array? Give example of each array type.

10 Marks Question

12. Create a Java class that stores original numerator and denominator of a fraction and then simplifies it to find numerator and denominator of simplified fraction. The class should have following details

Class name	Rationalclass
Data memebers/Instance variables	
numerator	to store numerator of original fraction (int type).
denominator	to store denominator of original fraction (int type).
hr	to store numerator of simplified fraction (int type)..
dr	to store denominator of simplified fraction (int type).
Methods	
simplify( )	simplifies the given fraction
gcd( )	determines the gcd of two passed numbers.
print( )	prints the fraction in original as well as simplified form.
constructor	receives two parameters and initialises the numerator and denominators.

Specify the class Rationalclass giving the details of the constructor, gcd(), print() and simplify(). Define the main() function to create object and call the functions accordingly to enable the task.

08

File Handling

TREND ANALYSIS 4 YEARS

File Handling

Average No. of Questions Across all Sets

Types of Questions	2024	2023	2020	2019
1 Mark	–	–	–	–
2 Marks	–	–	–	–
3 Marks	–	–	–	–
5 Marks	–	–	–	–
10 Marks	–	–	–	–

File handling is an integral part of nearly all programming projects. Files provide the means by which a program stores data, accesses data or appending data. In Java, file handling is simply a special case aspect of a larger concept because file I/O is tightly integrated into Java's overall I/O system.

There are two aspects of the I/O system that make this feature possible. The first is that, Java I/O system is build on a cohesive set of class hierarchies. The second is the stream. This stream ties together the file system.

You can read files using these classes:

(i) **FileReader** For text files in your system's default encoding.

(ii) **FileInputStream** For binary files and text files that contain 'weird' characters.

Java Stream Classes

In Java, I/O facility is based on streams. Stream is a continuous flow of data. The InputStream is used to read data from a source and the OutputStream is used for writing data to a destination. These two are the basic stream classes in Java.

The java.io package contains a large number of stream classes that provide capabilities for processing all types of data. Java stream classes may be categorised into two groups based on the data type on which they operate:

(i) **Byte Stream** Classes that provide support for handling I/O operations on bytes.

(ii) **Character Stream** Classes that provide support for managing I/O operations on characters.

These two groups may further be classified based on their purpose, as shown in figure:

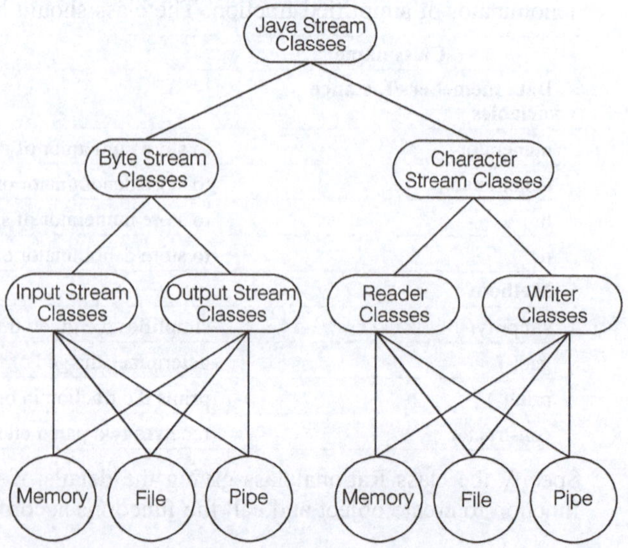

Classification of Java Stream Classes

Here, an object that outputs data to a byte stream belongs to one of the subclasses of the abstract class is **Output Stream** and objects that read data from a byte stream belong to subclasses is **Input Stream**.

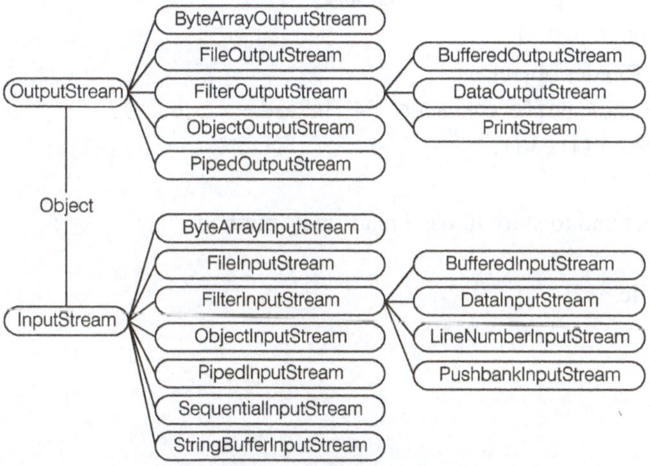

Hierarchy of Java Stream

Operations on Files

In Java, files can perform various operations such as file input, i.e. obtaining input from a file and file output i.e. writing output to a file, etc.

Buffering

Buffering is a process, used to hold data during communication. A buffer is a temporary storage used to hold data while it is being moved from one place to another.

- It can be used for both input and output.
- An **input buffer** is used for reading data from a stream.
- An **output buffer** is used to store data to be written to a stream.
- For byte stream classes, **BufferedInputStream** and **BufferedOutputStream** filters are used to add buffering.
- For character stream classes, **BufferedReader** and **BufferedWriter** filters are used to add buffering.

Character oriented I/O is performed on text files, while binary files are modified by byte oriented I/O stream.

Output to Text Files

To get the output from text files, we follow some basic steps:

***Step* 1** To write to a file, create a FileWriter object. The syntax of FileWriter is:

```
FileWriter <stream-object-name> =
    new FileWriter ("<filename>");
```

e.g.
```
FileWriter fout = new
    FileWriter("Output.txt");
```

***Step* 2** Next, link the FileWriter object to BufferedWriter. The syntax of BufferedWriter is:

```
BufferedWriter <stream-object-name>
        = new BufferedWriter
          (<FileWriterobject>);
```

e.g.
```
BufferedWriter bout = new
        BufferedWriter(fout);
```

***Step* 3** Next, we provide a link to BufferedWriter object with a PrintWriter object. The syntax is:

```
PrintWriter <Objectname>= new
  PrintWriter(<BufferedWriterobject>);
```

e.g.
```
PrintWriter pout = new
        PrintWriter(bout);
    //Object creation of PrintWriter
```

The stream is the combination of various character oriented stream, i.e. the PrintWriter stream will provide the necessary filtering, the BufferedWriter stream will provide the buffering and the FileWriter provides the content (text).

***Step* 4** Now, write any character or text from your program with PrintWriter object using either print or println methods as:

```
<PrintWriter object>.print(…);
<PrintWriter object>.println(…);
```

e.g.
```
pout.print("Sample");
pout.println("Program");
```

***Step* 5** After completing all these steps, we successfully close the stream chain of all stream objects, as

```
<Stream Object>.close();
```

e.g.
```
pout.close();
bout.close();
fout.close();
```

Appending to Text File

Appending to text files means, retaining the old contents and append the new contents.

For this just write like,

```
FileWriter <Object name> = new FileWriter
                      (<filename>,true);
```

Here, an object of FileWriter is created and true means that the new text will be appended to file and old data will be retained.

Input from Text Files

Input from text files means, read the text from a file. We need to follow some basic steps to read the content of a file:

***Step* 1** Create a FileReader stream object.

Syntax `FileReader <stream-object-name> = new FileReader("<File name>");`

e.g. `FileReader fread = new FileReader("Input.txt");`

***Step* 2** Next, link the BufferedReader stream object to FileReader object.

Syntax `BufferedReader <stream-object-name> = new BufferedReader (<FileReader object>);`

e.g. `BufferedReader brd = new BufferedReader(fread);`

Note BufferedReader improves the performance by buffering input.

***Step* 3** Now, you can read the text of BufferedReader object and to store it, used readLine() method.

Syntax `String txt = brd.readLine();`

Here, readLine() method reads the line of the text file.

***Step* 4** At the end, you need to close the file as

`<BufferedReader object>.close();`

e.g. `brd.close();`

Output to Binary Files

Here, we followed some steps to write data to a binary file as,

***Step* 1** Create FileOutputStream object.

Syntax `FileOutputStream <Objectname> = new FileOutputStream("<filename>");`

e.g. `FileOutputStream fop = new FileOutputStream("Demo.bin");`

***Step* 2** Next, java.io.DataOutputStream class is used to write primitive data types to connect with FileOutputStream.

Syntax
```
DataOutputStream <Objectname> = new
        DataOutputStream(<FileOutputStream object>);
```

e.g. `DataOutputStream dop = new DataOutputStream(fop);`

***Step* 3** Next, we can use to write() method or flush() method to write data in byte format on the file. Here, flush() method is used to write all the buffered data on to the file.

Syntax
```
   writeInt(int) //data type integer
or writeByte(byte) //data type byte
```

***Step* 4** Once through, close all the stream objects using close()

e.g.
```
dop.close(); //DataOutputStream is closed
fop.close(); //FileOutputStream is closed
```

Input from Binary Files

We need to follow some basic steps to read from an already existing binary file.

***Step* 1** To read a binary file, create an object of FileInputStream and connect it to an existing binary file.

e.g. `FileInputStream finp = new FileInputStream("Marks.dat");`

***Step* 2** Next, to read primitive data types from FileInputStream, we connect it with DataInputStream object.

e.g. `DataInputStream dinp = new DataInputStream(finp);`

***Step* 3** Now, read the data from DataInputStream object, using following read() methods.

```
readInt() //returns int
        or
readByte() //returns byte
        or
readLong() //returns long
```

***Step* 4** After reading the files, the input streams get automatically closed.

Stream Tokenizer

Stream tokenizer breaks up the InputStream into tokens that are delimited by sets of characters. The java.io.StreamTokenizer class takes an InputStream and parses it into 'tokens', allowing the tokens to be read one at a time. The StreamTokenizer can:

- Recognise identifiers, numbers, quoted string's and various comment styles.
- Uses the following declaration for java.io.StreamTokenizer class
  ```
  public class StreamTokenizer
  extends objects
  ```
- Create an instance of a class StreamTokenizer using
  ```
  java.io.StreamTokenizer.nextToken() method
  ```
- java.io.StreamTokenizer.nextToken() method parses the next token from the Input Stream of this tokenizer.

Stream tokenizer defines four int constants are TT_EOF, TT_EOL, TT_NUMBER and TT_WORD.

Obtaining Input using Scanner Class

The **Scanner** class is a class of java.util, which allows the user to read values of various types. A Scanner class:

- Breaks its input into tokens using a delimiter pattern, which by default matches with whitespace.
- A scanning operation may block waiting for input.

```
import java.util.*;
public class ScannerDemo
{
    public static void main(String[] args)
    {
        String s = "Hello World! 3 + 3.0 = 6";
        //create a new scanner with the
                    specified String object
        Scanner scanner = new Scanner(s);
        //print the text line of the string
        System.out.println("
                    "+scanner.nextLine());
        System.out.println("Closing Scanner…");
        scanner.close(); //close the scanner
        System.out.println("Scanner Closed.");
    }
}
```

The output will be

Hello World! 3 + 3.0 = 6
Closing Scanner…
Scanner Closed.

Methods of Scanner

Scanner class has retrieved tokens and converted them to the appropriate types using the following set of methods.

Methods of Scanner Class

Scanner Methods	Description
java.util.Scanner.hasNextFloat( )	Returns true, if the next token in this scanner's input can be interpreted as a valid float value using the nextFloat( ) method.
java.util.Scanner.hasNextDouble( )	Returns true, if the next token in this scanner's input can be interpreted as a valid double value using the nextDouble( ) method.
java.util.Scanner.hasNextBoolean( )	Returns true, if the next token in this scanner's input can be interpreted as a valid boolean value using a case insensitive pattern created from the string 'true/false'.
java.util.Scanner.hasNextInt( )	Returns true, if the next token in this scanner's input can be interpreted as a valid int value in the default radix using the nextInt( ) method.
java.util.Scanner.hasNext( )	Returns true, if this scanner has another token in its input. This method may block while waiting for input to scan.
java.util.Scanner.next( )	Finds and returns the next complete token from this scanner. A complete token is preceded and followed by input that matches the delimiter pattern.
java.util.Scanner.nextInt( )	Returns scanned next token of the input as an int. An invocation of this method of the form nextInt( ) behaves in exactly the same way as the invocation nextInt(radix), where radix is the default radix of the scanner.
java.util.Scanner.nextFloat( )	Scans the next token of the input as a float. This method will throw InputMismatchException, if the next token cannot be translated into a valid float value.

Printing in Java

Java provides various classes for obtaining input. It introduces classes for printing on printer through API. This class is represented by the java.out.printpackage. Printing is implemented with the help of one public interface—PrinterGraphic and one public class— PrinterJob, of AWT.

Java Printing API

In Java for printing API, it creates a PrintJob associated with a printer specifying the number of copies and user print dialog interaction. A PrintJob is a unit of work to be run on a printer and can consist of printing one or more files.

- Assign a unique job number to each job.
- Decide what to print and then ready printer for it.
- To create the printer job, used the following syntax

```
PrinterJob job = PrinterJob.getPrinterJob();
```

Rendering Models

It involves two types of printing modes i.e. Printable jobs and Pageable jobs.

Printable Jobs

(i) This model uses one page painter for the entire document.

(ii) All pages are arranged in sequence with numbering.

(iii) At the last page of print job, it returns NO_SUCH_PAGE value.

Pageable Jobs

(i) The pageable jobs are used where we have a collection of page with different formats.

(ii) For each page, painter will be assigned uniquely.

(iii) It can also covered the issue of Printable jobs i.e. if pages are skipped then it will cover it.

(iv) Pageable jobs allow you to print a large number of pages.

Interfaces, Classes and Exceptions inside java.awt.print Package

The java.awt.print consists of the following interfaces, classes and exceptions:

(i) **Interfaces** It includes following interfaces are:

(a) **Pageable** represents a set of pages to be printed.

(b) **Printable** implements a page painter.

(c) **PrinterGraphics** provides the getPrinterJob() method to obtain the printer job.

(ii) **Classes** This print package consists of following classes are:

(a) **Book** a collection of pages with different formats.

(b) **PageFormat** defines the orientation of the page i.e. landscape or portrait and page's size.

(c) **Paper** defines a physical characteristics of page.

(d) **PrinterJob** manages the print job by providing a sequence number, painter, etc.

(iii) **Exceptions** It involves following exceptions during processing are:

(a) **PrinterAbortException** indicates that an application has terminated the PrintJob while it was in the process of printing.

(b) **PrinterException** displays the message of the exception.

(c) **PrinterIOException** is used to indicate that an error of some sort has occurred while printing.

Pageable Interface

This interface is implemented by multipage documents. It includes three following methods:

(i) **int getNumberOfPages( )** returns number of pages.

(ii) **PageFormat getPageFormat(int pageIndex)** returns page format as specified by pageIndex.

(iii) **Printable getPrintable(int pageIndex)** returns the Printable instance responsible for rendering the page specified by pageIndex.

Note PrintIndex decides which page is to be printed.

Printable Interface

This interface is implemented by objects that always print a single page or multiple pages in a sequential order. It has one method and two values which are given below:

(i) **int print(Graphics graphics, PageFormat pageFormat, int pageIndex)** requests that the graphics handle using the given page format render the specified page.

(ii) **NO_SUCH_PAGE** is a constant value that returns to indicate that there are no more pages to print.

(iii) **PAGE_EXISTS** is a value that indicates that the page passed as a parameter to print() has been rendered and does exist.

Printer Graphics Interface

This interface is implemented by any graphics object that is passed to the print() method of a printable object. It uses the getPrinterJob() method and returns the PrinterJob for the rendering request.

Units of Measurement

This defines two types of classes as:

1. **PageFormat class** This class is a combination of a paper object that specifies page size and imageable area with a field that specifies the orientation of the page. It contains the following orientation values are:
   (i) **Portrait** The origin is at the top left, with the X-axis running from left to right and the Y-axis running from top to bottom.
   (ii) **Landscape** The origin is at the bottom left of the speed of paper with the X-axis running from bottom to top and the Y-axis running left to right.

The page format consists of following method:

Methods Name	Description
double getHeight( )	This method returns the page's physical height in points (1 inch = 72 points). If your page measure 8.5 by 11 inches, then the return value will be 792 points or 11 inches.
double getImageableHeight( )	This method returns the page's imageable height, of the print on which you may draw.
double getImageableWidth( )	This method returns the page's imageable width - the width of the print area on which you may draw.
double getImageableX( )	This method returns the X origin of the imageable area.
double getImageableY( )	This method returns the imageable area's of Y origin.
double getWidth( )	This method returns the page's physical width in points. If you print on letter-sized paper, the width is 8.5 inches or 612 points.
double getHeight( )	This method returns the page's physical height in point. e.g. letter sized paper is 11 inches in height or 792 points.
double getMatrix( )	This method returns a transformation matrix that translates user space into the requested page orientation. The returned value is in the format required by the AffineTransform constructor.
void setPaper(Paper paper)	This method sets the Paper object that will be used by the PageFormat class. PageFormat must have access to the physical page characteristics to complete this task .

2. **PrinterJob class** This PrinterJob class controls printing of Printable and Pageable objects. It defines following:

Class Methods

Modifier and Type	Method	Description
abstract void	cancel( )	Cancel a print job that is in progress.
PageFormat	defaultPage( )	Creates a new **PageFormat** instance and sets it to a default size and orientation.
abstract PageFormat	defaultPage(PageFormat page)	Clones the **PageFormat** argument and alters the clone to describe a default page size and orientation.
abstract int	getCopies( )	Gets the number of copies to be printed.
abstract String	getJobName( )	Gets the name of the document to be printed.
PageFormat	getPageFormat (PrintRequestAttributeSet attributes)	Calculates a **PageFormat** with values consistent with those supported by the current **PrintService** for this job (i.e. the value returned by **getPrintService()**) and media, printable area and orientation contained in attributes.
static PrinterJob	getPrinterJob( )	Creates and returns a **PrinterJob** which is initially associated with the default printer.

PrintService	getPrintService( )	Returns the service (printer) for this printer job.
abstract String	getUserName( )	Gets the name of the printing user.
abstract boolean	isCancelled( )	Returns **true** if a print job is in progress, but is going to be cancelled at the next opportunity, otherwise returns false.
abstract PageFormat	pageDialog (PageFormat page)	Displays a dialog that allows modification of a PageFormat instance.
PageFormat	pageDialog (PrintRequestAttributeSet attributes)	A convenience method which displays a cross-platform page set-up dialog.
abstract void	print( )	Prints a set of pages.
void	print (PrintRequestAttributeSet attributes)	Prints a set of pages using the settings in the attribute set.
abstract boolean	printDialog( )	Presents a dialog to the user for changing the properties of the print job.
abstract void	setJobName (String jobName)	Sets the name of the document to be printed.
abstract void	setPageable (Pageable document)	Queries **document** for the number of pages and the **PageFormat** and **Printable** for each page held in the **Pageable** instance **document.**
abstract void	setPrintable (Printable painter)	Calls **painter** to render the pages.
abstract void	setPrintable (Printable **painter**, PageFormat format)	Calls **painter** to render the pages in the specified **format.**
abstract PageFormat	validatePage (PageFormat page)	Returns the clone of **page** with its settings adjusted to be compatible with the current printer of this **PrinterJob.**

Printing Sequence

In Java, printing process usually takes two parts:

(i) **Job Control** It involves a creation of print job and specifying the number of copies with user print dialog interaction and manage content that spans pages.

(ii) **Page Imaging** Drawing contents to a page. To illustrate the process, follow these steps:

(a) **Creating PrintJob** Firstly, create a PrinterJob associated with printer. The declaration to create the PrintJob is

```
PrinterJob PrintJob = PrinterJob.getPrinterJob();
//name of printjob object of PrinterJob method
```

(b) **Render Content of Page for Printing** Next, implement the Printable interface by using print method of the current page painter, which is called by the printing system to render a page. The following declaration is used:

```
class HelloPrinter implements Printable
{
   ⋮
}
PrintJob.setPrintable(new HelloPrinter());
```

or, PageFormat can also set with the painter, syntax for this is

```
PrintJob.setPrintable(Painter, PageFormat);
```

(c) **Display printDialog** A print dialog shows the number of copies, page orientation or destination printer. By invoking printDialog() method *via* the PrintJob object,

```
boolean doprint = PrintJob.printDialog();
```

If doprint variable is true, then the application will request that the job be printed by calling the PrinterJob.print method.

```
if(doprint)
{
    try
    {
        job.print();
    }
    catch(PrinterException e)
    {
        //handle the error and thrown it
    }
}
```

Additional Questions

1. What are Java stream classes?

Ans In Java, I/O facility is based on streams. Stream is a continuous flow of data. The InputStream is used to read data from a source and the OutputStream is used for writing data to a destination.

The **java.io** package contains a large number of stream classes that provide capabilities for processing all types of data. Java stream classes may be categorised into two groups based on the data type on which they operate:

(i) **Byte Stream** Classes that provide support for handling I/O operations on bytes.

(ii) **Character Stream** Classes that provide support for managing I/O operations on characters.

2. Define appending to text file with example.

Ans Appending to text files means, retaining the old contents and append the new contents.

Syntax

```
FileWriter <Objectname> = new FileWriter(<filename>,true);
```

Here, an object of FileWriter is created and true means that the new text will be appended to file and old data will be retained.

3. Name the interfaces used inside the package of awt print.

Ans The java.awt.print consists of the following interfaces are:

(i) **Pageable** represents a set of pages to be printed.

(ii) **Printable** implements a page painter.

(iii) **PrinterGraphics** provides the getPrinterJob() method to obtain the printer job.

4. Explain the components of page imaging in printing sequence.

Ans It involves a creation of print job and specifying the number of copies with user print dialog. They include drawing contents to a page. Printing sequence consists of following steps are:

(i) **Creating Print Job** Firstly, you create a PrinterJob associated with printer. This includes declaration to create the PrintJob.

(ii) **Render Content of Page for Printing** Here, we implement the Printable interface by using print method of the current page painter, which is called by the printing system to render a page.

(iii) **Display printDialog** A print dialog shows the number of copies, page orientation or printer's destination. By invoking printDialog( ) method *via* the PrintJob object.

CHAPTER TEST

1 Mark Questions

1. Which of the following classes that provide support for handling I/O operations on bytes?
   (a) Character Stream (b) Byte Stream (c) Input Stream (d) Output Stream
2. ………… breaks up the InputStream into tokens that are delimited by sets of characters.
   (a) Stream Tokenizer (b) String Tokenizer (c) BufferedReader (d) BufferedWriter
3. How to get input from user using Scanner classes?

2 Marks Questions

4. Which operations are performed on files?
5. What is buffering?

3 Marks Questions

6. Explain file handling.
7. What are the methods of Scanner class? Explain with example.

5 Marks Questions

8. What is stream tokenizer?
9. Explain the method to get output to binary files.

10 Marks Question

10. Write about units of measurement in detail.

09

Inheritance, Interface and Polymorphism

TREND ANALYSIS 4 YEARS

Inheritance, Interface and Polymorphism

Average No. of Questions Across all Sets

Types of Questions	2024	2023	2020	2019
1 Mark	1	1	–	–
2 Marks	–	1	2	1
3 Marks	–	–	–	–
5 Marks	1	1	1	1
10 Marks	–	–	–	–

Inheritance is the ability to derive something specific from something generic. Inheritance aids in the reuse of code, i.e. a class can inherit the features of another class and also add its own properties.

The parent class is known as the **superclass** or **base class** and the newly created child class is known as the **subclass** or **derived class**. A subclass derives all the properties and methods of the superclass and can have attributes and methods of its own.

Need of Inheritance

Following are the major reasons for introducing inheritance:

(i) **Reusability** Using inheritance, one can add new features in an already existing class without even modifying it.

(ii) **Capability to Express the Inheritance Relationship** Inheritance makes the understanding of programming concepts because this is very much similar to the real-world relationships.

(iii) **Transitive Nature of Inheritance** Inheritance is transitive in nature. Suppose class2 inherits class1 and class3 inherits class2, then because of transitive nature class3 will automatically inherit class1.

Types of Inheritance

Depending on the nature and member of a class, inheritance is classified into the following forms:

(i) **Single Inheritance** In single inheritance, a derived class can inherit only from one base class. Figure shows a single inheritance relationship between two classes A and B.

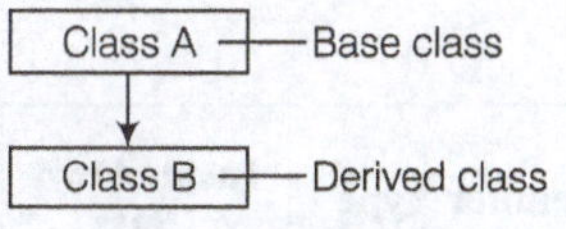

Single Inheritance

(ii) **Multiple Inheritance** In multiple inheritance, a class can inherit from more than one class. Java does not support multiple inheritance, as shown in figure:

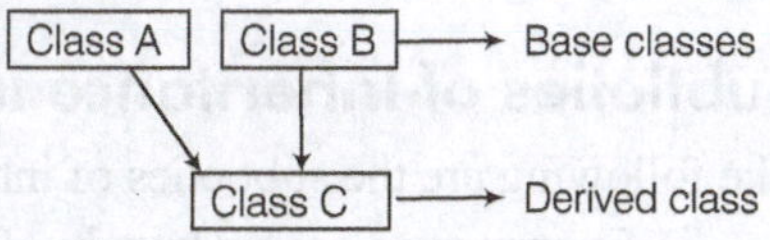

Multiple Inheritance

(iii) **Hierarchical Inheritance** In hierarchical inheritance, more than one derived class can inherit from a single base class, as shown in figure:

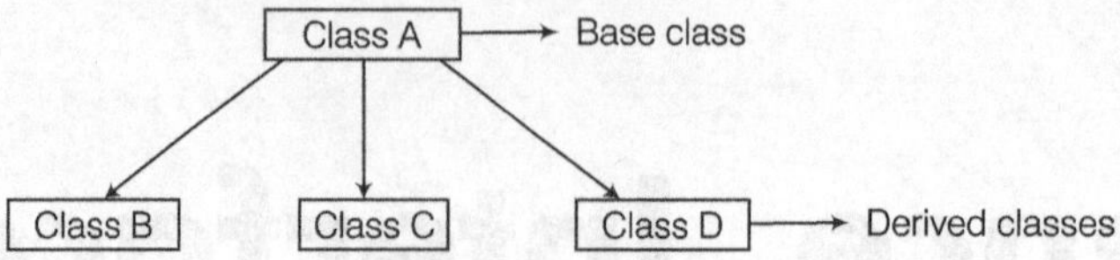

Hierarchical Inheritance

(iv) **Multilevel Inheritance** This form of inheritance is the implementation of transitive nature of inheritance. The following figure depicts multilevel inheritance:

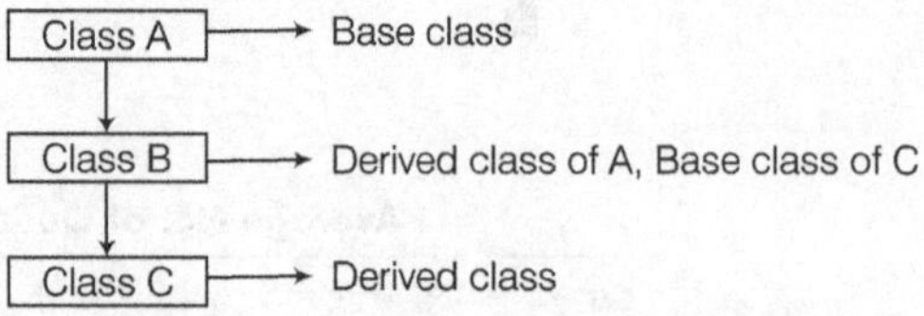

Multilevel Inheritance

In the above figure, class C will inherit class A transitively.

(v) **Hybrid Inheritance** This inheritance is a combination of two or more types of inheritance. When a subclass inherits from multiple base classes and all of its base classes inherit from a single base class, this form of inheritance is known as hybrid inheritance.

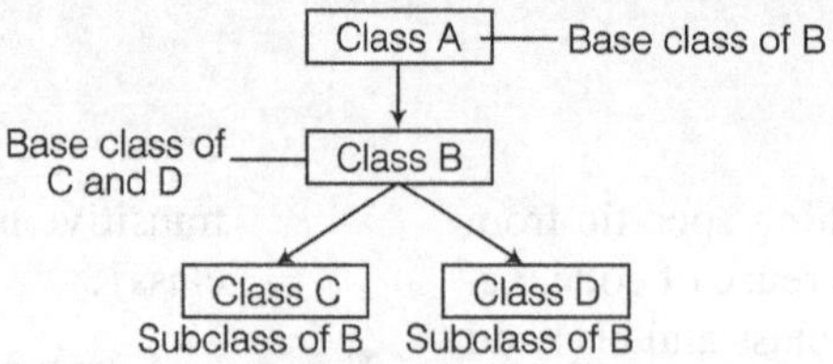

Hybrid Inheritance

Inheritance and Access Modifiers

Access modifiers or access specifiers are used to control the access of inherited members. It is also known as visibility mode because it shows the visibility of members.

public, protected, private and friendly access modifiers are the ones which cause difference in case of inheritance. The following table depicts the accessibility of access modifiers in case of inheritance:

Accessibility of Class Members

Member Type	Inside Own Class	Inside Subclasses		Inside Non-subclasses	
		In the Same Package	In Other Packages	In the Same Package	In Other Packages
public	Yes	Yes	Yes	Yes	Yes
protected	Yes	Yes	Yes	Yes	No
default (friendly)	Yes	Yes	Yes	No	No
private	Yes	No	No	No	No

Subtleties of Inheritance in Java

The following are the subtleties of inheritance in Java:

(i) Every new class in Java by default has one superclass.

(ii) Java allows only single, hierarchical and multilevel inheritance.

(iii) Every class in Java can have atmost one direct superclass but a class can have more than one subclasses.

(iv) Because of transitive property of inheritance, a subclass in Java inherits properties and behaviour of all the classes which are at higher level in inheritance hierarchy.

Overriding Methods

When a method in a subclass has the same name and same type signature as a method in its superclass, then the method in the subclass will override the same method of the superclass at the time of execution.

When an overridden method is called within a subclass, it will always refer to the version of the method defined by the subclass. The superclass version of the method is hidden.

Let us consider an example, where subclass B overrides the methods of class A.

```
class A
{
        int i = 0;
        void dooverride(int k) // method declaration with argument
        {
            i = k;
        }
}
class B extends A //class B inherits class A using extends keyword
{
        void dooverride(int k) // method overriding
        {
            i = 2 * k; // initialisation of i
            System.out.println("The value of i is : " +i);//print the value of i
        }
        public static void main(String args[])
        {
            B b = new B( );             // object creation
            b.dooverride(12);           // invocation of method dooverride( ) of B class
        }
}
```

Output

The value of i is: 24

Note
- Overriding is possible only if methods are accessible.
- The version of the hidden method that gets invoked depends on which class it is invoked.

Abstract Class and Methods

An abstract class is designed only to act as a base class, i.e. we cannot create object of an abstract class. Abstract classes cannot be instantiated. It contains one or more abstract methods that is declared but contains no implementation (i.e. no method body). Methods that are declared without any body within an abstract class is known as abstract method. The method body will be defined by its subclass.

Syntax `abstract class classname{ }`

Some key features of an abstract class are as follows:

- They cannot be instantiated but they can have a reference variable.
- A class can inherit only one abstract class, as multiple inheritance is not allowed amongst classes.
- They can have abstract methods as well as non-abstract methods.
- It is mandatory for a subclass to override the abstract methods of the abstract class, otherwise the subclass also need to declare itself as abstract.
- Abstract classes can have constructors and variables also.

Why do We Create Abstract Methods?

Abstract methods are usually declared, where two or more subclasses are expected to do a similar thing in different ways through different implementation. These subclasses extend the same abstract class and provide different implementation for the abstract methods.

e.g.

```
abstract class Animal                    // Name of abstract class
{
    String name;
    String species;
    void init(String n, String s)    // method with arguments
    {
        name = n;
        species = s;
    }
    void eat(String fooditem)        // method with argument
    {
        System.out.println(species+" "+name+"likes to have"+fooditem);
    }
    abstract void sound();           // declaration of abstract method
}
class Lion extends Animal                // subclass of abstract class
{
    Lion() // default constructor
    {
        init("Lion","Asiatic");
    }
    void sound()                     // implementation of abstract method
    {
        System.out.println("Lions Roar! Roar!");
    }
    public static void main(String args[])
    {
        Lion l = new Lion();         //object reaction
        l.eat("flesh");
        l.sound();
    }
}
```

Output

Asiatic Lion likes to have flesh

Lions Roar! Roar!

> **final Keyword**
>
> In Java, we use final keyword with variables to make its value not to be changed. The final keyword can be used in many content. Final can be
> (i) Final variable
> (ii) Final method
> (iii) Final class
> final keyword is used:
> - To declare constants.
> - To disallow method overriding.
> - To disallow inheritance i.e. you can not extend it.

Interfaces

Interfaces are basically a collection of methods which are public and abstract by default. These interfaces do not have any method body. The implementing classes have to override all the methods of the interface and provide implementation of all these methods. An interface is not a class. It contains behaviours that a class implement. The best part of an interface is that a class can inherit any number of interfaces, thus it allows multiple inheritance. 'Java does not support multiple inheritance among classes but interfaces allow Java to support this feature.'

It is important to know that interfaces cannot contain:

- Constants
- Fields (private data numbers)
- Constructors
- Static members

An interface is declared with the help of keyword **interface**. It is the responsibility of the implementing class to override the methods and provides the implementation for these methods.

Syntax

```
interface interfacename
{
    returntype methodname(argument list);
    ...
}
```

Difference between Class and Interface

Class	Interface
The members of a class can be declared as constant or variables.	The members of an interface are always declared as constant, i.e. their values are final.
The class definition can contain the code for each of its methods i.e. the methods can be abstract or non-abstract.	The methods in an interface are abstract in nature i.e. there is no code associated with them. It is later defined by the class that implements the interface.
It can be instantiated by declaring objects.	It cannot be used to declare objects. It can only be inherited by a class.
It can use various access specifiers like public, private or protected.	It can only use the public access specifier.

An interface defines a contract specifying a set of methods that a class implementing the interface must provide. Interfaces allow you to define methods without providing implementations for them. Then, classes can implement these interfaces, providing concrete implementations for the methods defined in the interface.

```
// Define an interface
interface Vehicle {
    void start();
    void stop();
}
// Implement the Vehicle interface through a class
class Car implements Vehicle {
    @Override
    public void start() {
        System.out.println("Car started");
    }
    @Override
    public void stop() {
        System.out.println("Car stopped");
    }
}
public class Main {
    public static void main(String[] args) {
        // Create an instance of the Car class
        Car myCar = new Car();
        // Call methods defined in the Vehicle interface
        myCar.start();
        myCar.stop();
    }
}
```

Output:

Car started

Car stopped

Your code defines an interface Vehicle with two methods start() and stop(). Then, it implements this interface in a class Car. In the Car class, both methods start() and stop() are overridden to provide specific behavior for a car.

Implementing interfaces in this manner allows for flexibility and code reusability in Java, enabling classes to adhere to common contracts while still providing their own specific implementations for the methods defined in the interfaces.

super Keyword

The super keyword refers to the reference variable that is used to refer immediate parent class object. Whenever you create the instance of subclass, an instance of parent class is created implicitly i.e. referred by super keyword.

It is used for the following three purposes:

(i) For calling methods of superclass.
Syntax `super.<superclass_method_name>( );`

(ii) For accessing the member variables of the superclass.
Syntax `super.<superclass_method_variable_name>( );`

(iii) For invoking the constructors of the superclass.
Syntax `super();`

Inheritance and Constructor

Class cannot only be determined by state and behaviour of object but also determined by each of its superclass. Due to that reason, it is not sufficient to execute a constructor of that class but also need to initialise each constructor of superclass. A superclass constructor must execute before a subclass constructor. So that, the state and the behaviour defined by the superclass may be correctly and completely initialised before a subclass constructor executes.

In Java, constructor of superclass with no argument gets automatically called in subclass constructor when the object of subclass is created.

But, if we want to call parameterized constructor of subclass, then we can call it using super keyword, as given below:

```
class Base
{
      int p;
      Base(int x) //parameterized constructor
      {
            p = x;
      }
}
class Derived extends Base
{
      int y;
      Derived(int a, int b)//parameterized constructor
      {
            super(a);
            y = b;
      }
      void display()
      {
            System.out.println("p = "+p+", y = "+y);
      }
}
```

```
public class Main
{
        public static void main(String args[])
        {
                Derived d = new Derived(10, 20);
                d.display();
        }
}
```

Output p = 10, y = 20

Note You cannot use both `super()` and `this()` at the same time in same constructor because both must appear as the first statement of the constructor.

Polymorphism

In the term polymorphism, poly means many and morphism means forms. Thus, polymorphism means something that can take many forms as shown in figure.

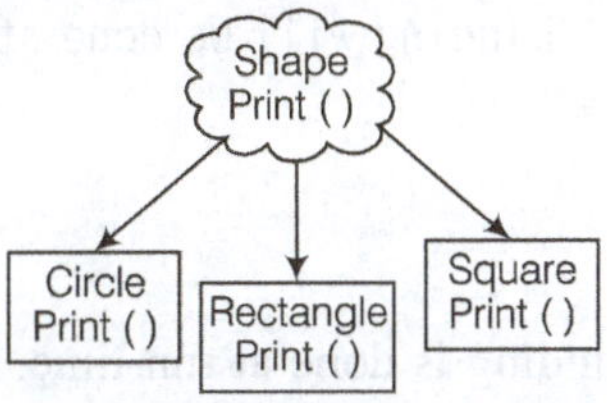

Polymorphism

Polymorphism is a characteristic of being able to assign different behaviours or values in a subclass, to something that was declared in a parent class. In other words, polymorphism means performing different behaviours using a common interface. 'Polymorphism means that one operation (method) can be implemented in different ways in different classes'.

Overloading

In Java, it is possible to create methods that have the same name but different parameter lists and different definitions. This is called method overloading. Method overloading is used when objects are required to perform similar tasks but using different input parameters.

When we call a method in an object, Java matches the method name first and then the number and type of parameters to decide which one of the definitions to execute.

Following are overloaded methods:

```
void area(int);
void area(float);
void area(int, int);
void area(int, float);
```

Overriding

When a method of superclass is redefined in its subclass, then it is called overriding. e.g.

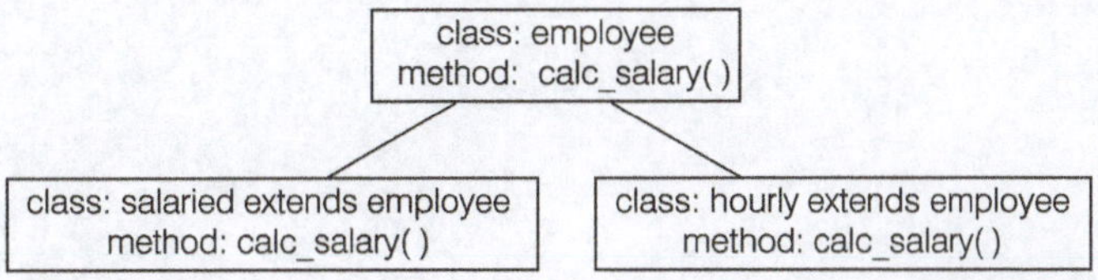

The benefit of overriding is the ability to define a behaviour that's specific to the subclass type which means a subclass can implement a parent class method based on its requirement.

Binding

Binding is the process of connecting a method call to its definition. The two forms of binding are static (or early) binding and dynamic (or late) binding.

(i) **Static Binding** When the binding is done at compile time (by the compiler), it is known as static binding. If there is any private, final or static method in a class, there is static binding.

e.g.
```
class Dog
{
    private void eat()
    {
        System.out.println("dog is eating…");
    }
    public static void main(String args[])
    {
        Dog d1 = new Dog();
        d1.eat(); //binding will be done at compile time
    }
}
```

Output
```
dog is eating…
```

(ii) **Dynamic Binding** When binding is done at run-time, it is known as dynamic binding. Since, object of the class is created at runtime, so in case of overriding, which class method will be called is decided at runtime.

e.g.
```
class Animal
{
    void eat()
    {
        System.out.println("animal is eating…");
    }
}
class Dog extends Animal
{
    void eat()
    {
        System.out.println("dog is eating…");
    }
    public static void main(String args[])
    {
        Animal a = new Animal();
        a.eat();
    }
}
```

Output
```
animal is eating…
```

PYQs Previous Years Questions

1 Mark Questions

1. State any one use of interfaces in Java. **ISC 2024**

Ans Interfaces are used in Java to achieve abstraction.

2. The keyword that allows multi-level inheritance in Java programming is **ISC 2023**

(a) implements
(b) super
(c) extends
(d) this

Ans (c) extends

3. Transitive nature of inheritance is implemented through **ISC SQP 2023**

(a) Single inheritance
(b) Multiple inheritance
(c) Hybrid inheritance
(d) Multilevel inheritance

Ans (d) Multilevel inheritance

4. The concept in Java to perform method overloading and method overriding is called **ISC 2022 (Sem II)**

(a) inheritance
(b) polymorphism
(c) data abstraction
(d) encapsulation

Ans (b) polymorphism

5. The interface in Java is a mechanism to achieve **ISC 2022 (Sem II)**

(a) encapsulation
(b) overriding
(c) polymorphism
(d) abstraction

Ans (d) abstraction

6. The keyword used by a class to acquire the properties of an interface is **ISC SQP 2022 (Sem II)**

(a) import (b) implements
(c) extends (d) include

Ans (b) implements

7. The ability of an object to take many forms is known as **ISC SQP 2022 (Sem II)**

(a) inheritance
(b) data abstraction
(c) overriding
(d) polymorphism

Ans (d) polymorphism

2 Marks Questions

1. Mention any two properties of the data members of an interface. **ISC 2023**

Ans (i) final keyword is always used to declare data members.

(ii) Data members cannot be change in due course of the program.

2. Define Interface with respect to data abstraction. **ISC SQP 2023**

Ans Interface has static constants and abstract methods. In Java, interface is a mechanism to achieve abstraction. There can be only abstract methods in the Java interface, not method body.

3. What is the significance of the keyword 'new' in Java? Mention the areas, where it is used. **ISC 2020**

Ans The keyword 'new' is used to create an instance of a class. It actually allocates memory for the object of the class and returns its reference. The new keyword is followed by a call to the class constructor, thus initializing the object.

'new' keyword is also used to instantiate an array.

4. What is an interface? How is it different from a class? **ISC 2020, 2019, 2017**

Ans Interfaces are basically a collection of methods which are public and abstract by default. These interfaces do not have any method body.

```
Syntax
interface interface_name
{
    returntype method_name(arg_list);
}
```

Differences between interface and class are as follows

Interface	Class
The members of an interface are always declared as constant i.e. their values are final.	The members of a class can be declared as constant or variables.
It cannot be used to declare objects. It can only be inherited by a class	It can be instantiated by declaring objects.

5. From the class declaration given below, state the nature of the identifiers *A*, *B*, *C* and *D*: class *A* extends *B* implements *C*, *D* **ISC 2016**

Ans From the class declaration,

Superclass = *B*
Subclass = *A*
Interfaces = *C*, *D*

6. Differentiate between this keyword and super keyword. **ISC 2015**

Ans The differences between this keyword and super keyword are as follows:

this Keyword	super Keyword
this keyword is a reference to the currently executing object on which the method or constructor was invoked.	super keyword is used to access methods or variables of an instance's superclass members.
It can not appear within static methods.	You can invoke the overridden method through the use of the keyword super.
It is also used to call another constructor in the same class.	It is also used to invoke super class's constructor.

7. State two advantages of using the concept of inheritance in Java. **ISC 2014**

Ans Following are the advantages of inheritance:

(i) Reuse the existing code and extend the functionality.
(ii) Add new members to the derived class to specialise the class.
(iii) Replace the implementation of existing methods by overriding a method that already exists in the base class.

8. Differentiate between the keywords extends and implements. **ISC 2012**

Ans Differences between the keywords extends and implements are as follows:

implements	extends
When a class implements an interface, that class needs to implement all the methods declared in the interface.	When a subclass extends a superclass, it may or may not override the methods included in superclass.
A class can implement multiple interfaces.	It can only extend from one superclass in Java.

9. How can we override a method in inheritance? **ISC 2011**

Ans Overriding is the ability to define a behaviour specific to the subclass type which means a subclass can implement a parent class method based on its requirement. Overriding means to override the functionality of an existing method.

Rules for Method Overriding

(i) The argument list should be exactly the same as that of the overridden method.
(ii) Instance methods can be overridden only if they are inherited by the subclass.
(iii) A method declared as final cannot be overridden.
(iv) A method declared as static cannot be overridden but can redeclared.

10. State the difference between an interface and a class. **ISC 2010**

Ans Refer to text on Page 281 (Difference between class and interface).

11. Define inheritance. How is it useful in programming? **ISC 2009**

Ans Inheritance is the ability to derive something from something generic. Inheritance aids in the reuse of code i.e. a class can inherit the features of another class and add its own modification.

The parent class is known as the superclass or base class and the newly created child class is known as the subclass or derived class.

In Java programming, inheritance is used as follows:

(i) **Similarities** Whenever there are similarities between two or more classes, apply inheritance.
(ii) **Extraction** If a new class to be defined has certain features in addition to the features of an existing class, use inheritance and code only the additional features of this new class.
(iii) **Combination** If a class is inherited from more than one class, it results in multiple inheritance. Multiple inheritance combines features from more than one existing class.

12. What is meant by visibility mode in the definition of derived classes in inheritance? Explain any two visibility modes available. **ISC 2007**

Ans Visibility mode in case of derived classes modifies the accessibility of the superclass members in the derived class. Two visibility modes available are explained below:

Protected Members are accessible inside their own class as well as in all subclasses of their class, regardless of whether subclasses exist in the same package or any other package.

Private Members are accessible only to the class in which it is defined.

4/5 Marks Questions

1. A super class EmpSal has been defined to store the details of an employee. Define a subclass Overtime to compute the total salary of the employee, after adding the overtime amount based on the following criteria.

- If hours are more than 40, then ₹ 5000 are added to salary as an overtime amount.
- If hours are between 30 and 40 (both inclusive), then ₹ 3000 are added to salary as an overtime amount.
- If hours are less than 30, then the salary remains unchanged. **ISC 2024**

The details of the members of both the classes are given below

Class name	EmpSal
Data members/Instance variables	
empnum	to store the name of the employee
empcode	integer to store the employee code
salary	to store the salary of the employee in decimal
Methods/Member functions	
EmpSal(...)	parameterised constructor to assign values to data members
void show()	to display the details of the employee
Class name	**Overtime**
Data members/instance variables	
hours	integer to store overtime in hours
totsal	to store the total salary in decimal
Methods/Member functions	
Overtime(...)	parameterised constructor to assign values to data members of both the classes
void calSal()	calculates the total salary by adding the overtime amount to salary as per the criteria given above
void show()	to display the employee details along with the total salary (salary + overtime amount)

Assume that the super class EmpSal has been defined. Using the concept of inheritance, specify the class Overtime giving the details of the constructor (...), void calSal() and void show().

The super class, main function and algorithm need NOT be written.

Ans

```
class EmpSal
{
   private String empnum;
   private int empcode;
   protected double salary;
   public EmpSal(String empnum, int empcode, double salary)
   {
      this.empnum = empnum;
      this.empcode = empcode;
      this.salary = salary;
   }
   public void show()
   {
      System.out.println("Employee name: " + empnum);
      System.out.println("Employee code: " + empcode);
      System.out.println("Employee salary: " + salary);
   }
}
class Overtime extends EmpSal
{
   private int hours;
   private double totsal;
   public Overtime(String empnum, int empcode, double salary, int hours)
   {
      super(empnum, empcode, salary);
      this.hours = hours;
   }
```

```
    public void calSal()
    {
        totsal = salary;
        if( hours>40 )
        {
            totsal += 5000;
        }
        else if( hours>=30 )
        {
            totsal += 3000;
        }
    }
    public void show()
    {
        super.show();
        System.out.println("Overtime hours: " + hours);
        calSal();
        System.out.println("Total Salary: " + totsal);
    }
}
public class Q10
{
    public static void main(String args[])
    {
        Overtime overtime = new Overtime("Lalita", 234122, 100000, 31);
        overtime.show();
    }
}
```

Output:

Employee name: Lalita
Employee code: 234122
Employee salary: 100000.0
Overtime hours: 31
Total Salary: 103000.0

2. A super class Demand has been defined to store the details of the demands for a product. Define a subclass Supply which contains the production and supply details of the products. The details of the members of both the classes are given below

Class name	**Demand**
Data members/Instance variables	
pid	string to store the product ID
pname	string to store the product name
pdemand	integer to store the quantity demanded for the product
Methods / Member functions	
Demand(...)	parameterised constructor to assign values to the data members
void display( )	to display the details of the product

Class name	**Supply**
Data members/Instance variables	
pproduced	integer to store the quantity of the product produced
prate	to store the cost per unit of the product in decimal

Methods / Member functions	
Supply(...)	parameterised constructor to assign values to the data members of both the classes
double calculation()	returns the difference between the amount of demand (rate × demand) and the amount produced (rate × produced)
void display( )	to display the details of the product and the difference in amount of demand and amount of supply by invoking the method calculation( )

Assume that the super class Demand has been defined. Using the concept of inheritance., specify the class Supply giving the details of the constructor(...), double calculation( ) and void display( ).

The super class, main function and algorithm need NOT be written. ***ISC 2023***

Ans

```
class Supply extends Demand
{
   private int pproduced;
   private double prate;
   public Supply(String id, String name, int demand, int produced, double rate)
   {
      super(id, name, demand);
      this.pproduced = produced;
      this.prate = rate;
   }
   public double calculation()
   {
      double demandAmount = pdemand * prate;
      double producedAmount = pproduced * prate;
      return demandAmount - producedAmount;
   }
   public void display()
   {
      super.display();
      System.out.println("Quantity produced: " + pproduced);
      System.out.println("Cost per unit: " + prate);
      System.out.println("Difference in demand and supply: " + calculation());
   }
}
```

3. A super class Bank has been defined to store the details of the customer in a bank. Define a subclass Interest to calculate the compound interest.

The details of the members of both the classes are given below:

Class name	**Bank**
Data members/Instance variables	
name	to store the name of the customer
acc_no	integer to store the account number
principal	to store the principal amount in decimals
Methods / Member functions	
Bank(...)	parameterized constructor to assign values to the data members
void display()	to display the customer details
Class name	**Interest**
Data members/Instance variables	
rate	to store the interest rate in decimals
time	to store the time period in decimals

Methods / Member functions	
Interest(...)	parameterized constructor to assign values to the data members of both the classes
double calculate()	to calculate and return the compound interest using the formula [$CI = P(1 + R/100)^N - P$] where, P is the principal, R is the rate and N is the time
void display( )	to display the customer details along with the compound interest.

Assume that the super class Bank has been defined. Using the concept of inheritance, specify the class Interest giving the details of the constructor(...), double calculate( ) and void display( ).

The super class, main function and algorithm need NOT be written. *ISC SQP 2023*

Ans
```
class Interest extends Bank
{
   private double rate;
   private double time;
   Interest(String name, int acc_no, double principal, double rate, double time)
   {
      super(name, acc_no, principal);
      this.rate = rate;
      this.time = time;
   }
   double calculate()
   {
      double CI = principal * Math.pow((1 + rate/100), time) - principal;
      return CI;
   }
   void display()
   {
      super.display();
      System.out.println("Compound Interest: " + calculate());
   }
}
```

4. A super class Item has been defined to store the details of an item sold by a wholesaler to a retailer. Define a subclass Taxable to compute the total amount paid by the retailer along with service tax.

Some of the members of both the classes are given below:

Class name	**Item**
Data members/Instance variables	
name	to store the name of the item
code	integer to store the item code
amount	stores the total sale amount of the item (in decimals)
Member functions/methods	
Item (……)	parameterized constructor to assign value to the data members
void show()	to display the item details

Class name	**Taxable**
Data members/Instance variables	
tax	to store the service tax (in decimals)
totamt	to store the total amount (in decimals)

Member functions/methods	
Taxable(……)	parameterized constructor to assign values to the data members of both classes
void cal_tax()	calculates the service tax @ 10.2% of the total sale amount calculates the total amount paid by the retailer as (total sale amount + service tax)
void show()	to display the item details along with the total amount

Assume that the super class Item has been defined. Using the concept of inheritance, specify the class Taxable, giving details of the constructor, void cal_tax() and void show(). The super class, main function and algorithm need NOT be written. ***ISC 2022 (Sem II)***

Ans

```
class Taxable extends Item
{
   double tax;
   double totamt;
   Taxable (String n, int c, double p)
   {
      super (n, c, p);
      tax = 0.0;
      totamt = 0.0;
   }
   void cal_tax()
   {
      tax=(amount*10.2)/100;
      totamt = amount + tax;
   }
   void show()
   {
      System.out.println("Name of the item:" + name);
      System.out.println("Item code:" + code);
      System.out.println("Sales amount:" + amount);
      System.out.println("Total amount:" + totamt);
   }
}
```

5. A super class Godown has been defined to store the details of the stock of a retail store. Define a subclass Update to store the details of the items purchased with the new rate and update the stock. Some of the members of both the classes are given below

Class name	**Godown**
Data members/Instance variables	
item	to store the name of the item
qty	to store the quantity of an item in stock
rate	to store the unit price of an item
amt	to store the net value of the item in stock
Member functions/Methods	
Godown(...)	parameterized constructor to assign value to the data members
void display( )	to display the stock details
Class name	**Update**
Data members/Instance variables	
pur_qty	to store the purchase quantity
pur_rate	to store the unit price of the purchased item

Member functions / Methods	
Update(...)	parameterized constructor to assign values to the data members of both the classes
void update( )	to update the stock by adding the previous quantity by the purchased quantity and replace the rate of the item, if there is a difference in the purchase rate. Also, update the current stock value as: (quantity * unit price)
void display()	to display the stock details before and after updating

Assume that the super class Godown has been defined. Using the concept of inheritance, specify the class Update giving details of the constructor, void update () and void display(). The super class, main function and algorithm need NOT be written. ***ISC SQP 2022 (Sem II)***

Ans

```
public class Update extends Godown
{
   private int pur_qty;
   private double pur_rate;
   public Update(String item, int qty, double rate, double amt, int pur_qty, double pur_rate)
   {
      super(item, qty, rate, amt);
      this.pur_qty = pur_qty;
      this.pur_rate = pur_rate;
   }
   public void update()
   {
      qty += pur_qty;
      if (rate != pur_rate)
      {
         rate = pur_rate;
      }
      amt = qty * rate;
   }
   public void display()
   {
      System.out.println("Stock details before updating:");
      super.display();
      update();
      System.out.println("Stock details after updating:");
      super.display();
   }
}
```

6. An interface Data is defined with a data member and a method volume() which returns the volume of the implementing shape. A super class Base has been defined to contain the radius of a geometrical shape. Define a sub class CalVol which uses the properties of the interface Data and the class Base and calculates the volume of a cylinder.

The details of the members of the interface and both the classes are given below :

Interface name	Data
Data member	
double pi	initialize pi = 3.142
Member function/Method	
double volume ()	

Class name	Base
Data member/Instance variable	
rad	to store the radius in decimal

Member functions/Methods	
Base (...)	parameterized constructor to initialize the data member
void show ()	displays the radius with an appropriate value
Class name	**CalVol**
Data member/Instance variable	
ht	to store the height to decimal
Member functions/Methods	
CalVol(...)	parameterized constructor to initialize the data members of both the classes
double volume()	calculates the volume of a sphere by using the formula (pi x radius^2 x height)
void show()	displays the data members of both the classes and the volume of the sphere with appropriate message

Assume that the interface Data and the super class Base has been defined.

Using the concept of inheritance, specify the class CalVol giving the details of the constructor(...), double volume() and void show().

The interface, super class, main function and algorithm need NOT be written. ***ISC 2020***

Ans

```
class CalVol extends Base implements Data
{
   double ht;
   public CalVol(double r, double h)
   {
      super(r);
      ht = h;
   }
   public double volume()
   {
      return pi * rad * rad * ht;
   }
   public void show()
   {
      super.show();
      System.out.println("Height: " + ht);
      double v = volume();
      System.out.println("Volume of cylinder: " + v);
   }
}
```

7. An interface Shape is defined with a method area() which returns the area of the implementing shape.

Create the classes Circle and Rectangle which implement the interface Shape. These classes have attributes which reflect their dimensions (radius- for a circle, height and width for a rectangle) which are set by their constructors.

The details of the members of the interface and both the classes are given below:

Interface name	**Shape**
Member function/Method	
double area()	returns the area of the implementing shape
Class name	**Circle**
Data member/Instance variable	
radius	to store radius of the circle in decimal

Member functions/Methods	
Circle(int r)	parameterized constructor to initialise radius=r
double area()	to calculate area of the circle [area of a circle is 3.14*radius*radius]
Class name	**Rectangle**
Data members/Instance variables	
length	to store length of the rectangle in decimal
breadth	to store breadth of the rectangle in decimal
Member functions / Methods	
Rectangle(int 1, int b)	parameterized constructor to initialize length=1, breadth=b
double area()	to calculate area of the rectangle [area of a rectangle is length*breadth]

Assume that the interface Shape has been defined. Using the concept of inheritance, specify the classes Circle and Rectangle giving details of their constructors and double area( ) respectively. The interface, main function and algorithm need NOT be written. ***ISC SQP 2020***

Ans

```
interface Shape
{
   double area();
}
class Circle implements Shape
{
   double radius;
   public Circle(double r)
   {
      radius = r;
   }
   public double area()
   {
      return 3.14 * radius * radius;
   }
}
class Rectangle implements Shape
{
   double length;
   double breadth;
   public Rectangle(double l, double b)
   {
      length = l;
      breadth = b;
   }
   public double area()
   {
      return length * breadth;
   }
}
```

8. A super class Record contains names and marks of the students in two different single dimensional arrays. Define a sub class Highest to display the names of the students obtaining the highest mark. The details of the members of both the classes are given below :

Class name	Record
Data members/Instance variables	
n[ ]	array to store names
m[ ]	array to store marks
size	to store the number of students
Member functions/Methods	
Record(int cap)	parameterised constructor to initialise the data member size = cap
void readarray( )	to enter elements in both the arrays
void display( )	displays the array elements

Class name	Highest
Data member/Instance variable	
ind	to store the index
Member functions/Methods	
Highest(...)	parameterised constructor to initialise the data members of both the classes
void find( )	finds the index of the student obtaining the highest mark and assign it to 'ind'
void display( )	displays the array elements along with the names and marks of the students who have obtained the highest mark

Assume that the super class Record has been defined. Using the concept of inheritance, specify the class Highest giving the details of the constructor(...), void find() and void display(). The super class, main function and algorithm need NOT be written. ***ISC 2019***

Ans

```
class Highest extends Record
{
   int ind;
   Highest(int cap)
   {
      super();
      ind=0;
   }
   void find()
   {
      int h=m[0];
      for(int i=0;i<=50;i++)
      {
         if(h>m[i])
         {
            h=m[i];
            ind=i;
         }
      }
   }
   void display()
   {
      super.display();
      System.out.println("List of students who are scoring highest
                                                         marks"+n[ind]);
   }
}
```

9. A super class Number is defined to calculate the factorial of a number. Define a sub class Series to find the sum of the series S = 1! + 2! + 3! + 4!+.......+n!

The details of the members of both the classes are given below:

Class name	Number
Data member/Instance variable	
n	to store an integer number
Member functions/Methods	
Number(int nn)	parameterised constructor to initialize the data member n=nn
int factorial(int a)	returns the factorial of a number (factorial of n = 1×2×3×......×n)
void display( )	displays the data members

Class name	Series
Data member/Instance variable	
sum	to store the sum of the series
Member functions/Methods	
Series(...)	parameterised constructor to initialize the data members of both the classes
void calsum( )	calculates the sum of the given series
void display( )	displays the data members of both the classes

Assume that the super class Number has been defined. Using the concept of inheritance, specify the class Series giving the details of the constructor(...),void calsum( ) and void display( ).

The super class, main function and algorithm need NOT be written. ***ISC 2018***

Ans
```
class Series extends Number
{
  int sum;
  Series (int n, int sum)
  {
    super (n);
    this.sum = sum;
  }
  public void calsum ()
  {
    int i, j, fact, sum = 0;
    for (i = 1; i < = n; i + +)
    {
      fact = 1;
      if (i!= n)
        System.out.println ("! + " + i);
      else
        System.out.println ("! = " + i);
      for (j = 1; j < = i; j + +)
      {
        fact = fact * j;
```

```
                sum = sum + fact;
            }
        }
    }
    public void display ()
    {
        super.display ();
        System.out.println ("Integer number = " + n);
        System.out.println (" Sum = " + sum);
    }
}
```

10. A super class Product has been defined to store the details of a product sold by a wholesaler to a retailer. Define a sub class Sales to compute the total amount paid by the retailer with or without fine along with service tax.

Some of the members of both the classes are given below

Class Name	**Product**
Data members/Instance variables	
name	stores the name of the product
code	integer to store the product code
amount	stores the total sale amount of the product (in decimals)
Member functions/Methods	
Product(String n, int c, double p)	parameterized constructor to assign data members name=n, code=c and amount=p
void show()	displays the details of the data members

Class Name	**Sales**
Data members/Instance variables	
day	to store number of days taken to pay the sale amount
tax	to store the services tax (in decimals)
totamt	to store the total amount (in decimals)
Member functions/Methods	
Sales (…)	paramaterized constructor to assign values to data members to both the classes
void compute( )	calculates the services tax @ 12.4% of the actual sale amount
	calculates the fine @ 2.5% of the actual sale amount only if the amount paid by the retailer to the wholesaler exceeds 30 days
	calculates the total amount paid by the retailer as (actual sale amount + service tax + fine)
void show( )	displays the data members of super class and the total amount

Assume that the super class Product has been defined. Using the concept of inheritance, specify the class Sales giving the details of the constructor(…), void compute() and void show().

The super class, main function and algorithm need NOT be written. ***ISC 2017***

Ans

```
class Sales extends Product
{
    int day;
    double tax;
    double totamt;
```

```
    Sales (String n, int c, double p, int d)
    {
        super (n, c, p);
        day = d;
        tax = 0.0;
        totamt = 0.0;
    }
    void compute( )
    {
        tax = (amount*12.4)/100;
        int fine = 0;
        if (day > 30)
            fine = (amount * 2.5)/100;
        totamt = amount + tax + fine;
    }
    void show( )
    {
        System.out.println("Name of the product:" + name);
        System.out.println("Product code :" + code);
        System.out.println("Sale amount of the product :" +amount);
        System.out.println("Total amount :" + totamt);
    }
}
```

11. A super class Bank has been defined to store the details of a customer. Define a sub-class Account that enables transactions for the customer with the bank. The details of both the classes are given below:

Class name	**Bank**
Data members/Instance variables	
name	stores the name of the customer
accno	stores the account number
p	stores the principal amount in decimals
Member function/Method	
Bank(...)	parameterised constructor to assign values to the instance variables

Class name	**Account**
Data member/Instance variable	
amt	stores the transaction amount in decimals
Member functions/Methods	
Account(...)	parameterised constructor to assign values to the instance variables of both the classes
void deposit( )	accepts the amount and updates the principal as p=p+amt
void withdraw( )	accepts the amount and updates the principal as p=p–amt If the withdrawal amount is more than the principal amount, then display the message "INSUFFICIENT BALANCE". If the principal amount after withdrawal is less than 500, then a penalty is imposed by using the formula $p = p - (500 - p) / 10$
void display( )	displays the details of the customer

Assume that the super class Bank has been defined. Using the concept of Inheritance, specify the class Account giving details of the constructor(...), void deposit( ), void withdraw () and void display( ). The super class and the main function need not be written. **ISC 2016**

Ans

```
class Account extends Bank
{
        double amt;
        public Account(String name, int accno, double p, double amt)
        {
            super(name, accno, p);
            this.amt = amt;
        }
        public void deposit()
        {
            p = p + amt;
        }
        public void withdraw()
        {
            if(amt > p)
                System.out.println("INSUFFICIENT BALANCE");
            else
            {
                p = p - amt;
                if(p < 500.0)
                    p = p - (500 - p)/10;
            }
        }
        public void display()
        {
            super.display();
            System.out.println(''Last transaction amount: Rs.'' +amt);
        }
}
```

10 Marks Questions

1. A line on a plane can be represented by coordinates of the two-end points p1 and p2 as p1(x1, y1) and p2(x2, y2).

   A super class Plane is defined to represent a line and a sub class Circle to find the length of the radius and the area of circle by using the required data members of super class.

   Some of the members of both the classes are given below:

Class name	Plane
Data members/Instance variables	
*x*1	to store the *x*-coordinate of the first end point
*y*l	to store the *y*-coordinate of the first end point
Member functions/Methods	
Plane(int n*x*, int n*y*)	parameterized constructor to assign the data members *x*1 = *nx* and *y*l = *ny*
void Show( )	to display the coordinates

Class name	Circle
Data members/Instance variables	
*x*2	to store the *x*-coordinate of the second end point
*y*2	to store the *y*-coordinate of the second end point
radius	double variable to store the radius of the circle
area	double variable to store the area of the circle

Member functions/Methods	
Circle(....)	parameterized constructor to assign values to data members of both the classes
void findRadius( )	to calculate the length of radius using the formula: $(\sqrt{(x2-x1)^2+(y2-y1)^2})/2$ assuming that $x1, x2, y1, y2$ are the coordinates of the two ends of the diameter of a circle.
void findArea( )	to find the area of circle using formula : πr^2. The value of pie (π) is 22/7 or 3.14
void Show( )	to display both the coordinates along with the length of the radius and area of the circle

Specify the class Plane giving details of the constructor and void Show(). Using the concept of inheritance, specify the class Circle giving details of the constructor, void findRadius(), void findArea() and void Show().

The main function and algorithm need not be written. ***ISC 2015***

Ans

```
class Plane
{
    int x1, y1;
    Plane(int nx, int ny)
    {
        x1=nx;
        y1=ny;
    }
    void Show()
    {
        System.out.println("First Coordinates are ("+x1+", "+y1+")");
    }
}
class Circle extends Plane
{
    int x2, y2;
    double radius,area;
    Circle(int nx1, int ny1, int nx2, int ny2)
    {
        super(nx1,ny1);
        x2=nx2;
        y2=ny2;
    }
    void findRadius()
    {
        int d=(x2-x1)*(x2-x1)+(y2-y1)*(y2-y1);
        radius=(Math.sqrt(d))/2;
    }
    void findArea()
    {
        area=3.14*radius*radius;
    }
    void Show()
    {
        super.Show();
        System.out.println("Second Coordinates are ("+x2+","+y2+")");
        System.out.println("Length of radius" +radius);
        System.out.println("Area of circle" +area);
    }
}
```

2. A superclass Stock has been defined to store the details of the stock of a retail store. Define a subclass Purchase to store the details of the items purchased with the new rate and updates the stock. Some of the members of the classes are given below:

Class name	Stock
Data members/Instance variables	
item	to store the name of the item
qty	to store the quantity of an item in stock
rate	to store the unit price of an item
amt	to store the net value of the item in stock
Member functions	
Stock (…)	parameterized constructor to assign values to the data members
void display ( )	to display the stock details

Class name	Purchase
Data members/Instance variables	
pqty	to store the purchased quantity
prate	to store the unit price of the purchased item
Member functions	
Purchase(…)	parameterized constructor to assign values to the data members of both the classes
void update( )	to update stock by adding the previous quantity by the purchased quantity (quantity * unit price)
void display( )	to display the purchase details before and after updation

Specify the class Stock giving details of the constructor and void display(). Using concept of inheritance, specify the class Purchase giving details of the constructor, void update() and void display(). The main( ) function and algorithm need not to be written. ***ISC 2014***

Ans

```
import java.io.*;
class Stock
{
    //starting of super class
    public String item;
    public int qty, rate, amt;
    public Stock(String ite, int qt, int r)
    {
        item=ite;
        qty=qt;
        rate=r;
        amt=qty*rate;
    }
    public void display()
    {
        System.out.println("Item name:" +item);
        System.out.println("Quantity of item:" +qty);
        System.out.println("Unit price of item:" +rate);
        System.out.println("Net value of item:" +amt);
    }
}
```

```
class Purchase extends Stock
{
    //starting of subclass
    public int pqty, prate;
    public Purchase(int pq, int pr, String ite, int qt, int r)
    {
        super(ite,qt,r);
        pqty=pq;
        prate=pr;
    }
    public void update()
    {
        qty = qty + pqty;
        if(rate!=prate)
        {
            rate = prate;
        }
        amt = rate * qty;
    }
    public void display()
    {
        System.out.println("Previous details:");
        super.display();
        update();
        System.out.println("New details:");
        super.display();
    }
}
```

3. A superclass Perimeter has been defined to calculate the perimeter of a parallelogram. Define a subclass Area to compute the area of the parallelogram by using the required data members of the superclass. The details are given below:

Class name	**Perimeter**
Data members/Instance variables	
a	to store the length in decimal
b	to store the breadth in decimal
Member functions	
Perimeter (...)	parameterized constructor to assign values to data members
double calculate ( )	to calculate and return the perimeter of a parallelogram as 2 * (length + breadth)
void show ( )	to display the data members along the perimeter of the parallelogram

Class name	**Area**
Data members/Instance variables	
h	to store the height in decimal
area	to store the area of the parallelogram

Member functions	
Area(...)	parameterized constructor to assign values to data members of both the classes
void doarea( )	compute the area as (breadth * height)
void show( )	display the data members of both classes along with the area and perimeter of the parallelogram

Specify the class Perimeter giving details of the constructor, double calculate() and void show(). Using the concept of inheritance, specify the class Area giving details of the constructor, void doarea() and void show().
The main( ) function and algorithm need not to be written. ***ISC 2013***

Ans

```
class Perimeter
{
    protected double a, b;
    Perimeter(int aa, int bb)
    {
        a = aa;
        b = bb;
    }
    double calculate()
    {
        double P;
        P = 2 * (a + b);
        return P;
    }
    void show()
    {
        double P = calculate();
        System.out.println("In perimeter of parallelogram with
        Length "+a+" and Breadth "+b+" is :" +P);
    }
}
class Area extends Perimeter
{
    double h, area;
    Area(int aa, int bb, int hh)
    {
        super(aa, bb);
        h = hh;
    }
    public void doarea()
    {
        area = b * h;
    }
    void show()
    {
        super.show();
        System.out.println("Height" +h+ "Area" +area);
    }
}
```

4. A superclass Detail has been defined to store the details of a customer. Define a subclass Bill to compute the monthly telephone charge of the customer as per the chart given below:

Number of Calls	Rate
1—100	Only rental charge
101—200	60 paisa per call + rental charge
201—300	80 paisa per call + rental charge
Above 300	1 rupee per call + rental charge

Details of both the classes are given below:

Class name	Detail
Data members/Instance variables	
name	to store the name of the customer
address	to store the address of the customer
telno	to store the phone number of the customer
rent	to store the monthly rental charge
Member functions	
Detail(...)	parameterized constructor to assign values to data members
void show( )	to display the details of the customer

Class name	Bill
Data members/Instance variables	
n	to store the number of calls
amt	to store the amount to be paid by the customer
Member functions	
Bill(...)	parameterized constructor to assign values to data members of both classes and to initialize amt = 0.0
void cal( )	calculate the monthly telephone charge as per the chart given above
void show( )	display the details of the customer and amount to be paid

Specify the class Detail giving details of the constructor and void show(). Using the concept of inheritance, specify the class Bill giving details of the constructor, void cal() and void show(). The main() function and algorithm need not to be written. ***ISC 2012***

Ans

```
class Detail
{
    protected String name, address;
    protected int telno;
    protected double rent;
    Detail(String n, String ad, int t, double r)
    {
        name = n;
        address = ad;
        telno=t;
        rent=r;
    }
    void show()
    {
        System.out.println("Name of customer "+name);
        System.out.println("Address of customer "+address);
        System.out.println("Telephone no. "+telno);
        System.out.println("Rent "+rent);
    }
}
```

```
class Bill extends Detail
{
    int n;
    double amt;
    Bill(String na, String a, int te, double re, int c)
    {
        super(na, a, te, re);
        n=c;
        amt=0.0;
    }
    void cal()
    {
        if(n>=1&&n<=100)
            amt=rent;
        else if(n>=101 && n<=200)
            amt = rent+(.60*(n-100));
        else if(n>=201 && n <= 300)
            amt = rent + (.60*100) + (.80 *(n-200));
        else
            amt = rent + (.60*100) +(.80 * 100) + (n-300)*100;
    }
    void show()
    {
        super.show();
        System.out.println("Amount to be paid =" +amt/100+" Rs");
    }
}
```

5. A superclass Record has been defined to store the names and ranks of 50 students. Define a subclass Rank to find the highest rank along with the name. The details of both classes are given below:

Class name	**Record**
Data members/Instance variables	
name[ ]	to store the names of students
rnk[ ]	to store the ranks of students
Member functions	
Record( )	constructor to initialize data members
void readvalues( )	to store the names and ranks
void display( )	to display the names and the corresponding ranks

Class name	**Rank**
Data member/Instance variable	
index	integer to store the index of the topmost rank
Member functions	
Rank( )	constructor to invoke the base class constructor and to initialize index = 0
void highest( )	finds the index/location of the topmost rank and stores it in index without sorting the array
void display( )	display the names and ranks alongwith the name having the topmost rank

Specify the class Record giving details of the constructor, void readvalues() and void display(). Using the concept of inheritance, specify the class Rank giving details of constructor, void highest() and void display().

The main() function and algorithm need not to be written. **ISC 2011**

Ans

```
import java.io.*;
class Record
{
    String name[];
    int rnk[];
    Record()
    {
        name = new String[50];
        rnk = new int[50];
    }
    void readvalues() throws IOException
    {
        BufferedReader b=new BufferedReader(new InputStreamReader(System.in));
        System.out.println("Enter the name and rank of 50 students");
        for(int i = 0;i < 50;i++)
        {
            name[i]= b.readLine();
            rnk[i] = Integer.parseInt(b.readLine());
        }
    }
    void display()
    {
        System.out.println("Name" + "\t" + "Rank");
        for(int i=0; i <= 49; i++)
        {
            System.out.println(name[i] + "\t" + rnk[i]);
        }
    }
}
class Rank extends Record
{
    int index;
    Rank()
    {
        super();
        index = 0;
    }
    void highest()
    {
        int h = rnk[0];
        for(int i = 1;i < 50;i++)
        {
            if(h > rnk[i])
            {
                h = rnk[i];
                index = i;
            }
        }
    }
    void display()
    {
        super.display();
        System.out.println("The student having the topmost Rank is " +name[index]);
    }
}
```

6. A superclass Worker has been defined to store the details of a worker. Define a subclass Wages to compute the monthly wages for the worker. The details/ specifications of both the classes are given below:

Class name	Worker
Data members/Instance variables	
Name	to store the name of the worker
Basic	to store the basic pay in decimals
Member functions	
Worker (...)	Parameterized constructor to assign values to the instance variables
void display( )	display the workers details

Class name	Wages
Data members/Instance variables	
hrs	stores the hours worked
rate	stores rate per hour
wage	stores the overall wage of the worker
Member functions	
Wages (...)	Parameterized constructor to assign values to the instance variables of both the classes
double overtime( )	Calculates and returns the overtime amount as (hours*rate)
void display( )	Calculates the wage using the formula wage = overtime amount + Basic pay and display it alongwith the other details

Specify the class Worker giving details of the constructor and void display(). Using the concept of inheritance, specify the class Wages giving details of constructor, double overtime() and void display(). The main() function need not to be written. ***ISC 2010***

Ans

```
class Worker
{
    String Name;
    float Basic;
    Worker(String n, float b)
    {
        Name=n;
        Basic=b;
    }
    void display()
    {
        System.out.println("Name is "+Name);
        System.out.println("Basic Salary is "+Basic);
    }
}
class Wages extends Worker
{
    int hrs,rate;
    double wage;
    Wages(int h, int r, String n, float b)
    {
        super(n,b); //using the constructor of base class
        hrs=h;
        rate=r;
    }
```

```
    double overtime()
    {
        return hrs*rate;
    }
    void display()
    {
        wage=overtime()+ Basic;
        super.display();
        System.out.println("Hours Worked ="+hrs);
        System.out.println("Rate per hour ="+rate);
        System.out.println("Total Wages ="+wage);
    }
}
```

7. A library issues books on rental basis at a 2% charge on the cost price of the book per day. As per the rules of the library, a book can be retained for 7 days without any fine. If the book is returned after 7 days, a fine will also be charged for the excess days as per the chart given below:

Number of Excess Days	Fine per Day (Rs.)
1 to 5	2.00
6 to 10	3.00
Above 10 days	5.00

Design a class Library and another class Compute to perform the task. The details of the two classes are given below:

Class name	Library
Data members/Instance variables	
name	to store name of the book
author	to store author of the book
p	to store price of the book in decimals
Member functions	
Library (...)	parameterized constructor to assign values to data members
void show( )	displays the book details

Class name	Compute
Data member/Instance variable	
d	number of days taken in returning the book to store the fine
Member functions	
Compute (...)	parameterized constructor to assign values to data members of both the classes
void fine ( )	calculates the fine for the excess days
void display( )	display the book details along with the number of days, fine and the total amount to be paid. Total amount is calculated as (.2% of price of book * total no. of days) + fine

Specify the class Library giving the details of the constructor and void show(). Using the concept of Inheritance, specify the class Compute giving the details of constructor, void fine() and the void display() functions. You need not to write the main() function.

ISC 2009

Ans

```
class Library
{
    String name;
    String author;
    float p;
    Library(String n, String a, float amt)
    {
        name = n;
        author = a;
        p = amt;
    }
    void show()
    {
        System.out.println("Book Name = "+name);
        System.out.println("Author Name = "+author);
        System.out.println("Price = "+p);
    }
}
class Compute extends Library
{
    int d;
    float f, total;
    Compute(String n, String a, float amt, int days)
    {
        super(n,a,amt);
        d = days;
        f = 0;
        total=(float)((.02*p)*d);
    }
    void fine()
    {
        if(d>7)
        {
            d=d-7;
            if(d<=5)
            {
                f=2*d;
            }
            else if(d<=10)
            {
                f=10+((d-5)*3);
            }
            else
            {
                f=10+15+((d-10)*5);
            }
        }
        d=d+7;
        total=total+f;
    }
    void display()
    {
        show();
        System.out.println("Book taken for = "+d+" days");
        System.out.println("Total fine = Rs." +f);
        System.out.println("Total amount to be paid = Rs."+total);
    }
}
```

8. A class Employee contains employee details and another class Salary calculate the employee's net salary. The details of the two classes are given below:

Class name	**Employee**
Data members/Instance variables	
empNo	to store the employee number
empName	to store the employee name
empDesig	to store the employee's designation
Member functions	
Employee ( )	default constructor
Employee (...)	Parameterized constructor to assign values to employee number, name and designation
void display ( )	display the employee details

Class name	**Salary**
Data member/Instance variable	
basic	float variable to store the basic pay
Member functions	
Salary (...)	parameterized constructor to assign values to data members
void calculate( )	calculate the employee's net salary according to following rules : DA = 10% of basic HRA = 15% of basic Salary = basic + DA + HRA PF = 8% of Salary Net salary = Salary – PF Display the employee details and the Net salary.

Specify the class Employee giving details of the constructors and members function void display(). Using the concept of inheritance, specify the class Salary giving details of constructor and the member function void calculate(). The main( ) function needs to be written. ***ISC 2008***

Ans

```
class Employee
{
    int empNo;
    String empName;
    String empDesig;
    Employee()
    {
        empNo = 0;
        empName = "";
        empDesig = "";
    }
    Employee(int n, String na, String ed)
    {
        empNo=n;
        empName=na;
        empDesig=ed;
    }
    void display()
    {
        System.out.println("Employee No:" +empNo);
        System.out.println("Employee Name:" +empName);
        System.out.println("Employee Designation:"+empDesig);
    }
}
class Salary extends Employee
{
    float basic, DA, HRA, PF, NS;
```

```
        Salary(float b, int n, String na, String ed)
        {
            super(n,na,ed);
            basic=b;
            DA=0;
            HRA=0;
            PF=0;
            NS=0;
        }
        void calculate()
        {
            DA=(float)(basic*(.1));
            HRA=(float)(basic*(.15);
            float s=basic+DA+HRA;
            PF=(float)(s*(.08));
            NS=s-PF;
            display();
            System.out.println("Net salary:"+NS);
        }
        public static void main(String args[])
        {
            Salary s1=new Salary(5000, 101, "Akash", "Manager");
            s1.calculate();
        }
    }
```

9. A class Student defines the personal data of a student while another class Marks defines the register number, name of subject and marks obtained by the student. The details of both the classes are given below:

Class name	Student
Data members/Instance variables	
name, sex	array of characters (string)
age	integer variables
Member functions	
void inpdetails1 ( )	to accept values for data members
void show1 ( )	to display personal data of student

Class name	Marks
Data members/Instance variables	
regnum, marks	integer type variables
subject	array of characters (string)
Member functions	
void inpdetails2 ( )	to accept values for data members
void show2 ( )	to display exam details (regnum, marks, subject)

(i) Specify the class Student giving details, if the functions void inpdetails1() and void show1().

(ii) Using the concept of inheritance, specify the class Marks giving the details of the functions void inpdetails2() and void show2(). The main( ) function need not to be written. ***ISC 2007***

Ans (i)
```
import java.io.*;
class Student
{
    String name,sex;
    int age;
    void inpdetails1() throws IOException
    {
```

```
        InputStreamReader in = new InputStreamReader(System.in);
        BufferedReader br=new BufferedReader(in);
        System.out.println("Enter student name");
        name = br.readLine();
        System.out.println("Enter sex");
        sex = br.readLine();
        System.out.println("Enter age");
        age = Integer.parseInt(br.readLine());
    }
    void show1()
    {
        System.out.println("Name" + name);
        System.out.println("Sex" + sex + "\nAge" +age);
    }
}
```

(ii)
```
class Marks extends Student
{
    int regnum;
    int marks;
    String subject;
    void inpdetails2()throws IOException
    {
        InputStreamReader in = new InputStreamReader(System.in);
        BufferedReader br = new BufferedReader(in);
        System.out.println("Enter reg.no");
        regnum = Integer.parseInt(br.readLine());
        System.out.println("Enter subject");
        subject = br.readLine();
        System.out.println("Enter marks");
        marks = Integer.parseInt(br.readLine());
    }
    void show2()
    {
        System.out.println("Reg no." + regnum + "\nSubject"
        + subject + "\nMarks" + marks);
    }
}
```

CHAPTER TEST

1 Mark Questions

1. The parent class is known as
(a) super class (b) sub class (c) derived class (d) child class
2. Which of the following form of inheritance is the implementation of transistive nature of inheritance?
(a) Hierarchical (b) Multilevel (c) Hybrid (d) Multiple
3. What do you mean by derived class?

2 Marks Questions

4. What do you understand with term overloading?
5. What do you mean by static binding?
6. What is the difference between polymorphism and inheritance?

3 Marks Questions

7. How does overloading differ from overriding?
8. Explain the significance of access modifiers in inheritance.

5 Marks Questions

9. What is polymorphism? How can be it achieved in Java?
10. What is inheritance? Explain the importance of multilevel inheritance in Java.
11. What are abstract classes? Differentiate between interfaces and abstract classes.
12. What is multiple inheritance? Does Java support multiple inheritance?

10 Marks Questions

13. Write a program to signify the concept of inheritance in Java.
14. Implement following class hierarchy:

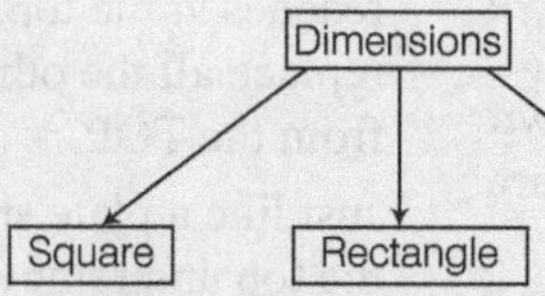

The specification of these classes are:
Dimensions (Data members: no_of_sides, sides[ ](stores the sides), area.
Methods: constructor, readSides ( ), calcArea( ))
Square, Rectangle, Triangle (Method: constructor, display( ), overridden calcArea( ))

10

Data Structures

TREND ANALYSIS 4 YEARS

Data Structures

Average No. of Questions Across all Sets

Types of Questions	2024	2023	2020	2019
1 Mark	1	–	–	–
2 Marks	1	2	2	2
3 Marks	1	1	1	1
5 Marks	–	–	–	1
10 Marks	–	–	–	–

Data structure is an inevitable part of any programming language. The whole programming depends upon the basic unit that is 'data' and the data structure is a specialised format for organising and storing data. Any data structure is designed to organise data to suit a specific purpose, so that it can be occured and worked within appropriate ways.

Types of Data Structures

The data structures can be classified into following two types:

1. **Simple Data Structure** Those data structures which are normally built from primitive data types like integers, real, characters, boolean values are known as simple data structures. Simple data structures are of two types: array and structure.
2. **Compound Data Structure** Simple data structures can be combined in various ways to form more complex structures called compound data structures. It is classified into two types:
   (i) **Linear Data Structure** A data structure is said to be linear, if its elements form a sequence e.g. stack, queue, linked list.
   (ii) **Non-Linear Data Structure** These are multilevel data structures. e.g. tree and graph.

Stack

A stack is a **Last In First Out** (LIFO) abstract data type and linear data structure. A stack is a list like structure, where stack items can only be added or removed from the end of the stack.

Consider the situation when there is a pile of 5 books on a table. You want to add one book to the pile. What do you do? You simply add the book on the TOP of the pile. But if you want the third book from the new 6 book pile then you lift each book one by one from the TOP until the third book reaches at the top. Then, you will take the third book and replace all the others back into the pile by adding them from the TOP.

Just like a plate stack in canteens, where plates are added to the top and removed from the top. Stacks are restricted data structures in which data could be added and retrieved only from one end (also known as the TOP of the stack). Elements are removed from the stack in the reverse order to the order of their addition.

Terms Regarding Stack

- **Push** Adding data to the stack or initialises the stack, if the stack is empty. This process is known as pushing.

- **Pop** Retrieving data from the stack. This process is known as popping.
- **Overflow State** If the stack is full and does not contain enough space to accept the given item, the stack is then considered to be in an overflow state.
- **Underflow State** It means no items are present in stack to be removed, i.e. the stack is empty.
- **Stack Top** It represents the top most position of data in stack.

Suppose, we insert 5, 6, 9 to the stack consecutively, then while retrieving the first one to be retrieved will be 9 then 6 and then 5. That is why, stacks are also known as Last In First Out (LIFO) structure.

e.g. Suppose, we have a stack represented by an array stack [10], which is empty in starting.

```
push(5)
Now, stack[10] = 5
push(10)
Now, stack[10] = 5, 10
pop() [it returns 10]
Now, stack[10] = 5
pop() [now it returns 5]
Now, stack[10] is again empty
```

In this way, a stack can grow and shrink over time.

Operations on Stack

Following operations can be implemented on a stack:

(i) **Insertion in Stack as an Array** Here, STACK is an array with MAX locations. TOP points to the top most element. The simplest form of this is:

```
if(TOP >= MAX)          [Check for overflow]
   Print "Overflow"
else
{
   TOP = TOP + 1
   STACK[TOP] = ITEM
   Print "Item Inserted"
}
```

(ii) **Deletion in a Stack as an Array** Here, STACK is an array with MAX locations. TOP points to the top most element. The simplest form of this is:

```
if(TOP == -1)           [Check for underflow]
   Print "Underflow"
else
{
   ITEM = STACK[TOP]
                        [Assign top of STACK to ITEM]
   TOP = TOP - 1            [Decrement TOP by 1]
   Print "ITEM deleted"
}
```

(iii) **Insertion in a Stack Implemented as a Linked List** Let us consider that TOP points to the top most node of the stack, Item represents the data part of the node and *n* is the data which we want to insert in the new node and next is the pointer pointing to the next node in sequence. The algorithm is:

```
NEWPTR = new Node
NEWPTR.Item = n , NEWPTR.next = NULL
if TOP = NULL then
   TOP = NEWPTR
else
{
   NEWPTR.next = TOP
   TOP = NEWPTR
}
```

(iv) **Deletion from a Stack Implemented as a Linked List** Let us consider that, START is a pointer variable which contains the address of first node. PTR will point to the current node and PREV will point to the previous node. REV will maintain the reverse list. The simplest form is:

```
if START = NULL then
   Print "Stack is Empty"
else
{
   REV = PREV
   PREV = PTR
   PTR = PTR.LINK
   PREV.LINK = REV
}
START = PREV
```

Applications of Stack

Stacks are used, whenever Last In First Out scheme need to be implemented. Here, we are going to discuss various applications of stack data structure.

Infix to Postfix Conversion

Stacks are widely used in the designing and implementation of compilers. e.g. they are used to convert arithmetic expressions from infix notation to postfix notation. An infix expression is one in which operators are located between their operands. This is how, we are accustomed for writing expressions in standard mathematical notation. In postfix notation, the operator immediately follows its operands. A useful feature of postfix is that the order in which operators are applied is always unambiguous, i.e. there is only a single interpretation of any postfix expression. This is not true in case of infix.

Here is the algorithm for infix to postfix conversion in which *I* is an arithmetic expression written in infix notation and *P* is the equivalent postfix expression that is generated by this algorithm.

***Step* 1** Push '(' left parenthesis onto stack.

***Step* 2** Add ')' right parenthesis to the end of expression *I*.

***Step* 3** Scan *I* from left to right and repeat Step 4 for each element of *I* until the stack becomes empty.

***Step* 4** If the scanned element is
- (i) an operand then add it to *P*.
- (ii) a left parenthesis then push it onto stack.
- (iii) an operator, then
  - (a) Pop from stack and add to *P* each operator which has the same or higher precedence then the scanned operator.
  - (b) Add newly scanned operator to stack.
- (iv) a right parenthesis, then
  - (a) Pop from stack and add to *P* each operator until a left parenthesis is encountered.
  - (b) Remove the left parenthesis.

  [End Step 4 If]

  [End of Step 3 For Loop]

***Step* 5** Exit.

Postfix Evaluation

Here, *P* is a postfix expression and this algorithm evaluates it

***Step* 1** Add ")" right parenthesis at the end of *P*.

***Step* 2** Scan *P* from left to right and repeat Steps 3 and 4 for each element of *P* until ")" is encountered.

***Step* 3** If an operand is encountered, push it onto stack.

***Step* 4** If an operator is encountered, then
- (i) Pop the top two elements from stack, where *A* is the top element and *B* is the next to top element.
- (ii) Evaluate *B* operator *A*.
- (iii) Place the result of (ii) back on stack.

  [End of Step 4 If]

  [End of Step 2 For Loop]

***Step* 5** Set VALUE equal to the top element on the stack.

***Step* 6** Exit.

Infix to Prefix Conversion

Algorithm for Infix to Prefix Conversion:

***Step* 1** Reverse the infix expression.

***Step* 2** Replace each opening parenthesis '(' with a closing parenthesis ')' and vice versa.

***Step* 3** Swap the positions of the operands for binary operators.

***Step* 4** Convert the modified infix expression to postfix expression using the stack-based algorithm.

***Step* 5** Reverse the postfix expression to obtain the prefix expression.

Balanced Parenthesis

Given an expression string named exp, the algorithm below examines whether the pairs and the orders of "{","}","(",")","[","]" are correct in exp. e.g. it would print true for exp = "[()]{}{[()()]()}" and false for exp = "[(])"

- Declare a character stack S.
- Now traverse the expression string exp.
  - (i) If the current character is a starting bracket ('(' or '{' or '['), then push it to stack.
  - (ii) If the current character is a closing bracket (')' or '}' or ']'), then pop from stack and if the popped character is matching the starting bracket, then find else parenthesis are not balanced.
- After complete traversal, if there is some starting bracket left in stack, then "not balanced"

Nested Function Calls

Nested function calls are those, where a method calls another method which in turn may call another method before returning and so on.

We have already learnt the concept of recursion which uses the stack data structure. The only difference between recursive function calls and nested function calls is that in recursion, a method calls itself while in nested function, a method calls another method. Rest the usage of stack remains same in both the cases.

Solving Maze Problem

A Maze is a network of paths and edges designed as a puzzle through which one has to find a way. It is viewed as a puzzle that must be solved and for solving it, any one of the many method can be used. This can be understood with the help of an example.

Here, given a Maze with one starting position and one ending position. You have to find your way from starting position to the ending position.

This is somewhat related to the recursive backtracker solving method described below and requires stack up to the size of the Maze.

When carving, be as greedy as possible and always carve into an unmade section, if one is next to the current cell. Each time you move to a new cell, push the former cell on the stack.

If there are no unmade cells next to the current position, pop the stack to the previous position. The Maze is done when you pop everything off the stack.

e.g. Consider the following Maze, where a player has to decide how to get from room *A* to room *B*. The player can move from room to room throw the corridors provided but has no way of telling, how many corridors a room is connected to until the reaches that room.

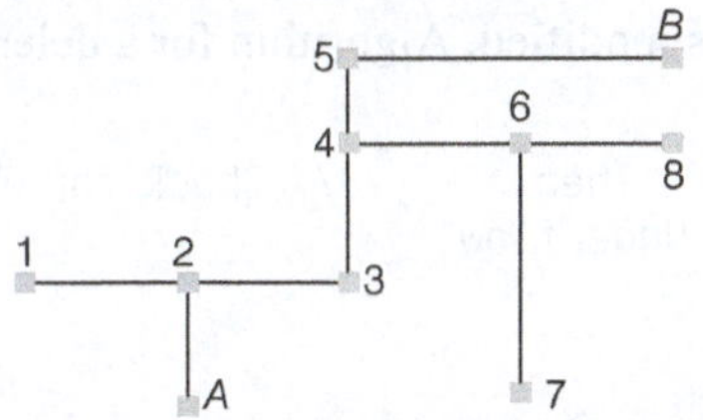

We will now see a sample session to understand the approach the player uses to solve the Maze.

(i) The player moves from room *A* to room 2, pushes to 2 into stack.

(ii) From here, he can move either to room 1 or 3, he chooses 1, pushes 1 into stack.

(iii) 1 is dead end, he pops 1 from stack and returns 2, then goes on to room 3, he pushes 3 into stack.

(iv) He has no choice so, move to room 4, pushes 4 into stack.

(v) From here given a choice between rooms 5 and 6, he chooses 6 and pushes 6 into stack.

(vi) Another choice between 7 and 8, he chooses 7 and pushes 7 into stack.

(vii) Dead end, pops 7 and returns to 6 and chooses 8.

(viii) Dead end again, pops 8 and return to 6 and see that he has exhausted his choose, then also pops 6.

(ix) He goes back to room 4 and choose 5 and pushes 5 into stack.

(x) He sees room *B*, move to it and solve the Maze.

Recursive Backtracker

This will find a solution, but it won't necessarily find the shortest solution. It focuses on you, is fast for all types of Mazes and uses stack space up to the size of the Maze.

Very simple: If you're at a wall (or an area you've already plotted), return failure, else if you're at the finish, return success, else recursively try moving in the four directions. Plot a line when you try a new direction and erase a line when you return failure, and a single solution will be marked out when you hit success. This method will always find a solution if one exists, but it won't necessarily be the shortest solution.

Queue

There's a huge crowd at your local groccry store. There are too many people trying to buy their respective items and the shopkeeper does not know from where to start. Everyone wants their job done quickly and the shopkeeper needs an efficient method to solve this problem. What does he do? He introduces a queue system based on the First Come First Serve (FCFS) system. The last person trying to buy an item stands behind the last person at the END of the queue. The shopkeeper however is present at the FRONT end of the queue. He gives the item to the person in FRONT of the queue and after the transaction is done, the person in FRONT of the queue leaves. Then, the person second in queue becomes the first person in the queue. Do you get the point here? Queue is a First In First Out (FIFO) data structure i.e. the element added first to the queue will be the one to be removed first.

In a FIFO data structure, the first element added to the queue will be the first one to be removed. Elements are always added to the back of the queue and removed from the front of the queue.

A queue is similar to a stack except that addition of data is done in the BACK end and deletion of data is done in the FRONT end.

By convention, we name the queue insert operation enqueue and the remove operation dequeue. A queue is like a line of people waiting for a bank teller. The queue has a front and a rear. Items enter in a queue at the **rear** and leave a queue at the **front**.

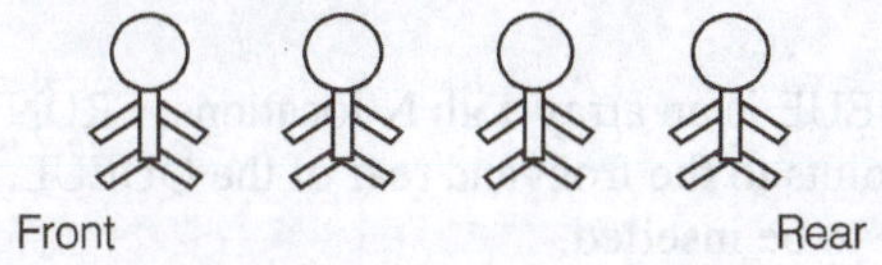

Types of Queue

A Queue can be divided into following categories:

(i) **Circular queue**

- When a new item is inserted at the rear, the rear pointer moves upwards.
- Similarly, when an item is deleted from the queue, the front pointer moves downwards.
- After a few insert and delete operations, the rear might reach the end of the queue and no more items can be inserted, although the items from the front of the queue have been deleted and there is space in the queue.
- To solve this problem, queues implement wrapping around. Such queues are called circular queues.
- Both the front and the rear pointers wrap around to the beginning of the array.
- It is also called as ring buffer.

(ii) **Double-ended queue (Dequeue)**

- Items can be inserted and deleted from either ends.
- More versatile data structure than stack or queue.
- e.g. policy-based application (e.g. low priority go to the end, high go to the front).

(iii) **Priority queue**

- More specialised data structure.
- Similar to queue, having front and rear.
- Items are removed from the front.
- Items are ordered by key value, so that the item with the lowest key (or highest) is always at the front.
- Items are inserted in proper position to maintain the order.

Operations on Queue

Following operations can be performed on a queue data structure:

Insertion in a Queue implemented as an Array

Here QUEUE is an array with N locations. FRONT and REAR points to the front and rear of the QUEUE. ITEM is the value to be inserted.

```
if(REAR == N)                  //Check for overflow
    Print "Queue Overflow"
else
{
    if(FRONT and REAR == 0)
                              //Then Check if QUEUE is empty
    {
        FRONT = 1
        REAR = 1
    }
    else
    {
        REAR = REAR + 1    //Increment REAR by 1
    }
    QUEUE[REAR] = ITEM
    Print "ITEM inserted"
}
```

Deletion from a Queue Implemented as an Array

Here QUEUE is an array with N locations. A deletion can occur at the 'Front' end only and with every deletion, the 'FRONT' gets modified. Algorithm for a deletion of a queue is:

```
if(FRONT == 0) Then            // Check for underflow
    Print "Underflow"
else
{
    ITEM = QUEUE[FRONT]
    if(FRONT == REAR)
                         //Check if only one element is left
    {
        FRONT = 0
        REAR = 0
    }
    else
    {
        FRONT = FRONT + 1    //Increment FRONT by 1
    }
    Print "ITEM deleted"
}
```

Applications of Queue

Typical applications of queue data structure are as follows:

(i) Operating systems often maintain a queue of processes that are ready to execute or that are waiting for a particular event to occur.

(ii) Computer systems must often provide a "holding area" for messages between two processes, two programs, or even two systems. This holding area is usually called a "buffer" and is often implemented as a queue.

(iii) For implementing any natural FIFO service, like ticket reservation, traffic flow, telephone enquiries.

(iv) For implementing any computational FIFO service, for instance, to access some resources like print job scheduling etc.

Our software queues have counterparts in real world queues. We wait in queues to buy pizza, to enter movie theaters, to drive on a turnpike and to ride on a roller coaster. Another important application of the queue data structure is to help us simulate and analyse such real world queues.

Single Link list (Algorithm and Programming)

Algorithm

Algorithm for the singly linked list operations:

1. Node Class

1. Define a class Node with two attributes: data to store the value and next to store the reference to the next node.

2. Singly Linked List Class

1. Define a class SinglyLinkedList with a private attribute head to point to the first node.
2. Implement a constructor to initialize the head to null.
3. Implement methods:
   i. **isEmpty():** Returns true if the list is empty, otherwise false.
   ii. **insertAtBeginning(int data):** Inserts a node with given data at the beginning of the list.
   iii. **insertAtEnd(int data):** Inserts a node with given data at the end of the list.
   iv. **delete(int key):** Deletes the node with data equal to the given key.
   v. **reverse():** Reverses the linked list.
   vi. **display():** Displays the elements of the list.

3. Main Class

1. Create an instance of SinglyLinkedList.
2. Demonstrate various operations such as insertion at the beginning and end, deletion, and reversal of the list.
3. Print the original list, list after deletion, and reversed list.

Program

```
class Node
{
  int data;
  Node next;

  Node(int data)
  {
     this.data = data;
     this.next = null;
  }
}
class SinglyLinkedList
{
  private Node head;
  SinglyLinkedList()
  {
     this.head = null;
  }
  // check wheather the list is empty or not
  public boolean isEmpty()
  {
     return head == null;
  }
  // Insertion at the beginning of the list
  void insertAtBeginning(int data)
  {
     Node newNode = new Node(data);
     newNode.next = head;
     head = newNode;
  }
  // Insertion at the end of the list
  void insertAtEnd(int data)
  {
     Node newNode = new Node(data);
     if (head == null)
     {
        head = newNode;
        return;
     }
     Node current = head;
     while (current.next != null)
     {
        current = current.next;
     }
     current.next = newNode;
  }
  // Deletion or extracting an element of a node
                                               by key
  void delete(int key)
  {
     Node temp = head;
     Node prev = null;
     if (temp != null && temp.data == key)
     {
        head = temp.next;
        return;
```

```
    }
    while (temp != null && temp.data != key)
    {
        prev = temp;
        temp = temp.next;
    }
    if (temp == null) return;
    prev.next = temp.next;
  }
  // Reverse the list
  public void reverse()
  {
    Node prev = null;
    Node current = head;
    Node next = null;
    while (current != null)
    {
        next = current.next;
        current.next = prev;
        prev = current;
        current = next;
    }
    head = prev;
  }
  // Display the list
  void display() {
    Node current = head;
    while (current != null)
    {
        System.out.print(current.data + " ");
        current = current.next;
    }
    System.out.println();
  }
}
public class Main
{
  public static void main(String[] args)
  {
    SinglyLinkedList list
                    = new SinglyLinkedList();
    System.out.println("Is the list empty? "
       + list.isEmpty()); // Output should be: true
    list.insertAtEnd(10);
    list.insertAtEnd(20);
    list.insertAtBeginning(5);
    list.insertAtEnd(30);
    System.out.println("Original list:");
    list.display();
    list.delete(20);
    System.out.println("List after deleting 20:");
    list.display();
    System.out.println("Original list:");
    list.display();
    System.out.println("Reversed list:");
    list.reverse();
    list.display();
  }
}
```

Output:

Is the list empty? true

Original list:

5 10 20 30 40 50

List after deleting 20:

5 10 30 40 50

Original list:

5 10 30 40 50

Reversed list:

50 40 30 10 5

Tree

A tree is a non linear data structure that represents data in hierarchical manner. It associates every object to a node in the tree and maintains the parent/child relationship.

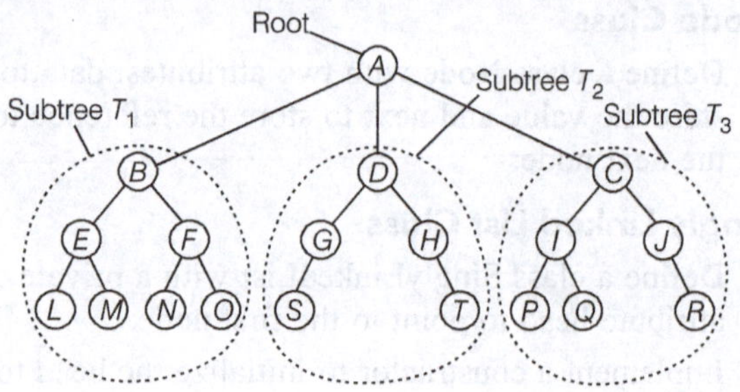

A tree is a finite set of one or more nodes such that:

- There is specially designated node called root.
- The remaining nodes are partitioned into $n(n>=0)$ disjoints sets $T_1, T_2 \ldots T_n$, where each of these sets is itself a tree called subtree. The given figures shows a general tree with parent child relationship.

Tree Terminology

- **Root Node** A node is said to be root node only if it does not have any parent. In the given tree, node '*A*' is the root node of the tree.
- **Subtree** Any part of the tree which follows the property of the tree is known as subtree of the tree, parts T_1, T_2 and T_3 are the subtree of the given tree.
- **Leaf Node or External Node** A node is said to be a leaf if it does not have any child. In given tree, nodes *L, M, N, O, P, Q, R, S* and *T* are leaf nodes.
- **Internal Node** A node is said to be an internal node, if the node have one or more children. In given tree, nodes *A, B, C, D, E, F, G, H, I* and *J* are the internal node.

- **Sibling** A node is said to be sibling of another node only if both the node have same parent. In given tree, *B*, *D* and *C* are siblings. *E* and *F* are siblings, *G* and *H* are siblings, etc.
- **Level or Depth** Level or Depth of a node is the distance from the root of the tree. In a tree, root is always at level 0, children of the root are at level 1, children of the nodes which are level 1, are in level 2 and so on. In given tree, if we assume a node *E*, it is at level 2.
- **Height of a Tree** Height of a tree is the maximum level of any node in the tree. In the given tree, the height of tree is 3.
- **Degree of a Node** The degree of a node is the number of children of that node. e.g. root node has 3 children. So, the degree of root node is 3. The node *B* has 2 children, so, the degree of *B* is 2 and so on.
- **Degree of a Tree** The maximum degree of any node is called the degree of a tree. In given tree, root node has the maximum degree 3. So, the degree of tree is 3.

Binary Tree

A binary tree is a tree, which is either empty or has at most two subtree (children), each of the subtrees also being a binary tree. It means each node in a binary tree can have 0, 1 or 2 subtree (children). In other words, we can say that a binary tree is a tree, in which maximum degree of each node is the 2. It is composed of three disjoint sets of node i.e. a root node, a binary tree called its left subtree, and a binary tree called its right subtree.

The figure shows a binary tree:

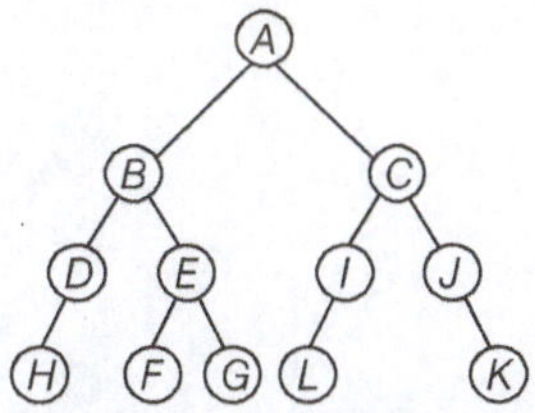

Each node has maximum 2 children. So, the above tree is a binary tree.

Completeness (Complete Binary Tree)

A complete binary tree is a binary tree in which all the levels are completely filled except possibly the lowest one, which is filled from the left.

The following binary tree is a complete binary tree.

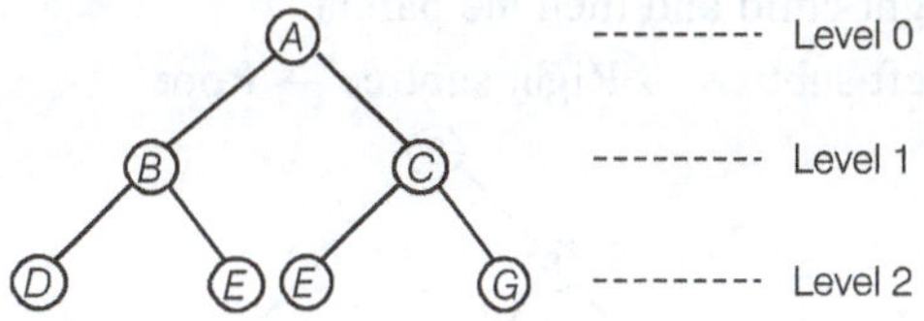

In the above figure, leaf nodes *D, E, F* and *G* are at level 2 i.e. at last level. So, it is a complete binary tree.

Balancing (Fully Binary Tree)

A binary tree is balanced or fully binary tree in which each node has exactly zero or two children or, if all the levels contain maximum possible node.

Following figure shows a fully binary tree:

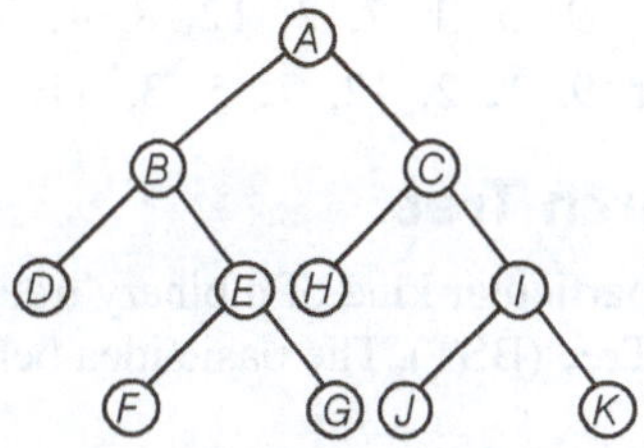

In the above figure, each node has either 0 or 2 children. So, it is a fully binary tree.

Binary Tree Node Structure

In a binary tree, every node contains two reference variables along with data, one of which points to left child node and the other one point to right child node. e.g. to create a binary tree containing integer data, we need to write like,

```
class NODE
{
   int data;
   NODE leftchild;
   NODE rightchild;
}
```

Traversals in Binary Tree

There are three types of tree traversals:

(i) **Preorder traversal** Visit the parent first and then left and right children.

Root → Left subtree → Right subtree

(ii) **Inorder traversal** Visit the left child first, then the parent and the right child.

Left subtree → Root → Right subtree

(iii) **Postorder traversal** Visit left child first, then the right child and then the parent.

Left subtree → Right subtree → Root

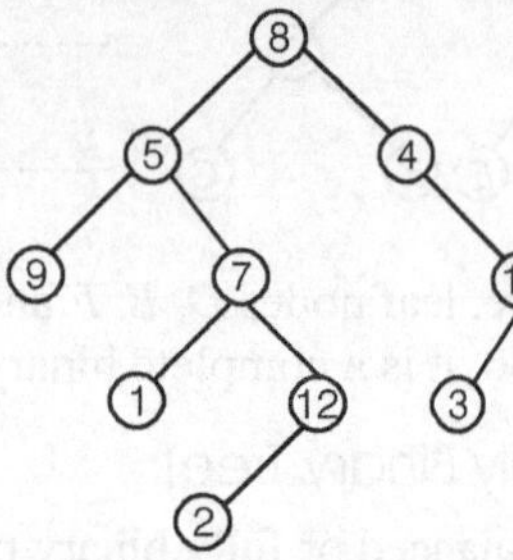

e.g. Consider the tree shown in figure and its three traversals

Preorder 8, 5, 9, 7, 1, 12, 2, 4, 11, 3

Inorder 9, 5, 1, 7, 2, 12, 8, 4, 3, 11

Postorder 9, 1, 2, 12, 7, 5, 3, 11, 4, 8

Binary Search Tree

We consider a particular kind of a binary tree called a Binary Search Tree (BST). The basic idea behind this data structure is to have such a storing repository that provides the efficient way of data sorting, searching and retrieving.

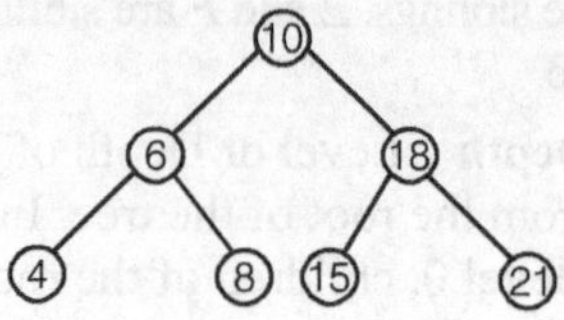

A BST is a binary tree where nodes are ordered in the following way:

(i) Each node contains one key (also known as data).

(ii) The keys in the left subtree are less than the key in its parent node, in short L < P.

(iii) The keys in the right subtree are greater than the key in its parent node, in short P < R.

(iv) Duplicate keys are not allowed.

In the given tree, all nodes in the left subtree of 10 have keys < 10 while all nodes in the right subtree > 10. Because both the left and right subtrees of a BST are again search trees, the above definition is recursively applied to all internal nodes.

PYQs Previous Years Questions

1/2 Marks Questions

1. **Assertion** Recursive data structure follows the LIFO principle.

   Reason Execution of recursive code follows the concepts of data structure Queue. **ISC 2024**

   (a) Both Assertion and Reason are true, and Reason is the correct explanation for the Assertion.
   (b) Both Assertion and Reason are true, but Reason is not the correct explanation for the Assertion.
   (c) Assertion is true but Reason is false
   (d) Assertion is false but Reason is true

Ans (c) Assertion is true but Reason is false

2. Convert the following infix notation to postfix form

   (P + Q * R – S) / T * U **ISC 2024**

Ans (P+Q*R-S)/T*U

Infix	Stack	Status
(	(	
P	(	P
+	(+	P
Q	(+	PQ
*	(+*	PQ
R	(+*	PQR
-	(-	PQR*+
S	(-	PQR*+S
)	)	PQR*+S-
/	/	PQR*+S-
T	/	PQR*+S-T
*	*	PQR*+S-T/
U		PQR*+S-T/U*

Postfix form: P Q R * + S - T / U *

3. Convert the following infix notation to prefix notation.

   *(A – B)/C * (D + E)* **ISC 2023**

Ans Given, expression is *(A – B)/C * (D + E)*

Step 1 Reverse the infix expression

)E + D (C/) B – A(*

Step 2 Make every '('as')' and every')' as '('

*(E + D) * C / (B – A)*

Step 3 Convert expression to postfix form

Infix	Stack	Status
(	(	
E	(	*E*
+	(+	*E*
D	(+	*ED*
)	–	*ED* +
*	*	*ED* +
C	*	*ED* + *C*
/	/	*ED* + *C**
(	/(	*ED* + *C**
B	/(	*ED* + *C*B*
–	/(–	*ED* + *C*B*
A	/(–	*ED* + *C*BA*
)	/	*ED* + *C*BA–*
		ED + *C*BA–/*

Step 4 Reverse the expression */– AB*C + DE*

4. Convert the following infix notation to postfix form.

   *((P/Q – R) * (S + T))* **ISC SQP 2023**

Ans Given, *((P / Q –R) * (S + T))*

Infix	Stack	Status
(	(	
(	((	
P	((	*P*
/	((/	*P*
Q	((/	*PQ*
–	((–	*PQ/*
R	((–	*PQ/R*
)	(	*PQ/R–*
*	(*	*PQ/R–*
(	(*(	*PQ/R–*
S	(*(	*PQ/R–S*
+	(*(+	*PQ/R–S*
T	(*(+	*PQ/R–ST*
)	(*	*PQ/R–ST+*
)		*PQ/R–ST+**

Result : *PQ / R – ST +**

5. Name a data structure that follows LIFO principle and one that follows FIFO principle. **ISC 2022 (Sem II)**

Ans Stack follows LIFO principle
Queue follows FIFO principle.

6. Convert the following infix notation to prefix notation **ISC 2022 (Sem II)**

$$P^* (Q-R)+S$$

Ans Given expression $(P^* (Q-R)+S)$

Step 1 Reverse the infix expression
$)S+)R-Q(*P($

Step 2 Make every '(' as ')' and every ')' as '('
$(S+(R-Q)*P)$

Step 3 Convert expression to postfix form

Infix	Stack	Status
(	(	–
S	(	S
+	(+	S
(	(+(	S
R	(+(	SR
–	(+(–	SR
Q	(+(–	SRQ
)	(+	SRQ –
*	(+*	SRQ –
P	(+*	SRQ – P
)		SRQ – P*+

Step 4 Reverse the expression
+* P – QRS

Result +*P – QRS

7. Convert the following infix notation to postfix notation
A * (B+C/D) – E/F **ISC SQP 2022 (Sem II)**

Ans Given, (A * (B + C/D) – E/F)

Infix	Stack	Status
(	(	
A	(	A
*	(*	A
(	(*(	A
B	(*(	AB
+	(*(+	AB
C	(*(+	ABC
/	(*(+/	ABC
D	(*(+/	ABCD
)	(*	ABCD/+
–	(–	ABCD/+*
E	(–	ABCD/+*E
/	(–/	ABCD/+*E
F	(–/	ABCD/+*EF
)		ABCD/+*EF/–

Result ABCD/+*EF/–

8. State the principle by which the stack data structure works. **ISC SQP 2022 (Sem II)**

Ans Last In First Out (LIFO)

9. Convert the following infix notation to postfix notation
A*(B/C)/E+F **ISC SQP 2022 (Sem II)**

Ans Given, A *(B/C)/E + F

Infix	Stack	Status
(	(	
A	(	A
*	(*	A
(	(*(	A
B	(*(	AB
/	(*(/	AB
C	(*(/	ABC
)	(*	ABC/
/	(/	ABC/*
E	(/	ABC/*E
+	(+	ABC/*E/
F	(+	ABC/*E/F
)		ABC/*E/F+

Result ABC/*E/F +

10. State the difference between binary tree structure and single linked list. **ISC 2020**

Ans Differences between binary tree structure and single linked list are as follows :

Binary Tree Structure	Single Linked List
• In a binary tree structure, each node can have 0, 1 or 2 sub nodes.	• In single linked list, the items are linked together through a single next pointer.
• Time complexity of Search : O(log (n)) Insert : O(log (n)) Delete : O(log (n))	• Time complexity of Search : O(n) Insert : O(1) Delete : O(1)

11. Convert the following infix notation to prefix form:

$(X+Y)/(Z*W/V)$ **ISC 2020**

Ans Given, expression is $(X+Y)/(Z*W/V)$.

Step 1 Reverse the infix expression

$)V/W*Z(/)Y+X($

Step 2 Make every '(' as ')' and every ')' as '('

$(V/W*Z)/(Y+X)$

Step 3 Convert expression to postfix form

Infix	Stack	Status
(	(	
(	((	
V	((	V
/	((/	V
W	((/	VW
*	((*	VW/
Z	((*	VW/Z
)	(	VW/Z*
/	(/	VW/Z*
(	(/(	VW/Z*
Y	(/(	VW/Z*Y
+	(/(+	VW/Z*Y
X	(/(+	VW/Z*YX
)	(/	VW/Z*YX+
)		VW/Z*YX+/

Step 4 Reverse the expression

$/+XY*Z/WV$

Result $/+XY*Z/WV$

12. Differentiate between stack data structure and queue data structure. **ISC SQP 2020**

Stack data structure	Queue data structure
It works on LIFO (Last In First Out) which implies that element which is inserted last would be the first one to be deleted.	It works on FIFO (First In First Out) which implies that element which is added first would be the first element to be removed from the list.
A stack is visualised as a vertical collection.	A queue is visualised as a horizontal collection.

13. Convert the following infix notation to postfix form:

$(A+B*C)-(E*F/H)+J$ **ISC 2019**

Ans Given expression, $((A+B*C)-(E*F/H)+J)$

Infix	Stack	Postfix
(	(	
(	((	
A	((	A
+	((+	A
B	((+	AB
*	((+*	AB
C	((+*	ABC
)	(	ABC*+
–	(–	ABC*+
(	(–(	ABC*+
E	(–(	ABC*+E
*	(–(*	ABC*+E
F	(–(*	ABC*+EF
/	(–(/	ABC*+EF*
H	(–(/	ABC*+EF*H
)	(–	ABC*+EF*H/
+	(+	ABC*+EF*H/–
J	(+	ABC*+EF*H/–J
)		ABC*+EF*H/–J+

Output $ABC*+EF*H/-J+$

14. State the difference between internal nodes and external nodes of a binary tree structure. **ISC 2019**

Ans Differences between internal nodes and external nodes are as follows

Internal nodes	External nodes
It is any node of a tree that has child nodes.	It is any node that does not have child nodes.
e.g. 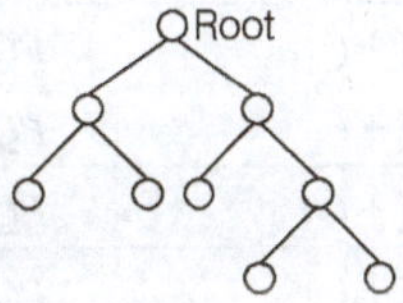	e.g. 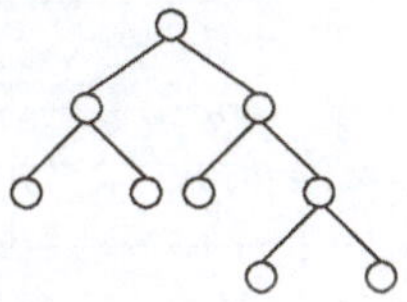
Internal nodes = 4	External nodes = 5

15. Convert the following infix notation to postfix form:

$A+(B-C*(D/E)*F)$ **ISC 2018**

Ans Given infix expression :

$(A+(B-C*(D/E)*F))$

Infix	Stack	Status
(	(	
A	(	A
+	(+	A
(	(+(	A
B	(+(	AB
–	(+(–	AB
C	(+(–	ABC

Infix	Stack	Status
*	(+(−*	ABC
(	(+(−*(	ABC
D	(+(−*(	ABCD
/	(+(−*(/	ABCD
E	(+(−*(/	ABCDE
)	(+(−*	ABCDE/
*	(+(−*	ABCDE/*
F	(+(−*	ABCDE/*F
)	(+	ABCDE/*F*−
)		ABCDE/*F*−+

Postfix expression is $ABCDE/*F*-+$

16. Convert the following infix expression to postfix form $P*Q/R+(S+T)$ **ISC 2017**

Ans Given, infix expression : $(P*Q/R+(S+T))$

Infix	Stack	Status
(	(	
P	(	P
*	(*	P
Q	(*	PQ
/	(/	PQ*
R	(/	PQ*R
+	(+	PQ*R/
(	(+(	PQ*R/
S	(+(	PQ*R/S
+	(+(+	PQ*R/S
T	(+(+	PQ*R/ST
)	(+	PQ*R/ST+
)		PQ*R/ST++

Result $PQ*R/ST++$

17. Convert the following infix expression to postfix form $A+B/C*(D/E*F)$ **ISC 2016**

Ans Given expression, $(A+B/C^*(D/E^*F))$

Infix	Stack	Postfix
(	(	
A	(	A
+	(+	A
B	(+	AB
/	(+/	AB
C	(+/	ABC
*	(+*	ABC/
(	(+*(	ABC/
D	(+*(	ABC/D
/	(+*(/	ABC/D
E	(+*(/	ABC/DE
*	(+*(*	ABC/DE/
F	(+*(*	ABC/DE/F
)	(+*	ABC/DE/F*
)		ABC/DE/F**+

∴ Postfix expression $ABC/DE/F**+$

18. Convert the following infix notation into postfix form: **ISC 2015**

$$X+(Y-Z)+((W+E)*F)/J$$

Ans Given infix expression is:

$$= X+(Y-Z)+((W+E)*F)/J$$
$$= X+(YZ-)+((WE+)*F)/J$$
$$= XYZ-++(WE+F*)/J$$
$$= XYZ-++WE+F*J/$$
$$= XYZ-+WE+F*J/+$$

The postfix expression is $XYZ-+WE+F*J/+$

19. State any two characteristics of a Binary tree. **ISC 2015**

Ans The two characteristics of a binary tree are as follows:

(i) In binary tree, each node can have maximum 2 children.

(ii) A unique path exists from the root to every other node.

20. State the sequence of traversing a binary tree in **ISC 2014**

(i) Pre-order (ii) Postorder

Ans (i) **Pre-order** To traverse a binary tree in preorder, following operations are carried out

Root → Left subtree → Right subtree

(ii) **Postorder** To traverse a binary tree in postorder, following operations are carried out

Left subtree → Right subtree → Root

21. Convert the following infix expression into postfix form. **ISC 2014**

$$(A/B+C)*(D/(E-F))$$

Ans In the above expression,

$$= (A/B+C)\ (D/(E-F))*$$
$$= (AB/+C)\ (D/(EF-))*$$
$$= (AB/C+)\ (DEF-/)*$$

After eliminating brackets, we get postfix form

$$= AB/C+DEF-/*$$

22. Convert the following infix notation to its postfix form. **ISC 2013**

$$E*(F/(G-H)*I)+J$$

Ans First, we eliminate bracket content and then convert it into postfix expression

$= E * (F/(GH-) * I) + J$

$= E * ((FGH-/)* I) + J$

$= E * (FGH-/I*) + J$

$= EFGH-/I**+J$

The postfix expression is

$= EFGH-/I**J+$

23. Write the algorithm for push operation (to add elements) in an array based stack. **ISC 2013**

Ans The algorithm for push operation to add elements in stack based on array,

Step 1 `if (top = size - 1)`
Step 2 `return false //overflow error`
Step 3 `else`
Step 4 `top = top + 1`
Step 5 `data [top]`
Step 6 `return true`

24. Convert the following infix notation to its postfix form. **ISC 2012**

$$(A+(B+C)+(D+E)*F)/G$$

Ans Given expression is

$((A+(B+C)+(D+E)*F)/G)$

Infix	Stack	Status
(	(	
(	((	
A	((	A
+	((+	A
(	((+(	A
B	((+(	AB
+	((+(+	AB
C	((+(+	ABC
)	((+	ABC+
+	((+	ABC++
(	((+(	ABC++
D	((+(	ABC++D
+	((+(+	ABC++D
E	((+(+	ABC++DE
)	((+	ABC++DE+
*	((+*	ABC++DE+
F	((+*	ABC++DE+F
)	(	ABC++DE+F*+
/	(/	ABC++DE+F*+
G	(/	ABC++DE+F*+G
)		ABC++DE+F*+G/

Result $ABC++DE+F*+G/$

25. State how a binary tree is a recursive data structure. **ISC 2012**

Ans A binary tree can be viewed as a recursive data structure. This means that trees are made up of subtrees as its children, as shown

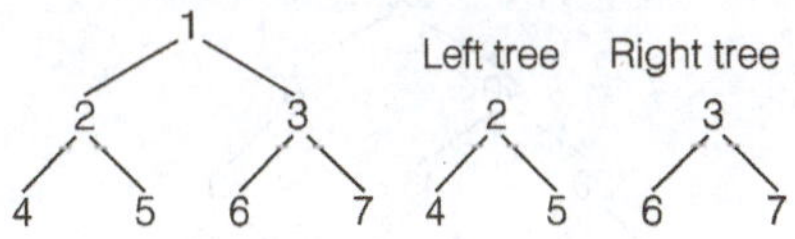

Here, 2 and 3 are children of 1 and 4, 5 are children of 2. So, it is concluded that a binary tree is a recursive tree.

26. Convert the following infix expression to its postfix form. $a+b*c-d/e$ **ISC 2011**

Ans From above expression brackets will be eliminated as per the operator precedence

$= a + b * c - (de/)$

$= a + (bc *) - (de/)$

Here, + and − both have same precedence, so we evaluate from left to right

$= (abc * +) - (de/)$

$= (abc * +) (de/) -$

The postfix form is

$= abc * + de/ -$

27. Convert the following infix notation to postfix notation. **ISC 2010**

$$(A+B)/C*(D+E)$$

Ans From above the expression, eliminate brackets as per operator precedence from left to right associativity,

$= (AB +) /C * (DE +)$

$= (AB + C/) * (DE +)$

$= (AB + C/) (DE +) *$

The postfix expression is

$= AB + C/DE + *$

28. Convert the following infix expression to its postfix form. **ISC 2009**

$$((P*Q)/(R/S+T))+U$$

Ans From the above expression, eliminate the brackets as per operator precedence from left to right associativity,

$= ((PQ *) / (RS/ + T)) + U$

$= ((PQ *) / (RS/T +)) + U$

$= (PQ * RS/T +/) + U$

$= PQ * RS/T +/ U +$

29. State a difference between linear and non-linear data structure. Give an example of each. **ISC 2009**

Ans Differences between linear and non-linear data structures

Linear data structure	Non-linear data structure
It is a set of similar values that are kept in a sequence to store.	It is used to hold similar values but not are in sequencing manner.
e.g. Array.	e.g. Linked list.

30. List the nodes in the tree given below **ISC 2008**
(i) Pre-order (ii) Postorder

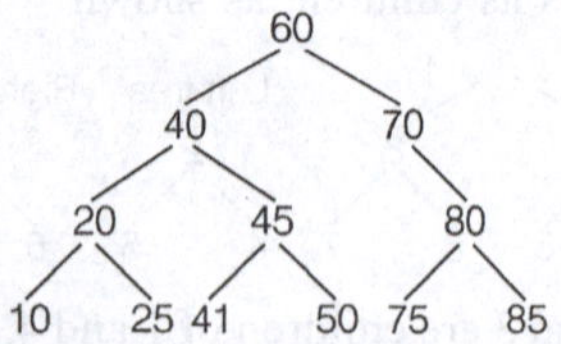

Ans (i) **Pre-order**

= 60, 40, 70
= 60, 40, 20, 45, 70, 80
= 60, 40, 20, 10, 25, 45, 41, 50, 70, 80, 75, 85

(ii) **Postorder**

= 40, 70, 60
= 20, 45, 40, 80, 70, 60
= 10, 25, 20, 41, 50, 45, 40, 75, 85, 80, 70, 60

31. What do LIFO and FIFO stand for? Name a data structure that follows LIFO principle and one that follows FIFO principle. **ISC 2008**

Ans LIFO : Last In First Out
FIFO : First In First Out
The data structure that follows LIFO principle is stack and the data structure that follows FIFO principle is queue.

32. Convert the following infix expression to its postfix form.

$$a/(b + c) + d * (e - f)$$ **ISC 2008**

Ans From the above expression, eliminate the brackets as per operator precedence from left to right associativity,

$((a /(b + c)) + (d* (e - f)))$
$= (a / (bc +)) + d * (e - f)$
$= (abc + /) + d * (e - f)$
$= (abc + /) + d * (ef -)$
$= (abc + /) (def - *) +$

The postfix expression is
$= abc + / def - * +$

33. Convert the following infix expression to its postfix form. **ISC 2007**

$$(A + B * C) / (C - (D * B))$$

Ans From the above expression, eliminate the brackets as per the operator precedence from left to right associativity,

$= (A + BC *) / (C - DB *)$
$= (ABC * +) / (CDB * -)$
$= ABC * + CDB * - /$

The postfix expression is $= ABC * + CDB * - /$

34. Explain any two standard ways of traversing a binary tree. **ISC 2007**

Ans Two standard ways of traversing a binary tree are:

(i) **Preorder Traversing** Preorder traversal prints the contents of a binary tree in preorder. In other words, the contents of the root node are printed first, followed by left subtree and finally the right subtree, as shown

Root → Left subtree → Right subtree

(ii) **Inorder Traversing** Inorder traversal prints the contents of a sorted tree are in inorder. In other words, the contents of the left subtree are printed first, followed by root and finally the right subtree, as shown

Left subtree → Root → Right subtree

35. Convert the following infix expression to its postfix form. **ISC 2006**

$$A + ((B + C) + (D + E) * F) / G$$

Ans Given expression is

$$(A + ((B + C) + (D + E) * F) / G)$$

Infix	Stack	Status
(	(	
A	(	A
+	(+	A
(	(+(	A
(	(+((	A
B	(+((	AB
+	(+((+	AB
C	(+((+	ABC
)	(+(	ABC +
+	(+(+	ABC +
(	(+(+(	ABC +
D	(+(+(	ABC + D
+	(+(+(+	ABC + D
E	(+(+(+	ABC + DE

Infix	Stack	Status
)	(+ (+	ABC + DE +
*	(+ (+ *	ABC + DE +
F	(+ (+ *	ABC + DE + F
)	(+	ABC + DE + F * +
/	(+ /	ABC + DE + F * +
G	(+ /	ABC + DE + F * + G
)		ABC + DE + F * + G /+

Postfix expression is $ABC + DE + F * + G / +$

36. Define a queue. How is a dequeue different from a queue? **ISC 2006**

Ans The queue can be formally defined as ordered collection of elements that has two ends named as front and rear, from the front end one can delete the elements and from the rear one can insert the elements.

A queue is a non-primitive linear data structure in which elements are inserted from one end and deleted from another end and in dequeue both insertion and deletion operations can perform at either end of the queue.

37. State the different applications of stack. **ISC 2005**

Ans The different applications of stacks are:

(i) Parsing
(ii) Recursive function
(iii) Calling function
(iv) Expression conversion (infix to prefix, prefix to infix, etc.)
(v) Tower of hanoi.

38. What is data structure? What are the different types of data structure? **ISC 2005**

Ans **Data structure** is a representation of the logical relationship between individual elements of data. In other words, a data structure is a way of organising all data items that considers not only the elements stored but also their relationship to each other.

Different types of data structure are arrays, stacks, queues, linked lists, trees etc.

39. Convert the following expression into postfix. **ISC 2005**

$$(A + B/C) + B - C * D + C$$

Ans Given expression is $((A + B / C) + B - C * D + C)$

Infix	Stack	Status
(	(	
(	((	
A	((	A
+	((+	A
B	((+	AB
/	((+/	AB
C	((+/	ABC
)	(	ABC /+
+	(+	ABC /+
B	(+	ABC /+B
–	(–	ABC /+B+
C	(–	ABC /+B+C
*	(–*	ABC /+B+C
D	(–*	ABC /+B+CD
+	(+	ABC /+B+CD *–
C	(+	ABC /+B+CD *–C
)		ABC /+B+CD *–C+

Postfix expression is $ABC / + B + CD * - C +$

3 Marks Questions

1. Answer the following questions based on the diagram of a Binary Tree given below **ISC 2024**

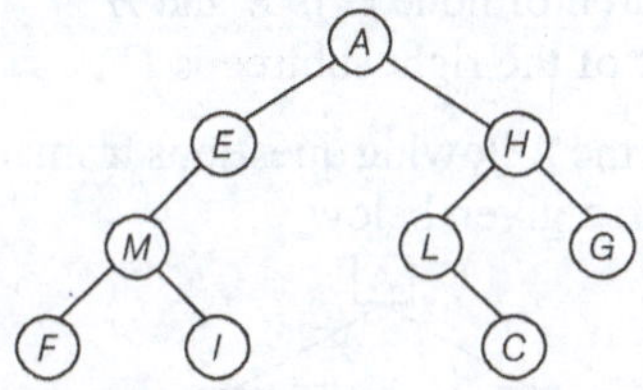

(a) Name the external nodes of the tree.
(b) State the degree of node M and node L.
(c) Write the *post-order* traversal of the above tree structure.

Ans (a) The external nodes of the tree-F I C G

(b) Degree of M = 2
Degree of L = 1

(c) The post-order traversal is F I M E C L G H A

2. Answer the following questions from the diagram of a binary tree given below:

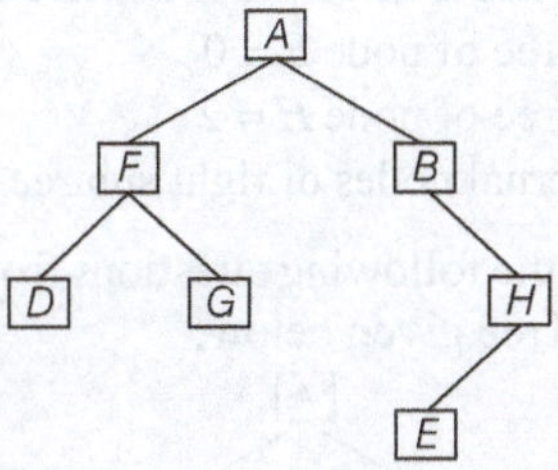

(a) Write the pre-order traversal of the above tree structure.
(b) Name the parent of the nodes *D* and *B*.
(c) State the level of nodes *E* and *F* when the root is at level 0. **ISC 2023**

Ans (a) *AFDGBHE*

(b) Parent of node *D* is *F*

Parent of node *B* is *A*

(c) Level of node *E* is 3, level of node *F* is 1.

3. Answer the following questions from the diagram of a Binary Tree given below:

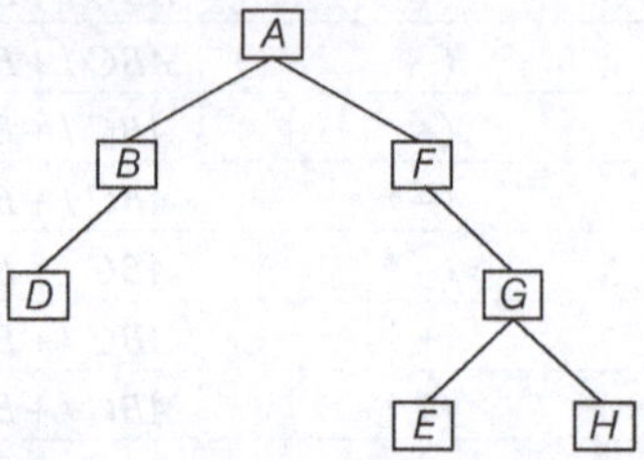

(a) Write the in-order traversal of the above tree structure.

(b) Name the children of the nodes *B* and *G*.

(c) State the root of the right subtree. **ISC SQP 2023**

Ans (a) *DBAFEGH*

(b) Children of node *B* is *D*

Children of node *G* is *E* and *H*

(c) Root of the right subtree is *F*

4. Answer the following questions from the diagram of a binary tree given below :

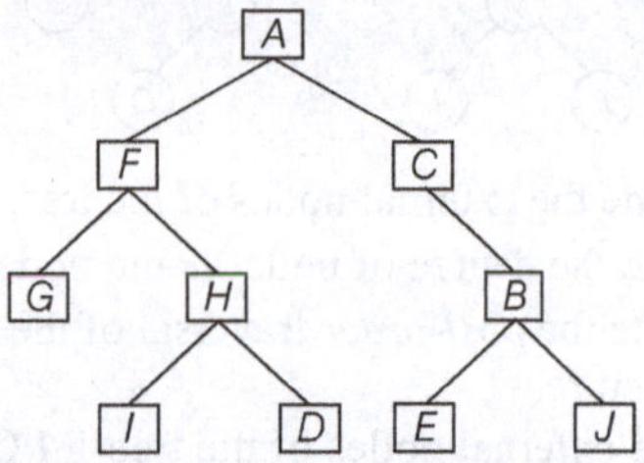

(i) Write the post order traversal of the left subtree of the above structure.

(ii) State the degree of the nodes *E* and *H*.

(iii) Mention the external nodes of the right subtree. **ISC 2020**

Ans (i) Post order traversal of the left subtree = *GIDHF*

(ii) Degree of node *E* = 0

Degree of node *H* = 2

(iii) External nodes of right subtree are *E* and *J*.

5. Answer the following questions from the diagram of a Binary Tree given below:

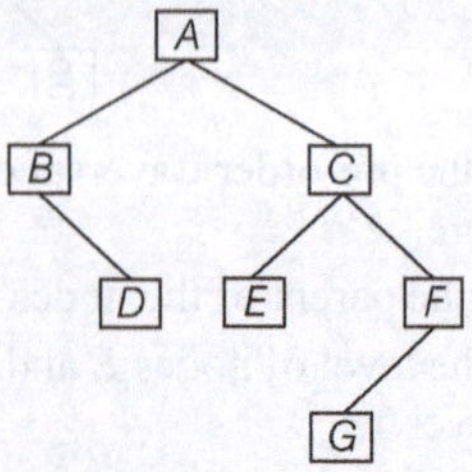

(i) Name the root and the leaves of the tree.

(ii) Write the post order traversal of the tree.

(iii) Separate the internal nodes and the external nodes of the tree. **ISC SQP 2020**

Ans (i) Root = *A*

Leaves of the tree are *D, E, G*

(ii) *DBEGFCA*

(iii) Internal nodes are *A, B, C, F*

External nodes are *D, E, G*

6. Answer the following questions from the diagram of a binary tree given below:

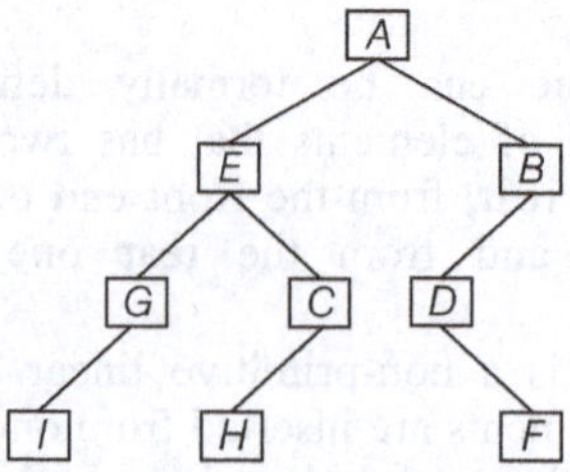

(i) Write the pre-order traversal of the above tree structure.

(ii) State the size of the tree.

(iii) Name the siblings of the nodes *E* and *G*. **ISC 2019**

Ans (i) Pre-order traversal = *AEGI CH BDF*

(ii) Size of the tree = 9

(iii) Sibling of node *E* is *B*.

Sibling of node *G* is *C*.

7. Answer the following questions from the diagram of a binary tree given below: **ISC 2018**

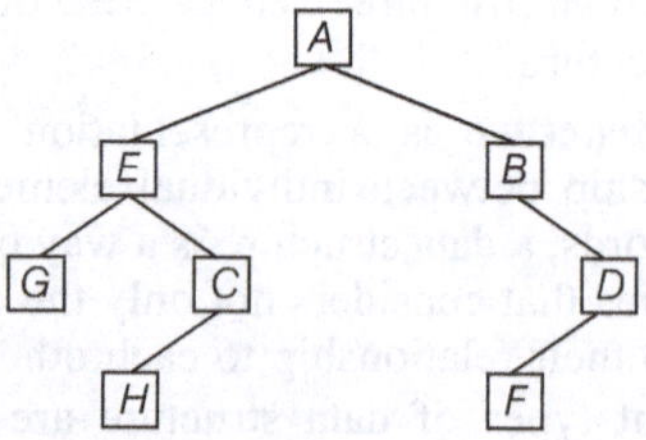

(i) Write the inorder traversal of the above tree structure.

(ii) State the height of the tree, if the root is at level 0 (zero).

(iii) List the leaf nodes of the tree.

Ans (i) Inorder traversal

GEHCABFD

(ii) Height of the tree is 3.

(iii) Leaves of the tree = *G, H, F*

8. Answer the following questions from the diagram of a binary tree given below **ISC 2017**

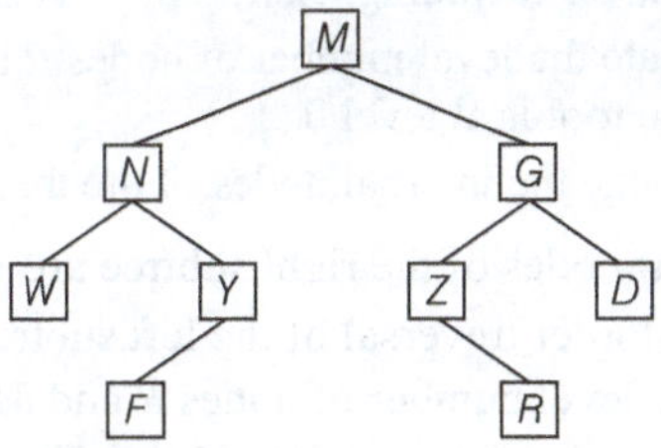

(i) Write the postorder traversal of the above tree structure.

(ii) State the level numbers of the nodes *N* and *R* if the root is at 0 (zero) level.

(iii) List the internal nodes of the right subtree.

Ans (i) Post order traversal of tree is

= *W F Y N R Z D G M*

(ii)

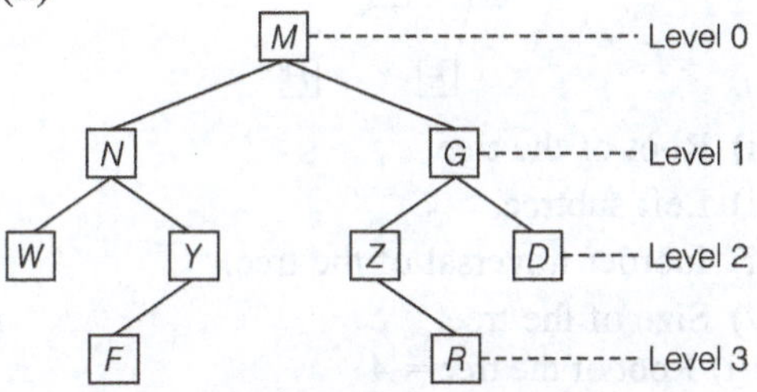

Level number of the node *N* = 1

Level number of the node *R* = 3

(iii) Internal nodes of the right subtree = *G, Z*

9. Answer the following questions from the diagram of a binary tree given below: **ISC 2016**

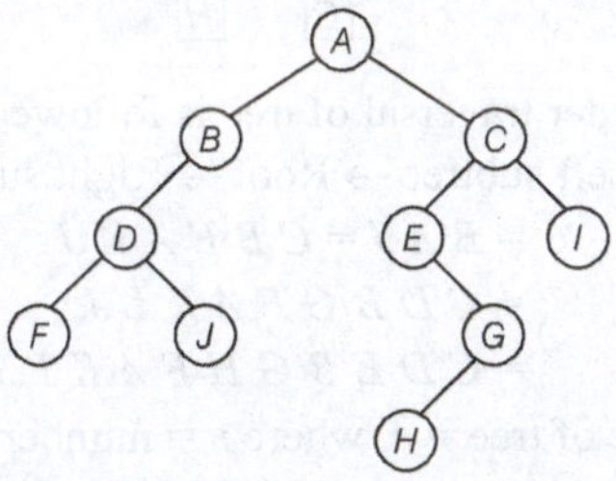

(i) Write the inorder traversal of the above tree structure.

(ii) Name the parent of the nodes *B* and *G*.

(iii) Name the leaves of the right subtree.

Ans (i) Inorder traversal *F D J B A E H G C I*

(ii) Parent node of *B* is *A*.

Parent node of *G* is *E*.

(iii) Leaves of the right sub tree are *H* and *I*.

4 Marks Questions

1. Answer the following questions from the diagram of a binary tree given below

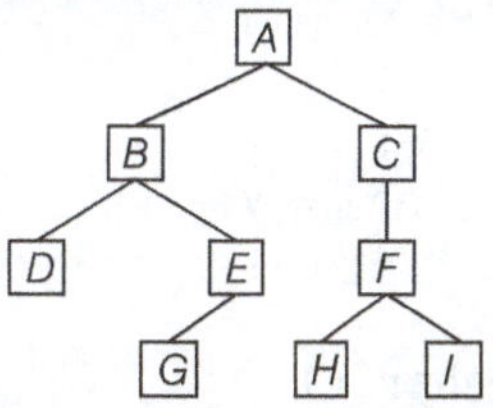

(i) State the siblings of the nodes *C* and *E*. Also, state the predecessor node(s) and successor node(s) of node *B*.

(ii) Write the inorder traversal of the left sub tree and the preorder traversal of the right sub tree.

ISC 2022 (Sem II)

Ans (i) Sibling of node *C* is *B*.

Sibling of node *E* is *D*.

Predecessor node of node *B* is *D*.

Successor node of node *B* is *G*.

(ii) Inorder traversal of the left subtree = *DBGE*

Preorder traversal of the right subtree = *CFHI*

2. A Stack is a kind of data structure which can store elements with the restriction that an element can be a added or removed from the top end only.

The details of the class Stack is given below

Class name	Stack
Data members/Instance variables	
cha[ ]	array to hold the characters
size	stores the maximum capacity of the stack
top	to point the index of the topmost element of the stack
Member functions/Methods	
Stack (int mm)	constructor to initialise the data member size = mm, top = –1 and create the character array
void push_char (char v)	to add characters from the top end if possible else display the message ("Stack full")
char pop_char()	to remove and return characters from the top end, if any, else returns '$'
void display()	to display elements of the stack

Specify the class Stack, giving the details, of void push_char(char) and char pop_char(). Assume that the other functions have been defined.

The main() function and algorithm need not be written. **ISC 2022 (Sem II)**

Ans
```
void push_char (char v)
{
  if (top == size)
    System.out.println("Stack full");
  else
  {
    top + +;
    cha [top] = v;
  }
}
char pop_char ()
{
  if (top ==-1)
    return '$';
  else
  {
    char c = cha [top] ;
    top - -;
    return c ;
  }
}
```

3. Answer the following questions on the diagram of a Binary Tree given below:

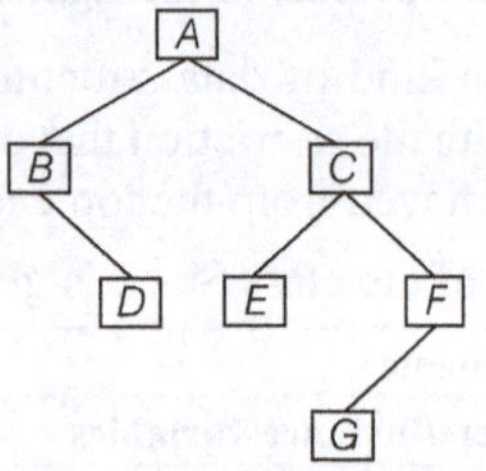

(i) State the degree of the nodes *C* and *G*. Also, state the level of these nodes when the root is at level 0.

(ii) Write the pre-order and post order traversal of the above tree structure. **ISC SQP 2022 (Sem II)**

Ans (i) Degree of node *C* is 2
Degree of node *G* is 0
Level of node *C* is 1
Level of node *G* is 3

(ii) Pre-order traversal *ABDCEFG*
Post order traversal *DBEGFCA*

4. Answer the following questions from the diagram of a binary tree given below:

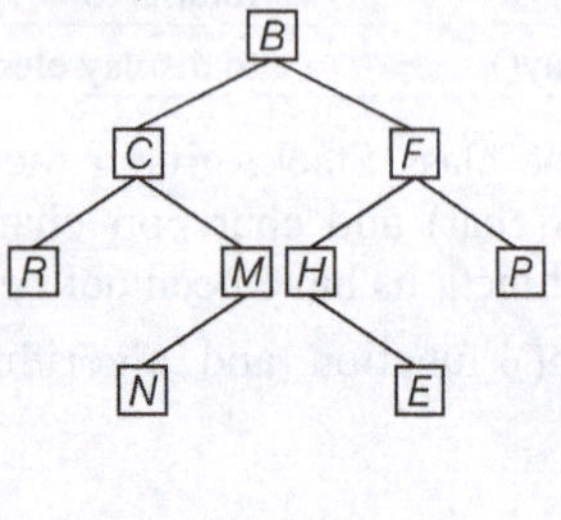

(i) Name the leaf nodes of the right subtree.

(ii) Write postorder traversal of the left subtree of node *B* including itself.

(iii) State the level number of nodes *R* and *M* when the root is at level 0.

(iv) Name the internal nodes of the tree. **ISC 2015**

Ans (i) Leaf nodes of the right subtree are *E* and *P*.

(ii) Postorder traversal of the left subtree: *RNMCB*.

(iii) The level number of nodes *R* and *M* is 2.

(iv) Internal nodes are *C, F, M* and *H*.

5. Answer the following questions from the diagram of a binary tree given below.

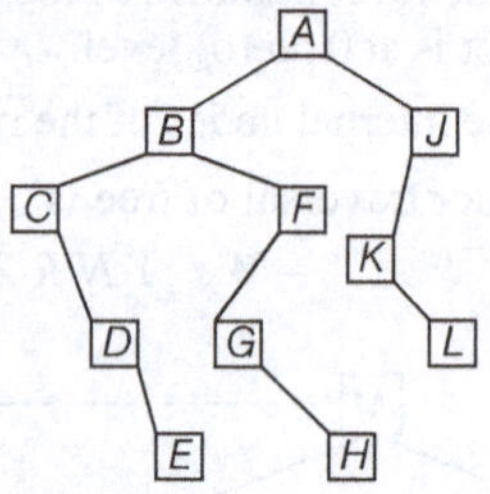

(i) Root of the tree.

(ii) Left subtree.

(iii) Inorder traversal of the tree.

(iv) Size of the tree. **ISC 2014**

Ans (i) Root of the tree = *A*

(ii) Left subtree is

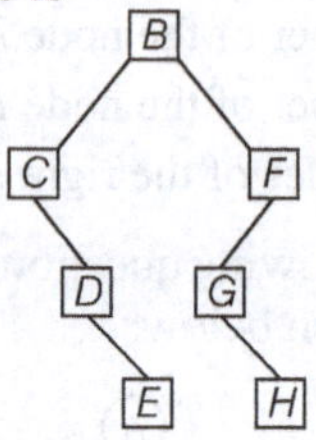

(iii) Inorder traversal of tree is followed as,
Left subtree → Root → Right subtree
$= B\ A\ J = C\ B\ F\ A\ K\ J$
$= C\ D\ B\ G\ F\ A\ K\ L\ J$
$= C\ D\ E\ B\ G\ H\ F\ A\ K\ L\ J$

(iv) Size of tree = *n*, where *n* = number of total nodes
= 11

6. Answer the following questions from the diagram of a binary tree given below **ISC 2013**

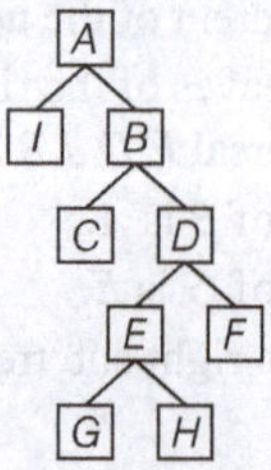

(i) Preorder traversal of tree.
(ii) Children of node *E*.
(iii) Left subtree of node *D*
(iv) Height of the tree when the root of the tree is at level 0.

Ans (i) Preorder traversal of tree

$= A\ I\ B$

$= A\ I\ B\ C\ D$

$= A\ I\ B\ C\ D\ E\ F$

$= A\ I\ B\ C\ D\ E\ G\ H\ F$

(ii) Children of node *E* = (*G*, *H*)

(iii) Left subtree of *D* =

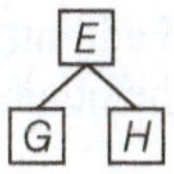

(iv)

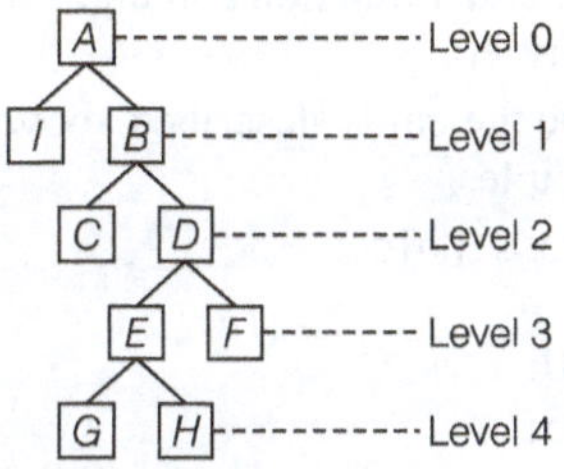

The height of tree = Number of level = 4

7. Answer the following questions from the diagram of a binary tree given below **ISC 2012**

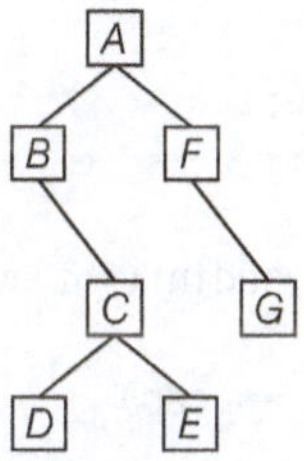

(i) External nodes of the tree.
(ii) Parent of node *D*.
(iii) Inorder traversal of the tree.
(iv) Right subtree of node *B*.

Ans (i) External nodes = *D*, *E*, *G*

(ii) Parent Node of *D* = *C*

(iii) Inorder traversal of tree is as follows:

$= B\ A\ F = B\ C\ A\ F\ G$

$= B\ D\ C\ E\ A\ F\ G$

(iv) Right subtree of *B* is

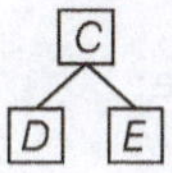

8. Answer the following questions from the diagram of a binary tree given below **ISC 2011**

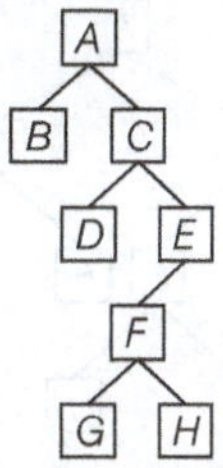

(i) Write the Postorder tree traversal.
(ii) Name the leaves of the tree.
(iii) Height of the tree.
(iv) Root of the tree.

Ans (i) Postorder traversal of tree is

$= B\ C\ A$

$= B\ D\ E\ C\ A$

$= B\ D\ F\ E\ C\ A$

$= B\ D\ G\ H\ F\ E\ C\ A$

(ii) Leaves of tree = *B*, *D*, *G*, *H*

(iii) Height of tree = Number of level = 4

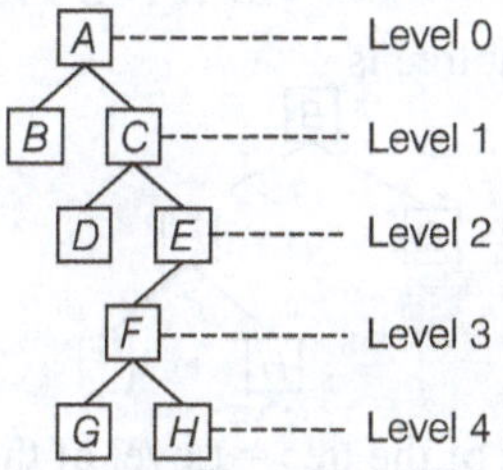

(iv) Root of the tree = *A*

9. Answer the following questions from the diagram of a binary tree given below **ISC 2010**

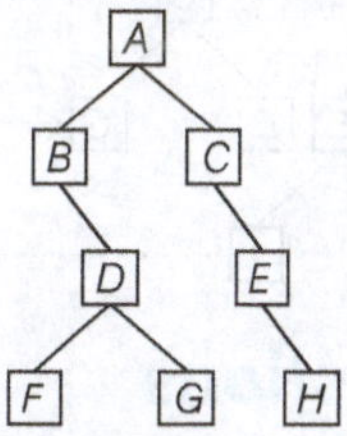

(i) Name the parent of node *E*.
(ii) Write the Postorder tree traversal.
(iii) Write the internal nodes of the tree.
(iv) State the level of the root of the tree.

Ans (i) Parent node of *E* = *C*

(ii) Postorder tree traversal is as

$= B\ C\ A = D\ B\ E\ C\ A$

$= F\ G\ D\ B\ H\ E\ C\ A$

(iii) Internal nodes of the tree are as

= *A*, *B*, *C*, *D*, *E*

(iv) The level of the root of the tree is 0.

10. Answer the following questions from the diagram of a binary tree given below **ISC 2009**

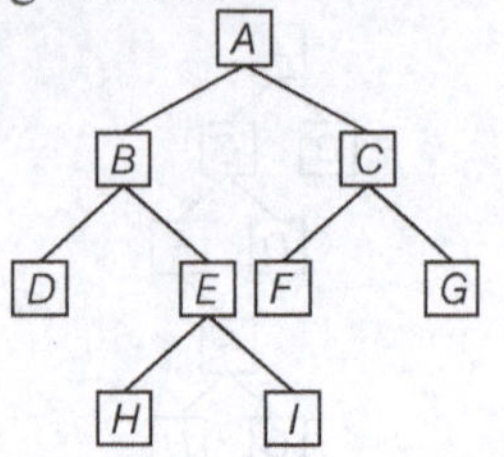

(i) Root of the tree.
(ii) External nodes of the tree.
(iii) List the nodes in the tree using Inorder traversal.
(iv) Left subtree.
(v) Height of the tree.

Ans (i) Root of the tree = *A*

(ii) External nodes of the tree are as

= *D, H, I, F, G*

(iii) Inorder traversal of the tree

= *B A C*

= *D B E A F C G*

= *D B H E I A F C G*

(iv) Left subtree is

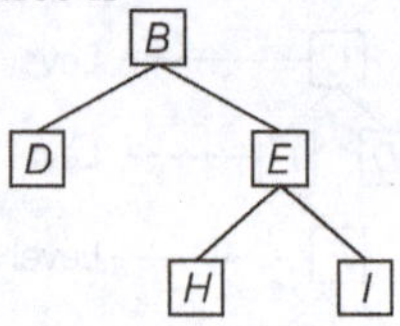

(v) Height of the tree = Level of the tree

= 3

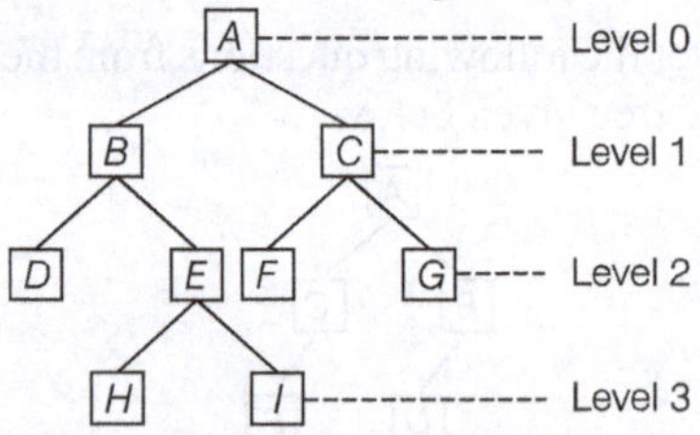

5 Marks Questions

1. Holder is a kind of data structure which can store elements with the restriction that an element can be added from the rear end and removed from the front end only.

The details of the class Holder is given below:

Class name	Holder
Data members/Instance variables	
Q[]	array to hold integers
cap	maximum capacity of the holder
front	to point the index of the front end
rear	to point the index of the rear end
Methods / Member functions	
Holder(int n)	constructor to initialize cap=n, front= 0 and rear=0
void addint(int v)	to add integers in the holder at the rear end if possible, otherwise display the message "HOLDER IS FULL"
int removeint()	removes and returns the integers from the front end of the holder if any, else returns-999
void show()	displays the elements of the holder

(i) Specify the class Holder giving details of the functions void addint(int) and int removeint(). Assume that the other functions have been defined.

The main() function and algorithm need NOT be written.

(ii) Name the entity described above and state its principle. **ISC SQP 2023**

Ans

```
public class Holder
{
  int[] Q;
  int cap;
  int front;
  int rear;
  public Holder(int n)
  {
    Q = new int[n];
    cap = n;
    front = 0;
    rear = 0;
  }
  public void addint(int v)
  {
    if (rear == cap)
    {
      System.out.println("HOLDER IS FULL");
      return;
    }
    Q[rear] = v;
    rear++;
  }
  public int removeint()
  {
    if (front == rear)
    {
      return -999;
    }
    int value = Q[front];
    front++;
    return value;
  }
}
```

2. A Queue is a linear data structure in which the operations are performed based on FIFO (First In First Out).

Define a class Queue with the following details:

Class name	Queue
Data members/Instance variables	
dat[ ]	array to hold the integer elements
cap	stores the maximum capacity of the queue
front	to point the index of the front
rear	to point the index of the rear.
Member functions/methods	
Queue(int max)	constructor to initialize the data member cap = max, front = rear=0 and create the integer array
void add_dat(int v)	to add integers from the rear index if possible else display the message("Queue full")
int pop_dat()	to remove and return elements from front, if any, else returns-999
void display()	to display elements of the queue

Specify the class Queue giving the details of void add_dat(int) and int pop_dat( ). Assume that the other functions have been defined.

The main( ) function and algorithm need NOT be written. *ISC SQP 2022 (Sem II)*

Ans

```
public class Queue
{
   private int[] dat;
   private int cap;
   private int front;
   private int rear;
   public Queue(int max)
   {
      cap = max;
      front = rear = 0;
      dat = new int[cap];
   }
   public void add_dat(int v)
   {
      if (rear == cap)
      {
         System.out.println("Queue full");
      }
      else
      {
         dat[rear] = v;
         rear++;
      }
   }
   public int pop_dat()
   {
      if (front == rear)
      {
         return -999;
      }
      else
      {
         int val = dat[front];
         front++;
         return val;
      }
   }
}
```

3. A linear data structure enables the user to add address from rear end and remove address from front. Define a class Diary with the following details. *ISC 2019*

Class name	Diary
Data members/Instance variables	
Q[ ]	array to store the address
size	stores the maximum capacity of the array
start	to point the index of the front end
end	to point the index of the rear end
Member functions	
Diary(int max)	constructor to initialise the data member size = max, start = 0 and end = 0
void pushadd(String n)	to add address in the diary from the rear end if possible, otherwise display the message "NO SPACE"
String popadd()	removes and returns the address from the front end of the diary if any, else returns "?????"
void show()	displays all the addresses in the diary

(a) Specify the class Diary giving details of the functions void pushadd(String) and String popadd(). Assume that the other functions have been defined.

The main function and algorithm need NOT be written.

(b) Name the entity used in the above data structure arrangement.

Ans. (a)

```
class Diary
{
   int Q[],size,start,end;
   Diary(int max)
   {
      size=max;
      start=0;
      end=0;
```

```
        Q=new int[size];
    }
    void pushadd(String n)
    {
        if(end==size-1)
            System.out.println("No Space");
        else
            Q[end++]=n;
    }
    String popadd()
    {
        if(end==start)
        {
            System.out.println(" ");
            return "?????";
        }
        else
            return Q[start++];
    }
}
```

(b) Queue

4. Register is an entity which can hold a maximum of 100 names. The register enables the user to add and remove names from the top most end only. *ISC 2018*

Define a class Register with the following details:

Class name	Register
Data members / Instance variables	
stud[ ]	array to store the names of the students
cap	stores the maximum capacity of the array
top	to point the index of the top end
Member functions	
Register (int max)	constructor to initialize the data members cap = max, top = –1 and create the string array
void push(String n)	to add names in the register at the top location if possible, otherwise display the message "OVERFLOW"
String pop( )	removes and returns the names from the top most location of the register if any, else returns "$$"
void display( )	displays all the names in the register

(a) Specify the class Register giving details of the functions void push(String) and String pop(). Assume that the other functions have been defined.

The main function and algorithm need NOT be written.

(b) Name the entity used in the above data structure arrangement.

Ans (a)
```
class Register
{
    String stud [];
    int cap,top, ctr;
    Register (int max)
    {
        stud = new String [max];
        cap = max;
        top = -1;
        ctr = 0;
    }
    void push (String n)
    {
        if (top > = cap - 1)
            System.out.println ("Overflow");
        else
        {
            top + +;
            stud [top] = n;
            ctr + +;
        }
    }
    String pop ()
    {
        String S = " ";
        if (top < 0)
            System.out.println("$$");
        else
        {
            S= stud [top];
            top --;
            ctr --;
        }
        return S;
    }
}
```

(b) The entity used in above data structure arrangement is LIFO (Last In First Out).

5. Queue is an entity which can hold a maximum of 100 integers. The queue enables the user to add integers from the rear and remove integers from the front. *ISC 2017*

Define a class Queue with the following details

Class Name	Queue
Data members/Instance variables	
Que[ ]	array to hold the integer elements
size	stores the size of the array
front	to point the index of the front
rear	to point the index of the rear
Member functions	
Queue (int mm)	constructor to initialize the data size = mm, front = 0, rear = 0
void addele(int v)	to add integer from the rear, if possible else display the message "Overflow"

Class Name	Queue
int delele( )	returns elements from front if present, otherwise displays the message "Underflow" and return-9999
void display( )	displays the array elements

Specify the class Queue giving details of ONLY the functions void addele(int) and int delele (). Assume that the other functions have been defined.

The main function and algorithm need NOT be written.

Ans

```
class Queue
{
    int Que[];
    int size, front, rear;
    Queue(int mm)
    {
        Que = new int [mm];
        size = mm;
        front = 0;
        rear = 0;
    }
    void addele (int v)
    {
        if (rear = = – 1)
        {
            front = 0;
            rear = 0;
            Que [rear] = v;
        }
        else if (rear + 1 < Que.length)
            Que [++rear] = v;
        else
            System.out.println("Overflow")
;
    }
    int delele ( )
    {
        int element;
        if (front = = 0)
        {
            System.out.println("Underflow");
            return –9999;
        }
        else if (front = = rear)
        {
            element = Que [front];
            front = rear = 0;
            return element;
        }
        else
            return (Que [front ++]);
    }
}
```

6. A bookshelf is designed to store the books in a stack with LIFO(Last In First Out) operation. Define a class Book with the following specifications: ***ISC 2016***

Class name	Book
Data members/Instance variables	
name[ ]	stores the names of the book
point	stores the index of the topmost book
max	stores the maximum capacity of the bookshelf
Methods/Member functions	
Book(int cap)	constructor to initialise the data members max = cap and point = – 1
void tell( )	displays the name of the book which was last entered in the shelf. If there is no book left in the shelf, displays the message "SHELF EMPTY"
void add(String v)	add the name of the book to the shelf if possible, otherwise displays the message "SHELF FULL"
void display( )	displays all the names of the books available in the shelf

Specify the class Book giving the details of ONLY the functions void tell() and void add(String). Assume that the other functions have been defined. The main function need not be written.

Ans

```
class Book
{
    String name[];
    int point, max;
    Book(int cap)
    {
        name=new String[cap];
        max = cap;
        point = – 1;
    }
    public void tell()
    {
        if(point  = = – 1)
            System.out.println("SHELF
                                     EMPTY");
        else
            System.out.println("Last
                        entered:"+name[point]);
    }
    public void add(String v)
    {
        if(point = = max)
            System.out.println("SHELF
                                      FULL");
        else
            name[+ +point] = v;
    }
}
```

10 Marks Questions

1. WordPile is an entity which can hold maximum of 20 characters. The restriction is that a character can be added or removed from one end only. ***ISC 2015***

Some of the members of class are given below:

Class name	WordPile
Data members/Instance variables	
ch[ ]	character array to hold the character elements
capacity	integer variable to store the maximum capacity
top	to point to the index of the topmost element
Methods/Member functions	
WordPile(int cap)	constructor to initialise the data member capactiy = cap, top = -1 and create the WordPile
void pushChar(char v)	adds the character to the top of WordPile if possible, otherwise output a message "WordPile is full"
char popChar( )	returns the deleted character from the top of the WordPile if possible, otherwise it returns '\\'

(a) Specify the class WordPile giving the details of the constructor, void pushChar(char) and char popChar(). The main() function and algorithm need not be written.

(b) What is the name of the entity described above and state one of its application?

Ans (a)

```
public class WordPile
{
    char ch[ ];
    int capacity,top;
    WordPile(int cap)
    {
        capacity=cap;
        top=-1;
        ch =new char[20];
    }
    void pushChar(char v)
    {
        if(top==capacity)
            System.out.println
                ("WordPile is full");
        else
        {
            top++;
            ch[top]=v;
        }
    }
    char popChar()
    {
        if(top==-1)
            return '\\';
        else
        {
            char c = ch[top];
            top--;
            return c;
        }
    }
}
```

(b) The entity described above is stack and it is used to add or remove data which is stored at last i.e. based on LIFO (Last In First Out) technique. It can also be used for string reversal, postfix evaluation, etc.

2. A stack is a linear data structure which enables the user to add and remove integers from one end only, using the concept of LIFO (Last In First Out). An array containing the marks of 50 students in ascending order to be pushed into the stack.

Define a class Array_to_Stack with the following details: ***ISC 2014***

Class name	Array_to_Stack
Data members/Instance variables	
m [ ]	to store the marks.
st [ ]	to store the stack elements.
cap	maximum capacity of the array and stack.
top	to point the index of the topmost element of the stack.
Member functions	
Array_to_Stack (int n)	parameterised constructor to initialise cap = n and top = –1.
void input_marks ( )	to input the marks from user and store it in the array m [ ] in ascending order and simultaneously push the marks into the stack st[ ] by invoking the function pushmarks( ).
void pushmarks (int v)	to push the marks into the stack at top location if possible, otherwise display "not possible".
int popmarks ( )	to return marks from the stack if possible, otherwise returns-999.
void display ( )	to display the stack elements.

Specify the class Array_to_Stack giving the details of the constructor(int), void input_marks(), void pushmarks(int), int popmarks() and void display(). The main() function and algorithm need to not be written.

Ans

```
import java.io.*;
class Array_to_Stack
{
    public int m[];
    public int st[],top;
    public static int cap;
    public Array_to_Stack(int n)
    {
        cap = n;
        top = -1;
        m = new int[n];
        st = new int[n];
    }
    void input_marks()throws IOException
    {
        BufferedReader br = new
                    BufferedReader(new
            InputStreamReader(System.in));
        int i;
        System.out.println("Enter array
                        element:");
        for(i =0; i<cap;i++)
        {
            m[i]=Integer.parseInt
                    (br.readLine());
        }
        int len = m.length;
        int j, small, p, temp;
        for(i=0; i<len; i++)
        {
            small = m[i];
            int pos = i;
            for( j =i + 1; j<len;j++)
            {
                if(m[j]<small)
                {
                    small = m[j];
                    pos = j;
                }
            }
            temp = m[i];
            m[i] = m[pos];
            m[pos] = temp;
            pushmarks(m[i]);
        }
    }
    void pushmarks(int v)
    {
        if(top<cap)
        {
            top++;
            st[top] = v;
            System.out.println("Element"
                +v+ "is pushed to stack!");
        }
        else
        {
            System.out.println("not
                            possible");
        }
    }
    int popmarks()
    {
        if(top >= 0)
        {
            int x = st[top];
            top--;
            return x;
        }
        else
        {
            return -999;
        }
    }
    public void display()
    {
        if(top>= 0)
        {
            System.out.println("Elements
                        in stack :");
            for(int i=0; i<= top; i++)
            {
                System.out.println(st[i]);
            }
        }
    }
}
```

3. Link is an entity which can hold a maximum of 100 integers. Link enables the user to add elements from the rear end and remove integers from the front end of the entity. Define a class Link with the following details: ***ISC 2012***

Class name	**Link**
Data members/Instance variables	
lnk[ ]	entity to hold the integer elements.
max	stores the maximum capacity of the entity.
begin	to point to the index of the front end.
end	to point to the index of the rear end.

Member functions	
Link (int mm)	constructor to initialise max = mm, begin = 0, end = 0.
void addlink(int v)	to add an element from the rear index, if possible otherwise display the message "OUTSIDE OF SIZE...".
int dellink ( )	to remove and return an element from the front index, if possible otherwise display the message "EMPTY..." and return-99.
void display ( )	display the elements of the entity.

(i) Specify the class Link giving details of the constructor(int), void addlink(int), int dellink() and void display().

The main() function and algorithm need not to be written.

(ii) Which type of data structure is the above entity?

Ans (i)
```
class Link
{
    int lnk[], max, begin, end;
    Link(int mm)
    {
        max=mm;
        begin= 0;
        end = 0;
        lnk = new int[max];
    }
    void addlink(int v)
    {
        if(end == max-1)
            System.out.println("Outside of
                                      size");
        else
            lnk[end++]=v;
    }
    int dellink()
    {
        if(end == begin)
        {
            System.out.println("Empty");
            return -99;
        }
        else
            return lnk[begin++];
    }
    void display()
    {
        for(int i=begin; i< end; i++)
        {
            System.out.println(lnk[i]);
        }

    }
}
```

(ii) In above, we used queue as a data structure.

4. Stack is a kind of data structure which can elements with the restriction that an element can be added or removed from the top only. ***ISC 2011***

The details of the class Stack is given below:

Class name	Stack
Data members/Instance variables	
st [ ]	the array to hold the names.
size	the maximum capacity of the string array.
top	the index of the topmost element of the stack.
ctr	to count the number of elements of the stack.
Member functions	
Stack ( )	default constructor
Stack(int cap)	parameterized constructor to initialise size = cap and top = –1
void pushname (String n)	to push a name into the stack. If the stack is full, display the message "OVERFLOW".
String popname ( )	removes a name from the top of the stack and returns it. If the stack is empty, display the message "UNDERFLOW".
void display ( )	display the elements of the stack.

(i) Specify class Stack giving details of the constructors, void pushname(String), String popname() and void display().

The main() function and algorithm need not to be written.

(ii) Under what principle does the above entity work?

Ans (i)
```
class Stack
{
    String st[];
    int size, top, ctr;
    Stack()
    {
        top = -1; ctr = 0; size = 0;
    }
    Stack(int cap)
    {
        st = new String[cap];
        size = cap;
        top = -1;
        ctr = 0;
    }
    void pushname(String n)
    {
        if(top >= size- 1)
            System.out.println("Overflow");
```

```
        else
        {
            top++;
            st[top]= n;
            ctr ++;
        }
    }
    String popname ()
    {
        String S = " ";
        if (top < 0)
            System.out.println("Underflow");
        else
        {
            S = st[top];
            top--;
            ctr--;
        }
        return S;
    }
    void display()
    {
        for(int i = 0; i <= top; i++)
            System.out.println(st[i]);
    }
}
```

(ii) Stack works on LIFO (Last In First Out) principle.

5. Define a class Repeat which allows the user to add elements from one end (rear) and remove elements from the other end (front) only. ***ISC 2010***

The following details of the class Repeat are given below:

Class name	**Repeat**
Data members/Instance variables	
st [ ]	an array to hold a maximum of 100 integer elements.
cap	stores the capacity of the array.
f	to point the index of the front.
r	to point the index of the rear.
Member functions	
Repeat (int m)	constructor to initialise the data members cap = m, f = 0, r = 0 and to create the integer array.
void pushvalue(int v)	to add integers from the rear index, if possible else display the message ("OVERFLOW").
int popvalue ( )	to remove and return elements from the front. If array is empty, then return -9999.
void disp ( )	display the elements present in the list.

(i) Specify the class Repeat giving details of the constructor(int), member functions void pushvalue(int), int popvalue() and void disp(). The main() function need not to be written.

(ii) What is the common name of the entity described above?

(iii) On what principle does this entity work?

Ans (i)
```
class Repeat
{
    int st[];
    int cap;
    int f,r;
    Repeat(int m)
    {
        cap = m;
        f = 0;
        r = 0;
        st = new int[100];
    }
    void pushvalue(int v)
    {
        if(r == cap-1)
        {
            System.out.println("OVERFLOW");
        }
        else if(r == 0)
        {
            f = r = 1;
            st[r]=v;
        }
        else
            st[++r] =v;
    }
    int popvalue()
    {
        if(f == 0)
        {
            System.out.println("EMPTY");
            return -9999;
        }
        else if(f == r)
        {
            int k = st[f];
            f = r = 0;
            return k;
        }
        else
            return(st[f++]);
    }
    void disp()
    {
        for(int i = f;i<= r; i++)
        {
            System.out.print(st[i]+" ");
        }
    }
}
```

(ii) The common name of the entity described above is queue.

(iii) This entity works on FIFO (First In First Out) principle .

CHAPTER TEST

1 Mark Questions

1. Which of the following is/are linear data structure?

(a) Stack (b) Queue (c) Linked list (d) All of these

2. Items enter in a queue at the

(a) rear (b) front (c) top (d) None of these

3. What is a queue?

2 Marks Questions

4. What is a binary search tree?

5. Convert the following infix notation to postfix form $(A+B*C)/(D-E)*F$

3 Marks Question

6. Answer the following questions from the diagram

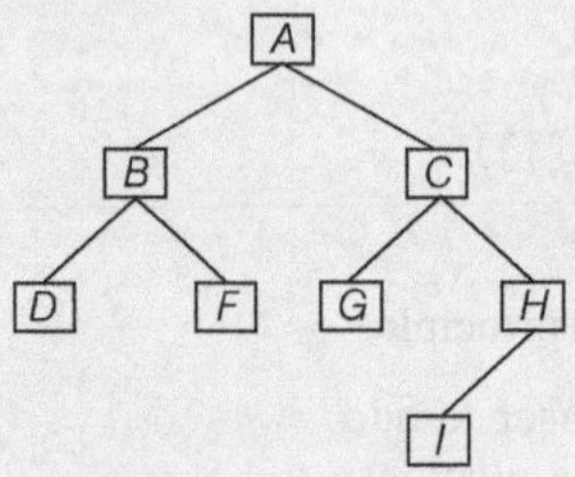

(i) Write the pre-order traversal of the above structure.

(ii) State the level of *G* and *B*, if the root is at level 0.

(iii) Mention the internal nodes of the above tree.

5 Marks Questions

7. A queue is a linear data structure which works on the principle of FIFO, enables the user to enter data from the rear end and remove data from the front end. Define a class Queue with the following details

Class name	Queue
Data member/Instance variable	
cq[ ]	array to store the integers
cap	stores the maximum capacity of the array
front	to point the index of the front end
rear	to point the index of the rear end
Member functions/Methods	
Queue (int max)	constructor to initialize the data member cap=max, front=0 and rear=0
void push(int n)	to add integer in the queue from the rear end if possible, otherwise display the message "QUEUE IS FULL"
int pop( )	removes and returns the integer from the front end of the queue if any, else returns – 9999
void show( )	displays the queue elements

(a) Specify the class Queue giving details of the functions void push(int) and int pop( ). Assume that the other functions have been defined. The main function and algorithm need NOT be written.

(b) How is a linear queue structure different from a circular queue structure?

10 Marks Question

8. TestSeries is an entity which can hold a maximum of 200 names. The series enables the user to add and remove names from the top most end only.

Define a class TestSeries with the following details:

Class name	**TestSeries**
Data members / instance variables	
name[ ]	array to store the names of the students
cap	stores the maximum capacity of the array
top	to point the index of the top end
Member functions	
TestSeries (int max)	constructor to initialize the data member cap = max, top = – 1 and create the string array
void push(String n)	to add names in the series at the top location if possible, otherwise display the message "OVERFLOW"
String pop( )	removes and returns the names from the top most location of the series if any, else returns "-999"
void show( )	displays all the names in the series

Specify the class TestSeries giving details of the constructors, functions void push(String), String pop( ) and void show(). Define the main( ) function to create objects and call the functions accordingly to enable the task.

11

Computational Complexity

TREND ANALYSIS 4 YEARS

Average No. of Questions Across all Sets

	Types of Questions	2024	2023	2020	2019
Computational Complexity	1 Mark	–	–	–	–
	2 Marks	–	–	1	–
	3 Marks	–	–	–	–
	5 Marks	–	–	–	–
	10 Marks	–	–	–	–

An algorithm is a well-defined list of steps for solving a particular problem. It is a sequence of computational steps that transform the input into the output. The complexity of an algorithm is the function which gives the run time and/or space in terms of input size. The performance of a program is measured through its complexity.

Computational complexity, focuses on the amount of computing resources needed for a particular algorithm to run efficiently. The efficiency of a program can be measured in terms of space and time.

Space Complexity

The space complexity of an algorithm is the amount of memory required for its execution.

Time Complexity

The time complexity of an algorithm is the amount of time required for its execution. Sometimes, the choice of program involves a time-space trade off : by increasing the amount of space for storing the data, one may be able to reduce the time needed for processing the data or *vice-versa*.

Estimating Complexity of Algorithm

To choose the best algorithm, we need to check efficiency of each algorithm. The efficiency can be measured by computing time complexity of each algorithm. Actual runtime of an algorithm depends upon speed of computer, amount of RAM, operating system and the compiler being used. Hence, we cannot use actual runtime of algorithms for comparison between two algorithms. So, for time complexity estimation of an algorithm, we need to count the number of elementary instructions that executes this algorithm. This number is computed with respect to the size n of the input data.

Big-O Notation

It is a method of representing the upper bound of algorithm's running time. It is also known as Omega Notation. Using Big-O notation, we can give longest amount of time taken by the algorithm to complete. e.g. if we have two algorithms having time complexity $O(N)$ and $O(N^2)$ respectively then by varying value of N, we can easily check which algorithm is more efficient, i.e. which one takes less time to run.

Classification of Different Order of Growth

Class Name	Order of Growth	Description	Example
Constant	1	As input size grows, we get larger running time.	Scanning array elements.
Logarithmic	log n	The algorithm does not consider all its input, divided into smaller parts on each integration.	Performing binary search.
Linear	n	The running time of algorithm depends on the input size n.	Performing sequential search operation.
n log n	n log n	Some instance of input is considered for the list of size n.	Merge sort or quick sort.
Quadratic	n^2	When the algorithm has two nested loops then this type of efficiency occurs.	Scanning matrix elements.
Cubic	n^3	It occurs when algorithm has three nested loops.	Performing matrix multiplications.
Exponential	2^n	When the algorithm has very faster rate of growth then it occurs.	Generating rebuts of n inputs.

Dominant Term

The concept of the dominant term generally refers to the term with the highest degree in an algorithm's time complexity analysis. Understanding the dominant term and its significance is crucial for assessing the efficiency of algorithms and predicting how their performance will scale with input size.

Reason why the dominant term is important in Java (or any programming language):

1. **Performance Prediction** The dominant term largely determines how an algorithm will perform as the input size grows. Algorithms with lower-order dominant terms (e.g., O(n), O(log n)) tend to be more efficient than those with higher-order dominant terms (e.g., $O(n^2)$, $O(2^n)$) for large inputs.
2. **Algorithm Selection** By analyzing the dominant term, developers can choose the most efficient algorithm for solving a particular problem. For example, if an algorithm has a dominant term of $O(n^2)$ and another has O(n log n), the latter would generally be preferred for large inputs due to its better scalability.
3. **Optimization** Developers can focus their optimization efforts on improving the efficiency of the dominant term, as improving lower-order terms in the algorithm's complexity might not significantly impact overall performance.
4. **Resource Allocation** Understanding the dominant term helps in making informed decisions about resource allocation. For instance, if an algorithm's dominant term is $O(n^2)$, it might require more memory or computational resources compared to an algorithm with a dominant term of O(n log n) for handling large datasets.
5. **Comparative Analysis** When comparing algorithms, focusing on the dominant term allows for a fair and meaningful comparison, especially when dealing with different input sizes or scenarios.

Calculating Complexity

For finding out the time complexity of a piece of code, we need to consider for loops, nested loops, if-then-else, consecutive statements and logarithmic complexity.

for loop

e.g.

```
for (i= 0; i< N; i++)
{
    count++;
}
```

Every time this statement will take constant time i.e. 'C' for execution.

Loop will execute for i values from 0 to $N-1$.

Total time = CN i.e. O(N) [Linear]

for nested loop

e.g.

```
for(i= 0; i< N; i++)
{
      for(j= 0; j< N; j++)
      {
            count++; //will take constant      } Inner loop will execute N times
            time 'C' to execute.
      }
}                                              } Outer loop will execute N times
```

i.e. whenever outer loop condition will be true inner loop will execute *N* times.

Since, outer loop is executing total *N* times hence, inner loop will execute $N \times N$ times.

$$\text{Total time} = C * N * N = CM^2, \text{ i.e. } O(N^2)$$

if-then-else statement

e.g.

```
if(amt > cost+ tax) → c0 time
  {
        count = 0; → c1 time
        while(count < n)
        {
              amt = (cost + tax); → c2 time     } will execute N times
              count++; → c3 time
        }
        System.out.println("Capacity:" + count); → c4 time
  }
  else
        System.out.println("Insufficient funds"); → c5 time
```

Total time $= c_0 + c_1 + n * (c_2 + c_3) + c_4 + c_5$, i.e. $O(n)$.

consecutive statement

e.g.

```
for(i= 0; i< n; i++)
{
      A[i]= (1- t) * X[i]+ t * y[i]; //constant time c0    } will execute N times
      B[i]= (1- s) * X[i]+ s * y[i];
}
for(i= 0; i< n; i++)
{
      for(j= 0; j< n; j++)
      {                                                      Inner loop will execute N times
            c[i, j]= j * A[i]+ i * B[j]; //constant time c1
            z= z+ 1; //constant time c2
      }
}                                                            } outer loop will execute N times
```

So, Total time $= n * c_0 + n^2 c_1 + c_2$, i.e. $O(n^2)$

logarithmic complexity

Algorithm taking logarithmic time are commonly found in operations on binary trees or when using binary search. An algorithm is said to take logarithmic time if,

$$T(n) = O(\log n)$$

Best, Average and Worst Case Complexity

There are three cases to analyse algorithm complexities:

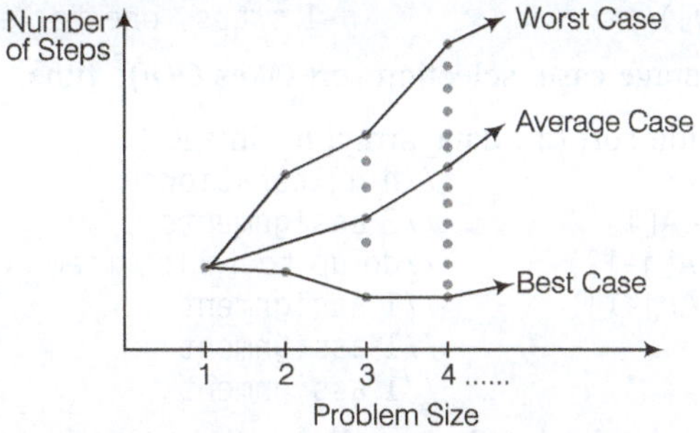

Best, Worst and Average Case Complexity

In **best case complexity**, we calculate lower bound of running time of an algorithm. We must know, the case that cause **minimum number of operations** to be executed. It describes an algorithm's behaviour under optimal conditions.

In **worst case complexity**, we calculate upper bound of running time of an algorithm. We must know, the case that causes **maximum number of operations** to be executed.

In **average case complexity**, we consider all possible inputs and calculate computing time for all of the inputs.

Running Time Complexity

It determines how much times does each function require?

Running Time Complexities

$O(1)$	Fast
$O(\log(n))$	Fast
$O(n)$	Fast for some things, slow for others
$O(n*\log(n))$	Fast–compared to $O(n^2)$
$O(n^2)$	Slow for most things
$O(2^n)$	Intractable
$O(n!)$	Intractable

Analysing Algorithms

Analysing an algorithms, means predicting the resources that the algorithm requires. Now, we consider following examples of sortings and searchings to analysis the algorithm.

(i) Bubble Sort

```
BubbleSort (a : data_array; n : integer)
  for i ← 1 to n do
    for j ← n to i + 1 do
      if a[j] < a[j - 1] then
        swap( a[j], a[j - 1])
```

In best, worst and average case, bubble sort takes $O(n)^2$ time.

(ii) Selection Sort

```
SelectionSort (a : data_array; n : integer)
  for i ← 1 to n - 1 do              loop executes n - 1 times
    low ← j
```

```
for j ← i + 1 to n do                Number of comparisons
  if a[j] < a[low] then              n-1, then n-2, ...,
     low ← j
swap(a[i], a[low])                   n-1 swaps, one for each value of i
```

In best, worst and average case, selection sort takes $O(n)^2$ time.

(iii) **Insertion Sort** Insertion sort (a : data_array; n : integer)

```
for i ← 2 to n do              //n-1 iterations
    j← i, tmp ← A[i]           //2 assignments
    while(tmp < A[j-1])        //do up to i list item comparisons
        A[j] ← A[j-1]          //1 assignment
        j ← j-1                //1 assignment
    A[j] ← tmp                 //1 assignment
```

Best Case When the array is already sorted, insertion sort takes $O(n)$ time.

Worst Case In worst case insertion sort takes $O(n^2)$ time.

We start by presenting the insertion sort procedure with the time cost of each statements and the number of times each statement is executed. For each j = 2, 3... n, where n = length [A], we let t_j be the number of times the while loop test in line 3 is executed for that value of j. When a for or while loop exits in the usual way (i.e. due to the test in the loop header), the test is executed one time more than the loop body.

(iv) **Linear Search** A linear search is a sequential search. A linear search sequentially moves through your collection looping for a matching value.

```
LinearSearch(int arr[], int val)
i ← 1                            //1 assignment
while(i ≤ n and val ≠ arr[i])    //2 comparisons each time
     i ← i + 1                   //1 assignment each time
if i ≤ n then location ← i       //1 comparison and 1 assignment
else location ← 0
```

Best Case val must be present in the first position on the list (named arr [ ]). In this case, two comparisons of while loop and one comparison of if statement will be required. Hence, complexity is $O(1)$ i.e. constant.

Worst Case for unsuccessful search (i.e. when value to be searched will not be there in list), total number of comparisons would be $2n + 2$ and for successful search (i.e. when the required element will be the last element in the list), total number of comparisons required will be $2n + 1$. Hence, complexity is $O(n)$.

(v) **Binary Search**

```
BinarySearch(x : int a1, a2,..., an, int in)
i ← 1                        //left endpoint to search interval(1 assignment)
j ← n                        //right endpoint of search interval(1 assignment)
i ← j                        //1 assignment
in ←[(i + j) / 2]
if x > an then i ← n + 1     //1 comparison and 1 assignment
else j ← n
or
if x = a1 then location ← i  //1 comparison and 1 assignment
else location ← 0
```

Best Case Binary search gives best case when the element to be searched is the middle element. Best case time complexity of binary search is $O(1)$, i.e. constant.

Worst Case In worst case as well as in average case binary search takes $O(\log n)$ time.

PYQs Previous Years Questions

1 Mark Questions

1. List any two cases to analyse algorithm complexities. **ISC 2015**

Ans Two cases to analyse algorithm complexities are worst case and average case.

2. What is the worst case complexity of the following code segment? **ISC 2010**

```
for(int i = 0; i < N; i ++)
{
  sequence of statements; //Statement 1
}
for(int j=0; j<M; j ++)
{
  sequence of statements; //Statement 2
}
```

Ans The first loop will execute N times, so the worst case complexity of the first loop is $O(N)$. The second loop will execute M times, so the worst case complexity of the second loop is $O(M)$. So, total time complexity of the code segment would be $O(N+M)$.

3. How would the complexity change if the second loop went on N instead of M? **ISC 2010**

Ans If the second loop went to N instead of M then, the complexity will become $O(N)$, because both loops will execute N times each.

2 Marks Questions

1. With the help of an example, briefly explain the dominant term in complexity. **ISC 2024**

Ans The dominant term is the term that gets biggest (i.e. dominates) as N gets bigger.

e.g.: $O(N^2+3N+2) \rightarrow$ eventually equals (N^2), because as N gets larger N^2 dominates the other two terms and determines the complexity.

2. State the two factors which determine the complexity of an algorithm. **ISC 2020, 2018**

Ans Two factors which determine the complexity of an algorithm

(i) **Space complexity** The space complexity of an algorithm is the amount of memory required for its execution.

(ii) **Time complexity** The time complexity of an algorithm is the amount of time required for its execution.

3. (i) What is the worst case complexity of the following code segment? **ISC 2017**

```
for (int x = 1; x <=a; x++)
{
    statements;
}
for (int y = 1; y <=b; y++)
{
    for (int z = 1; z <= c; z++)
    {
        statements;
    }
}
```

(ii) How would the complexity change, if all the three loops went to N instead of a, b and c?

Ans (i) In the given code, first loop will execute c times and its sequence will take constant time t_1. So, execution time will be $c * t_1$.

Second loop is nested loop. The outer loop of second loop will execute a times and inner loop will execute b times and sequence of statements will take constant time i.e t_2. So, execution time will be $a * b + t_2$.

Hence, total time $= c * t_1 + a * b + t_2$

Worst case complexity $= O(c + ab)$

(ii) If all the loop execute N times, the body of the loop get executed $N-1$ times, the condition will evaluate to false and loop terminated without executing the body. So, the time complexity for such code would be :

Total time $= c * N = cN$ i.e. $O(N)$

4. What is the worst case time complexity of the following code segment? **ISC 2013**

```
for(int p=0; p<N; p++)
{
    for(int q=0; q<M; q++)
    {
        sequence of statements;
                                //Statement 1
    }
}
for(int r  =  0; r < X; r++)
{
    sequence of statements;
                                //Statement 2
}
```

Ans In the given code first loop is nested loop. The outer loop of first loop will execute N times and inner loop will execute M times and sequence of statements will take constant time i.e. c_1. So, total execution time of this outer loop would be $N * M * c_1$. And, second loop will execute X times and its sequence statement 2 will take constant time c_2. So,

$$\text{Total time} = N * M * c_1 + X * c_2 = O(NM + X)$$

5. How would the complexity change, if all the loops went upto the same limit N? **ISC 2013**

Ans Refer to Question 3 (ii) (2 Marks Questions).

6. What is the role of constants in complexity? Explain briefly with an example. **ISC 2012**

Ans **Role of Constants in Complexity** Constant Time $O(1)$ function needs fixed amount of time to execute program of algorithm. It does not depend upon number of inputs.

e.g. You want to write a function that returns true or false based on the value of first element in an integer array. Program needs input of an integer array. If first element in array is greater than 0, function must return true. In all other conditions, function must return false.

In the above example, function execution time does not depend on number of elements. It just check the first element and returns the result. It does not matter if function get array of 1 integer or 1 million of integers.

Hence, we can say that the running time of this function is constant. This function can be represented as $O(1)$ time complexity.

7. Distinguish between worst case and best case complexity of an algorithm. **ISC 2011**

Ans Differences between worst case and best case complexity of an algorithm:

Worst Case Complexity	Best Case Complexity
It is the function defined by the maximum number of steps taken on any instance of size n.	It is the function defined by the minimum number of steps taken on any instance of size n.
In the worst case analysis, we calculate upper bound on running time of an algorithm.	In the best case analysis, we calculate lower bound on running time of an algorithm.
The worst case time complexity of linear search would be $O(n)$.	The time complexity in the best case of linear search would be $O(1)$.

CHAPTER TEST

1 Mark Questions

1. Which of the following complexity of an algorithm is the amount of memory required for its execution?
   (a) Space (b) Time
   (c) Memory (d) None of these
2. What do you mean by time complexity?

2 Marks Question

3. How to calculate the complexity of if-then-else statement?

3 Marks Question

4. What is the worst case complexity of each of the following code fragments?

```
for (i=0; i<N; i++)
{
    sequence of statements;
}
for (j=0; j<M; j++)
{
    sequence of statements;
}
```

5 Marks Questions

5. Given an array B of appropriate size, what is the complexity in terms of n?

```
int j=n, x=0;
while(j>0)
{
    j--;
    x+=B[i][n-j];
}
```

6. What is the computational complexity of following fibonacci sequence?

```
int Fibonacci(int n)
{
    if(n <= 1)
        return n;
    else
        return Fibonacci(n - 1)+ Fibonacci(n - 2);
}
```

10 Marks Question

7. What do you understand by best case, worst case and average case complexities? When are they considered?

ISC
SAMPLE PAPER 1

Unsolved

COMPUTER SCIENCE-XII

Time : 3 hrs | Max. Marks : 70

General Instructions

1. Candidates are allowed additional 15 minutes for only reading the paper. They must NOT start writing during this time.
2. Answer all questions in Part I (compulsory) and **six** questions from Part II, choosing **two** questions from Section-A, **two** from Section-B and **two** from Section-C.
3. All working, including rough work, should be done on the same sheet as the rest of the answer.
4. The intended marks for questions or parts of question are given in brackets [ ].

Part I (20 Marks)

(Answer all questions)

While answering questions in this part, indicate briefly your working and reasoning, wherever required.

1. (i) Commutative law is represented by **[1]**

(a) $X+Y=Y+X$

(b) $X+(Y+Z)=(X+Y)+Z$

(c) $X\cdot(Y+Z)=XY+XZ$

(d) $X+X\cdot Y=X$

(ii) **Assertion** In Boolean algebra, the OR operation is commutative. **[1]**

Reason The commutative property states that changing the order of operands in an operation does not affect the result.

(a) Both Assertion and Reason are true, and the Reason is the correct explanation of the Assertion.

(b) Both Assertion and Reason are true, but the Reason is not the correct explanation of the Assertion.

(c) Assertion is true, but the Reason is false.

(d) Assertion is false, but the Reason is true.

(iii) The dual of $(A'+B)(1+B')$ is **[1]**

(a) $(A+B)(1+B)$

(b) $(A'\cdot B)+(0\cdot B')$

(c) $A\cdot B+0\cdot B'$

(d) $A\cdot B+B'$

(iv) The Boolean equation which holds true for the Involution Law is **[1]**

(a) $A'+1=1$

(b) $((A+B)')'=A+B$

(c) $(A+B)'=A'\cdot B'$

(d) $A\cdot(B+C)=(A+B)\cdot C$

(v) Write the minterm of $F(A,B,C,D)$ when $A=1$, $B=0$, $C=0$ and $D=1$. **[1]**

(a) $AB'C'D$ (b) $A'B'CD$

(c) $ABC'D'$ (d) $A'BCD'$

(vi) **Assertion** In Boolean algebra, the AND operation is distributive over the OR operation.

Reason The distributive property states that A AND (B OR C) is equivalent to (A AND B) OR (A AND C), where A, B, and C are logical variables. **[1]**

(a) Both Assertion and Reason are true, and the Reason is the correct explanation of the Assertion.

(b) Both Assertion and Reason are true, but the Reason is not the correct explanation of the Assertion.

(c) Assertion is true, but the Reason is false.

(d) Assertion is false, but the Reason is true.

(vii) Obtain the simplest form of a Boolean expression using Karnaugh map

$F(w,x,y,z)=\Sigma(2,3,6,10,11,14)$ **[1]**

(viii) Write the truth table for a 2 inputs disjunction in a propositional logic. **[1]**

(ix) What are the differences between class and object? **[1]**

(x) State any one purpose of using the keyword this in Java programming. **[1]**

2. (i) Convert the following infix expression to postfix form: $A + B * (C - D) / E$ **[2]**

(ii) A matrix of $2D$ array defined as $A[4, \cdots 7][-1, \cdots +3]$ requires 2 words of storage space for each element. If the array is stored in row major form, calculate the address of $A[6, 2]$ given the base address as 100. **[2]**

(iii) The following function month() is a part of some class.

```
void month(String n, int R)
{
    if(R < 0)
        System.out.print(" ");
    else
    {
        System.out.println(n.charAt(R) + ".");
        month(n, R - 1);
    }
}
```

(a) What will be the output of the function month() when the value of *n* is 'JANUARY' and the value of *R* is 5? **[2]**

(b) Show the dry run/working. **[1]**

(iv) The following function is a part of some class. Assume num is a positive integer. Answer the given questions along with dry run/working.

```
int Status (int num)
{
    int i, j = 0;
    if (num % 2 = = 0)
    {
        i = num/2;
        j = 1;
    }
    else
    {
        j = num;
        num --;
        i = num/2;
    }
    while (i > 0)
    {
        j = j * i * num;
        i --;
        num --;
    }
    return j;
}
```

(a) What will be returned by Status (6)? **[1]**

(b) What is being computed by Status (int num) when num is odd? **[2]**

Part II

(50 Marks)

Answer six questions in this part, choosing two questions from Section A, two from Section B and two from Section C.

Section A

(Answer any two questions)

3. (a) Given the Boolean function $F(A, B, C, D) = \Sigma(0, 1, 2, 6, 8, 9, 10)$

(i) Reduce the above expression by using 4-variable Karnaugh map, showing the various groups (i.e. octet, quads and pairs). **[4]**

(ii) Draw the logic gate diagram for the reduced expression. Assume that the variables and their complements are available as inputs. **[1]**

(b) Given the Boolean function $F(A, B, C, D) = \Pi(3, 4, 5, 7, 11, 12, 13, 14, 15)$

(i) Reduce the above expression by using 4-variable Karnaugh map, showing the various groups (i.e. octet, quads and pairs). **[4]**

(ii) Draw the logic gate diagram for the reduced expression. Assume that the variables and their complements are available as inputs. **[1]**

4. (a) A committee has three general members and a group head, Mr. Amazing. The three general members are Mr. Big, Ms. Creative and Ms. Dynamic. According to the rule, a motion passes only when,

- The group head and atleast anyone general member vote yes or,
- All three general members vote yes.

Let us assume that

Inputs	
A	Denotes Mr Amazing's vote (1 indicates yes and 0 indicates no)
B	Denotes Mr Big's vote (1 indicates yes and 0 indicates no)
C	Denotes Ms Creative's vote (1 indicates yes and 0 indicates no)
D	Denotes Ms Dynamic's vote (1 indicates yes and 0 indicates no)

Output

M - Denotes the passes of a motion.
(1 indicates the motion passes and 0 indicates the motion does not pass)

Draw the truth table for the inputs and output given above and write the SOP expression for the result of the motion $M(A, B, C, D)$. **[5]**

(b) What are the NAND gate? Explain with logic diagram and truth table. **[3]**

(c) Explain XNOR gate with logic diagram. **[2]**

5. (a) What do you understand by a multiplexer? State any one application of a multiplexer circuit. **[2]**

(b) Draw the logic diagram and truth table for 4×1 multiplexer. **[5]**

(c) Verify if the following proposition is valid

$(P \Rightarrow Q) \wedge (P \Rightarrow R) = P \Rightarrow (Q \wedge R)$ **[3]**

Section B

(Answer any two questions)

Each program should be written in such a way that it clearly depicts the logic of the problem. This can be achieved by using mnemonic names and comments in the program. (Flowcharts and Algorithms are not required.)

The programs must be written in Java.

6. A class called Number has been defined to find the frequency of each digit present in it and the sum of the digits and to display the results. Some of the members of the class number are given below:

Class name	Number
Data member	
num	long integer type
Member functions/methods	
Number( )	constructor to assign
Number(long n)	constructor to assign *n* to num
void digitFrequency( )	to find the frequency of each digit and to display it
int sumDigits( )	to return the sum of digits of the number

Specify the class name Number giving the details the constructors and functions void digitFrequency() and int sumDigits(). Define the main() function to create an object and call the functions accordingly to enable the task. **[10]**

7. A class FactorPrime contains an array of 100 integers. Some of the members of the class are given below:

Class name	FactorPrime
Data members/Instance variables	
n [ ]	array to store integers
freq [ ]	array to store the frequency of prime factors of numbers
Member functions	
FactorPrime ()	constructor to initialise array elements to 0
void input ()	to enter values into array n [ ]
void freq ()	to determine the frequency of prime factors of the number stores in n [ ] and assign it to freq [ ]
void show ()	to show the array

Specify the class FactorPrime giving the details of constructor, void input (), void freq () and void show (). Also, define the main () function to create an object and call the method's accordingly to enable the task. **[10]**

8. Design a class Convert to perform string related operations. The details of the class are given below:

Class name	Convert
Data members/Instance variables	
stg	stores the word
newstg	stores the changed word
len	stores the length of the word
Member functions/Methods	
Convert( )	default constructor
void character( )	to accept a word
char caseconvert(char ch)	converts the case of the character and returns it
void reconvert(int)	extracts character using recursive technique and changes it case using caseconvert( ) and form a new word
void output( )	displays both the words

Specify the class Convert giving details of the constructor, member functions void character(), char caseconvert(char), void reconvert(int) and void output(). Define the main() function to create an object and call the functions accordingly to enable the above change in the given word. **[10]**

Section C

(Answer any two questions)

Each program should be written in such a way that it clearly depicts the logic of the problem stepwise. This can be achieved by using comments in the program and mnemonic names or pseudo codes for algorithms. The programs must be written in Java and the algorithms must be written in general/standard form, wherever required/specified. (Flowcharts are not required)

9. Define a class Sequence which allows the user to add elements from one end (rear) and remove elements from the other end (front) only. The following details of the class sequence are given below:

Class name	Sequence
Data members/Instance variables	
stk [ ]	an array to hold a maximum of 50 integers elements
max	stores the capacity of the array
f	to point the index of the front
r	to point the index of the rear
Member functions	
Sequence (int n)	constructor to initialise the data members max = n, f = 0, r = 0 and to create the integer array
void pushEle (int e)	to add integers from the rear index, if possible else display the message "Overflow"
int popEle ()	to remove and return elements from the front. If array is empty, then return-99
void show ()	show the elements present in the list

(i) Specify the class Sequence giving details of the functions void pushEle (int) and int popEle (). Assume that the other functions have been defined. **[4]**

The main() and algorithm need NOT be written.

(ii) What is the common name of entity describe above? **[1]**

10. A super class Employee has been defined to store the details of an employee. Define a subclass Income to compute the monthly income of the employee. The details specifications of both the classes are given below:

Class name	Employee
Data members/Instance variables	
name	to store the name of the employee
about	to store the basic pay in decimals
Member functions/Methods	
Employee (......)	parameterised constructor to assign values to the instance variables
void output( )	displays the employee detail
Class name	**Income**
Data members/Instance variables	
time	stores the hours worked
rate	stores the rate per hour
wages	stores the overall wage of the worker
Member functions/Methods	
Income (......)	parameterised constructor to assign values to the instance variables of both the classes
double overtime( )	calculates and returns the overtime amount as (time * rate)
void output( )	calculate the wage using the formula wage = overtime amount + Basic pay and displays it alongwith the other details

Assume that the super class Employee has been defined. Using the concept of inheritance, specify the class Income giving details of the constructor (......), double overtime() and void output().

The super class and the main() function need not be written. **[5]**

11. (a) State the two factors which determine the complexity of an algorithm. **[2]**

(b) Answer the following questions from the diagram of a binary tree given below:

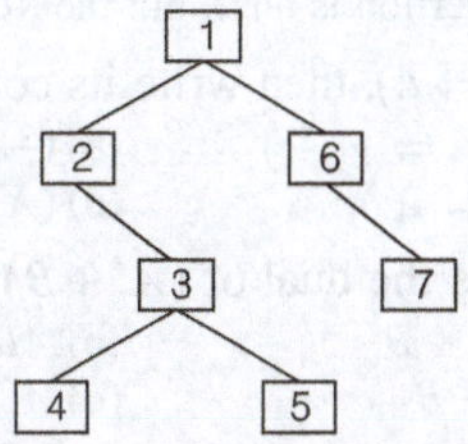

(i) Write the inorder traversal of the above tree structure. **[1]**

(ii) Name the parent of the nodes 4 and 7. **[1]**

(iii) Draw the right subtree of node 2. **[1]**

ISC SAMPLE PAPER 2

Unsolved

COMPUTER SCIENCE-XII

Time : 3 hrs

Max. Marks : 70

General Instructions See Sample Paper 1.

Part I (20 Marks)

(Answer all questions)

While answering questions in this part, indicate briefly your working and reasoning, wherever required.

1. (i) Which of the following are used to determine all the possible truth values regarding a propositional variable? **[1]**

(a) Well Formed Formula
(b) Truth Table
(c) Connectives
(d) Variables

(ii) **Assertion** Boolean algebra and Binary number system are different from each other. **[1]**

Reason There are some basic operations like AND, OR and NOT which are performed in Boolean algebra.

(a) Both Assertion and Reason are true, and the Reason is a correct explanation of the Assertion.
(b) Both Assertion and Reason are true, but the Reason is not a correct explanation of the Assertion.
(c) Assertion is true, but the Reason is false.
(d) Assertion is false, but the Reason is true.

(iii) If $(X \Rightarrow 4)$, then write its contra positive **[1]**

(a) $(\neg Y \Rightarrow \neg X)$ (b) $(\neg X \Rightarrow \neg Y)$
(c) $(Y \Rightarrow X)$ (d) $(X \Rightarrow \neg Y)$

(iv) What is the dual of $(A'+B)\cdot(1+B')$? **[1]**

(a) $A'B + B$ (b) $AB' + B$
(c) $A' + B$ (d) $A' \cdot B$

(v) The representation of the Boolean function $F(A, B) = p(1, 3)$ in canonical form is **[1]**

(a) $(A'+B)\cdot(A+B)$ (b) $S(0, 2)$
(c) $A'B + AB$ (d) $(A+B')\cdot(A'+B')$

(vi) **Assertion** In boolean algebra, the OR operation returns a true value if any of the input variables is true.

Reason The OR operation follows the logical rule that if any of the inputs is true, the output will be true. **[1]**

(a) Both Assertion and Reason are true, and the Reason is a correct explanation of the Assertion.
(b) Both Assertion and Reason are true, but the Reason is not a correct explanation of the Assertion.
(c) Assertion is true, but the Reason is false.
(d) Assertion is false, but the Reason is true.

(vii) Mention any one property of the data members of an interface. **[1]**

(viii) Given the function

$$F(A, B, C) = \Sigma(0, 2, 3, 4, 6)$$

Reduce it using Karnaugh's Map. **[1]**

(ix) What do you mean by inheritance? **[1]**

(x) What is the use of implements keyword? **[1]**

2. (i) Each element of an array $A[-20 \cdots 20], [10 \cdots 35]$ requires one byte of storage. If the array is stored in column major order beginning location 500, determine the location of $A[0, 30]$. **[2]**

(ii) Convert the following infix expression into postfix form. **[2]**

$$(p + q * r - s / t)$$

(iii) The following function someFn() is a part of any class. Assume that arguments a and b are greater than 0, when the function is invoked. Show the dry run/working.

```
int someFn(int a, int b)
{
    //assume that a > 0 and b > 0
```

```
int ans, sm, la;
if(a < b)
{
      sm = a;
      la = b;
}
else
{
      sm = b;
      la = a;
}
ans = la;
while(ans%sm! = 0)
  ans+ = la;
return ans;
}
```

(a) What will the function someFn (7, 5) return? **[2]**

(b) In one line state, what is the function someFn doing? **[1]**

(iv) The following functions show() and calling() are a part of some class. Assume that the parameter n is greater than 1 when the function is invoked. It returns the value 1 when true otherwise it returns 0. Show the dry run/working.

```
void calling (int i)
{
   int f = 2;
   show (n, f);
}
int show (int n, int f)
{
   if (n = = f)
      return 1;
   else if (n%f = = 0 || n = = 1)
      return 0;
   else
      return show (n, f + 1);
}
```

(a) What will the function show() return when the value of n is 11? **[2]**

(b) In one line state, what the function show (...) is doing? **[1]**

Part II (50 Marks)

Answer six questions in this part, choosing two questions from Section A, two from Section B and two from Section C.

Section A

(Answer any two questions)

3. (a) Given the Boolean function

$F(A,B,C,D) = \Sigma(1,6,7,8,9,10,14,15)$.

(i) Reduce the above expression by using 4-variable Karnaugh Map, showing the various groups (i.e. octet, quads and pairs). **[4]**

(ii) Draw the logic gate diagram for the reduced expression. Assume that the variables and their complements are available as inputs. **[1]**

(b) Given the Boolean function

$F(A, B, C, D) = \Pi(2, 3, 4, 5, 11, 12, 13)$.

(i) Reduce the above expression by using 4-variable Karnaugh map, showing the various groups (i.e. octet, quads and pairs). **[4]**

(ii) Draw the logic gate diagram for the reduced expression. Assume that the variables and their complements are available as inputs. **[1]**

4. (a) A family consists of father, mother, son and daughter. They want to build a voting machine according to the following rules. A motion is carried if:

- Both father and mother vote yes.
- Father, mother and anyone of the children vote yes.
- Mother and both the children vote yes.
- All vote yes.

Let us assume that

Inputs	
F	Denotes father's vote (1 indicates yes and 0 indicates no).
M	Denotes mother's vote (1 indicates yes and 0 indicates no).
S	Denotes son's vote (1 indicates yes and 0 indicates no).
D	Denotes daughter's vote (1 indicates yes and 0 indicates no).

Output

R – Denotes the result of the motion (1 indicates it is carried and 0 indicates it is not carried).

Draw the truth table for the inputs and output given above and write the SOP expression for the result of the motion $R(F, M, S, D)$. **[5]**

(b) Find the complement of the following using DeMorgan's laws **[2]**

$$X.(Y'.Z' + Y.Z)$$

(c) Explain NAND and NOR gates with logic diagram. **[3]**

5. (a) Verify if the following proposition is valid

$(a \Rightarrow b) \wedge (a \Rightarrow c) = a \Rightarrow (b \wedge c)$ **[3]**

(b) Draw the logic gate diagram for 3 × 8 decoder circuit with its truth table. **[5]**

(c) Define logic gates. How many types of logic gate are available? **[2]**

Section B

(Answer any two questions)

Each program should be written in such a way that it clearly depicts the logic of the problem.

This can be achieved by using mnemonic names and comments in the program.

(Flowcharts and Algorithms are not required.)

The programs must be written in Java

6. A class **Employee** contains the following members:

Class name	Employee
Data members/Instance variables	
String ename	to store the name of employee
int ecode	to store the employee code
double basicpay	to store the basic pay of employee
Member functions/methods	
Employee(– – – –)	an argumented constructor to assign name, employee code and basic salary to data members/instance variables
double salCalc( )	to compute and return the total salary of an employee
void display( )	to display ename, ecode, basicpay and calculate salary

The salary is calculated according to the following rules

Salary = Basic pay + HRA + DA + TA.

where, HRA = 20% of basic pay

DA = 25% of basic pay

TA = 10% of basic pay

if the ecode ≤ 100, then a special allowance (20% of salary)will be added and the maximum amount for special allowance will be ₹2500.

if the ecode > 100, then the special allowance will be ₹1000. Hence, the total salary for the employee will be calculated as

Total Salary = Salary + Special Allowance

Specify the class Employee giving the details of the constructor, double salCalc() and void display().

Define the main() function to create an object and call the functions accordingly to enable the task. **[10]**

7. A class Record contains the enrollment numbers of 50 students. Some of the data member and member functions are given below:

Class name	Record
Data member/Instance variable	
EnRoll [ ]	integer array to store enrollment numbers
Member functions	
Record ()	constructor to initialise the array elements
void Enter ()	to accept the elements of the array in ascending order
int binSearch (int l, int u, int v)	to search for a particular enrollment number (v) using binary search and recursive technique and returns 1 if found otherwise returns-1

Specify the class Record giving details of the constructor, void Enter () and int binSearch (int, int, int). Define the main () to create an object and call the functions accordingly to enable to task. **[10]**

8. Design a class Reverse to accept a sentence and the first alphabet with last alphabet for each word in the sentence with single letter word remaining unchanged. The words in the input sentence are separated by a single blank space and terminated by a full stop.

e.g. **Input** Do your best

Output Od ruoy tseb

Some of the data members and member functions are given below:

Class name	Reverse
Data members/Instance variables	
line	to store the sentence
rev	to store new sentence
size	to store the length of the sentence
Member functions/methods	
Reverse( )	default constructor
void readInput( )	to accept the sentence
void exfirstlast( )	to extract each word and interchange the first and last alphabet of the word and form a new sentence rev using the change words
void output( )	displays the original sentence along with the new changed sentence

Specify the class Reverse giving details of the constructor, void readInput(), void exfirstlast() and void output(). Define the main() function to create an object and call the functions accordingly to unable the task. **[10]**

Section C

(Answer any two questions)

Each program should be written in such a way that it clearly depicts the logic of the problem stepwise. This can be achieved by using comments in the program and mnemonic names or pseudo codes for algorithms. The programs must be written in Java and the algorithms must be written in general/standard form, wherever required/specified.
(Flowcharts are not required.)

9. Chain is an entity which can hold at the most 50 integers. The chain enables the user to add and remove integers from the both the end, i.e. front and rear. Define a class Chain with the following details:

Class name	Chain
Data members/Instance variables	
ele[ ]	the array to hold the integer elements
cap	stores the maximum capacity of the array
front	to point the index of the front
rear	to point the index of the rear
Member functions/Methods	
Chain(int max)	constructor to initialise the data cap = max, front = rear = – 1 and to create the integer array
void pushfront(int v)	to add integers from the front index, if possible else display the message ("full from front")
int popfront( )	to remove the return elements from front. If array is empty then return-999
void pushrear(int v)	to add integers from the front index, if possible else display the message ("full from rear")
int poprear( )	to remove and return elements from rear. If the array is empty then return-999

(i) Specify the class Chain giving details of the constructor and only the functions void pushfront(int) and int poprear(). Assume that the other functions have been defined. The main() function need not to be written. **[4]**

(ii) Name the entity described above and state its principle. **[1]**

10. A super class Inventory has been defined to store the details of the Inventory of a retail store. Define a sub class Sell to store the details of the produce selled with the new rate and updates the Inventory. Some of the members of the classes are given below:

Class name	Inventory
Data members/Instance variables	
product	to store the name of an item
qty	to store the quantity of an item
rate	to store the unit price of an item
amt	to store the net value of the item in stock
Member functions/Methods	
Inventory (– – –)	parameterised constructor to assign values to the data members
void display( )	to display the inventory details
Class name	**Sell**
Data members/Instance variables	
sqty	to store the sell quantity
srate	to store the unit price of a seller item
Member functions/Methods	
Sell(……)	parameterised constructor to assign values to the data members of both classes
void update( )	to update the inventory
void display( )	to display the stock details of inventory before and after updation

Assume that the super class Inventory has been defined. Using concept of inheritance, specify the class Sell giving details of the constructor and methods void update() and void display(). The super class and main() function need not to be written. **[5]**

11. (a) Distinguish between worst case and best case complexity of an algorithm. **[2]**

(b) Answer the following questions from the diagram of a binary tree given below.

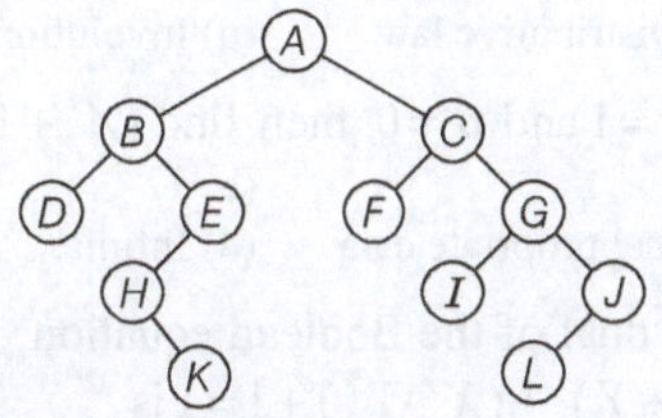

(i) Root of the tree. **[1]**

(ii) Children of node *B*. **[1]**

(iii) List pairs of siblings. **[1]**

ISC SAMPLE PAPER 3

Unsolved

COMPUTER SCIENCE-XII

Time : 3 hrs | Max. Marks : 70

General Instructions See Sample Paper 1.

Part I

(Answer all questions) (20 Marks)

While answering questions in this part, indicate briefly your working and reasoning, wherever required.

1. (i) If $(X \Rightarrow Y)$, then what is converse? **[1]**

(a) $(Y \Rightarrow X)$ (b) $(\neg Y \Rightarrow \neg X)$
(c) $(\neg X \Rightarrow \neg Y)$ (d) $X \Rightarrow Y$

(ii) **Assertion** The complement of a variable in boolean algebra is its inverse value. **[1]**

Reason The complement operation changes the value of a variable to its opposite value (true to false or false to true).

(a) Both Assertion and Reason are true, and the Reason is a correct explanation of the Assertion.
(b) Both Assertion and Reason are true, but the Reason is not a correct explanation of the Assertion.
(c) Assertion is true, but the Reason is false.
(d) Assertion is false, but the Reason is true.

(iii) $X \cdot (X+Y) = X$ is represented by **[1]**

(a) Commutative law (b) Absorption law
(c) Distributive law (d) Involution law

(iv) If $A = 1$ and $B = 0$, then find $(A'+1) \cdot B$ **[1]**

(a) 0 (b) 1
(c) Inappropriate data (d) Infinite

(v) The dual of the Boolean equation $(X+Y)' + (X' \cdot Y') + 1 = 1$ is **[1]**

(a) $(X \cdot Y)' \cdot (X' + Y') \cdot 0 = 0$
(b) $(X+Y) \cdot (X' \cdot Y') + 1 = 1$
(b) $(X \cdot Y) \cdot (X+Y) \cdot 0 = 0$
(d) $(X \cdot Y)' \cdot (X' + Y') \cdot 1 = 1$

(vi) **Assertion** A ^ B = B ^ A. **[1]**

Reason The AND operation (^) is commutative.

(a) Both Assertion and Reason are true, and the Reason is a correct explanation of the Assertion.
(b) Both Assertion and Reason are true, but the Reason is not a correct explanation of the Assertion.
(c) Assertion is true, but the Reason is false.
(d) Assertion is false, but the Reason is true.

(vii) State and verify Distributive law using the truth table. **[1]**

(viii) Find the complement of $F(A, B, C, D)$ using DeMorgan's laws. Also, show the relevant reasoning, **[1]**
where, $F(A, B, C, D) = a + ((b+c) \cdot (b' + d'))$. **[1]**

(ix) What is recursion? **[1]**

(ix) Define universal gates. Give one example and show how it works as an OR gate. **[1]**

2. (i) Convert the following infix notation to its postfix form.

$$(A + (B * C)) / (C - (D * B))$$ **[2]**

(ii) Each element of an array A[−15, …20] [20, …45] requires 2 bytes for storage. Find the address of A[20] [30], if the base address is 100 in Row Major Wise. **[2]**

(iii) With reference to the code given below, answer the questions that follow along with dry run/working.

```
void confusing(int x, int y)
```

```
{
    if( x > 1 )          // base case
    {
        if( x % y == 0 )
        {
            System.out.print( y + " " );
            confusing(x/y, y);
        }      // end of inner if
        else
            confusing( x,y+1);
    }      // end of outer if
}
```

(a) What will be the function confusing (int, int) return when the values of *x* and *y* are greater than 0? **[2]**

(b) What is the method confusing() performing? **[1]**

(iv) In the following, function Test is a part of some class. Assume that the arguments *a* and *b* are greater than 0 when the function is invoked.

Show the dry run/working.

```
int Test (int a, int b)
{
    if(a>=b)
    {
        a=a-b;
        return Test (a, b);
    }
    else
    {
        return b;
    }
}
```

(a) What will function Test (20, 5) return? **[2]**

(b) In one line state, what the function Test(...) is doing? **[1]**

Part II (50 Marks)

Answer six questions in this part, choosing two questions from Section A, two from Section B and two from Section C.

Section A

(Answer any two questions)

3. (a) Given the Boolean function $F(A, B, C, D) = \Pi(3, 4, 6, 7, 11, 12, 13, 14, 15)$.

(i) Reduce the above expression by using 4-variable K-map, showing the various groups (i.e. octet, quads and pairs). **[4]**

(ii) Draw the logic gate diagram of the reduced expression. Assume that the variables and their complements are available as inputs. **[1]**

(b) Given the boolean function $F(A, B, C, D) = \Sigma(0, 1, 2, 5, 8, 9, 10)$.

(i) Reduce the above expression by using 4-variable K-map, showing the various groups (i.e. octet, quads and pairs). **[4]**

(ii) Draw the logic gate diagram of the reduced expression. Assume that the variables and their complements are available as inputs. **[1]**

4. (a) The past Pupil Association of R. K. University Computer Science Department is organising a reunion function at the campus. The invitation card is to be issued to a person if

- The person is an ex-student of the department and had passed out in 1995.

or

- The person is not an ex-student of the same department but passed out from the University in 1995 and has made a contribution of 1000.

Inputs	
E	The person is an ex-student of the department.
U	The person is not an ex-student of the department but a student of the same university.
P	The person passed out in 1995.
C	The person contributes ₹ 1000.

Output

I–Denotes the Invitation Card is issued (1 indicates it is issued and 0 indicates it is not issued).

Draw the truth table for the inputs and output given above and write the SOP expression for $I(E, U, P, C)$. **[5]**

(b) Draw the truth table to prove the following proportional logic expression

$A <=> B = (A <=> B) \wedge (B => A)$ **[3]**

(c) State differences between a tautology and a contradiction. **[2]**

5. (a) Draw a logic diagram for the following function using only NAND gate. **[2]**

$F(A, B, C) = (A' + B') \,.\, (B + C') \,.\, (C' + A)$

(b) Using a truth table, verify if the following proposition is valid or invalid. **[3]**

$(a \Rightarrow b) \wedge (b \Rightarrow c) = (a \Rightarrow c)$

(c) From the logic circuit diagram given below, name the outputs (1), (2) and (3). Finally derive the boolean expression and simplify it. **[5]**

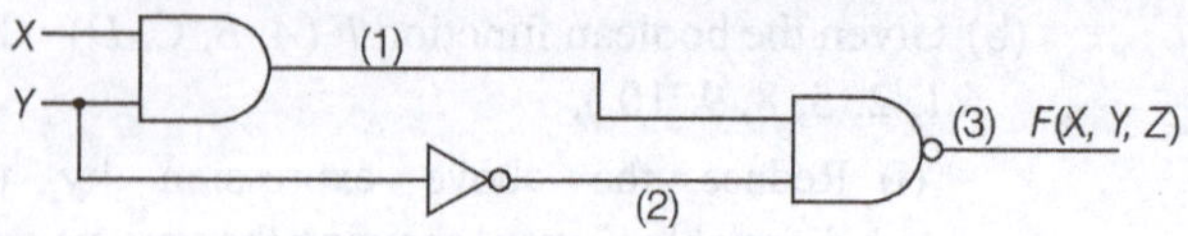

Section B

(Answer any two questions)

Each program should be written in such a way that it clearly depicts the logic of the problem.
This can be achieved by using mnemonic names and comments in the program.
(Flowcharts and Algorithms are not required.)
The programs must be written in Java

6. A class called LCM has been defined to find the LCM of two integers. Some of the data members and functions of the class LCM are given below:

Class name	LCM
Data members/Instance variables	
n1, n2	integers whose LCM is to be found
large, sm	integers to store the largest and the smallest from *n*1, *n*2
lcm	integer to store the LCM of the *n*1 and *n*2
Member functions/methods	
LCM( )	constructor to assign initial values to the data members
void acceptData( )	to accept the value of *n*1 and *n*2
int getLCM( )	to find the LCM of n1 and n2 using the recursive technique and store it in lcm. Return the value of lcm
void printData( )	to print the numbers *n*1, *n*2 and the LCM

Specify the class LCM giving details of the constructor and functions void acceptData(), int getLCM() and void printData(). Also, write the main() function to create an object and call the member functions accordingly. **[10]**

7. A class MyArray contains an array of *n* integers (*n*<=100) that are already arranged in ascending order. The subscripts of the array elements vary from 0 to *n*-1. Some of the member functions of the class are given below:

Class name	MyArray
Data members/instance variables	
arr[ ]	an array of n integers
n	size of the array
Member functions/methods	
MyArray( )	constructor to initialise 0 in each memory location of the array arr[ ]
void readArray( )	to read *n* integers that are arranged in ascending order
void displayArray( )	to display the n integers of the array arr[ ]
int binarySearch(int)	to search for the value taken as parameter in the array using the binary search technique. It returns the subscript of the array element if the value is found, otherwise it returns -999

Specify the class MyArray giving the details of the function void readArray(), void displayArray() and int binarySearch(int). Define the main() function to create an object and call the methods accordingly to enable the task. **[10]**

8. Write a Java program to input a sentence from the user in lowercase and remove the first and the last characters of every word in it.
e.g.
Input i love java for school
Output ov av o choo

Some of the data members and member functions are given below:

Class name	Remove
Data members/Instance variables	
sent	stores the sentence
rem	stores the new sentence
size	stores the length of the sentence
Member functions/methods	
Remove( )	default constructor
void readsentence( )	to accept the sentence
void remfirstlast( )	to extract each word and remove the first and the last alphabet of the word and form a new sentence **'rem'** using the changed words
void display( )	to display the original sentence alongwith the new changed sentence

Specify the class Remove giving details of the constructor Remove() functions, void readsentence(), void remfirstlast() and void display(). Define the main() function to create an object and call the functions accordingly to enable the task. **[10]**

Section C

(Answer any two questions)

Each program should be written in such a way that it clearly depicts the logic of the problem stepwise.

This can be achieved by using comments in the program and mnemonic names or pseudo codes for algorithms. The programs must be written in Java and the algorithms must be written in general/standard form, wherever required/specified. (Flowcharts are not required).

9. A Queue is a linear data structure in which the operations are performed based on FIFO (First In First Out).

Define a class Queue with the following details:

Class name	Queue
Data members/Instance variables	
dat[ ]	array to hold the integer elements
cap	stores the maximum capacity of the queue
front	to point the index of the front
rear	to point the index of the rear.
Member functions/methods	
Queue(int max)	constructor to initialize the data member cap=max, front = rear = 0 and create the integer array
void add_dat(int v)	to add integers from the rear indexd if possible else display the message("Queue full")
int pop_dat( )	to remove and return elements from front, if any, else returns-999
void display( )	to display elements of the queue

(i) Specify the class Queue giving the details of void add_dat(int) and int pop_dat(). Assume that the other functions have been defined.
The main() function and algorithm need NOT be written. **[4]**

(ii) Name the entity described above and state its principle. **[1]**

10. A class Student defines the personal data of a student while another class Marks defines to the roll number, name of subject and marks obtained by the student. The details of classes are as follows:

Class name	Student
Data members/Instance variables	
name, sex	string variables to store name and gender male/female
age	integer variable to store age of the student
Member functions/methods	
Student( )	constructor to assign initial values to the data members
void inputDetails( )	to accept values for data members
void show( )	to print personal data of student

Class name	Marks
Data members/Instance variables	
rollno, marks	integers to store roll number and marks
subject	string variable to store name of subject
Member functions/methods	
Marks( )	constructor to assign initial values
void readDetails( )	to accept values for data members
int point( )	to return the point obtained according to the following

Marks	Point
>=90	1
70-89	2
50-69	3
40-49	4
<40	5

void show( )	to display name, sex, age, rollno, marks, subject and point of the student by invoking suitable function

Assume that the super class Student has been defined. Using the concept of inheritance, specify the class Marks giving the details of the constructor (.....), void readDetails(), int point() and void show(). The super class and the main() function need not be written. **[5]**

11. (a) What is the role of constants in complexity? Explain briefly with an example. **[2]**

(b) Answer the questions below for the given binary tree:

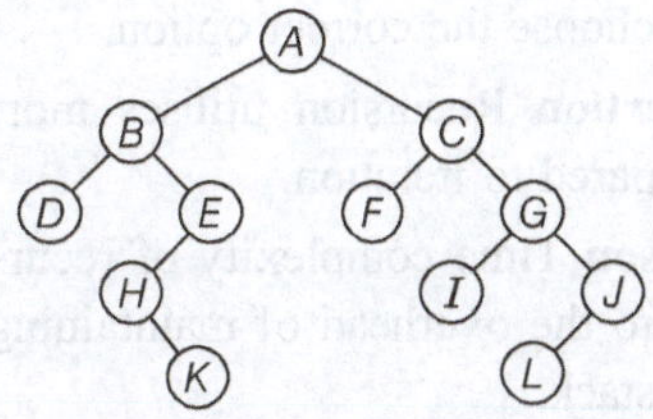

(i) List the internal nodes of the binary tree. **[1]**

(ii) List the leaf nodes of the binary tree. **[1]**

(iii) Write preorder traversal of the binary tree. **[1]**

ISC

Latest Specimen Question Paper

Fully Solved

COMPUTER SCIENCE-XII

Time : 3 hrs Max. Marks : 70

General Instructions

1. You are allowed **additional 15 minutes** for **only** reading the question paper.
2. You must **NOT** start writing during the reading time.
3. This question paper has **12** printed pages.
4. It is divided into **two parts** and has **11 questions** in all.
5. **Part I** is compulsory and has **two** questions. Answer **all** questions.
6. **Part II** is divided into **three sections**: A, B and C.
7. While attempting **Multiple Choice Questions** in Part I, you are required to **write only ONE option as the answer.**
8. **Each section in Part II** has **three questions. Any two** questions have to be attempted from each section.
9. The intended marks for questions are given in brackets [ ].

Part I (20 Marks)

(Answer all questions)

While answering questions in this part, indicate briefly your working and reasoning, wherever required.

1. (i) The compliment of the Boolean expression $A' \bullet (B \bullet C' + B' \bullet C)$ *(Application)* **[1]**

(a) $A' \bullet (B + C + B' + C)$
(b) $A + (B + C') \bullet (B + C')$
(c) $A + (B' + C) \bullet (B + C')$
(d) $A' \bullet (B' + C' + B' \bullet C)$

(ii) Given below are two statements marked Assertion and Reason. Read the two statements carefully and choose the correct option.

Assertion Recursion utilises more memory as compared to iteration.

Reason Time complexity of recursion is higher due to the overhead of maintaining the function call stack. **[1]**

(Analysis)

(a) Both Assertion and Reason are true and Reason is the correct explanation for Assertion.
(b) Both Assertion and Reason are true but Reason is not the correct explanation for Assertion.
(c) Assertion is true and Reason is false.
(d) Assertion is false and Reason is true.

(iii) According to the Principle of duality, the Boolean equation $(A' + B) \bullet (1 + B) = A' + B$ will be equivalent to: *(Application)* **[1]**

(a) $(A + B') \bullet (0 + B) = A + B'$
(b) $(A' \bullet B) + (0 \bullet B) = A' \bullet B$
(c) $(A' \bullet B) + (0 \bullet B) = A' + B$
(d) $(A' + B) \bullet (0 + B) = A' + B$

(iv) Distributive law states that: *(Recall)* **[1]**

(a) $A + B \bullet C = (A + B) \bullet (A + C)$
(b) $A + (A \bullet B) = A$
(c) $A \bullet (B + C) = (A \bullet B) + (B \bullet C)$
(d) $A + B \bullet C = A \bullet B + A \bullet C$

(v) The complement of the reduced expression of $F(A, B) = \Sigma(0,1,2,3)$ is: *(Application)* **[1]**

(a) 1 (b) $A \bullet B$
(c) 0 (d) $A' + B'$

(vi) Study the given propositions and the statements marked Assertion and Reason that follow it. Choose the correct option on the basis of your analysis.

p = I am a triangle
q = I am a three-sided polygon
$s_1 = p \rightarrow q$
$s_2 = q \rightarrow p$

Assertion s_2 is converse of s_1

Reason Three-sided polygon must be a triangle. ***(Analysis)*** **[1]**

(a) Both Assertion and Reason are true and Reason is the correct explanation for Assertion.
(b) Both Assertion and Reason are true but Reason is not the correct explanation for Assertion.
(c) Assertion is true and Reason is false.
(d) Assertion is false and Reason is true.

(vii) Given below are two statements marked Assertion and Reason. Read the two statements carefully and choose the correct option.

Assertion In Java, the String class is used to create and manipulate strings, and it is immutable.

Reason Immutability ensures that once a String object is created, its value cannot be changed. ***(Analysis)*** **[1]**

(a) Both Assertion and Reason are true and Reason is the correct explanation for Assertion.
(b) Both Assertion and Reason are true but Reason is not the correct explanation for Assertion.
(c) Assertion is true and Reason is false.
(d) Assertion is false and Reason is true.

(viii) Consider the following statement written in class Circle where pi is its data member.

```
static final double pi = 3.142;
```

Which of the following statements are valid for pi?

I. It contains a common value for all objects class Circle.
II. Its value is non-changeable.
III. At a time two access modifiers, static and final, cannot be applied to a single data member pi. ***(Application)*** **[1]**

(a) I and II (b) II and III
(c) I and III (d) Only III

(ix) For Big O notation, state the difference between O(n) and O(n^2). ***(Analysis)*** **[1]**

(x) A full adder needs five gates and those are 3 AND gates, 1 OR gate and 1 XOR gate. When a full adder is constructed using 2 half adders, it also requires 5 gates. State the names along with the quantity those gates. ***(Analysis)*** **[1]**

2. (i) Convert the following infix notation to prefix form. ***(Create)***

$(A - B) / C * (D + E)$ **[2]**

(ii) A matrix M[-6 ...... 10, 4 ...... 15] is stored in the memory with each element requiring 4 bytes of storage. If the base address is 1025, find the address of M[4][8] when the matrix is stored in column major wise. ***(Application)*** **[2]**

(iii) The following function getIt() is a part of some class. Assume x is a positive integer, f is the lower bound of arr[ ] and l is the upper bound of the arr[ ].

Answer the questions given below along with dry run/working.

```
public int getIt(int x,intarr[],int f,int l)
{
  if(f>l)
    return -1;
  int m=(f+l)/2;
  if(arr[m]<x)
    return getIt(x,m+1,l);
  else if(arr[m]>x)
    return getIt(x,f,m-1);
  else
    return m;
}
```

(a) What will the function getIt( ) return if arr[ ] = {10,20,30,40,50} and x=40? ***(Analysis)*** **[2]**

(b) What is function getIt( ) performing apart from recursion? ***(Analysis)*** **[1]**

(iv) The following is a function of class Armstrong. This recursive function calculates and returns the sum of the cubes of all the digits of num, where num is an integer data member of the class Armstrong.

[A number is said to be Armstrong if the sum of the cubes of all its digits is equal to the original number].

There are some places in the code marked by ?1?, ?2?,?3? which may be replaced by a statement/expression so, that the function works properly.

```
public int sumOfPowers(int num)
{
  if (num == 0)
    return ?1?;
  int digit = ?2?;
  return (int) Math.pow(digit, 3) + ?3?;
}
```

(a) What is the expression or statement at ?1? *(Analysis)* [1]

(b) What is the expression or statement at ?2? *(Analysis)* [1]

(c) What is the expression or statement at ?3? *(Analysis)* [1]

Part II (50 Marks)

Answer six questions in this part, choosing two questions from Section A, two from Section B and two from Section C.

Section A

(Answer any two questions)

3. (i) A shopping mall announces a special discount on all its products as a festival offer only to those who satisfy any one of the following conditions.

- If he/she is an employee of the mall and has a service of more than 10 years.

Or

- A regular customer of the mall whose age is less than 65 years and should not be an employee of the mall.

Or

- If he/she is a senior citizen but not a regular customer of the mall.

The inputs are :

INPUTS	
E	Employee of the mall
R	Regular customer of the mall
S	Service of the employee is more than 10 years
C	Senior citizen of 65 years or above

(In all the above cases, 1 indicates yes and 0 indicates no.)

Output *X* - Denotes eligible for discount [1 indicates YES and 0 indicates NO in all cases]

Draw the truth table for the inputs and outputs given above and write the SOP expression for $X(E,R,S,C)$. *(Application)* [5]

(ii) Reduce the above expression $X(E,R,S,C)$ by using 4-variable Karnaugh map, showing the various groups (i.e. octal, quads and pairs).

Draw the logic gate diagram for the reduced expression. Assume that the variables and their complements are available as inputs. *(Create)* [5]

4. (i) (a) Reduce the Boolean function $F(P,Q,R,S)=(P+Q+R+S)\cdot(P+Q+R+S')\cdot(P+Q+R'+S)\cdot(P+Q'+R+S)\cdot(P+Q'+R+S')\cdot(P+Q'+R'+S)\cdot(P+Q'+R'+S')\cdot(P'+Q+R+S)\cdot(P'+Q+R+S')$ by using 4-variable Karnaugh map, showing the various groups (i.e. octal, quads and pairs). *(Application)* [4]

(b) Draw the logic gate diagram for the reduced expression. Assume that the variables and their complements are available as inputs. *(Create)* [1]

(ii) From the given logic diagram :

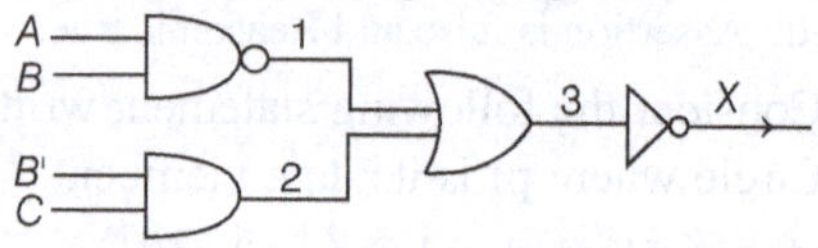

(a) Derive Boolean expression and draw the truth table for the derived expression. *(Application)* [4]

(b) If *A*=1, *B*=0 and *C*=1 then find the value of *X*. *(Application)* [1]

5. (i) Draw the logic circuit to decode the following binary number (0001, 0101, 0111, 1000, 1010, 1100, 1110,1111) to its hexadecimal equivalents. Also state the Hexadecimal equivalents of the given binary numbers. *(Application & Analyse)* [5]

(ii) Verify if the following proposition is valid using the truth table:

$(X \wedge Y) \Rightarrow Z = (Y \Rightarrow Z) \wedge (X \Rightarrow Y)$ *(Application)* [3]

(iii) Answer the following questions related to the below image:

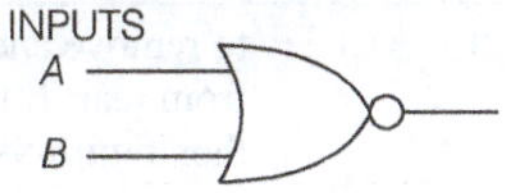

(a) What is the output of the above gate if input $A = 0, B = 1$? *(Analysis)* [1]

(b) What are the values of the inputs if output =1? *(Application)* [1]

Section B

(Answer any two questions)

Each program should be written in such a way that it clearly depicts the logic of the problem. This can be achieved by using mnemonic names and comments in the program. (Flowcharts and Algorithms are not required.)

The programs must be written in Java.

6. Given are two strings, input string and a mask string that remove all the characters of the mask string from the original string.

Example

INPUT

ORIGINALSTRING: communication

MASK STRING: mont

OUTPUT cuicai

A class StringOp is defined as follows to perform above operation.

Some of the members of the class are given below:

Class name	:	**StringOp**
Data members/instance variables		
str	:	to store the original string
msk	:	to store the mask string
nstr	:	to store the resultant string
Methods / Member functions		
StringOp()	:	default constructor to initialize the data member with legal initial value
void accept( )	:	to accept the original string str and the mask string msk in lower case
void form()	:	to form the new string nstr after removal of characters present in mask from the original string
void display( )	:	to display the original string and the newly formed string nstr

Specify the class StringOp giving details of the constructor( ), void accept( ), void form() and void display( ). Define a main( ) function to create an object and call all the functions accordingly to enable the task. *(Create)*

7. A class Mixarray contains an array of integer elements along with its capacity (More than or equal to 3). Using the following description, form a new array of integers which will contain only the first 3 elements of the two different arrays one after another. [10]

Example: Array1: { 78, 90, 100, 45, 67 }

Array2: {10, 67, 200, 90 }

Resultant Array: { 78, 90, 100, 10, 67, 200}

The details of the members of the class are given below:

Class name	:	**Mixarray**
Data members/instance variables		
arr[]	:	integer array
cap	:	integer to store the capacity of the array
Member functions/methods		
Mixarray (int mm)	:	to initialize the capacity of the array cap=mm
void input( )	:	to accept the elements of the array
Mixarray mix(Mixarray P, Mixarray Q)	:	returns the resultant array having the first 3 elements of the array of objects P and Q
void display( )	:	to display the array with an appropriate message.

Specify the class Mixarraygiving details of the constructor(int), void input( ), Mixarray mix(Mixarray,Mixarray) and void display( ). Define a main( ) function to create objects and call all the functions accordingly to enable the task. *(Create)*

8. A class LCM has been defined to find the Lowest Common Multiple of two integers. [10]

Some of the data members and member functions are given below:

Class name	:	**LCM**
Data members/instance variables		
n1	:	to store an integer number
n2	:	to store an integer number
large	:	integer to store the largest from n1,n2
sm	:	integer to store the smallest from n1,n2
l	:	to store lcm of two numbers

Methods / Member functions		
LCM( )	:	default constructor to initialize data members with legal initial values
void accept( )	:	to accept n1 and n2
int getLCM( )	:	returns the lcm of n1 and n2 using the recursive technique
void display( )	:	to print the numbers n1, n2 and lcm

Specify the class LCM giving details of the constructor( ), void accept( ), int getLCM() and void display( ). Define a main ( ) function to create an object and call the member functions accordingly to enable the task. ***(Create)***

Section C

(Answer any two questions)

Each program should be written in such a way that it clearly depicts the logic of the problem stepwise. This can be achieved by using comments in the program and mnemonic names or pseudo codes for algorithms. The programs must be written in Java and the algorithms must be written in general/standard form, wherever required/specified. (Flowcharts are not required)

9. Recycle is an entity which can hold at the most 100 integers. The chain enables the user to add and remove integers from both the ends i.e. front and rear.

Define a class ReCycle with the following details:

Class name	:	**ReCycle**
Data members/instance variables		
ele[ ]	:	the array to hold the integer elements
cap	:	stores the maximum capacity of the array
front	:	to point the index of the front
rear	:	to point the index of the rear
Methods / Member functions		
ReCycle (int max)	:	constructor to initialize the data cap = max, front = rear = 0 and to create the integer array.
void pushfront(int v)	:	to add integers from the front index if possible else display the message("full from front").
int popfront( )	:	to remove the return elements from front. If array is empty then return-999.
void pushrear(int v)	:	to add integers from the front index if possible else display the message("full from rear").
int poprear( )	:	to remove and return elements from rear. If the array is empty then return-999.

(i) Specify the class ReCycle giving details of the functions void pushfront(int) and int poprear( ). Assume that the other functions have been defined.

The main( ) function and algorithm need NOT be written. ***(Create)*** **[4]**

(ii) Name the entity described above and state its principle. ***(Understanding)*** **[1]**

10. A library issues books on rental basis at a 2% charge on the cost price of the book per day. As per the rules of the library, a book can be retained for 7 days without any fine.

If the book is returned after 7 days, a fine will also be charged for the excess days as per the chart given below:

Number of excess days	**Fine per day (Rs.)**
1 to 5	2.00
6 to 10	3.00
Above 10	5.00

A super class Library has been defined. Define a sub class Compute to calculate the fine and the total amount. The details of the members of both the classes are given below:

Class name	:	**Library**
Data members/instance variables		
name	:	to store the name of the book
author	:	to store the author of the book
p	:	to store the price of the book (in decimals)
Methods / Member functions		
Library(...)	:	parameterized constructor to assign values to the data members
void show( )	:	displays the book details
Class name		**Compute**
Data members/instance variables		
d	:	number of days taken in returning the book
f	:	to store the fine (in decimals)

Methods / Member functions:		
Compute(...)	:	parameterized constructor to assign values to the data members of both the classes
void fine( )	:	calculates the fine for the excess days as given in the table above
void show( )	:	displays the book details along with the number of days, fine and the total amount to be paid. Total amount is (2% of price of book * total no of days) + fine

Assume that the super class Library has been defined. Using the concepts of Inheritance, specify the class Compute giving the details of constructor, void fine ( ) and void show ( ) functions.

The super class, main function and algorithm need NOT be written. **(Create)**

11. (i) A linked list is formed from the objects of the class Node. The class structure of the Node is given below: **[2]**

```
class Node
{
  int n;
  Node link;
}
```

Write an Algorithm OR a Method to search for a number from an existing linked list.

The method declaration is as follows:

`void FindNode( Node str, int b)` ***(Analysis)*** **[2]**

(ii) Answer the following questions from the diagram of a Binary Tree given below:

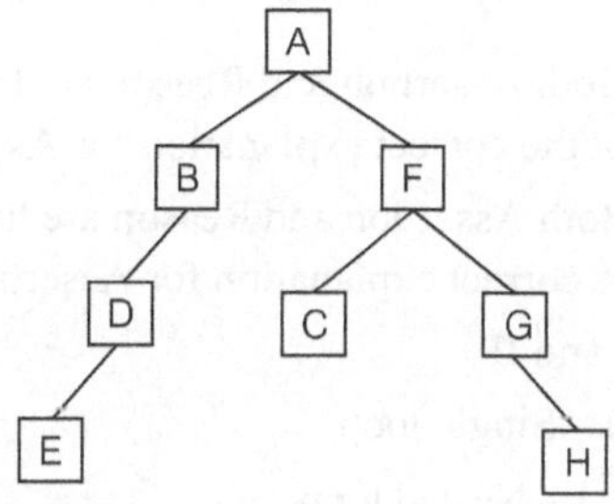

(a) Name the root of the left sub tree and its siblings. ***(Understanding)*** **[1]**

(b) State the size and depth of the right sub tree. ***(Understanding)*** **[1]**

(c) Write the in-order traversal of the above tree structure. ***(Understanding)*** **[1]**

Answers

1. (i) (c) $A+(B'+C)\bullet(B+C')$

(ii) (b) Both Assertion and Reason are true but Reason is not the correct explanation for Assertion.

(iii) (b) $(A'\bullet B)+(0\bullet B)=A'\bullet B$

(iv) (a) $A+B\bullet C=(A+B)\bullet(A+C)$

(v) (c) 0

(vi) (b) Both Assertion and Reason are true but Reason is not the correct explanation for Assertion.

(vii) (a) Both Assertion and Reason are true and Reason is the correct explanation for Assertion.

(viii) (a) I and II

(ix) O(n) – Single loop

$O(n^2)$ – Nested loop

(x) 2 AND gates, 1 OR gate and 2 XOR gates

2. (i) $*/-ABC+DE$

(ii) Address of

$M[4][8]=B+W*[(J-L_c)*M+(I-L_r)]$

$=1025+4[(8-4)17+4-(-6)]$

$=1025+4(68+10)$

$=1025+4*78$

$=1025+312$

$=1337$

(iii) (a) 3

(b) Function getIt( ) is performing binary search on arr [ ]

(iv) (a) 0

(b) num%10

(c) sumOfPowers(num/10)

3. (i)

E	R	S	C	X
Employee of the mall	**Regular customer of the mall**	**Service of the employee is more than 10 years**	**Senior citizen of 65 years or above**	**Output**
0	0	0	0	0
0	0	0	1	1
0	0	1	0	0
0	0	1	1	1
0	1	0	0	1
0	1	0	1	0
0	1	1	0	1
0	1	1	1	0
1	0	0	0	0
1	0	0	1	1
1	0	1	0	1
1	0	1	1	1
1	1	0	0	0
1	1	0	1	0
1	1	1	0	1
1	1	1	1	1

$X(E,R,S,C)=\Sigma(1,3,4,6,9,10,11,14,15)$

$=E'R'S'C+E'R'SC+E'RS'C'+E'RSC'$

$+ER'S'C+ER'SC'+ER'SC+ERSC'+ERSC$

(ii)

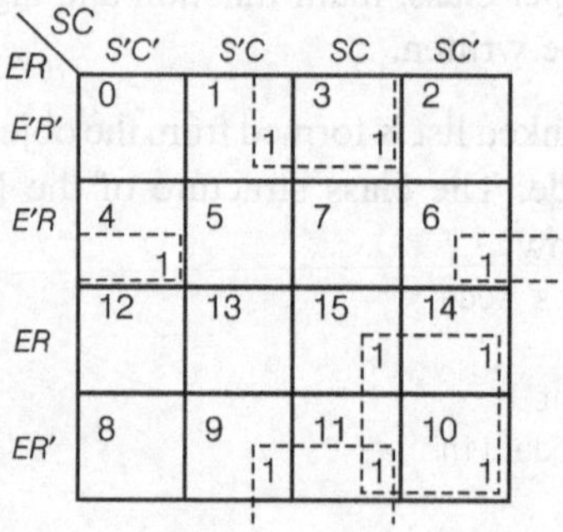

There are two quads and a pair:

Quad 1 $(m_1+m_3+m_9+m_{11})=R'C$

Quad 2 $(m_{10}+m_{11}+m_{14}+m_{15})=ES$

Pair $(m_4+m_6)=E'RC'$

Hence $F(E,R,S,C)=R'C+ES+E'RC'$

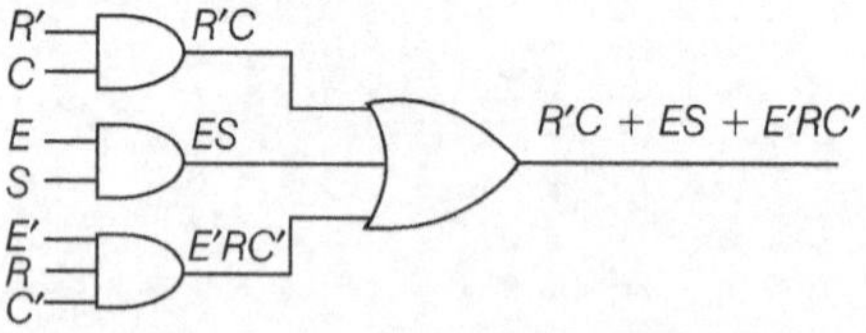

4. (i) (a)

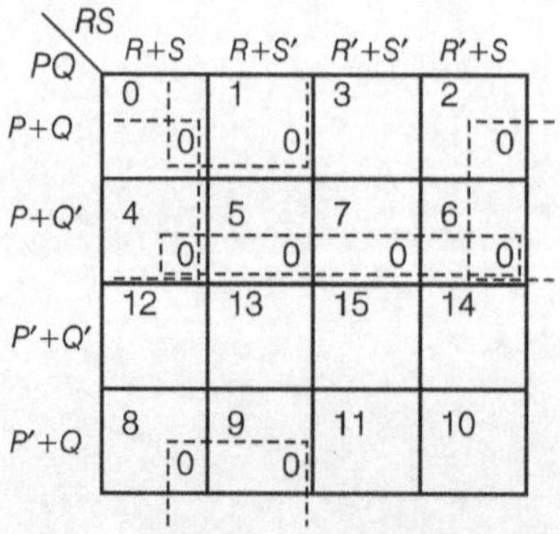

There are three quads :

Quad 1 $(M_0 \cdot M_1 \cdot M_8 \cdot M_9) = Q + R$

Quad 2 $(M_4 \cdot M_5 \cdot M_6 \cdot M_7) = P + Q'$

Quad 3 $(M_0 \cdot M_2 \cdot M_4 \cdot M_6) = P + S$

Hence

$F(P,Q,R,S) = (Q+R).(P+Q').(P+S)$

(b) 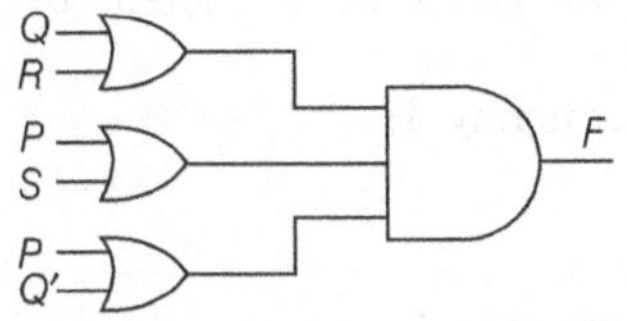

(ii) (a) $[(A.B)'+B'\cdot C]'$

A	B	C	B'	$B'.C$	$(A\cdot B)'$	$(A\cdot B)' + B'\cdot C$	$[(A\cdot B)' + B'\cdot C]'$
0	0	0	1	0	1	1	0
0	0	1	1	1	1	1	0
0	1	0	0	0	1	1	0
0	1	1	0	0	1	1	0
1	0	0	1	0	1	1	0
1	0	1	1	1	1	1	0
1	1	0	0	0	0	0	1
1	1	1	0	0	0	0	1

(b) 0

5. (i) 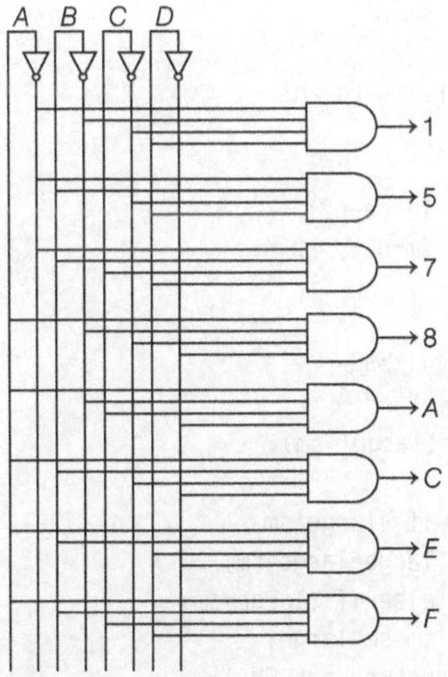

(0001) = 1
(0101) = 5
(0111) = 7
(1000) = 8
(1010) = A
(1100) = C
(1110) = E
(1111) = F

(ii)

X	Y	Z	X^Y	(X^Y =>Z	Y=>Z	X => Y	(Y => Z) ^(X=>Y)
0	0	0	0	1	1	1	1
0	0	1	0	1	1	1	1
0	1	0	0	1	0	1	0
0	1	1	0	1	1	1	1
1	0	0	0	1	1	0	0
1	0	1	0	1	1	0	0
1	1	0	1	0	0	1	0
1	1	1	1	1	1	1	1

Invalid

(iii) (a) 0 (b) A=0, B=0

6.
```
import java.util.*;
class StringOp
{
  String str;
  String nstr;
  String msk;
  Scanner sc=new Scanner(System.in);
  StringOp()
  {
     str="";
     nstr="";
     msk="";
  }
  void accept()//to accept the original and mask
                                            string
  {
     System.out.println("Enter the original word");
     str=sc.next()+sc.nextLine();
     System.out.println("enter the mask string");
     msk=sc.next();
  }
  void form() //formation of a new string
                     according to the requirement
  {
     int l1=str.length();int l2=msk.length();
     for (int i=0;i<l1;i++)
     {
       int fr=0;char c1=str.charAt(i);
       if (msk.indexOf(c1)==-1)
       nstr=nstr+c1;
     }
  }
  void display() //display original and newly
                                  formed string
  {
```

```
        System.out.println("original string: "+str);
        System.out.println("changed string: "+nstr);
    }
    public static void main()
    {
        StringOp ob=new StringOp();
        ob.accept();
        ob.form();
        ob.display();
    }
}
```

7.
```
import java.util.*;
class Mixarray
{
    int arr[];
    int cap;
    static Scanner sc=new Scanner(System.in);
    Mixarray(int mm)
    {
        cap=mm;
        arr=new int[cap];
    }
    void input()
    {
        System.out.println("Enter the content of the
                                          array");
        for (int i=0;i<cap;i++)
        arr[i]=sc.nextInt();
    }
    void display()
    {
        for (int i=0;i<cap;i++)
        System.out.print(arr[i]+" ");
        System.out.println();
    }
    Mixarray mix(Mixarray P,Mixarray Q)
    {
        Mixarray res=new Mixarray(6);
        int k=0;
        for (int i=0;i<3;i++)
        res.arr[k++]=P.arr[i];
        for (int i=0;i<3;i++)
        res.arr[k++]=Q.arr[i];
        return res;
    }
    public static void main()
    {
        System.out.println("enter the capacity of
                                    both the array");
        int c1=sc.nextInt(); int c2=sc.nextInt();
        Mixarray ob1=new Mixarray(c1);
        Mixarray ob2=new Mixarray(c2);
        System.out.println("Enter the content of
                                        Ist array");
        ob1.input();
        System.out.println("Enter the content of
                                        2nd array");
        ob2.input();
        Mixarray r=new Mixarray(c1+c2);
        Mixarray res=r.mix(ob1,ob2);
        System.out.println("content of the combined
                                            array");
        res.display();
    }
}
```

8.
```
import java.util.*;
class LCM
{
  int n1,n2;
  int large,sm;
  int l;
  static Scanner sc=new Scanner(System.in);
  void accept()
  {
    System.out.println("enter 2 different
                                   integers:");
    n1=sc.nextInt();
    n2=sc.nextInt();
    if (n1>n2)
    {
      large=n1;
      sm=n2;
    }
    elseif (n2>n1)
    {

      large=n2;
      sm=n1;
    }
  }
  int getLCM()
  {
    if(large!=sm)
    {
      if (large>sm)
      large=large-sm;
      else if (large<sm)
      sm=sm-large;
      return getLCM();
    }
    else
    return (n1*n2)/large;
  }
  void display()
  {
    l=getLCM();
```

```
    System.out.println("LCM of "+n1 +"and
                                  "+n2+"="+l);
  }
  public static void main()
  {
    LCM ob=new LCM();
    ob.accept();
    ob.display();
  }
}
```

9. (i)
```
class ReCycle
{
  void pushfront(int v)
  {
    if(front !=0)
      q[front--]=v;
    else
    System.out.println("FULL FROM FRONT");
  }
  int poprear()
  {
    if(front !=rear)
      return(q[rear--]);
    else
      return -999;
  }
}
```

(ii) Entity is dequeue and works on the principle of FIFO

10.
```
class Compute extends Library
{
  private int d;
  private double f;
  public Compute(String name, String author,
                               double p, int d)
  {
    super(name, author, p);
    this.d=d;
    f=0.0;
  }
  public void fine( )
  {
    int d1=d-7;
    if(d1>=1 && d1<=5)
      f = d1*2;
    else if(d1>=6 && d1<=10)
      f = d1*3;
    else
      f = d1*5;
  }
  public void show( )
  {
    super.show( );
    System.out.println("Fine =" +f);
    System.out.println("Total amount ="+
                              ((0.02*p*d)+f));
  }
}
```

11. (i) **Algorithm**

Step 1 Start

Step 2 Set temporary pointer to the first node

Step 3 Repeat steps 4 and 5 until the pointer reaches null. Display number not found

Step 4 check for number, if found display, exit

Step 5 Move pointer to the next node

Step 6 End algorithm

Method

```
void FindNode(Node str, int b)
{
  Node temp=str;
  while(temp.link!=null)
  {
    if (temp.n == b)
    {
      System.out.prinln(b+" is found ");
        break;
    }
    temp=temp.link;
  }
  if (temp.link= =null)
  System.out.prinln(b+" is not found ");
}
```

(ii) (a) **Root** B

Sibling F

(b) **Size** 4

Depth 2

(c) E D B A C F G H

ISC

Examination Paper 2025

Fully Solved

COMPUTER SCIENCE-XII

Time : 3 hrs

Max. Marks : 70

General Instructions

1. You are allowed an **additional fifteen minutes** for **only** reading the question paper.
2. You must NOT start writing during the reading time.
3. This question paper has **15 printed pages and one blank page**.
4. It is divided into **two parts**: **Part I** and **Part II**.
5. It has **11 questions** in all.
6. **Part I** is compulsory and has **two** questions.
7. While attempting **Multiple Choice Questions** in **Part I**, you are required to **write only ONE option as the answer**.
8. **Part II** is divided into **three sections**: **A, B and C**.
9. **Each section in Part II** has **three questions**. **Any two** questions have to be attempted from each section.
10. The intended marks for questions are given in brackets [ ].

Part I **(20 Marks)**

(Answer all questions)

While answering questions in this part, indicate briefly your working and reasoning, wherever required.

1. (i) The complement of the Boolean expression $(A \cdot B') + (B' \cdot C)$ is:

(a) $(A + B') \cdot (B' + C)$

(b) $(A' \cdot B) + (B \cdot C')$

(c) $(A' \cdot B) \cdot (B + C')$

(d) $(A \cdot B') + (B \cdot C')$

(ii) Given below are two statements marked, Assertion and Reason. Read the two statements carefully and choose the correct option.

Assertion The expression $\sim (X \vee Y)$ is logically equivalent to $(\sim X \wedge \sim Y)$

Reason The commutative property of logical operators states that the order of the operands does not change the result of a binary operation.

(a) Both Assertion and Reason are true, and Reason is the correct explanation for Assertion.

(b) Both Assertion and Reason are true but Reason is not the correct explanation for Assertion.

(c) Assertion is true and Reason is false.

(d) Both Assertion and Reason are false.

(iii) According to the principle of duality, the Boolean equation $(1 + Y) \cdot (X + Y) = Y + X'$ will be equivalent to:

(a) $(1 + Y') \cdot (X' + Y') = Y' + X$

(b) $(0 \cdot Y) + (X \cdot Y) = Y \cdot X'$

(c) $(0 + Y) \cdot (X + Y) = Y + X'$

(d) $(1 \cdot Y) + (X \cdot Y) = Y \cdot X'$

(iv) The associative law states that:

(a) $A \cdot B = B \cdot A$

(b) $A + B = B + A$

(c) $A \cdot (B + C) = A \cdot B + A \cdot C$

(d) $A + (B + C) = (A + B) + C$

(v) Consider the following code statement:

```
public class Person
{
  int age;
  public Person (int age)
  {
    this.age = age;
  }
}
```

Which of the following statements are valid for the given code?

I. The keyword **this** in the constructor refers to the current instance of the class.

II. The keyword **this** differentiates between the instance variable age and the parameter age.

III. The keyword **this** can be used only in constructors.

(a) Only I and II (b) Only II and III
(c) Only I and III (d) Only III

(vi) Given below are two statements marked, Assertion and Reason. Read the two statements carefully and choose the correct option.

Assertion The break statement prevents fall through effect in switch case construct.

Reason The break statement enables unnatural exit from the loop.

(a) Both Assertion and Reason are true and Reason is the correct explanation for Assertion.
(b) Both Assertion and Reason are true but Reason is not the correct explanation for Assertion.
(c) Assertion is true and Reason is false.
(d) Both Assertion and Reason are false.

(vii) The canonical expression of $F(P, Q, R) = \pi\ (2, 5, 7)$ is:

(a) $(P + Q' + R) \cdot (P' + Q + R') \cdot (P' + Q' + R')$
(b) $(P \cdot Q' \cdot R) + (P' \cdot Q \cdot R') + (P' \cdot Q' \cdot R')$
(c) $(P' + Q + R') \cdot (P + Q' + R) \cdot (P + Q + R)$
(d) $(P' \cdot Q \cdot R') + (P \cdot Q' \cdot R) + (P \cdot Q \cdot R)$

(viii) Study the given propositions and the statements marked, Assertion and Reason that follow it. Choose the correct option on the basis of your analysis.

P — It is a holiday,

Q — It is a Sunday

Assertion If it is not a Sunday, then it is not a holiday. $(Q' \Rightarrow P')$

Reason Inverse is formed when antecedent and consequent are interchanged.

(a) Both Assertion and Reason are true and Reason is the correct explanation for Assertion.
(b) Both Assertion and Reason are true, but Reason is not the correct explanation for Assertion.
(c) Assertion is true and Reason is false.
(d) Both Assertion and Reason are false.

(ix) For the given code segment, write Big O notation for worst case.complexity.

```
for (int i = 1; j < = P; i + +)
{Statements}
for (int j = 1; j < = P; + + j)
for (int k = 1; k < = Q; k + +)
{Statements}
```

(x) Write the minterms in canonical form for the Boolean Function $X(A, B)$, from the truth table given below:

A	*B*	*X*
0	0	1
0	1	0
1	0	0
1	1	1

2. (i) Convert the following infix notation to postfix form.

$$(A - B / C) + (D * E / F) * G$$

(ii) A matrix M [-1...10,4....13] is stored in the memory with each element requiring 2 bytes of storage. If the base address is 1200, find the address of M[2][7] when the matrix is stored Row Major Wise.

(iii) The following function int solve( ) is a part of some class. Assume 'm' and 'n' are positive integers. Answer the questions given below with dry run / working.

```
int solve (int m, int n)
{
  int k = 1;
  if (m < 0)
    return – k;
  else if (m = = 0)
    return m;
  else
    return k + (solve (m – n, n + 2));
}
```

(a) What will the function solve( ) return if:
(1) m = 16, n = 1
(2) m = 9, n = 1

(b) What is the function solve( ) performing apart from recursion?

(iv) The following function duck( ) is a part of some class which is used to check if a given number is a duck number or not. There are some places in the code marked by ?1?, ?2?, ?3? which may be replaced by a statement / expression so that the function works properly.

A number is said to be Duck if the digit zero (0) is present in it.

```
boolean duck (int a)
```

```
{
  int f = -1;
  if (a = = 0)
    return true;
  for (int i = a; i! = 0; ?1?)
  { int c = i% 10;
    if (c = = ?2?)
    { f = 1; break;}
    }
  return (f = = ?3?)? false: true;
}
```

(a) What is the expression or statement at ?1?

(b) What is the expression or statement at ?2?

(c) What is the expression or statement at ?3?

Part II

(50 Marks)

Answer six questions in this part, choosing two questions from Section A, two from Section B and two from Section C.

Section A

(Answer any two questions)

3. (i) A superhero is allowed access to a secure Avengers facility if he/she meets any of the following criteria:

- The superhero has Avengers' membership and possesses a high-security clearance badge

Or

- The superhero does not have Avengers membership, but holds a special permit issued by S. H. I. E. L. D. along with a high-security clearance badge

Or

- The superhero is not a recognised ally but holds a special permit issued by S. H. I. E. L. D. along with a high-security clearance badge

The inputs are:

INPUTS	
A	Superhero has Avengers membership.
S	Superhero holds a special permit issued by S. H. I. E. L. D.
C	Superhero possesses a high-security clearance badge
L	Superhero is a recognised ally

(In all the above cases, 1 indicates YES and 0 indicates NO)

Output X - Denotes allowed access [1 indicates YES and 0 indicates NO in all cases]

Draw the truth table for the inputs and outputs given above. Write the POS expression for X (A, S, C, L).

(ii) Reduce the above expression X (A, S, C, L) by using 4-variable Karnaugh map, showing the various groups (i.e., octal, quads and pairs).

Draw the logic gate diagram using NOR gates only for the reduced expression. Assume that the variables and their complements are available as inputs.

4. (i) (a) Reduce the Boolean function F(P, Q, R, S) $= \sum(0, 1, 2, 5, 7, 8, 9, 10, 13, 15)$ by using 4-variable Karnaugh map, showing the various groups (i.e., octal, quads and pairs).

(b) Draw the logic gate diagram using NAND gates only for the reduced expression. Assume that the variables and their complements are available as inputs.

(ii) From the logic gate diagram given below:

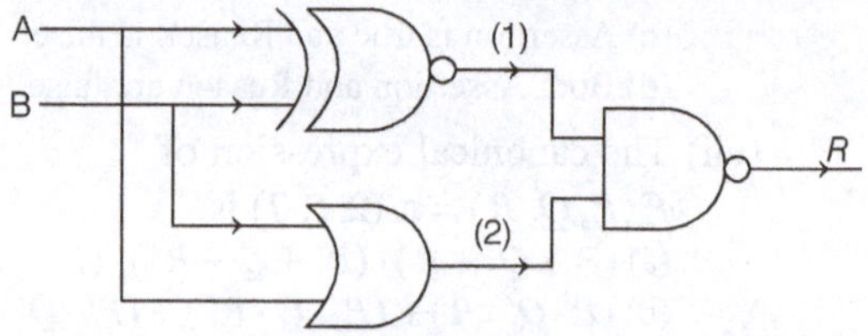

(a) Derive Boolean expression for (1), (2) and R. Reduce the derived expression.

(b) Name the logic gate that represents the reduced expression.

5. (i) What is an encoder? Draw the logic gate diagram for an octal to binary encoder. State one application of a decoder.

(ii) By using truth table, verify if the following proposition is valid or not.

$(\sim X \Rightarrow Y) \wedge X = (X \wedge \sim Y) \vee (X \wedge Y)$

(iii) Study the logic gate diagram given below and answer the questions that follow:

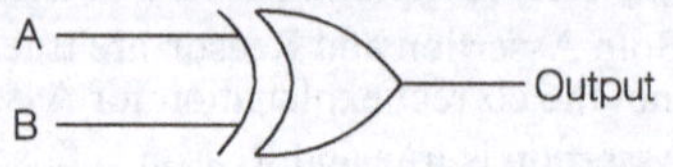

What will be the output of the above gate when:

(a) $A = 1, B = 0$

(b) $A = 1, B = 1$

Section B

(Answer any two questions)

Each program should be written in such a way that it clearly depicts the logic of the problem. This can be achieved by using mnemonic names and comments in the program. (Flowcharts and Algorithms are not required.)

The programs must be written in Java.

6. A class Perni has been defined to accept a positive integer in binary number system from the user and display if it is a Pernicious number or not.

[A pernicious number is a binary number that has minimum of two digits and has prime number of 1's in it.]

Examples

- 101 is a pernicious number as the number of 1's in 101 = 2 and 2 is prime number.
- 10110 is a pernicious number as the number of 1's in 10110 = 3 and 3 is prime number.
- 1111 is a NOT a pernicious number as the number of 1's in 1111 = 4 and 4 is NOT a prime number.

The details of the members of the class are given below:

Class name	**Perni**
Data member/instance variable	
num	to store a binary number
Methods/Member functions	
Perni( )	constructor to initialise the data member with 0
void accept( )	to accept a binary number (containing 0's and 1's only)
int countOne (int k)	to count and return the number of 1's in 'k' using recursive technique
void check( )	to check whether the given number is a pernicious number by invoking the function countOne( ) and to display an appropriate message

Specify the class Perni giving the details of the constructor( ), void accept( ), int countOne (int) and void check( ). Define a main( ) function to create an object and call the functions accordingly to enable the task.

7. Design a class Colsum to check if the sum of elements in each corresponding column of two matrices is equal or not. Assume that the two matrices have the same dimensions.

Example

Input

Matrix A

2	3	1
7	5	6
1	4	2

Matrix B

7	4	2
1	3	1
2	5	6

Output Sum of corresponding columns is equal.

The details of the members of the class are given below:

Class name	**Colsum**
Data members/instance variables	
mat[ ][ ]	to store the integer array elements
m	to store the number of rows
n	to store the number of columns
Member functions/methods	
Colsum (int mm, int nn)	parameterised constructor to initialise the data members m = mm and n = nn
void readArray( )	to accept the elements into the array
boolean check(Colsum A, Colsum B)	to check if the sum of elements in each column of the objects A and B is equal and return true otherwise, return false
void print()	to display the array elements

Specify the class Colsum giving details of the constructor(int, int), void readArray( ), boolean check(Colsum, Colsum) and void print( ). Define the main() function to create objects and call the functions accordingly to enable the task,

8. A class Flipgram has been defined to flip the letters of the left and right halves of a non-heterogram word. If the word has odd number of characters, then the middle letter remains at its own position.

A heterogram is a word where no letter appears more than once.

Example 1 : INPUT : BETTER
OUTPUT : TERBET

Example 2 : INPUT : NEVER
OUTPUT : ERVNE

Example 3 : INPUT : THAN
OUTPUT : HETEROGRAM

The details of the members of the class are given below:

Class name	**Flipgram**
Data member/instance variable	
word	to store a word
Methods/Member functions	
Flipgram(String s)	parameterised constructor to assign word = s
boolean ishetero( )	to return true if word is a heterogram else return false
String flip( )	to interchange the left and right sides of a non-heterogram word and return the resultant word
void display( )	to print the flipped word for a non-heterogram word by invoking the method flip(). An appropriate message should be printed for a heterogram word

Specify the class Flipgram giving the details of the constructor(String), boolean ishetero( ), String flip( ) and void display( ). Define a main( ) function to create an object and call the functions accordingly to enable the task.

Section C

(Answer any two questions)

Each program should be written in such a way that it clearly depicts the logic of the problem stepwise. This can be achieved by using comments in the program and mnemonic names or pseudo codes for algorithms. The programs must be written in Java and the algorithms must be written in general/standard form, wherever required/specified. (Flowcharts are not required)

9. A circular queue is a linear data structure that allows data insertion at the rear and removal from the front, with the rear end connected to the front end forming a circular arrangement.

The details of the members of the class are given below:

Class name	**CirQueue**
Data members/instance variables	
Q[ ]	array to hold integer values
cap	maximum capacity of the circular queue
front	to point the index of the front
rear	to point the index of the rear
Methods/Member functions	
CirQueue(int n)	constructor to initialise cap = n, front = 0 and rear = 0
void push(int v)	to add integers from the rear index if possible else display the message "QUEUE IS FULL"
int remove( )	to remove and return the integer from front if any, else return-999
void print( )	to display the elements of the circular queue in the order of front to rear

(i) Specify the class CirQueue giving the details of the functions void push(int) and int remove( ). Assume that the other functions have been defined.

The main( ) function and algorithm need NOT be written.

(ii) State one application of a circular queue.

10. A superclass Flight has been defined to store the details of a flight. Define a subclass Passenger to calculate the fare for a passenger.

The details of the members of both the classes are given below:

Class name	**Flight**
Data members/instance variables	
flightno	to store the flight number in string
dep_time	to store the departure time in string
art_time	to store the arrival time in string
basefare	to store the base fare in decimal
Methods/Member functions	
Flight (...)	parameterised constructor to assign values to the data members
void show( )	to display the flight details
Class name	**Passenger**
Data members/instance variables	
id	to store the ID of the passenger
name	to store the name of the passenger
tax	to store the tax to be paid in decimal
tot	to store the total amount to be paid in decimal
Methods/Member functions	
Passenger(...)	parameterised constructor to assign values to the data members of both the classes
void cal( )	to calculate the tax as 5% of base fare and total amount (base fare + tax)
void show()	to display the flight details along with the passenger details and total amount to be paid

Assume that the super class Flight has been defined. Using the concepts of Inheritance, specify the class Passenger giving the details of constructor(...), void cal () and void show( ).

The super class, main function and algorithm need NOT be written.

11. (i) A linked list is formed from the objects of the class Cell. The class structure of the Cell is given below:

```
class Cell
{
  char m;
  Cell right;
}
```

Write an Algorithm OR a Method to print the sum of the ASCII values of the lower case alphabets present in the linked list.

The method declaration is as follows:
void lowercase(Cell str)

(ii) Answer the following questions based on the Binary Tree given below:

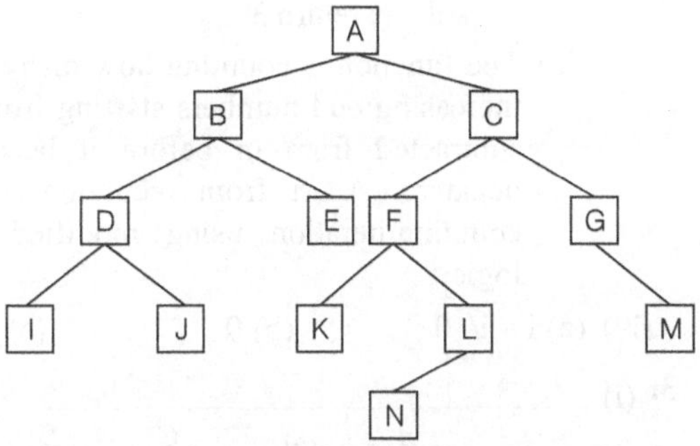

(a) Write the in-order traversal of the right subtree.

(b) State the depth of the entire binary tree and depth of node E.

(c) Name the external nodes of the left subtree and internal nodes of the right subtree.

Answers

1. (i) (c) $(A' \cdot B) \cdot (B + C')$

(ii) (b) Both Assertion and Reason are true but Reason is not the correct explanation for Assertion.

(iii) (b) $(0 \cdot Y) + (X \cdot Y) = Y \cdot X'$

(iv) (d) $A + (B + C) = (A + B) + C$

(v) (a) Only I and II

(vi) (a) Both Assertion and Reason are true and Reason is the correct explanation for Assertion.

(vii) (a) $(P + Q' + R) \cdot (P' + Q + R') \cdot (P' + Q' + R')$

(viii) (c) Assertion is true and Reason is false.

(ix) $O(P * Q)$

(x) Boolean function $X(A, B)$

Minterms = $\overline{A}\,\overline{B} + AB$

2. (i) Infix notation = $(A - B / C) + (D * E / F) * G$

S.No.	Expression	Stack	Postfix
0	(	(	
1	A	(	A
2	-	(-	A
3	B	(-	A B
4	/	(-/	A B
5	C	(-/	A B C
6	)		A B C / -
7	+	+	A B C / -
8	(	+(	A B C / -
9	D	+(	A B C / - D
10	*	+(*	A B C / - D
11	E	+(*	A B C / - D E
12	/	+(/	A B C / - D E *
13	F	+(/	A B C / - D E * F
14	)	+	A B C / - D E * F /
15	*	+*	A B C / - D E * F /
16	G	+*	A B C / - D E * F / G
17			A B C / - D E * F / G * +

Hence postfix expression is $A\ B\ C / - D\ E * F/G * +$

(ii) Given, $B = 1200$, $W = 2$ bytes, $i = 2$, $j = 7$,

$U_r = 10, U_c = 13, L_r = -1, L_c = 4$

n (number of columns) $= U_c - L_c + 1$

$= 13 - 4 + 1 = 10$

According to row major wise

$= B + W[n(i - L_r) + (j - L_c)]$

$= 1200 + 2[2 - (-1) * 10 + (7 - 4)]$

$= 1200 + 2[(3) * 10 + 3]$

$= 1200 + 2(30 + 3) = 1200 + 2(33)$
$= 1200 + 66 = 1266$

(iii) (a) (1) m = 16, n = 1
solve() return 4
(2) m = 9, n = 1
solve() return 3

(b) The function is counting how many successive increasing odd numbers starting from n can be subtracted from m before it becomes 0 or negative. Apart from recursion, it performs counting/iteration using modified arithmetic logic.

(iv) (a) i = i/10 (b) 0 (c) – 1

3. (i)

	A	*S*	*C*	*L*	*X*
0	0	0	0	0	0
1	0	0	0	1	0
2	0	0	1	0	0
3	0	0	1	1	0
4	0	1	0	0	0
5	0	1	0	1	0
6	0	1	1	0	1
7	0	1	1	1	1
8	1	0	0	0	0
9	1	0	0	1	0
10	1	0	1	0	1
11	1	0	1	1	1
12	1	1	0	0	0
13	1	1	0	1	0
14	1	1	1	0	1
15	1	1	1	1	1

POS expression

$(A+S+C+L)\cdot(A+S+C+\overline{L})\cdot(A+S+\overline{C}+L)\cdot$
$(A+S+\overline{C}+\overline{L})\cdot(A+\overline{S}+C+L)\cdot(A+\overline{S}+C+\overline{L})\cdot$
$(\overline{A}+S+C+L)\cdot(\overline{A}+S+C+\overline{L})\cdot(\overline{A}+\overline{S}+C+L)\cdot$
$(\overline{A}+\overline{S}+C+\overline{L})$

(ii) From K-map

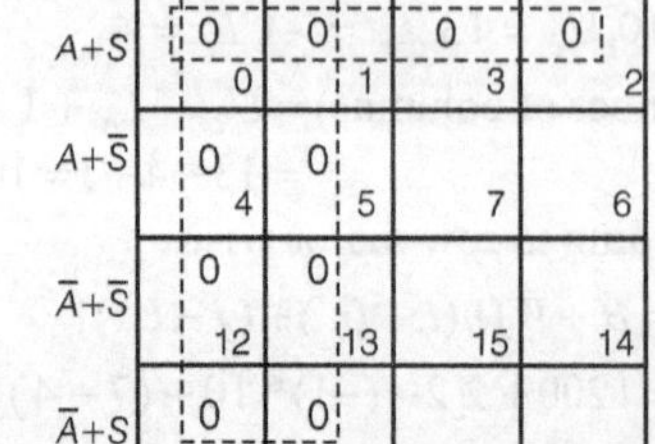

We conclude,

Quad $(M_0 \cdot M_1 \cdot M_3 \cdot M_2) = A + S$

Octet $(M_0 \cdot M_1 \cdot M_4 \cdot M_5 \cdot M_8 \cdot M_9 \cdot M_{12} \cdot M_{13}) = C$

Hence, the final reduced expression

$F(A,S,C,L) = (A+S)\cdot C$
$= C\cdot(A+S)$

The logic circuit diagram for the reduced expression is given below:

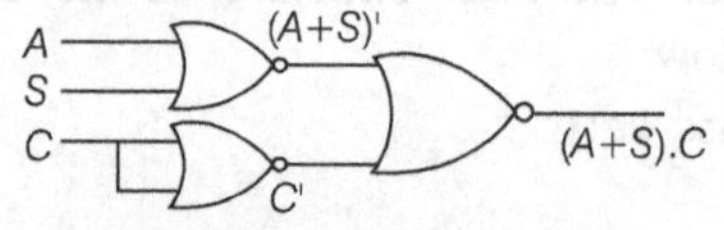

4. (i) (a) Karnaugh map $F(P,Q,R,S) = \Sigma(0, 1, 2, 5, 7, 8, 9, 10, 13, 15)$

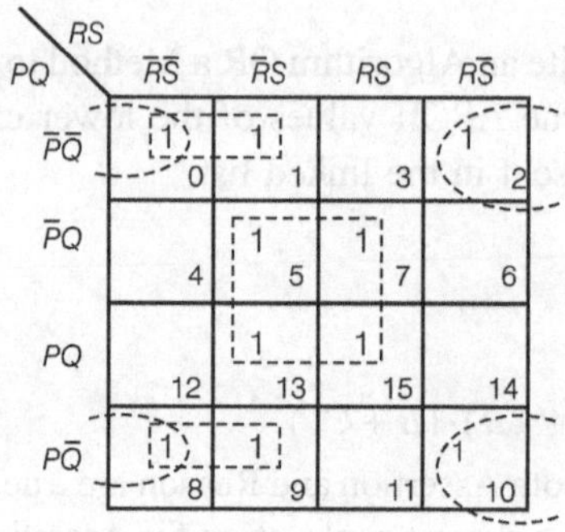

Given expression,

$F(P, Q, R, S) = \Sigma(0, 1, 2, 5, 7, 8, 9, 10, 13, 15)$

There are three quads,

First Quad $(M_5 + M_7 + M_{13} + M_{15}) = QS$

Second Quad $(M_0 + M_1 + M_8 + M_9) = \overline{Q}\,\overline{R}$

Third Quad $(M_0 + M_2 + M_8 + M_{10}) = \overline{Q}\,\overline{S}$

Reduced expression $= QS + \overline{Q}\,\overline{R} + \overline{Q}\,\overline{S}$

(b) The logic gate diagram for the reduced expression using NAND gate only is given below:

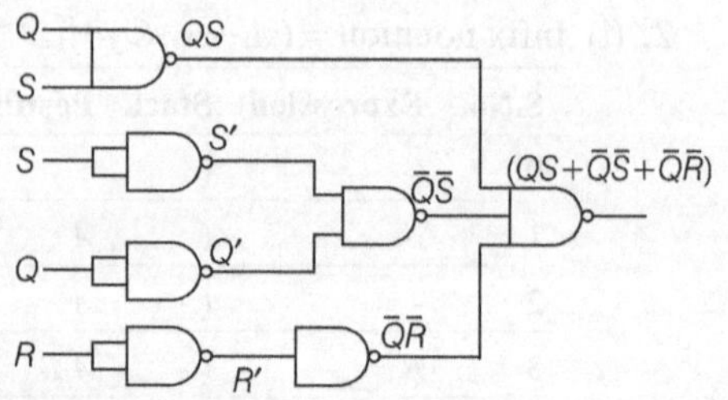

(ii) (a) 1. $(A \oplus B)'$

2. $(A+B)$

$R = [(A \oplus B)'\cdot(A+B)]'$

Step 1 Expand XOR

$A \oplus B = A'B + AB'$

$\Rightarrow (A \oplus B)' = (A'B + AB')'$

Apply De Morgan's Law:

$\Rightarrow (A'B)' \cdot (AB')' = (A + B') \cdot (A' + B)$

Step 2 Substitute in original expression

$R = [\ (A + B') \cdot (A' + B) \cdot (A + B)\ ]'$

Step 3 Simplify the inner expression

$(A + B') \cdot (A' + B) = AB + A'B'$

Then, $(AB + A'B') \cdot (A + B) = AB + A'B'$

Step 4 Final reduction

$R = (AB + A'B')'$

We know that, $AB + A'B' = (A \oplus B)'$

$\Rightarrow R = ((A \oplus B)')' = A \oplus B$

Final Answer:

$R = A \oplus B$

(b) Since the reduced expression is $A \oplus B$, the logic gate is: XOR Gate (Exclusive OR Gate)

5. (i) An encoder is a digital circuit that performs the inverse operation of a decoder. An encoder has 2n (or less) input lines and n output lines.

The output lines generate the binary code corresponding to the input value. An example of an encoder is the octalto-binary encoder, whose truth table is given below.

Truth Table for Octal-to-binary Encoder

Input								Output		
D_7	D_6	D_5	D_4	D_3	D_2	D_1	D_0	A_2	A_1	A_0
0	0	0	0	0	0	0	1	0	0	0
0	0	0	0	0	0	1	0	0	0	1
0	0	0	0	0	1	0	0	0	1	0
0	0	0	0	1	0	0	0	0	1	1
0	0	0	1	0	0	0	0	1	0	0
0	0	1	0	0	0	0	0	1	0	1
0	1	0	0	0	0	0	0	1	1	0
1	0	0	0	0	0	0	0	1	1	1

The encoder can be implemented with OR gates whose inputs are determined directly from the truth table.

Output A_0 =1 if the input octal digit is 1 or 3 or 5 or 7. Similar conditions apply for other two outputs.

These conditions can be expressed by the following Boolean functions:

$A_0 = D_1 + D_3 + D_5 + D_7$

$A_1 = D_2 + D_3 + D_6 + D_7$

$A_2 = D_4 + D_5 + D_6 + D_7$

The encoder can be implemented with three OR gates.

Octal-to-binary Encoder

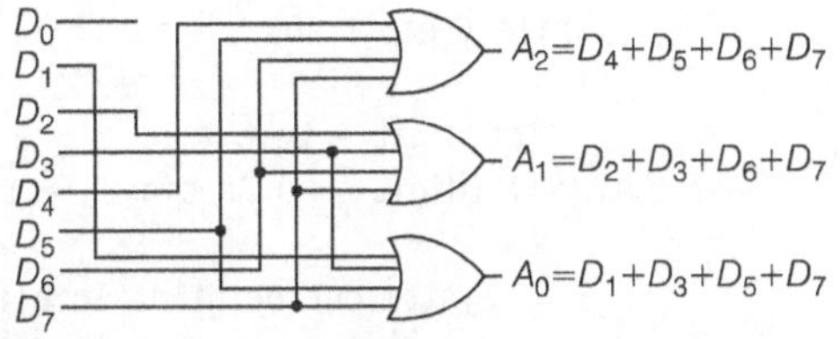

Application One key application of a decoder is in memory addressing, where it selects a specific memory location based on a binary input address.

(ii)

X	Y	$\overline{X}$	$\overline{X} \to Y$	$\overline{X} \to Y \wedge X$	$\sim Y$	$X \wedge \sim Y$	$X \wedge Y$	$(X \wedge \sim Y \vee X \wedge Y)$
0	0	1	0	0	1	0	0	0
0	1	1	1	0	0	0	0	0
1	0	0	1	1	1	1	0	1
1	1	0	1	1	0	0	1	1

From the above truth table, we can see that both LHS and RHS posses same truth values. So, it is a valid proposition.

(iii)

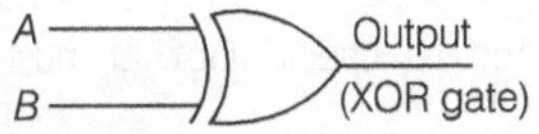

(a) $A = 1,\ B = 0$

Output = 1

(b) $A = 1,\ B = 1$

Output = 0

6.

```
import java.util.Scanner;
public class Perni
{
  int num; // to store the binary number
  // Constructor to initialize num with 0
  public Perni()
  {
    num = 0;
  }
  // Function to accept a binary number (0's
                                    and 1's only)
  public void accept()
  {
    Scanner sc = new Scanner(System.in);
    boolean valid = false;
    while (!valid)
```

```
    {
        System.out.print("Enter a binary number
                         (0s and 1s only): ");
        num = sc.nextInt();
        int temp = num;
        valid = true;
        // Validate binary input
        while (temp != 0)
        {
            int digit = temp % 10;
            if (digit != 0 && digit != 1)
            {
                System.out.println("Invalid binary
                             number! Try again.");
                valid = false;
                break;
            }
            temp /= 10;
        }
    }
}
// Recursive function to count number of 1's in k
public int countOne(int k)
{
    if (k == 0)
        return 0;
    int digit = k % 10;
        return (digit == 1 ? 1 : 0) + countOne(k / 10);
}
// Function to check whether num is a
                              pernicious number
public void check()
{
    int count = countOne(num);
    if (isPrime(count))
    {
        System.out.println(num + " is a PERNICIOUS
                                     number.");
    }
    else
    {
        System.out.println(num + " is NOT a
                         pernicious number.");
    }
}
// Helper function to check if a number is prime
private boolean isPrime(int n)
{
    if (n <= 1)
        return false;
    for (int i = 2; i <= Math.sqrt(n); i++)
    {
        if (n % i == 0)
            return false;
    }
    return true;
}
// Main method to run the program
public static void main(String[] args)
{
    Perni obj = new Perni();
    obj.accept();
    obj.check();
}
}
```

Output

Enter a binary number (0s and 1s only): 101

101 is a PERNICIOUS number.

Enter a binary number (0s and 1s only): 1111

1111 is NOT a pernicious number.

7.

```
import java.util.Scanner;
public class Colsum
{
    int mat[][]; // 2D array to store matrix elements
    int m, n;    // m = number of rows, n = number
                                      of columns
    // Parameterized constructor
    public Colsum(int mm, int nn)
    {
        m = mm;
        n = nn;
        mat = new int[m][n];
    }
    // Method to accept elements into the array
    void readArray()
    {
        Scanner sc = new Scanner(System.in);
        System.out.println("Enter elements for
              matrix (" + m + " x " + n + "): ");
        for (int i = 0; i < m; i++)
        {
            for (int j = 0; j < n; j++)
            {
                mat[i][j] = sc.nextInt();
            }
        }
    }
    // Method to display the array elements
    void print()
    {
        System.out.println("Matrix:");
        for (int i = 0; i < m; i++)
        {
            for (int j = 0; j < n; j++)
            {
```

```
            System.out.print(mat[i][j] + "\t");
        }
        System.out.println();
    }
}
// Method to check if sum of elements in each
              column of both matrices is equal
boolean check(Colsum B)
{
    for (int j = 0; j < n; j++)
    {
        int sumA = 0, sumB = 0;
        for (int i = 0; i < m; i++)
        {
            sumA += mat[i][j];
            sumB += B.mat[i][j];
        }
        if (sumA != sumB)
            return false;
    }
    return true;
}
// Main function
public static void main(String args[])
{
    Scanner sc = new Scanner(System.in);
    System.out.print("Enter number of rows: ");
    int r = sc.nextInt();
    System.out.print("Enter number of columns: ");
    int c = sc.nextInt();
    Colsum A = new Colsum(r, c);
    Colsum B = new Colsum(r, c);
    System.out.println("Enter elements for
                                    Matrix A:");
    A.readArray();
    System.out.println("Enter elements for
                                    Matrix B:");
    B.readArray();
    A.print();
    B.print();
    if (A.check(B))
    System.out.println("Sum of corresponding
                              columns is equal.");
    else
    System.out.println("Sum of corresponding
                           columns is NOT equal.");
}
}
```

Output

Enter number of rows: 3
Enter number of columns: 3
Enter elements for Matrix A:
2 3 1
7 5 6
1 4 2
Enter elements for Matrix B:
7 4 2
1 3 1
2 5 6
Matrix:
2 3 1
7 5 6
1 4 2
Matrix:
7 4 2
1 3 1
2 5 6
Sum of corresponding columns is equal.

8.

```
import java.util.*;
class Flipgram
{
    String word;
    // Constructor
    Flipgram(String s)
    {
        word = s;
    }
    // Check if the word is a heterogram
                          (no repeating letters)
    boolean ishetero()
    {
        word = word.toUpperCase();
        for (int i = 0; i < word.length(); i++)
        {
            char ch = word.charAt(i);
            if (word.indexOf(ch) !=
                          word.lastIndexOf(ch))
                return false;
        }
        return true;
    }
    // Flip the left and right halves of the word
    String flip()
    {
        int len = word.length();
        int mid = len / 2;
        if (len % 2 == 0)
        {
            String left = word.substring(0, mid);
            String right = word.substring(mid);
            return right + left;
        }
        else
```

```
        {
            String left = word.substring(0, mid);
            String midChar = word.substring(mid,
                                            mid + 1);
            String right = word.substring(mid + 1);
            return right + midChar + left;
        }
    }
    // Display the result
    void display()
    {
        if (ishetero())
        {
            System.out.println("OUTPUT: HETEROGRAM");
        }
        else
        {
            String flipped = flip();
            System.out.println("OUTPUT:"+ flipped);
        }
    }
    // Main function
    public static void main(String[] args)
    {
        Scanner sc = new Scanner(System.in);
        System.out.print("INPUT: ");
        String input = sc.nextLine();
        Flipgram ob = new Flipgram(input);
        ob.display();
    }
}
```

Output

INPUT: BETTER
OUTPUT: TERBET
INPUT: NEVER
OUTPUT: ERVNE
INPUT: THAN
OUTPUT: HETEROGRAM

9.
```
class CirQueue
{
    private int[] Q;
        // array to hold integer values
    private int cap;
        // maximum capacity of the circular queue
    private int front;
        // to point the index of the front
    private int rear;
        // to point the index of the rear
    private int size;
        // current number of elements in the queue
        // constructor to initialize cap = n,
                                front = 0 and rear = 0
    public CirQueue(int n)
    {
        cap = n;
        Q = new int[cap];
        front = 0;
        rear = 0;
        size = 0;
    }
    // to add integers from the rear index
                                            if possible
    // else display the message "QUEUE IS FULL"
    public void push(int v)
    {
        if (size == cap)
        {
            System.out.println("QUEUE IS FULL");
        }
        else
        {
            Q[rear] = v;
            rear = (rear + 1) % cap;
            size++;
        }
    }
    // to remove and return the integer from front
    // if any, else return -999
    public int remove()
    {
        if (size == 0)
        {
            return -999;
        }
        else
        {
            int removedElement = Q[front];
            front = (front + 1) % cap;
            size--;
            return removedElement;
        }
    }
    // to display the elements of the circular
                queue in the order of front to rear
    public void print()
    {
        if (size == 0)
        {
            System.out.println("Queue is empty");
            return;
        }
        System.out.print("Queue elements: ");
        int current = front;
        for (int i = 0; i < size; i++)
        {
            System.out.print(Q[current] + " ");
            current = (current + 1) % cap;
        }
        System.out.println();
    }
    public static void main(String[] args)
```

```
    {
        CirQueue cq = new CirQueue(5);
        // Create a circular queue with capacity 5
        cq.push(10);
        cq.push(20);
        cq.push(30);
        cq.print(); // Output: Queue elements:
                                            10 20 30
        int removed1 = cq.remove();
        System.out.println("Removed: "+ removed1);
          // Output: Removed: 10
        cq.print(); // Output: Queue elements: 20 30
        cq.push(40);
        cq.push(50);
        cq.print(); // Output: Queue elements:
                                         20 30 40 50
        cq.push(60); // Queue is now full
        cq.print(); // Output: Queue elements:
                                      20 30 40 50 60
        cq.push(70); // Output: QUEUE IS FULL
        int removed2 = cq.remove();
        System.out.println("Removed: "
               + removed2); // Output: Removed: 20
        cq.print(); // Output: Queue elements:
                                         30 40 50 60
        cq.push(80);
        cq.print(); // Output: Queue elements:
                                      30 40 50 60 80
        int removed3 = cq.remove();
        int removed4 = cq.remove();
        int removed5 = cq.remove();
        int removed6 = cq.remove();
        int removed7 = cq.remove();
        System.out.println("Removed: " + removed3);
          // Output: Removed: 30
        System.out.println("Removed: " + removed4);
          // Output: Removed: 40
        System.out.println("Removed: " + removed5);
          // Output: Removed: 50
        System.out.println("Removed: " + removed6);
          // Output: Removed: 60
        System.out.println("Removed: " + removed7);
          // Output: Removed: 80
        cq.print(); // Output: Queue is empty
        int removed8 = cq.remove();
        System.out.println("Removed: " + removed8);
          // Output: Removed: -999
    }
}
```

Output:
Queue elements: 10 20 30
Removed: 10
Queue elements: 20 30
Queue elements: 20 30 40 50
Queue elements: 20 30 40 50 60
QUEUE IS FULL
Removed: 20
Queue elements: 30 40 50 60
Queue elements: 30 40 50 60 80
Removed: 30
Removed: 40
Removed: 50
Removed: 60
Removed: 80
Queue is empty
Removed: -999

10.

```
class Passenger extends Flight
{
    String id;        // Passenger ID
    String name;      // Passenger name
    double tax;       // Tax to be paid
    double tot;       // Total fare
    // Parameterized constructor
    Passenger(String fno, String dep, String arr,
            double base, String id, String name)
    {
        super(fno, dep, arr, base); // call to
                             superclass constructor
        this.id = id;
        this.name = name;
        this.tax = 0.0;
        this.tot = 0.0;
    }
    // Method to calculate tax and total fare
    void cal()
    {
        tax = 0.05 * basefare;
        tot = basefare + tax;
    }
    // Method to display details
    void show()
    {
        super.show(); // show flight details
        System.out.println("Passenger ID: " + id);
        System.out.println("Passenger Name: " + name);
        System.out.println("Tax: " + tax);
        System.out.println("Total Fare: " + tot);
    }
}
```

11. (i)

```
class Cell
{
   // Assuming 'cell' in the image refers to a
            class, likely for a linked list node
  char m;
    // To store a character
```

```
    Cell right;
    // To point to the next Cell in the linked list
    public Cell(char m)
    {
        this.m = m;
        this.right = null;
    }
}
public class LowercaseSum
{   // Class name reflecting the functionality
    // Method to calculate the sum of ASCII
   values of lowercase characters in a linked list
   public static void lowercaseSum(Cell str)
   {
       int sum = 0; // Initialize sum to 0
       Cell temp = str; // Use 'temp' instead of
                        't' for better readability
       while (temp != null) { // Iterate through
                                   the linked list
         if (Character.isLowerCase(temp.m))
        { // Check if the character is lowercase
            sum += (int) temp.m;
          // Add the ASCII value to the sum
         }
         temp = temp.right; // Move to the
                                        next node
       }
           System.out.println(sum);
          // Print the final sum
       }
       public static void main(String[] args)
       {
           // Example usage (assuming you have a way
              to create a linked list of Cells)
           // Create a sample linked list:
                                     a → B → c → D
           Cell a = new Cell('a');
           Cell B = new Cell('B');
           Cell c = new Cell('c');
           Cell D = new Cell('D');
           a.right = B;
           B.right = c;
           c.right = D;
           lowercaseSum(a); // Call the method with
              the head of the list.  Output should be
                                        196 (97 + 99)
       }
   }
```

(ii) (a) In order traversal of the right subtree is –KFNLCGM

(b) Depth of the entire binary tree – 4

Depth of node E – 2

(c) External nodes of the left subtree – IJE

Internal nodes of the right subtree – CFLG